AMERICAN POWER, THE NEW WORLD ORDER
AND THE JAPANESE CHALLENGE

American Power, the New World Order and the Japanese Challenge

William R. Nester
Assistant Professor of Political Science
St. John's University of New York

St. Martin's Press   New York

First published in the United States of America in 1993

Printed in Great Britain

ISBN 0–312–08991–0

Library of Congress Cataloging-in-Publication Data
Nester, William R., 1956–
American power, the new world order, and the Japanese challenge /
William R. Nester.
p.   cm.
Includes bibliographical references and index.
ISBN 0–312–08991–0
1. United States—Foreign economic relations—Japan.   2. Japan–
–Foreign economic relations—United States.   3. United States–
–Commercial policy.   4. Japan—Commercial policy.   5. International
economic relations.   I. Title.
HF1452.5.J3N47   1993
337.73052—dc20   92–28897
                                                              CIP

Contents

Introduction 1

PART I   LIBERALISM, NEOMERCANTILISM AND THE
         NEW WORLD ORDER 13

1 Power and the Changing Nature of International Relations 15

2 American Liberalism: Triumph and Tragedy 56

3 Japanese Neomercantilism: The New Hegemony 90

PART II   POLITICAL ECONOMIC BATTLEGROUNDS 121

4 The Shifting Balance of Economic Power 123

5 The Shifting Balance of Political Power: Hearts, Minds and
   Policies 154

6 American Policy Toward Japan: The Sisyphean Dilemma or
   What is the Sound of One Hand Clapping? 195

7 The Mature Industry Front 228

8 The Foreign Investment Front 280

9 The High Technology Front 312

10 The Financial Front 371

PART III   WHAT IS TO BE DONE? 393

11 America and Japan into the 21st Century 395

Notes 438

Bibliography 461

Index 488

With deepest love to my grandparents, Evelyn and Bill, Josephine and Mark

Introduction

Are international relations evolving into a "New World Order" in which, according to President George Bush, "diverse nations are drawn together in common cause to achieve the universal aspirations of Mankind: peace and security, freedom and the rule of law"?[1] Although the concept remains vague, the world has changed remarkably over the past several years. The most startling event was the Cold War's finale as President Gorbachev essentially admitted defeat, the Soviet empire rapidly broke up, Germany reunited under Bonn's leadership, and the Eastern European countries and the former Soviet Union struggled to create free political and economic systems. But the Soviet bloc is only the most recent region to experience revolutionary political and economic change. From Nicaragua to South Korea, and Nepal to Algeria left and right wing governments are falling to mass democratic revolutions. Throughout the 1980s, virtually every Latin American country shook off military dictatorship and embraced democracy, while into the 1990s similar pressures are mounting across Africa, the Middle East, and Asia.

There is a virtuous relationship between political and economic freedom – the transition into political democracy is at once stimulated by and stimulates greater economic freedom. Political philosophers from Aristotle to Jefferson have argued that democracy is best rooted in a middle class society. But how do states create a viable middle class society? Inspired by "economic miracles" in Japan, South Korea, Taiwan and Singapore, increasing numbers of governments have rejected both pure free market and state ownership of production strategies as inadequate means of creating and distributing wealth. Instead, they are carefully managing rather than outright controlling or completely freeing their economies: strategic industries are targeted for development, public corporations are privatized, markets partially opened, trade promoted.

As more states rely on increased trade to create more wealth, geoeconomic problems are rapidly overshadowing geopolitical conflicts as the number one agenda issue in international relations. Global and regional economic interdependence deepens annually. Over 110 nations are members of the international free trade organizations, the General Agreement on Tariffs and Trade (GATT) and the International Monetary Fund (IMF), and dozens more are clamoring to join. In 1992 the European Community (EC) and the European Free Trade Association (EFTA) joined in abandoning all their internal trade barriers to create an

1

enormous market of 380 million people, while a North American free
trade bloc is evolving through international treaties and an East and
Southeast Asian trade bloc under Japan's domination is emerging through
more subtle means.

With the Cold War's demise, nations can increasingly devote their
collective energy, time, and resources to combating such global problems
as poverty, disease, natural disasters, overpopulation, and, perhaps the
most catastrophic problem of all, the rapidly worsening greenhouse effect
which may eventually transform much of the earth to desert. The most
dramatic recent example of international cooperation, however, was the
United Nations' authorization of economic sanctions and a military
alliance to first drive Iraq out of Kuwait, and then ensure that Iraq's
nuclear, chemical, and biological warfare capacity is destroyed.

Where does the United States fit into this "New World Order"? In his
1991 State of the Union address, President Bush spoke boldly of "the next
American century" and a "renewed America" which "can shape the
future".[2] Bush's celebration of American power seemed fulfilled by the
dazzling victory of American-led forces over Iraq in the Gulf War. The
public was mesmerized by film of pinpoint accurate cruise missiles
destroying Iraqi command and control centers and burned out Iraqi
tanks strewn across the desert, as well as immensely relieved that the
victory cost little more than 150 American lives. President Bush summed
up the feelings of most Americans over the decisive victory against Iraq
when he exclaimed: "By God, we've kicked the Vietnam syndrome once
and for all!"[3]

Bush's hopes for the continuation of America's pre-eminent position in
global affairs, however, may be extremely optimistic. His speeches, like
President Reagan's before him, are filled with visions of American power
and prosperity that do not correspond to reality. The outpouring of
American patriotism and support for the Gulf War – at one point Bush's
popularity rating soared to 89 per cent – is certainly understandable. After
two decades of failed presidencies, foreign policy debacles, and accelerating
economic decline and social problems, Bush's successful assertion of
American military power in the Gulf seemed like a godsend to most
Americans. But the "lessons" drawn from the Gulf victory, such as the
viability of "solving" complex issues with military means, may be as
ultimately self-defeating as the "lesson" of Vietnam which stressed a
continued military buildup while avoiding the use of force.

Any American celebration of the military triumph is undercut by
deteriorating conditions at home. Headlines blare such tragic realities
as: 2.3 million violent crimes in 1990, a 3.4 per cent rise from 1989; one in
eight children or over 5.5 million go hungry each day while an additional
6 million are underfed; America's public and private debt tripled from

$3.4 trillion in 1981 to $10.6 trillion in 1990; in 1980 the average corporate executive made 25 times more money than the average worker, in 1990 executive salaries averaged 85 times greater than those of workers; America's literacy rate is barely 75 per cent; over 35 million Americans subsist without health insurance; the country is scarred by thousands of bleeding toxic waste sites; bridges, roads, ports, and inner cities crumble; hundreds of tons of smuggled drugs continue to feed millions of addicts. America's domestic tragedies are mirrored by a steady decline in its global economic power. During the 1980s, the United States was transformed from the world's greatest creditor to worst debtor country; suffered horrendous trade and payments deficits which in 1990 remained above $100 billion; saw its leadership in one product and technology after another overtaken by foreign rivals while its economic growth remained among the lowest and gap between rich and poor among the highest of the industrial democratic countries.

Chalmers Johnson succinctly captured perhaps the most significant result of the Soviet Empire's collapse and America's decline: "The Cold War is over – Japan won!" The United States won the Cold War with the Soviet Union while it lost the economic war with Japan. The next century may well be Japan's rather than America's. By most measures, Japan has replaced the United States as the world's most dynamic economic power. Japan's average annual economic growth rate of about 10 per cent between 1950 and 1973 was four times America's 2.5 per cent average, while its 4.5 per cent average since then has been double America's 2.2 per cent. In 1990, Japan's economy grew 4.7 per cent, twice America's 2.3 per cent, while its inflation and unemployment rates of 2.6 per cent and 2.2 per cent respectively, were far less than America's 4.4 per cent and 5.7 per cent rates. Although the United States remains the world's largest economy, Japan's economy is already 70 per cent the size of America's and will surpass it in fifteen years if current growth rates hold. This represents an extraordinary development achievement and shift in economic power. In 1960 America's GNP was 33 per cent of global GNP while Japan's was only 3 per cent; in 1990, America's percentage of global GNP had dropped to 21 per cent while Japan's had risen to 15 per cent. Japanese are now wealthier than Americans – in 1990, Japan's per capita income was $24 500 while America's was $20 500. When Japan's GNP eventually equals that of the United States, with only half the population, Japanese will be twice as wealthy as Americans.

Japan has surpassed the United States by most financial, manufacturing, and technological standards. Japan is now the world's banker while the United States has deteriorated into the world's largest debtor nation. The world's eight largest banks, and 14 of the top 25 banks, are now Japanese, and Japanese banks hold more than twice the assets of their

American counterparts. Of American banks only Citicorp at number 14 was ranked among the world's top 25; the next largest, Chase Manhattan, was a distant 36th.[4] Of the world's top 1000 corporations in 1990, 333 were Japanese whose $2.649 trillion in assets accounted for 39.3 per cent of the world total compared to America's 329 firms worth $2.288 trillion or 33.3 per cent. Altogether Japanese corporations ranked among six of the top ten, 14 of the top 25, and 31 of the top 50 corporations in the world while American firms were only three of the top ten, 9 of the top 25, and 22 of the top 50 corporations.[5] Japanese direct investments in the United States totaled $78.5 billion in 1990, compared to only $7 billion of American investments in Japan. Although Japan's investments still trailed those of the British with $122.1 billion of the total, it is estimated that at current investment rates, Japan will surpass Britain as the largest foreign invester in the United States in 1995 and by 1999 will own more American assets than Britain, the Netherlands, and Canada combined![6] Japan has technologically leapfrogged the United States. A 1990 Commerce Department study revealed that of twelve emerging technology sectors, Japan was leading in 10 and running neck and neck with the United States in the other two.[7]

Japan has clearly surpassed the United States by almost every economic measure. How significant are all these figures? Does Japan now dominate the world economically if not politically? And will it eventually inherit the throne from the United States as the leader of the global political economy? Is American decline as severe as it seems? Is it reversible?

Throughout the 1980s and into the 1990s, a growing tide of Congressional debates, business and academic seminars, books, journals, magazines, and newspapers have raised the specter of American decline and Japanese ascendance over the global political economy. Both the public and intellectuals are split over the issue. Popular views about American decline are predictably volatile. The Gulf War dramatically decreased the number of Americans who believe that the United States is a declining power. Before the War, according to a New York Times/CBS poll conducted in June 1989, only 44 per cent of respondents believed the United States remained a world power, only 25 per cent thought government did the right thing most or all of the time, and only 34 per cent thought things would get better over the next five years. In a similar poll taken in March 1991, those who believed that the United States was still a world power had risen to 73 per cent, 51 per cent felt things would get better over the next five years, and 47 per cent claimed the government did the right thing almost always or most of the time. In June 1989, exactly half of Americans believed that Japan would surpass the United States and become the world's leading economic power in the 21st century; in March 1991 only 43 per cent thought so.[8]

Historians have been debating reasons for the rise and fall of the great powers since Thucydides. Startling as the economic measurements of Japan's rise and America's decline appear, analysts are deeply divided over their significance. The debate involves a struggle between two diametrically opposed world views – optimists which include neoclassical economists and political conservatives who argue that no decline has occurred and that unfettered markets and high military spending are the only road to wealth and power, and revisionists who argue that by virtually any measure America's relative decline has been swift and will eventually become absolute if Washington fails to adopt rational foreign, trade and industrial policies that create wealth and power.

Optimists tend to dismiss the economic measurements of America's decline. Robert Gilpin writes:

> . . . although the relative power of the United States has declined, it remains the dominant world economy. The scale, diversity, and dynamics of the American economy will continue to place the United States at the center of the international economic system. The universal desire for access to the huge American market, the inherent technological dynamism of the American economy, and America's additional strength in both agriculture and resources – which Europe and Japan do not have – provide a cement which will be sufficient to hold the world economy together and keep the United States at its center. The continued dependence of Europe and Japan on America for their security provides the United States with a strong lever over the economic policies of each.[9]

Samuel Huntington concurs, arguing that "if hegemony means having 40 per cent or more of world economic activity (a percentage Britain never remotely approximated during its hegemonic years), American hegemony disappeared long ago. If hegemony means producing 20–25 per cent of the world product and twice as much as any other individual country American hegemony looks quite secure."[10] Citing CIA statistics which indicate that the United States actually increased its share of global GNP from 25 per cent in 1975 to 26 per cent in 1988, while manufacturing as a percentage of GNP remained constant at 21 per cent, Joseph Nye agrees that the United States has not really lost any ground economically since the mid-1970s, and that the "decline of US power was steepest from 1950 to 1973, the period often identified as 'the period of American hegemony',"[11] Nye even argues that Washington "never enjoyed a general hegemony after the war, so hegemony can be neither lost nor regained in the future."[12]

Yet, most analysts dismiss the opinion that America remains as powerful as ever as based more on wishful thinking than careful analysis. Paul

Kennedy argues that much of the optimists' (or revivalists as he calls them) beliefs are shaped, not by empirical evidence, but by the unwillingness to accept that the United States could ever be anything less than "number one". In analyzing a spate of recent revivalist publications, Kennedy writes that:

> Those who hate the very idea of American 'decline' will welcome these publications; those who are convinced the nation is in deep trouble will be unconvinced . . . (the argument) is a classic example of a debate in which one expert can assemble (seemingly impressive) evidence for 'decline', whereas another expert can produce (apparently equally impressive) evidence for 'revival' . . . Certain writers are claiming that the 'container' of American power is now half empty; others that it is half full. Virtually everyone seems to agree that the present position of the United States in world affairs has changed from that of 1945, even if there is disagreement over how far it has changed, and what that change implies . . . The 'half empty' school inclines to believe that a further diminution will occur. The 'half full' school . . . inclines toward believing that much of the decrease was natural, that the level has now stabilized, and that there are prospects for that level being maintained indefinitely if certain reforms are undertaken.[13]

Kennedy then pointedly reminds us that "the greatest cause for the decline of empires was hubris".

Who is right? Has Japan replaced the United States as global hegemon? Just what are the qualifications for global leadership, and how well do the United States and Japan fulfill those responsibilities?

Leadership or hegemony over the global political economy means managing, funding and defending the system. Thus, any aspiring leader must have the political will and ability to lead, and the manufacturing, financial and technological power to generate annual balance of payments surpluses with which to supply both the long-term credit necessary to finance and the military forces to defend the system. As the recent Persian Gulf War revealed, the United States still retains the political will and military muscle for leadership, but had to pass the cup to its allies to finance the War. America has clearly lost its manufacturing, financial, and technological leadership to Japan. Without overwhelming economic power, Washington is finding the system's management increasingly difficult. Tokyo, meanwhile, is not interested in taking over global leadership since such responsibilities would mean abandoning the neo-mercantilist policies which have transformed Japan from mass poverty into the world's most dynamic economic superpower. Leadership requires genuine sacrifice – open markets for foreign products and investments, untied foreign aid, trade deficits with developing countries, technology transfers to potential competitors, deep involvement in global and regional political problems, a military powerful enough to successfully intervene in such economically strategic regions as the Panama Canal and Persian Gulf. Even though Japan is now the world's greatest creditor nation and America the world's worst debtor nation, Tokyo will continue its policy of relying on the United States to bear the major costs of upholding the system.

Some relative decline in American economic power over the past forty years was not only inevitable but actually necessary for the prosperity of both the United States and the world economy. The United States was the only major industrial country to emerge from the Second World War with its economy not only intact but enhanced by the conflict. Determined not to return to the era of global depression and protectionism that characterized the 1930s, Washington has devoted its postwar international economic policy to first creating and then maintaining a world economy based on the principles of free trade. To rebuild the shattered economies of its trade partners and reintegrate them into the world economy, the United States had to open its own markets and extend tremendous amounts of foreign aid. In the immediate postwar decades, free trade largely meant the virtually unlimited access of foreign products to the vast American market, while the United States tolerated foreign trade and investment barriers that nurtured overseas economic development. America's economic prosperity and security depended on global prosperity and interdependence. While a prosperous world economy was good in itself, it also helped contain the Soviet Union; communism's appeal weakens with mass prosperity.

This policy was an enormous success in building a dynamic world economy. Today, Western Europe and Japan are as wealthy as the United States, and a host of Newly Industrializing Countries (NICs) are scrambling to join the rich countries' ranks. World trade continues to expand at a rate of 7 per cent a year, and its benefits are increasingly diffused throughout both industrial and developing countries. The world economy is solidly built on a web of both formal and informal institutions that shook off the blows of OPEC's quadrupling of oil prices in 1974 and further doubling in 1979 and has so far managed to contain the debt crisis.

Although some decline was clearly inevitable, why and how did the United States allow Japan to take its place as the economic, financial, and technological powerhouse of the world economy? Most analysts agree that America's foreign policy grasp has simply exceeded its reach; that the means of American foreign policy have fallen far short of the ends. Great powers which fail to accord their goals with the means accelerate their decline as the increasing costs – economic, political, psychological – of overseas commitments drain the country of resources which could be better utilized to increase that nation's wealth.

America's decline relative to Japan occurred to a large extent because Washington has not understood and thus not adapted to the tremendous changes in the nature of international relations and power since 1945 – changes that Washington was largely instrumental in stimulating. Since 1947 Washington has consistently subordinated its genuine geoeconomic interests to real and imagined geopolitical interests. Policymakers lost touch with the reality that military power has to be financied. In the almost forty-five years since the wartime alliance with the Soviet Union collapsed into the Cold War, American foreign policy has focused on containing a perceived Soviet military and ideological threat. All other national needs were subordinated to Washington's single-minded determination to prevent communism's spread at all costs. Containment involved not just tying much of the world together in military alliances but in also recreating a viable global political economy in which communism could not take root. The economic and military costs of containing the Soviet Union and building and protecting the global political economy were, and remain, exhorbinant. However, Washington failed to pursue policies which would generate more wealth and maintain America's global economic power. In other words, the United States bankrupted itself in its successful post-1945 policies of containing the Soviet threat and creating a dynamic world political economy.

While the United States was preoccupied with the enormous financial, human and psychic costs of hegemony, Japan essentially got a free ride into an economic superpower. The relative economic success of Japan and the United States reflects their different economic orientations. Tokyo has mastered a superior way to develop, distribute, and secure wealth, and assert political economic power around the world. Japan's success rests on the rejection of both communist-style state ownership of the economy and the neoclassical belief that free markets and minimal state interference is the answer. Instead, Tokyo uses neomercantilist policies which target strategic industries for development and declining industries for protection, and nurtures those industries through a dynamic mixture of corporate collusion and competition. Industrial policies are implemented with a range of subsidies, cartels, import barriers, technology infusions and export promotions. These policies follow a similar pattern:

> Japan imports a technology . . . from the West. It then protects the industry . . . from foreign competition to whatever extent and by whatever means may be required while it gains scale, experience, cost parity, and momentum in Japan itself – the world's second largest and fastest growing market, exporting aggressively, further enhancing its

cost position. Gradually it converts a part of its cost advantage into improved product quality. At some point the Japanese producer is able to offer a better product, profitability, and lower price.[14]

Japan's policymakers constantly added new, higher technology strategic industries to its older targets. Thus the ranks of heavy industries like steel, shipbuilding, automobiles, textiles and petrochemicals targeted in the 1950s, were swelled in the 1960s by computers and consumer electronics, in the 1970s by semiconductors, aerospace and robots, in the 1980s by biotechnology, fifth generation computers, and superconductors, and in the 1990s by sixth generation computers, virtual reality, and microrobots. Behind these industrial policies designed to create global champions was another set of industrial policies that propped up inefficient, high employment sectors like farming, distribution, and construction. These sectors were targeted with immense protection and subsidies because they represented huge voting blocs of support for the conservative ruling party, the Liberal Democratic Party (LDP). By pursuing two sets of rational industrial policies, one that targeted potential global champions and the other large voting blocs, the LDP achieved a virtuous circle of political power; economic growth and the widespread distribution of that growth resulted in continual LDP political triumphs during elections which in turn allowed the LDP to continue its successful industrial policies, and so on.[15]

Relations between Washington and Tokyo have worsened steadily over the past two decades as America's power declined and Japan's rose. The many trade, financial, technological, and military issues tearing at the bilateral relationship are deeply entrenched, interrelated and heavily weighted in Japan's favor. Japan enjoys not only vast trade surpluses with the United States, which remained a mind-boggling $41 billion in 1990, but the trade's composition is essentially one of Japanese manufactured goods for American agricultural and natural resource products. Japanese businessmen easily sell and invest in the United States; American businessmen who sell and invest in Japan, if at all, are plagued by webs of restrictions. Japan has easy and cheap access to American technology; American access to Japanese technology is highly restricted. The United States spends 6.5 per cent of GNP on defense and expends enormous treasure and sometimes blood to protect Japanese interests in Northeast Asia, the Gulf region, and elsewhere; Japan spends only 1 per cent of its GNP on defense and refuses to send even token amounts of its forces overseas. Japanese government and business lobby groups annually spend an estimated $400 million in the United States influencing American national, state and local policies to Japan's advantage; American ability to lobby Tokyo is extremely limited.

Does Japan's economic superpower pose a threat to the United States? Americans overwelmingly recognize a Japanese threat. A 15–19 March 1991 Harris survey revealed that 72 per cent of Americans thought Japan's economic threat and only 20 per cent of Americans felt the Soviet military threat was a more serious challenge to America's future.[16]

Some analysts have argued for some time that the Japanese rather than the Soviet challenge has been the more pressing and that the United States must drastically revise its policies toward both countries. A stable military balance of power with the Soviet Union has existed since the 1960s while the economic balance of power has steadily shifted in Japan's favor. Prestowitz states bluntly that "the real challenge to American power is not the sinister one from the Eastern bloc, but the friendly one from the Far East".[17] Harrison and Prestowitz write that "even before the Berlin Wall fell, it was increasingly apparent that the fundamental challenge facing the United States is not Soviet military might. Rather, it is the danger of economic insolvency, reflected in budget deficits, an eroding industrial base, and the growing American inability to compete with newly formidable economic rivals, especially Japan".[18]

Neoclassical economists dismiss these issues and the apparent shift in power as insignificant, and maintain that Japanese dumping and the trade deficit are good because they raise America's standard of living. It is true that the Japanese dumping of steel, televisions, VCRs, semiconductors, automobiles, loans, and other products allows some American consumers to pay less in the short run. The trouble is that by driving American industries, and thus well paying jobs, out of business, America's growth rate and standard of living are much lower over the long run than they would have been without Japanese neomercantilism. The United States then has even less money to address deep rooted socioeconomic problems – highways and bridges continue to crumble, teenagers graduate from high school who cannot read, people are afraid to walk city streets, once dynamic businesses are driven to bankruptcy or bought out by foreign firms, and drugs destroy entire neighborhoods. The United States is more deeply trapped in a vicious socioeconomic cycle whereby continued trade deficits further weaken or bankrupt American firms which in turn worsens such problems as the trade deficit, unemployment, deteriorating savings, investment, research and development, and infrastructure, and increased crime, which further undermines America's ability to compete.

However, contrary to the fears of some and a recent elaborate but largely fanciful book, the Japanese threat does not and will never include a military dimension.[19] Tokyo was the first government to understand that military power becomes increasingly irrelevent in an increasingly interdependent world. Global power depends on the ability of a nation's banks and corporations to capture market share and eliminate foreign rivals; a large military industrial complex hobbles a nation's ability to compete in commercial markets. A major element of Japan's successful neomercantilist strategy involves free riding on global markets, technologies, and defense. Tokyo has transformed Japan from mass poverty into an economic superpower by maintaining a minimal defense force and concentrating its human, financial, and production resources on developing strategic industries which takeover global markets and bring immense wealth back to Japan which is then reinvested in those strategic industries.

Although Japanese nationalism is growing ever more emotional, Tokyo will never do anything to jeopardize its growing power over the global political economy. For both psychological and practical reasons, Japan's political leadership and mass public are thoroughly against any significant military buildup, let alone its use for overseas military adventures. There is absolutely no chance that Japanese will ever abandon their deep-rooted pacificism. After all, Japan's political elite and mass public were overwelmingly against sending even minesweepers to the Gulf War. And even if somehow a miracle happened and Japan's government and public did support a massive military buildup, to what end would it serve? The Cold War against the Soviet Union is over and Japan will continue to win countless victories in the economic war it has been waging against the United States and other countries for the past four decades by political economic means. With its huge population densely packed into a small area, Japan would be quickly devastated in any war against the United States. Tokyo will continue to maintain the neomercantilist policies which have brought Japan such wealth and power. It will spend about 1 per cent of GNP on defense for the foreseeable future but will confine its conventional forces to protecting Japan and will never develop a nuclear force. American troop levels in Japan may be reduced but the bilateral treaty will remain in force. Tokyo needs the alliance far more than Washington – the alliance diverts Washington's attention, energy, and resources from confronting Japan's economic threat.

Tokyo, however, wants the rest of the world to believe that it could become militaristic if the foreign pressure on Japan to abandon neomercantilism and genuinely liberalize its economy becomes too great. "Don't push us too hard", Japanese spokespeople mutter darkly, "or you may get another Pearl Harbor!" The success of this message varies from one audience to the next. The White House naively believes that Japanese militarism is a possibility and thus avoids demanding genuine reciprocity. Most European leaders, however, are well aware that the Japanese are bluffing and do not hesitate to act tough, thus blunting Tokyo's neomercantilist strategy within the European Community.

How has the White House responded to the reality of declining American power? Throughout the 1980s, the White House reaction to America's decline recalls Nero's alleged fiddling while Rome burned. Eight years of Reaganomics resulted in a tripling of the national debt and the transformation of the United States from the world's greatest banker to world's worst debtor, while Japan soared ahead into the world's most dynamic economy. The Bush Administration, in keeping with the Reaganomic policies of the 1980s, does nothing to alleviate America's decline. The White House continues to fail not only to acknowledge a Japanese threat, but does not even enforce American trade law which could blunt some of Japan's dumping offenses and trade barriers. Meanwhile, the White House and Congress continued to haggle over such superfluous issues as prayer in public schools, flag burning, and public funding of the arts.

How important is all this? What does it matter if the United States continues to run deficits while Japan enjoys huge surpluses, and surpasses America in manufacturing, financial, and technological power? So what if Japan spends over $400 million annually to influence American policies in its favor? How does continuing American liberalism and Japanese neomercantilism, and the related tremendous shift in the balance of economic power from the United States to Japan affect American security? What is the nature of the Japanese threat? Are the United States and Japan really at war? If so, what kind of war, who is winning, how are they winning, and what is at stake?

Why has the United States declined so precipitously and Japan risen into an economic superpower? Can America's decline be reversed? This book systematically explores those and related questions. Chapter 1 attempts to put America's decline and Japan's rise in perspective by analyzing the continuities and changes in international relations and power throughout the modern era. Chapters 2 and 3 then examine in detail American liberalism and Japanese neomercantilism, respectively, focusing on their dynamic interaction and powerful effect on America's decline and Japan's rise. Chapters 4 and 5 document Japan's growing economic and political power over the United States, respectively. Chapters 6, 7, 8, 9 and 10 analyze first the overall trade duel between the two countries, then specific industrial, foreign investment, financial, and high technology issues. The last chapter attempts to provide answers to the question: What should be done? Chapter 11 presents a plan for overhauling America's policy making system so that it can create and implement rational industrial and foreign policies that enhance rather than undermine American wealth and power. Any reversal of American power must include a complete reform of American policy toward Japan that will make Tokyo an equal partner with the United States in managing the global political economy, and ensure genuine economic and political reciprocity between the two countries.

Part I

Liberalism, Neomercantilism and the New World Order

1 Power and the Changing Nature of International Relations

A global political economy did not begin to emerge until Portuguese navigators first rounded the vast African continent and sailed to South and Southeast Asia over 500 years ago. Competing European powers soon sent out their own trade and war ships to the world's far ends in search of riches and Christian converts. In 1522 the fifteen surviving members of the Magellan expedition sailed into Cadiz, becoming the first human beings to circumnavigate the world, thus symbolically globalizing Europe's geopolitical and geoeconomic struggles, and knitting the first tentative strand in an increasingly dense global political economic web that today binds every state and virtually every human being to all others.

A succession of great powers have struggled for and sometimes briefly achieved dominance over the global political economy in the five centuries since those first intrepid navigators set sail. The dominant global power or hegemon was not necessarily the dominant European power. Although Portugal played a peripheral role in European politics, a combination of far-sighted, ambitious kings, merchants, and sea captains, a strong centralized state, the ability to adapt new navigation techniques and ship designs, a geographic location on Europe's remote southwestern end, and the Turk's cutoff of traditional trade routes through the Middle East to the spices and treasures of the Far East allowed Portugal to become the first global power. Subsequent global powers – Spain, Holland, France, Britain and the United States – have varied greatly in the tenure and degree of their dominance, yet all became great powers by skillfully converting human, industrial, financial, technological, maritime, and diplomatic resources to their advantage. Each great power has in turn experienced a similar pattern of rise, maturity and decline as the initial burst of dynamism and ambition, and the wealth and power it brought, was slowly transformed into political complacency, economic sluggishness, and often, defeat in war. Eventually that great power finds itself over-shadowed by yet another.

Over the past five centuries, the global political economy has passed through two development stages and appears to be entering a third. Until the late 19th century, states followed mercantilist policies whereby they attempted to increase their wealth and power by maximizing exports and minimizing imports. Trade between mercantilist states was carefully managed and thus relatively limited as each side tried to avert any drain of gold and wealth to the other side while doing everything possible to entice its inward flow. Most trade, and the only "free" trade, was between a power and its overseas colonies. During the mercantilist era the virtuous cycle of power and wealth revolved around states investing much of their wealth into large military forces with which to conquer rich distant lands whose wealth was carried back to the state, which then converted much of it into more military power for further conquests, and so on. By the late 19th century, although the Western hemisphere had achieved independence, virtually all of Africa and Asia had been carved up among the European powers, the United States, and Japan.

Ironically, even when imperialism was at its height, the world's greatest power, Britain, was championing a vastly different form of political economy based on free rather than managed trade. Several forces stimulated Britain's policy shift from mercantilism to liberalism. Britain had initiated the industrial revolution and most of its manufactured goods had an overwelming comparative advantage. The rise of Britain's empire and industrialization led to the shift in power from agrarian to trade and industrial interests in Parliament. Britain thus had a compelling interest in promoting liberalism over mercantilism. As home to such political economists as Adam Smith, David Ricardo, Jeremy Bentham and John Stuart Mill, Britain had a powerful theoretical voice to match the economic and political interests pushing for free trade.

Although as a result of Britain's efforts increasing amounts of world trade did become unfettered from prohibitive tariffs, quotas and imperial preferences, it would be an exaggeration to describe the global economy as predominantly liberal anytime before the 1960s. It took the trauma of a global depression in the 1930s, World War II and a deepening Cold War to convince Washington to pick up and wave Britain's fallen free trade banner. Washington's efforts to promote liberalism went well beyond Britain's. American markets were not only opened wide but in addition Washington led the creation of such institutions as the General Agreement on Tariffs and Trade (GATT), the International Monetary Fund (IMF), and the World Bank designed to facilitate world trade and punish mercantilists.

By the early 1990s, Washington had largely realized its vision of a dynamic, prosperous, and predominantly free global political economy. Western Europe and Japan compete now with the United States for industrial supremacy, the East Asian states are rapidly industrializing, and increasingly important sectors of most other nation's economies operate along free market principles. Meanwhile, the Soviet empire and communism crumbled in the late 1980s and early 1990s under the dead weight of communism's inability to stimulate any meaningful development or distribute anything other than poverty.

Yet, ironically in this moment of triumph, increasing numbers of American and foreign analysts were concluding that the United States may have won the Cold War only to lose the geoeconomic war with Japan for supremacy over the global political economy. In the over four decades while the United States largely opened its markets to the world, and expended trillions of dollars on managing and defending the global political economy against the Soviet and other geopolitical challenges, Japan perfected a new geoeconomic strategy – neomercantilism – which has proven superior to liberalism as the best means of creating wealth and power. Neomercantilism differs from mercantilism only in the importance of military power. In an interdependent world of sovereign states, military power is an increasingly ineffective means of promoting a state's national interests. Instead, states invest the wealth generated by targeting strategic industries for development, maximizing exports, and minimizing competitive imports to develop further the economy and "buy" greater access for their products in overseas markets. Neomercantilist states like Japan and its emulators South Korea, Taiwan and Singapore enjoy growth rates more than double and income distributions far more egalitarian than states following free trade policies.

The world political economy seems to be entering a new era characterized by neomercantilism. As traditionally liberal states like the United States wallow in immense and intractable trade and payments deficits with all growth stalled except for debt, and watch in impotent disbelief as neomercantilist states like Japan surpass them industrially, financially and technologically, they are increasingly coming to the conclusion that "if you can't beat 'em, join 'em". Managed rather than free trade is the secret to the dazzling success of Japan and other neomercantilist countries, and their successful strategy is increasingly being emulated by other states. The claims by liberal theorists that world trade would collapse if every state followed neomercantilist policies is highly unlikely. World trade and wealth will continue to expand but states will increasingly manage their industrialization and trade to prevent other neomercantilist states from determining it for them.

This book explores the nature of power in a changing world by focusing on America's relative decline and Japan's rise to global political economic supremacy. But what is power? What does it mean to call the United States and Japan superpowers and to say one nation's power is in decline and the other's in ascendance? Is power itself, however defined, unchanging or has its nature evolved with the modern and increasingly postmodern world? Do some states at some times acquire enough power that they achieve a hegemony over the global system? If so, how is that power measured and how do they achieve, manage, and eventually lose that status? America's relative decline and Japan's dazzling rise in economic power largely reflect their governments' very different abilities to understand and creatively respond to the nature of power and super-power in a rapidly changing world.

POWER

Power is the ability to get others to do things they normally would not do. Powerful states are those which shift the outcomes of conflicts in their favor. States achieve power by mobilizing all their available human and natural resources toward realizing their objectives in any given conflict. A state's power is always relative to that possessed by other states. Power resources and the distribution of power among states vary greatly from one issue and relationship to another, while the outcomes of each are seldom certain. Outcomes depend on how skillfully each state involved in a given conflict mobilizes all its potential resources. Outcomes, however, can be ambiguous. A military victory can be a political defeat as the Americans found out with the 1968 Tet Offensive. Power is thus a relative concept which involves both outcomes and resources. A state's actual power at any given time can only be measured by the outcomes of the conflicts in which it is involved; until then power is only potential.

Morganthau describes power as "anything that establishes and maintains control of man over man, and covers all social relationships which serve that end, from physical violence to the most subtle of psychological ties by which one mind controls another".[1] Thus a state's use of power can be blatantly coercive, as with marching an army to another state's frontier or cutting off all economic ties and demanding concessions, or persuasive, as with extracting the same concessions through rational and/or moral arguments. Power can also be wielded virtually unnoticed. The more successful leaders are experts at mobilizing mass emotions by manipulating the state's moral and psychological authority manifested through national institutions and symbols. People may simply and unthinkingly obey their president, priest or father if they believe that authority is legitimate.

Karl Deutsch has explored in depth the concept of power, and the changing array of tangible and intangible resources that can shape a state's power in any conflict. He identifies a domain, range and scope of power, in which a state's power domain includes both internal tangible and intangible resources as well as international contraints and opportunities; its power range includes the spectrum and severity of coercion and persuasion a state could employ against its opponent; and power scope the institutional framework with which a state employs its power domain and range.[2]

It is the relative importance of the array of tangible and intangible resources that states can mobilize to acheive their goals – the power domain – that has changed over time. Tangible power traditionally rested on three pillars – population, territory and natural resources. The more people, territory, and natural resources within a state, the more potential that state had to become a great power. Yet, raw size in territory, people or natural resources has rarely been decisive in an international conflict. Some of the mightiest nations in history have been among the smallest. Macedonia under King Philip and later Alexander was not only able to conquer the Greek polities but actually overran the Middle East and extended its empire to the Indus River. Relatively small countries on the periphery of Europe like Portugal, Holland and Britain were able to defeat larger European powers like Spain and France and for a while become the world's leading naval powers. Within a decade, Japan defeated the vast empires of China and Russia and acquired its own empire in Northeast Asia. What has continually proved decisive is the skill with which a state mobilizes its tangible resources against others.

The quality of a state's territory is more important than its size, while a state's location is as important as its topography. A large territory can as much hinder as enhance a nation's strength if it lacks natural borders, is spare of population, infrastructure, fertile soil and water, or is broken by desert or mountain wasteland. Natural boundaries, a temperate climate, fertile soil and a topography allowing easy transportation and communication can be important components of national power. England and Japan are relatively small in territory, but as fertile island kingdoms they enjoy huge natural moats to help deter foreign invasion, while their reliance on the sea for their livelihood made them natural naval powers. With ocean views on two thirds of its frontiers, and military midgets Mexico and Canada bordering the rest, the United States is virtually an island country. Even a conqueror powerful enough to seize the Eurasian landmass would hesitate before attempting to vault the Atlantic or Pacific to invade the United States.

Bigger is also not necessarily better when a state's population is factored into its potential power. Military history continually records nations with smaller populations but well-trained, well-led armies defeating nations with much larger populations. China and India are the world's most populous countries but because most of those people are poverty-stricken and illiterate, they undermine rather than enhance those countries' potential power. Large, literate, technically adept, affluent and loyal populations enhance a state's power. Market power, the ability to reward or deny the access of other states to one's domestic market as well as allow domestic industries to gain large scale production to bring down prices and improve efficiency, is an increasingly vital pillar of contemporary geoeconomic power. By defending itself with a bewildering maze of import barriers, Japan brilliantly uses its vast market power – with 120 million people the world's second largest consumer market – to develop its industries into global leaders and simultaneously weaken foreign industries by denying them equal access.

In the premodern era, when military technology was relatively simple, the most important natural resources were fertile, well-watered lands with which to grow crops to feed a large population; small deposits of iron ore generally were adequate to supply enough steel to arm a state's soldiers. But the industrial revolution was fueled by immense amounts of natural resources, and the ability to control those raw materials essential for industrial production, such as coal, iron ore, and oil, became an important source of power from the early industrial age up through 1945. European imperialism in the late 19th century and Japanese imperialism in the 1930s was stimulated in part by the perceived need to capture vast quantities of overseas natural resources that were unavailable at home.

Directly owning natural resources is no longer an essential component of power in an interdependent global political economy. For example, although Japanese continually bemoan the fact that their country has few natural resources, it is actually to Japan's competitive advantage to buy natural resources at the cheapest global price rather than outright owning them. Few countries enjoy abundant, easily extracted natural resources; most must expend enormous human, financial and technological efforts to extract domestic natural resources that yield relatively small profits. Buying at the cheapest global source is a blessing in disguise since it allows a country to concentrate on continually developing new consumer products.

The potential is very limited for countries rich in natural resources to withhold their products from the global market in order to reap higher profits. Stockpiling, greater industrial efficiency, developing alternate sources and subsitutes, and the need for resource rich countries to export them in exchange for other products makes the natural resource weapon an illusory and ultimately self-defeating option. Oil is probably the only resource that can cause widespread global economic disruption if the supply is disrupted and price boosted. OPEC's quadrupling of prices in 1973 and further doubling of prices in 1979 severely damaged all oil dependent countries in the short run. But greater industrial efficiency, the discovery and exploitation of new oil fields and cheating by OPEC members brought the real price of oil down to levels below that of 1972 in the late 1980s.

A state's power can also be greatly augmented by its ability to work in concert with others. There is safety in numbers – both physical and moral. "Burden sharing" with allies spreads the costs and risks of military action. Great powers which attempt to go it alone risk losing their power since even military victory can be pyrrhic if the material and psychological losses are too great. The Gulf War of 1990–91 is a model of a great power skillfully forging an alliance of states with similar interests and negotiating either significant or symbolic contributions from them all. The United States alone could have militarily defeated Iraq, but the political and economic costs for a unilateral American assault would have been devastating to the United States, even if Washington had succeeded in its goal of getting President Hussein to withdraw from Kuwait. The Bush administration knew that Iraq's defeat would not only be easier with 37 nations contributing troops, but more importantly, the war's political costs would be lightened with United Nations approval, and economic costs by financial contributions.

Alliances are even more vital to the success of relatively weak nations. "Classic" international relations revolved around the attempts by states to protect and enhance their national interests by maintaining a "balance of power" in which weaker states allied with other weak states to protect themselves against any state that attempted to acheive hegemony over the system. This assumption that states "have no permanent allies, only permanent interests" and "the enemy of my enemy is my friend" remain important to international relations. The entire Cold War was based on such assumptions as both the United States and Soviet Union set aside their respective ideals in trying to court potential allies. Washington would support virtually any country that claimed to be anti-Soviet, even if it was a repressive dictatorship or a communist country like Yugoslavia or China; Moscow would do likewise even if the regime crushed the local communist party. Regional conflicts in the Middle East or Southeast Asia are also models of the traditional balance of power. Although all the Arab states claim to be anti-Israel, some secretly collaborate with Tel Aviv against their Arab rivals. Just as Moscow aids Vietnam to help contain China, Beijing aids the Khmer Rouge to help contain Vietnam, despite the fact that they are all communist countries.

The balance of power's importance to international relations will continue. Balance of power strategies, however, may be increasingly applied to geoeconomic rather than geopolitical conflicts. The Cold War's demise and subsequent co-operation between Washington and Moscow rather than competition in regional conflicts has reduced the use of geopolitical balance of power. Meanwhile, Tokyo's successful neomercantilist policies have provoked calls for the United States, EEC, and other states whose economies have been bashed by Japanese

protectionism and predatory exports to "contain Japan". Tokyo meanwhile is solidifying its hegemony in Southeast Asia in order to offset the
potential power of a united trade front by North American and European
trade blocs.

Tangible resources such as a state's control over a large, prosperous and
dynamic territory, population, natural resources and economy, and
skillful use of alliances, may not be decisive in deciding a conflict's
outcome. There is often a vast gap between potential and actual power,
and it is power's intangibles that explain the difference. Power involves
more than capability, it depends on the will and strategy of those in
charge. A well-organized, well-led state with the ability to mobilize its
economic, political, social and moral power resources towards fulfilling its
interests will always have the edge over states with similar resource
endowments but weak national organization and leadership. Skillful use
of such intangible resources as intelligence, negotiation, propoganda, and
mass opinion against one's opponets can make the difference in a conflict.
A state with fewer tangible resources can prevail in an issue if its opponent
is either preoccupied with what it perceives as other more important
matters, is ignorant of the potential power it can mobilize, and/or lacks
the will to assert its interests in that particular issue.

History is filled with examples of small yet well-led and organized states
defeating ones with far larger territories, populations, natural resources,
economies or alliances. Seemingly powerful states – those with advanced
economies, large populations, and huge military forces – can be defeated
by seemingly weak states, as the Americans learned in Vietnam, and the
Russians in Afghanistan. "Liberation" movements with relatively few
human, financial, or military resources can acheive independence against
colonial powers with vast resources, as the British discovered in America
and the French in Vietnam and Algeria. A study of 164 conflicts between
1816 and 1976 in which military force was either threatened or used
revealed that victory usually went to the side with a qualitative rather
than quantitative advantage.[3] The most important ingredient of power in
all these conflicts was resolve – the will to win.

Sometimes a country can enhance its national interests and powers by
maintaining a low political profile rather than directly challenging the
existing power hierarchy. "Free riding" on the open markets, technology
and military commitments of other great powers is a very sensible –
perhaps the most sensible – national strategy to follow in an increasingly
interdependent world. It is certainly the most cost-effective way to
accumulate wealth and expand global economic power, which in turn
can be translated into political power. The United States surpassed
Britain as the world's largest industrial nation at the beginning of the
20th century, and had a population three times larger and national

territory thirty times larger, yet declined to challenge Britain for leadership over the global political economy. Why did the United States not attempt to actualize its vast potential power? Essentially because its interests were fulfilled by playing an obsequious rather than assertive role in international affairs. America's accumulation of wealth was all the greater by following a strategy of maximizing its position in global markets while allowing other states to flush immense wealth down the drain of relatively unproductive military and colonial commitments. Pulled temporarily into the maelstrom of international politics during World War I and the Versailles Conference, Washington withdrew once again into its continental isolation and single-minded pursuit of wealth during the 1920s and 1930s. Japan has followed the same strategy since 1945; by "free-riding" the coattails of America's vast financial, technological, material, and human sacrifices toward maintaining the global political economy, Japan eventually succeeded in economically surpassing the United States.

Conflicts, whether they be military or economic, are as much over hearts and minds as tangible geoeconomic or geopolitical issues. National leaders must increasingly play to the galleries of public opinion, both domestic and global. How does a nation's mood or morale affect national power? Government policies have always been strengthened by mass compliance and weakened by dissent. The "public", or those members of society considered to have a legitimate voice in government, has steadily expanded over the millenium from absolute monarchs ruling agrarian kingdoms into the mass publics of today. Ideology and mass communications have forced even totalitarian governments to convert their mass subjects into mass citizens, whose compliance must be carefully groomed. Peasants still revolt for bread and land, but their struggles are now shaped by democratic or Marxist ideals, and linked by satellite to similar rebellions around the world. Liberal democratic systems are so attuned to the public pulse that the result is often government by mass opinion survey. The late 20th century emergence of the "global village", stimulated by such institutions as the UN and CNN, and linked by television antennas sprouting from even the world's poorest and most remote dwellings, has forced every government to at least listen to if not heed the voice of global elite and mass opinion. Even authoritarian governments keep one eye not just on their own streets, but on public squares around the world.

Mass opinion may well be the decisive factor in victory or defeat. To believe that one's country or religion is inately superior to others can be a powerful motivation and justification for action. With God on their side, fervent adherents of Christianity and Islam carved out vast empires. The American belief that the United States is a "city on a hill" whose

"manifest destiny" was to show the light to others helped justify and
motivate the country's expansion across a continent and beyond, and still
underlines much American foreign policy. Similarly, the "white man's
burden" helped justify European imperialism in the late 19th century.
Marxist-Leninism and nationalism gave Vietnamese the psychologial edge
with which to win long, bloody wars against first the French and then the
Americans. America's vast military might was defeated, not on the
battlefield, but by mass opposition both in Vietnam and at home. The
White House seems to have learned Vietnam's lessons; President Bush
unleashed the American military against Iraq only after he had received
overwelming United Nations and Congressional approval.

But mass opinion can be a double edged sword. Ideologies can be self-
defeating if there is too large a gap between belief and reality. The ability
to hoodwink the public into unwavering support can lead a government to
disaster. During World War II, the Japanese believed that their nation's
"spirit" (*Yamatodamashi*) would triumph over all – a notion that left almost
3 million Japanese and 20 million Asians dead during 14 years of Japanese
aggression. Even in the summer of 1945, after suffering three years of
continual military defeats and the firebombing of its cities, Tokyo had so
indoctrinated the Japanese that they were prepared to fight to the last old
man, woman and child against the American invaders, and with bamboo
spears and human wave attacks at that. Only the atomic bombings
convinced Japan's government that it had no choice but to surrender.
War between Iraq and Iran lasted eight years, in part, because the
governments were able to convince their respective populations that
death on the battlefield was the express route to an Islamic heaven.
The Reagan Administration's genius for packaging and selling the
President's genial, all-American image blinded an adoring public to
policies which tripled America's national debt within eight years. Most
Americans still believe that minimizing the government's role in the
economy is the best means of growth even though some countries like
Japan that carefully manage their markets have grown as much as four
times faster than the United States. The enduring hold on policymaker's
imaginations of the "magic of the marketplace" has prevented the United
States from creatively confronting its relative economic decline. In the
long run, mass support empowers a state only if its policies serve rather
than undermine national interests. Thus, a nation's belief system can
sometimes either enhance or detract from a nation's total power potential.

Yet another intangible but important potential source of a state's power
is the ability to set the parameters of an international issue. Nye writes
that it is "just as important to set the agenda and structure the situations
in world politics as it is to get others to change in particular situations."[4]
This involves:

"co-optive" rather than "command" power; the power of the "attraction of one's ideas or on the ability to set the political agenda in a way that shapes the preferences that others express . . . If a state can make its power legitimate in the eyes of others, it will encounter less resistance to its wishes. If its culture and ideology are attractive, others will more willingly follow. If it establishes international norms that are consistent with its society, it will be less likely to have to change. If it can help support institutions that encourage other states to channel or limit their activities in ways the dominent state prefers, it may not need as many costly excercises of coercive or hard power in bargaining. In short, the universalism of a country's culture and its ability to establish a set of favorable rules and institutions that govern areas of international activity are critical sources of power.[5]

Unlike imperial states which rely on "hard" military power to force other states to their will, hegemonic states use such "soft power" resources as culture, ideology and institutions to sway other states to their side. In their respective tenures as hegemons, Britain and the United States led the global political economy through the universal appeal of aspects of their national cultures, the propagation of a liberal economic ideology, and the creation of a range of international organizations designed to realize that free trade ideology. Washington's creation of the GATT and IMF structured the global political economy in a way that enticed other states to at least partially liberalize their own economies.

Success breeds success – sometimes. A nation's reputation for winning conflicts can attract allies and inhibit opponents, and thus become a self-fulfilling prophecy. Cities across Eurasia usually chose to surrender rather than resist the Mongolian onslaught because of Gengis Khan's reputation for slaughtering his opponents. Likewise, states with reputations for duplicity are unlikely to find willing allies or favorable international agreements. Since the early 1960s, Japan has repeatedly claimed to have "liberalized" its markets so that they are now the world's most open – foreign firms supposedly do not sell more in Japan because they do not try hard enough and their products are inferior. In reality, Japan's markets remain carefully managed and foreign access strictly limited by webs of import barriers. Foreign governments realize this and thus dismiss Tokyo's "significant market opening steps" as elaborate but transparent public relations stunts, thus undercutting their effectiveness as means of diverting foreign pressure.

Fate, finally, is the most intangible of all a state's potential power sources and one to which a state can not control but only respond. How long would Alexander's empire have lasted had he not died from either disease or poison at age 32? What would have been Russia's fate if the

Germans had not sent Lenin home in a sealed train? Would war have engulfed Europe between 1939 and 1945 if that stray shell had killed rather than spared Hitler in 1916? Power underlines all history's "what if's".

WEALTH AND POWER

Wealth is power's bottom line. There has always been a dynamic relationship between a state's wealth and power. The wealthier a state, the more potential power it has to prevail in conflicts – it all depends on how that wealth is invested. Traditionally, power flowed from the thrust of a sword, or more recently, the barrel of a gun. States diverted wealth into large armies and navies with which to defend or expand the realm, and the economic resources at its disposal. Thus, the skillful use of power can in turn enhance a state's wealth, part of which can then be invested in wielding power. The relationship between wealth and power, both geopolitical and geoeconomic, has increased dramatically since the industrial revolution. Since the industrial revolution, the most powerful state has generally been the one with the largest and most advanced industrial base.

The key to wealth, and thus power, can be a state's ability to utilize a technological breakthrough. Paul Kennedy's monumental study, *The Rise and Fall of the Great Powers*, convincingly argues that economic and technological vitality is the ultimate source of power in the global system: "major shifts in the world's military power balances have followed alterations in the productive balances".[6] According to Kennedy, although the rise and fall of the Great Powers "has usually been a consequence of lengthy fighting . . . it has also been the consequence of the more or less efficient utilization of the state's productive economic resources in wartime, and . . . the way in which that state's economy has been rising or falling, relative to the other leading nations, in the decades preceding the actual conflict."[7]

In the 15th century, China not only had the world's largest population and territory, but it possessed such technologies as a printing press, gunpowder and ships capable of navigating the world. Yet, China remained isolated and backward while the smaller Western powers created an ever growing world economy based on trade and colonialism which eventually engulfed China itself. Tiny Portugal used new navigation and sailing techniques to gather wealth and assert power around the world. Eventually, however, a technology and the power it brings will become diffused. Great Powers must retain their status by leading the cutting edge of technology and mobilizing that technology into the range of military, economic, diplomatic means of achieving its national interests.

In an increasingly interdependent world, power is manifested through market shares and deep financial pockets rather than state of the art weaponry. The power of a state is measured by its ability or inability to buy rather than fight its way into the possession of foreign markets, technology, and capital. Wealth and power become increasingly synonymous. Wealth is used to create more wealth.

But how is wealth created? Three theories dominate contemporary discussions of wealth's creation and distribution – Marxism, liberalism, and neomercantilism. There are still many people around the world who for either sentimental, neurotic, or cynical reasons claim allegiance to Marxism. But at best, Marxism's focus on state ownership and direction of the means of production has simply redistributed poverty and been used as a highly effective means whereby a tiny elite exploits a captive, impoverished population; at worst, Marxism, in the Soviet Union, China, Kampuchea and elsewhere, has led to the mass murder and starvation of tens of millions of human beings. Marxism is thoroughly discredited both theoretically and practically. The wave of mass revolutions against Marxist regimes in Eastern Europe, the Soviet Union, and elsewhere is rapidly relegating communism to history's dust heap.

Although the other two theories have been relatively successful in creating and distributing wealth, they differ greatly in their theoretical and applied power. Liberal (neoclassical) economic theory is composed of a very simple set of assumptions about the world which are adhered to with almost religious fervor by believers.[8] Economic liberalism's central belief is the less government, the more economic development. Government, according to Adam Smith, should have:

> only three duties . . . first, the duty of protecting the society from the violence and invasion of other independent societies; secondly, the duty of protecting, as far as possible, every member of the society from the injustice or oppression of every other member, or the duty of establishing an exact administration of justice; and thirdly, the duty of erecting and maintaining certain public works and certain public institutions, which it can never be for the interest of any individual, or small number of individuals.[9]

Less is more. Why? According to liberal theory, individual consumers and producers, not the state, should be the primary economic units. The needs and wants of consumers and skills of producers vary considerably, and everyone should be free to consume and produce what they want. Goods are demanded by consumers and thus created by entrepreneurs who realize they can profit by that demand. Government simply gets in the way of these natural forces of supply and demand.

Government's economic role should be minimal not only within but between states. Consumer demands and producer supply are enhanced through international trade. The concept of comparative advantage presumes that all nations, like all individuals, have certain unique economic strengths and weaknesses. Natural, technological and human resources vary greatly from one country to the next, and it is no more rational for a nation to attempt to produce everything it consumes than it is for an individual to attempt to do the same. Instead, all nations, and thus all consumers, would benefit if they specialize in what they best produce and then trade those products for what can be better produced elsewhere. Adam Smith wrote that "what is prudence in the conduct of every private family can scarcely be folly in that of a great kingdom. If a foreign country can supply us with a commodity cheaper than we ourselves can make it, better buy it of them with some part of our own industry."[10] According to Samuelson, "free trade promotes a mutually profitable division of labor, greatly enhances the potential real national product of all nations, and makes possible higher standards of living all over the globe."[11] Trade barriers are thus inimical to economic development. Liberal economists go so far as to assert that in an asymmetrical trade relationship in which country A's markets are relatively open and country B's markets protected, country's A's economy will develop while country B's stagnates.[12]

Alas, there is often a severe gap between theory and reality. It is a pity that Lewis Carroll is not alive to write about Alice's adventures in the mythical land of liberal economic theory. The gap between liberal economic theory and reality is so vast that one sometimes suspects that its adherents have been imbibing the White Rabbit's magic potion. Liberal economic theory is deeply flawed. Attractive as economic liberalism appears at first glance, its Utopian assumptions and tenets are rarely if ever duplicated in the real world: consumers and producers supposedly enjoy "perfect knowledge"; markets are shaped by "perfect competition"; the comparative advantage of a nation's goods and services is determined by natural endowments; technology is stagnant; there is no unemployment, foreign trade, politics, or government. This is the world in which neoclassical economists busily construct the two dimensional equations, graphs, and maxims which are then used to shape American economic policy and outlook.

Henry Clay exposed the emptiness of liberal theory when he wrote: "The call for free trade is as unavailing as the cry of a spoiled child in its nurse's arms for the moon or stars or the glitter in the firmament of heaven. It never has existed. And never will."[13] There are no free markets in the modern world; politics and economics are intricately intertwined. Every government manages its economy; economic management differs only in its skill, degree, and direction from one country to the next. Countries like Japan, South Korea, Taiwan, and Singapore which have carefully managed their economies by targeting strategic industries have grown the fastest, while the United States, which more than any other major economy has tried to restrain the role of government in managing the economy, has grown the slowest of the OECD countries. Yet, even Washington, despite its free trade pretensions, interferes deeply in the economy, picking winners and losers. The winners, however, are the loudest whiners – those with the most political clout enjoy the most protection. Robert Kuttner writes that liberal economic theory "to most of the world . . . seems utopian and the practice hypocritical. America seems to practice a chaotic *ad hoc* mercantilism – weapons procurement, farm price supports, textile quotas, and various 'voluntary' restraints extracted from trading partners – while it stridently preaches free trade."[14] Neoclassical economists have blinded themselves to these basic realities.

Liberalism posits a static notion of comparative advantage in which nations produce only those things in which they have a "natural" advantage and import everything else. The theory does not differentiate between the different development levels among states and the resulting implications for future development. This argument was perhaps best summed up by Friedrich List, a nineteenth-century German political economist. After studying the economy of Great Britain, the world's first industrial state to champion free trade, List advised Germany against free trade, arguing that:

> . . . free competition between two nations which are highly civilized can only be mutually beneficial in case both of them are in a nearly equal position of industrial development, and that any nation which owing to misfortunes is behind others in industry, commerce, navigation . . . must first of all strengthen her own individual powers, in order to fit herself to enter into free competition with more advanced nations.[15]

John Spanier elaborates the argument:

> the free market may well be a superior mechanism for allocating goods, when those competing and exchanging goods are of approximately equal power. When one nation is clearly more advanced economically however, free trade benefits it more because it is able to penetrate the markets of weaker countries. The laws of the free market are not neutral. Power is the 'invisible hand' determining the distribution of wealth. Among nations that are equal in economic power, economic relations may well breed interdependence, as in the EEC and relations between them and the United States. But between the economically

strong and the economically weak, the inevitable result is the
dependence of the latter.[16]

The theory also assumes that all products are of equal importance to a
nation's economy – that either surfboards or satellites will do if their
production value is the same. David Ricardo, for example, argued in 1817
that Britain and Portugal should concentrate on producing cloth and
wine, respectively, since that is what each produces best. But simply
focusing on a product's production value while failing to differentiate
between the effect of products on the entire economy can hobble a nation's
development. If, for example:

> the Portugese follow the Western theory of comparative advantage,
> they are sacrificing long-term growth for short-term gains and
> implicitly accepting a lower standard of living than the British . . .
> the . . . implications for a (liberal) economic strategy are likely to lead
> to second rate performance at best . . . To stick with these natural
> advantages is to accept a lower rate of growth and technology
> development simply because it is a "natural state of affairs," for
> which, unfortunately, there is no remedy.[17]

Industries and products vary considerably in the ripple effects their
production has in stimulating or retarding the rest of the economy. A
nation's comparative advantage in steel or semiconductors, for example,
can also provide a comparative advantage for a range of other heavy and
high technology industries, respectively. Pet rocks, mood rings and
dancing flowers were undoubtedly very profitable to their "creators",
but were of questionable value in promoting America's economic development.

The trouble with economic liberalism is that in a

> world of static comparative advantage free trade favors the rich and the
> strong – those with natural resources and high levels of productivity in
> major growth industries. They can undersell newcomers in less-
> fortunate or less-developed countries and maintain their favored
> position. The issue is not so much "exploitation" of the weak as a
> "natural state of affairs" governed by an efficient impersonal market-
> place. It is not surprising that the leading advocates of free trade have
> been those who were strong at the time, first the United Kingdom, then
> the United States . . . Free trade, like free competition, has political as
> well as economic content: taken literally it is a system that enhances the
> power of the powerful and makes it all the more difficult for the poor to
> catch up.[18]

Nations do not have to confine themselves fatalistically to the products in which they seem "naturally" best endowed. Comparative advantage can be created. In their book, *Politics and Productivity: the Real Story of Why Japan's Economy Works*, Johnson, Zysman and Tyson present a systematic, devastating attack on liberal theory, and its "new trade" variant.[19] The authors argue that although markets may reflect present efficiencies, they are unable to predict future products and industries, let alone which will be most profitable and dynamic. Of course, no one can predict the future with certainty, but it is obvious which future industries and products will be dynamic cores of an increasingly complex economy. The trouble is that the development costs of "strategic transformative industries" like micro-electronics, superconductors, new materials, and biotechnology, to name a few, are beyond the means of even the largest corporations. Only the government has the financial and organizational power to advance these industries. Yet, despite this reality, liberals continue to assert that only impersonal markets and not governments should pick economic winners and losers. This attitude's grip on Washington policymakers is the biggest obstacle to any revival of American power.[20]

Paradoxically, liberal theory does allow states to protect "infant industries" until they have been nurtured into industries capable of competing in global markets. But "infant industry" protection raises many questions which liberal economists cannot answer. Should protection from the market's magic be extended to every new industry proposed by entreprenuers? If not, what new industries should a state protect? And how does picking winners and losers jive with the notion that governments should not do so? Entrepreneurs would presumably not venture into an new industry unless they received protection from the first blueprints. Thus, governments would have to protect the industry from conception to maturity. And, using the logic that comparative advantage can be created, if the state can protect "infants" why not "ailing" industries that have temporarily lost their comparative advantage if the owners promise to revitalize those industries? The liberal notion of infant industry protection reveals deep contradictions in liberal theory – government is bad except when it protects infant industries; the market, not government should pick winners and losers, unless it happens to be an infant industry.

Other weaknesses in liberal theory abound. Although the consumer is supposedly king in a free market economy, in reality, demand is often created by the producers themselves through slick advertizing campaigns that appeal to the human need to be either like everyone else or the "first on their block" to have something new. Likewise, although liberal economists make the consumer king, they talk little about workers or producers. Liberal theory's "exclusive focus on the consumer tended to obscure the other side of the equation. Never calculated were the expense of retraining and moving displaced workers or of unemployment compensation, lost tax revenue, and social costs such as stress related health care and family and marriage counseling".[21] Gilpin points out a related flaw: "although traditional trade theory maintains that the benefits of trade and specialization will always be greater than its costs, it has assumed a relatively slow rate of change . . . so that displacement of workers is gradual and associated adjustment costs are low".[22] If the assumptions on which liberal theory is based are not valid, the theory itself is questionable at best.

Neomercantilism is not an abstract theory, it is a very real strategy for achieving economic development and political power. The strategy assumes that comparative advantage can be created and does not have to be fatalistically inherited as liberal theory maintains. Trade is a zero-sum game in which one state's gains are another's loss – states accumulate wealth by running continual trade surpluses. It also assumes that industries vary according to what they contribute to overall economic development. Steel or semiconductors are considered more important to the economy than surfboards or skateboards, even if their market value is identical, because those "strategic industries" represent value-added products which form the foundations for scores of other industries and provide high paying jobs for white and blue collar workers.

Strategic industries are targeted for development with a range of incentives that can include loans, grants, or tax reductions, cartels, technology infusions, import restrictions and export incentives. "Industrial policy" can be defined as any government initiatives "that will improve growth, productivity, and competitiveness", including "increasing the economy's supply potential (that is, increasing resources, and labor supply and capital stock), developing technology, fostering industrial development, and improving mobility and structural adaptation" or "a complex set of trade, financial, and fiscal policies, conducted within a political environment, with outcomes at variance from market solutions."[23]

But every industry has some value, and all are protected in varying ways and degrees. Consequently, neomercantilist states only import essential raw materials and intermediate goods that cannot be produced at a reasonable cost are allowed unrestricted entry. Protected at home from competitive foreign imports, firms dump their excess production abroad to capture markets, thus achieving ever greater scale production which reduces costs, and increases profits and comparative advantage, while it correspondingly weakens foreign rivals. The conquest of foreign markets is assisted through investments by the neomercantilist's firms in foreign strategic sectors, huge payoffs to key political and economic leaders who open more gates for even deeper penetration, and, for developing countries, aid tied to purchases of the donor country's goods and services.

Wealth, thus, is used to create yet more wealth and the political power that accompanies it. New industries and thus new wealth are amassed that would not have existed with free trade. International trade and power, in a neomercantilist world, is shaped by bilateral rather than multilateral agreements, with the balance of benefits varying according to the relative power of the states involved. If the states have roughly equal power the economic relationship will be mutually beneficial, but if power is unequal, the stronger state will exploit the weaker state.

Neomercantilist theory differs from classic mercantilist theory on one key point – the importance of the military. Neomercantilist states only maintain a military large enough to deter attacks on their home territory. Any military force large enough to project power overseas is considered a waste of valuable economic assets and actually diminishes a state's overall power as key technological, intellectual and financial resources are diverted from export or mass consumer good industries that fuel economic growth and prosperity.

A liberal state will not survive long in a global trade system in which most states practice neomercantilist policies because it would run continual, devastating trade deficits and either end up bankrupt, protectionist, or both. On the other hand, a neomercantilist state's survival in a liberal system would depend on the willingness of other states to tolerate such policies, which in turn depends on how disruptive those policies are to the international system as a whole.

All states use industrial policies – the difference is whether they are created through predominately *ad hoc* political means as in the United States or comprehensive planning as in Japan. States also vary considerably in the success of their industrial policies. Scott and Lodge's comparison of the five leading industrial countries revealed that Japan was the only country whose industrial policies were consistently successful. Between 1967 and 1981, Japan gained market share in thirteen of twenty industries targeted for development, remained the same in three, and lost out in four. The four losers were all chemical industries which did fine until their "created" comparative advantage was undercut by the quadrupling of oil prices in 1973. In comparison, the four other key industrial countries – the United States, France, Germany, and Britain – stagnated or lost ground.[24]

What are the effects of neomercantilism on global trade? The shift from a largely liberal to neomercantilist global political economy will not affect global trade volume, which will continue to expand at the 6–8 per cent annual rate of the late 1980s. Transactions will increasingly be based on managed rather than the free trade. Even the United States is increasingly mixing managed with free trade policies in specific threatened sectors. In 1975, only 8 per cent of American imports were protected; in 1985, about

25 per cent were protected. Although all this is anathema to liberal economists, Reich argues that free trade should not be "an end in itself, but a means to a higher living standard for the world's people. Government interventions that make economic transitions smoother, more equitable, and more efficient can serve precisely this purpose".[25]

HEGEMONY

Some analysts identify a succession of states whose power was so vast that they overshadowed the power of all other states and thus dominated and shaped the evolution of the global political economy. "Hegemons" share the ability "to dictate, or at least dominate, the rules and arrangements by which international relations, economic and political, are conducted . . . Economic hegemony implies the ability to center the world economy around itself. Political hegemony means being able to dominate the world militarily".[26] Hegemony clearly must involve "productive, commercial, and financial as well as political and military power".[27]

How do states become hegemons? Although a hegemon does not necessarily need to have the world's largest economy, it must excel in controlling vital sources of capital, markets, raw materials and technology, thus allowing a comparative advantage in the production of highly valued goods. Countries with well-developed financial markets can supply their industries and allies with cheap credit and deny it to rivals. A hegemon also needs a large domestic market in which its products can achieve economies of scale, while foreign access to that market can be used to either reward compliance or punish transgressions of the hegemon's policies. A hegemon does not necessarily have to own the supplies of essential raw material and energy resources that fuel its industries, and agriculture which feeds its people, but it must have unhindered access to cheap, diversified, dependable supplies. Hegemons maintain a comparative advantage for their products by leading in the creation and application of technology. Comparative advantage does not mean that the hegemon exports everything but that it produces and exports the most profitable products and those that will provide the basis for producing even more advanced goods and services in the future.[28] A hegemonic state must also possess enough military power to be able to protect the global political economy from challengers. The final ingredient of hegemony is political will, or the desire to make and enforce the rules governing the global political economy, and pay most of the political, economic, military costs of its upkeep. The United States, for example, held predominant economic and military power following World War I, but lacked the will to maintain the global political economy.

How do hegemons assert their influence over other states and the global political economy? Why do most states follow the hegemon's policies most of the time? Like any other assertion of power, the hegemon bends other states to its will through a combination of coercion and persuasion. The hegemon's ability either to reward or deny another state markets, aid, investments, finance, technology, and/or military assistance are key elements of command. But perhaps the most important ingredient of hegemonic power is the hegemon's ability to create and impose an ideology on the global political economy which justifies and explains the system, and elicits other states' compliance. According to Ikenberry and Kupchan, "elites in secondary states buy into and internalize norms that are articulated by the hegemon and therefore pursue policies consistent with the hegemon's notion of international order".[29]

The ability of hegemons to socialize other states into the system is strongest after wars and political crises which discredit the existing international and national systems. Hegemons socialize other states into the system by linking the extension or denial of material benefits with a coherent ideology. This socialization process "leads to a consolidation of hegemonic power; rule based on might is enhanced by rule based on right. Furthermore, it is less costly; the hegemon can expend fewer economic and military resources to secure compliance".[30] Successful hegemonic leadership thus depends on a dynamic "intertwining of socioeconomic, political, and ideological structures" embedded in a particular economic system, which "limit the bounds of what is understood to be legitimate policy choice, thereby securing" the hegemon's continued dominance.[31]

Although most analysts agree on these basic requirements for and assertion of hegemony, they are split over a range of other key questions. What states were hegemons? Analysts are divided. Chase Dunn, for example, identifies three hegemons of the modern age: Holland, 17th century; Britain, 19th century; and United States, 20th century; while Modelski identifies five: Portugal, 16th century; Holland, 17th century; Britain twice, 18th & 19th centuries; and the United States, 20th century.[32]

How much power does it take to achieve hegemony? When does a state's power become and when does it cease to be hegemonic? All the analysts are foggy over how and when a state wins and loses the hegemony title. A comparison of British and American power illustrates the vagueness of hegemony's requirements. Gilpin points out that at Britain's peak of power in 1860, its GNP exceeded that of its nearest European rival, Russia, by only 12 per cent. By contrast, in 1950, America's aggregate economic output was 173 per cent greater than that of the Soviet Union, the second largest economic actor, and 327 per cent greater than that of Britain, the third largest actor.[33] In addition, Britain was never as superior in productivity to the rest of the world as the United States was after 1945, nor was the United States ever as dependent on foreign trade and investment as Britain. Also, while America's economic partners were also its military allies, Britain's chief trading partners were its major military and political rivals. The comparison is further clouded by asking Gilpin how he determined Britain's power peaked in 1860 – why not 1914?

The analytical confusion is deepened further when other "hegemons" are examined. Portugal was the first power to establish trading posts on the shores of Africa and Asia, but why does that make it a hegemon when similar posts were soon established by the Spanish on those same shores as well as throughout much of the Western Hemisphere? Holland was certainly a feisty naval power throughout the mid-17th century, humbling Britain and Spain in several world-wide naval wars and establishing small colonies in Sumatra, the Carribean and elsewhere. But why does that make Holland a hegemon? And why is not 17th century Spain with its vast empire in the Western hemisphere, global trade routes, and immense riches considered a hegemon?

The notion that hegemony is achieved through persuasion rather than coercion makes questionable the assumption that hegemons have existed since a global trade system was first knit together in the 15th century. During the age of mercantilism, each great power maintained its own global trade regime centered on trade with its colonies; there was little economic intercourse between the trade powers within Europe or overseas. Thus, the major naval power may have been able to conquer its rivals' possessions and carve out new ones but was unable to dominate all trade relations within the expanding global economy. Hegemonic and imperial power differ greatly. While an imperial power uses coercion to force others to comply to a largely exploitative system, a hegemon cannot make and enforce rules without a certain degree of consent from other sovereign states in a system that is mutually beneficial. Thus, hegemons must accomplish by persuasion what imperial powers achieve by coercion. In a hegemonic system, power is primarily consensual – the hegemon must convince others that every state that participates in the system will benefit.[34]

Gilpin dismisses the claims that any hegemons bestrode the global political economy before the 19th century.[35] Until then the great powers carved out empires for their largely exclusive reserve, and any trade between them was limited by mercantilist policies whereby each state attempted to maximize exports and minimize imports. Thus, there was not one unified global political economy but as many systems as there were great powers. Since hegemons are distinguished from imperial powers by dominating a system by persuasion and example rather than force, Gilpin maintains that the first global hegemon was Great Britain when it attempted to convince the other great powers to abandon mercantilism and embrace liberalism as the basis of the global system. Through its consistent, strenuous efforts throughout the 19th century, Britain was eventually able to mesh each of the half dozen great power systems into one.

However, it can be argued that if we distinguish between imperial and hegemonic power, only the United States can be considered a true hegemon since the power of all previous "hegemons", including Britain, had imperial roots. American power, in contrast, has largely depended on Washington's ability to persuade rather than coerce other states into following its lead in participating in a liberal global political economy and defending it from the Soviet Union.

Washington has actively championed free trade since the Roosevelt Administration took office in 1932. Roosevelt was determined to pull the United States and world out of a depression largely caused when Congress passed the 1930 Smoot Hawley Act which boosted tariffs 50 per cent and imposed quotas on competitive imports. American hegemony begins with the passage of the 1934 Reciprocal Trade Agreements Act which authorized the President to negotiate free trade treaties with other nations. Although the White House signed 34 bilateral trade agreements between 1934 and 1945, its most important action was to sponsor the international conference attended by 44 nations at Bretton Woods, New Hampshire in 1944. The conference's objective was to create international organizations which would revive and manage the global political economy and prevent the beggar thy neighbor policies which collapsed world trade in the 1930s. Treaties were signed creating the International Bank for Reconstruction and Development (IBRD, World Bank) and International Monetary Fund (IMF), institutions designed to aid postwar reconstruction and overcome balance of payments problems, respectively.

Congress renewed the President's authority to negotiate tariff reductions in 1945. That December an international conference in Washington called for future multilateral negotiations to conclude a tariff reduction treaty. In February 1946, the UN resolved that a conference should be formed to draft a International Trade Organization (ITO) charter. Washington published a draft charter for such an organization, and in October 1946 a committee first met in London to refine the proposal. At the third charter meeting in Geneva in October 1947, the representatives of 23 countries continued working on the charter and signed the General Agreement on Tariffs and Trade (GATT). The charter for the ITO was completed and signed in Havana in 1948. Unfortunately, a Republican dominated Congress refused to ratify the ITO and the other signatories refused to form an ITO without American participation.

GATT was only supposed to be a treaty, not an organization, but with the ITO's demise GATT became the central international organization promoting trade liberalization. GATT is based on the most favored nation (MFN) principle, in which any trade barriers that a contracting party negotiates with another country must be granted to all other contracting parties. There are some significant exceptions to this principle. GATT does allow the existence of regional and other types of trade arrangements which are considered to enhance world trade. The twelve nation European Community (EC) free trade region and UNCTAD in which industrial countries allow developing countries special tariff reductions for their products are the two most prominent MFN exceptions.

GATT has had a major if not decisive effect on stimulating global trade expansion. Since its founding, GATT has conducted eight intensive rounds of tariff and other trade barrier reduction negotiations, of which the last three, the Kennedy (1962–67), Tokyo (1973–79) and Uruguay (1986–90) were the most significant. The average tariff cut during the Kennedy Round was 35 per cent on $40 billion worth of trade and Tokyo Round was 34 per cent on $155 billion of trade.[36] The Uruguay Round, in contrast, broke up in December 1990 deadlocked over agricultural subsidies and intellectual property issues. Despite the disappointing results of the last round, GATT has negotiated the reduction of tariffs to today's average 4.7 per cent, as well as attempted to alleviate predatory export practices such as dumping and subsidies, nontariff barriers, trade in services and agriculture, and balance of payment problems There are currently 107 contracting parties with most other countries eager to join. Impressive as these accomplishments are, over 60 nations and at least a quarter of world trade falls outside of MFN principles.[37]

America's economic hegemony, however, was shortlived – at most from World War II to perhaps the early 1970s. During that time Washington largely achieved its goals: it created and nurtured a range of institutional pillars of the global political economy, including the UN, GATT, IMF and World Bank; encouraged the growth of the European Community and transformed Japan into an economic superpower; convinced most developing countries to join the global economy; and through its containment policies prevented the Soviet empire from undermining the system. But the economic, political, military, and psychological costs of these achievements was exorbitant, and Washington was unable to prevent the steady erosion of American economic power to the point where Japan has deposed the United States from the throne of economic hegemony. Even America's vast military power has not been supreme. Washington's power to promote its national interests has varied considerably from one region to the next and in many regions has been virtually nonexistent. Despite its vast nuclear and conventional military power, the web of alliances it forged and the many times its troops intervened overseas, Washington was never able to dominate the world militarily.

There were always constraints on the exercise of American military power, even in nearby Cuba or Central America.

Why do hegemons rise and fall? Hegemony involves a dilemma. A hegemon's prosperity depends on an open global trade system in which its corporations can sell their products and thus increase the nation's wealth and power. Yet, in order to entice other states into joining the system, the hegemon must make its own markets, technology and capital freely available to its economic rivals. Inevitably, some states enjoy "free" or "cheap" economic and defense rides while refusing to reciprocate. By tolerating these free riders, the hegemon inevitably sows the seeds of its future decline. The more powerful the free rider, the more rapid the hegemon's economic decline. In the early 20th century, the United States free rode itself to hegemony on the back of Britain's tremendous economic, political, and military burdens; Japan, in turn has supplanted American hegemony with its own through its neomercantilist policies since 1945.

A hegemon's tenure over the global political economy depends on its ability to root its global commitments in economic dynamism. A hegemon declines when its commitments exceed its ability to pay for them. Nye succinctly summarizes "imperial overreach" as when "a Great Power becomes exhausted through the protection of its far flung interests. International commitments sap its strength at home, while rising challengers profit from the public order, global economic growth, and diffusion of the hegemon's technology. Eventually, the hegemon is replaced by a rising challanger which may be a military opponent or one of its former allies".[38] Wallerstein identifies a hegemon's economic deterioration as the key reason for its decline: "the overall productivity edge relative to that of the closest rival states . . . had begun to fritter away because of aging plant (in the loosest sense of this term) and rising comparative costs of the factors of production, combined with the high economic costs of political and military imperium which led to rising taxation levels".[39]

Although Washington's policies since 1945 provide a classic example of a state's inability to overcome the hegemon's dilemma, Rosecrance and Taw write that, historically, every hegemon has pursued policies that ultimately undermined its own power and wealth:

> in the seventeenth century, Holland did not bargain effectively with England, and . . . did not close its markets despite the discrimination it suffered under the latter's navigation acts. Great Britain did not bargain with Germany or France to open continental markets after 1860, and generally remained on a free-trade standard until 1931. The United States allowed – indeed even encouraged – considerable European and Japanese discrimination against itself in the period

immediately following World War II. Moreover, the U.S. did not greatly curtail its markets in the 1970s and 1980s when exportation of its agricultural and industrial products was limited by Europe and Japan. In all three cases, the result was the leader declined rapidly under the burden of maintaining the system.

The fact is that the old hegemonic leader greatly assisted the rise of the new. Dutch capital largely financed British commercial and industrial growth at the end of the seventeenth century and the beginning of the eighteenth century. Similarly, British investments provided an essential stimulus to the growth of the United States . . . (and) the growing British market – the dominant consumer market of the time – helped spur both German and American industrial development . . . The United States provided not only a great deal of economic aid to Japan in the aftermath of the war, but also sustained the latter's growth through offshore procurement of Japanese goods . . . Finally, the US offered a crucial market in the 1970s and 1980s, when the rest of the world could not absorb the surging output of Japanese factories.[40]

The authors add one final zinger to these tales of hegemonic decay: "The paradox is rendered more acute when one recalls that the decaying hegemonic leaders – Holland, England, and the United States – were well aware of what was happening to them."[41]

THE CHANGING NATURE OF INTERNATIONAL RELATIONS

As far back as 1795, Immanuel Kant predicted in his "Essay on Perpetual Peace" that the global political economy would eventually evolve into a system in which conflicts are resolved by peaceful cooperation rather than war.[42] Kant foresaw three developments which would lead to a "perpetual peace": (1) the conversion of authoritarian states into liberal democracies (republicanism); (2) the evolution of international law and organization into an authoritative system which binds all sovereign states (federalism); and (3) economic development and interdependence (hospitality). Is the manifestation of international power changing as global interdependence steadily deepens, the Cold War abruptly ends, and democratic states are taking root amidst the rumble of a collapsed Soviet empire? Scholars are divided over these and related questions.

Many scholars continue to maintain a geopolitical or "realist" world view in which international relations are characterized as a "war of all against all" as states continually battle for scarce territorial, economic, and natural resources. States, at a minimum, "seek their own preservation, and, at a maximum, drive for universal domination".[43] But whether states either attempt to protect or disrupt the international status quo, they are regardless obsessed with ensuring national survival. In an anarchic system, states are constrained only by their interaction with other states in the system. There is a clear hierarchy of issues in a "realist" world as "high political" issues of security and diplomacy push aside "low political" issues of commerce and welfare. Power is determined by prowess either on the battlefield or at the negotiating table, with the use or threat of the use of military force usually the deciding factor. War determines the actual ratio of power; bargaining, either the perceived or actual ratio of power. Yet, paradoxically, this reliance on force creates a "security dilemma" whereby the insecurity of all states in the system compels each to strive for greater security by engaging in a constant scramble for increased power; policies designed to increase one's own power by definition decrease the security of others, thus driving others to increase their power. The result is a perpetual arms race and constant tension.[44]

International relations is largely dominated by the great powers, and it is the distribution of power among them that determines the system's structure, major processes, and general evolution. Shifts in the balance of power alter the system's structure, and change every state's behavior. Competition continues but the new distribution of power leads to new alignments. There is no such thing as peace at any price; peace is subordinate to, first, national security interests, and, second, balance of power interests. The balance of military power determines the balance of economic power. When the distribution of power and international political relations change, corresponding changes may be expected to take place in global economic relations.[45] Gilpin writes that "every economic system rests on a particular political order; its nature cannot be understood aside from politics".[46]

This classic view of international relations is rejected by a growing body of analysts with a geoeconomic outlook. While acknowledging that geopolitics may have dominated past international relations, the geoeconomists assert that as the world becomes increasingly tightly bound by a web of economic, nuclear, moral, and environmental relations, conflicts are increasingly over economic and human welfare rather than territory and ideology. Instead of a world whose relations are characterized by violence and anarchy, there is instead an increasingly orderly world in which the nature and effectiveness of power varies according to what the issue is, how other issues and priorities are related to it, and how skillfully the participants bargain.[47] According to this view, state goals remain the same: states strive for strategic and economic security. But the means to achieve those ends have greatly changed. Rosecrance neatly summarizes the differences between a geopolitical and geoeconomic outlook:

in a power world states act as coherent units, force is a usable instrument of policy and there is a hierarchy of international issues dominated by questions of military security. Interdependence refers to a world in which states can no longer fully regulate policy, there are multiple channels of access between societies, no hierarchy of issues, and force is generally unusable. The difference between these two systems concerns the means that are used to advance state interests.[48]

Although geopolitical and geoeconomic systems differ greatly in the way power is massed and utilized, success in both systems depends on governments skillfully entering a virtuous circle of power and wealth. States in a territorial system enhance their power and wealth through military aggression, by using force to maximize their self-sufficiency in population, natural resources and land, which in turn is mobilized into an ever stronger military. States in a trade system enhance their power and wealth through economic aggression by using economic force in global markets to accumulate wealth which is then reinvested in strategic industries which lower costs, increase technology inputs, and thus capture even larger market share.

Other scholars have concisely characterized these two parallel systems. Nye sees the world political economy as composed of a range of "systems" each having a different distribution of power, making such broad characteristics of the world as bipolar or multipower increasingly meaningless. He writes that:

> different issues in world politics have different distributions of power. Military power, particularly at the nuclear level, remains largely bipolar . . . But in trade . . . power is multipolar. Ocean resources, money, space, shipping and airlines each have somewhat different distributions of power. The power of states varies as well, as does the significance of nonstate actors in different issues . . . (S)pecifying the context is increasingly important in estimating the actual power that can be derived from power resources. More than in previous times, one must ask the question, 'Power for what'?[49]

Brown also sees complex interdependence creating a condition of global polyarchy, or

> a situation of many communities, spheres of influence, hegemonic imperiums, interdependencies, and trans-state loyalties . . . that exhibit no clearly dominant axis of alignment and antagonism and has no central steering group or agency . . . (m)ajor participants in the widest variety of coalitions and joint or multilateral ventures . . . would have

the largest supply of usable political currency – in effect . . . support on one issue in return for support on another.[50]

International relations has always been overwelmingly shaped by geoeconomics, or conflict management through peaceful means. Although wars will always grab the headlines, the "realists" are anything but realistic in their highly selective account of international relations since they obscure and outright distort the reality that most states are at peace most and sometimes all the time. How do the realists explain the virtual absence of international war in Latin America following independence in the 1820s? The Latin American states presumably could have resorted to war to protect or expand their national territory or other interests. Why didn't they? Even in Europe – until 1945 the world's most war prone area – many states have opted out of the balance of power. After 1713, Holland, and 1815, Spain and Sweden dropped out of the great power game, not from military defeat, but because of their respective leadership's conviction that national interests could be much better served through peaceful rather than military means. Other states such as Denmark, Switzerland and Portugal have also tried and largely succeeded in refusing to get caught up in Europe's balance of power system.

It is simply no longer true – if it ever was – that international relations is characterized by constant threats to a state's sovereignty by other states. The so called "realist" view is just not very realistic. Wars or threats of war may make front page news, but most countries are at peace most of the time. Geoeconomic, not geopolitical, conflict is now the norm in contemporary international relations.

How did these tremendous changes in international relations occur? These changes first began to manifest themselves not in 1945, but in 1789. In the old, simple Europe of feudal levies and economies, security was viewed in narrow territorial and military terms. Differences in geographical location, and population and resource endowments determined a state's foreign policy. The era of the French revolution introduced new forces into international relations: nationalism, mass politics and expansionist political ideologies. Since then, these forces have become increasingly important factors in balance of power calculations and served to demolish the realist assertion that states are monolithic actors whose roles are solely determined by the distribution of power. The demands of nationalism, mass politics and ideology shape a nation's foreign policy in ways that often conflict with a pure power politics orientation. States with similar power endowments may have completely different foreign policies. A state's foreign policy reflects the interaction of its domestic political, economic, and cultural system with the international environment. Different national characteristics result in different "world views" and "national styles." This determines the way a policymaking elite interprets and interacts with the world.[51]

The rise of the democratic industrial state brought a shift from a "high politics" emphasis on military security issues to a "low politics" emphasis on welfare; geoeconomic interests have eclipsed geopolitical interests in importance for most democratic states. Democratic countries have never warred against each other. Why? A common democratic ideology and economic interdependence prevents democratic states from going to war against each other. The implications of this are profound. Levy states that the "absence of war between democracies comes as close as anything we have to an empirical law in international relations".[52] It follows that, as more states become democratic, the possibility of war decreases accordingly, and if all states were genuine democracies, war would cease to plague humankind, thus fulfilling Kant's dream.

Encouraging as the propensity for peace among democratic states is, Levy points out that "democratic states have been involved proportionately in as many wars as nondemocratic states".[53] According to Doyle, the reason for continued armed conflict between democratic and authoritarian states is that "the very constitutional restraint, shared commercial interests, and international respect for individual rights that promote peace among liberal societies can exacerbate conflicts in relations between liberal and nonliberal societies".[54]

Thus, the democratic revolutions sweeping Eastern Europe, Latin America, and elsewhere in the late 1980s and 1990s, the corresponding demise of communism's appeal, and the Cold War's end bring the promise of ever more peaceful relations among states. Marxism-Leninism is an imperialistic ideology which advocates the overthrow of all governments and imposition of communist rule. As the first communist regime and a great military power, the Soviet Union proclaimed itself to be the leader of the communist movement and subsequently, incorporated Eastern Europe into its empire, threatened the West with a massive military buildup, and formented revolution across the Third World. Communist countries warred and competed not just against the democratic West, but against each other, as the conflicts between the Soviet Union and China, and China and Vietnam revealed. Communism also wars against the people upon which it is imposed, as the "revolutionaries" simply replace one exploitive, parasitic ruling elite with one led by themselves, and in so doing utterly fail to develop the country. Washington's containment policy combined with communism's internal contradictions and failure to develop made its eventual destruction inevitable.

No place better symbolized the stark choices and titanic struggle between liberal democracy and communism than cruelly divided Berlin – the West prosperous, creative, free, and beseiged; the East occupied, sullen, crumbling, exploited. On 9 November 1989, the Cold War symbolically ended with the Berlin Wall's destruction. Germany itself was soon reunited while mass democratic movements toppled communist dictatorships throughout East Europe. One year after the Berlin Wall crumbled, the Conference on Security and Cooperation in Europe (CSCE) met at Versailles on 19–21 November 1990. The 34 participants, including the NATO and Warsaw members, lauded Germany's reunification, encouraged faster disarmament, and institutionalized the gathering with the objective of accelerating and easing the revolutionary changes taking place. On 30 June and 1 July 1991, respectively, with surprisingly little fanfare, the economic and military chains of Moscow's domination over East Europe – Comecon and the Warsaw Pact – ceased to exist. Global peace is greatly enhanced with communism's destruction, the Warsaw Pact's demise, the breakup of the Russian empire and Moscow's rapid reduction of its vast military industrial complex.

The rise of democracy and demise of communism is only one major reason for transformation of international relations from geopolitical to largely geoeconomic conflicts. War is becoming increasingly obsolete as an foreign policy means because the costs in most cases far exceed the benefits. Before the political and industrial revolutions, wars were fought by small professional armies, destruction was relatively limited, and territorial gains directly translated into power gains as a state incorporated more potential soldiers and peasants into its realm. But the French Revolution initiated the modern era of mass warfare fought as much for ideological as territorial objectives, and the industrial revolution vastly expanded war's destructiveness. Wars between the great powers remained rational foreign policy tools, however, up through 1945 since the conquest of territory could enhance a state's power by the incorporation of more people, natural resources, farms, and factories.

Nineteen forty-five was the great divide for the use of military power. Gilpin writes that

> it was not until after 1945 that the threat of an all out military conflict (including the use of nuclear and thermonuclear bombs) became catastrophic so that such wars as did occur took on a more limited character. The risks of trying to take new territory through military invasion mounted while the alternative of development through rational industrial and trade policies heralded new rewards for a peaceful strategy. This shift . . . has largely escaped notice in the study of international politics.[55]

The nuclear balance of terror (Mutually Assured Destruction, MAD) prevented the United States and Soviet Union from going over the brink to war when, given their vastly conflicting geopolitical and ideological difference, they most certainly would have gone to war had such weapons not existed. Between 1945 and 1949, the United States was the only country to possess atomic power, and from then, when the Soviets exploded their first atomic bomb, until the late 1960s when the Soviet ICBM fleet achieved a rough parity with that of the United States, Washington had an overwelming superiority in nuclear power. Yet despite almost a quarter century of nuclear hegemony, the White House never seriously considered using its nuclear power to resolve any crisis or war, let alone the Cold War with the Soviet Union.

Nuclear superiority, however, may well have prevented at least ten crises from escalated into war. In his book, *Nuclear Blackmail and Nuclear Balance*, Richard Betts carefully examined those times when Washington's nuclear superiority either probably prevented war or protected American interests in four crises – Cuba (1962), Berlin (1948), Korea (1953) and Taiwan (1955), and were of uncertain value in the another six – Berlin (1958–1961), Middle East (1973), Suez (1956), Lebannon (1958), Taiwan (1958), and the Gulf (1980).[56] Nye, however, argues that American nuclear superiority may not have been a decisive factor in any of these crises. He writes: "American efforts to use nuclear influence was affected more by the balance of interests (that is, which state had the higher stakes in the status quo) than by the balance of power. The decline in the number of US nuclear threats is striking, but it says more about Soviet policies and nuclear learning in both countries than it does about a decline in American power."[57]

In fact, ever since Moscow launched Sputnik in 1957, many Americans have perceived a Soviet nuclear superiority. John Kennedy in 1960 and Ronald Reagan in 1980 both won the presidency in part by claiming the United States was suffering a "missile gap" or "window of vulnerability" with the Soviets. Once in office both presidents embarked on massive military buildups that severely strained the American economy. The Reagan Administration tripled the size of the defense budget – and America's national debt – between 1981 and 1988. Yet all these efforts were in vain – there was no Soviet nuclear superiority then or at any time. And even if the Soviets had been superior, there was no window of vulnerability. Even if the Soviets launched a first strike and destroyed both of America's land based ICBMs, one American nuclear submarine could have then destroyed two hundred Soviet cities. Although the United States could have "won" a nuclear war at least up through the mid-1960s, MAD would have devastated not only the Soviet Union and United States, but through nuclear winter possibly destroyed all human life.

Likewise, there has been a stable conventional balance of power between NATO and the Warsaw Pact. Any Soviet tank or artillery advantage was offset by NATO air superiority and the advantages of being on the defensive. Perhaps the most important NATO advantage was that its members could be relied upon to fight in the event of a war. Moscow had a genuine fear that the Polish or Hungarian army might as easily turn its guns on the Russians as on NATO troops. Moscow backed away from the brink of war during the first (1948–49) and second (1958–59) Berlin crises, and the Cuban missile crisis because it well knew that it would lose a conventional war with NATO.

Although a nuclear and conventional balance of power among the superpowers may well have prevented war from breaking out between them, it did not inhibit either Washington or Moscow, as well as many other powers from intervening throughout the Third World since 1945. But the effectiveness of great power military interventions in the Third World is increasingly questionable. Gunboat diplomacy is just not cost-efficient anymore. Effective use of nationalism, modern arms, the mass media, and international organizations like the United Nations have empowered Third World countries to successfully resist Great Power intervention. India, Pakistan, Israel and South Africa are already thought to have nuclear weapons while others like Iraq may acquire that capacity within a decade. At least twenty Third World countries including Iraq and Libya either already employ or could employ chemical weapons. Countries like Brazil, South Africa and Israel are major arms exporters. As the Americans found out in Vietnam and the Russians in Afghanistan, the diffusion of military technology to the Third World and the ability to mobilize entire populations behind "people's wars" make the costs of Great Power intervention excruciatingly painful and ultimately fruitless. For example, Washington stood largely impotent in the 444 days following the seizure of the American embassy in Iran in 1979. The rescue attempt resulted in disaster. Nye points out that in 1953 Washington used covert means to restore the Shah to power in Iran, then asks "how many troops would have been needed to restore the Shah in the socially mobilized and nationalistic Iran of 1979".[58]

The threat to use force was often much more effective in serving American interests than the actual use of force. Nye then argues that it is as important to study the times when Washington did not intervene overseas even when important interests were at stake, as to examine those few times when American troops did go into action. Between 1945 and 1973, Washington militarily intervened only four times – Korea (1951–53), Lebanon (1958), Dominican Republic (1965) and Vietnam (1961–72), and from 1974–89 only twice – Grenada (1982) and Lebanon (1984). He then cites a study that identifies 149 situations between 1945 and 1973 in which American interests were threatened but Washington did not intervene.[59] These situations include 31 cases where a Communist government threatened to come to power in a country of strategic interest; 13 cases where Communist countries threatened other countries; 35 threats by Communist governments to strategic regions; 8 situations of conflict on the frontiers of Communist states; 9 conflicts within Communist states; and 53 situations where American military intervention might have propped up friendly regimes. A variety of reasons may explain the non-use of military force in these situations. In some cases, political constraints within the United States or elsewhere may have inhibited American intervention at any level while in other cases Washington may have found diplomatic, economic, and/or covert means, or the use of proxy forces more effective. But regardless, America's four military interventions, only two of which involved fighting, must be put in the perspective of almost 150 situations in which the White House rejected a military option.

Nye goes on to cite Blechman and Kaplan's study of 215 incidents between 1945 and 1975 in which Washington used the threat of force or proxy military forces to protect American interests.[60] Half of the cases involve the movement of naval forces while another large category includes movement of ground or air forces. Washington's threats were not very successful – about one out of five resulted in a favorable outcome for the United States. Overall Washington was more successful in situations where Moscow was not involved.

To be credible any threat must be backed by the other side's belief that if it does not concede it will suffer an attack. Empty threats only encourage aggression. Nye points out that in 1853 Commodore Perry forced Japan and its 30 million people into the world economy by threatening to either blockade Edo or reduce it to ashes if the Shogunate did not comply. Washington could not "effectively threaten force to open Japanese markets today".[61] Unfortunately, many leaders lock themselves into the use of force when diplomatic and economic pressure might be more effective. President Hussain, for example, only worsened his country's problems by invading Kuwait on 2 August 1990.

War is clearly not obsolete. During the 1980s, the United States invaded Grenada and Panama, bombed Libya, and patrolled the Persian Gulf, while in 1990–91, Washington forged a military alliance of 37 nations and fought a war to destroy Iraq's military power after it invaded Kuwait. The value of each of these military actions is questionable. The invasions of Grenada and Panama may have toppled unsavory regimes, but tiny Grenada did not have any strategic importance despite Reagan Administration arguments to the contrary while the multibillion dollar cost of rebuilding Panama makes many wonder if some other means could have been found to silence Noriega. Even conservatives were split over Bush's response against Iraqi aggression. Some advocated a hands off, isolationist policy, arguing that oil prices would rise regardless, but widespread fighting in the Gulf would cause an even worse disruption to the global economy.[62] In retrospect, the bombing of Libya was probably the most cost-effective although the action was widely criticized at the time. The near miss on Kadafi seems to have quelled his penchant for sponsoring international terrorism.

Outright aggression – the invasion of one country by another – is a steadily diminishing phenomena in international relations. The invasions of Panama and Kuwait make the headlines but most wars are civil rather than international conflicts. Conflict will increasingly be within rather than between states. In 1990, while there was only one international conflict that could be called a "war", Iraq's invasion of Kuwait, there were at least a score of other countries torn by civil war, usually in which a subject nation was trying to achieve independence. But that leaves at least 150 states which were not experiencing any military conflict. Outright aggression, such as Iraq's invasion of Kuwait, will become increasingly rare as the costs of such aggression increasingly exceed the benefits. The Cold War's end has meant greater co-operation among not just the Great Powers, but among most nations. The United Nations passed a series of resolutions condemning Iraqi aggression and calling for economic sanctions.

Economic interdependence is as important as nuclear interdependence and the diffusion of military power throughout the world in inhibiting the use of force in conflicts. The industrial revolution affected international relations as profoundly as did the French Revolution. Initially, the industrial revolution strengthened the traditional need for new resources and population filled territories to fuel modern mass armies. The European powers and the United States acquired vast overseas empires during the 19th century – in part to obtain the markets and raw materials vital to industrial growth. But the advent of nuclear weapons and less resource-intensive high technology weapons and mass consumer goods made territory and population far less important to power calculations.

Meanwhile, virtually all the countries in the world have become increasingly dependent on the world economy. It is the relative balance or imbalance of economic power that is the most important source of power in the world today. Economic power has assumed an importance in international relations that military power once held. Interdependence, or a relative balance of economic power among states, gives each state an opportunity to negotiate issues on relatively equal grounds. Dependence, or a relative imbalance in economic power among states allows the more powerful states an opportunity to extract far more concessions than they give up to less powerful states. For example, the IMF and World Bank have the power to force member states to completely change their domestic policies in return for low interest loans. Despite the humiliation in having to give up policy autonomy, states continue to remain members since the costs in lost economic growth from nonmembership would be considerably higher. Almost every country is a member of these international economic organizations including China and former communist states like Hungary, and Poland. Even the Soviet Union has applied for membership.

Economic power, just like military power, has spread to the Third World. The expression "Third World", itself, is simply a convenient category for any country that was not an industrial democracy or part of the Soviet bloc. Economic power within the Third World is so diverse that the term "Third World" is increasingly meaningless when it groups relatively wealthy countries like Taiwan, Singapore, South Korea, South Africa or Israel which have achieved incomes comparable to Portugal or Greece with abysmally poor countries like Bangladesh, Vietnam, Bolivia, or Central Africa. The wealthier countries clearly have a greater range of power resources to achieve their interests than the poorer ones, such as their own multinational corporations which often work in concert with their governments to achieve national interests. By banding together in OPEC, the oil rich countries were able to quadruple oil prices in 1973 and further double them in 1979. Huge debtor countries like Mexico and Brazil regularly use the threat of defaulting and, thus, drag the world into a deep recession to extract concessions from creditor countries.

The Third World has clearly developed, although some countries have developed far more quickly than others and a few have actually declined. According to Bairoch, the Third World's share of world manufacturing more than doubled over a 28 year period, starting 5.3 per cent in 1953, and rising to 8.5 per cent in 1963, 9.98 per cent in 1973, and 12 per cent in 1980.[63] The CIA etimated that the Third World's share in global GNP rose just as steadily from 11.1 per cent in 1960 to 12.3 per cent in 1970 to 14.8 per cent in 1980.[64] The discrepancy between the industrialized world and Third World, and within the Third World, however, was vast. In 1980, the average GNP per capita in the industrialized countries was $10,660, while the middle income country average of $1,580 was little more than 10 per cent of the wealthy country level, and the very poorest countries averaged $250 per capita.[65]

The more dependent every country, wealthy and poor alike, becomes on the global political economy, the less inclined they will be to attempt to resolve conflicts with force. In an increasingly interdependent global political economy, states can much more cheaply achieve their national objectives through such peaceful means as diplomacy and trade rather than force. National power no longer depends on the outright ownership of natural mineral and energy resources – it is enough merely to be able to buy them in the world marketplaces.

In a 1945 speech, President Truman clearly distinguished between the traditional and contemporary nature of power and security in international relations: "The fundamental choice is whether countries will struggle against each other for wealth and power, or work together for security and mutual advantage."[66] But the choice is not quite that clear-cut. The greater the interdependence, the greater the costs and lower the benefits of using military means to resolve international conflicts. Thus geoeconomic conflicts involving manufacturing, financial, technological competition are becoming increasingly prevalent in international relations while geopolitical conflicts involving territorial and ideological competition, although they continue to grab the headlines, steadily weaken in importance.

Many argue that the United States could have secured its interests in the Gulf region through diplomatic and economic maneuvering rather than war. Economic sanctions have been just as effective – or ineffective – as the threat of military force in achieving Washington's foreign policy goals. According to Hufbauer and Schott, Washington's economic sanctions were effective in 17 of 32 cases between 1944 and 1973, while only 7 of 34 cases were successful between 1974 and 1984.[67] The lower success rate after 1973 can be attributed to a more ambitious American policy agenda – twenty cases involved human rights or nonproliferation compared to only two cases before 1973. The steady diffusion of power, military and economic, throughout the world, particularly after 1973, is another important but difficult to measure factor. Geoeconomic and geopolitical issues and power, however, are linked – wealth and power must be created and skillfully wielded to ensure both geoeconomic and geopolitical security.

The growth of international norms of morality and organizations which are supposed to personify them, like the United Nations, is yet another powerful strand of complex interdependence. The world is simply not as anarchic as the "realists" claim. While a world government does not exist and international law remains limited in its effectiveness, states generally follow both explicit and implicit international norms of acceptable behavior. Hopkins writes that "statesmen nearly always perceive themselves as constrained by international principles and rules that prescribe and proscribe behavior", and that these "international norms are more important than countervailing power in constraining states".[68] Such factors as transnational elite ties, world opinion expressed through and shaped by mass media, and a growing international political culture increasingly govern and channel most states' foreign policy. States are socialized by the international system. Even revolutionary states eventually settle down and accept international behavior norms. Policymakers must weigh in the effects of adverse national and international opinion with the decision of whether or not to go to war. Every modern state, whether democratic or authoritarian, must to varying extents be sensitive that the power it wields and policies it promotes are legitimate in the eyes of the masses. States like Iraq or Burma can still attempt to monopolize power through coercion rather than persuasion, but, as the history of revolution and civil war dramatically reveal, these policies are self-defeating over the long run.

Interdependence is mostly a result of the virtuous cycle between trade and wealth, the greater a state's participation in the global trade system, the more wealthy it becomes and thus more dependent on trade. Thus, no rational leadership would ever do anything to jeopardize the benefits of its state's position in the global economy. The 170 sovereign states are increasingly knit together by a range of other interrelated institutions, issues and viewpoints as well as trade. International organizations designed to address a mushrooming of global concerns have proliferated throughout the 20th century, and these in turn represent a global consensus that problems exist and are best addressed collectively. Drugs, AIDS, mass starvation, terrorism are recent concerns that affect all nations to varying extents.

Yet, even these problems pale before the global environmental break-down which includes the interrelated catastrophies of the "Greenhouse Effect", depletion of the ozone layer, desertification and destruction of the tropical forest, pollution of air and water and unbridled population growth. States are finally realizing that it is in their interests to set aside their geopolitical and geoeconomic squabbles and collectively address these global environmental disasters before it is too late. Fortunately, Washington and Moscow are addressing the most potentially catastrophic threat to the global environment – nuclear winter. In a world facing environmental catastrophe, national survival and global survival are intricately linked. Cooperation rather than confrontation becomes the only rational policy for states on most issues.

CONCLUSION

Historians and political scientists tend to focus on the drama of war in shaping international relations. The so-called "realist" school of political science, in particular, argues that war and the balance of power are central to international relations. Those who assume that international relations is mostly characterized by geopolitics, or the threat or use of force to resolve conflict, are simply wrong.

In reality, the nature of international relations has dramatically changed in the postwar era. Power itself, the ability to get others to do things they normally would not do, remains just as important as the basis of international relations. The nature of power, however, has changed dramatically. Although conflicts between states are endemic and growing with interdependence, the use of force in international conflicts is growing increasingly rare. In most cases, war's political and economic costs have far exceeded its benefits since 1945. The age of empire has ended, with the great powers eventually either voluntarily or through force extending independence to their former colonies. The last great empire, the Russian, is finally breaking down from the internal contradictions of Marxism-Leninism and the growing nationalism of the nations within its vast territory. Communism, an imperialist ideology, is thoroughly discredited on theoretical and practical grounds, and will play a steadily diminishing role in international relations. Wars of conquest – Iraq's invasion of Kuwait notwithstanding – are obsolete in the contemporary world. The American and Soviet acquisition of nuclear weapons and subsequent possibility of mutually assured destruction prevented the Cold War from escalating into a world war between the two blocs. Elsewhere, as the Americans found out in Vietnam and the Russians in Afghanistan, it is almost impossible to defeat a mass guerrilla "war of liberation" with conventional military power. The diffusion of military technology to the Third World has meant that any great power intervention will be generally very costly and the results uncertain.

Interdependence is deepening; the greater the global interdependence, the greater the costs and thus the lower the likelihood of military conflict. Military force is becoming increasingly obsolete as a means to deal with such pressing global problems. International relations is increasingly based on geoeconomic rather than geopolitical conflict. The advantages of an interdependent world, to Rosecrance, are clear: "a new 'trading world' of international relations offers the possibility of escaping such a vicious cycle (war) and finding new patterns of cooperation among nation-states . . . the benefit of trade and cooperation today greatly exceeds that of military competition and territorial aggrandizement. States, as Japan has shown, can do better through a strategy of economic development based on trade than they are likely to do through military interventions in the affairs of other states".[69] It can be indeed claimed that "the new world that is unfolding contrasts very sharply with comparable periods of major historical transition. Unlike those earlier periods, no major new military threat is likely to replace the old one anytime soon".[70]

Why? Rosecrance writes that previously, "it was cheaper to seize another state's territory by force than to develop the sophisticated economic and trading apparatus needed to derive benefit from commercial exchange".[71] This is no longer true. Throughout the post World War II years, the costs for a state of using military power to advance its interests have increasingly exceeded the benefits. The greater a nation's dependence on the global political economy, the greater the costs and fewer the benefits of using military force to fulfill national interests.

Yet, the world will probably never know genuine peace and tranquillity. Although conflict between states will continue to subside, conflict within states will continue and probably increase as the oppressed nations in multinational states increasingly assert their rights. And another world war cannot be categorically ruled out. After all, the world was experiencing fundamental changes in 1914 when Europe plunged into war.

How do all these developments affect the United States? Japan has surpassed the United States by most economic measurements. What accounts for America's relative economic decline and Japan's rise?

Over the past forty-five years, the United States faced not one threat but two. The United States won the Cold War with the Soviet Union only to lose the economic war with Japan. While Washington was concentrating its efforts on offsetting the military and ideological Soviet threat, Japan was steadily developing itself into an economic superpower. The heart of Japan's neomercantilist policies involved rational industrial policies that targeted strategic industries for development with an array of subsidies, cartels, technology, import barriers, and export promotion. The success of Japan's neomercantilist policies was dramatically boosted by Washington's Cold War policies. The United States continued to rely on liberal economic policies, oblivious to the reality that the neomercantilist policies of Japan and other countries resulted in growth rates two to four times greater, and subsidized exports that battered American industries. Trillions of dollars and many of America's best minds were committed to building arcane and often unreliable and unnecessary weapons systems rather than better televisions, automobiles, and mousetraps while Japan's resources were concentrated on transforming itself into an economic superpower.

Harrison and Prestowitz concisely capture some of the reasons behind America's decline relative to Japan:

> the continuing shift of economic power to East Asian competitors has been due in significant measure to the single-minded American focus on security concerns in the Asia-Pacific region. Since the Truman adminstration, sucessive presidents have subordinated US economic interests to perceived geopolitical requirements. As the price for their military and diplomatic cooperation, the United States has actively promoted the economic power of its East Asian allies. Critical American technology and industrial know-how have repeatedly been transferred at little or no cost. Washington has accepted trade and investment relationships based on an implicit understanding that US

markets would be relatively open while those of its partners would be much more restrictive. Whenever this asymetry has caused economic diputes to reach a crisis the United States has generally avoided pressing the issue to a conclusion.[72]

Japan's neomercantilist policies have overwhelmingly outperformed America's largely free market policies. Tokyo's industrial policies fueled an average annual economic growth over three times that of the United States before 1973, and over twice the growth rate since; they have allowed Japanese firms to first catch up to and then leapfrog their American rivals in one industry after another until finally Japan itself pushed the United States aside and took over the throne as manufacturing, financial and increasingly technological leader of the world economy. Tokyo clearly understood and rode the wave of the revolutionary changes in the basis of power and international relations since 1945. And consequently, Japan is rapidly becoming the new hegemon over the global political economy.

2 American Liberalism: Triumph and Tragedy

America's philosophical, institutional, and cultural foundations are classically liberal. In no country are individual rights more honored and protected or power more decentralized and restrained than in the United States. Building upon democratic traditions that had been evolving over 150 years and driven by the principles that the "government that governs least governs best" and "the more power is decentralized the less chance it will be abused", the Constitution's architects created a political system in which power was divided between the executive, legislative and judicial branches, and federal, state and local governments, all to the end of guaranteeing individual liberty and rights.

Noble as these liberal principles are, the central theme of American history has been the continuous struggle to fulfill them. It was not until a half century after the Revolution that property qualifications were waived and all men, or at least all white men, were allowed to vote. Slavery was not abolished until 1865, and legal discrimination against African Americans continued until the 1965 Voting Rights Act. Women did not receive the vote until 1920. Congress passed the Freedom of Information Act in 1975 to curb the abuse of rights by the FBI, CIA, and other government agencies. Although tremendous progress has been made over the past two centuries, discrimination and violations of human rights continue sporadically if not systematically. Meanwhile, power may have been decentralized, but its abuse continues. During the 1980s, a mere decade after Watergate, the Reagan Administration's Iran/Contragate and Savings and Loan scandals, however devastating to America's moral and economic well-being, shared headlines with countless lesser tales of corruption at all levels across the country.

Continuing corruption and discrimination, however, may not so much reflect flaws in America's political system as it does flaws in human nature itself. Abuse of power will exist, to varying extents and ways, wherever there are people. What is significant about America's liberal system is not that there is so much corruption, that but there is so little. More important than the reality that over 225 Reagan Administration officials resigned, were indicted, or imprisoned for unlawful or unethical acts is the fact that these abuses were uncovered and most of the violators punished.

There has been just as noticeable a gap between liberal economic ideals and reality. Every president, from Washington through Bush, has claimed allegiance to free trade. Yet, from the Republic's birth, the government

56

has sporadically aided some businesses through tariffs and the general economy through building such infrastructure as canals, railways, and highways. Starting with the Antitrust Act of 1894, the government has attempted to curb the worst abuses of business. Roosevelt's "New Deal" and Johnson's "Great Society" stimulated massive expansions of government economic regulation and social welfare. Yet, both Presidents justified their policies with claims they were simply fulfilling Adam Smith's call for justice and public works. In word if not deed, Reagan's policies were rooted in the axion that "government was not the solution, it was the problem", and he promised repeatedly that his administration would "get government off the people's backs". Despite this rhetoric, the federal government's share of GNP actually rose one percentage point under the Reagan administration, from 24.5 per cent to 25.5 per cent.

The failure of American economic liberalism to create and distribute wealth as dynamically as those countries which pursue rational noemercantilist and industrial policies has been painfully evident throughout the postwar era. Hobbled by its *laissez-faire* philosophy and politically-shaped economic policies, America's growth rate lumbered along at around 2.5 per cent between 1945 and 1973, and 2.0 per cent since, while its competitors raced along at paces two to four times faster. Like all other nations, the United States has industrial policies which favor some over others. But, unlike those of its competitors, Washington's industrial policies are shaped by the industries and their political representatives with the most clout rather than by those industries which can contribute the most to American wealth and power. A related difference is that since industrial policies conflict with liberal theory, the "if it ain't broke, don't fix it" crowd of politicians and economists pretend they do not exist. Of course, many aspects of American policymaking system and policies need "fixing", but the first step is admitting that they do.

The constraints on America's economic development imposed by liberalism have been exacerbated by Washington's leadership of the global political economy since 1944. The United States in the twentieth century has followed the classic pattern of a country's rise to hegemony, its attempts to create a global political economic system in its own image, and its subsequent decline under the burden of maintaining the system and loss of comparative advantage to its economic rivals. A global leader must give more than it takes from the world political economy. Washington expended vast sums of wealth on defense and foreign aid, opened its own markets to its economic rivals while allowing them to keep theirs shut, intervened militarily and clandestinely around the world, and created and led a web of economic and military alliances. In so doing, Washington nurtured forces which would eventually lead to its own relative decline. While America's relative economic decline was inevitable, its absolute decline and displacement by Japan as the dynamic financial and technological core of the world economy was not. Blinded by its liberal economic outlook, Washington failed to prevent America's relative economic decline from becoming absolute. Over the past thirty years, Washington remained obsessed with a rapidly diminishing Soviet military challenge while ignoring Japan's rapidly building economic challenge.

America's hegemony was shortlived. Economically it can be dated from the 1944 Bretton Woods conference; politically from Truman's March 1947 containment policy. When did American hegemony end? Certainly by the mid-1970s, symbolically either 15 August 1971 when President Nixon took the United States off the gold standard and forced the other industrial powers to revalue their currencies or late 1973 when Washington was unable to prevent OPEC's quadrupling of oil prices.

America's relative decline, however, turned into a rout during the Reagan era. Previous Administrations had failed to adjust American policy to Japan's rise into an economic superpower. The Reagan Administration's inept political economic policies, however, vastly accelerated America's relative economic decline. Vowing to make America the world's most powerful country again and obsessed with the "Soviet threat", the White House launched a trillion dollar defense buildup, while at the same time cutting taxes and pushing up the dollar's value as a sign of American power. The combination of loose fiscal and tight monetary policies, and supply-side macroeconomic policies produced average yearly budget deficits of $200 billion. Meanwhile, President Reagan's firm belief in *laissez-faire* economics led to record trade deficits. Although Reagan took pride in a strong dollar as "a symbol of a strong America", it resulted in the loss of two to three million export-dependent jobs, hundreds of billions of dollars worth of sales for American firms at home and abroad, and tens of billions of dollars in lost revenues. These severe trade deficits are estimated to have reduced GNP growth one and a half to two percentage points a year. In 1985, the United States became the world's greatest debtor country while Japan became the global banker.[1]

This chapter will analyze the related industrial and foreign policies which have shaped and reflected American power within the global political economy, with a section analyzing how the Reagan Administration's misguided policies accelerated America's relative economic decline.

AMERICAN INDUSTRIAL POLICIES, POLICYMAKERS AND POWERS

Liberalism won out over neomercantilism in the early federal era when Congress soundly rejected Treasury Secretary Alexander Hamilton's 1791

Report on Manufacturers, which warned that if left unchecked, foreign mercantilist policies would severely damage and impede American economic development. In his report, Hamilton condemned *laissez-faire* economics, arguing that "Capital is wayward and timid in lending itself to new undertakings and the state ought to excite the confidence of capitalists, who are ever cautious and sagacious, by aiding them overcome the obstacles that lie in the way of all manufactures".[2] Hamilton wrote that "certain nations grant bounties (subsidies) on the exportation of particular commodities, to enable their own workmen to undersell (dump) and supplant all competitors, in the country in which the commodities are sent. Hence the undertakers of a new manufacture have to contend not only with the natural disadvantages of a new undertaking, but with the gratuities and renumerations which other governments bestow".[3] Although Hamilton was largely referring to British policies, his account today perfectly describes Japanese neomercantilism. According to Hamilton, the only sensible policy was to counter foreign predatory trade practices with systematic American industrial and trade policies targeting strategic industries for development. One can only wonder at America's development had Hamilton's proposals been accepted.

Although Hamilton's sweeping plan promoting strategic industries with government subsidized national infrastructure projects and protection from competitive imports was rejected, bits of it have become reality in the two hundred years since. The result is a patchwork quilt of trade and industrial policies which are largely determined by political expediency rather than cool rational analysis of America's long-term interests.

Trade has been a vital element of American prosperity from the first English settlements, and the struggle within Congress and more recently between Congress and the President over trade policy dates to the war of independence. America's first significant foreign trade treaty was with France in 1778 which included a most favored nation clause. It was not until the 1816 Tariff Act, however, that the United States imposed its "first distinctly protectionist tariff . . ., and it has been claimed that the threat to American industries from English dumping . . . was an important influence contributing to this, as well as subsequent, protectionist legislation".[4] American tariffs have been imposed in a roller coaster fashion since, averaging 60 per cent during the early 1800s, dropping to a low of 20 per cent during the 1850s, then climbing again to around 50 per cent between 1860 and 1914, being cut sharply during the Wilson era (1914–20) then steadily climbing once again to peak with Smoot Hawley in 1930.[5]

In addition to protecting infant industries with tariffs, Washington also took the lead in promoting huge infrastructure projects that united what became a vast nation sprawling from the Atlantic to the Pacific oceans. It was largely government rather than private money and initiative which built the canal network in the early 19th century, the railroads of the late 19th century, and the highway and airport systems of the late 20th century.

Yet, despite all this, Washington's industrial and trade policies have largely been irrationally conceived and executed, and self-defeating. America's economic future depends on its ability to build the world's best satellites, computers and semiconductors, not producing wheat, coal, clothes and shoes. But in a decentralized political system presided over by a series of presidents steeped in liberal economic ideology, industrial policies are made by the most powerful political interests without regard to America's economic future. Washington continues to protect agriculture and textiles while allowing strategic industries like machine tools or semiconductors to largely fend for themselves. Why? Traditional industries like agriculture and textiles have deeply entrenched political clout stretching back into the 18th century while the more recently established high technology industries are still trying to find a political voice.

For example, the United States has negotiated over 1000 textile agreements with 38 countries. Virtually all these agreements protect America's textile industry from cheap imports. With American textile hourly wages averaging $9.31 compared to $0.31 in China, the industry would be quickly destroyed under free trade conditions. It is estimated that existing import restrictions cost American consumers $20.3 billion annually, or $238 for every American household, a subsidy which costs $70 000 for every job in the textile industry. In October 1990, President Bush vetoed a protectionist textile bill designed to limit the growth of textile imports to 1 per cent a year and freezing footwear imports at 1989 levels, an action that would have cost about $160 billion over five years, effectively taxing every family of four $2600. An attempt to overide Bush's veto on 10 October came very close to success; 275 representatives voted for an overide and only 152 for its defeat, ten short of the two-thirds vote required. Congress passed the textile bill despite the fact that America's textile industry has rarely been healthier – in 1989, domestic sales were up 7 per cent and exports 27 per cent. The bill would have violated GATT, the Multifiber Arrangement, and 38 bilateral agreements.[6]

Like all industrialized countries, the United States protects agriculture more than any other economic sector. For example, Washington subsidies support peanut prices 60–80 per cent above production costs, which costs American consumers an additional $553 million annually. Although the Reagan White House *laissez-faire* policies and, at times, outright collusion with foreign governments against some American producers (machine tools) may have allowed many strategic industries to whither on the vine, some groups with large political power did benefit. One of the biggest beneficiaries of the Reagan era was farmers, whose subsidies rose enormously throughout the 1980s. In 1982, less than 30 per cent of corn farmers received subsidies; in 1990, 88 per cent did.[7]

Washington's export policies have, at times, been just as self-defeating. Jefferson's embargo of 1807–09 was merely the first of a series of national trade measures enacted with high purpose but which ultimately harmed the United States more than its enemies. Determined not to fulfill Lenin's prediction that the West would sell the Soviet Union the rope with which to hang the capitalist world, Congress passed the Export Control Act of 1949 vastly empowering the White House to control the export of technology and products deemed strategic to Soviet bloc and other communist countries. Washington pressured its allies to adopt similar export restraints and formed the Co-ordinating Committee on Multi-lateral Export Controls (Cocom) to co-ordinate the boycott. But the 16 other Cocom members only reluctantly went along, and many corporations continue to find evasion easy and highly profitable. Meanwhile, American exporters are hobbled by webs of bureaucratic red tape; the Commerce Department's list of dual use products is 128 pages long and includes 40 per cent of all American industrial exports. Over 200 000 applications for permission to export are filed each year. Although the license process takes less than two months and only 2 per cent of applications are rejected, it is one more hurdle Americans face in attempting to compete. Japanese turn the same application around in three days. Noted political economist, Robert Kuttner, has described America's export controls as "an industrial policy in reverse".[8] Estimates of the annual loss the restrictions cost the United States range from $9 billion to $50 billion. The Cold War's end may allow Washington to stem this hemorrhage of wealth and jobs. In June 1990, Cocom agreed to ease restrictions on the Soviet Union and phase out all controls on shipments to Eastern Europe.

Yet, the Soviet empire's collapse has not allowed consumer goods to edge out military production in priority in the eyes of conservative leaders. On 17 March 1991, President Bush asked Congress to authorize the Export–Import Bank to underwrite sales of military products for the first time since 1974. Bush claimed that an additional $1 billion in export credits would even the playing field with America's foreign competitors which blatantly subsidize their arms exports. But with a fixed budget, the $1 billion for financing military exports means $1 billion less to finance nonmilitary exports. American military exports in 1989 were $10.8 billion of that year's $31.8 billion global market, yet only 2.5 per cent of America's $250 billion in exports.[9]

Irrational as these policies appear, they simply mirror the disarray of the ideals and institutions of America's policymaking system which reflects

the liberal belief that the depth of democracy parallels the decentralization of power. Unfortunately, any theoretical gain the check and balance
system may achieve in detering potential abuses of power is offset by
concrete losses in the country's potential economic development and
ability to compete in an increasingly interdependent global economy.

How is economic policy made? Glenn Fong described America's formal
policymaking system as

> fragmented by a separation of powers, federalism, bicameralism, the
> congressional committee system, judicial independence, autonomous
> bureaus, and undisciplined, nonprogramatic political parties. Jurisdic-
> tion over industry matters is spread willy-nilly throughout the govern-
> ment departments, including regulatory commissions, the Council of
> Economic Advisors, the Office of Management and Budget, the Office
> of the US Trade Representative, and the Departments of Commerce,
> Defense, Justice, Labor and Treasury. The policies that emerge from
> such a decentralized setting are unco-ordinated, can work at cross
> purposes, and often have counterproductive effects on industrial
> competitiveness.[10]

Cohen agrees, stating that American international economic policies are

> shaped not systematically, but almost by accident. It is the least
> common denominator worked out, as some have so aptly put it, by a
> kind of guerrilla warfare among the Departments of State, Treasury,
> Agriculture, Commerce, the Fed, and a whole host of other executive
> branch agencies . . . Key U.S. international economic policy has been
> made on a highly idiosyncratic basis. Some were quickly devised in
> crisis situations, others grew by inertia . . . All too often policies have
> been reactive. There is an inability to get the problem identified far
> enough in advance. Policy makers are on the defensive putting out a
> series of brush fires. There is a lack of any firm guidelines from the
> White House and the bewildering array of co-ordinating committees,
> working groups, and task forces complicate the problem. The result is a
> cumbersome system in which an inordinate amount of time and energy
> is consumed in intragovernment debates which pass through a multi-
> stage process.[11]

This Hobbesian system is further confused by America's adversarial
legal system which values winning ahead of truth or national interests,
and by the virtually unlimited access of national and foreign interest
groups with large bundles of cash to plead their cases to key policymakers.
Foreign interests enjoy a level playing field with national interests, even if

their ends undermine American power. There is a revolving door of high administrative officials going to work for foreign interests. A 1986 General Accounting Office survey revealed that 76 former federal officials had become registered foreign agents, among which were 20 personal assistants to the president, six senators, nine representatives, twelve senior Senate staff, five senior House staff, and four retired generals. These ex-officials altogether represented 166 foreign clients from fifty-one countries and two international organizations. One third of these ex-officials worked for Japanese interests. But the GAO report did not include the hundreds of former officials who lobbied for the domestic affiliates of foreign corporations. Consultants and advisors who do not lobby do not have to register with the Justice Department.[12]

As if this free-for-all were not chaotic enough, without firm national leadership, each of the fifty states is forced to develop its own industrial policies. The result is that foreign governments and corporations can play off one state against the others, forcing the states into Faustian bargains whereby they surrender immense tax, subsidy, and land advantages to foreigners in return for the often miniscule employment increases brought by those foreign investments. Recently, some states have tried to work together to lessen the ability of foreign governments to play them off against each other. The Mid–South Trade Council of six states – Alabama, Arkansas, Mississippi, Tennessee, Kentucky and Louisiana was set up in 1983; the Council of Great Lakes Governors of Michigan, Illinois, Wisconsin, Minnesota, Indiana, Ohio, Pennsylvania and New York in 1988; the economics panel of the New England Conference in 1985. All these associations represented attempts to bargain collectively with foreign powers for better investments at home and sales for their industries abroad. The rational policy void in Washington even stimulated an international coalition between American states and Canadian provinces called the Pacific Northwest Legislative Leadership Forum of Washington, Oregon, Montana, Alaska, British Columbia and Alberta. Yet these regional attempts to promote rational trade and investment policies have been no more successful than the solitary states in cutting better deals with foreign governments and corporations.[13]

This multistranded economic policy tug of war is exacerbated over international issues, in which the President and Congress seem in constant conflict. The Constitution authorizes the President to enforce the laws, serve as commander-in-chief of the armed forces, and enjoy virtually unlimited power to conduct foreign affairs. In the 1936 case, The United States v. Curtiss Wright Export Co., the Supreme Court ruled that the President has certain inherent rights over foreign affairs that even transcend the Constitution. The President can also negotiate executive agreements with foreign governments that do not require Congressional approval. The distinction between executive agreements and treaties is more semantic than real; foreign governments do not distinguish between the two. Yet, in one foreign policy area, trade, the President's powers are severely curtailed and must be delegated by Congress. Article I, Section 8, of the Constitution grants to Congress the power to "regulate trade with foreign nations" and to "lay and collect taxes, duties, imposts, and excises". In addition, all treaties must be submitted to the Senate for approval and can only be passed by a two-thirds affirmative vote. Congress can delegate some responsibilities to the President to negotiate international agreements affecting trade. Yet, no President took any interest in leading trade policy until President Roosevelt asked Congress to grant him temporary powers to negotiate trade barriers reductions with foreign countries. Congress complied with the 1934 Reciprocal Trade Agreement Act, whose powers to negotiate international trade agreements have been renewed and expanded fourteen times since. Since 1935, the Supreme Court has never ruled such a delegation of power unconstitutional, so long as the delegation contains an "intelligible principle" on which the executive can act.[14]

Despite this transfer of power, the United States is the only major industrial country that does not have a separate department charged with the overall direction of trade policy. Theoretically, American trade policy is led by the United States Trade Representative (USTR, originally called the Special Trade Representative) and the International Trade Commission (ITC), which were created in 1962 by the Kennedy Administration to lead America's negotiations in the GATT negotiations then about to begin. In 1974, Congress upgraded the USTR to cabinet and ambassador rank. The USTR heads a 150 person agency which is responsible for creating and implementing trade policy, and chairs the many committees dealing with trade issues including the Trade Staff Committee and cabinet-level Trade Policy Committee. Despite the urgency of Japan's geoeconomic challenge, only two of the USTR staff concentrate on Japanese relations. The ITC is composed of six commissioners appointed for 9 year terms whose responsibility is to investigate any petition for injury filed by an American firm, industry, or other interested party against foreign corporations or governments.

The USTR and ITC remain the neglected stepchildren of the executive branch. For example, if the ITC finds that foreign predatory trade practices have injured an American firm, it forwards the case to the President who decides on political grounds whether or not to retaliate. President Reagan acted on only 11 of the 32 recommendations for retaliation he received.[15] The Secretaries of State and Treasury rather than the USTR or Commerce Secretary usually accompany the President to economic summit meetings. As political appointees, most USTRs stay in office for a year or two then depart for greener pastures. As a result, there is no continuity in experience or knowledge in dealing with Japan and other predatory traders. Choate writes that "America does not have one trade policy: it has dozens, each of which reflects the limited bureaucratic concerns of individual federal agencies. In principle, the Office of the USTR has the responsibility to assemble an overall US trade policy and co-ordinate America's trade negotiations. But it has little authority to enforce consistent or even supportive action by other agencies".[16]

Although the Commerce and Agriculture Departments, and Central Intelligence Agency usually line up beside the USTR, they are outgunned by the State, Treasury and Defense Departments, National Security Council and Council of Economic Advisors which invariably subordinate geoeconomic to geopolitical issues, particularly as regards Japan. Institutional, ideological, and policy extremists are the the the Council of Economic Advisors which always takes a dogmatic neoclassical position on any economic issues, and defends it with bulldog ferocity, and the Agriculture Department which Prestowitz calls America's closest version of MITI, since it creates and implements realistic industrial policies for agriculture. Yet, each issue can inspire a different lineup. The Treasury Department, for example, is generally liberal on all international trade issues but finance, while Prestowitz describes the Defense Department as schizophrenic in regard to the Japan challenge. On one hand the Defense Department values the alliance with Japan as the top priority yet worries that Japanese neomercantilism is destroying America's strategic industries and thus its national security. The CIA generally takes a realistic view of Japanese neomercantilism and its destructive effects on American national security but offers no alternative policies to the present drift, and, regardless, is ignored.[17]

Ultimately, the President can cut through these divisions and impose a coherent trade policy. American trade laws give the President enormous clout in remedying trade deficits and retaliating against predatory trade nations. Unfortunately, all the Presidents have neglected systematically to use these vast powers. Congress' dissatisfaction with the White House's handling of trade issues led it to pass the 1962 Trade Act granting the President some authority to retaliate against the predatory trade strategies of America's trade rivals. These powers were enhanced by the 1974, 1979, 1984 and 1988 Trade Acts. The sharpest arrow in the President's quiver of retaliatory powers is Section 301 of the 1974 Trade Act (strengthened in 1984 and 1988) allowing American firms, citizens or other interested parties including the government to petition formally the Administration for redress of foreign neomercantilist trade tactics. Under this act Congress authorized the President to retaliate against "unjustifiable, unreasonable, or discriminatory acts of foreign governments that burden or restrict United States commerce" including actions such as "dumping" and export subsidies.[18]

The 1984 Trade and Tariffs Act was the first major trade act which the White House opposed. In 1982, Senators Lloyd Bentsen and John Danforth introduced the Reciprocal Trade and Tariff Act into Congress, which, after much debate and footdragging by the Reagan Adminstration, was passed two years later. Disgusted with the Reagan Administration's appeasement of foreign neomercantilism, Congress shifted responsibility for acting on complaints from the President to the USTR and requires it to prepare "an annual accounting of major foreign barriers to US exports of good, services, and foreign direct investment".[19] Additional provisions include: "Foreign barriers not removed through negotiation or enforcement of the GATT could be offset by the US through withdrawal of prior concessions, imposition of duties, and other restrictions available under the present law . . . of particular interest is the clarification of the President's authority to impose fees and restrictions on foreign services or suppliers of those services".[20] The President now can retaliate against foreign economic aggression even before actual injury to American firms has occurred. These powers, however, are offset by the loophole which allows the USTR to decide which countries and barriers are harmful enough to be publicly identified. It also seems to allow the USTR to take countries at their word on the existance of trade and investment barriers. For example, the 1986 report on Japan made the extraordinary claim that that country had no investment barriers.

After four years of continued Reagan Administration appeasement, Congress attempted to close off some loopholes by passing the 1988 Omnibus Trade and Competitiveness Act. Written largely with Japanese neomercantilist practices in mind and over 1,300 pages long, the 1988 Bill represented a vast undertaking of over 200 legislators from twenty-two separate committees and subcommittees. The Act empowers the President to retaliate against "unfair trade practices" which are intended to "destroy or substantially injure an industry . . . or to prevent the establishment of such an industry, or to restrain or monopolize".[21] The Act extended from five to eight years the limit for protective measures and also changed Section 337 so that an "injury test" is no longer a prerequisite for restricting imports of products from corporations that have stolen American intellectual property such as patents, trademarks and copyrights. Section 1310, amended to Section 301, includes in the list of "unreasonable" foreign neomercantilist policies which can invite American retaliation is the "toleration by a foreign government of systematic anticompetitive activities by private firms or among private firms in the foreign country that have the effect of restricting . . . access of

United States goods to purchasing by such firms".[22] The ITC must investigate any petition within 12 to 18 months after its submission. The President, however, can overrule the Commission's conclusions.

How effectively have these vast powers been used? Section 301 has been frequently utilized by American industries targeted by foreign trade predators. Between the 1974 Trade Act and April 1989, there were at least seventy petitions under Section 301 accepted by the USTR, of which 30 were eventually settled by bilateral agreement, 21 were still pending, and only 10 involved American retaliation.[23] The petition process itself is considered very effective since the petition "carries an effective threat of potential retaliation, combined with the threat of adverse publicity and a general souring of trade relations. These potential ramifications alone may bring the offending government to the bargaining table . . . Section 301 works through feints and threats rather than through formal legal processes".[24]

Yet, problems remain. Jackson argues that the retaliation provisions are too refined and that domestic industries seeking relief

find that in many circumstances they are not eligible under United States law for that relief although they might well be eligible for such relief if the GATT language were the applicable legal standard . . . United States law and procedures have led the United States to decline to utilize the explicit measures of escape clause relief in cases (such as the automobile case) where clearly other governments would not be so inhibited . . . (S)uch restraints leads to pressure on the United States government to evade its own law in applying safeguard measures that are not explicitly provided for in the statutes.[25]

Governments can pursue neomercantilist trade policies by a variety of means. "Dumping" is a neomercantilist policy whereby a firm or industry sells its products overseas at a lower price than its production cost. America's first legislation enacted to counter foreign dumping was in 1916, strengthened with the 1921 Anti-dumping Act but not overhauled again until legislation in 1974 and 1979. Since 1974, complaints are simultaneously filed with the Commerce Department which decides whether dumping exists and ITC which must determine within 45 days whether injury occurred. If dumping and injury are found, the Commerce Department can then issue a tariff increase on the offending products. If the foreign companies do not release production information, Commerce can use the "best evidence" to calculate the dumping margin. Between 1979 and 1988, there were 420 petitions to the Commerce Department, of which eight were suspended, 120 found to have suffered injury, about 150 withdrawn when the dumping was alleviated, and another 150 cases still pending.[26] Yet, in some respects, America's dumping law favors foreign over domestic firms. If a domestic firm is found to have infringed on another firm's patents, it must halt its sales of the product and pay damages. A foreign firm, however, can continue to exploit another firm's patents without penalty if no serious loss of sales or profits occurs.[27]

Another neomercantilist strategy is for governments to subsidize their nation's exports. Here again, the White House has ample retaliatory powers either to deter or defeat such attacks, but rarely uses it. A 1897 law empowered the Treasury Department to retaliate with countervailing duties against foreign government subsidies to their industries. In 1980, Congress transferred the power to impose countervailing and antidumping duties from the Treasury to the Commerce department because of the former's timidity in retaliating against foreign neomercantilism. Between 1979 and September 1988, the United States imposed about 300 counter-vailing duties on the products of foreign corporations which were heavily subsidized by their governments.[28]

A little known weapon of US trade law is Section 232 of the 1962 Trade Expansion Act which empowers the President to limit imports of certain products that undermine American security. This statute was further strengthened by the Trading with the Enemy Act and 1979 Export Administration Act which empower the President to restrict trade with foreign adversaries of any products deemed vital to American security. Between 1962 and 1988, only 18 petitions for relief were received under this statute, of which all but three were for petroleum products. The most famous case was the 1985 petition by Houdaille Corporation to limit Japan's dumping of machine tools in the United States which, if left unhindered, could have destroyed America's machine tool industry, thus severely undermining American security. President Reagan rejected the Houdaille petition although Tokyo eventually agreed to "voluntary" export restraints.

Washington first introduced an escape clause, allowing the imposition of temporary protectionist measures under adverse circumstances, in a 1943 trade treaty with Mexico. As his Administration was negotiating the texts of GATT and ITO, President Truman signed an executive order requiring the United States to include an escape clause in those and all subsequent trade agreements. "Escape" measures can include increased tariffs, quotas, and orderly marketing agreements. Escape clauses have remained an important but overlooked aspect of US statutory law ever since.

Strangely, Presidents have forgone these vast legal powers to retaliate against foreign neomercantilist trade practices for such extralegal measures as negotiating "voluntary export retraints" (VERs) or "orderly marketing agreements" (OMAs) in which quotas are imposed on the predatory industries and corporations. Quotas, however, are self-defeating because they are usually imposed only after the predatory industry has conquered huge market share and severely weakened their American rivals. The predatory industry can thus use the quotas to solidify its market share within which it raises prices to recoup profit losses incurred from its earlier dumping campaign. Quotas actually reward rather than deter predatory trade practices.

Washington has been little more effective at promoting exports as it has been defending against foreign dumping, subsidized exports, and other neomercantilist strategies. American exports can be financed through a range of government programs including the Export–Import Bank, Domestic International Sales Corporation, Commodity Credit Corporation, Overseas Private Investment Corporations, and smaller programs of the Commerce and Agriculture Departments. The Export–Import Bank and Commodity Credit Corporation extend loans to foreigners to buy American goods. The Overseas Private Investment Corporation extends insurance to American foreign investments against such losses resulting from expropriations or law. The Domestic International Sales Corporation (DISC) provisions of the Internal Revenue Code allow deductions of up to half of profits from export sales by domestic corporations. In addition, the Commerce Department's International Trade Administration and Agriculture Department's Foreign Agriculture Service promote exports.

These vast trade powers are nothing without a President which understands American geoeconomic interests and is willing to defend and promote them.

AMERICAN FOREIGN POLICY (1776–1980)

American foreign policy has been characterized by as severe a gap between rhetoric and reality as have America's economic policies, with the inevitable, tragic results. Every President has preached, if rarely practiced, Jefferson's ideal that America's "interests soundly calculated will never be found inseparable from our moral duties".[29] American leaders from George Washington to George Bush have extolled the virtues of American democracy and the need for all other nations to be free. Jefferson expressed this vision when he wrote that the United States was the "solitary republic of the world, the only monument of human rights . . . the sole depository of the sacred fire of freedom and self government, from hence it is to be lighted up in other regions of the earth."[30] President Wilson expressed America's vision of international relations before the Senate in January 1917, when he proclaimed: "There must be, not a balance of power, but a community of power; not organized rivalries, but an organized common peace".[31] In his Fourteen Points, President Wilson articulated the creation of a new global political economy based on such principles as open diplomacy, democracy, free trade, disarmament, self-determination for all nationalities, a lenient peace with Germany, the resolution of conflict through co-operation rather than force, and the creation of a League of Nations to manage these sweeping changes. Wilson accurately predicted that unless peace were based "on the higest principles of justice, it would be swept away by the peoples of the world in less than a generation".[32] President Roosevelt revived and developed Wilson's ideals during the 1930s and early 1940s, with the Atlantic Charter essentially reiterating Wilson's fourteen Points and calling for a peace in which all people everywhere enjoy the four freedoms – freedom of speech and expression, freedom of worship, freedom from want, and freedom from fear.

Yet ironically until 1941, despite acknowledging America's unique mission to spread democracy, most Presidents followed largely isolationist policies. Washington's Farewell Address, written by Hamilton, most succinctly expresses American policy, which:

> in regard to foreign nations is, in extending our commercial relations, to have with them as little political connection as possible . . . it must be unwise . . . to implicate ourselves by artificial ties in the ordinary vicissitudes of her (Europe's) politics, or the ordinary combinations and collisions of her friendships or enmities. Our detached and distant situation invites and enables us to pursue a different course . . . to steer clear of permanent alliances with any portion of the foreign world . . . and to safely trust to temporary alliances for extraordinary emergencies.[33]

In his own farewell address, Jefferson argued that "Commerce with all nations, alliance with none, should be our motto".[34]

American foreign policy is the outcome of the struggle between contradictory idealist and realist, isolationist and interventionist arguments. Because most Americans believe that the assertion of national interests must be compatible with "making the world safe for democracy", the White House gains public support for its policies by cloaking brutal assertions of power with idealistic bunting, often making for a very awkward fit. Isolation from the Byzantine political struggles of Europe did not prevent the United States from trading with virtually all sides of conflicts, and enriching itself in the process. Americans proudly waved banners of democracy and freedom as they marched West to the Pacific and beyond, leaving scores of American Indian nations trampled and imprisoned in their wake. Stripped of their pleas for political and economic freedom, the Monroe Doctrine (1823) and Open Door Policy (1898) respectively asserted America's exclusive sphere of influence in the Western Hemisphere and a place at the imperialist banquet table in East Asia. Few Presidents have been quite as honest as President Roosevelt's answer as to why the United States supported the corrupt, brutal rule of Nicaragua's Samoza: "He may be a son-of-a-bitch, but he's our son-of-a-bitch".[35] Instead, anti-American democracies and dictatorships alike from Chile to Iran have been toppled with the curious logic that reached a surrealistic height during the Vietnam War as articulated by a lieutenant: "We had to destroy the village, in order to save it".

Contradictions aside, until recently Washington's foreign policies have largely been enormously successful in promoting American power and wealth. During its first 150 years, the United States largely practiced the same strategy that Japan has since 1945: trade everywhere, expand against the weak, undermine the strong, try to hold everyone at political arms length, and only form alliances as a last resort. Although politics and economics are inseparable, Washington like Tokyo tried and largely succeeded in maintaining as low a political profile as possible; all the while its soldiers and settlers quietly expanded to and then across the Pacific Ocean and its merchants bought and sold in the globe's far corners. Like Japan, the United States got rich while the other great powers periodically devastated themselves in war and bankrupted themselves through the race to gobble up more foreign lands. Despite witnessing democratic governments beseiged by aggressors in two World Wars, the United States languished nervously on the sidelines until it was directly attacked, then emerged from both wars all the more powerful and its rivals all the weaker.

There are, however, sharply significant differences in how Washington and Tokyo executed these grand strategies. Despite tariffs and spurts of energetic canal and railway construction, Washington's trade and industrial policies were and remain largely shaped by free economic and political marketplaces. Tokyo's trade and industrial policies, in contrast, are created by corporatist politics and single-minded neomercantilist policies of import barriers, export promotion, and carefully managed markets. America's expansion before 1945 was both geopolitical and geoeconomic; land was conquered and administered both directly by arms and indirectly by finance. Japan's expansion since 1945 has only been geoeconomic; its rapidly expanding overseas empire is of invisible but no less powerful financial rather than overt political control.

World War II was the watershed in American foreign policy –
Washington finally assumed a global political role commiserate with its
vast economic power. No state has ever held greater relative power than
the United States immediately after World War II.[36] The United States
also possessed or controlled the three main sources of economic power in
the modern world: comparative advantage in high technology products,
monetary reserves and petroleum. American factories produced over 50
per cent of the world's industrial output, its banks held almost 50 per cent
of the world's monetary reserves, and its oil companies controlled the non-
communist world's supply of oil.[37]

Despite this enormous power, the decision to assume global leadership
was not an easy one – Washington was still torn between isolationists and
internationalists. It was the isolationists that had a quarter century earlier
yanked Wilson off the political stage at Versailles and forbade American
membership in the League of Nations. It was the isolationists that had
authored the Smoot Hawley legislation in 1930 which sparked a world
trade war and depression. Isolationist voices in Congress remained
powerful; the call for America's retreat into its political shell, into the
creed that "the business of America is business", was highly appealing to
many.

President Roosevelt had picked up the internationist reins earlier
dropped by Wilson. In 1934, Roosevelt made the first tentative
internationalist step when he got Congress to grant him the power to
negotiate free trade agreements with other countries and followed it up
with the 1936 Tripartite monetary agreement and the 1938 Anglo-
American Trade Agreement, which attempted to pull down the
currency blocks and other barriers that hobbled global trade. During
World War II, Washington and Britain signed the 1941 Atlantic
Charter committing their countries to promote both free trade and
freely chosen government around the world, while with the signing of
the 1942 Mutual Aid Pact, Britain promised to end its imperial
preference trade system. The most important step was the Bretton
Woods Conference in 1944, when forty-four nations committed themselves to free trade and began negotiating what would become the three
major institutional pillars of the global political economy – the International Bank for Reconstruction and Development (IBRD or World
Bank), the International Monetary Fund (IMF) and the General
Agreement on Tariffs and Trade (GATT). The United Nations was
created on the ruins of the League of Nations, with the high hopes that
World War II was the war to end all wars and that henceforth
international conflicts could be settled peacefully.

It was the outbreak of the Cold War which tipped the balance between the internationalists and isolationists decisively in favor of the former. By early 1947, a political consensus had been forged in Washington around the fear that the "iron curtain" the Soviet Union had heavily drawn across Eastern Europe would eventually be expanded to encompass all of Europe and East Asia, then the rest of the world. Diplomat George Kennan's long telegraph from Moscow and later *Foreign Affairs* article presented both the nature of the Soviet threat and a strategy to overcome it.[38] Kennan argued that any Soviet expansion would be through the appeal of communism rather than the force of arms. Communism can appeal to those without; the greater and more obvious the gap between the politically and economically deprived and the elite, and the greater the numbers of the former and smaller the latter, the greater communism's potential appeal. Conversely, communism's appeal shrivels when wealth is both created and distributed; political philosophers since Aristotle have argued that democracy can florish only in a middle class society. Thus, Soviet expansion would be contained if the war-devastated and poverty-stricken countries were transformed into prosperous liberal democracies. Containment, however, did not mean containing every nation against communism. Kennan's containment policy was confined largely to strategic countries and regions – West Europe, Japan and the Middle East. Economic growth and political stability in these core countries would inevitably spill over into peripheral countries, even if they temporarily went communist.

President Truman used Kennan's ideas as the basis for the containment policy he announced in March 1947, in which he promised that the United States would help any country threatened by a communist takeover. He then used his doctrine to immediately extend military and economic aid to the anti-communist forces in Greece and Turkey. In June 1947 the Marshall Plan was announced whereby the United States would massively aid Europe's stalled economic recovery – the bill eventually topped $14 billion or $175 billion by today's value. Washington was no less vigorous in building up Japan as the "workshop" of Asia to contain further Soviet expansion in the Far East. Altogether the United States: (1) extended Japan $2.2 billion in aid; (2) completely revamped its political economy with revolutionary constitutional, land, labor and industrial reforms; (3) allowed Japanese products virtually unlimited access to American markets; (4) tied aid to Southeast Asia to purchases of Japanese products; (5) bought tens of billions of military procurements from Japan; (6) and assumed the burden of defending Japan. American policies were responsible for the eventual "economic miracle" in both Europe and Japan.

The Cold War increased in intensity. The Soviets attempted to starve Allied controlled West Berlin into surrender by blockading it for nine months in 1948 and 1949 but finally backed off when the airlift succeeded in keeping the city supplied. In 1949, the creation of the North Atlantic Treaty Organization (NATO) showed Washington's resolve to defend West Europe against a Soviet invasion. That same year, however, the Soviet explosion of an atomic bomb and communist party victory in China simultaneously seemed to tip the military and Asian balances of power in Moscow's favor. But it was not until North Korea's invasion of South Korea in June 1950, that the brinksmanship and sabre-rattling burst into war. Washington responded not only by forging a United Nations coalition and sending an American-led army into the peninsula, but also sailed the 7th Fleet into the Taiwan Straits, thus saving Chiang Kaishek's Nationalist Party (Koumintang, KMT) from inevitable conquest by China. General MacArthur's drive north to North Korea's Yalu River border with China provoked a massive Chinese counterattack which swept the Allied forces back to South Korea..

The North Korean attack and Chinese intervention seemed to realize the West's worst fears that it faced a monolithic communist bloc that was willing to expand through invasion as well as subversion, which seemingly made Kennan's selective containment policy woefully inadequate. President Eisenhower's Secretary of State, John Foster Dulles, began shifting American policy from a selective to a cross-the-board defense of noncommunist governments everywhere, regardless of their geopolitical or geoeconomic value – a mentality that would eventually lead the United States into the quagmire of Vietnam. Washington forged much of the noncommunist world into a web of military and economic alliances, of varying longevity and strength. This burden of upholding the global political economy and containment against the Soviet Union increasingly wore heavily on the United States throughout the 1960s. The United States got bogged down in an unwinnable war in Vietnam which was exacerbating a range of socioeconomic problems at home. The Soviet Union had achieved nuclear parity with the United States and was formenting insurrections throughout the Third World. Meanwhile, Washington's attempts to convert West Europe and Japan into loyal, prosperous and stable American allies, and thus help stimulate the revival of the global political economy, seemed so successful that increasing numbers of industries from those countries were now challenging their American rivals for global supremacy. The United States began to suffer a number of economic problems including trade deficits, high inflation and slower growth.

President Nixon understood these tremendous changes in international relations and the consequent challenges they posed for the United States. He attempted to realign America's international commitments with its relatively diminishing power. He tried to alleviate East–West tensions while simultaneously stimulating tensions between China and the Soviet Union by pursuing detente with both countries. His Nixon Doctrine of 1969 declared that the United States would continue to aid friendly countries in squashing communist insurgencies, but only if their troops did the actual fighting. Nixon then slowly withdrew American troops and handed over fighting to the South Vietnamese while negotiating a peace agreement with Hanoi.

Nixon clearly understood the significance of the shift in the balance of geoeconomic power away from the United States. In July 1971, he identified five centers of world economic power – the United States, Japan, Western Europe, the Soviet Union, and China – and proclaimed that "these are the five that will determine the economic future, and because economic power will be the key to other kinds of power, the future of the world in other ways in the last third of this century".[39] Acting on this understanding, Nixon attempted to turn around America's relative economic decline so that it could better pay for its existing commitments. On 15 August 1971, the President announced a 10 per cent tariff on all imports, took the United States off the gold standard, introduced legislation creating a Domestic International Sales Corporation (DISC) which would finance exports, and imposed price controls on certain products. President Nixon partly justified his August 1971 actions under GATT Articles XII, XIII, and XIV allowing temporary MFN relief to correct balance of payments difficulties. Nixon also threatened to invoke the "Trading with the Enemy Act" against American importers if Japan and other countries did not follow his policies. In December 1971, the major industrial countries agreed to revalue their currencies, and, in March 1973, Nixon allowed the dollar to float against other currencies.

Richard Nixon was the only President who clearly understood the vast changes in the nature of international relations, and tried to pursue detente with the Soviet Union while pressuring Japan to open its markets and contribute more to the world economy. Nixon's efforts only temporarily arrested America's economic decline. Watergate swept him from power and the Ford and Carter Administrations continued the traditional Cold War policy of increased military spending and open American markets without foreign reciprocity. OPEC's quadrupling of oil prices in 1973 and further doubling in 1979, sharply cut down economic growth and stimulated high inflation in all countries, but America's free market economy was much less equipped to adjust to these crises than the much stronger governments in other industrial countries. Geopolitically, the United States seemed also to steadily lose ground. Indochina fell to the communists in 1975; Nicaragua to the communists, Iran to Islamic fundamentalism, and Afghanistan to the Soviet Red Army, all in 1979.

THE REAGAN ERA (1981–PRESENT): RETREAT INTO ROUT

During the 1980 Presidential campaign, disillusioned with the White House's impotent, hand wringing response to a series of foreign and domestic policy defeats of the 1970s, including the disgrace of Watergate and Nixon's resignation, the fall of Saigon and Kabul, the quadrupling and then further doubling of oil prices, the seizure of the Teheran embassy, and persistent stagflation, Americans were desperate for anyone on a white horse with promises for a better future. Ronald Reagan proved to be that man. Reagan captured the support of many Americans when he simply asked them if they were better off today than four years ago, while his campaign slogans promised that his White House would unleash the "magic of the marketplace" and usher in a "new morning" of American power and prosperity. His "next-door-neighbor", sunny personality and incessant optimism contrasted with Jimmy Carter's pessimism. Even then, many Americans were still leary of Reagan's hardline anti-Soviet stance, and polls indicated a neck and neck race with Carter to the November election. Ultimately, Reagan won, possibly because his campaign staff struck a secret deal with Teheran not to release the hostages until after the election in return for shipments of military equipment.[40]

But once entrenched in the White House, the Reagan Administration's misguided policies transformed the retreat of American power into a rout. Under President Reagan's "watch" (or "doze" as many assert), the United States sank from the world's greatest banker to worst debtor nation brought on in part by deepening budget and international payments deficits, a bankrupt savings and loan industry that will cost at least $500 billion to revive, and a banking system teetering on the edge of insolvency. Meanwhile, America's cities remain hostages to worsening plagues of crime, drugs, AIDS and homelessness, the country's education systems are battered by declining test scores and revenue, and everywhere basic public services are slashed and roads and bridges are crumbling. And although the Reagans retired to Bel Air in 1989, the Reagan era continues through the Bush Administration attitude of fervently believing that America's diseased economy will revive through faith and good wishes alone.

What went wrong? The Jeffersonian maxim that the less government, the better may be appropriate for individual rights, but is disastrous when applied to a modern economy in a neomercantilist world. Promoting a free market economy when one's rivals are carefully managing theirs is like entering a boxing ring with one's feet and hands tied together.

Some argue that the Reagan Administration's legacy goes far beyond simple economic mismanagement. Benjamin Friedman, in his book *Day of Reckoning*, argues that the Reagan "revolution" involved breaking faith with a central tenet of American culture, that one should not live beyond one's means. In Friedman's words, it "violated the basic moral principle that had bound each generation of Americans to the next to the founding of the republic: that men and women should work and eat, earn and spend, both privately and collectively, so that their children and their children's children would inherit a better world".[41] The Reagan era represents the triumph of image over reality, in which America's "sense of economic well being was an illusion, an illusion based on borrowed time and borrowed money . . . (O)ur prosperity was a false prosperity, built on borrowing from the future".[42]

In October 1980, Reagan promised a Chicago audience that: "We can do it. We must do it. We must do all three together: balance the budget, cut tax rates, and build our defenses". In the summer of 1981, Reagan again promised that "starting next year, the deficits will get smaller until in just a few years the budget can be balanced. And we hope we can begin whittling at that almost $1 trillion debt that hangs over the future of our children".[43] According to Reagan, these policies would result in unparalleled prosperity and growth, a balanced budget and revival of American power. How was this supposed to occur? Reagan and other "supply siders" claimed it was all quite simple – tax cuts would stimulate consumers and corporations with incentives to work and save more. Increased work means increased productivity and thus growth, which would in turn stimulate even greater work and savings. Increased savings would bring lower interest rates which would stimulate greater investments and thus more productivity, growth, and savings. Increased growth would eventually bring in more tax revenues which would balance the budget.

Most observers dismissed supply-side theory as deeply flawed. While running against Reagan for the Republican nomination, George Bush denouced these supply side ideas as "voodoo economics". According to Bush, cutting taxes while increasing military spending would worsen the budget deficit which would cause interest rates to rise as the govenment and private sector competed for funds, and thus cut economic growth. Bush, of course, was right, although after becoming Vice President he turned a blind eye to the mayhem set loose on the American economy by Reaganomics, and has continued these policies as President.

Once in office, the Reagan Administration turned a deaf ear to such protests and soon fulfilled his promise to sharply cut taxes. Enacted in August 1981, the Kemp–Roth bill (euphemistically called the "Economic Recovery Act") cut taxes by 5 per cent in September 1981, 10 per cent in July 1982, and a further 10 per cent in July 1983. The average American family of four saw their taxes reduced from 24 per cent to 18 per cent of income. Individual taxes were lower by $32 billion in 1982, $75 billion in 1983, $113 billion in 1984, $135 billion in 1985, and $160 billion in 1986, while corporate taxes were slashed by corresponding amounts.[44]

Tragically, the promised transformation of America's economy never occurred. The White House vastly overestimated the resulting economic growth, while, ironically, having taken power by severely castigating the Democrats for running huge national deficits, Reagan tripled the national debt while in the White House. Whether the Reagan Administration truly believed that their policies would fulfill all they had promised, or that their policies were cynically designed to create a debt crisis which would force the reduction of the government's role in American life is unclear. The reality remains that Reaganomics was a dismal failure that severely weakened American political economic power.

As a percentage of GNP, the United States never borrowed as much during peacetime as it did during the 1980s. Throughout American history the government has only run large deficits during wartime, then spent the postwar years trying to pay back its debts. The United States first went into debt to finance its War of Independence against Britain. By 1790, the government owed creditors $79 million. During the next seventy years the debt fluctuated as the government financed another war against Britain (1812–15) and the Mexican War (1846–48), but paid back much of the principal during peacetime. By 1860, the national debt was only $65 million. Although Washington borrowed the then extraordinary amount of $2 billion to finance the Civil War (1861–65), it then ran continual budget surpluses from 1866 to 1893 during which it was able to pay back three-fourths of that debt. World War I cost the United States $31 billion but government surpluses during the 1920s retired about $8 billion of that debt. The government borrowed $25 billion to offset revenue loses and finance the New Deal during the great depression and World War II ran up the national debt to $242 billion. But fiscal conservatism during the postwar era restrained the national debt's growth. By 1970, despite the costs of the Great Society and Vietnam War, the debt had grown to only $285 billion. Although increased government spending and the mid-decade recession caused the debt to balloon to $743 billion by 1980, the debt only represented 26 per cent of GNP. In the century between 1870 and 1980, although the national debt had fluctuated wildly, it had averaged about 25 per cent of GNP during peacetime. Eight years (1981–89) of Reagan spend and borrow policies tripled the national debt from $914 billion to $2.6 trillion, or 35 per cent of GNP, and converted the United States from the world's greatest creditor nation to the worst debtor nation.

How did this occur? Although Reagan continually blamed Congress for the deficit, the total amount of the budgets he submitted to Congress remained largely intact. In 1981, the Office of Budget and Management estimated that the budget would be $849 billion in 1986 – actual spending was $854 billion, only $5 billion more. Furthermore, Friedman points out that "Republicans controled the senate from Reagan's first day in office until January 1987, and . . . in his first seven years in office Reagan vetoed only seven spending bills out of nearly a hundred that Congress passed".[45] Military spending was the major reason for the increase in government spending. During the Reagan Administration's first three years military spending almost doubled from $134 billion to $210 billion, and finally peaked at $295 billion in 1988. Military spending rose from 5.0 per cent to 6.4 per cent of GNP. In contrast, the after inflation growth of spending for all nondefense programs other than interest on the national debt rose only 0.5 per cent per annum in the 1980s compared to 1.7 per cent in the 1950s, 7.2 per cent in the 1960s, and 6.9 per cent in the 1970s. The real flaw was revenue projections which predicted a balanced budget by 1984, and surpluses thereafter. Instead the annual budget deficits surged to a peak of $221 billion in 1986, a mindboggling 5.3 per cent of GNP.

How did the United States finance its debt? Having ruled out tax increases the White House could only borrow the money, much of which came from foreign investors. During the 1980s, foreign borrowing averaged 3.0 per cent of GNP – the highest sustained borrowing as a percentage of GNP in American history. In 1986, for example, the United States borrowed $144 billion, nearly two-thirds of that year's federal deficit and twice the net investment in plant and equipment, and in 1987 borrowed $157 billion from overseas. Much of that foreign capital was Japanese, and America's financial dependence on Japan will rapidly deepen in the decades ahead leading to even more tremendous transfers of wealth west across the Pacific.

The United States originally became a net creditor country in 1915, and its net surplus rose steadily over the course of the century to peak at $141 billion in 1981. In that year, the United States had $720 billion in overseas assets while foreigners held $579 billion in the United States. America's last surplus year was 1984 when its $896 billion in overseas assets exceeded the $892 billion in foreign assets in the United States by only $4 billion. And even that surplus was extremely shaky since over half of America's overseas assets in 1984 were in outstanding loans, and over half of those to developing countries which were experiencing repayment difficulties.

Reaganomics, between 1981 and 1985, wiped out the entire net foreign asset position that had taken over 75 years to accumulate, then ran up America's net foreign debt over the next five years to $670 billion in 1990. In early 1985, the United States became a net debtor nation, and by the year's end the net debt had swelled to $112 billion, a sum greater than the debt of either Mexico or Brazil. The debt mountain soared. In 1986, America's debt of $264 billion was larger than the combined debt of the next three largest debtor countries – Mexico, Brazil, and Argentina![46]

Even worse than the amount of debt accumulated during the Reagan years was the way those foreign borrowings were spent. In a complete break with tradition, the United States borrowed foreign money to finance consumption rather than investment. The Reagan inspired consumption boom contrasted sharply with the only other unusually large period of foreign borrowing. During the 1860s and 1870s, the United States borrowed 2.2 per cent of its GNP from foreign lenders; in 1873 America's accumulated net foreign debt of $1.8 billion was about 25 per cent of GNP. The debt peaked at $3.3 billion in 1896, then declined rapidly until the United States became a net creditor country in 1915. But these loans were invested in infrasture like railroads, canals, and ports, or industries like steel, petroleum and shipbuilding.

Under Reaganomics, consumers not only spent their tax rebates, but dipped deeply into their savings to spend even more. Between 1950 to 1980, individual savings after taxes averaged 7.2 per cent of GNP, then fell steadily to just 3.7 per cent of GNP in 1987. Net private savings (households and businesses) averaged 7.5 per cent (personal 4.7 per cent, business 2.8 per cent) during the 1950s, 8.2 per cent (4.8 per cent personal, 3.4 per cent business) during the 1960s, and 8.0 per cent (5.5 per cent personal, 2.5 per cent business) during the 1970s.

What was the effect of the government's immense debt on interest rates? In early 1981, Reagan declared that the government "has only two ways of getting money other than raising taxes. It can go into the money markets and borrow, competing with its own citizens and driving up interest rates . . . or it can print money." Reagan apparently either forgot or overlooked this simple economic principle during the 1984 televised debate with Walter Mondale when he said simply that: "The connection has been made between the deficit and the interest rates. There is no connection."[47]

The Federal Reserve was locked in a paradox – it needed to raise interest rates to attract money to finance the deepening deficits while it needed to lower interest rates to stimulate the economy out of the 1982 recession. Thus, although Treasury Bill rates eventually fell from 16 per cent in May 1981 to about 8 per cent by late 1982, real interest rates (the inflation rate subtracted from the nominal rate) remained high. Once again, Reaganomics sharply broke with tradition. During the 1950s, real interests rates on short term business loans were only 0.22 per cent, the 1960s 1.9 per cent, and 1970s 0.24 per cent, for an average of 0.79 per cent between 1950 and 1980. During the 1980s, this rate rose to 4.95 percent!

During the 1980s, the federal deficit averaged 4.2 per cent and private savings 5.7 per cent (3.9 per cent personal savings and 1.8 per cent business) of GNP, as compared to an average federal deficit of 1.8 per cent of GNP during the 1970s and a net private savings rate of 8.0 per cent.

Thus the Reagan Administration had to borrow the equivalent of almost three fourths of private savings to pay for its debts. The federal deficits are somewhat undercut by state and local surpluses. If all government deficits are subtracted from net savings, the remainder left for private investors averaged 7.1 per cent during the 1950s, 7.8 per cent during the 1960s, and 7.0 per cent in the 1970s. The massive federal deficits caused by Reagan-omics meant that only 2.8 per cent of GNP was available to private investors during the 1980s. Higher interest rates were largely a result of the fierce competition between the government and private investors for this reduced savings pool.

Thus, public and private investments alike – which are vital to stimulating increased productivity, growth and competitiveness – languished. The share of federal spending devoted to enhancing America's economic infrastructure like roads, bridges, ports, dropped steadily from a peak of 6.9 per cent of GNP in 1952 to average 1.5 per cent during the 1970s and a miniscule 1.2 per cent during the 1980s. The stock of public capital annually grew 3.5 per cent between 1950 and 1980, but only 0.9 per cent since. Although gross investment rose steadily from 9.6 per cent of GNP in the 1950s, 9.9 per cent in the 1960s, 10.8 per cent in the 1970s, and 10.9 per cent in the 1980s, net investment averaged 3.0 per cent in the 1950s, 3.5 per cent in the 1960s, and 3.3 per cent in the 1970s, for an average of 3.3 per cent between 1950 and 1980, it plunged to only 2.3 per cent during the 1980s. Between 1950 and 1980, the average capital stock per worker rose steadily from $26,000 to $43,100, but in 1987, had only slightly risen to $45,900. Net business investment in plant and equipment and additions to inventory averaged 4.1 per cent between 1950 and 1980; during the 1980s it fell to an average 2.7 per cent. The net housing investment averaged 2.9 per cent up through 1980 and 1.9 per cent since. Although manufacturing productivity rose at an annual average 4.1 per cent, most of this increase resulted from the net loss of 1.5 million jobs rather than investments.

Reaganomics did not increase real corporate wealth – by 1987 American corporations did not own any more tangible real assets than in 1980. Most wealth created during the Reagan years was paper wealth which, instead of being reinvested in capital equipment or research and development was instead used to finance acquisitions, leveraged buyouts, and stock repurchases. Between 1984 and 1987, American corporations raised $116 billion through new issues of common and preferred stock while retiring $432 billion and taking on $726 billion of new debt (net of repayment of old debt). This massive substitution of debt for equity forced American businesses to divert 56 per cent of available earnings just to pay interest. In the 1950s and 1960s, the average percentage of earnings to interest payments was only 16 per cent while during the 1970s it was 33 per cent. The corporate debt to equity ratio thus steadily rose and varied from a high of 78 per cent in 1982 to a low of 57 per cent in April 1987, considerably higher than the average 45 per cent average for the fifties and sixties though below the postwar high of 105 per cent in 1974.

Friedman points out that

> stock repurchases, leveraged buyouts, and other acquisitions all represent the use of a corporation's funds (whether generated internally or borrowed in the credit market) for purposes other than investment in new plant and equipment. No new refineries were built because Chevron spent $13 billion to buy Gulf. Nor did GE's $6 billion purchase of RCA put any new electronics factories, nor Burrough's $4 billion acquisition of Sperry put any new computer plants in place. In each case, the money went to the acquired company's previous shareholders. The $730 million that GM paid to Ross Perot and his group to buy back their stock built no new auto plants, nor will the billions of dollars GM will pay to whichever of its other shareholders accept its offer to buy back an additional 20 per cent of its stock by 1990. In each of these kinds of transactions, the money leaves the corporate sector altogether.[48]

Despite all the promises, economic growth was actually lower during the Reagan era. Between 1980 and 1990, American GNP grew at an annual rate of 2.4 per cent, considerably less than the 3.3 per cent annual average increase between 1950 and 1980. Reaganomics initially pushed the United States into its worst depression since the 1930s; during 1981–82 11 per cent of Americans were unemployed while industry utilization of capacity fell to only 69 per cent in comparison to a postwar average of 82 per cent. But eventually the deficit spending and tax cuts stimulated the economy, with consumer spending leading the way as it rose from an average 62.9 per cent during the 1970s to 65.1 per cent during the 1980s. Real income, however, trailed far behind spending; consumer spending increased 24.7 per cent between 1980 and 1987 while real income increased only 19.8 per cent. The result was a deepening consumer debt. Reaganomics left most Americans running even harder to stay in place. By 1987, 49 per cent of all married couples were working couples, up from 42 per cent in 1980. But real medium family weekly income fell from $516 in 1979 to $501 in 1990.

Although the Reagan Administration boasted of all the new jobs created, the estimated 13 million net new jobs created during the 1980s was well short of the 20 million created during the 1970s. Business simply was not expanding at its previous rates; the number of new businesses incorporated each year rose by only 3.7 per cent between 1980 and 1987 compared to an average 6.0 per cent between 1950 and 1980. Of new jobs created during the 1980s, 36 per cent have provided workers with less than half of what the average worker made in 1973.[49] Manufacturing jobs declined by 1.7 million during the 1980s. Part-time work has grown one and a half times that of full time work. The shift to a service based economy has contributed to the deterioration in the real income of Americans. Service jobs do pay far less than manufacturing or construction jobs. In 1987, the average service job paid $179 per week compared to $406 in manufacturing and $477 in construction.

Why did America's trade deficit balloon during the 1980s, with devastating consequences for America's economy? The most important reason was the overvalued dollar which rose from 209 against the yen in December 1980 to 260 in early 1985, thus imposing a 30 per cent tax on American exports and granting a 30 per cent subsidy to Japanese imports. And why did the dollar rise so precipitously during this time? Higher real interest rates to attack inflation and attract foreign money to pay for the deepening deficits were the primary cause of the dollar's rise, exacerbated by the White House policy of talking up the dollar because of their quaint belief that a "strong dollar represents a strong America". From 1976 to November 1980, real interest rates overseas exceeded those in the United States, thus reducing the dollar's demand and thus its value. Starting in 1980, the Federal Reserve imposed a tight monetary policy to attack inflation, which caused America's real interest rates to rise. The Reagan Administration's massive deficits and consequent need to borrow caused real interest rates to skyrocket and far exceed those of its foreign industrial rivals.

Higher interests rates delivered a double whammy to America's economy. Real interest rates in the United States rose compared to those of its overseas industrial rivals, thus raising the cost of money for American investors and the dollar's value which overpriced American goods at home and abroad. The demand for dollars raised the dollar's value by almost 50 per cent between 1981 and 1985. The increased demand for dollars caused it to steadily rise in value by 74 per cent between 1980 and 1985, or 64 per cent after subtracting international differences in inflation. The prices of goods abroad fell an average 20 per cent while the prices of American made goods rose 12 per cent, for an average 32 per cent price advantage for foreign goods and corresponding penalty for American goods. Foreign holders of American dollars have increasingly reinvested their money in the United States instead of exchanging it for their own currency, thus keeping the demand for dollars keeps the price high.

The result was a deepening trade deficit. America's trade deficit increased almost six times between 1980 and 1987, from a $26 billion to $159 billion deficit. This deficit devastated scores of American industries and thousands of American companies. Even the agricultural surplus declined from $29 billion in 1980 to $6 billion in 1986, thus creating the farm crisis which bankrupted tens of thousands of farm families. The payments balance likewise suffered a horrifying decline. In 1980, the United States still enjoyed a payments surplus because the return ($73 billion) on overseas investments such as stocks, bonds, bank deposits and profits exceeded the return ($42 billion) on foreign investments in the United States. The United States earned an additional $13 billion from royalties and licensing fees on technology while foreigners earned only $5 billion from such sales to Americans. The relative decline of American manufacturing is also reflected in the greater percentage of American products requiring protection. The percentage of total imports restricted doubled from 12 per cent in 1980 to 23 per cent in 1987.[50]

By the mid-1980s, it was clear to most observers that Reaganomics was drastically undermining America's economy. Even the White House was torn between neoclassical ideologues and realists. An administrative shakeup in early 1985 which allowed realist Jim Baker to head the Treasury Department while making ideologue Don Regan chief of staff led to a reversal of the high dollar policy. Baker engineered an agreement at New York's Plaza Hotel in September 1985 among the finance ministers of the United States, Japan, Germany, Britain and France to devalue the dollar. Although no previous efforts to devalue the dollar had been as extensive since President Nixon's efforts in August and December 1971, the major reason for the dollar's decline was the decline in the interest rate differential between the United States and other industrial giants. Foreign central banks raised their interest rates while the Federal Reserve lowered its rates. By 1986, America's real interest rates once again fell below those of other industrial countries and by 1987 they were an average one percentage point lower, and the dollar fell accordingly as the demand for dollars shifted to other currencies. Between 1985 and 1988, the dollar devalued by over 50 per cent against the yen, from 265 to 125.

But in the short term, the J-curve effect caused America's trade deficit with its major trade partners to peak at a $59 billion trade deficit with Japan, a $20 billion deficit with the European Community, of which $16 billion was with West Germany, and a $34 billion deficit with the four newly industrializing countries (NICs) – South Korea, Taiwan, Singapore and Hong Kong. America's trade deficits have lessened in the three years since. In 1990, although it continued to suffer an overall trade deficit of $95 billion, the United States actually enjoyed a $10 billion trade surplus with the European Community, while its deficit with both Germany and the NICs halved to $8 billion and $17 billion, respectively. In stark and disturbing contrast to America's improved trade position with its other industrial rivals was its $41 billion trade deficit with Japan in 1990, nearly

45 per cent of its total deficit. Japan's surplus with the United States remained immense and debilitating despite the yen's almost doubling in value over the previous four years. The efforts to devalue the dollar may have been too little too late. The overvalued dollar's damage to America's economy has already been devastating. Although the dollar's devaluation did eventually help reduce America's trade deficit, it also allowed Japanese and other foreign investors to buy up American economic assets at bargain basement prices.

Thus, Reaganomics retarded rather than stimulated economic growth. The high dollar and high interest rates chopped several percentage points off growth that would have occurred with a low dollar and interest rates. Friedman's assessment of Reaganomics is stark: "Reagan's fiscal policy has achieved none of its advertised economic objectives . . . The assets we have dissipated are gone. The debts which we occured are real".[51] Paying only the interest on the debt, let alone the principal, will mean the transfer of immense amounts of American wealth abroad for the foreseeable future. Americans are becoming increasingly pessimistic about the future of themselves and the nation. Most no longer believe they will do better than their parents; most would be content to even equal their parent's socioeconomic achievements.

CONCLUSION

In his philosophical and political duel with Alexander Hamilton, Thomas Jefferson asserted that American democracy would be upheld by yeoman farmers and merchants, and undermined by the Treasury Secretary's industrial policy schemes which envisioned government assisted development. Jeffersonian liberalism soon triumphed over Hamiltonian state-led industrialization. But who really won in the long term?

American liberalism may largely guarantee individual liberty but is a woefully inadequate means of acheiving economic development. The United States became the global hegemon despite rather than because of its liberal system. America's growth rate has lumbered along at around two per cent a year throughout most of the 19th and 20th centuries. Other industrial states grew faster but sqandered their wealth through imperialism and two devastating world wars. Safe in the Western Hemisphere, the United States continued to trade with almost all sides of both struggles until it was directly attacked. After World War I, the United States set aside its great power crown and not only returned to political isolation, but toppled the global trade system by initiating a trade war in 1930.

The Roosevelt Administration, which came to power in 1933, recognized America's responsibility for not only collapsing the global economy but refusing to uphold it as its most powerful state. But while the Roosevelt White House had the will to assume hegemony, it took the devastation of the other industrial powers during World War II for the United States to achieve overwhelming economic and military superiority. American hegemony lasted only a quarter century. By the late 1960s, the revitalization of other industrial powers had eliminated American comparative advantage in most products, and America's trade balance steadily worsened. Although President Nixon's New Economic Policy of 1971 signaled a shift from a predominantly liberal to increasingly interventionist policy, it proved too little too late. America's relative economic decline continued and in 1985 Japan snatched the crown and throne of hegemony from the United States.

The reasons for American decline are clear. American foreign policy since 1945 has concentrated on maintaining a balance of power with the Soviet Union and a liberal global political economy. The cost of a continuing Cold War arms race and hot wars against 'Soviet surrogates' in Korea and Vietnam has been heavy. The 'military industrial complex' has not only drained the American economy of trillions of dollars and many of its best minds, but has also locked up much of its high technology for 'security purposes.' America's comparative advantage in high value mass consumer products has suffered a corresponding steady decline. Numerous studies have revealed that the greater a country's defense spending the lower its productivity.[52] Kennedy bluntly asserts that the diversion of the best scientists, engineers, and vast financial resources into defense-oriented production rather than commercial exports

> will hurt economic growth . . . Large scale armaments spending . . . can benefit specific industries; but it can also lead to a diversion of resources from other groups in society, and it can make that national economy less capable of handling the commercial challenges of other states . . . A large military establishment may, like a great monument, look imposing to the impressionable observer; but if it is not resting upon a firm foundation (in this case, a productive national economy), it runs the risk of a future collapse . . . A top heavy military establishment may slow down the rate of economic growth and lead to a decline in the nation's share of world manufacturing output, and therefore wealth, and therefore power, the whole issue becomes one of balancing the short-term security afforded by large defense forces against the longer-term security of rising production and income.[53]

A related reason has been allowing America's economic rivals to pursue protectionist foreign economic policies and relatively unrestricted access to the United States market. Nye writes that "the political context of the miltary balance limited US ability to wield its economic power . . . Economic issues were rarely linked explicitly to military ones . . . The United States often subordinated economic interests during the period of the supposed Pax Americana because it was concerned about the high politics of the global balance and the challenge of Soviet power".[54] In the early postwar era, this was necessary to revitalize the war-ravaged industrial powers and integrate them into the international trade system. Still, some of the Cold War successes may not have been as effective as is commonly thought. For example, Charles Maier argues that American aid contributed only about 10 to 20 per cent of Europe's capital needs during the late 1940s, and regardless doubts Europe would have gone communist even if Washington had not made the effort.[55] Washington has continued these policies despite increasingly severe balance of trade payments. America's traditional *laissez-faire* orientation has prevented it from pursuing rational industrial policies that would enable it to compete with its economic rivals.

America's decline was vastly accelerated during the Reagan Administration whose spend and borrow policies devastated the economy. Although Reagan repeatedly promised to cut overall government spending, it actually increased since he took office from about 24 per cent of GNP to over 25 per cent, largely the result of a trillion dollar defense build-up. The huge government spending increases and tax cuts led to budget deficits of over $200 billion a year and a tripling of the national debt in eight years; it had taken the United States over 200 years to run up a national debt of $1 trillion, it took the Reagan Administration just eight years to push the national debt to $3 trillion. The federal budget deficit rose steadily from an average one per cent of GNP in the 1960s to 2 per cent in the 1970s to 4.5 per cent in the 1980s while America's net personal savings rate declined from 7.9 per cent in the 1970s to 2.1 per cent between 1985 and 1987. By 1987, the budget deficit absorbed two-thirds of net private savings forcing the United States to make up the difference by borrowing from foreign and largely Japanese creditors. During that time, 60 per cent of net national investment was financed from abroad. The Reagan Administration locked itself into a very vicious economic cycle in which it had to raise interest rates to attract foreign capital which in turn undermined America's economy, forcing the government to borrow yet more money to make up for the lack of savings, which led to yet higher interest rates, a vastly overvalued dollar, and even greater budget deficits. As if all this were not debilitating enough, Reagan budget cuts, devastating such important economic programs as Eximbank, the National Science Foundation, and grants for private research and development, proved the equilvalent of unilateral geoeconomic disarmament. The administration's high dollar policy which pushed the exchange rate from about 200 yen to a dollar in 1980 to as high as 270 yen to the dollar in 1985 gave Japanese manufacturers tremendous windfall comparative advantages and profits at the expense of their American rivals. America's trade deficit with Japan shot up over six times in as many years, from about $8 billion in 1980 to $60 billion in 1986.

During the 1980 and 1984 Presidential races, Ronald Reagan repeatedly turned toward the television cameras and asked the American people if they were better off today than they were four years before. If the viewers had been able to resist the patriotism and good neighbor emotions evoked by the Reagan Administration public relations machine and carefully examined the facts, most Americans would have discovered that in 1984 they were not only worse off than four years earlier but that their real incomes had dropped considerably since the early 1970s.

During the Reagan era the rich certainly did get richer while most other Americans either kept up or fell behind. Reaganomics allowed the richest 1 per cent of the population to enjoy 60 per cent of the new wealth created during the 1980s. The next 19 per cent gained an additional 29 per cent, for a total gain among the richest 20 per cent of 89 per cent! The second and third quintiles received meager 9 per cent and 4 per cent gains, respectively, while the bottom two quintiles lost 1 per cent and 9 per cent, respectively. The percentage of Americans in the middle class shrank steadily from 71.2 per cent in 1969 to 63.3 per cent in 1989.[56]

But Reaganomics simply accellerated a downward trend which began in the early 1970s. Median weekly family earnings from wages and salaries dropped from $516 in 1979 to $471 in 1981, then rose to $537 in 1988, then dropped again to $501 in 1990. The real median hourly pay for the average worker was $8.52 in 1973, $7.66 in 1982, $7.83 in 1988, and $7.46 in 1990. Despite an average annual 4 per cent productivity rise through the 1980s, median factory wages dropped from $8.65 in 1985 to $8.00 in 1990. However, Reaganomics did clearly boost the incomes of the wealthiest 20 per cent of Americans, although the incomes of the remaining 80 per cent either stagnated or declined. The real median income of the top quintile rose from $73 764 in 1981 to $92 663 in 1990.

What accounts for the stagnant or declining real income for most Americans since the early 1970s? Most economists point the figure the 1973 quintupling of oil prices and further doubling of prices in 1979. But American productivity and capital investments had declined throughout the 1960s and early 1970s – the oil price rises only exacerbated the problem. During this period, America's manufacturing corporations steadily located more of their production overseas or bought foreign components to bring down costs with the cheaper overseas labor. Thus the wealth generated by American manufacturing was spread around the world rather than kept in the United States where consumers could benefit from the higher wages, government from higher tax receipts, and ulitimately, business from the lower interests rates from increased savings and higher profits from increased consumption.

But this production shift in search of cheaper wages was not inevitable – in 1990 Japan's overseas production still accounted for only 5 per cent of its total manufacturing output compared to 20 per cent of America's despite the fact that Japan's per capita income is higher than that of the United States. What explains for this difference? One key goal of Japan's rational industrial policies has been to keep as much manufacturing, and thus wealth, in Japan as possible while shedding only the most heavily polluting or basic production overseas. Neoclassical economics would claim that this strategy would be ultimately self-defeating since Japan's higher cost labor would lead to higher cost production, and thus a steady loss of competitive advantage. But as always, Japan's economy, let alone the real world, does not conform to neoclassical economic's simplistic assumptions. Webs of import barriers, cartels, and subsidies prevented competitive foreign products from challenging the market shares of Japanese corporations, which thus received windfall profits from selling their products at highly inflated prices to captive Japanese consumers. Japan's corporations achieved immense scale production and profits from sole access to 120 million consumers, and these huge production scales and profits were further boosted by concerted Japanese dumping of production in foreign markets to capture market share and drive foreign rivals out of business. If Washington had pursued neomercantilist rather than liberal policies, America's economic growth, industries, and wage earners would have similarly benefited.

Although Washington continues to cling to anachronistic measures of power, some top officials are beginning to understand the revolutionary changes in international relations and the power balance. Assistant Secretary of State Richard Solomon stated in 1990 that: "We now face a future in which technological and commercial capabilities more than military strength are the significant determinants of state power and influence. National security is ever more reckoned in terms of economic and environmental concerns".[57] From 1945 to late 1960s when it was the world's sole economic power, the United States not only could afford an unequal playing field, it had to accept one in order to help revive the other industrial countries and the global political economy. But continued adherence to liberal principles in a neomercantilist world is devastating America's economy and accelerating the country's decline. While liberalism should remain at the heart of the country's political system, America's leadership and public must adopt a range of economic policies based on the real world rather than on discredited liberal ideals.

3 Japanese Neomercantilism: The New Hegemony

The Japanese have mastered a superior way of creating and distributing wealth. How do they do it?

Japanese spokespeople, their well-paid foreign lobbyists, and neoclassical economists propogate the view that Japan's economic miracle results from strict adherence to free market principles. The reality is quite different – Japanese shun liberal theory as an economic plague. Neomercantilism, not liberalism, accounted for an average Japanese growth rate four times that of the United States before 1973, and twice America's rate since, and a population whose per capita wealth is greater and distribution more egalitarian than that of the United States. Neomercantilism not liberalism converted Japan from wartime ruin and mass poverty into the world's most dynamic banking, technological, and manufacturing superpower. Neomercantilism, not liberalism, will make the 21st century the "Japan Century". Tokyo's economic policies violate every liberal tenet. Japan's markets are carefully managed, not free. Policies, not "natural endowments", created the comparative advantage for most Japanese products. The government, not markets, determines the ever more sophisticated industrial profile of Japan's economy.

The dazzling success of Japanese neomercantilism thoroughly discredits neoclassical economic theory. Liberal economists cannot explain Japan's rise through the two-dimensional maxims of their creed – although that has not stopped them from trying. If Tokyo had followed liberal rather than neomercantilist policies since 1945, Japan would today be poor rather than rich, politically volatile rather than stable. If free markets had prevailed, Japan's economy today would be built around labor-intensive industries like toys, textiles, and consumer electronics. Any entrepreneurial efforts to create capital-intensive industries like automobiles, computers, semiconductors, steel, shipbuilding, aerospace or biotechnology, to name a few, would have been wiped out by inexpensive, high quality American or European imports. To develop their economy, Tokyo turned for inspiration not to Smith's or Ricardo's liberal maxims, but to Schumpeter's microindustrial theories. According to a Ministry of International Trade and Industry (MITI) official:

MITI decided to establish in Japan industries which require intensive employment of capital and technology, industries that in consideration of comparative cost of production should be the most inappropriate for Japan, industries such as steel, oil-refining, industrial machinery of all sorts, and electronics . . . From a short run, static viewpoint, encouragement of such industries would seem to conflict with economic rationalism. But, from a long-range viewpoint, these are precisely the industries where income elasticity of demand is high, technological progress is rapid, and labor productivity rises fast. It was clear that without these industries it would be difficult to employ a population of 100 million and raise their standard of living to that of Europe and America with light industries alone; whether right or wrong (in a neoclassical economic sense), Japan had to have these heavy and chemical industries . . . (the government) has been able to concentrate its scant capital in strategic industries.[1]

Miyohei Shinohara, former head of the economics section of the Economic Planning Agency (EPA), justifies the rejection of a free market for Japan's development by pointing out that although by liberal standards MITI's industrial policies "were wrong," they

achieved unprecedented success by going against modern economic theory . . . The lesson we have learned . . . is that perfunctory theories framed in a surrealistic and hypothetical world, in the years when Adam Smith and David Ricardo were predominant, are no longer workable . . . Should Japan have entrusted its future . . . if the Japanese economy had adopted the simple doctrine of free trade . . . it would almost permanently have been unable to break away from the Asian pattern of stagnation and poverty, and would have remained the weakest link in the free world, thereby becoming a problem area in the Far East.[2]

THE JAPANESE WORLD VIEW

Japanese neomercantilism is not just a set of nationalist policies, it is a way of life that is deeply interwoven in Japan's culture, institutions, and psychology.[3] Rimei Honda, a Tokugawa philosopher, wrote in the 18th century that "foreign trade is a war in that each party seeks to extract wealth from the other".[4] The idea that Japan is locked in a perpetual trade war with the outside world is the spiritual engine of Japanese neomercantilism that single-mindedly drives virtually all Japanese, from the highest minister to lowest factory worker, to devote themselves to Japan's success.

Nationalism is boiling within Japan's elite and mass public alike. Chalmers Johnson expresses the fever of Japanese nationalism very colorfully: "from about 1941 to 1961 the Japanese economy remained on a war footing. The goal changed from military to economic victory, but the Japanese people could not have worked harder, saved more, or innovated more ruthlessly if they had actually been engaged in a war for national survival".[5] Japan's bureacrats are considered fiercely nationalistic, with MITI and other officials favoring expressions such as *joi* (expulsion of the foreigners), *iteki* (barbarians), and hairy Chinese (*keto*) when discussing Japan's trade rivals, and see their function in life as the protection of Japanese industries from "foreign pressures".[6] Even Foreign Ministry officials, usually described as the least nationalistic of Japan's bureaucrats, display "an impatient, defiant, and cocky attitude of self-assertion, with heavy nationalist overtones" which "is more than a mood and will affect the general orientation of Japanese foreign policy – including the controversial issues of national security and rearmament – in important ways in the years to come . . . Today's Young Turks may be beginning to fight against postwar pacifism and 'economic diplomacy' in the name of an independent foreign policy".[7]

Japanese sharply and continuously distinguish between themselves and the rest of humanity, and see themselves as a "pure, unique race." Japan's response to such international calamaties as war, poverty, disease, starvation, environmental degradation, and other human-made and natural disasters is revealed by the Japanese expression *taigan no kaji*, or "fire on the other side of the river"; in other words, those are other people's problems, not Japan's. Tokyo's response to foreign pressure to act responsibly in the global political economy thus follows a consistent pattern. International appeals for Japan to open its markets, stop dumping, untie its aid, or make larger contributions to the Western alliance are fiercely resisted until the foreign pressure (*gaiatsu*) subsides. Japanese make a "concession" only when faced with a credible threat of retaliation, and even then it will be some token gesture that is hoped will allay criticism. These "concessions" are make not because they are long overdue but because they help Japan's image.

What is the origin of this fierce nationalism? Japanese society is based on the group rather than the individual – in premodern days the village or clan, today the company. The group gives individual members security and identity in return for undying loyalty. Individuals attain their identity mostly from the successes and failures of their group rather than themselves. Rather than follow their own preferences, individuals must conform to group norms and policies. Failure to do so can result in ostracism (*mura hachibu*) with the resulting trauma of lost identity and security. Although Japanese groupism may appear totalitarian to Western observers, Japanese are socialized from birth in these norms and most simply conform without thinking. Prestowitz points out that "in the United States, everything is allowed unless specifically prohibited, while in Japan, everything is prohibited unless specifically allowed".[8]

There is no equality within Japan; every individual and group is considered to be either above or below all others. In the premodern era, one's social place was theoretically fixed; society was organized into four classes with samurai at the top followed by farmers, artisans, and merchants. Each class was divided by countless groups with each slightly above or below the others. Society continues to be hierarchial today, although now individuals and groups can rise or fall in the social hierarchy according to their efforts. Japanese see international relations as also shaped by hierarchy rather than equality; like individuals and groups within Japan, states rise or fall within the international system based on their efforts. Japan's racist world view was succinctly captured by a 1983 statement by an NTT official that Japan "can manufacture a product of uniformity and superior quality because the Japanese are a race of completely pure blood, not a mongrelized race as in the United States".[9] A 1983 survey revealed that 53 per cent of Japanese felt "superior" to Westerners and only 8 per cent felt "inferior" to Westerners, a sharp contrast from survey results thirty years earlier in which only 20 per cent of Japanese felt superior, while 28 per cent inferior.[10] That a public survey would ask such a question of relative superiority or inferiority among nations is revealing in itself. It is difficult to imagine such a survey question being asked in any other democratic industrial country.

Japanese ethics are determined by the group's needs rather than a universal standard of right and wrong. Anything goes if it advances one's group, and thus a group's behavior can vary greatly from one situation to the next (*tsukaiwake*). The Japanese word for "fair" (*kohei*) suggests unequal benefits flowing from an unequal distribution of power, a meaning far different from the English concept. Japanese tend to be meek toward the strong and arrogant toward the weak. This partly reflects the pressures of competition both within and between groups. Haitani declares that "Japanese tend to be impervious to arguments based on logic or universal principles. The arguments based on free-trade principles carry little weight in a particularistic society . . . Because the Japanese are anxious to preserve domestic harmony at all costs – except, of course, at the cost of compromising national survival – they cannot allow anyone to be injured much, which they must do if the external economic frictions are to be significantly reduced".[11]

Groups sublimate their internal struggles with all the fiercer competition against other groups. Rival groups are often considered outright enemies. Yet if faced with a common enemy, Japanese groups can cooperate by forming even larger groups even while competing (*Kyoruku shi nagara kyoso*). The ultimate group is Japan itself. Japan's countless groups unite into a fierce nationalism when faced with a real or imagined foreign threat. Foreign criticism of Japanese neomercantilist policies, no matter how well-reasoned or documented, is fiercely denounced as "racist" and "Japan bashing". Foreign pressure on Japan to abandon its neomercantilist policies invariably provokes a highly nationalistic reaction. Japanese have angrily denounced virtually all such American efforts to reform Japan, from the Occupation reforms of the late 1940s through to the Structural Impediments Initiatives of the early 1990s, as revisits of Commodore Perry's "Black Ships" which in 1854 forced Japan into the global political economy.

Japan's ability to play a martyr scapegoated by a racist world was epitomized by the reaction when, in April 1988, Congress imposed limited sanctions on Toshiba for its sell-out of technology to the Soviet Union that would enable Russian submarines to run more quietly and cost the United States an estimated $30–40 billion to overcome. Toshiba's guilt and the costs to the United States were clearly established. MITI Minister Hajime Tamura articulated the views of virtually all Japanese when he accused Congress of "racial discrimination and anti-Japanese sentiment".[12] Japan's "we can do no wrong" outlook is a major obstacle to the mutual understanding that Japanese claim to desire.

Tokyo's need to find foreign scapegoats to distract attention from its own neomercantilist policies is reflected in the powerful anti-semitism which has swept Japan over the last half dozen years. Masami Uno's *If You Understand Jews, You Can See the Whole World* has sold over 540 000 copies since it was published in 1986, while over 100 books were published about Jews in 1990 alone, of which the *Counterattack of Hitler* which was advertized on the front page of the *Asahi Shimbun* and has sold 30 000 to date, claimed that the Holocaust was a myth. Most of these books luridly claim that a Jewish conspiracy rules the world. Neil Sandberg, Director of the American Jewish Committee's Pacific Rim Institute, met with Japan's leading publishers over the issue in 1990. He said that he found the Japanese publishers puzzled by the protests, and wondered why the Jews were not instead flattered to be thought so powerful: "They told us, 'You're members of a superior race and you come from a successful group, and we're surprised this material concerns you'".[13] Japan's Foreign Ministry has been concerned that Japanese anti-semitism could cause a backlash among American Jews. In 1989, it urged Japan's publishers to be more sensitive since the "Japanese government regrets to see that the label of Japanese anti-semitism has taken root among American Jews".[14]

Japanese neomercantilism, which has brought the country such vast wealth and rapid development, is intractably mired in Japanese culture, and thus can not be significantly liberalized despite all the sustained foreign pressures and subsequent Tokyo promises. Japanese groupism translates into trade and investment exclusionism. Economic transactions between firms are determined by the relationship between buyer and seller rather the product's price or quality. Ronald Dore asserts that in Japan "there are no markets, only a network of established customer relations", a phenomena which he describes as "relational contracting".[15] This careful market management allows even the weak firms to cling to small market shares.

This attempt to protect the weak and not disrupt the economy does not extend to foreign firms. Either they will be attacked unmercifully until they either sell-out or declare bankruptcy, or, if politically expedient, will be confined to tiny market slivers. In Haitani's words: "when giant Japanese firms compete for a market share or ranking in an overseas market and foreign competitors are crushed, few Japanese become alarmed. Foreigners, being outsiders, are not the object of Japanese concern. Japanese . . . are culturally conditioned to think only in terms of their group interest and foreigners fall outside of the boundary of their relevant group."[16] No amount of foreign pressure or Tokyo promises will change this basic socioeconomic reality. Few foreign producers with a comparative advantage for their goods and services will ever achieve a market share in Japan comparable to their penetration elsewhere. Japan's values of groupism, hierarchy, conformity, cooperation, competition, xenophobia, status-obsession, and balance of power among organizations will continue to nourish Tokyo's neomercantilist policies into the future.

JAPAN'S POWER ELITE

On November 12, 1990, Emperor Akihito was formally installed as Japan's 125th emperor. Wearing a morning coat instead of the traditional robes, Emperor Akihito pledged to "observe the Constitution of Japan and discharge my duties as a symbol of state and unity of the people".[17] By virtually any standard, Japan is a well functioning liberal democracy.[18] Japan's American-imposed Constititution guarantees the full spectrum of human rights and regular elections within a parliamentary political system. Although conservative parties have ruled Japan for all but nine months since 1945, they reflect the people's will.

There is a wide gap, however, between official and actual sources of policy, budget and law making. Although the Constitution declares Japan's parliament the highest authority, it is the bureaucrats who continue to draft as well as implement the vast majority of Japan's policies, budgets and laws. Japan's political economic system is built on corporatist foundations in which the state organizes and regulates conflict between society's most important interests. The central players in this system are a "governing triad" composed of the ministries, ruling Liberal Democratic Party (LDP) and big business interests. The triad is knit together in a tight web of mutual interests in which:

> the LDP depended on the bureaucracy for technical expertise and legislative initiative; the bureaucracy depended upon the LDP for parliamentary majorities in favour of government legislation, and for jobs on retirement; the LDP depended upon big business for electoral funding; big business depended upon the LDP for political backing, advantageous policies and political stability; big business depended upon bureaucracy for favors in the drawing up and implementing of legislation; the bureaucracy depended upon big business for jobs upon retirement.[19]

Much of the elite is tied together by graduation from Tokyo University and marriage. Other business interests such as farmers, contractors and distributors play an important role in determining protectionist policies for their respective sectors, but have no significant impact on general policies, while other groups like the opposition parties, labor, consumers and environmentalists play little more than a symbolic role in Japanese policymaking. The mass media can be very critical of specific government policies, but firmly supports Japan's neomercantilist and industrial policies.

Policy is shaped by continuous consultation among the relevant interests. There are as many policymaking processes and actors as their are policies. On most issues, Japan's policy making has shifted from a bureaucracy-dominated into a joint ministry–LDP system (*jimin-kancho kongotai*). Policy councils (*shingikai*) and their working groups (*konronkai*) composed of representatives of all relevant interests in a policy area are essential for forming an elite consensus behind specific policies. Although the bureaucracy continues to write up most bills, the LDP is playing an increasingly important role in initiating and shaping policy. Ministry bills are sent to appropriate bureaus in the LDP's Policy Affairs Council (PARC, *Seichokai*), and are then approved by the Executive Council, which then sends it on to the appropriate Diet Committees then onto the floor where it usually becomes law. Increasingly important in policy-making, however, are party caucuses (*zoku*) of LDP politicians grouped around specific issues who pressure the ministries to write up the bills on their behalf. Smooth as this process seems from the outside, it is actually characterized by fierce turf battles between and within each triad leg and other relevant interests. The number of new interests gaining access to the policymaking process has steadily increased to the point where the government often experiences "policy gridlock". Japan's footdragging on such international issues as dismantling its trade barriers or contributing more defense, aid or disaster relief is as much the result of policymaking stalemate as neomercantilism.

The lines between those who make and those who implement policy are extremely blurred in Japan. Gaikaku Dantai are groups composed of bureaucrats, politicians, and private citizens, and formed to implement government policies. For example, MAFF uses the agricultural groups (Nokyo) to administer the Food Control, Livestock Stabilization, Feed Demand and Supply Stabilization, and Dairy Farming Promotion laws. Such responsibilities can include targeting and distributing subsidies, implementing land and irrigation improvement schemes, and offering technical and information assistance. Japan's official government thus appears limited while its semiofficial government is virtually unlimited in its ability to micromanage the economy.[20]

The ministries battle constantly over either defending or expanding their turf (*nawabari arasoi*). The two most important "policy ministries" (*seisaku kancho*) are the Ministry of Finance (MOF) and Ministry of International Trade and Industry (MITI), in which the former shapes the broad macroeconomic policies and the latter determines most industrial policies, although both have a powerful say in each other's policy bailiwick. Johnson identifies MITI as the "general economic staff" of Japanese neo-mercantalism, and asserts that "the history of MITI is central to the economic and political history of modern Japan", and "single-mindedly turned the Japanese industrial structure from light, labor–intensive industries to steel, ships and automobiles, of which Japan is today the leading producer. To find comparable achievements by bureaucracies in other nations, one would have to look to cases like America's wartime Manhattan Project or NASA's sending a manned rocket to the moon".[21] Prestowitz writes that an American version of MITI would have to include the "Departments of Commerce and Energy, the Office of the US Trade Representative, the Export–Import Bank, the Small Business Administration, the National Science Foundation, the Overseas Private Investment Corporation, the Environmental Protection Agency, and parts of the Departments of Defense and Justice."[22] With legal authorization (*kyoninka*) in over 2000 areas, MITI is responsible for managing the entire economy, and as such is not beholden to any one industry. Other ministries, however, like the Ministry of Posts and Telecommunications (MPT), Ministry of Construction (MOC), Ministry of Transportation (MOT), Ministry of Health and Welfare (MHW), Ministry of Justice (MOJ), and Ministry of Agriculture,

Forestry and Fisheries (MAFF) dispense enormous patronage to specific industries, making foreign penetration of those markets all but impossible. The power of MITI and the other ministries is furthur enhanced by the lack of independent appeals procedures and a strong judiciary. According to Prestowitz, the ministries "write the laws, then write the interpretative ordinances, administer the laws, and handle most complaints arising from them".[23]

Although the challenge of other ministries to MITI's power has grown steadily over time, competition among the LDP factions has always been fierce. Japan has been ruled by conservative parties for all but nine months since 1945. In 1955, the conservative Liberal and Democratic parties combined to form the LDP. Split by a half dozen competing factions, the ruling party is often described as a minature party system itself. Every cabinet is composed of representatives from the factions in proportion to their Diet representatives. The factions are built around the personalities and, most importantly, the seemingly bottomless money purses of their leaders rather than any specific issues or ideas. The constant one-upmanship and division of the spoils prevents any one group from consolidating power.

How have the conservatives managed to stay in power for so long? The LDP is locked into a virtuous cycle of power in which its neomercantilist policies create and distribute more wealth. Then, during elections a satisfied near majority of Japanese continues to send them back to office, which in turn allows the LDP to continue those policies. The LDP's conservatism has been pragmatic rather than ideological. Although gerrymandered election districts in favor of conservative rural districts remain important, the LDP would never have retained power if the government's neomercantilist policies had not converted Japan from poverty into wealth in little more than two generations. In addition to farmers, the LDP has captured such huge voting blocks as constructors and distributors through highly protectionist policies. And although the government's primary focus remains creating and distributing wealth, the LDP has coopted popular opposition party ideas on public health, welfare, and the environment, while cutting deals and payoffs with the opposition behind the scenes to ensure no more than verbal protests on virtually all issues. The Japan Socialist Party (JSP), Democratic Socialist Party (DSP), and Clean Government Party (CGP) vote with the LDP on 90 per cent of all bills and the Japan Communist Party (JCP) on 75 per cent of all bills.

Japan's corporate world (*zaikai*) is intensely organized to maximize its ability to shape and implement policy. The Federation of Economic Organizations (FEO, Keidanren) represents the *zaikai*'s interests in all relevant policy areas. Its membership includes 117 trade associations which represent virtually every industry in Japan, as well as 839 leading corporations. Other national business federations include the Council for Economic Development (CED, Keizai Doyukai), Chamber of Commerce (Shoko Kaigisho), and Japan Federation of Employers Association (Nikkeiren). The efforts of these four corporate associations are in turn complemented and implemented by the over 22 000 industrial and enterprise associations.

Officially Keidanren annually gives the LDP over $100 million, and individual companies hundreds of millions of dollars more. In the 1990 Diet election, the LDP raised over $1 billion from Keidanren and individual corporations, while two years earlier the LDP officially raised over $2 billion while the unofficial figure is estimated to be twice that. In contrast, the 1988 US Presidential, Senate, and House elections cost $803 million, which means that Japan's corporate contributions are about ten times that of American firms on a per capita basis.[24]

The pillars of Japan's political economy, however, are the industrial groups (*keiretsu*), which include a range of related industrial corporations which are financed by the group's bank, insurance firm, and trading company. Although there are scores of keiretsu of varying sizes and compositions, the big six – Mitsubishi, Sumitomo, Mitsui, Fuyo, Daii-chi-Kangyo, and Sanwa – alone account for about 25 per cent of Japan's economy. Each group competes to match the range of enterprises of its rivals, a phenomenon known the "one set principle" (*wan setto-shugi*). Keiretsu company presidents meet monthly (*shacho-kai*) to co-ordinate the group's broad strategy and exchange information. Keiretsu are further bound by the "interlocking stock ownership" (*kabushiki mochiai*) of its member firms in each other, cozy business ties which "keep each other warm" (*hada o atatame-au*) under the philosophy "protect your own castle" (*jibun no shiro wa jibun de mamore*), thus simultaneously keeping other firms, particularly foreigners, out in the cold. Cross-shares vary from 15 to 30 per cent of each keiretsu, but when combined with other "stable share-holders" (*antei kanushi*) such as financial institutions, comprise between 60 and 80 per cent of each corporation's total outstanding shares, forming an impregnable defense against hostile takeovers. These shares are rarely traded, but simply used for defense, stable stock prices and long term appreciation.

Japan's corporate world is feudalistic in both structure and behavior. Of the roughly 6.5 million companies, only 0.7 per cent have more than 300 employees, while the other 99.3 per cent are described as medium or small firms.[25] Each keiretsu member sits atop a vast pyramid of sometimes hundreds of medium- and small-sized component manufacturers and distributors (vertical keiretsu, tatewari gyosei), whose ties are close as the horizontal keiretsu. Japan's vertical keiretsu vary greatly in assets, numbers of affiliated firms, and group shares as a percentage of the total shares. Japan's ten largest groups by total assets in 1990 begins with Mitsubishi's 529 firms, 7.7 trillion yen in assets, and 44.8 per cent group shares; Toyota's 168 firms, 5.3 trillion yen, and 68.9 per cent shares; Mitsui's 640 firms, 4.9 trillion yen, and 62.1 per cent shares; Hitachi's 224 firms, 3.3 trillion yen, and 68.2 per cent shares; Nissan's 270 firms, 3.1 trillion yen, and 63.0 per cent shares; Nippon's 180 firms, 3.0 trillion yen, and 29.8 per cent shares; Matsushita's 435 firms, 2.9 trillion yen, and 77.5 per cent shares; Orix's 77 firms, 2.8 trillion yen, and 76.1 per cent shares; Toshiba's 246 firms, 2.7 trillion yen, and 74.2 per cent shares; and NEC's 188 firms, 2.4 trillion yen, and 65.7 per cent shares.[26] Superficially the vertical keiretsu appear to be one big extended happy family, with "parent firms" (*oya-gaisha*) nurturing "child firms" (*ko-gaisha*) with capital, technology, managerial expertise, and guaranteed markets in return for the suppliers' undying loyalty. But the parents squeeze their "children" during economic downturns.

Clustered around the triad are two auxiliary institutions which play important supporting roles in Japan's neomercantilist policies. The Fair Trade Commission (FTC) is perhaps Japan's most vivid example of windowdressing (*tatemae*) to give foreigners the illusion that Japan operates under free trade principles. Lapdog rather than watchdog, the FTC is essentially MITI's handmaiden; the FTC and the anti-monopoly law is supposed to promote free trade but actually provides absolutely no deterence to anti-market activities. From April to October 1990, the FTC investigated 209 cases, of which it proved 7 cartels composed of 146 firms existed. The members were collectively fined 892 million yen ($5.5 million). Trifling as these efforts appear, the figures are up from the 279 cases it examined in 1989, of which 6 cartels involving 54 firms were proven and fined 892 million yen ($5 million), while at the same time it followed MITI's "advice" and exempted 265 cartels.[27] The civil penalties are trivial – companies are required to pay 0.05–2 per cent of their sales during the period the cartel existed, an amount simply written off as a minor business expense. The FTC has only brought criminal charges once in its entire history – in 1974 against the oil companies. One of Tokyo's promises in the Structural Impediments Initiative (SII) negotiations, concluded in April 1990, was to beef up the FTC's investigatory staff from 25 to 154 and its enforcement powers. Japan's economy runs on hundreds of interlocking cartels. The FTC is unlikely to ever become anything more than a minor irritant to Japan's corporate world.

Japan's mass media is as nationalistic as its bureaucrats. Newspapers and televisions consciously spotlight any defective foreign products while covering up Japanese products failures, thus reinforcing the Japanese misconception that foreigners cannot sell more in Japan because their products are of inferior quality. Higashi claims that, "the Japanese mass media are . . . always ready to exaggerate even the smallest sign of United States pressure. In the resulting highly charged emotional atmosphere, Japanese government officials and negotiators find it difficult to respond to even the most reasonable United States expectations".[28] De Mente relates a typical example of the press's nationalism and parochialism:

> foreign politicians who go to Tokyo and make what they feel are rational, reasonable, and practical dissertations on Japan's "invisible trade barriers," pointing out example after example, are often stopped cold when a ranking Japanese journalist gets up and says something like, "Senator, what we really want to hear is what you think about the Japanese people . . ." The journalists go on to write that foreign businessmen have trouble getting into the Japanese market because they are not willing to do things the Japanese way, not because of any barriers blocking their entry.[29]

Virtually every group in Japan supports Tokyo's neomercantilist policies in varying ways to varying degrees. Anti-LDP appearances and rhetoric notwithstanding, the opposition parties, labor unions, consumers, and environmentalists may be quiet but no less enthusiastic Japanese nationalists.

The political opposition is fragmented among four significant parties – the Japan Socialist Party (JSP), Japan Communist Party (JCP), Democratic Socialist Party (DSP) and Clean Government Party (CGP). In the House of Representatives election of 1989, the JSP received 19 per cent of the vote, JCP 9 per cent, DSP 6 per cent, and CGP 7 per cent. The JSP and DSP have traditionally based much of their funding and electoral support from organized labor. But union membership as a percentage of the workforce peaked at 55.8 per cent in 1950, and has declined steadily ever since to 25.9 per cent in 1989, and is expected to drop as low as 14 per cent by 2000.[30] Unions have failed to use Japan's growing labor shortages as an opportunity to increase their bargaining power. Part time workers, females, and service workers continue to undermine labor's ability to organize.

Likewise, Japan's consumer groups continue to be impotent even as Japan's per capita income steadily rises. The number of Japanese consumer groups and members has dropped steadily from its peak of over 5,000 groups with 25.3 million members in 1978 to 4,636 groups with 21.43 million members in 1988. Formidable as these numbers seem, no national organization unites them, and their efforts are thus fragmented and often contradictory. Few of these organizations have any political or economic clout. About 60 per cent of these groups have an annual income of less than 500,000 yen, 35 per cent have fewer than 100 members and 34 per cent under 1,000 members. At least one third of the "consumer groups" are simply front organizations for industrial, agricultural, and distribution interests which advocate higher not lower prices. Other organizations are concerned with "peace" and "cultural" issues, which often means they are anti-American, or simply social groups for bored housewives. Those consumer groups actually interested in lower prices and greater safety are hobbled by Japan's rule by relationships rather than law. Tokyo deliberately limits the number of judges, lawyers, and lawsuit awards to minimize litigation. There are no class action suits or specific product liablity laws to protect Japan's consumers, thus few groups ever bother suing a Japanese cartel or producer of a dangerous product. Consumer "protection" responsibilities are scattered among 18 government agencies, including such seemingly diametrically opposed organizations as MITI and the Environmental Protection Agency.[31]

INDUSTRIAL AND TRADE POLICY

There is tremendous overlap between macroeconomic, industrial and trade policies. Although macroeconomic policies are those which affect the entire economy, and industrial policies those which affect specific sectors or firms, in fact the impact of macroeconomic policies can vary considerably from one sector and firm to the next while the ripple effects of industrial policies spread across the entire national economy and beyond. All Japanese economic policies, whether they have predominantly macro or micro effects, are at once both because they simultaneously boost a specific sector, industry or firm and Japan's entire economy.

Tokyo's macroeconomic policies have centered on achieving as high a savings/investment ratio and as undervalued a yen as possible. Both policies have been enormously successful. Although many Japanese will claim that their country's high household savings rate flows from a cultural disposition to frugality and long-term outlook, government policies are the real reason. Between 1890 and 1945, national savings averaged 5 per cent of GNP, a rate comparable to other industrial countries.[32] After 1945, by deliberately spending little on welfare, education and social security programs while restricting consumer credit and alternative investments at home or abroad, Tokyo forced households to save a large percentage of their income – around 30 per cent in the 1950s and about 14 per cent at present. Why did Japanese endure these forced savings? The power of Japanese groupism for its members to conform without question to the group's dictates was reinforced, according to Horne by the fact that although "personal savers consistently received a real return on their savings close to zero . . . they benefited from regular, significant increases in real wage incomes".[33]

MOF and MITI then targeted these vast cash reserves into Japan's strategic industries. The means was "window guidance" (*madoguchi no shido*), in which firms would request a loan, which would then be granted only if that firm were a strategic member of a strategic industry targeted by the government for development. The interest rate on that loan would vary considerably depending on just how strategic the firm's industry. By paying low interest rates to savers, Tokyo was able to keep interest rates and capital costs low for Japan's strategic industries, giving them a significant advantage over their foreign rivals.

Likewise, although MOF's undervalued yen policy is predominantly macroeconomic, it has had significant industry specific effects. In April 1949 the exchange rate was set at 360 yen to a dollar, which was about 10 per cent lower than the 330 yen to a dollar rate that was widely held to be the appropriate rate.[34] The yen remained fixed between then and August 1971, when Nixon forced its revaluation. During those twenty-two years, the yen became increasingly devalued as Japan's economy grew at an average 10 per cent annual rate. Tokyo was the last major industrial country to revalue its currency and has continued to keep the yen devalued even after the major currencies began to float in March 1973.

Tokyo uses a variety of means to keep the yen severely undervalued. The Bank of Japan (BOJ) intervenes in global currency markets to buy dollars when the yen starts to strengthen, a policy which has steadily diminished in effectiveness as private funds have swamped public funds in global financial markets. More effective has been Tokyo's policy of loosening the reins on Japanese foreign investment while restricting the investment opportunities for foreigners, thus keeping Japanese demand for dollars strong and foreign demand for yen weak. Tokyo also refuses to denominate a significant portion of Japan's trade in yen. Over 80 per cent of the demand for and supply of yen in international currency markets is financial-flow-oriented while only 20 per cent is related to trade. In 1990, yen-denominated transactions still accounted for only about 35 per cent of Japan's exports and about 14 per cent of its imports. By contrast, 60 to 80 per cent of export sales and 30 to 50 per cent of imports of other industrial countries use their own national currency.[35]

In his classic book, *MITI and Japan's Economic Miracle*, Chalmers Johnson argues that Japan's postwar industrial policies are a continuation of the wartime controls, associations, and institutions formed between 1925 and 1945.[36] Until World War II's end, Japan's industrial policies were largely failures, a reflection of the struggle for power between the ministries and bureaucratic interests, the lack of business competition which contributed to economic inefficiency and poor quality products, and the economy's mobilization for military rather than economic war. Ironically, it was the American Occupation (1945–52) which revolutionized Japan's economic policymaking regime and policies into the rational neomercantilist macroeconomic, industrial and trade policies that transformed Japan from mass poverty into mass affluence and global power.

How did MITI achieve this "economic miracle"? MITI was given sweeping responsibilities and powers over Japan's economy when it was created in 1949, and those powers have been since reinforced by literally hundreds of laws and directives. For example, the Foreign Exchange and Foreign Trade Control Law (FECL) of 1949 gave MITI absolute powers to control trade and allocate scarce foreign exchange to targeted industrial sectors, while the Foreign Investment Law of 1950 gave MITI similar powers to control foreign investment. The Export–Import Bank (Eximbank) and Japan Development Bank (JDB) were created in 1951 to enhance MITI's financial powers. The Enterprise Rationalization Promotion Law of 1952 was the first of 58 separate MITI sponsored policy laws and 50 administrative directives passed up through 1965 related to industrial and trade policy, that gave MITI enormous, wide-ranging powers to restructure the designated industry. The Law enpowered MITI to provide direct subsidies to firms buying new equipment, plus tax exemptions for all R & D investments. It also authorized designated strategic industries to depreciate the costs of installing new equipment by 50 per cent during the first year. Finally it commited both the central and local government to build the infrastructure – ports, highways, railroads, electric power grids, industrial parks – vital for economic development at public expense, and made them available to these industries.

These formal laws were backed by MITI's powers of administrative guidance, whereby the ministry would issue such things as directives (*shiji*), requests (*yobo*), warnings (*keikoku*), suggestions (*kankoku*), and encouragements (*kansho*), and guidance through policy statements (*shido yoko*), all of which were not legally binding, but were nevertheless followed just as closely by the affected industry. Although firms were theoretically free to do as they pleased, in reality they had to conform. Those few firms which attempted to buck MITI's commands quickly saw their markets and resources dry up and eventually buckled.

MITI guides the economy's broad development through a series of "visions" (*bijon*) and five year plans worked out with the EPA. These visions and plans indicate the government's priorities, and manufacturers and financiers adjust their business strategies accordingly. According to Johnson, industrial policy implementation tools have included:

on the protective side, discriminatory tariffs, preferential commodity taxes on national products, import restrictions based on foreign currency allocations, and foreign currency controls, on the development side they include the supply of low interest funds to targeted industries through governmental fianancial organs, subsidies, special amortization benefits, exclusion from import duties of designated critical equipment, licensing of imported foreign technology, providing industrial parks and transportation facilities for private business through public investments, and administrative guidance by MITI and other ministries.[37]

In the 1950s and early 1960s, MITI's system of nurturing a new industry generally included the following steps: First, an investigation was made and a basic policy statement drafted within MITI on the need for the industry and its prospects for success. Next, foreign currency allocations were made. Third, licenses were granted for the importation of foreign technology. Fourth, the nascent industry was designated "strategic" in order to give it special and accelerated depreciation on its investments. Fifth, it was provided with improved land on which to build its installations, either free of charge or at nominal cost. Sixth, the industry was given key tax breaks. Seventh, MITI created an "administrative guidance cartel" to regulate competition and coordinate investment among the firms in the industry.[38] The series of currency liberalizations since the mid–1960s have removed MITI's foreign currency allocation controls, but MITI's use of control over the other "nurturing" steps has remained essentially the same.

Cartels have been a vital part of Japan's industrial policies. Schmeligower writes that the government has "tolerated, encouraged, and occasionally even coerced thousands of cartels since 1945 to restrict imports, counteract recessions, promote technology diffusion, and restructure industries. MITI and the Japanese public do not share the faith that free market ideologues hold in the market to solve complex economic and social development problems, and therefore do not feel the same anxiety about departures from neoclassical models of the world".[39] In other words, managed competition is necessary to control the evils of "excess (free) competition". This attitude was most clearly summed up in the Enterprises Bureau-sponsored, cabinet-level Deliberation Council on the Future Status of the Anti-monopoly Law. The Council's final report issued in 1958 stated that "the public interest is not best served by the legal maintenance of a free competitive order." It recommended instead a new law that would allow MITI to openly co-ordinate investment and various cartels to overcome "excessive competition".[40] Japan's keiretsu and cartels are often referred to euphemistically as "friendship clubs" (*nakayoshi kurabu*) built within Japan's "village society" (*mura shakai*) and around "inside information" (*tsuka*).

MITI nurtures and oversees a systematic strategy whereby Japanese corporations master technologies, produce goods, and then conquer overseas markets. In their book, *The Second Wave: Japan's Global Assault on Financial Services*, Richard Wright and Gunter Pauli identify six steps in this strategy.[41] The first step involves intensive market research and the identification of key underserved product niches usually at the lower end of the market. The next step is to form a joint venture with a foreign firm to gain access to the technology and knowledge necessary to develop products for that niche. This is followed by mass producing the products and selling them through extensive domestic distribution channels in Japan. During this time the government provides a web of import barriers to prevent foreign rivals from seizing part of the market. After establishing large economies of scale which reduce prices and improve quality the firm then "dumps" its product in the targeted foreign market through a carefully constructed foreign distribution system and marketing strategy. Under this barrage of cheaply priced imports the affected foreign firm then runs to its government for protection. Often long after the Japanese firms have seized huge market shares in the product area, a "voluntary export restraint" (VER) or "orderly marketing agreement" (OMA) setting up formal import quotas is struck between the foreign government and Tokyo. With its now dominant market share, the Japanese firm then raises prices to recoup losses incurred from its earlier dumping offensive, and uses the windfall profits to invest in higher-value-added products, with which the same procedure is used to capture those niches as well. During this time the Japanese firm sets up factories in the targeted country to allay continued criticism of unfair trade tactics. During the final stage the Japanese firm buys up its by now severely weakened rivals and the takeover is complete.

Japanese trade policies are a vital aspect of its industrial policies. The objectives are quite simple – maximize exports and minimize competitive imports. Japan has been overwhelmingly successful at achieving these objectives. Trade barriers have limited competitive imports either completely or to tiny market slivers while export offensives have driven foreign rivals bankrupt.

Japan's government and businesses work closely together to maximize exports through a variety of means. By passing the Export Import Transaction Law and Export Trade Control Ordinance in 1952 allowing Japanese firms to form export cartels, Tokyo gave Japanese firms the legal authority to dump their products overseas both to build up economies of scale at home and to undermine foreign rivals. Indirectly, dumping is encouraged by industrial policies which base the subsidies, technologies, tax holidays and other benefits Tokyo awards firms on their market share, thus stimulating each firm to overinvest and overproduce. Firms then dump their excess production overseas. The eternally undervalued yen remains, of course, another major government export policy.

Japan's wave after wave of dumping campaigns designed to destroy foreign competitors causes enormous damange and resentment in the targeted countries. As early as 1952, Tokyo was skillfully staving off European complaints about Japan's "unfair trade competition . . ., unethical use of . . . industrial designs and trademarks, and excessive Japanese government aid to shipping, shipbuilding and other industries connected with exports".[42] How does Tokyo handle the inevitable protests? Prime Minister Yoshida captured the essence of Japan's managed trade policies of dividing markets and fixing prices: "where competition between them might seem unavoidable, (foreign) and Japanese manufacturers should co-operate in developing markets through a judicious arrangement of the outlets and types of goods to be reserved for each country".[43]

Japan's corporations can afford to dump because they are protected at home; dumping is subsidized by gouging domestic consumers with high prices. Superficially, Japan's markets are the world's most open. Japan's average tariff rates are now only 2.6 per cent, the lowest of the OECD countries, while its official quotas were reduced from 466 in 1962 to 21 at present. Although Japan's quotas are much higher than America's 7, Germany's 4, or Britain's 3, they are less than half France's 46 and the number will probably slowly lessen over time. For example, Tokyo will completely abolish all its remaining quotas on beef and raw fruit by April 1991, and oranges by April 1992.

Yet, tariffs and quotas are only the two outer walls of as many as a dozen concentric walls surrounding every Japanese product and industry. Japan's markets continue to be carefully managed by hundreds of unofficial import quotas; market, price, production, import, export, and distribution cartels; government and private "buy Japan" policies; discriminatory standards and certification procedures; negative lists of approved ingrediants; "lot" or "unit" import approval instead of the "type" approval of other industrial countries; inadequate intellectual protection; and the sole agent import system. Although the Japanese government vigorously denies it, Tokyo is responsible for the continued existance of all these barriers, either by directly administering them or by failing to enforce antitrust laws and free trade agreements.

Numerous studies have proven that Japan's import barriers remain the major reason for its immense export surplus. Comparing American sales in Japan with other markets is one indication of the depth of Japanese protectionism. A study by Stephen Krasner found that American exports exceeded Japanese exports to third markets in eighteen of twenty-three products, yet not one of the eighteen products in which America enjoyed a comparative advantage had a similiar market share in Japan.[44] Prestowitz reveals a range of products in which American firms held a comparative advantage yet were denied access to Japan's markets, including soda ash which was 20 per cent cheaper; tire valves with a 60 per cent global share; blood plasma which although it had a 70 per cent market share (Japanese abhor donating blood), could only be shipped and distributed by Japanese firms; and plywood in which Japan sold more than it bought from the United States, even though it bought its logs in North America.[45] In a survey of 62 firms in April–May 1988, of which 20 were Japanese, 22 American and 20 European, Mordechai Kreinin found that the American and European firms bought their capital equipment from the lowest cost source on the basis of competitive bids regardless of its national origin while 15 of the Japanese corporations do not use competitive bids at all and instead bought either all or 80 per cent of their capital equipment from related Japanese firms even if there was a less expensive substitute.[46] Ironically, declining American sales in third markets and steady sales in Japan can also indicate how managed Japan's markets are. For example, America's share of Japan's semiconductor market has mysteriously held steady at around 10 per cent over the past decade, despite the fact that America's global market share has declined from about 70 per cent to 35 per cent.

Official American government studies repeatedly reveal that Japan's markets remain highly protected despite Tokyo's contrary claims. A 1982 Commerce Department study revealed that the United States could annually sell an additional $20 billion in Japan if Americans had market shares in Japan similar to in third markets.[47] A November 1984 report said that although Japan had taken five successive market opening measures from December 1981 to April 1984, "significant barriers to trade still remain in Japan".[48] The report cited unsolved problems in such areas as telecommunications equipment, agricultural products, communications satellites, tobacco, services and investment – in short in nearly all areas of bilateral trade. Former US Trade Representative William Brock said, "there are 8 to 10 depressed industries in Japan but the import penetration is less than 1 per cent . . . and we have a better product at a better price than you do in each of those industries".[49] Other protected industries in which the United States has a strong comparative advantage include pulp and paper products, fruit, livestock and leather, computers, computer parts, computer peripherals, heavy electrical machinery, medical and diagnostic equipment, petrochemicals, urea manufacturing, ferosilicon, cardboard paper, ammonia, phosphoric acid, aluminum, copper, naptha, caustic soda, processed foods, and fertilizer. These industries have costs 20 per cent or more higher than their American competitors. Japan not only protects these products, but exports them despite the fact that the United States has a comparative advantage in all of them except steel. This type of targeting not only restricts the ability of the United States to export the products in which it has a comparative advantage, but also leads to pressure in the United States to protect industries in which Japan has a comparative advantage.

Japan's low rate of manufactured imports is another sign of persistent Japanese trade barriers. As a share of total imports, Japan's did rise from 22.8 per cent in 1980 to 49.0 per cent in 1988, but still lagged well behind America's increase in manufactured imports from 56.8 to 81.6 per cent, Germany's 58.3 to 74.5 per cent, Britain's 67.2 to 79.7 per cent, France's 57.7 to 77.9 per cent, or Italy's 49.7 to 69.6 per cent during the same eight years. During the same period, Japan's ratio of imported manufactured goods as a percentage of GNP rose only slightly from 2.9 to 3.5 per cent, compared to America's rise from 5.1 to 7.5 per cent, Germany's from 13.3 to 14.8 per cent, and the European Community's from 5.3 to 5.8 per cent.[50] An extensive study by Robert Lawrence of the Brookings Institute found that Japan's manufactured imports remain 40 per cent lower than they would have been if its markets had been as open as other OECD countries, and attributes this discrepancy to trade barriers and buyers preferences.[51]

Who is hurt by Japanese neomercantilism? Tokyo's policies allow Japanese firms to gouge Japanese consumers unmercifully. One major indicator is the relative prices Japanese must pay for goods compared to their counterparts in other leading industrial countries. In 1988, the OECD estimated that Japan's trade barriers were largely responsible for Japanese prices being an average 57 per cent higher than those in the United States.[52] This was despite the yen's rise in value from 265 yen to the dollar in 1985 to 125 to the dollar in 1988. High prices inhibit consumer spending. In 1988, Japanese private consumption per capita was only $7623 compared to America's $12 232 despite the fact that the two country's per capita incomes were roughly equal. American automobiles or golf balls cost about 50 per cent more in Japan than they would in the United States, thus pricing them out of the market. Japanese cameras and stereos cost about half as much in New York as they do in Tokyo, thus undercutting any equivalent American products which are already priced out of Japan. Denied the freedom of choice at home, Japan's consumers are increasingly shopping overseas for an astonishing 2.3 per cent of total consumption. The average Japanese tourist brought back $2200 worth of foreign goods.[53]

Japanese neomercantilism severely damages America's economy, as its protectionism and dumping offensives essentially steal American jobs, wealth, and development. These devastating effects of Japan's neomercantilism were succinctly captured by an American corporate executive writing in *Businessweek* in 1982: "The strategic leverage provided to the selected Japanese industries by the initial protection has been crucial . . . By denying US companies access to Japan's rapidly expanding markets while simultaneously exploiting Japan's free access to the US market, Japan, in case after case, has preempted the lion's share of the available market growth and all the cost productivity benefits that go with it".[54] Economists estimate that about 35 000 jobs are lost for every $1 billion of a country's trade deficit. In 1990, America's trade $41 billion deficit with Japan cost 1 435 000 Americans their livelihood. The amount of wealth that would have remained in the United States far excceeds the $41 billion figure, which does not take into account the multiplier effects of those decreased sales throughout America's economy. The result is that Japan's wealth and security increases enormously at America's expense.

FOREIGN POLICY

Nations are said to have not permanent friends, but permanent interests. This maxim has guided Japan's leaders since Perry's gunboats first steamed into Tokyo Bay in 1853 and demanded that Japan be opened to the world. Japan's government has single-mindedly pursued four national goals over the last 140 years: (1) territorial integrity and sovereignty; (2) rapid and balanced political economic development; (3) global political economic power; and (4) international recognition of these accomplishments.

The means to achieve these ends have varied little since 1853. Masayoshi Hotta, the Shogun's confidant, offered the chilling advice in 1957 that "our policy should be to . . . conclude friendly alliances, to send ships to foreign countries everywhere and conduct trade, to copy the foreigners where they are at their best and so repair our own shortcomings, to foster our national strength and complete our armaments, and so gradually subject the foreigners to our influence until in the end . . . our hegemony is acknowledged throughout the globe".[55] Prime Minister Yoshida restated this strategy succinctly a century later when he said that Japan's destiny "was to be a global power, and the expansion as well as the security of the state was best guaranteed by close alliance with the dominant Western power in Asia and the Pacific . . . just as the United States was once a colony of Great Britain but is now the stronger of the two, if Japan becomes a colony of the United States it will eventually become the stronger".[56]

Although before 1945, Japan attempted to achieve global power through imperialism and since then through neomercantilism, Tokyo's foreign policy strategy of hitch-hiking to global power on the backs of its allies has essentially remained unchanged. Japan used its alliances with Britain after 1902 and America after 1951 to enhance its military security through both strength in numbers and shared technology from its allies. Preoccupied with threats elsewhere, both London and Washington failed to prevent Japan from using its alliances with them eventually to leapfrog them in global power at a minimal price. Kanji Nishio candidly points out that America's obsession with containing the Soviet Union at all costs had allowed Japan to "conduct a diplomacy that exploited and totally used the US. Even if Japan was asked to take some responsibility, we could get away with avoiding it and simply pursue our own economic interests".[57]

Japan's foreign relations were milked for their trade and technology wealth. The government sent the 48-man Iwakura Mission to the United States and Europe during 1872–73, ostensibly to negotiate treaty revisions, but also to examine those countries' "courts, prisons, schools, trading firms, factories and shipyards, iron foundaries, sugar refineries, paper plants, wool and cotton spinning and weaving, silver, cutlery, and glass plants, coal and salt mines".[58] Meiji leader Ito Hirobumi stated his mission's goals clearly in a speech before the city fathers of Sacremento: "We come to study your strength, that, by adopting widely your better ways, we may hereafter be stronger ourselves . . . We shall labor to place Japan on an equal basis, in the future, with those countries whose modern civilization is now our guide".[59] In addition to its foreign mission, Japan hired foreign advisors– about 3,000 between 1854 and 1890 – to guide all aspects of its development drive including creating a constitution, educational system, agriculture, railroads, military, and legal system. The advisors were sent home as soon as Japan had absorbed the knowledge.

Japan's strategy between 1853 and 1931 was a brilliant success. By 1919, when Japan was seated as one of the Big Five powers at the Versailles Peace Conference ending World War I, it had overwhelmingly achieved its goals of sovereignty, development, global power, and international recognition. Japan had rapidly industrialized, carved out a small empire encompassing the Ryukyu Islands, Taiwan and Korea in Northeast Asia, and was capturing markets around the world. Unfortunately, Japan's elite and public lost sight of the reality that these remarkable achievements had been gained through careful strategies of maintaining a relatively low political profile while manipulating the global power balance for every advantage. Increasingly drunk with their nation's dazzling rise to global power, Japanese became as arrogant and aggressive during the 1920s and 1930s as they had been self-effacing and meek when first humbled by Western imperialism. Japan had achieved equality with the West through imperialism; now the "pure Japanese race" would surpass the West by fulfilling its destiny to "free Asia for the Asians" and rule the "world's eight corners". Japan's invasion of Manchuria in 1931 was the first step in its fourteen year attempt to conquer all of East and Southeast Asia.

Japan's defeat in 1945 was psychologically and physically devastating. The once seemingly invincible imperial army and navy had suffered continual routs since 1942, while Japan's cities had been systematically destroyed. Yet, until the atomic bombing of Hiroshima and Nagasaki in August 1945, Tokyo was still mobilizing Japan's entire adult population to die, bamboo spears in hand, charging the inevitable American invasion. Even then the Cabinet was split over whether or not to continue the struggle. But Emperor Hirohito realized that Japanese spirit could not resist atomic power, and convinced the Cabinet to surrender.

Since 1945, although Japan's goals remain constant, the means have shifted dramatically from imperialism to neomercantilism. Japanese were the first to understand that as the world's economic, humanitarian, cultural, and environmental interdependence deepens, global power will increasingly be based on the country which can build the best automobile rather than tank. Prime Minister Takeo Fukuda expressed this succinctly when he said, "We wish to employ our economic strength to gain an increasing voice in the international community. The tradition once was that a nation used its economic power to become a military power, but that is not the case today".[60] Other Japanese leaders have been equally candid in describing Japan's neomercantilist policies. Former MITI Vice Minister Naohiro Amaya distinguishes between "samurai" states like the United States and Soviet Union and "merchant" states like Japan. While the world appears to "belong to the samurai . . . in reality it is owned by the merchants".[61] According to Amaya, for "a merchant to prosper in samurai society, it is necessary to have superb information-gathering ability, intuition, diplomatic skill, and at times the ability to be a sycophant (*gomasuri noryoku*) . . ." and even go so far as to maximize Japan's wealth and power by "beg(ging) for oil from the producing countries, grovel on bended knee before the samurai".

Japan's neomercantilist strategy has been overwhelmingly successful, and its leaders intend to continue it indefinitely despite having already achieved global wealth, power, and prestige. According to Japanese political scientist, Masataka Kosaka, a neomercantist nation "has wide relations with many alien civilizations, makes differing use of various different principles of behavior, and manages to harmonize them with each other".[62] For Kosaka benefits flowing from the strategy whereby Japan "simply takes advantage of international relations created by stronger states" and enjoys "the advantages of being an ally and the benefits of non-involvement" far outweigh the "hypocrisy" (*gizen*) of the strategy and fact that it "is not a popular role in the international order, since it is regarded as selfish and immoral".

Japan's broad foreign policy guidelines since 1945 have been relatively simple – trade with everyone and avoid any international conflicts. But the implementation of these "omnidirectional diplomacy" (*zenhoi gaiko*) or "separation of economic and politics" (*seikei bunri*) principles has been as richly sophisticated, subtle and complex as it has been successful. Japan's foreign policy has evolved through three phases since 1945 and has entered a fourth: Occupation (1945–52); Economic Miracle (1952–73); Comprehensive Security (1973–85); and Global Hegemony (1985–future). Each phase is simply a more elaborate version of its predecessor.

Japan's foreign policy during the American Occupation was almost exclusively shaped by Prime Minister Yoshida who brillantly achieved the restoration of Japan's sovereignty, military security, and trade relations. Yoshida capitalized on Washington's preoccupation with the Cold War and subsequent need to build up Japan economically and militarilly by extracting enormous amounts of aid, technology and foreign markets, and negotiating a defense treaty in which the United States guaranteed Japan's security. On issues like trade with China and Japanese rearmament where Tokyo and Washington interests clashed, Yoshida got his way – trade with China continued while Japan's rearmament was strictly limited.

Japan's foreign policy during its "economic miracle" phase elaborated Yoshida's strategy. Japan succeeded in expanding its market shares around the world while keeping its own markets firmly locked against competitive imports. Tokyo and Washington worked together to override the protests of many other members and gain Japan membership in GATT (1955) and OECD (1964). In both organizations, although it was required to open its markets as the entry fee, Tokyo broke its promise and actually built up even more elaborate protectionist walls. Japan began giving foreign aid during this period, but virtually all its aid was tied to purchases of Japanese goods and services and thus acted as an export subsidy for Japan's economy. Meanwhile, Tokyo shrugged off Washington's periodic pressures to increase the size of its military forces. Despite the yen's continual undervaluing since it was first set at 360 to the dollar in 1949, Tokyo resisted any revaluation until the Smithsonian Conference of December 1971, and floating until March 1973, long after other industrial nations had revalued their currencies. During this period, Japan began to reconstruct its economic empire in East and Southeast Asia, achieving trade, investment and aid dominance in virtually every nation in the region. Tokyo attempted to assert leadership with its creation of the Asian Development Bank in 1964, and restored relations with South Korea in 1965 and China in 1972.

Japan's steady march into a regional then global economic superpower received a sharp setback with OPEC's quadrupling of oil prices in

November 1973. With 99 per cent of its oil needs imported and 70 per cent of its oil coming from the Middle East, Japan's economy plunged into recession and inflation. Tokyo now clearly understood that the strategy of strictly separating economics and politics would be increasingly difficult; as it became more powerful, the demands on Japan to give more and take less from the world would increase. The result was Japan's comprehensive security policy (*sogo anzen hosho*) which is simply a more sophisticated version of Japanese neomercantilism. The assumptions of both neomercantilism and comprehensive security are identical – in an increasingly interdependent world geoeconomic threats to one's security are far more important than geopolitical threats, while geoeconomic power is far more important than geopolitical power in securing national interests. Comprehensive security simply entails spreading Japan's geoeconomic interests more widely and entrenching them more deeply, thus reducing their vulnerability and enhancing their security. Japan's dependence on foreign resources, energy, and markets are minimized by diversifying those sources as widely as possible and playing them off against each other to achieve the lowest prices and easy, long-term access, while simultaneously making those sources dependent on Japanese trade, finance, investments, and technology. Meanwhile, MITI poliices transform Japan's economy with strict conservation and energy efficiency measures. This policy has been enormously successful. For example, Japan's dependence on petroleum as a percentage of its total energy needs has plunged from its peak of 71.1 per cent in 1973 to 24.9 per cent in 1988, while Tokyo has reduced its dependence on Middle East oil from about 80 per cent of total oil imports in early 1970s to 46.6 per cent in 1986, and oil from Iran and Iraq represented only 6.3 per cent of Japan's total oil supply.[63]

Since 1973, instead of shunning regional conflicts, Tokyo attempts to mediate those conflicts, thus allowing Japan to continue trading with both sides of the diplomatic fence. Japan played the diplomatic go-between in conflicts between ASEAN and Vietnam, North and South Korea, Iraq and Iran, and the Arab states and Israel. Although it remains largely tied to purchases of Japanese goods and services, Tokyo's aid increasingly flows to front line states in regional conflicts like Turkey, Egypt, Pakistan and Thailand, to simultaneously promote both stability and Japan's economic penetration of those large, growing markets. Tokyo, of course, continues to make its alliance with Washington the cornerstone of its geopolitical security, while making limited, grudging contributions to its upkeep.

During the 1980s, as Japan leapfrogged the United States as global banker, technological and manufacturing leader, Tokyo tentatively appeared to be entering yet another foreign policy phase distinguished by an increased assertiveness and independence on many issues. The turning point in the "Hegemony" policy phase may well have been 1985

when the United States became the world's worst debtor nation and
Japan the global banker. Prime Minister Kaifu articulated this new stance
in a September 1989 speech at San Francisco, where he declared that US–
Japanese relations had ceased to be one of "teacher–student," and instead
advocated a "global partnership" between the two countries. The
preceding year Japan's premier diplomat, Ryohei Murata, encouraged
a more blatant use of Japanese power when he wrote that "after economic
strength grows to a certain size, it inevitably becomes political".[64]

One area of increased Japanese assertiveness is foreign aid. Japan is now
the world's largest aid donor. In 1990, Tokyo extended about $10 billion
in aid, and is increasingly using its aid clout to shape the policies of
recipient countries. A government white paper issued on 5 October 1990,
declared that Japan would withhold aid from countries with excessive
amounts of military spending or which followed economic development
models not favored by Japan. Although Tokyo will continue its policy of
aiding friendly governments in strategic regions like the Middle East, it
has increasingly distanced itself from Washington's policies. For example,
on 15 April 1991, Tokyo protested Washington's write-off of $7 billion of
Egypt's debt and $5 billion of Poland's as fiscally irresponsible.

Yet, Japan's aid policies are open to criticism since most of it remains
tied to the purchase of Japanese goods and services, thus acting chiefly as
an export subsidy for Japanese corporations. Shoji Ochi, deputy president
of the Japan Center for International Finance, a private banks' research
institution established to analyze country risks, admits that Tokyo's aid
policy is still basically neomercantilist: "Japan's ODA has so far been
export-oriented, aimed at increasing Japan's exports to developing
nations".[65] The Asahi Shimbun reports that even if loans are officially
designated as untied, in reality "the bidding is open only to companies
from Japan and firms of the recipient nations." Since Japanese companies
are more competitive than the domestic firms they land such contracts
"almost 100 per cent of the time".[66] The actual quality of Japanese aid
remains dismally low. Tokyo's aid still remains skimpy compared to its
economic power – in 1990, Japan's ODA was only 0.32 per cent of GNP
and ranked 12th among OECD members. In 1988, only 47 per cent of
Japan's ODA was estimated to be genuinely untied compared to 78 per
cent for France, 90 per cent for the United States and 99 per cent for
Britain.[67] Typical was Tokyo's extension of $1 billion in aid to the
Philippines in 1989, of which 85 per cent was in yen-credit loans that
must be paid with 3.5 per cent interest and are tied to purchases of
Japanese goods and services.[68]

Japan's aid power was nicely symbolized when many presidents of the
poor countries attending Emperor Akihito's enthronement on 13 November 1990 used the opportunity to press Tokyo for greater aid or trade

concessions. Yet, all the presidents, including those of such desperate countries as Pakistan, Bangladesh, the Philippines, Romania, and Hungary, who had lined up, hats literally in hand, for more aid were politely refused except for one – Peru's President, Alberto Fujimori, of Japanese descent.[69]

Tokyo is also trying to strengthen its economic hegemony over East and Southeast Asia to offset the European and North American trade blocks. At the June 1988 Toronto summit meeting of the seven leading industrial nations Prime Minister Takeshita attempted to speak on behalf of East Asia against American and European protectionism while his entourage hinted broadly that Tokyo was considering an East Asian trade zone to counter those of North America and the European Community. Thus, Takeshita skillfully shifted East Asian criticism of Japan's continuing trade surplus and closed markets to the United States and EC which have trade deficits with the region while their markets are largely open. Tokyo has taken a similar position at subsequent Group of Seven meetings and other international conferences. It has also tried to develop Asia–Pacific Economic Cooperation (APEC) organization into the regional equivalent of the OECD, with Japan assuming a dominant role. Japan's government is currently debating a Foreign Ministry proposal to create an Asian Pacific Security Forum which would attempt to resolve regional disputes such as in Indochina, as well as strengthen existing forums such as ASEAN and APEC.

A regional trade bloc is clearly emerging. In 1989, the region's internal trade amounted to $256 billion or 40 per cent of the global total, a ratio that could rise to 55 per cent by 2000. Although Japan dominates the region in terms of trade, investment, and aid volume and direction, the composition of Japanese economic relations with the region is rapidly changing. Up through the early 1980s, Japan primarily exported manufactured products for natural resources and components, but with the yen's rise after 1985, about 60 per cent of Japan's imports from the region have become manufactured goods, although virtually all of these came from either Japanese subsidiaries or subcontractors – NIC manufacturers remain largely excluded from Japan's carefully managed markets. Between 1985 and 1989, Japan's annual trade with the NICs and ASEAN doubled to $118 billion.[70]

Tokyo's aspirations for regional leadership, however, face both internal and external obstacles. While every country in the region welcomes Japanese money, memories linger of Japan's brutal imperialism during World War II which left over 20 million Asians dead and those countries devastated. The governments of the region vary in their welcome for greater Japanese involvement. In May 1990, Thailand Prime Minister Chatichai Choonhavan proposed to the visiting Japan Defense Agency minister that the two countries conduct joint naval exercises and planning in the South China Sea to fill the void left when the United States withdraws from the Philippines. Tokyo said it would "study" the proposal, and it was quickly rejected after other ASEAN members protested.[71]

Yet, while most regional governments are leery of any Japanese military presence, a consensus is forming around the need to institutionalize the regional trade bloc. In January 1991, Malaysian Prime Minister Mahathir asked visiting Prime Minister Kaifu to create and lead a new East Asian economic bloc embracing Japan, China, South Korea, Taiwan, Hong Kong and the six ASEAN countries. Although he promised to "study" the proposal, Kaifu reiterated Japan's commitment to APEC, which includes the United States, Canada, Australia and New Zealand. Kaifu and the government were embarrassed by Mahathir's request, since it would have spotlighted Tokyo's systematic creation of just such an economic block.[72] Potential Japanese domination of APEC, however is further undercut by the fact that the United States, Canada and Australia are also members and would resist a Japanese takeover. Tokyo would also be unwilling to shoulder the responsibilities for leadership of a trade bloc if it meant running trade deficits with the poorer countries. If Tokyo somehow were able to wrest political control over APEC and use it to counter European and American protectionist policies, Japan would have to absorb the diversion of Western Pacific trade that would normally flow to America and Europe. Meanwhile Japan's ambitions for a Asian Pacific Security Forum are stalled by those who object that such a forum could be used to reduce American naval forces in the Pacific or evoke fears of a revival of Japanese power.

Economically, Japan also faces limitations in its quest for complete regional hegemony. Although Japan dominates the imports of every country in the region, more than twice as many regional exports go to the United States than to Japan, while about four-fifths of the region's trade is denominated in dollars. The yen accounts for only about 10 per cent of the region's currency reserves while dollars average 63.3 per cent. With its exports dependent on America's vast market, no country would stand by Japan in an economic shootout with the United States. Likewise, the Asian countries are reluctant to tie their currencies to the yen because of the resulting loss of economic independence. If the yen strengthens, that country's currency correspondingly strengthens which harms its trade and payments balances. There is no serious talk of creating a common tariff union. Although the per capita income gap between Japan and the NICs will narrow to 3.3 times by the year 2000, less than the 5 fold gap between Germany and Portugal, Japan's per capita income is ten times higher than the ASEAN members and 25 times higher than China's.

CONCLUSION

On 5 July 1990, MITI's Industrial Structure Council unveiled its latest "vision" for Japan's future. Despite being shaped by over 100 meetings between MITI and a range of prominent businessmen, politicians, academics, and media leaders, the "vision" typically offered grand ideas but few specifics of how they would be accomplished. MITI promised that Japan would no longer be "a passive follower" but will "take creative initiatives in the interests of world prosperity and stability" and "emulate the role that the United States played in world development after World War II". MITI promised to improve the quality of life as well as standard of living for Japanese and foreigners alike. Two ideas seemed to clash: MITI asserted that Japan would continue its industrial and trade drive while seeking "trustworthiness" from abroad.[73]

Will Japan's neomercantilism continue? During the 1980s, Tokyo made ten "significant" market opening packages of reduced tariffs, quotas and government barriers. Japanese and their foreign spokespeople claim that Japan's markets are the world's most open, that Japanese firms do not dump their products overseas, that foreigners do not sell more in Japan because their goods are inferior and they do not try hard enough, while Japan continually enjoys immense trade surpluses because its products are superior in quality and low priced. Is this true?

Japanese neomercantilism has not receded, but has instead become more subtle and sophisticated. While outer barriers like tariffs, quotas, and the more obvious government restrictions have been reduced, Tokyo has simply strengthened the half dozen or so less obvious nontariff barriers around each product or industry. Japanese dismiss any example of Japanese trade barriers as mere "anecdotes". But the "anecdotes" are the reality; there are countless anecdotes for every foreign firm which has ever tried selling or investing in Japan.

Japanese actions constantly belie their words. A controversy broke out in Spring 1990 when Tokyo said it would not allow its projected current account surplus of $56 billion for the year to fall under 2 per cent of GNP. Tokyo argued that it had to maintain a surplus of at least 2 per cent of GNP in order to extend finance to needy deficit countries including the United States. What Tokyo officials and their well-paid foreign spokespeople neglected to mention is that in the zero-sum game of international trade if some nations enjoy surpluses other nations must suffer corresponding deficits. If Japan's accounts were balanced, the accounts of other nation's would be greatly relieved and hence a reduced need for them to borrow funds to finance their deficits. And cannot every country make the same argument? Japanese seem to operate under a double standard whereby the wealth and advantages they frenzily amass are somehow invalid for others. The argument is also weakened by the reality that the United States remains the world's second largest lender despite the fact that it suffers continual payments deficits. In other words, it is not necessary to run an account surplus in order to be an international lender, although to do so means higher interest rates for both domestic and foreign lenders. Tokyo's argument that it intends to maintain a surplus equal to 2 per cent of GNP is also a tacit admission that it still has the power to carefully manage Japan's economy and its global activities.

Change is unlikely. Kent Calder describes Japan as a "reactive state" which "fails to undertake major independent foreign economic policy initiatives when it has the power and national incentives to do so and responds to outside pressures (*gaiatsu*) . . . erratically, unsystematically, and often incompletely".[74] Calder characterizes Japanese foreign policy-making as a "complex mixture of strategy, hesitancy, and pragmatism".[75] Iron triangles among the different ministries, industrial associations, and LDP "policy tribes" will guarantee the continuation of neomercantism.

Will the global political economy survive a Japanese hegemony characterized by neomercantilism? Probably. Japan's transition into a global hegemon will unfold gradually. Tokyo will continue to cooperate as much as it confronts the United States on international issues. With Japan's relatively greater dependence on the global economy, Tokyo will pull back from the brink of a total trade war. But as Japan's economic prowess soars as America's continues to decay, Tokyo will increasingly determine the outcome of international conflicts in Japan's favor at the expense of the United States and others.

Part II

Political Economic Battlegrounds

4 The Shifting Balance of Economic Power

In an interdependent world, nations still struggle to defend and expand national security and prosperity. But power flows, not out of gun barrels, but from bank vaults, laboratories, boardrooms, factory floors and classrooms. Nations tip the balance of power in their favor, not with vast military forces, but with vast trade surpluses. Armies are equipped with business suits, calculators, and flowcharts rather than khaki, rifles and tanks. Superpower rests on corporate rather than nuclear power.

The Japanese understand this. Since 1945 Tokyo has singlemindedly driven Japan to be "number one", the world's political economic superpower. They have succeeded. Japan enjoys immense trade surpluses with virtually all its trade partners and is the world's banking, corporate and technological leader. Japan's banks and corporations float happily atop cash oceans.

How did Tokyo do it? Why did America fail? Self-defeating as its policies are, America's economic decline is not predominantly the result of an overvalued dollar, immense budget deficits or other macroeconomic policies. More profoundly, American decline reflects the inability of a largely free market, mass production economy to compete in a neomercantilist world. Likewise, Japan's economic supremacy is not merely the result of dumping and trade barriers, but reflects Tokyo's systematic mobilization and organization of the entire nation behind a strategy to that end. Japan's leapfrogging of the United States in technology, manufacturing, and finance represents an entirely new way of creating and distributing wealth.

In their book, *Politics and Productivity: The Real Story of Why Japan's Economy Works*, Johnson, Zysman and Tyson argue that the United States until recently and Japan now and into the future became political economic superpowers by mastering a new means of production and innovation, or "technoeconomic paradigm".[1] America's economic supremacy throughout most of the 20th century resulted from its ability to create then master two dynamic innovations: mass production and the hierarchial, multidivisional corporation. America led the world in manufacturing high quality, inexpensive products, and other industrial nations scrambled to emulate its system. Since 1950, Japan has mastered a technoeconomic paradigm which represents a fundamentally different,

123

superior way of production and technological innovation, and thus is leading a third industrial revolution which will guarantee its economic supremacy for the foreseeable future as thoroughly as Britain's mastery of steam power did throughout the 19th century and America's mass production did throughout much of the 20th century.

Japan's neomercantilist strategy of nurturing "strategic" industries and technologies with subsidies, cartels, import barriers, and export promotion is a far superior means of achieving political economic power than America's liberal reliance on limited government regulation of free markets. "Strategic industries" are the dynamic cores around which constellations of countless other related industries gain sustenance; they are the industries which provide the value-added products, high paying jobs, high profits, exports, and product and technology spin-offs that are vital to a nation's economic development. "Strategic transformative" technologies like microelectronics, new materials, superconductivity, and biotechnology are those which "radically transform the products and production sectors that employ them and thus have a profound effect on the competitiveness of national producers in a wide variety of world markets".[2] The development costs of these industries and technologies are often beyond that of even the richest corporations. Tokyo's systematic development of both strategic industries and technologies through organizing and financing research, production, and market cartels, amassing the latest foreign technology advances, imposing import barriers against competitive products, and promoting the capture of overseas markets, is the heart of its technoeconomic paradigm.

How is economic power determined? A state's potential economic power has traditionally been measured by its GNP and per capita income, but Knorr reminds us that "just as army divisions per se are not military power, so GNP or national wealth per se is not economic power".[3] Potential economic power can rest on a nation's geographic centrality, innovative technologies, sufficient investment capital, diversified capital intensive agriculture, human capital, a unified representative ruling class, the ability to extract taxes, egalitarian and pluralist politics, a large home market, asymmetrical trade ties (the dependence of other states) or owning the source of vital resources, markets, or technology. According to Knorr, economic power is the ability of a state to enrich itself while harming others. National economic power is actualized when wealth and economic policy are used deliberately to modify the behavior or capabilities of other states. The ability to shut off valuable markets, to preempt sources of supply, to stop investments, or reduce economic aid would constitute elements of national economic strength comparable to military strength. According to Knorr, economic power can be actualized in three ways: 1) A applies economic power directly; 2) A threatens B with economic attack; 3) B anticipates the threat and adjusts according to A's wishes.[4] International economic power is largely a zero sum calculation, in which one country masters a virtuous cycle and others fall into vicious cycles of economic and political power. As Japan rises further, the United States falls lower. Japan's trade surpluses and America's trade deficits reflect a tremendous shift in manufacturing, financial, and techological power from the United States to Japan. Global economic power means global political power. Tokyo is using its vast economic power to influence politics in both the United States and elsewhere to extract yet more advantages and concessions to Japan's corporations, which deepens further their economic power and thus ability to armtwist foreign governments.

ECONOMIC SIZE, GROWTH AND PRODUCTIVITY POWER

There is a virtuous cycle of economic well-being. The larger and more affluent a population, the greater the opportunity for domestic firms to establish economies of scale, bring down prices and sell more, thus generating more employment and wealth. Vigorous, rapid, relatively egalitarian, noninflationary economic growth in turn generates political stability which enhances the environment for even more economic growth, and so on.

America's growth has lumbered along at an annual rate of about two per cent since the late 19th century. The American economy benefited enormously from World War II, growing from $88.6 billion in 1939 to $135 billion in 1945 as measured in constant 1939 dollars, and to $220 billion in current dollars. Productive capacity and output expanded 50 per cent, and American production accounted for half of global GNP, and one third of global exports. America's gold reserves of $20 billion were two thirds the global total of $33 billion.[5] American economic power has declined steadily from this peak; its economy has continued to grow but other countries have simply grown faster. American international financial reserves fell from 49 per cent of the world total in 1950 to 21 per cent in 1960, and 7 per cent in 1976; exports fell from 18 to 16 to 11 per cent of the world total for the same years; American petroleum production fell from 53 per cent of the world total in 1950 to 33 per cent in 1960 and 14 per cent in 1976. United States labor productivity declined from almost three times the world average in 1950 to only about one and a half times the world average in 1977. In 1971, the United States incurred a trade deficit – a trade deficit of $2.1 billion – for the first time since 1893.[6]

Although the United States remains the world's largest economy, between 1950 and 1990, its share of global GNP fell from about 33 per cent to 23 per cent while Japan's rose from about 5 to 15 per cent.[7] This dramatic shift in global economic weight reflected the vastly different growth rates in the United States and Japan. Between 1950 and 1973 Japan's GNP grew at an average annual rate of about 10.5 per cent, four times America's 2.5 per cent rate; between 1974 and 1990, Japan's GNP grew at an annual rate almost twice that of the United States – 4.4 per cent compared to 2.7 per cent. Between 1980 and 1990, Japan's economy grew 69.1 per cent in real terms while America's grew only 16.4 per cent! In 1990, Japan's economy grew 6.1 per cent, while its inflation was 1.5 per cent, and unemployment only 2.2 per cent, while America's barely grew at 1.0 per cent while it suffered a 4.2 per cent inflation rate and 6.3 per cent unemployment rate. Although its economy remains only 70 per cent the size of America's, Japan's economy will surpass that of the United States within twelve years if present growth rates hold. With less than half the population, Japanese will then be more than twice as wealthy as Americans. Japanese already are richer than Americans: in 1989 Japan's per capita income stood at $23,296 compared to $20,768 in the United States. Japan's wealth is spread much more equitably than that of the United States – the income ratio between the top and bottom 20 per cent of the population is about 6 in Japan and 11 in the United States.

These vastly different growth rates were the result of vastly different economic strategies. America's liberal policies emphasized consumption and low savings while Japan's neomercantilism policies emphasized production, high savings, and low consumption. A central pillar of Tokyo's policies has been to channel funds from consumers to strategic industries at minimal interest rates. Japan's dazzling economic growth rates have been based, in part, on Tokyo's ability to force Japanese households to save large amounts of their income which is then channeled into strategic industries, whose production creates more wealth which is then reinvested. Between 1960 to 1982, for example, the ratio of fixed capital formation to GNP was 18 per cent in the United States and 32 per cent in Japan. Although Japan's household savings rate has fallen from its height of over 25 per cent in the 1950s, to 15.1 per cent in 1989, it remains the second largest of the OECD countries. Between 1980 and 1988, America's net disposable savings as a percentage of disposable income averaged 5.5 per cent compared to Japan's 16.4 per cent.

From 1950 until 1973, the annual average growth of output in American manufacturing was 2.7 versus 9.9 per cent in Japan, 6.5 per cent in Germany, and 5.1 per cent elsewhere in Europe. During 1973 to 1980, America's annual average manufacturing productivity growth dropped to 1.2 per cent, Japan's to 5.7 per cent, Germany's to 3.7 per cent and the other Western European countries to 3.3 per cent. Between 1980 and 1985, largely because of massive layoffs, America's manufacturing output increased at an annual average of 4.1 per cent compared to Japan's 5.9 per cent increase, West Germany's drop to 3.5 per cent, and the other Western European countries' rise to 4.6 per cent.[8] Much of this drop, however, resulted from the shift to a service economy which accounts for 68 per cent of GNP and 71 per cent of all jobs. According to some measurements, American manufacturing productivity actually increased from 21 to 22 per cent in the 1980s, with an annual productivity growth of 2.8 per cent.[9] In 1990, there were only 19 million manufacturing workers compared to 21 million in 1979.[10]

The productivity of Japan's strategic industries has been two to three times faster than that of America's. How do they do it? Japan's vast productivity gains flow from its corporations' ability to master flexible manufacturing systems (FMS) in which production lines and machines can be rapidly reprogrammed to make entirely new products. In the mid–1980s, the average number of parts made by a Japanese FMS was 93, almost ten times more than the American average of 10; the annual volume per part in Japan was 258, in the United States 1,727.[11] Japan's 219,667 robots in 1989 were almost six times greater than America's 36,977 and ten times more numerous than West Germany's 22,395.[12]

Thus, the contrasting images of Japan as an industrial and export superpower managed by a lean farsighted government while a spendthrift American government and public leeches off a small industrial base are not inaccurate. In 1987, Washington accounted for 20.6 per cent of consumption compared to Tokyo's 9.6 per cent, while Americans consumed 67.0 per cent of GNP while Japanese bought only 58.1 per cent. While America's government and public were engaging in a consumer orgy, Japan's corporations invested almost twice as much in fixed capital (28.9 per cent of GNP) as American firms (15.0 per cent), while Japanese exports (12.8 per cent) were one and a half times greater as a percentage of GNP than America's (7.4 per cent). Not surprisingly, Japan's industrial sector accounted for about one third (32.6 per cent) of GNP while America's was less than one quarter (24.3 per cent). In contrast, financial services made up 45.5 per cent of America's economy and only 37.1 per cent of Japan's, while, despite all the complaints about Japan's inefficient distribution system, wholesale and retail trade was only 13.3 per cent of Japan's economy and 17.2 per cent of America's. One third (33.8 per cent) of Japanese are employed in the industrial sector and only 58.7 per cent in services and 7.6 per cent in agriculture compared to one quarter (26.0 per cent) of Americans in industry, a whopping 71.2 per cent in services, and 2.9 per cent in agriculture.

CORPORATE POWER

Power brings publicity. Dozens of Japanese corporations are now household words. Toyota, Honda, Mitsubishi, Hitachi or Nomura are as familiar to Americans as GM, IBM, Zenith or Paine Webber. Front page reports detail Matsushita's takeover of Paramount or Bridgestone's of Firestone. Sony President Akio Morita's autobiography becomes a bestseller. Scores of books and articles annually appear exploring the principles of Japanese management, documenting the global rise of specific corporations, or analyzing the threat to America of the Japanese neomercantilist juggernaut.

How powerful are Japan's corporations? In both numbers and market value Japanese firms trail American firms. In 1991, 309 Japanese firms with a combined market value of $2.246 trillion (33.4 per cent of the total assets) ranked among the world's largest 1000 firms, compared to 359 American firms with a combined market value of $2.559 trillion (38.0 per cent of total assets). Five Japanese and four American firms ranked in the world's top ten firms in market value, 11 each among the top 25 firms, and 19 Japanese firms and 23 American firms ranked in the world's top fifty firms. The Japanese corporations had a price/earnings of 60 compared to an American rate of 22, a yield of 0.7 per cent compared to one of 3.1 per cent, and return on equity of 8.6 per cent compared to 19.1 per cent. Reflecting their sales orientation, the top five sales firms and seven of the top fifteen were Japanese and five were American, while, reflecting their quarterly profit orientation, the top four profits firms and eight of the top 15 were American and only two were Japanese.[12]

Heartening as these statistics may appear to concerned Americans, they may actually represent a temporary anomaly caused by the Tokyo Stock Market's 40 per cent decline in 1990. Japan's 1991 rankings represented a considerable drop from the previous year in which Japan's firms surpassed America's in both numbers and assets. Of the world's top 1000 corporations in 1990, 333 were Japanese whose $2.649 trillion in assets accounted for 39.3 per cent of the world total compared to America's 329 firms worth $2.288 trillion or 33.3 per cent.[13] NTT, with a market value of $118.79 billion, was the world's largest. IBM and and the Industrial Bank of Japan jousted for second place, with IBM's market value of $68.89 billion slightly edging out the Industrial Bank's $67.61 billion. Altogether Japanese corporations ranked among six of the top ten, 14 of the top 25, and 31 of the top 50 corporations in the world while American firms were only three of the top ten, 9 of the top 25, and 22 of the top 50 corporations. The Japanese corporations had an average price/earning ratio of 69, yield of 0.5 per cent, and return on equity of 9.2 per cent compared to American price/earnings ratio of 19, yield of 3.5 per cent, and return on equity of 18.0 per cent.

Throughout the postwar era, Tokyo's neomercantilist policies have allowed Japan's banks and corporations to excel in the ability to raise capital at minimal prices, thus giving Japanese corporations an enormous capital advantage over their American rivals. Capital costs for strategic Japanese industries are about 20 per cent lower than their American counterparts. For example, in the months following the October 1987 stock market crash, while American banks raised $5.7 billion in equity, just eight Japanese banks raised more than $22 billion. In 1989, Japan's corporations raised $115 billion in new shares and convertible bonds while American firms raised a mere $37 billion. In 1990, Matsushita Electric had estimated cash reserves of $15 billion, enough to have paid twice the $7.5 billion it settled on for MCA; Toyota had $15.9 billion reserves; Hitachi $15.9 billion.[14]

How do Japanese firms and banks do it? One reason for the ability of Japanese corporations to raise so much capital so easily and quickly is the different reserve requirements and debt equity ratios. The average Japanese bank reserves are only 2.5 per cent compared to 5 per cent for American banks, while Japanese stock prices trade on average more than 40 times earnings compared to only 10 times earnings for American firms. Thus, Japanese firms can raise the same amount of funds by issuing only one quarter the amount of new shares, a practice which simultaneously allows a tighter control over a firm's ownership. Between 1986 and 1989, Japanese firms paid an average 5–6 per cent rate for new equity, less than half the 12–13 per cent rate for American firms. Japan's low interest and inflation rates also keep borrowing costs low. Japanese banks can own up to five per cent in other corporations while American banks are barred from shareholding in other companies unless the business is directly related to their own.[15]

TRADE POWER

Perhaps no sign of a nation's power is more revealing than the composition, balance, and direction of its trade and payments, and that trade's percentage to GNP.[16] States achieve enormous potential power by maximizing the benefits of trade while minimizing the potential vulnerabilities of dependence on foreign markets and products for a significant percentage of GNP. The more a state's GNP is generated by a huge, affluent domestic market and resources, the less vulnerable it is to trade disruptions. Yet, as the world becomes increasingly interdependent, all nations must "export or die". The most economically powerful nations are those which enjoy continual trade surpluses generated by their ability to seize global markets for the widest possible range of value-added products. States enhance their power by making other states dependent on their manufacturing, financial, natural resources, and service products while spreading the sources of important imports as widely as possible to play off one source against the others for cheap, long term, stable deals.

America's economic decline is sadly evident in its trade and payments balances. At one time, the United State enjoyed both a strong currency and persistent trade surpluses, but no more. America's overall trade balance was positive from 1893 to 1970, but has been negative and getting worse since 1971. As recently as 1981, however, the United States still had a current account surplus of $10 billion. Since then both the trade and current accounts have plunged deeply into the red, peaking at $171.2 billion and $160.2 billion, respectively in 1987. America's current account deficit has dropped to $110 billion in 1989, and $99.3 billion in 1990, the smallest since 1984.

Boosted by the weak dollar, American manufactured exports grew rapidly throughout the late 1980s and into the 1990s – almost everywhere except, of course, to Japan. Between 1986 and 1990, American aircraft sales increased 99.4 per cent, electrical machinery 133.1 per cent, cars and trucks 61.4 per cent, computers and office machines 69.5 per cent, and small manufactured goods 145.9 per cent. Encouraging as was the performance of these sectors, America's trade deficit of nearly $100 billion in 1990 reveals the country's decline and the bankruptcy of its *laissez-faire* policies.

Japan's economic superpower is largely based on its ability to maximize its economic growth and exports and minimize imports. Japan has enjoyed almost continuous and steadily mounting trade and account surpluses since 1965, but the Reagan White House's high dollar policy caused Japan's surpluses to skyrocket during the 1980s. Between 1982 and 1985, Japan's trade surplus rose from $18.6 billion to $55.9 billion, and its current account surplus from $6.8 billion to $49.1 billion. Then in 1986, Japan's trade and current account surpluses almost doubled to $92.8 billion and $85.8 billion, followed by a moderate increase to $96.3 billion and $87.0 billion, respectively, in 1987.

The September 1985 Plaza Accord, in which the major industrial powers agreed to devalue the dollar, did not begin to take significant effect until several years later. In 1988, Japan's payments and trade surpluses decreased slightly to $79.6 billion and $95.0 billion. Then Japan's payments and trade surpluses shrank more rapidly from $56.975 billion and $77.13 billion in 1989 to $35.79 billion and $52.064

billion in 1990. But the drop represented a temporary adjustment to a strengthened yen and subsequent outflow of capital as Japanese corporations gobbled up foreign assets at fire sale prices. The current account surplus will remain at about two per cent of GNP for the foreseeable future as Japanese corporations further cut costs and increase productivity, thus enlarging their global market shares and more profits are reinvested in Japan to take advantage of higher interest rates.

Obviously, the less dependent a nation is on trade, the less vulnerable it is to trade disruptions. Ideally, a nation will enjoy immense trade surpluses while its trade remains relatively low as a percentage of GNP. Both the United States and Japan rely on their vast markets for the creation of most of their wealth, thus enjoying a relatively low vulnerability to global economic disruptions. Of all the industrial powers, Japan and the United States are the least trade dependent. Japan's trade to GNP ratio of 17.1 per cent in 1989 was slightly higher than America's 16.4 per cent, and both were well below Germany's 50.8 per cent, France's 36.5 per cent, Britain's 42.0 per cent, or Italy's 34.2 per cent. Not surprisingly, the importance of imports and exports in each country's GNP were a mirror image of each other. Imports (9.4 per cent) were a larger percentage of America's GNP than its exports (7.0 per cent), while Japan's exports (9.7 per cent) were more important than its imports (7.4 per cent).

More important than a nation's trade volume is its composition. Ideally, a nation will export the widest possible range of manufactured products while importing mostly raw or semi-finished materials from as wide a variety of sources as possible. America's trade composition is more characteristic of an underdeveloped than industrial country. In 1989, America's four largest exports to Japan were lumber, coal, grain, and seafood while its four largest imports were motor vehicles, finished electronics goods, electronics components, and general machinery. In contrast, Japan's trade composition revealed a manufacturing giant. The four largest categories of Japan's total exports in 1989 were: transportation equipment 24.2 per cent (passenger cars 14.1 per cent); electrical equipment, 23.4 per cent (VCRs 2.2 per cent, semiconductors 5.1 per cent); general machinery, 22.2 per cent; and metal production 7.8 per cent. The four largest categories of Japan's total imports were: other, 27.4 per cent (textiles 6.3 per cent, gold 1.7 per cent); fossil fuels, 20.4 per cent; chemicals 15.4 per cent; and foods 14.7 per cent.

Japanese and their foreign lobbyists constantly bemoan the fact that Japan is relatively poor in natural resources and use it to justify neomercantilist economic policies. In reality, Japan's dependence on foreign raw material sources is not unique, it is comparable to all the European countries, while in energy only Britain and Norway have significant though rapidly declining domestic sources. Furthermore, a lack of domestic raw materials or energy in an interdependent, well-developed global economy can actually be an advantage rather than a curse. Japanese corporations can search the world for the cheapest sources and further pressure down prices by playing off one supplier against another, thus giving them a tremendous cost advantage over foreign rivals that must depend on much more expensive domestic resources. For example, American steel producers largely rely on domestic iron ore whose extraction and transportation costs are excessive. As important a measure of Japan's power has been its ability to spread its imports of key energy and raw materials across several sources to reduce the vulnerability to any supply disruptions while simultaneously making those sources dependent on Japanese finance, technology, markets, and intermediate goods.

Geography remains a factor in shaping a nation's potential political economic power, but the actual benefits and costs of geography are not always apparent. For example, the United States seems to enjoy a clear advantage is being the focal point of both the Altantic and Pacific basin trade systems, while Japan's position in the far Northwest corner of the Pacific would seem to be a disadvantage. Yet, Japan's small size and range of excellent natural ports give Japanese producers a significant transportation cost advantage over their American rivals which must contend with shipping across the vast American continent. It is actually cheaper to send automobiles from Yokahama to Los Angeles than from Detroit to Los Angeles.

A key pillar of Japan's neomercantilist policies has been to maximize exports of manufactured goods while minimize imports of competitive manufactured goods. This policy has been an enormous success. Japan's ratio of manufactured imports to its total is the OECD's lowest. Japan's imports of manufactured goods represent only 3 per cent of GNP compared to 7 per cent in the United States, 14 per cent for West Germany, and 21 per cent in South Korea.[17] Although Japan's percentage of manufactured imports to its total more than doubled from 22.8 per cent in 1980 to 50.4 per cent in 1989, it remained well below America's 80.2 per cent, Germany's 76.1 per cent, Britain's 80.0 per cent, France's 77.8 per cent, and Italy's 69.1 per cent. For example, foreign made machine tools account for only 6 per cent of Japan's market in 1989 compared to about 50 per cent of Germany's. The volume of Japan's manufactured imports more than doubled from $40.1 billion in 1985 to $106.1 billion in 1989, but most of these were imported from Japan's overseas investments. Throughout the 1980s, the United States generally absorbed over half of newly industrializing exports while Japan took an average seven per cent. Of all the developing world's exports in 1987, the United States bought 52.6 per cent, the European Community 26.1 per cent, and Japan only 9.1 per cent.[18]

Although Japanese spokesmen declare repeatedly with straight faces that these differences are simply the result of Japan's superior quality products, it is clear that Japan will not buy foreign manufactured products in anything more than token amounts even when the foreign producer has an overwhelming comparative advantage. A Brookings Institute study found that in 1987, Japan would have imported more than $40 billion of additional manufactured goods if its markets had been free rather than carefully managed to prevent just such a possibility.[19]

What is "competitiveness"? The President's Commission on Industrial Competitiveness defines it as a nation's ability to successfully export in free global markets while expanding real domestic income, in other words, a nation's ability to balance trade without devaluing its currency and thus its citizen's real incomes.[20] Nations usually devalue their currencies when their industries lose their competitiveness. This prevents those industries from complete collapse but raises prices somewhat for consumers. The American dollar became increasingly overvalued throughout the 1960s as America's industrial rivals grew faster. President Nixon's devaluation of the dollar in 1971 reflected the steady competitive loss for many American industries. But the dollar was not devalued enough and America's trade continued to deteriorate throughout the 1970s; it then went into a tailspin during the 1980s because of Reagan's high dollar policy.

By the standard definition, Japan's competitiveness is inflated since Japan's economic growth has traditionally been fueled by exports subsidized by a chronically undervalued yen. A recent measure of Japan's economic prowess, however, is its industry's ability to compete even though the yen doubled in value between 1985 and 1988, when it reached a historic high in January at 120.45 to the dollar. Although Japan's trade surplus was trimmed, most industries claimed they could compete even if the yen rose to 100 or even 90 to the dollar. Unfortunately the yen declined instead to 160 yen to a dollar in late 1989 and early 1990, and has hovered at around 135 yen to a dollar from late 1990 through 1991. The yen thus remains grossly undervalued despite the dollar's recent devaluation, and Japan's much exploited consumers and foreign producers continue to suffer. Although Japan's per capita income is higher than America's, its purchasing power parity is about 50 per cent lower reflecting the undervalued yen and high living costs. Japan's ability to subsidize its industries by squeezing its consumers has been a major pillar of its neomercantilism.

A balance of trade power can be measured several ways. The most important measure of a nation's trade power is its account with its most significant rival. Trade is a zero sum game in which one nation's gain is another's loss. The United States first began suffering trade deficits with Japan in 1965 and they have worsened steadily since, then skyrocketed throughout the 1980s because of the Reagan Administration's inept policies. America's trade deficit with Japan was $15.8 billion in 1981, rose slightly to $16.7 billion in 1982 and $19.3 billion in 1983 then soared as the dollar gained almost 35 per cent in value to $33.6 billion in 1984, $46.2 billion in 1985, $55.0 billion in 1986 and peaked at $56.3 billion in 1987. The cheaper Japanese goods became, the more Americans bought them. American imports from Japan were $37.6 billion in 1981 and only slightly higher at $37.7 billion in 1982, but shot up to $41.2 billion in 1983, $57.1 billion in 1984, $68.8 billion in 1985, $81.8 billion in 1986, $84.6 billion in 1987, $89.8 billion in 1988, to peak at $93.5 billion in 1989, and then decline slightly to $89.6 billion in 1990. Japan's exports to the United States remain strong despite the yen's doubling in value since 1985, revealing that Japanese corporations exploited the dollar's over-value in the early 1980s to weaken or outright destroy their American rivals and carve out virtually impregnable market shares. American exports to Japan have risen considerably since the 1985 Plaza Accord, but will never balance trade with Japan unless the yen is revalued to less than 100 to the dollar and other powerful managed trade measures are taken. After falling from $21.8 billion in 1981 to $21.0 billion in 1982, American exports to Japan rose slowly to $28.2 billion in 1987, then leapt to $37.7 billion in 1988, $44.5 billion in 1989, and $48.6 billion in 1990.

Although the trade deficit has declined since 1987, in 1990, the United States still transferred a mindboggling $41 billion of wealth, jobs, technology and dynamism to Japan. America's increased exports to Japan were virtually all low-technology areas like raw materials, agriculture, and energy. For example, American wood and cork products increased from $0.93 billion in 1987 to $2.69 billion in 1990; ores and scrap iron from $0.41 billion to $1.02 billion; coal from $0.06 billion to $0.53 billion; nonferrous metals from $0.95 to $1.12 billion; and paper from $0.09 billion to $0.28 billion. Meanwhile, America's high technology deficit with Japan continues to deepen. Between 1987 and 1990, America's deficit in office machines, computers, and electrical generating equipments rose by $2.3 billion. Japanese producers have already captured almost all of America's consumer electronics markets, over half of the machine tool market, about 20 per cent of the semiconductor market, and 30 per cent of the automobile market.

Although the trade balance is the most important indicator of power, a potential source of power is the relative dependence of each country on each other as a percentage of its total trade. If one country depends on its major rival for more of its trade, it is more vulnerable in a trade war. The Achilles heel of Japan's economic superpower – one which American policymakers have refused to take advantage of – is its overwhelming dependence on the United States. Between 1985 and 1989, Japan's foreign trade amounted to $1.958 trillion, of which 30.1 per cent was with the United States, 14.1 per cent with Europe, 13.7 per cent with the NICs, 9.5 per cent with ASEAN, 3.7 per cent with China, and the remaining 28.9 per cent with the rest of the world. Japan's $93.188 billion in exports to the United States in 1989 represented 33.9 per cent of its total exports of $275.175 billion, while its $48.246 billion was only 22.9 per cent of its total imports of $210.847 billion. In comparison, only 21.1 per cent of America's trade in 1989 was with Japan.

Japan's vulnerability is even greater when Japan's high export dependence on specific products and the United States is revealed: 58.1 per cent for automobiles (28.4 per cent to America), 48.7 per cent for consumer electric equipment (23.4 per cent to America), 49.1 per cent for electric goods and parts (18.5 per cent to America), 48.5 per cent for other machines and equipment (17.6 per cent to America), 25.9 per cent for electronic and communications equipment (15.5 per cent to America), 38.6 per cent non-steel and non-steel products (13.3 per cent to America), 41.9 per cent steel (12.4 per cent to America). In contrast, America's dependence on some of its largest exports is relatively small: 17.0 per cent forestry of which 7.0 per cent goes to Japan, 3.9 per cent fisheries (3.1 per cent to Japan), 17.9 per cent agriculture (3.1 per cent to Japan), 32.0 per cent electronic/electronic parts (2.6 per cent to Japan), 23.7 per cent other transportation machines (2.4 per cent to Japan), 20.6 per cent non-steel and non-steel products (2.4 percent), and 18.3 per cent chemicals (2.2 per cent to Japan).

Bilateral trade statistics do not tell the entire story. Any analysis of American economic decline must increasingly include Japanese exports from direct foreign investments. In 1990, for example, America's consumer electronics deficit with Japan fell 8 per cent or $400 million while its imports from Thailand totaled $310 million, a 4,326 per cent rise since 1988. Since 1985, 46 Japanese electronics firms have set up shop in Thailand.[21] America's relative economic decline is severe by virtually any trade measure.

FOREIGN INVESTMENT POWER

Washington's "free trade" obsession is perhaps the major reason for America's relative decline and Japan's rise to global economic superpower. According to neoclassical economic theory, the free flow of foreign investments is good; any restrictions on investments bad. Foreign investment in one's economy provides not only jobs and capital, but a general upgrade of the economy's technology and managerial expertise. Neoclassical economists justify their dogma by pointing to America's industrial development during the late 19th century which was largely fueled by foreign investments in canals, railroads, ranches, and other key industries. The Reagan Administration summed up this outlook on foreign investments in the United States in a 1983 statement: "We believe that there are only winners, no losers, and all participants gain from it."[22]

Enticed by Washington's liberal policies and America's vast markets, foreign investments have steadily mounted from a total of $107 million in 1970 to an estimated $1.5 trillion in 1987. Of this total, an estimated 80 per cent was in government and private portfolio investments, which included as much as 15 to 20 per cent of America's national debt, $445 billion in bank assets, $300 billion in diversified stocks and bonds, $100 million in real estate, and $200–300 billion in direct investments of factories, warehouses, and assembly plants. Foreign holdings of American bank assets rose from $32 billion in 1973 to $445 billion in 1986, or an estimated 16 percent of total assets. About one third of California's banking assets are foreign owned while 40 per cent of the business loans in New York are foreign. More than half of America's cement industry and four of the largest chemical corporations are foreign owned. Foreign governments own an estimated 20 per cent of all foreign holdings in the United States.[23]

Direct foreign investments in the United States also rose very rapidly during the same period. The average annual value of new foreign direct investments in the United States rose from an average $7 billion in the 1970s to $20 billion in the early 1980s, to $25 billion in 1986. Between 1981 and 1986, foreign holdings of American assets rose from $579 billion to $1.3 trillion, of which stock holdings increased from $64 billion to $167 billion, bank deposits from $192 billion to $476 billion, US Treasury securities and corporate bonds from $154 billion to $415 billion, and direct investments from $109 billion to $209 billion.[24] These foreign holdings, however, represented only 6 per cent of all American corporate stock.[25]

Japanese investments spearheaded the wave of foreign investments into the United States during the 1980s. Between 1951 and 1989, Japanese directly invested $104.4 billion in the United States, of which almost one-third or $32.54 billion was invested in 1989 alone! The vital importance of the American market to Japan is further underlined by the fact that 41.1 per cent of Japanese direct foreign investments are in the United States. Japan's investments represented 17.6 per cent of all foreign investments, and represented 6000 American companies in which Japanese owned over 10 per cent, which is considered to be a controlling interest.[26] These investments represent the tip of the iceberg – it is estimated that at least half of all foreign investments in the United States go unreported.[27] Although Japan's investments still trailed those of the British with $122.1 billion, or 30.5 per cent of the total, it is estimated that at current investment rates, Japan will surpass Britain as the largest foreign investor in the United States in 1995 and by 1999 will own more American assets than Britain, the Netherlands and Canada combined.[28]

In stark contrast, of $15.654 billion in accumulated direct investments in Japan in 1990, Americans accounted for $7.91 billion or 49.3 per cent of the total, but only about ten per cent of Japan's investments in the United States. Of the total foreign investments in Japan, manufacturing investments were $9.03 billion or 70.6 per cent while nonmanufacturing was $3.764 billion or 29.4 per cent of the total. In early 1987, foreign-owned manufacturing firms in Japan accounted for about 4 per cent of the assets of all manufacturing firms in Japan, although one third of those foreign assets were concentrated in the oil refinery industries.[29] But foreign direct investment in Japan accounted for only 1 per cent of all corporate assets compared to 9 per cent in the United States, 14 per cent in Britain, and 17 per cent in West Germany. In 1990, American firms had only directly invested $17 billion in Japan compared to almost $85 billion of Japanese investments in the United States.[30] American and European financial firms have been unable to translate their comparative advantage in sophisticated financial products into market success in Japan – their investments were largely money-losers. In 1982, foreign banks held only 4.2 per cent of Japan's loan market, but this share shrank to 2.2 per cent as of August 1987. Over a quarter of the 79 foreign banks in Japan are losing money. This decline for foreign financial institutions in Japan's market is matched by equally dramatic losses elsewhere.[31]

BALANCE OF DEBT POWER

A nation "becomes a "net debtor" when it owes foreigners more money than foreigners owe it. Debtors can become subject to the will of their creditors as their economic policies are shaped by creditors to protect their financial stake in that country. America's national debt in 1980 was $914.3 billion, interest payments on the national debt $52.5 billion, and the budget deficit $59.6 billion. Five years of Reaganomics doubled the national debt to $1.823.1 trillion, and more than doubled the annual interest payments on the national debt to $129.0 billion, while the 1985 budget deficit of $202.8 billion was almost four times the 1980 figure, which presidential candidate Ronald Reagan had, at the time, persistently and harshly criticized. In 1989, America's budget deficit reached $220.4

billion or 4 per cent of GNP, barely missing the record $221.4 billion deficit reached in 1986. A $30 billion shortfall in anticipated revenues plus $58.1 billion or 4.6 per cent of total government outlays earmarked for the savings and loan bailout accounted for the 45 per cent increase over the $152 billion deficit in 1989. America's total public and private debt tripled from $3.4 trillion or 142.7 per cent of GNP in 1981 to $10.6 trillion in 1990 or 193.2 per cent of GNP.[32]

Much of this debt is owed to foreigners. Between 1917 and 1985, the United States was a net creditor country. America's net foreign investments peaked at $141 billion in 1981, then rapidly declined. In the first half of 1985, the United States became a net debtor nation when its surplus of $28 billion became a deficit of $35 billion. Total foreign holdings of treasury notes increased from $100 billion of $864.7 billion in 1980 to $201.3 billion of $1.799 trillion in 1985, or about 15 per cent of the total. By 1990 Americans owned $1.764 trillion in foreign assets while foreigners owned $2.176 trillion in American assets, causing a net American foreign debt of $412 billion in 1990 which equalled 7.5 per cent of the $5.465 trillion GNP. America's debt now far exceeds most of the Third World's combined debt, let alone countries like Brazil with $105 billion in debt or Mexico with $95 billion.[33]

America's vast debt must eventually be paid back. By 1992, interest payments on the debt alone will represent almost 25 per cent of the national budget, surpassing the military to become the largest budget category, and will require over $250 billion a year to service. This represents an incredible waste of money which could have been invested in strategic American industries and infrastructure. The United States is mortgaging its future to pay for contemporary excesses. Wealth that could have been reinvested in the United States is being sent overseas as interest payments while dynamic businesses that could have helped revive America's economic decline are being sold off to cash-rich foreign corporations, with the profits remitted to their own countries. Future generations of Americans will be transferring tremendous amounts of wealth to foreign countries just to meet interest payments.

While America descended to the world's worst debtor nation, Japan became the world's third largest financier in 1982, and in 1985 the world's largest banker. America's net foreign debt is expected to reach $1.3 trillion by 1995, while Japan's net surplus will surpass $650 billion! During the early 1980s, Japan financed increased amounts of America's annual government debt. Japan's lending to the United States throughout the early 1980s paralleled its ever growing payments surpluses and peaked with the net purchase of $50.7 billion of American securities in 1986. The amount has declined sharply since then with net purchases of around $38 billion in 1987, $36 billion in 1988, and $25 billion in 1989.[34]

America's huge debt forces the United States to become increasingly dependent on foreign capital and vulnerable to the political power that accompanies that debt. How vulnerable is the United States to Japan's financial power? Japanese ownership of American debt gives it enormous potential leverage over America's political economy, and Tokyo increasingly uses the threat of diverting its investments to exact concessions from Washington that further enrich Japan. America's interest rates are increasingly determined by Tokyo. Japan's mere threat of withholding the purchase of new treasury bills forces the Department of the Treasury to raise interest payments and lower the terms. In May 1987 Japanese investors refused to bid on the sale of $29 billion in treasury bills, thus forcing the US Treasury Department to raise interest rates and reduce the price. Only then did the Japanese buy nearly half the $9.3 billion in thirty year bonds offered. Tokyo frequently jerks on the financial chain around America's throat by hinting that it would withdraw its funds if Washington did not retreat from threats of retaliation against Japanese neomercantilism. By 21 February 1989, Tokyo's pressure on the White House became so intense that President Bush warned that if Americans did not stop criticizing Japan's trade barriers Tokyo might stop funding the deficit.[35]

In 1984, the Continental Bank of Illinois collapsed after Japanese investors withdrew their funds after hearing rumors of the Bank's poor loans to the energy sector. Tokyo pressured the United States into bailing out Continental Illinois in order to protect Japan's remaining investments in that bank.[36] Washington complied.

Overall, however, Japan's power is more psychological than anything else. It is unlikely that Tokyo would ever completely pull out its huge investments in the United States. Firstly, Japan would have difficulty finding places to invest all that money, and secondly, with interdependence the collapse of America's economy would also mean the collapse of Japan's. For example, Japan's 1990 stock market crash which wiped out 41 per cent of the market's value, and the subsequent rise in interest rates caused Japanese investors many to dump their American securities in favor of Japanese investments. In the first six months of 1990, Japanese investors were net sellers of American securities for a deficit of $8.9 billion, a remarkable drop from the $17.4 net purchases in the last six months of 1989.[37] The cutback in Japanese finance did not cause the economic disaster for the United States that many had predicted. The Bank of Japan stepped in with its own purchases of bonds to fill some of the gap left by the pullout of Japanese corporations. Interest rates remain higher than they would have had all the Japanese funds been available, thus exacerbating the recession.

America's corporations have become almost as dependent on foreign and particularly Japanese capital as has Washington. Foreign loans to

America's private sector rose from 1.3 per cent in 1980 to 4.48 per cent in 1986.[38] Heavily indebted American corporations are increasingly looking to Tokyo for bail-outs. During the 1980s, Japan's cash flush financial institutions became big players in America's leveraged corporate buyouts (LBO) and mergers and aquistions (M&A), supplying more than half of all deals. Between 1984 and 1987, the number of M&A in which Japanese participated increased five times. Japanese banks have been involved in every major American buyout since April 1986, and own more than 30 per cent or $50 billion of LBO debt. For example, Southland Corporation sold a 75 per cent stake to Ito-Yokado for $400 million. The deal is subject to the restructure of $1.8 billion in junk bonds Southland had acquired when its LBO failed, saddling the corporation with debt it could not finance. NKK, Japan's second largest steel firm, paid $147 million for 20 per cent of National Steel, and will eventually acquire an additional 20 per cent in return for its agreement to pay back. In January 1990, the Japanese resturant chain, Kyotaru, paid $110 million for 85 per cent of Resturant Associates Industries equity. Kyotaru will pump in another $35 million over the next few years to finance $90 million in high-yield debt the American firm accumulated from a leveraged buyout. But the largest deal to date was the consortium of 17 Japanese banks which loaned more than $6.1 billion to Kohlberg Kravis Roberts & Co. to help finance the RJR Nabisco deal. The Japanese got burned in some of these investments. For example, Japanese banks supplied more than half of the initial $4.2 billion in loans for Campeau Corp.'s acquisition of Federated, a deal that is widely considered to be overpriced since the value of Federated's assets do not cover the loans.[39]

More significant than Japan's participation in these LBOs and M & Es is the increased dependence of American entrepreneurs on Japanese firms to finance their ventures. America's vast corporate debt forces most American venture capitalists to be very selective about their investments while the seemingly bottomless pockets of Japanese investors allow them to be far less discriminating. Prestowitz criticizes America's venture capital market for encouraging "bright engineers to desert their companies for seemingly greener pastures. This syndrome creates a proliferation of small companies, without financial staying power, which are tempted to sell their technologies for short term financing."[40] The result of these tie-ups is a classic Faustian bargain in which the American entrepreneurs sell out their technology to their Japanese financiers.

Are the Japanese investors riding into town wearing black or white hats? The Materials Research Corporation was one of America's most advanced semiconductor manufacturing equipment producers. In 1989, the corporation faced a dilemma when it could not borrow enough money to finance the next generation of equipment. Instead, the firm sold out to

Sony Corporation. Seldon Weinig, chairman and cheif executive of the Materials Research Corporation, expressed the dilemma of many American entrepreneurs when America's irrational industrial policies leave them vulnerable to foreign takeover. Weinig bitterly remarked that "after we were purchased by Sony there was an outcry about how M.R.C. had slipped into the hands of a foreign company. No one said we were a national treasure before we were sold."[41] He then went on to describe Sony as a "white knight", and asks what would have happened "if we were not sold? Would our brilliant team of scientists and engineers still be together, working on the next generation of processing machines and improved materials?" The answer, of course, is no, not in America's free market system. In Japan, however, the government would have arranged for a Japanese corporate "white knight" to purchase any failing "national treasure" – it would have never allowed it to fall into foreign hands. Neomercantilism continues to triumph over liberalism.

Material Research Corporation's experience was positive. Increasing numbers of American firms are crying foul against Japanese "white knights". The experience of Ardent Computer, a Silicon Valley-based superminicomputer maker, is increasingly common. In 1986 it sold a large equity position to Kubota Corporation, the immense Japanese farm and industrial equipment maker. In July 1990, Ardent filed suit against Kubota, charging that the Japanese company had swindled the American entrepreneur. In 1988, Ardent merged with another venture company, Stellar Computer Inc. of Massachusetts to create a new company, Stardust Computer Inc. Kubota followed by acquiring a large stake in the new company and thus solidified its controls.[42] The image of Pac Man-like Japanese corporations gobbling up America's high technology and industrial jewels may become the predominant pattern in the 1990s and beyond.

FINANCIAL POWER

Japan's rise and America's economic decline are vividly revealed by a comparison of the power of their respective banking and securities industries. Protected by a vast range of cartels, subsidies, and artificially low interest rates, Japanese banks in particular operate with very low capital requirements and profit margins, giving them a decisive advantage over their American counterparts which must struggle to survive in highly competitive markets without government backing. Japan's banks account for about 40 per cent of global banking assets and American banks only about 25 per cent. Tokyo is second only to London as the world's largest lending center, and if current growth rates hold will be number one by the mid-1990s.

America's banking power has deteriorated and Japan's has risen rapidly over the past several decades. America leads only in the sheer number of financial institutions – in 1990, there were 12,926 American banks and 2,898 savings and loans compared to 154 Japanese banks and institutions similar to savings and loans.[43] Although American banks and savings and loans are much more numerous, Japan's are much more powerful. The vast majority of America's banks and savings and loans are tiny state institutions teetering on the brink of insolvency. In 1970, there were nine American banks among the world's top 30, today there is only one, Citibank. As of 31 March 1990, Japan had the world's eight largest banks, 16 of the top 25 banks, and 23 of the top 50 banks; in sharp contrast, only four American banks ranked among the world's top 50 banks, with the largest, Citicorp, in tenth place, and the second largest, Chase Manhattan, a distant thirty-sixth.[44] Yet, despite its vast power, Japan's private banks in turn are dwarfed by Japan's postal savings system which has four times the assets of Japan's 12 largest commercial banks combined!

American banks have been a prime target of Japanese investors, which are trying to position themselves for the 1991 repeal of the McFadden-Douglas Act that has restricted inter-state banking since the 1930s and has been a severe drag on American bank expansion, and thus international power. By early 1990, Japanese banks controlled 14 per cent of all American banking assets, and 25 per cent of California's, including five of the ten largest California banks. With the strong yen and open American markets Japanese firms are gobbling up American firms and banks for a pittance. For example, the 1987 $750 million takeover of California Union Bank cost the Bank of Tokyo 97.5 billion yen; if they had bought it two and a half years earlier it would have cost 165 billion yen. What Japanese banks do not directly own they often indirectly influence. In August 1987, a consortium of nine Japanese banks bailed out the Bank of America with a $130 million loan. In stark contrast, American banks have only a 1–1.5 per cent share of Japan's total banking assets; Japanese have bought over a dozen American banks while no Japanese banks are foreign owned.

The power to give is also the power to deny. In April 1989, the Japanese-owned Union Bank of California agreed to provide T. Boone Pickens company, Mesa, with an unrestricted, revolving $50 million credit line. But when it was announced that Pickens had bought a 20 per cent stake in the Toyota subsidiary, Koito Manufacturing, and was requesting three Board of Director seats, Union Bank broke the agreement.[45]

Japan's securities firms are just as powerful. The world's four largest securities corporations are Japanese, with Nomura number one with 1990 equity assets of $14.7 billion, followed by Daiwa with $7.9 billion, and Nikko and Yamaichi with $6.1 billion each. The largest American firm, Merrill Lynch, with $3.2 billion in equity, was less than one quarter

Nomura's size and one half Nikko's size. The next biggest American securities firms were Salomon Brothers with $2.8 billion and Shearson Lehman with $2.0 billion. The Japanese Big Four securities companies – Nomura, Daiwa, Nikko, and Yamaichi – account for 20 per cent of trading in US Treasury securities and 10 per cent of all activity on the New York Stock Exchange.[46] Al Alletzhauser's book, *The House of Nomura*, reveals how powerful that corporation and other Big Four members are in manipulating both the stock market and politics.[47] In 1990, Nomura alone had assets worth $47 billion in 1990, and controls 20 per cent of Tokyo stock exchange trading and 30 per cent of investment funds.

Japan's securities firms are rapidly taking over America's industry. Nomura purchased a $100 million 20 per cent stake in Wasserstein-Perella; Nippon Life a $538 million 13 per cent share in Shearson Lehman; Yasuda Mutual Life Insurance a $300 million 18 per cent share in Paine Webber; Yamaichi Securities a $100 million 25 per cent stake in the Lodestar Group; Sumitomo paid $500 million 14 per cent interest in Goldman Sachs; and Nikko a $100 million 15 per cent of the Blackstone Group. Japanese daily trading on the New York Stock Exchange regularly accounts for 10 to 25 per cent of the total. By owning such a significant chunk of America's banking and securities industries, Japanese corporations not only enjoy prestige, market access, and money management techniques, but are positioned to extract sensitive information on the financial conditions, investments, and strategies of America's manufacturing firms. They can then use their "power of the purse" to undercut the dynamic, independent American firms and reward those which sell out to their Japanese rivals.

America's financial dependence on Japan was brutally illustrated on Monday, 19 October 1987, when New York's stock market crashed 508 points, nearly one-quarter of the market's value, a drop far surpassing the 31 point (13 per cent) drop of 1929. Investors lost over half a trillion dollars on Black Monday alone and altogether over $1 trillion before the market bottomed out. Nicholas Brady, who had headed the presidential panel that investigated the October stock market crash, revealed on 22 April 1988 that: "What was it that blew it off on the 19th of October? Was it the twin (trade and budget) deficits? I don't think it was any of those things . . . The real trigger was that the Japanese came in for their own reasons and sold an enormous amount of US government bonds and drove the 30-year government bond up through 10 per cent . . ." The resulting fears of inflation drove the huge financial institutions to dump their stocks thus panicking everyone with a stake in the market.[48]

How do Japan's stock markets compare to America's? The Tokyo and Osaka stock markets sandwich New York stock exchange as the world's first and third largest. The Tokyo Stock Market's (TSE) growth and resilience has been phenomenal. In 1976, the TSE was worth only $180 billion eleven years later, on 30 April 1987, the TSE surged past Wall Street to become the world's largest with a capitalization of $2.997 trillion or 39 per cent of the world's total compared to Wall Street's $2.581 trillion or 34 per cent share, and London's $625 billion or 8 per cent share. By 24 November 1988 the TSE share had risen to $3.950 trillion or 45 per cent share compared to Wall Street's $2.390 trillion or 27 per cent share and London's $745 billion or 9 per cent share. Despite the market's vast value, the TSE remains far more exclusive than the New York Stock Exchange – only 114 members compared to 555. The TSE is not just powerful in assets; since 1968 the stock market has only dropped twice on an annual basis, in 1974 by about 14 per cent and in 1982 by about 1 per cent; it has absorbed three huge sell-offs of Nippon Telephone and Telegraph stock without a tremor and quickly shook off the October 1987 crash.[49]

Like all its other markets, Japan's stock markets are carefully managed through cartels, insider trading, and government protection. Japanese corporations own each other, both within and between the industrial groups (Keiretsu). Among listed corporations, the average amount of stock in friendly hands was 67.4 per cent in 1989 compared to a mere 15.5 per cent in 1949 following the Occupation reforms.[50] These interlocking shareholdings make it virtually impossible for a hostile takeover to occur. Insider trading is pervasive. The Big Four securities firms account for about 80 per cent of all trading.

Until recently, except for the Asian Development Bank, Tokyo has not played a significant role in creating or leading an international organization. But Tokyo is now using its power of the purse as global banker to subtly shape the operations of international organzitions to favor Japanese interests. For example, in May 1990, the IMF agreed to raise its financial resources from $120 billion to $180 billion, and increased the quota so that Japan will share second billing with Germany in voting power while Britain and France occupy the third tier. Japan's power within international economic organizations will continue to rise steadily.

TECHNOLOGY POWER

Americans have lead the world in technology for over two centuries, inventing machines and processes that converted raw materials into products for mass consumption and destruction alike. Schoolchildren around the world are familiar with Benjamin Franklin's lighting rod, Eli Whitney's cotton gin, Robert Fulton's steamboat, Alexander Graham Bell's telephone, Thomas Edison's lightbulb, John Ford's assembly line, to name a few creators and their creations. Throughout the 20th century, however, the lone genius inventor has been replaced by vast institutions dedicated to creating a better mousetrap – Bell Laboratories, NASA, Lawrence Livermore. But regardless of whether the technology flows from a Steven Jobs tinkering in his garage or armies of white coated scientists in a huge laboratories, there is a heroic edge to much of this inventiveness – new vaccines, satellites or aircraft can improve both the length and quality of life.

America's power in creating the processes and inventions of the modern world declined precipitously over the past generation until it was eclipsed by that of Japan during the 1980s.[51] As early as 1984, a US Defense Science Board Task Force concluded that "Japan has created technological momentum that will broaden their present-day lead over the United States in some fields and will enable their long-term commitment to technology innovation to be successful".[52] According to the National Science Foundation, the United States has steadily declined in world export shares of technology intensive products from 27.0 per cent in 1970 to 22.9 per cent in 1980 and 20.9 per cent in 1986 while Japan's share increased from 10.9 per cent to 14.3 per cent to 19.8 per cent in those same years. During this time, America's surplus in technology trade dropped from $6 billion to $1 billion. Americans accounted for 65.7 per cent of US patents in 1970 but only 54 per cent in 1986.[53] A 1987 National Academy of Engineering study revealed that Japan had surpassed the United States in twenty-five of thirty-four key areas of high technology including artificial intelligence, optoelectronics, and systems engineering and control, while of 25 key semiconductor technologies, Japanese producers led in 12, were equal in eight, and were rapidly closing the gap in five.[54] A study by the Council on Competitiveness issued on 20 March 1991 revealed that of 94 technologies, the United States led in 25, was running neck and neck in 29, was falling behind in 21, and was either on the verge or had completely lost out in 19, while a Commerce Department study revealed that of twelve emerging technology sectors, Japan was leading in 10 and running neck and neck with the United States in the other two.[55]

Japan's leapfrogging of America in technology is reflected in the number of patents awarded to Japanese and American corporations, with the Japanese enjoying a significant lead. Japan has surpassed the United States in the number of patents granted to its citizens. In 1967 the Patent Office granted 13,877 patents to Japanese nationals; in 1984 it granted 51,690. In contrast, the number of patents granted by Washington to American citizens actually declined from 51,274 in 1967 to 38,363 in 1984. The amount of patents issued to foreigners doubled in the United States from 14,378 in 1967 to 28,837 in 1984; in Japan the comparative figures were 6,896 and 10,110, respectively. There is a large patent imbalance between the United States and Japan: in 1984 Japan accounted for 20 per cent of patents issued in the United States, while Americans accounted for only 7 per cent of patents issued in Japan. Of the ten leading winners of US patents in 1987, four were Japanese and four American. The top three patent winners – Canon (847), Hitachi (845), and Toshiba (823) and ninth Mitsubishi (518) were Japanese, while General Electric ranked fourth (779), Westinghouse fifth (652), IBM sixth (591) and RCA tenth (504).[56]

High technology's central pillar is the microelectronics industry. Every high technology industry from aerospace to biotechnology has an electronic core, including, of course, electronics products themselves. In 1989, global electronics production surpassed $740 billion, of which $218 billion of computers ran on a $57 billion semiconductor industry which in turn was produced by a $19 billion semiconductor materials and equipment industry. America's electronics industry is the country's largest, producing $295 billion of goods and services in 1989 compared to $250 billion for the automobile industry, $106 billion for aerospace, and $61 billion for steel. The electronics field is also a job rich industry. In 1989, over 2.6 million Americans were employed in electronics compared to 900 000 in the automobile indusry, 800 000 in aerospace, and only 300 000 in steel. America's microelectronics pillar has steadily crumbled throughout the last decade, thus cracking related high technology fields. America's $8 billion electronics trade surplus in 1980 steadily declined to a $10 billion deficit in 1989, and American jobs disappeared along with this deficit as American electronics firms increasingly invest overseas to tap cheap labor and leap trade barriers. In 1980, there were roughly 80 000 more Americans than foreigners employed in American electronics firms; in 1989, foreigners outnumbered Americans employed by American electronic firms by over 100 000.

America's decline in computers has been steady but less drastic than in the other two segments. In 1984, seven American firms were in the top ten, IBM (first), DEC (second), Burroughs (third), Sperry (fourth), Control Data (sixth), NCR (seventh), and HP (eigth), and only two Japanese firms, Fujitsu (fifth) and NEC (sixth). Siemens was tenth. In 1989, only four American firms were in the top ten, IBM (first), DEC (second), Unisys (fifth), and HP (seventh), while three Japanese firms placed, NEC (third), Fujitsu (fourth), and Hitachi (sixth). Three European firms, Groupe Bull, Siemens, and Olivetti took the eight, nineth, and tenth places, respectively. American global share fell from 78 per cent to 59 per cent, while Japan's rose from 11 per cent to 25 per cent.

Semiconductors are as important to the microelectronics industry as steel is to the automobile industry. American producers dominated the production of semiconductors throughout the 1960s and up to the late 1970s. But, according to Inman and Burton, by 1980 Japanese companies had surpassed US merchant semiconductor firms in the design and manufacture of the latest generation of semiconductor devices. By 1983 Japanese-based firms held a share of the market equal to that of American based firms. By 1986, the Japanese had taken 65 per cent of the world market for memory products, while the US share had fallen to under 30 per cent. In 1988, Japan held 85 per cent of the market for one-megabit memory chips, while the American share (not including IBM, which makes memory chips for it own use) had dwindled to 8 per cent.[57]

In 1980, there were five American firms in the top ten semiconductor manufacturers, of which Texas Instruments (TI) was first, Motorola second, National fourth, Intel eighth, and Fairchild ninth, while Japan's NEC, Toshiba, and Hitachi placed fourth, sixth and seventh respectively, and Europe's Philips and Siemens placed third and tenth, respectively. In 1989, Japan's firms controlled six of the top ten slots, with NEC, Toshiba, Hitachi, Fujitsu, Mitsubishi, and Matsushita placing first, second, third, fifth, seventh and ninth, respectively, while only three American firms made the list, Motorola fourth, TI sixth and Intel eighth. Philips placed tenth. In 1980, American firms enjoyed a 57 per cent global market share and Japanese only 27 per cent; in 1989, the Japanese had captured a 52 per cent global market share while the Americans had plunged to 35 per cent.[58] In 1979–80, the United States held a lead over Japan in 14 of 25 semiconductor technologies, parity in four, and lagged in five; in 1986–87, America's lead over Japan dropped dramatically to five, while parity rose to six, and the lag to 13 semiconductor technologies![59]

Any nation that dominates the technology food chain's base – the semiconductor manufacturing equipment industry – has the power to dominate all the other links up the chain. During the 1980s, the Japanese took over America's leadership in the semiconductor equipment segment. In 1980, nine of the ten largest firms making semiconductor equipment were American; in 1990, only Applied Materials remained in the top ten, behind Tokyo Electron and Nikon. Applied Materials has survived in part by its strategy of fighting its Japanese competitors in Japan as well as in the United States and Europe. It established a wholly owned subsidiary in Japan in 1979.[60] America's global market share in 1980 was 75 per cent and Japan's 16 per cent; in 1989, America's share had dropped to 47 per cent and Japan's had risen to 42 per cent. Although the United States maintained a slight overall lead in 1989, its share of key segments of the industry dropped alarmingly. Of the equipment industry, Americans produced only 20 per cent of the microlithography, 32 per cent of packaging, and 36 per cent of diffusion furnaces, while American firms were almost completely wiped out of the materials industry, clinging to a 2 per cent share of both the silicon wafers and mask blanks and 3 per cent of ceramic packages.

Given Japan's conquest of world's semiconductor industry, it comes as no surprise to learn that American industries are increasingly dependent on Japanese corporations for their components. For example, Japanese components comprised 20 per cent of the original Apple II computer introduced in 1977, but 70 per cent of Apple's Next Inc. computer introduced in 1988.[61] Japanese firms are the leading suppliers of flat liquid crystal display screens which normally account for over 25 per cent of the laptop computer's costs. The Defense Department revealed that in 1988 twenty-one American weapons systems were dependent on Japanese producers for all their semiconductors.[62]

The greater an American firm's dependence on Japanese components and/or finance the greater the vulnerability to Japanese blackmail involving the transfer of technology or markets.

Japan's most blatant use of its technology power has been to withhold or delay selling key equipment to American manufacturers while supplying it to their Japanese rivals. American firms have been complaining about the practice for years, but quietly for fear that the Japanese firms will withhold even more equipment. On 6 May 1991, Sematech, an American consortium of 14 chip and computer makers publicly denounced Japan's hoarding of essential equipment for as long as 6 to 18 months and then selling it at prices 20 to 30 per cent higher than Japanese firms pay in an attempt to damage the American firms as much as possible. The equipment identified included Nikon advanced steppers, Tokyo Eletron Ltd and Kokusai precision heating equipment, and Hitachi ion implanters. Likewise, America's remaining supercomputer producer, Cray, is dependent on Japanese suppliers for most of its key components, and the Japanese have not hesitated to exploit this dependency: in 1986, Hitachi delayed shipping a key component that Cray had actually designed, giving its own computer group a one-year lead time designing it into its own supercomputers.[63]

There are many reasons why Japan has surpassed the United States in creating and applying technology. Technology power tips not necessarily to the nation that invents new technologies but to the nation that can apply that technology into high value-added mass products. Between 1950 and 1980, Japanese firms signed over 30 000 technology licenses worth about $10 billion with American firms which had spent between $500 billion and $1 trillion to develop those technologies.[64] Despite – or because – of all its technological leadership, Japan continues annually to import more technology than it exports. In 1988, Japanese firms sold $1.785 billion of technology but bought $2.263 billion.

Another major reason is that Japan has simply outspent the United States. American research and development averaged 1.8 per cent of GNP during the 1970s and 1980s compared a Japanese average of 2.8 per cent.[65] Japan continues to outspend the United States in research and development as a percentage of GNP and as a percentage of private efforts. In 1989, Japan spent $76.249 billion or 3.35 per cent of GNP on R&D, of which government financed only 18.4 per cent while the United States spent $126.115 billion or 2.89 per cent of GNP, of which the government chipped in almost half (48.0 percent). Whether it is basic or applied, Japan's R&D expenses are characterized by being virtually all commercially oriented, while 70 per cent of America's government funds are military-oriented.[66]

A Japan Science and Technology Agency (STA) White Paper published in 1983 nicely illustrated the differences in R&D spending priorities between the two countries. In 1981 69.2 per cent of Japanese R&D funds came from industry, 25.0 from the government, and 5.8 per cent from the universities. From these sources industry spent 66.4 per cent of the total, the government 11.8 per cent, and universities 20.5 per cent. In comparison, of American funds only 49.0 per cent were raised by industry, 47.3 per cent by government, and 3.8 per cent from the universities. From these sources industry spent 71.2 per cent, government 13.0 per cent, and universities 15.8 per cent.[67] The biggest difference is how the government R&D funds are used. A 1982 OECD study revealed that in 1980 only 16.8 per cent of Japanese government funds went to defense and aerospace, while agriculture and industry consumed 25.4 per cent, energy and infrastructure 34.4 per cent, health and welfare 11.2 per cent, and the advancement of knowledge 3.5 per cent, for a total percentage of GNP of 0.56 per cent. In comparision, 63.7 per cent of American government R&D funds went to defense and aerospace, while agriculture and industry enjoyed a mere 3.0 per cent, energy and infrastructure 14.2 per cent, health and welfare 15.2 per cent, and the advancement of knowledge 3.0 per cent, for a government R&D as percentage of GNP of 1.11 per cent.[68] These spending patterns have remained constant; in 1988 69 percent of American government R&D funds went to the military compared to 13 per cent for West Germany and less than 5 per cent for Japan.

Another important difference between American and Japanese government spending involved the relative shares that government and industry would contribute to specific projects. While the United States usually provided all of the funds (*itakuhi*), more than 60 per cent of Japan's government funds were only partial expenses (*hojokin*) which had to be matched by industry, thus ensuring business would make an all-out effort to recoup its investment. Japan's microelectronic corporations now spend more on research and development than on plant and equipment. In 1989, Hitachi spent more than $2 billion on R&D (10 per cent of sales), NEC $1.8 billion (9.2 per cent of sales), Toshiba $1.4 billion (7.1 per cent of sales), and Fujitsu $1.3 billion (10.9 per cent of sales).[69] America's 1988 rate of return required to cover financing for R&D expenses was 20.3 per cent compared to Japan's 8.7 per cent ratio.[70]

There is an enormous education gap between the United States and Japan. Tokyo's education polices targeting the creation of mass armies of scientists and engineers and America's education policies opening its best universities and laboratories to the world are two more important reasons behind Japan's technology ascendance. Japanese students consistently score first or second in the world in subjects like math and science while American students are just as consistently toward the bottom of industrial country rankings. One major reason for the education gap is that Japanese students simply spend more time in school, 220 days a year and 41.5 hours a week compared to 180 days and 26.2 hours for American students. By the time Japanese students graduate from high school they will have spent the equivalent of four more years in school than their American counterparts! Japanese students also study more, 19.0 hours a week compared to 3.8 hours for American students. Only 75 per cent of American students finish high school compared to 95 per cent of Japanese students. In 1990, Japanese high school seniors ranked 4th in chemistry and physics, and 10th in biology while American students languished at 9th, 11th and 13th in those subjects, and 14th of 17 countries. In 1982 Japanese engineering students numbered 73,593 or about 20 per cent of all university students, compared to 66 990 in the United States or about 4 per cent of the total, giving Japan over twice as many Japanese engineers per capita as in the United States. Japan now has more than 5000 technical workers per million people compared to 3500 in America, and 2500 in West Germany. But the imbalance is not just confined to sheer numbers of scientists and engineers, but how they are employed. Japan's best minds are employed in its top corporations dedicated to creating mass consumer and capital goods. The number of American scientists and engineers doubled from 1978 to over 4.6 million in 1988, but many argue that they are inefficiently employed doing abstract and often overlapping work in research facilities.[71]

Brilliant as Japan's education system has been in creating a literate, docile, and diligent workforce, Japanese still look to American universities and laboratories for the most innovative basic scientific education and research. In any year there are 10 times more Japanese studying at American universities than Americans on Japanese campuses; in 1990, 20 000 Japanese students were enrolled at American universities and only

1800 Americans at Japanese universities. And, as might be expected, there is also a huge imbalance in the exchange of engineering students and professors between the two countries. Between 1957 and 1973, 1097 Japanese engineers and 7,207 natural and physical scientists studied in the United States for a month or longer; the American figures for the same period were 65 and 317, respectively, while by 1988 the number of Japanese scientists and engineers studying and working in the United States had risen to 52 000! Since 1945, Bell Labs alone has been the launching pad for the careers of 30 leading Japanese scientists. In 1986, there were more than 300 Japanese scientists working at the US National Institute of Health (NIH), most with American government support; in contrast there were only three American NIH workers in Japan.[72]

Yet another reason for Japan's seizure of global technology leadership involves the relative size of American and Japanese high tech corporations. American microelectronics industry is splintered among hundreds of small entrepreneur firms which lack the financial and marketing clout to support their inventions. In contrast, Japan's "big six" computer firms

> with annual revenues of more than $10 billion and with close links with other major Japanese industries, produce approximately 85 per cent of Japanese semiconductors, 80 per cent of Japanese telecommunications equipment, and 60 per cent of Japanese consumer electronics. A single $2 billion firm, Fanuc (Fujitsu Automatic Numerical Control), controls 80 per cent of the domestic market and 40 per cent of the world market for machine tool electronic control systems. Fanuc is also the world's largest robot producer and is 40 per cent owned by Fujitsu, Japan's largest computer manufacturer . . . the equity and debt of Japanese high technology firms and many of their suppliers are closely held within the major industrial groups. These groups, which are led by the world's largest banks and trading companies, each comprise more than 100 companies with total revenues of $100 billion or more. For instance, the leading companies in the Sumitomo group own not only 19 per cent of NEC, whose corporate revenues total more than $15 billion, but also almost 10 per cent of Matsushita, a $40 billion electronics firm. Large manufacturers, in turn, control many subcontractors: Two firms, one of them 51 per cent owned by NEC and the other 22 per cent owned by Fujitsu, control 90 per cent of Japanese production of semiconductor test equipment.[73]

Assuming that Japanese and American scientists are familiar with this vast statistical evidence of Japan's technological leapfrogging of the United States, one might expect Japanese elation and American alarm. Recent polls, instead, indicate typical Japanese modesty and American

Pollyannaish optimism over the results. A Spring 1989 Nihon Keizai Shimbun survey of 301 members of Japan's Science Council revealed that Japan's leading scientists thought that they led in only two of 47 major technologies – advanced robotics and ferromagnetic materials, although they felt that by 2000 they could possibly lead in seven other technologies.[74] It is probable that the results were skewed by Japanese humility and/or a desire not to panic their American rivals. The response of Lewis Branscomb, Professor of Science and Technology Policy at Harvard, was typical: "Come on, my friends, you are better than that and you know it. I don't think they really believe that America is ahead".[75] A similar STA survey conducted four years earlier of 83 current and future high technology areas may have revealed the true perspectives of Japanese scientists who believed they were ahead in 20 technologies, behind in 30 and about even in the rest.[76]

In contrast to the more recent bleak assessment by Japanese of their technology capabilities, a joint survey conducted from 29 October through 8 November 1990 of 150 leading American engineers, with 50 each from government agencies, academic institutions, and corporations revealed a generally optimistic view of American technological superiority.[77] Although an overwhelming 78.6 per cent said the United States would be able to maintain its technology lead into the 21st century, 82.0 per cent said bilateral competition would become greater, 75.4 per cent that technology protection would increase, and 62 per cent that Japan continued to enjoy an "easy ride" on taking foreign technology without reciprocating. Over two-thirds (68.7 percent) welcomed the creation of Japanese research facilities in the United States and 58 per cent said they would like to work at such facilities. The scientific community's reliance on defense spending was revealed by 50.0 per cent claiming that defense cutbacks would moderately affect research and 16.7 per cent saying it would be a great hindrance. The questionaire then cited twelve high technology fields in which it was asked whether the United States would be able to maintain its lead into the 21st century. The engineers conceded a possible future Japanese lead in only three of the twelve fields – memory semiconductors, consumer electronics and next generation computers. The assumption, however, that the United States already led in those twelve fields, which included artificial intelligence, new industrial materials, semiconductors, and fifth generation computers, among others, is highly questionable and may have skewed the results.

Which perspective is correct, the masses of statistics that clearly prove Japan's technological leadership or the views of the scientific community? Perhaps the views of both Japanese and American scientists would have changed greatly if the survey had been accompanied by the dozen studies cited above. Industries are related to each other on technology and product food chains. Japan's strategy has been to capture key links in those technology and product chains, with which they amass enormous profits, scale economies, and learning scales with which to expand systematically, link by link, their control over entire industries and technologies in the chain. Many analysts are concluding that Japan's technological superiority may threaten American national security and prosperity. Charles Ferguson consisely captures the dangers inherent in America's loss of technological leadership to Japan.

> technological revolutions often contribute to shifts in wealth and geopolitical influence by changing the sources of industrial and military success . . . As this transformation progresses, the United States is being gradually but pervasively eclipsed by Japan . . . (a development that could lead to American) decline and dependence on Japan . . . (and) major economic and geopolitical consequences . . . [W]hile Japan is a military ally . . . American policy must recognize that Japan is also a closed, highly controlled, and systematically predatory actor in the international economy . . . (and) a statist, strategically cohesive free rider in the world techological system . . . The simultaneous need to preserve the military-diplomatic alliance while responding to Japan's technoeconomic Prussianism will therefore prove a critical challenge for US policy . . . the United States must learn that . . . [the] issue of high technology and Japanese industrial policy, not just Soviet warheads, will determine the future national security of the United States.[78]

Liberal Democratic Party leader, Shintaro Ishihara, bluntly asserted the use of Japan's technology power for political ends. In his book, "The Japan That Can Say No!", Ishihara shrilly advocates using America's growing high technology dependence on Japan to extract political concessions: if Japan sold "microprocessor chips to the Soviet Union and stopped selling them to the United States, this would upset the entire military balance . . . The more technology advances the more the US and Soviet Union will become dependent upon the initiative of the Japanese people".[79]

Ishida's chilling words capture the essence of the application of economic power. By virtually all indicators, Japan's economic power far surpasses America's, and Japan's government and corporations are increasingly wielding their power to extract yet more benefits for Japan at America's expense.

5 The Shifting Balance of Political Power: Hearts, Minds and Policies

There is a reciprocal relationship between economic power – the ability to capture markets; play off raw material, capital and component suppliers against each other to extract the lowest possible price; and technologically leapfrog, financially outspend, undersell and eventually bankrupt rivals – and political power. Money buys access to political power which can then be used to promote policies favoring the buyer, which allows even greater resources with which to buy more political power.

Japan's use of economic power to extract political concessions from Washington and state and local governments is becoming increasingly blatant. What political objectives do Japan's government and business hope to achieve in the United States? Japan's objectives are quite simple – to keep America's political economy as open and Japan's as closed as possible. Tokyo's most strenuous efforts are focused on keeping America's vast market of 250 million consumers open to Japanese products and strategic American assets open to purchase by Japanese corporations. Meanwhile, the Japan lobby undercuts any White House and Congressional attempts to negotiate any genuine opening of Japanese markets or retaliate if Tokyo's neomercantilist policies persist. Tokyo's ultimate objective is to so deeply entangle America's political economy into dependence on Japan's that it becomes virtually impossible for Washington not only to retaliate against Japanese neomercantilism but even to formulate any policy that serves American rather than Japanese national interests.

What are the means by which Japan succeeds in accomplishing these goals? Tokyo skillfully uses three powerful resources – money, organization and message – to arm-twist the White House, Congress, American firms, state and local governments, and the mass public into granting massive concessions to Japanese corporations. Several analysts have explored Japan's deepening political power over the United States. It was a conversation with Senator Jim Sasser of Tennessee, whose opponent in the 1986 election had received substantial support from Nissan to counter Sasser's initial support for a domestic content bill for all automobiles sold in America, that inspired Martin and Susan Tolchin to write *Buying Into America*, their exposé of the increasing power that foreign and particularly Japanese multinationals have over America's political economy.[1] Even more disturbing was Pat Choate's *Agents of Influence*, in which he revealed, after years of extensive investigation of Japanese political power in the United States, that Japan annually spends an estimated $400 million at the national, state and local levels to buy the services of a mercenary army of hundreds of lawyers, former high ranking public officials, political consultants and even former presidents to promote Japanese over American national interests.[2]

Japan's massive efforts have been an enormous success. Since the mid–1960s, Tokyo has scored repeated successes in co-opting the White House into undermining any Congressional attempts to systematically address America's worsening trade deficit with Japan. Washington seems increasingly resigned to blindly accepting annual $50 billion trade deficits with Japan as a permanent and "natural" characteristic of the relationship. The White House accepts Japanese promises to open up its markets rather than increased sales of American products and a steadily diminishing trade deficit as the criteria for the successful conclusion of negotiations. As a result, Tokyo has chalked up victory after victory in such fields as "consumer electronics, supercomputers, machine tools, ball bearings, optical fibers, satellites, rice, biotechnology, air transport, telecommunications, semiconductors, legal and financial services, among dozens of others".[3] American producers once enjoyed comparative advantages in all these fields, but were devastated by Tokyo industrial policies that targeted their Japanese rivals with a range of cartels, subsidies, import protection, and export promotion. At best, the White House succeeded in getting Tokyo to agree to give up some of its industrial policy tools in each industry. But these "concessions" were always too little too late; the American industry had already been battered, often beyond repair, by Tokyo's neomercantilism.

Why is Japan beating the United States politically as well as economically? The political playing field between the United States and Japan is just as decisively tilted in Tokyo's favor as the economic playing field. Choate argues that "America tolerates foreign interference in its domestic affairs, Japan does not. This is the basic reason why Japan's trade negotiators and companies succeed, while America's fail".[4] American government is as open as American markets. Just as the largest market shares are won by the firms with the lowest priced products, those political economic forces – foreign or domestic – which can offer the highest prices to those in or near power have the most potential influence over government policy. Japan's government, in stark contrast, is not for sale; its former government leaders do not lobby for American interests nor are its politicians or political parties allowed to accept foreign financial donations. The Education Ministry ensures that it, and not foreigners, will determine Japan's elementary, high school and university curriculum.

The result is a massive transfer of wealth from the United States to Japan that would not have taken place if a level playing field had prevailed. Thus the United States has even less financial resources with which to deal with such debilitating problems as the trade and budget deficits, crumbling infrastructure, crime, drugs, and poverty. Locked in this vicious political economic circle, America's relative economic decline will continue to snowball. This chapter explores in detail the ends, means, and extent of Japanese political power in the United States.

JAPAN'S LOBBYING NETWORK IN AMERICA: FROM THE WHITE HOUSE TO PEORIA

There are restrictions on foreign lobbying in the United States. The Federal Election Campaign Act of 1974 specifically prohibits foreign nationals from contributing to political campaigns. The law states that "a foreign national shall not directly or through any other person make a contribution in connection with a convention, caucus, primary, general, special or run-off election in connection with any local, state, or federal public office". In addition, the Foreign Agents Registration Act requires any firm or individual engaged in "political activities", public relations counselling, or managing funds for such purposes to register with the Justice Department.

These laws, however, are riddled with loopholes and widely evaded. Japan's lobbying army still has plenty of room to maneuver. Although foreign individuals, corporations, and governments are legally prohibited from contributing money to candidates in any local, state, or national election, they sidestep this restriction by creating an American subsidiary which then operates under the same laws as any American firm. The subsidiary can then form political action committees (PACs) which can contribute up to $5,000 for any one candidate in an election, as well as spend an unlimited amount of money supporting any candidate or cause as long as the candidate does not directly receive that money. Thus, despite the unambiguous clarity with which the campaign contribution law is written, the Federal Election Commission (FEC) has interpreted the law to exempt subsidiaries controlled by foreign corporations, governments, or political parties from any reporting requirements if they are not directly or indirectly supervised, controlled, financed or subsidized by the parent organization. Furthermore, the civil fines of $5,000 for failure to register, material omission, and false statement are so insignificant that they actually encourage rather than deter continued circumvention of the law. The head of the Justice Department Foreign Agent Registration Bureau pointed out that many lobbyists "are exempt from registration requirements because they do simple legal representation, as opposed to direct lobbying, or are actually employed by exempted domestic affiliates of Japanese companies".[5] It is estimated that only about 5 per cent of foreign agents actually register.

Japan's vast lobbying network which extends literally from the White House to the 50 state houses and beyond makes a mockery of these foreign lobbying rules. According to Choate, dozens of Japanese government agencies and hundreds of corporations annually spend an estimated $400 million to shape national, state, and local American policies in its favor – more than the combined total expenditures of the 1988 Congressional elections and the combined budgets of America's major business lobby groups. Tokyo uses this money to buy the services of a mercenary army of hundreds of lawyers, former high ranking public officials, political consultants, and even former presidents to promote Japanese over American national interests. Roughly a quarter of this vast wealth is spent in Washington. In 1988 alone, 152 Japanese firms and government agencies hired 113 Washington firms to lobby Congress and the White House. Their recorded fees of over $100 million were greater than the combined budgets of the US Chamber of Commerce, the National Association of Manufacturers, The Business Roundtable, the Committee for Economic Development and the American Business Conference – the five most influential American business organizations in Washington. In 1990, Japan employed one and a half times more Washington lobbying, public relations and law firms (92) to promote its interests as Canada (55), twice as many as Britain (42), and thirteen times as many as Holland (7).[6]

The ranks of these Japanese lobby groups are filled with more than 100 former senior American officials including veterans of Congress, the White House, and even the Office of the United States Trade Representative. Representative Howard Wolpe characterizes the Federal government as "a finishing school for lobbyists for foreign interests . . . Can you conceive of masses of top administrators and prime minister's staffers in Japan going to work for Americans? It'd be a scandal there and it ought to be a scandal here". One of the most remarkable switches is former Under-secretary of Commerce Lionel Olmer who was once a tough critic of Japan's unfair trade practices, but now represents NTT.[7] Some of the other big name hired guns include Richard Whalen, former special assistant to President Nixon; Stuart Eisenstadt, head of President Carter's domestic policy staff; the former CIA chief Bill Colby; and Richard Allen, former National Security Advisor for President Reagan.

As a result, in Choate's words, "Japan may now have the best political intelligence system in America. Certainly it rivals the information gathering efforts of the Soviet KGB. It is comprehensive and systematic. It employs thousands of Americans, many of whom have direct access to the most intimate political information of virtually every important organization or network in this country. This intelligence . . . enables the Japanese to know when, how, and with whom to act".[8] In his book on the CIA, *Veil*, Bob Woodward reveals two startling cases of moles in American agencies leaking classified information to Tokyo. National Security Agency (NSA) intercepts of Mitsubishi cables on 13 and 29 July 1983 revealed their possession of the top-secret National Intelligence Daily briefs of 7, 9 and 26 July which the corporation had obtained from an undisclosed employee of an American intelligence service. Other intercepts revealed the Japanese embassy's running of an agent in the State Department who passed on America's trade negotiation strategies even before other relevant departments obtained access to them.[9] Choate reveals that in late 1988, Tokyo knew that Carla Hills was the leading candidate for the US Trade Representative weeks before any American newspapers had gotten the scoop, and they knew of her appointment at least a week prior to its announcement when a Japanese official even bragged that "the lady" would be "most acceptable" to Japan. A Japanese newspaper broke the news of her appointment two days before President Bush announced it.[10]

The Japanese embassy in Washington helps co-ordinate Japan's vast lobbying network which includes 9 diplomatic consulates, 8 trade centers, 18 Japan societies, 11 nonprofit organizations and hundreds of private corporations.[11] The embassy has 80 officials, most of which are constantly mobilized to sell Japanese interests in Washington while MITI has a huge office in New York. Japan's consulates and trade offices are located in America's most important cities. The Foreign Ministry's nine consulates are located in New York, Boston, San Francisco, Los Angeles, Seattle, Chicago, Houston, Kansas City and New Orleans. MITI's trade and investments promotion agency is the Japan External Trade Organization (JETRO), whose responsibilities include intelligence gathering, lobbying officials, public relations, and helping Japanese corporations to sell and invest more. JETRO's eight offices in the United States are located in New York, San Francisco, Chicago, Los Angeles, Houston, Atlanta, Denver and San Juan. Tokyo frequently "guides" Japan's corporations into boosting its public relations efforts. For example, in February 1990, the Foreign Ministry "requested" 300 of Japan's largest corporations to greatly increase their local donations in the United States to help stave off Congressional attempts to counter Japanese neomercantilism, and sweetened the order by allowing any donations to be tax deductible.[12]

But because of their deep financial pockets and ability to singlemindedly focus on specific projects and issues, the lobbying efforts of

Japan's corporations, collectively and individually, are far more significant that those of the government. Japan's corporate world uses a range of channels to lobby Washington and influence elections. The Federation of Economic Organizations (FEO, Keidanren) is the Japanese corporate world's collective voice and muscle in influencing policy and elections. It is composed of Japan's leading 120 industrial associations and 960 corporations. In 1988 Keidanren founded what became known as the Council for Better Corporate Citizenship in the United States (CBCCIUS) designed to promote such public relations activities as aiding charities and financing chairs at universities. Individual Japanese industrial associations are very effective in pushing their interests. Meanwhile, virtually every large Japanese corporation has organized its own PAC as well as twisted the arms of its American affiliates to form their PACs to represent Japanese interests. In addition to these efforts, Japanese firms have joined all the important American trade associations and thus subvert their policies. Finally, some of Japan's most effective lobbying forces are its front organizations masquerading as American interest groups.

Of the 3,000 Japanese companies in the United States, there are 70 formal philanthropic programs and 23 company foundations. The official amount of lobbying funds from Japan's industrial associations, corporations and other front organizations has risen steadily from $23 million in 1985 to $145 million in 1988, while the unofficial amount is estimated to be several times that.[13]

The Electronics Industries Association of Japan (EIAJ), composed of over 600 of Japan's electronics corporations, has been the most active of the industrial associations. In 1985, Sony President Akio Morita became chairman of the EIAJ and shaped a comprehensive public relations and lobbying strategy for manipulating America's political system in Japan's favor. Morita's strategy includes: (1) managing local debates and seminars; (2) staging local events with local Japanese investments; (3) publishing local newsletters and magazines; (4) instituting exchanges with state universities and think tanks; (5) pressuring state economic development bureaus, local chambers of commerce, and state offices of U.S. senators and representatives; (6) cooperating with local consumer groups; (7) co-opting the local media; and (8) sponsoring student exchanges. Through these channels EIAJ would continually drum away at four themes: (1) Japanese investment creates jobs in America; (2) Japanese investments help rebuild depressed American communities; (3) Japanese investments provide products that satisfy American consumers; and (4) the American and Japanese economies are so deeply interdependent that any retaliation would hurt the United States just as badly.[14]

Fronts have probably been the single most effective Japanese institutions for manipulating American policy. For example, the Auto Dealers and Drivers for Free Trade (AUTOPAC) is a front organization for Japan's automobile corporations and American vehicle-importers, and has been highly effective in derailing any significant attempts by Congress to impede Japan's inroads into the domestic market. In the 1988 election, AUTOPAC raised $4.5 million from American foreign vehicle dealers then spent $2.57 million on elections and the rest on such administrative costs as a newsletter, political polls, and staff. AUTOPAC spent $1.4 million on just seven races in 1988, of which six of its seven candidates won, five of which were Republicans.[15] Tokyo does not hesitate to arm-twist American firms that are dependent on Japanese components and/or attempting to do business in Japan to back its policies in Washington and elsewhere or else. Employees of Japanese firms which have invested in the United States are pressured to lobby their Congressman to back greater concessions for Japan. The growing dependence of the American economy on Japan, is vividly illustrated by the statement by Robert McElwaine, President of the American International Automobiles Dealers Association for over 17 years, which represents Japanese automobile manufacturers in the United States: "We don't feel we lobby for the Japanese. We lobby for 8,500 American businessmen". Those American businessmen annually sell about $30 billion worth of Japanese cars in the United States. It is estimated that there are 250,000 Americans, earning $4.5 billion annually, directly employed by the imported car industry.[16]

Global USA Inc., with over $1 million in annual fees, is Japan's largest lobbying firm. Its clients include such blue-chip Japanese firms as Hitachi, Komatsu, All Nippon Airways, Fanuc, Yamazaki-Mazek and Kyocera. The firm is led by Stanton Anderson, a key State Department official in the Nixon Administration, William Timmons, the chief congressional lobbyist for the Nixon Administration, William Morris and Bo Denysk from the Commerce department and John Nugent from the Energy Department in the Ford Administration. Another prominent firm, Tanaka Ritger & Middleton, is led by William Tanaka, who previously represented the Electronic Industries Association of Japan, the Japanese Automobile Association, and the Japan Tire Manufacturer's Association for over two decades.

Another influential Japanese front organization has been the United States–Japan Council which for twenty years had represented itself as an independent trade association until the Justice Department filed a civil suit against it in 1976. The Council is actually fronting MITI. Its most substantial victory was in 1973 when it played a key role in getting Congress to eliminate the "buy America" clause in the legislation authorizing the Alaska pipeline. The Council's American director, Noel Hemmendinger, perhaps as an act of contrition for selling out his country, issued a statement admitting that from its creation in 1957, the Council "has acted as an agent of the Japanese government, and . . . has never been . . . a trade association, nor has it been governed by its members . . . The Council receives almost all of its funds from the Japanese government, which exercises general supervision and has ultimate control over its activities".[17]

In 1990 Tokyo created the Japan Center for Global Partnership and armed it with $375 million to disburse to foreign groups. Starting in 1992, the Center spread $25 million among numerous influential American groups, having gotten such prominent Americans as former Secretary of State George Schultz, former ambassador to Japon, Mike Mansfield, and former Chase Manhattan Bank Chairman, David Rockefeller to serve on its board. Perhaps most disterbing are the Japanese contributions to America's mass media. The Center allocated $200 000 to American Public Radio in Minneapolis, $55 000 for the Roper Center for Public Opinion Research at the University of Connecticut to develop a Japanese public opinion data base.[18]

Several other Japanese front organization have been highly effective in undermining American interests. The Political Public Relations Center is a small but influential Japanese public relations organization that has employed such influential Americans as ex-CIA Director, William Colby, former Nixon and Ford official, Harold Malmgren, and Special Trade Representative in the Nixon Administration, William Eberle. The Council for World Trade (CWT) has been influencing American policy since the 1970s. During the hearings over the 1988 Omnibus Trade Bill, its representatives testified before Congress six times. Their lobbying effort was reinforced by the International Electronics Manufacturers and Consumers of America, Inc. (IEMCA), which was formed in March 1987 by the American divisions of thirteen Japanese electronics corporations, along with JC Penney and the National Office Machine Dealers Association. The umbrella organization for all these Japanese front organizations is the Pro Trade Group (PTG), which has committees working to overturn such specific tenets of US trade law as Super 301 (market access), 201 (import relief), anti-dumping, and countervailing duties. The PTG and other Japanese front organizations continued to lobby hard even after the 1988 Omnibus Trade Bill passed. In 1989, it succeeded in pressuring the USTR to limit its investigation of Japanese neomercantilism to only three of literally hundreds of industries – supercomputers, satellites, and lumber – and the following year helped score a resounding victory in getting Japan dropped from the "unfair trade nation" list, thus rendering impotent the 1988 Trade Bill, which was designed to open foreign markets and promote reciprocity.

Japanese investments in American corporations can bring political as well as economic power. For example, Nikko Securities' $100 million purchase of 20 per cent of the Wall Street brokerage firm, the Blackstone

Group, bought the loyalty of three former White House officials: Peter Peterson was Commerce Secretary in the Nixon Administration; David Stockman headed the OMB under Reagan, and Roger Altman was assistant Treasury Secretary in the Carter Administration and advisor to Michael Dukukis in his 1988 presidential bid. These men still have the power to whisper in the ears of White House officials and influence general policy. Peterson, for example, heads both the Council on Foreign Relations and the Institute for International Economics; these think tanks mute any criticism of Japan while promoting "free trade" polices. Holstein reveals how Japanese money may have shaped the views of Peterson as well as two other prominent former White House officials – Fred Bergsten and Stephen Bosworth – who now lead influential think-tanks and make speeches favoring Japan's interests, although he is careful to note that there is no evidence that these men "have changed their public policy pronouncements simply because they either profit or obtain funding from Japanese-related sources".[19] In 1988, Peterson's Institute for International Relations received $280,000 of its $3.6 million budget from Japanese sources including the US–Japan Foundation, founded by former war criminal Ryoichi Sasakawa and dedicated to influencing American public opinion in favor of Japan's agenda.

In 1990, Tokyo created the $375 million Global Partnership Center, an endowment fund which would annually generate about $30 million with which to support academic, journalist, and cultural exchanges with the United States. Those familiar with Japan's public relations machine immediately called for the government to sever its relations with the Center. Susan Berresford, vice president of the Ford Foundation, said that she would "be very candid. Many knowledgeable people feared the fund would set back US–Japan relations rather than advance them. They fear that it will be set up and run with the express purpose of polishing the Japanese image rather than being a legitimate philanthropy in the US tradition". Tadashi Yamamoto, president of the Japan Center for International Exchange admitted that: "Much of Japanese corporate money and government money is, bluntly speaking, PR oriented. There is very little money on the Japanese side for substantive policy oriented intellectual joint studies".[20]

The most effective Japanese lobbyists are those which actually make American policy. Japan's lobbyists have deeply penetrated both the White House and Capital Hill. Choate asserts that with agents working in virtually every important political economic institution in Washington, Tokyo is now "a major force in staffing the executive branch"; Japanese apologists are increasingly entrenched while revisionists are purged.[21]

The ability of Japanese agents to infiltrate presidential policy and personnel committees has been particularly disturbing. Three examples reveal the depth of Japan's penetration of American policymaking. Richard Allen is a top paid Japan lobbyist who worked for Nixon and briefly served as National Security Advisor to the Reagan Administration until his links with Tokyo were revealed. While with the Nixon Administration, Allen encouraged Tokyo to create an American-led lobbying machine in the United States and actually passed them confidential information including a proposal to restrict licensing agreements and technical information about videocassette recorders, an industry that was still dominated by American firms. James Lake was an important political consultant for the Republican Party in its 1980, 1984 and 1988 election victories, and is a particularly close friend of former Trade Representative, Clayton Yeutter, while simultaneously representing Mitsubishi Electric, the Japan Auto Part Industries Association, and Suzuki. He is credited with undermining the American position in the market-oriented sector-selective (MOSS), getting Reagan to rescind his sanctions placed on Japan's electronic organizations, and helping Mitsubishi steal the highly innovative fusion technology from the American company, Fusion Systems. Former Assistant Secretary of State, Richard Fairbanks, chaired the Asia-Pacific task force for George Bush's 1988 presidential campaign while simultaneously representing Fujitsu, then went on to represent the Japanese parts manufacturer Koito in its struggle with T. Boone Pickens to prevent him from having a board seat even though Pickens owned 23 per cent of the company.[22]

Perhaps even more disturbing is the revolving door between United States Trade Representative officials and Japan's lobbying groups. Choate reveals that between 1973 and 1990, one-third of the USTR officials who held principal positions left to become registered foreign agents, most of them for Japan. In 1989 alone, the top three American trade positions – the USTR and the two senior deputy USTRs – went to work for Japanese interests. The Commerce Department's International Trade Administration (ITA) is responsible for implementing the policies that the USTR formulates, and as such is privy to such secret information as special industry analyses, the confidential reports of the private industry advisory councils, classified information from the intelligence agencies, and, in some complex trade negotiations, even corporate plans. In the 1980s, two of the four heads of this bureau went to work for Japanese corporations. One particularly outrageous case of a former American trade official selling out to Tokyo was that of David Olive who had helped draft the State Department position on high technology trade negotiations, attended interagency meetings, had access to confidential information shared by American companies, and knew the American negotiating strategy inside out. In 1990, Olive resigned from the State Department in the middle of the negotiations and went to work for Fujitsu Ltd, a Japanese computer behemoth.[23]

Even American presidents have not been immune to the enticement of Japanese cash. Former President Ronald Reagan has been, to date, the best paid Japanese lobbyist. In October 1989, he earned over $2 million plus an all-expense paid nine day trip to Japan sponsored by the Fujisankei Communications Corporation. As always, Reagan read well the lines carefully prepared by others. In return for his huge fee, Reagan delivered speeches lauding Japan and criticizing the critics of Japan's neomercantilist policies. According to Reagan, trade friction was the fault of the "trade protectionists" in Washington – the Japanese were blameless. Presidents Reagan and Carter received over $3 million and $1 million in Japanese money, respectively, for their presidential libraries. Choate writes that the Founding Fathers "did not anticipate that sitting Presidents would seek foreign money to fund their private projects. They certainly could not have foreseen that ex-Presidents might turn to blatant commercialism after leaving office. Nor could they have imagined that ex-Presidents would seek funds from foreign powers to support their post-retirement activities".[24]

AMERICA'S LOBBYING EFFORT IN JAPAN: SCRATCHING AT CLOSED DOORS

Japan's political system is as closed as its economy. Few of Japan's bureaucrats, politicians, and businessmen can be bought. When bought, as in the Lockheed affair, it is only to favor one foreign firm over another, never for a foreign firm over a Japanese firm. Foreigners are trying to hire retired bureaucrats, but their success has been limited. Free trade arguments account for nothing in Japan. Foreign corporations attempting to disrupt Japan's cozy cartel arrangements are denounced at "impertinent" (*namaiki*) and lacking in "sincerity" (*sei'i*); when they avoid Japan's web of trade and investment barriers they are accused of not trying hard enough. While Japan's lobbying army in Washington and across the United States annually spends an estimated $400 million paying off hundreds of powerful Americans to serve Japanese interests, the ability of American and other foreigners to lobby Japan's national and local government is extremely limited.

Disheartening as these formidable obstacles are, foreign governments and business interests are playing a louder if not more effective role in attempting to influence Japanese policies. After over a decade of neglect under Ambassador Mansfield (who many angrily claimed worked more for Japanese than American interests), the American Embassy under Ambassador Michael Armacost has pressured Tokyo to grant equal opportunity for American firms, but the results have been as meager as the efforts have been enormous. Representatives of some powerful American companies like IBM Japan and Fuji Xerox have been allowed on ministerial councils, committees and subcommittees, and study groups, but their presence is purely symbolic; they have no influence on Japanese policy. In addition, thirty-eight states now have offices in Tokyo, and are increasingly trying to boost exports to Japan as well as attract Japanese investments. The American Chamber of Commerce and United States industrial associations like the American Electronics Association continue to press the interests of their affiliated firms, but with little success. Emulating the strategy of its Japanese rivals in the United States, IBM did endow a $120 million four year chair at Keio University. But unlike American university laboratories, Japan's are not at technology's cutting edge, so the payback is more public relations than technological or political influence.

One possibility to increase their now insignificant political presence is for American and other foreign firms to hire retiring influential bureaucrats (*amakudari*). This option, however, is limited. Unlike their American counterparts, few Japanese bureaucrats, and certainly not the most influential ones, would want to sellout their country for a foreign paycheck, particularly when the retirement opportunities are so lucrative financially and psychologically with a Japanese firm. Between 1986 and 1990, 989 or about ten per cent of all mid- to high-level bureaucrats parachuted into private firms, of which only a dozen or less than 0.01 per cent went directly to foreign companies. American influence remains minimal – a 1986 Keio University study revealed that less than 20 per cent of foreign firms had a government relations specialist and only 2 per cent had contact with Diet members.[25]

With three times as many companies and more Japanese employees, it would appear that American electronic firms have much more lobbying potential in Tokyo than Japan's electronic firms have in Washington. In 1989, 384 American electronics producers employed 72,137 Japanese employees while 113 Japanese electronics firms employed 69,480 American employees. Unfortunately, America's electronic industries' economic presence has not translated into political access. The American Electronics Association (AEA) in Japan was founded in 1984 and has since had only limited success in lobbying Tokyo to reduce its discrimination against foreign firms. AEA President, John Stern, points out the imbalance between the easy access of Japanese firms to Washington policymakers and highly restricted access of foreign firms to Japanese policymakers, citing Japanese nationalism as a major impediment. According to Stern, "a Japanese lobbying for the American side is like a turkey rooting for Thanksgiving. It's just not credible to other Japanese. If a former official of a ministry challenged that ministry's policy in a meeting, bureaucrats would say: 'What's wrong with you? You're Japanese. Which side are you on?"[26] In contrast, all too many former American government officials are, alas, more concerned about their bank accounts than their country.

Perhaps the only effective way to influence Japanese policy is to play off one ministry against the other in their turf battles. For example, in 1987 Washington succeeded in derailing a MITI attempt to strip software of copyright protection by temporarily allying with the MOE which was opposed only because it would reduce the expansion of its copyright responsibilities. Throughout the mid-1980s, Washington sided with MITI against MPT over the telecommunications market; MPT wanted to keep it firmly closed and under its control while MITI wanted it deregulated so it could play a larger role in shaping policy.

SETTING AMERICA'S POLITICAL AGENDA

Tokyo's massive lobbying efforts and negotiating skills have been an enormous success in manipulating America's political process to Japan's advantage. Tokyo has mastered the art of trade war brinksmanship, stonewalling on each issue, no matter how trivial, wearing down White House negotiators until in desperation they threaten sanctions, then offering a last minute symbolic concession which the Americans gratefully accept. But in return for its largely symbolic concessions, Tokyo skillfully extracts genuine American concessions in virtually all the issues negotiated. At best, the White House succeeds in getting Tokyo to agree to give up some of its industrial policy tools in each industry. But these "concessions" are always too little too late – usually the targeted American industry has already been battered into irreversible decline by Tokyo's neomercantilism. Since the Ford Administration, Tokyo has succeeded in coopting the White House into undermining any Congressional attempts to systematically address America's worsening trade deficit with Japan. Washington seems increasingly resigned to blindly accepting annual $40–50 billion trade deficits with Japan as a permanent and "natural" characteristic of the relationship. The White House unquestioningly accepts Japanese promises to open up its markets rather than weighing those promises against any real penetration of American products into Japan's still carefully managed markets and the trade deficits subsequent steady reduction as the criteria for a negotiation round's successful conclusion.

As a result, Tokyo has essentially set America's economic agenda, and in doing so has scored victory after victory in scores of fields.[27] American producers enjoyed comparative advantages in all these fields but were devastated by Tokyo industrial policies that pumped up their Japanese rivals with such neomercantilist steroids as cartels, subsidies, import protection, and export promotion. Japanese corporations thus continue either to leapfrog or rapidly catch up to their American rivals in all these fields. At worst, as in television or machine tools, Tokyo manipulated the White House into actually reinforcing its neomercantilist policies against American firms. According to Choate, "Japan now plays a critical role in devising the policies which will determine which US industries will survive and which will not, which parts of the country will grow and which will decline, which jobs will remain and which will disappear".[28]

Tokyo's brilliant deployment of its American lobbying army and constant media refrains that it was the victim, rather than victimizer, in the conflict reinforces the power of its negotiators. American negotiators find themselves outfought front and rear. For example, MITI initially responded to the 1989 "unfair trader" designation by decrying it as "racist" and threatening to file a complaint with GATT against the United States "because the US action seriously undermines the spirit of free trade".[29] This clever maneuver caused considerable disruption among America's trade representatives. Carla Hills had to spend considerable time and effort defending the decision to try to open Japan's markets rather than actually negotiating their opening. As usual, Tokyo was successful in turning any criticism of Japanese neomercantilism inside out and then hurling it at the critic.

By all accounts, Japan's lobbying efforts have been extremely successful. Representative Sander Levin said that "Judging from the results . . . it's certainly one of the most effective lobbies". Examples of Japan's immense lobbying power abound. Although it passed the House of Representatives, the domestic content legislation for automobiles was killed in the Senate, due in part to the extensive lobbying led by Japan's automobile manufacturers. In 1983, Prime Minister Nakasone was able to use the "Ron-Yasu" friendship to convince President Reagan to reject ITC recommendations that the President impose retaliatory tariffs against Japan's machine tool industry for dumping its products in the United States to destroy America's machine tool industry.[30] In 1986, Japanese corporations and their army of lobbyists on Capital Hill warned Congress that they would curtail their investments in the United States if a proposed repeal of investment tax credits were passed. The measure did not pass. That same year, Japan's electronic manufacturers pressured Speaker of the House Jim Wright to delete a provision imposing a one-year ban on the import of digital audio taping equipment. When Japanese investment houses wanted to persuade the Federal Reserve to allow them to become primary dealers, they hired Stephan Axelrod who formerly served as Federal Reserve chief of staff for policy. The Fed allowed two Japanese securities firms to begin dealing shortly thereafter. When the US semiconductor industry won a complex dumping case, the Commerce Department imposed tough restrictions on imports of Japanese semiconductors. The Japanese responded with an intensive lobbying campaign that included many hired big guns. As a result, the White House forced the Commerce Department to scale back the restrictions to a mere symbolic slap on the wrist. Japanese corporations which have set up shop in the United States are becoming adept at using America's political system against American industry. For example, in April 1991, the Japanese firm Brother Industries asked the ITC to impose duties on the imports of typewriters by the Singapore subsidiary of the American company, Smith Corona, claiming they were being dumped. Smith Corona claimed that Brothers was simply trying to obscure the investigation of the typewriters it was dumping in the United States from Japan.

One of Tokyo's most symbolic victories was in helping defeat the 1987 Bryant Amendment to that year's Trade Bill which would have required foreign investors to register all real estate and other business purchases with the government. As a result, Japanese interests prevailed over the American public's right to know. In 1986, Representative Jim Bryant of Texas introduced the "Foreign Investment and Disclosure and Reciprocity Act" which would have required all new foreign investments to be registered with the Department of Commerce, imposed severe penalties on anyone using dummy corporations, and prohibited foreign investors from countries which discriminated against American investors. Bryant's intention was to force "Japanese businessmen to go home and complain to their government to let our businesses invest".[31]

Japanese and other foreign lobby groups immediately launched a massive attack on the Bill, threatening to pull out their investments if the Bill passed. The Bill was defeated and a new version submitted which eliminated the reciprocity clause. With the teeth of the Bill knocked out, the measure's sole purpose became the public disclosure of foreign investments. Even that seemingly innocuous purpose was deemed too powerful for foreign investors and, under immense pressure, Congress rejected the Bill in 1987. Representative Tom Harkin, Democrat of Iowa, expressed his dismay at the Bill's defeat:

> I cannot imagine why a Honda or Toyota or other legitimate business would be afraid of disclosing this kind of information which . . . is no more or less than we require of US publically owned companies. The short term advantages of foreign investment should not prevent us from considering the potential long-term effects on our economy and our national security. Over time, as ownership of our assets is transferred overseas, so is the authority to make important business and economic decisions affecting the prosperity and independence of our nation.[32]

But the most remarkable display of Japan's lobbying power occurred after June 1987 when it was revealed that Toshiba Machine had sold technology to the Soviet Union that would enable their submarines to run quietly thus giving them an advantage in the event of nuclear war. It is estimated that the United States must now spend between $30—40 billion dollars to regain its lead over the Soviet submarine fleet. Rightfully incensed at this devious act of treachery the Senate resolved 94 to 0 to ban Toshiba from its $2.5 billion a year American market, while the House resolved to prohibit the sale of Toshiba products in the United States and at American overseas bases. These resolutions were non-binding but bills were soon submitted that would have given them the force of law.

Toshiba responded with a two-pronged attack. On the public relations front, Toshiba repeatedly claimed it had no knowledge of the sale, although it did send a letter of apology to Congress and its president and chairman resigned. Behind the scenes, Toshiba assaulted Congress with a vast multi-million dollar lobbying campaign that Senator Jake Garn described as the most intense of his 14 years in the Senate. Toshiba forced any American manufacturers dependent on Toshiba components or state or local governments with Toshiba facilities to lobby Washington on its behalf, including such influential American firms such as Apple, Westinghouse, and Honeywell. A senior executive from a company that helped Toshiba lobby explained that "We were outraged by what Toshiba had done and told them so. Half of our products, however, contained Toshiba components. The only alternative sources were made in Japan by Japanese companies. We looked quietly for other suppliers in Japan, but no one would sell to us . . . Like it or not, we had to lobby against the sanctions. Otherwise we could have been put out of business".[33] Toshiba spent an estimated $20 million and its American allies an additional $30 million to overturn the Congressional resolution, a small price considering that it faced losing $3 billion annually aslong as the sanctions would be in force.[34] This lobbying blitz was enormously successful as the final version of the Trade Bill reduced penalties against Toshiba to a slap on the wrist. Toshiba Machine would be barred from United States sales for only three years and its parent company barred from federal contracts for the same period. The total price tag for all three years was estimated at $200 million rather than the original $2.5 billion a year that would have lasted indefinitely.[35]

As if Toshiba's submarine technology sell-out to the Soviets was not horrific enough, the Defense Intelligence Agency and Central Intelligence Agency in September 1987 revealed two additional sales of strategic technology to the Soviet bloc. Toshiba sold: (1) in 1979, an entire computer-chip making plant to Czechoslovakia; and (2) in 1986, an advanced computer chip assembly plant to East Germany. A proposed

1987 sale of additional advanced semiconductor technology to East Germany was abandoned after the submarine technology sale was revealed. As part of the then Soviet empire, the technology acquired by Czechoslovakia and East Germany would be quickly passed on to Moscow.

Tokyo and Toshiba responded by calling its critics "racists" and "Japan bashers" and accusing the CIA of pursuing a vendetta against Japan. Embarrassed by the revelations, the Reagan Administration championed Tokyo's line that the transactions had never occurred. In February 1988 Assistant Defense Secretary Richard Armitage sent Congress a letter renouncing its earlier assertion that Toshiba's initial sale would cost the United States an estimated $30–40 billion and instead claimed that it was difficult to assess the damage and that the Soviets had been researching advanced propeller technology as early as 1979. What Armitage did not mention was that the Soviets could not have produced the quiet propellers without the Japanese technology. On 29 March 1988, State Secretary George Shultz, Commerce Secretary William Verity, and Defense Deputy Secretary William Taft IV sent Congress a letter in which they claimed that any retaliation "could have a chilling effect on the excellent cooperation we are now receiving from the governments of Japan and Norway in uncovering past diversions and halting illegal exports".[36]

Although it is clear how Toshiba was able to blackmail American corporations and Congress, just how Tokyo arm-twisted the White House into bowing once again to Japanese rather than American interests remains secret. Tokyo could have used such threats as not financing the budget deficit, withholding components from American producers, or even turning a blind eye to even more sensitive sales to the Soviet bloc. As usual, the White House simply and quietly surrendered without attempting to use its own power to serve American interests. If the Congressional retaliatory measure had passed and Tokyo responded by cutting back its finance or components to the United States, the White House would certainly have been justified in imposing severe tariff restrictions on Japanese exports or even threatening to nationalize Japanese holdings in the United States. Since Japan's exports and investments to the United States are much greater than America's in Japan, Tokyo would have had to have backed down. As usual, the White House failed to consider its own considerable power and instead kneeled to Tokyo's claims that any retaliation would severely disrupt bilateral relations. The Reagan Administration quickly agreed to help Tokyo derail the congressional sanctions.

Japan's array of negotiators, lobbyists, and public relations specialists have been just as effective at the state and local level. Savvy as to where the real power lies, thirty-eight states now have offices in Tokyo, more than in Washington. In Tokyo, the state representatives frenzily elbow and undercut each other to attract Japanese investments. States sell not just the favorable economic climate and the special benefits they will provide to the Japanese investor, but also the political power of their representatives and senators in Washington. Facilities are often located in the districts of representatives who sit on trade committees, or in the same district as their competitors thus forcing the local Congressman to represent both the domestic and foreign companies. Lee Iacocca commented that "with each plant, the Japanese have tried to get two senators".[37]

The Japanese have been just as active in the states as they have in Washington in setting up a range of public relations front organizations to promote Japanese interests. Most states now have friendship associations with Japan which were established and financed with Japanese money and fronted by high profile state representatives like the governor. Tokyo has also created regional organizations like the Japan–US Midwest Association, Japan–US Southeast Organization, and so on. Japanese corporations carefully weigh in political with economic objectives when making an investment in the United States, carefully playing one state off against all the others. Once entrenched, the Japanese investors use their deep pockets and threat to invest elsewhere to arm-twist the governor into protecting them against their American rivals. For example, YKK, the world's largest zipper manufacturer with about 60–65 per cent of global market share, has $200 million invested in facilities employing 1,140 in Georgia. In 1975, Talon, a domestic manufacturer, filed a complaint with the International Trade Commission (ITC) that YKK was hurting domestic industry. Governor George Bushbee lobbied on behalf of YKK and the ITC ended up ruling in the Japanese firm's behalf.

During his tenure in office, Tennessee Governor Lamar Alexander was a particularly effective Japanese ally. In 1986, he went so far as to promote a Japan Week celebration, publish a book entitled, *Friends: Japanese and Tennesseans*, and create the Japan–Tennessee Society to promote Japanese interests. Over two-thirds of the financing for the highly effective Japanese lobby group, the Tennessee–Japan Friends in Commerce (TJFC), comes directly from Japanese sources with the rest mostly from Japanese affiliates. The TJFC sponsors a range of forums designed to promote "friendship" and business between the two cultures. About thirty Japanese firms representing 12 per cent of total Japanese manufacturing in the United States, have invested in Tennessee. Most of the credit goes to Governor Lamar Alexander's skillful lobbying, the hundreds of millions of dollars of give aways, and the state's generally good investment climate. But the Tolchins argue that the Japanese also weighed in the importance of investing in the home state of Senator Howard Baker and International Trade Representative Bill Brock, both of whom had repeatedly urged Tokyo to invest more to allay criticism of Japan's vast trade surplus.[38] In fulfilling the Faustian bargain made by giving away hundreds of millions to attract Japanese investments, Tennessee and other states must then lobby for Japanese interests in Washington. For example, Tennessee launched an extensive campaign in 1985 on Washington to remove steel quotas all in an attempt to further aid companies like Bridgestone and Komatsu in more easily importing components from Japan.[39]

Tokyo's most dramatic success at the state level has been its ability to force the statehouses to repeal their unitary taxes which are based on a corporation's worldwide sales rather than simply the amount of sales within the state. In 1984, twelve states had unitary taxes. Two years later after an extensive campaign led by Akio Morita and the FEO only three states, Montana, Alaska and North Dakota, continued to maintain the tax. The other states had buckled under the Japanese threat to withdraw their investments, thus losing hundreds of millions in lost tax receipts.

Sony Corporation spearheaded the anti-tax drive in two states, Florida and Indiana, capping its high pressure campaign with threats to withdraw from those states. The state legislatures of both Florida and Indiana repealed their unitary taxes shortly after Morita applied the screws.[40] Indiana was particularly quick to bow to Morita. The day after Morita visited Indianapolis the Governor announced he would repeal the tax. The following day Morita announced he would add a new 300 worker plant in the state. Morita bluffed and huffed Indiana officials into giving away an immense source of state revenue for an investment that had undoubtedly long been planned.

California, with its huge market and wealth, proved the toughest unitary tax nut for Japan's corporate legions to crack.[41] Morita and Keidanren commenced their lobbying assault in 1984, and for the next two years swarmed over the Capitol armed with threats, promises, and huge wads of cash. A massive public relations campaign skillfully twisted the issue inside out so that it appeared that a repeal of the unitary tax would mean a vast wave of new foreign investments and a failure to repeal would mean the loss of hundreds of millions of investments and tens of thousands of jobs. Keidanren publicized a survey which purported to show that 99 Japanese firms would invest $1.4 billion worth 10,000 jobs in California if only there were no unitary tax. In late 1985 shortly after Oregon repealed its unitary tax Fujitsu announced it would build two plants in that state despite the fact that it already had four in California. Other Japanese firms including Kyocera, Nippondenso, NEC, and Epson America also announced similar plans to build plants in Oregon. The Japanese defeated an attempt led by State Senate Minority Leader Jim Nielsen to link a repeal to greater assess for American firms to Japanese markets. Only Washington has the clout to negotiate reciprocity with Japan, but has continually failed to do so. Nielsen's efforts were heroic but Quixotic given Japan's vast power. The Japanese contributed $108,000 to the campaigns of 53 senators, while Sony alone contributed $29,000. Key senators were flown to Japan on all expense paid trips. As if this pressure were not enough, the Reagan Administration joined with the Japanese in threatening states with Congressional action if they did not repeal the tax. In 1986, Keidanren then created and led a coalition of sixteen countries to overturn the tax. Altogether foreign lobby groups officially spent nearly $550,000 to repeal the tax.

Japan's multinationals and their foreign allies proved far more powerful than their American rivals. Although the tax's repeal would have given foreign firms a huge advantage over American multinationals which would still be taxed on dividends earned abroad, the efforts of domestic corporations to repeal the dividend tax fell on deaf ears. The Tolchins point out that with their huge investments "foreign multinationals . . . had become the political equals of the domestic multinationals. In the eyes of their representatives, foreign companies deserved the same protection as American companies; if they located in a district they deserved the same right to lobby as American companies".[42]

Finally, in 1986, overwelmed by this massive Japanese-led lobbying assault, California's legislators knuckled under and repealed the tax, thus dumping on its citizens the burden of making up the estimated annual $300 million in lost revenues. The Tolchins write that the "real surprise in the unitary issue is how much was given away without concrete data to buttress the notion that those losses would be replenished. The promise of future investment is a slim reed on which to hang a $300 million annual tax loss".[43] They go on to point out that states which repealed the tax had no large influx of foreign investment. State Senator Tom Hayden states that California's political economy "has mentally been colonized. There's a servility around investment. Some of it is ignorance; some a misguided understanding of the marketplace; some of it is the power of money. There are intense anti-Japanese feelings around the trade issue. It's a typical colonial mentality. One moment servile, the next angry. The mythology is that if you give up your right to participate in public policy decisions about the taxation of multinationals, then the international hand would bless you by showering investments on Califoria. This is voodoo economics revisited".[44] California is the nation's largest recipient of foreign investment because it has a huge market, skilled workforce, excellent infrastructure, and state of the art technology. Foreign corporations would have continued to invest in California whether or not there were a unitary tax. Yet, like Washington, Sacramento failed to realize its immense power to resist Japan's lobbying onslaught or horse trade the unitary tax for the dismantlement of Japan's vast web of trade and investment barriers.

Tokyo is undermining America's natural environment as well as continually lightening America's wallet. A Japanese owned pulp mill in Sitka, Alaska, which had a reputation for being a world-class polluter, played a leading role in the 1984 Congressional defeat of the Clean Water Act.[45] Sitka's investment dates to an Eisenhower Administration's invitation for Japanese investors to open a pulp mill in Alaska and export their products back to Japan. It has been exporting logs to Japan ever since and remains one of two corporations awarded monopoly powers by the National Forest Service to harvest the Tongass National Forest. American taxpayers have subsidized Sitka's investments for over thirty years; the Forest Service loses $171 for every 1,000 board feet sold to the mill. In addition, the mill received $14.9 million in government aid from 1976 to 1981 to help it comply with the Clean Air Bill requirements.[46] Sitka has built up enormous clout in Washington, repeatedly derailing Congressional attempts to impose pollution controls, raise timber cutting fees, regulate timber cutting, and has been able to limit its payments to the government to only $1.48 per thousand board feet of Tongass timber when the market price is more than $200 per thousand board feet.[47]

Sitka threatened to pull out its investment when Congress proposed strengthening the Clean Water Bill in 1986. Senator Frank Mukowski helped lead the fight on behalf of his Japanese interests, justifying his actions by pointing out that there "were 1,200 jobs in the two mills, plus 2,500 loggers" and summarized his argument by stating bluntly: We have Japanese capital . . . and we are selfish enough to want to keep it".[48] Ironically, Murkowski was honest enough to admit the Faustian bargain he and others had struck with Japanese capital: "Once they own your assets they own you." Sitka's victory was short-lived since the Clean Water Bill was renewed the following year. Sitka promptly applied for a $7 million federal subsidy for pollution equipment. Fortunately, the Senate voted down the demand by 70–26 on 17 October 1985. In voting against Sitka's demand, Senator Robert Stafford noted that it would be unfair to subsidize the Japanese firm when: "other mills of the same type owned by American companies have been forced to install the required technology. They cannot compete fairly with the Japanese mill, which presently enjoys a $30–40 per ton advantage".[49] Sitka's ability to enjoy over three decades of enormous subsidies renders insignificant its Clean Air Bill setback, and thus serves as one prominent study of countless outrageous examples whereby Japanese corporations manipulate America's political system to undermine American national interests.

HEARTS AND MINDS: BUYING MESSENGERS AND SELLING THE MESSAGE

In an increasingly interdependent world in which mass opinion powerfully shapes public policy, a government's ability to sell its positions to foreign elites and mass publics is an increasingly vital source of power.[50] No country has been more successful in propogating its positions abroad than Japan. The essence of Tokyo's message is simple: Japan's immense trade surpluses and the difficulty that foreigners experience selling or investing in Japan are simply a result of "misunderstandings." Japan not only has a liberal economy but is arguably the world's most open economy. Foreign corporations do not sell or invest more in Japan simply because they do not try hard enough and their goods are of inferior quality. Conversely, Japanese products have captured enormous market shares abroad, not because they have often been dumped at below production costs, but because they are of superior quality. Pat Choate identifies six additional assertions of Japan's public relations offensive in the United States and elswhere: (1) Japan creates jobs for Americans; (2) Japan's critics are racists; (3) the economic conflicts are America's fault; (4) Japan is internationalizing; (5) Japan is unique; (6) Japan is changing into a liberal economy.[51]

By what means is this message propagated? Tokyo's most effective means of propogating Japan's "liberal" image is systematically to condemn any alternative view. Japan's army of spokespeople will viciously denouce anyone who criticizes Japanese neomercantilism – no matter how well documented and argued the analysis – or promotes American over Japanese interests, as a "Japan basher" and "racist." Tokyo and its well-paid foreign spokesmen have actually identified a "gang of four" – Chalmers Johnson, Clyde Prestowitz, James Fallows and Pat Choate – as the worst "Japan bashers".[52] The "crime" of these scholars is to carefully analyze and expose Japanese neomercantilism for what it is, arguing that Japan's neomercantilism remains essentially unchanged despite many superficial trade "concessions." Their heavily documented analyses expose Tokyo's constant mantra that "Japan's markets are the world's most open" as simply propaganda.

These well orchestrated accusations effectively subvert any meaningful discussion of Japanese neomercantilism and America's woefully inadequate response to it. The "gang of four" and some lesser known analysts aside, many scholars attempting any objective analysis of the bilateral relationship find themselves increasingly censoring their own conclusions, thus leaving the field to Japan's public relations allies to loudly trumpet the same tired myths that Japan's economy is the world's most open and that foreigners do not sell more simply because they do not try hard enough. Wolfren writes that the term "Japan Bashing" which was "introduced into the US journalistic bloodstream by the Japanese spokesmen, is very effective for killing any kind of serious discussion. It intimidates those who have views at variance with the officially sanctioned position of Japan's bureaucrats".[53] According to Choate, "Japan's hiring of Americans gives it effective insulation against criticism. Just as many academics are reluctant to risk losing funding or vital access by offering real criticism, so do American critics of the Japan Lobby tend to tone down their comments because they are afraid to challenge the prominent, well-connected, and powerful American bankers, academics, and politicians who are Japan's representatives".[54] US Trade Representative official Glenn Fukushima admitted in a speech before the American Chamber of Commerce in Tokyo in September 1985 that "if you are a foreigner who is too critical of Japan, your sources of information, funding, or friends dry up".[55] After his book, *Trading Places*, was published, Clyde Prestowitz was told by hosts in five different cities that Japan's local consul general had discouraged them from inviting him to be a speaker at their programs.[56]

One would have to go back to the McCarthy era, when anyone who offered any criticism of the United States was immediately labeled "anti-American," to find as effective a means of silencing or undercutting critics. And the Japanese have skillfully appropriated the charge of McCarthyism by turning its meaning inside out; now the author of any objective analysis of Japanese neomercantilism is not only a "racist" and "Japan basher," but is engaging in "McCarthyism" as well. For example, when in December 1989, reporters asked Gary Saxonhouse about being a paid consultant to the White House Council of Economic Advisors while simultaneously acting as an "unpaid" advisor on MITI's Research Institute of International Trade and Industry (RIITI), Saxonhouse accused those who criticized such a outrageous conflict of interest of being "McCarthyite".[57] Saxonhouse is credited with using his influence with the Council of Economic Advisors to scuttle government plans to support the US Memories project and high definition television (HDTV). Meanwhile, Saxonhouse's contributions to RIITI are reimbursed by Tokyo's covering all his expenses while in Japan. Other prominent Japanese allies in the United States such as Hobart Rowen, John Makin and George Packard have also not hesitated to smear critics of Japanese neomercantilism with the same brush.

Who would sell out their country for Japan? Japan uses three types of influential Americans to advance its national interests: sentimental Japan hands, neoclassical economists, and cynical opportunists just in it for the money.

In the Western academic tradition, any proclaimed expert on any subject must base his or her views on objective analysis rather than sentiment. Of course, given the subjective nature of interpreting reality, a purely objective analysis is an ideal which can only be approximated. It is extremely difficult at once to step back far enough from any subject to gain perspective on it while at the same time immersing oneself thoroughly in the subject in order to gain an intimate understanding. This balance of

   In the over four decades since 1945, the ranks of such sentimentals or apologists have grown, and their collective voices have become increasingly powerful in shaping American policy and perceptions toward Japan. Yet until recently, despite its effectiveness in promoting Japanese interests, the so called "Chrysanthemum Club" has evaded criticism. One reason might be the seeming naïveté of many sentimentalists. Kevin Kearns, a State Department official who served at the American embassy in Tokyo, wrote that the Chrysanthemum Club's members "fail to see the trail from predatory Japanese policies, to lost markets, to destroyed industries, to large outflows of wealth in the form of trade deficits, and finally to the resultant decline of American power and influence".[60]

   A classic example of the shallowness and emotionalism of the apologist's attempts to shape American views of Japan was revealed in a recent taped "debate" over Japanese neomercantilism between Karl Van Wolferen and former ambassador to Japan, Edwin Reischauer, on Boston radio station WHRB. The debate's airing was cancelled when Reischauer attacked Van Wolferen's position on emotional rather than analytical grounds. Van Wolferen reported that "Reischauer said that Americans should be more patient, that fundamental changes are taking place in Japan. When I said this was the picture created by the media – one that does not reflect reality – his response was that too many Japanese love American for us to worry about a real crisis between the two countries".[61] When Van Wolferen offered other criticism of Japan's neomercantilist policies, Reichauer replied, "You know what you are saying is racist, don't you".[62] Lacking substantive analytical arguments, accusing the critic of racism is the ultimate Japanese defense against any criticism of Japan's policies.

   The Chrysanthemum Club's influence on policy is relatively indirect – mostly atmospheric. Japan's strongest allies in the United States are neoclassical economists, since they are often able to directly shape American policies. The belief – which would be quaint if it had not proven to be so devastating to America's national security – that free markets are the best means of developing an economy has immobilized American economic policy in the face of the Japanese challenge. Charles Schultze, chairman of the Council of Economic Advisors under President Carter, wrote the extraordinary statement that "Japan does not owe its industrial success to its industrial policy. Government is unable to devise 'a winning' industrial structure".[63] Herbert Stein, CEA Chairman in the Nixon administration, went even further. In 1989, he wrote that Americans should forget about their trade deficit because it does no harm. According to Stein, "the inflow of capital and ownership of assets in the US by foreigners is not a cause of dangerous dependence that is a political or security danger to us".[64] In 1990, he argued that it was irrelevant whether or not the United States had become the world's number two economic power.[65]

Tokyo uses American universities as yet another channel for propagating its "liberal" image. Money, as always, buys influence. Chalmers Johnson estimates that over 80 per cent of the 336 American colleges and universities which offer Japanese studies programs receive Japanese funding; others estimate the figure may be as high as 90 per cent.[66] A number of large Japanese corporations are donating large sums of money to key American technological institutes in order to win both a better image and access to key technology and researchers. Hitachi was one of 11 Japanese firms that have so far endowed permanent chairs at MIT, which included $1.5 million in combined grants to its Sloan management school from Daiichi Kangyo and Mitsuibishi. The largest single Japanese gift was $1.5 million to endow a chair in electrical engineering. Nomura has endowed chairs at both MIT and New York University.

As if simply funding Japanese studies or high technology programs were not enough, starting in the late 1980s, Japanese universities began buying up financially troubled American colleges and transforming them into bases to "internationalize" both Japanese and American students. For example, Teikyo University merged with Salem College in West Virginia, Post College in Connecticut and Westmar College in Iowa, and in 1990 dispatched 183 students to Salem and 105 to Westmar. Teikyo's deal with Salem included paying off the school's $5 million debt, establishing a $7.5 million endowment, raising faculty salaries and creating a scholarship for Appalachian high school students. The curriculum has been completely revamped to emphasis American and Asian studies.[67]

Branch campuses of American universitites in Japan are largely financed by Japanese corporations and are thus vulnerable to charges that they will end up dispensing "public relations" rather than objective analysis of Japan's political economy. For example, City University of New York's $50 million branch campus in Japan was entirely paid for by Japanese investors. Other American universities with branches include Temple University, South Illinois, the University of Nevada, Minnesota State and Lehman College.[68]

A classic example of how American universities can be used as platforms for selling Japanese "liberalism" was a 27 November 1990 conference at St. John's University sponsored by the "student organization", the Japan Forum. Entitled "Cross Cultural Equity: A Japanese-American Dialogue", the conference was advertized as "a discussion of the most fundamental problems confronting Japanese-American relationships". In reality, the conference was merely an elaborate public relations forum in which the Japanese and American speakers railed against "Japan bashing," and insisted that the intractable trade problems were all a misunderstanding, that Japan's markets were the world's most open and American firms simply needed to try harder and take a long term outlook.

The conference received mass media exposure and a crowd of several hundred people. The original source of the impetus, funding, and organizational ability of the Japan Forum remains unknown, although under pressure the Japan Forum later admitted it was affiliated with the Japanese consulate. The ability of this "student club" to pull together a conference of this kind within six weeks of its founding is certainly remarkable. The keynote speaker was Representative Stephen Solarz and the others were all businessmen – no academics who might have given a much more in-depth, objective view of the issues were invited.

Tokyo has targeted secondary teachers as an additional source for promoting Japan's national interests. Throughout the 1980s, Tokyo brought over 300 elementary and high school teachers to Japan for an all expenses paid "education" in Japan's world view, and gave them a range of materials on Japan to use not only in the classroom, but in the teacher's presentations before civic organizations, churches, and other local organizations.[69]

Tokyo has also made effective use of America's television networks to propagate its world view. Choate reports that "TeleJapan produced shows for the Christian Broadcasting Network in 1983, for the USA Cable Network in 1984 and for the public television stations in 1986. In 1984, Cable News Network (CNN) began showing *This Week in Japan*, a show paid for by the Japan Center for Information and Cultural Affairs (JCICA)".[70] TeleJapan is a broadcasting arm of MITI while JCICA is linked with the Foreign Affairs Ministry. The Japan Broadcasting Corporation (NHK) launched its *Japan Today* program on American television in 1989. The Japanese financed US–Japan Foundation has sponsored a number of programs on American television through its "Japan Project," which established a US–Japan Public Television Program Council composed of Japanese and American public television representatives. The US–Japan Foundation has also sponsored a number of radio programs, and since 1987 has annually given $100 000 to National Public Radio (NPR) to support the Tokyo reporting for *Morning Edition* and *All Things Considered*. One independent producer of public affairs programs bluntly revealed that "in the last half of the 1980s, the Japan Project had a chilling effect on those of us who wanted to do programs that might be critical of Japan. The participating stations were reluctant to offend potential Japanese sponsors. Consequently, Japan was able to buy a decade of inattention".[71]

The documentary series *Faces of Japan* hosted by Dick Cavett on PBS in Spring 1986 was a typically sophisticated public relations program. Billed as a "candid look at the Japanese people . . . produced by an American crew", an investigation revealed that the show was actually produced by

TeleJapan whose president, Junichi Shizunaga, is a key LDP member, and the show was actually funded by 20 Japanese corporations whose efforts were coordinated by Keidanren. Both Prime Minister Nakasone and MITI conferred extensively with TeleJapan on both the content and budget for the series. TeleJapan relies heavily on funds from both the government, corporations, and wealthy conservatives like Ryoichi Sasakawa, a former war criminal and suspected organized crime leader. Several of the American crew were forced to quit after TeleJapan constantly overruled them on content.[72]

Tokyo has not stopped at merely trying indirectly to supress objective reporting on Japan while sponsoring Japanese public relations programs. In 1986, MITI budgeted $200 000 to pay American reporters to write favorable stories about Japan. The "Moonlighter Plan" aimed at putting on its payroll one reporter, editor, or local chamber of commerce director in each of ten states. Two of the states, Michigan and Missouri, contained leading Congressional critics of Japan's neomercantilist policies – Representatives Richard Gephardt and John Dingell, and Senators John Danforth and Donald Riegle. The media agents would also collect information that would help Japan's corporations expand their operations. MITI abandoned its plan when Congress got wind of it and in an outrageous deception claimed that the plan was not intended to "manipulate American attitudes through deployment of US reporters . . . or buy a positive image by buying American journalists and opinion makers".[73] In reality, MITI intended to achieve these very objectives.

Japan's government and business have been extremely effective at boosting Japan's image with specific issues and groups. For example, in response to growing complaints about Japanese investments and labor practices in the United States, Tokyo and Keidanren have carefully coordinated a massive corporate charity campaign which rose from $85 million in 1987 to $140 million in 1988. This rapid increase is stimulated by efforts by the Foreign Affairs Ministry which co-sponsored with Keidanren a seminar in Tokyo in April 1988 on public relations abroad attended by over 100 corporations. Keidanren's Council for Better Investment in the United States is designed to advise firms on ways to improve their image.

Japan's huge corporate lobby has become very effective at damage control. For example, when Prime Minister Nakasone remarked that America's economic difficulties were attributable to the low intelligence of American Blacks, Hispanics, and other minorities, the corporate world stepped in with large, highly publicized grants to a variety of organizations including the United Negro College Fund, the National Association for the Advancement of Colored People, and the Congress of Racial Equality in order to soften any possible black boycott against Japanese products. When Honda was sued for discrimination over hiring practices at its Ohio plant, it settled out of court by immediately hiring some 370 blacks and other minorities, donated $50 000 to the Clara Hale House in Harlem, which cares for children born addicted to drugs, and started a scholarship for minority students at Drake University.[74]

Hitachi launched a massive public relations campaign after it pleaded guilty to buying stolen IBM secrets in 1983 followed by the embarrassing publication of a 1985 memo ordering distributors to cut prices to destroy their American competitors. First it set up the Hitachi Foundation in Washington in 1985 with an endowment of $25 million targeted on high profile charities, and chaired by former Nixon cabinet member, Elliot Richardson. Then it promised to buy $350 million worth of American goods a year and increase production in its United States plants. In addition, Hitachi has set aside 1.5 per cent of its pretax profits to be distributed to local charities by community action committees at each of its American plants. Hitachi has also made large donations to the University of Oklahoma located adjacent to its plant in Norman. These efforts have paid off. Representative David McCurdy of Oklahoma helped Hitachi avoid high tariffs on its imports of computer products while Representative Wes Watkins was roundly condemned by the Oklahoma press when he voted in favor of the Omnibus Trade Bill in 1988.[75]

Japanese firms have been effective at managing public relations even when they were not directly responsible for their bad image. For example, Flat Rock, Michigan convinced Mazda Motor Manufacturing to open a plant in return for a 100 per cent tax rebate for 12 years and a $120 million incentive package. Public criticism began to mount when the infrastructure investments severely strained the local community. Mazda responded by promising to donate $100 000 a year for 12 years, added another $1 million to complete the sewer project, and amidst great fanfare, donated $70 000 to the United Way.[76]

JAPANESE HEARTS AND MINDS: THE POWER OF PERCEPTION

Every society is torn, in varying degrees and ways, by the vast gulf between appearance and reality. Mass literacy and an endless cornucopia of information in democratic industrial nations seemingly enables individuals an unprecedented opportunity to distinguish fact from fancy. Yet, paradoxically, as the modern world's complexity deepens, most people retreat further into carefully manufactured contemporary and traditional myths. Unpleasant political, business, or social realities are masked by elaborate "public relations" campaigns. The ambitious seize power through the strength of their charisma rather than rational arguments on pressing issues. "Citizens" shrug off media warnings of savings and loan bankruptcies, greenhouse effects, drug and AIDS epidemics, and crime sprees. President Reagan consistently received high popularity ratings during his eight year tenure despite the fact that most Americans disagreed with him on most issues. George Bush became President in 1988 in part because of his staff's skill in wrapping him in the flag and associating Michael Dukakis with Willie Horton, while sidestepping such issues as America's rapid economic and environmental decay, and persistent poverty, crime, racism and ignorance.

Although the ability of emperors with "new clothes" to hoodwink both the people and themselves is universal, in no democratic industrial country is this phenomena more true than in Japan. Japanese are well aware of this split, conveyed by the words *tatemae* (appearance) and *honne* (reality). Yet, for Japanese, awareness simply exacerbates the gap. The fate of whistle blowers almost everywhere is bleak – firings, blacklistings, sometimes even violence. But in Japan those committed to the truth often lack even the psychological haven of knowing that their cause was just; finger pointers are considered as shameless as the naked emperors they target.

In 1945, Tokyo mobilized virtually every Japanese man and woman to greet the expected American invasion with human wave charges armed with bamboo spears, and mainland Japanese were just as prepared to emulate the actions of their compatriots on tiny volcanic and coral islands thousands of miles away, and fling their lives away for Japan. Today, Tokyo has mobilized the Japanese people almost as effectively for the economic war it is waging against the world. Unlike Japan's wartime frenzy, however, the new nationalism threatens foreign livilihoods rather than lives, and is completely painless for Japanese. But Japan's contemporary nationalist slogans and perceptions are every bit as shallow and unfounded as those of World War II. Sugimoto and Mouer have intensively studied Japan's new nationalism and argue that, "Japanese elites have found it advantageous to push the image of Japan's uniqueness abroad to ward off Western criticism. The more Japan is viewed as unique, the less it will have to abide by Western rules of negotiations and fair play. At home, the advantage of selling the view that Japanese society is an integrated, harmonious whole are obvious for a ruling class bent on maintaining its domination".[77] For example, foreign criticism of Japanese import barriers or unethical business practices is increasingly viewed by Japanese as an attack on their culture, and thus, racist.

Japan's schools, mass media, workplaces, and government pronoucements have socialized virtually all to believe, at least with the right side of their brains, that Japan strictly adheres to a neoclassical economic model, that its markets are the world's most open and thus foreign firms do not sell more because they do not try hard enough and their goods are inferior. Prime Minister Zenko Suzuki spoke for a nation in 1983 when he asserted that, "Our market in Japan is as open as American or European markets;" more recently Sony Chairman Akio Morita declared that, "I believe Japan's market is very easy for foreign countries to enter. I cannot understand why this wonderful market is left untouched. I believe that foreign industry should be more serious and make a real effort to sell in Japan".[78]

In a letter to the New York Times published on 25 April 1991, Professor Yoshi Tsurumi spoke for virtually all Japanese when he severely critized Washington's pressure on Tokyo to contribute more to the Persian Gulf War.[79] Tsurumi argued that Japanese considered the "payment as colonial taxes without representation levied by the United States", and subsequent Bush administration actions toward Japan as "serious diplomatic blunders that have seriously unraveled United States-Japanese relations." He concludes by warning that the "United States cannot afford to continue treating relations with Japan as if the United States dictates and Japan obeys".

The recent book, *The Japan That Can Say "No"*, by senior LDP leader Shintaro Ishihara and Sony president Akio Morita relects the thinking of most Japanese on international trade issues.[80] Across several chapters, Morita unwittingly shows the vast gap between Japanese public relations claims (*tatemae*) and Japan's neomercantilist reality (*honne*), when he repeatedly mixes claims that Japan's markets are the world's most open with example after example in which the government carefully manages Japan's markets in order to develop the economy. Ishida's chapters were even more candid in expressing the virulent emotionalism and anti-Americanism with which Japanese see the world. Ishida makes a range of such bizarre, unfounded, and irresponsible claims as "the roots of the US–Japan friction lie in the soil of racial prejudice", "Americans behave more like mad dogs than watchdogs", "the only reason why they could use the atomic bomb on Japan was because of their racial attitude toward Japan", "the US Congress is too hysterical to trust", or "Americans suggest the possible physical occupation of Japan in case Japan engages in semiconductor trade with the Soviet Union".[81] Recently, Ishihara recently described Washington as "an appalling place," and American legislators as "lazy, ignorant, and insensible".[82]

Other Japanese target minority groups within the United States as the culprits in bilateral conflicts. In 1986, Prime Minister Nakasone claimed that American economic decline was mostly a result of the low intelligence of American blacks and Hispanics. Although Nakasone later apologized and claimed his remarks were misunderstood, Japanese racism is becoming increasingly overt. The Japanese criticism of Nakasone revolved around giving foreigners a glimpse into how Japanese see others rather than the verity of his assertion.[83] On 21 September 1990, Justice Minister Seiroku Kajiyama likened foreign prostitutes in Tokyo to American blacks since, in his words: "It's like in America when neighborhoods become mixed because blacks move in and whites are forced out", thus "bad money drives out good money".[84] Under severe American criticism, Kajiyama retracted the statement several days later but the controversy continued. The resulting uproar forced Prime Minister Kaifu on 3 October 1990 officially to scold Kajiyama for his statement, but the justice minister was not forced to resign. Kajiyama did not get around to issuing his own "deep apologies" to the American people until 17 October and promised to send a letter to the Black Congressional Caucus. Kajiyama then followed up his apology with the extraordinary claim that "in Japan there is no discrimination against any races".

Japanese increasingly view Washington's continued demands as arrogant and agressive. Japan's academics are largely mobilized behind Japanese neomercantilism. Paul Krugman writes that he even found private economists who "refuse to acknowledge that the rice policy is costly, even in informal conversations. When pressed hard, they explained that they did not feel it was their place to criticize the government to a foreigner".[85] Any Japanese who fails to rally around the flag is open to accusations of acting as an agent of national dishonor (*kokujoku mono*).

In his article entitled "US Demands lead Japan in search for itself," Masahiko Ishizuka, editorial writer for the *Nihon Keizai Shimbun*, writes that "bitterness remains. The Japanese are asking themselves, 'If American demands are basically right, why did we not initiate the changes ourselves? Are we a people who cannot make our own affairs until somebody tells us, in a forceful manner, to do so?' The Japanese, therefore, are angry both at Americans and themselves – at the former for their apparent rudeness, and at the latter for lack of capacity to act on their own".[86] Here again is the Japanese tendency to martyr themselves and scapegoat the foreigner who points out the difference between Japanese ideals (*tatemae*) and reality (*honne*).

Mass support of a government's policies is a vital source of national power. The uniformity with which Japan's elite and most of its population perceive trade conflicts morally justifies Tokyo's bitter tenacity in negotiations in which it automatically dismisses any foreign requests that trade barriers be dismantled as unreasonable interference in Japan's domestic affairs. Washington's recent attempts to enlist Japanese consumers behind its market opening pressure has failed miserably.

Why does Japan continue to enjoy a $50 billion trade surplus with the United States? A March 1990 *Newsweek* poll found that almost four of five Japanese (77 per cent) believe that the trade imbalance simply reflects the superiority of Japanese products; little more than one in ten (12 per cent) thought Japanese trade barriers were to blame.[87] Thus, two out of three Japanese (64 per cent) believe that any criticism of alleged Japanese barriers is simply Washington's unfair scapegoating of Japan for its inability to resolve America's own problems. What are the reasons for America's economic problems? 57 per cent of Japanese agree with Nakasone and other Japanese leaders that "too many racial and ethnic groups" are an important reason for America's economic problems. But even more Japanese attributed "lazy workers" (66 per cent) and "drugs and alcohol addiction" (93 per cent) to America's economic decline. Will bilateral relations get worse or better? Over half of Japanese (55 per cent) thought it was likely (45 per cent "somewhat", 9 per cent "very") that the two countries would once again become "enemies".

A *Businessweek* poll of 1000 Japanese in November 10–14, 1989 similarly revealed a very mixed view of the United States and bilateral conflicts.[88] Although only 21 per cent thought America's decline was irreversible, Japanese were largely optimistic that their country would take America's place as the world's leading economic and political power, with 42 per cent agreeing and only 35 per cent disagreeing. Most Japanese thought little or nothing of the United States (41 per cent, 13 per cent) and even less of Americans (45 per cent, 18 per cent). Japanese had harsh views of American society, attributing America's decline to too many minorities (42 per cent), a lazy work force (35 per cent), disinterest in exporting (29 per cent), and obsession with short-term returns (25 per cent), although only 15 per cent thought America's poor educational system and 11 per cent incompetent management were chief causes.

Despite this prevalent anti-Americanism, Japanese did see both sides at fault for the trade conflict: inferior American products (54 per cent) and efforts (52 per cent), unfair Japanese trade barriers (55 per cent). Japanese were also willing to allow a certain amount of American goods into Japan (45 per cent), reform the distribution system (64 per cent), and remove the ban on imported rice (39 per cent). Although most Japanese (57 per cent) thought the United States was unfairly pressuring Japan to open its markets, even more (62 per cent) thought Japan could make some further concessions.

Japanese were split evenly on following Ishida's advice on forming closer ties with Moscow if relations with Washington deteriorated, with 41 per cent favoring such a strategy and 40 per cent opposed, while 55 per cent agreed that Japan's technology leadership gives Tokyo more clout in dealing with the Americans and 52 per cent thought Japan should rely less on the United States for defense.

Yet, like people elsewhere, Japanese are able to simultaneously hold two or more contradictory opinions. Paradoxically, while believing Japan's markets are wide open and foreigners do not sell more because they do not try hard enough, many Japanese also support the dismantling of Japan's trade barriers and understand that they would be the primary beneficiaries. A Nihon Keizai poll of 6,186 Japanese conducted on 16–19 March 1990 found that more agreed (46.4 per cent) than disagreed (39.5 per cent) that Washington's position was valid, and an overwelming 85.9 per cent thought that Tokyo should at least listen to Washington while only 5.0 per cent said there was no need to listen at all.[89] Almost half (47.4 per cent) believed that Japan should open its markets to foreign products – 9.0 per cent "totally," 38.4 per cent "basically." Over half (51.7 per cent) thought the major reason for opening markets was to improve Japanese lifestyles while 42.2 per cent said reforms should be made to improve bilateral relations. Two thirds said that Japan should open its rice markets – 12.3 per cent "completely", 50.7 per cent "partially" – while less than one third (31.1 per cent) said the market should remain shut. Finally, Japanese overwhelmingly believe that current aimable bilateral relations will continue despite the current tensions (83.8 per cent) while only 6.8 per cent thought there would be a breakdown in the relationship.

How can the discrepancies between different surveys be explained? Perhaps partially because any "loyal Japanese" will continue to spout the government line (*tatemae*) when any discussion of trade conflicts arise while quietly understanding (*honne*) that their government essentially exploits them as consumers in order to expand Japan's geoeconomic power. Foreign travel exposes Japanese to the descrepancy between their government's position that Japan's markets are the world's most open and the reality that consumer prices in Hong Kong or New York are at least half and as much as five times lower than Japanese prices. In 1989, the 9.6 million Japanese who traveled abroad brought back an average $2200 worth of goods with them.[90]

During the Structural Impediments Initiative (SII) negotiations, the White House attempted to justify its position in the name of Japanese consumer rights. As heartening as the Nihon Keizai poll must have been to the White House, there is no correlation between the views of Japanese consumers and the thousands of groups that claim to lobby Tokyo on their behalf. No significant Japanese consumer groups backed the American position. Once again Washington wrongly assumed Japan's economic orientation was the same as America's, and that Japanese consumer groups would have the same goals as their American counterparts. The reality, as always, is far different. It is estimated that at least half Japan's "consumer" groups are merely fronts for industrial and agricultural interests which explains why they advocate more rather than less regulation and continued cartel administered high prices rather low global market prices.[91]

Not only is Japan blameless in contemporary trade wars, but was also the victim rather than victimizer in the Second World War. Emotionally, Japanese increasingly feel the war began with the atomic bombing of Hiroshima and ended a few days later with Nagasaki's destruction – Japan's 14 year war of aggression which left an estimated 20 million East Asians dead is an increasingly hazy and irrelevant memory for most Japanese. Periodic protests from East Asian governments and international scholars have failed to rein in Japan's rewriting of history through school textbooks, books, and films. Japan's attempts to deny the past and rewrite history were revealed at the national outcry when Nagasaki mayor Hitoshi Motoshima suggested in August 1990 that the emperor and Japan bore some responsibility for World War II, its victims and the atomic bombings. The LDP was so incensed that one of its members would so brazenly assert that Japan may have been the wartime victimizer rather than victim that Prime Minister Kaifu removed Motoshima as a party advisor, withdrew another LDP candidate in an election so that the opposition parties would be united against him, and has cut off government funds to Nagasaki. To stack the deck further against Motoshima, a gunman shot him. Despite all this, Motoshima courageously continues to uphold his beliefs and office. There are very few Japanese like Motoshima.

AMERICAN HEARTS AND MINDS: THE POWER OF PERCEPTION

How effective is the Japan lobby in shaping mass American attitudes toward Japan? Surveys vary considerably in their results. Not only are there significant differences between surveys of business leaders and the mass public, but each group varies considerably over time in its answers to similar questions. Overall, each country's view of the other has deteriorated, with conflicting views over the most important reasons for the trade deficit.

How differently do Japanese and American see the bilateral conflicts? Who is at fault? Is the United States still number one or has Japan taken the title? A *Washington Post*/ABC poll conducted in February 1989 indicated that 54 per cent of Americans thought Japan was now the world's greatest economic power while only 29 per cent felt the United States still retained the title.[92] In contrast to this mass pessimism about American power were the views of 301 American, 90 Japanese, and 201 European business executives in a survey conducted in July 6–14, 1990 by *Businessweek*/NHK/Harris.[93] The poll may tell more about national character than anything else, with Americans as usual wildly optimistic about their own future, Japanese pessimistic about theirs, and Europeans tough realists. Only one quarter of Americans thought Japan was currently number one (28 per cent) and even less thought Japan's global share would increase in the future (25 per cent), almost three quarters of Americans (71 per cent) thought Japan was not number one while almost half (47 per cent) thought its current global power would decrease and one quarter (27 per cent) thought it would stay the same. Japanese were even more pessimistic about their present status, with only 13 per cent claiming they were the number one global economic power and 84 per cent disagreeing, although they were much more optimistic about their growth prospects over the next decade, with 54 per cent predicting an increase in global market share, and 31 per cent the same level, while only 13 per cent foreseeing a decrease. Exactly half of Europeans (50 per cent) polled think Japan is the number one economic power while 46 per cent disagreed; 36 per cent predict Japan's global power will increase, 31 per cent stay the same, and 31 per cent decrease.

There were widely differing views of the role of industrial policy in fueling Japan's continued expansion, with 49 per cent of Americans, 27 per cent of Europeans, and 10 per cent of Japanese believing it was decisive, while the figures were reversed for those who believed that technological leadership was the key: 91 per cent of Japanese, 49 per cent of Europeans, and only 24 per cent of Americans. American and Europeans rated higher than Japanese both the importance of management (32, 46 and 20 per cent) and skilled labor (20, 20 and 16 per cent) in contributing to Japan's continued economic success. Two thirds of Americans (67 per cent) thought Japan's workers were not sharing in Japan's enormous creation of wealth compared to only 35 percent of Europeans and 26 per cent of Japanese, while less than one third of Americans (31 per cent) thought Japanese workers were sharing the country's wealth compared to 56 per cent of Europeans and 69 per cent of Japanese.

Japanese generally dismissed the complaints of Americans and Europeans over Japanese protectionism. About one third of Americans (37 per cent) and Europeans (31 per cent) cited Tokyo's controls over the economy as a major barrier to entry for foreign firms compared to only one of five Japanese (20 per cent). About half of Americans (50 per cent) and Europeans (46 per cent) thought Japanese cartels were a major problem compared to only 20 per cent of Japanese. There were large difference in the perceived political support for Japanese protectionism, with 60 per cent of Americans, 47 per cent of Europeans, and only 14 per cent of Japanese citing it as important. In contrast, a much greater percentage of Japanese (43 per cent) than Americans (20 per cent) or Europeans (28 per cent) thought the high investment costs of land and commodity price were the most important barriers.

Yet, after largely dismissing European and American claims that Japan's markets were carefully managed by government regulations, business cartels, and politicians, Japanese executives contradicted themselves by overwhelmingly voicing support for Japan's abandonment of neomercantilist policies. More Japanese (76 per cent) than Europeans (65 per cent) or Americans (63 per cent) called on Japan to open its markets, increase its foreign aid (58, 39 and 34 per cent), increase its financial support to international organizations (32, 19 and 29 per cent) transfer its technology (54, 29, 27 per cent), promote global free trade (71, 43, 58 per cent), or open itself to more cultural and ethnic diversity (90, 65 and 71 per cent. A greater percentage of Americans and Europeans than Japanese thought Japan should contribute more in only two areas, defense (34 per cent, 9 per cent, and 4 per cent) and open capital markets (41 per cent, 39 per cent, and 29 per cent).

There were wide differences over possible obstacles to Japan's economic growth. Japanese (73 per cent) identified labor shortages and an aging workforce as the most serious challenge (23 per cent European, and 21 per cent American), while both Japanese (43 per cent) and Europeans (41 per cent) thought growing protectionist in European and North American trade blocs would be important constraints compared to only 27 per cent of Americans, who also thought (40 per cent) that growing criticism of Japan's neomercantilist trade practices were most important compared to only 30 per cent of Europeans and 9 per cent of Japanese. Almost equal amounts of Americans (41 per cent) and Europeans (40 per cent) thought the newly industrializing countries of East Asia would be a serious challenge for Japan, while only 9 per cent of Japanese thought so.

Mass opinion polls vary greatly in addressing such questions. Despite all the outcry by Japanese and their foreign lobbyists about "Japan bashing," a *Businessweek* poll of 1,250 Americans in July 1989 revealed a much more positive view of Japan than Japanese held of the United States.[94] Most Americans felt either a "great deal" or "some" admiration for Japan as a nation (25 per cent, 48 per cent), and even more as a people (32 per cent, 48 per cent), while almost four of five Americans lauded Japan's economy (49 per cent, 29 per cent). Although they deeply admired Japan, 66 per cent of Americans thought Japan's economic threat was more dangerous than the Soviet military threat (22 per cent). Americans overwhelmingly viewed that year's $55 billion trade deficit with Japan as "very serious" (69 per cent) or somewhat serious (23 per cent). Americans thought Japanese trade barriers (68 per cent) were the major reason for the deficit, followed by higher American prices (57 per cent), and poor quality (38 per cent). Americans were also overwhelming in favor of retaliating against Japan's trade barriers by requiring a certain amount of American goods be sold in Japan (79 per cent), limiting Japanese imports (69 per cent), imposing higher tariffs on Japanese goods (61 per cent), and restricting US technology flows to Japan (59 per cent). Americans also believed that American goods (45 per cent) were superior to Japanese goods (32 per cent), and were willing to pay more (66 per cent) for American goods even if they were of equal quality to Japanese goods.

A May–June 1990 poll jointly conducted by Tokyo Broadcasting Company and *New York Times*/CBS seemed to indicate considerate success for Japan's public relations machine.[95] It found that 68 per cent of Japanese and 44 percent of Americans thought the United States was blaming Japan for its own problems. Only 38 per cent of Americans and 26 per cent of Japanese thought the unfair tactics of Japanese companies were. But the results may have been skewed without questions dealing with the role of Japanese industrial policies and trade barriers in the persistent trade deficits. Most Japanese and Americans still felt friendly toward each other despite the entrenched trade deficits and American criticism of Japanese neomercantilism, with three of four (75 per cent) of Americans and two of three (66 per cent) Japanese had "generally friendly" feelings toward the other side. Less than one in five Americans had "generally unfriendly" feelings toward Japan while almost one of three (30 per cent) Japanese had such feelings towards the United States.

A *Washington Post* survey in September 1990 also indicated continued favorable American views of Japan, although the proportion fell from 70 to 61 per cent, while those holding an unfavorable view rose from 27 to 39 per cent between May 1987 and May 1990.[96] The drop in Japan's favorable rating was particularly sharp among well-educated people annually making more than $40 000, Republicans holding free market principles, and Americans living on the West Coast. During the same period, the Soviet Union's image rose dramatically, from 25 per cent holding favorable view to 51 per cent and those an unfavorable view falling from 71 percent to 44 per cent.

There is often a vast gap between perceptions and reality, and often beliefs shape reality. A November 1990 *Economist* poll revealed that even though three of four Americans have generally friendly feelings toward Japan, Japanese perceive that Americans are highly anti-Japanese.[97] Only 19 per cent of Japanese thought most Americans looked up to Japan while over 70 per cent thought Americans looked down on their country. Again, the American results were far less extreme. Almost half of Americans (48 per cent) thought Japanese looked down on the United States while little more than one-third (36 per cent) thought Japanese looked up to their country.

It is ironic but not surprising that a greater percentage of Japanese have negative feelings toward the United States than Americans have toward Japan despite enjoying vast and continual trade surpluses with the United

States. Tokyo has been very effective in socializing most Japanese and many Americans to see any criticism of Japanese neomercantilism as "Japan bashing," which accounts for the large and growing resevoir of anti-American feeling in Japan, and the perception that most Americans are anti-Japanese. According to Japan's world view, it is not Japan which is "bashing" other countries with neomercantilist policies and persistent trade surpluses, but it is the foreigners which are "bashing" Japan by criticizing Japan's neomercantilist policies. It is no surprise that most Japanese unquestioningly accept this view, but the increasing numbers of foreigners who also accept this view is surprising. Tokyo's public relations campaigns have been highly effective in shifting many to Japan's world view. Even through the percentage of those Americans polled holding a positive image of Japan has dropped throughout the 1980s, the drop would undoubtedly have been far steeper if Tokyo's public relations campaign had not been as effective.

Japan suffered a serious public relations setback during the Gulf War. A 15–19 March 1991 Harris poll revealed that about 73 per cent of Americans agreed that Japan "got away without contributing their fair share" while only 22 per cent thought Japan's financial contribution was sufficient.[98] As a result, 56 per cent of Americans thought more negatively about Japan and only 11 per cent more positively. While only 20 per cent of Americans identified the Soviet military threat, 72 per cent of Americans thought Japan's economic threat posed the greatest challenge to the United States. What should be done about the Japanese threat? Over two-thirds of Americans (68 per cent) felt the United States should take a tougher line on trade with Japan while only 28 per cent disagreed. This immense sentiment for pushing for a level playing field with Japan, however, is only a source of power if the president actually taps into it to assert American interests *vis-à-vis* Japan. Although a dip in America's view of Japan during the Gulf War can be expected, overall, Japan's image has worsened as the controversy over Japan's perennial immense trade surplus, purchases of landmark American companies and skyscrapers, and manipulation of America's political system continue to plague the headlines.

CONCLUSION

Economic and political power are closely intermeshed. Japan's political victories have at once built upon and built up its economic victories. Just as Washington's liberal economic philosophy and policies severely disadvantage American firms against their Japanese rivals which are massively supported by their government's systematic neomercantilist policies, America's open political system in which anyone can buy access for a price means Japan's vast lobby can manipulate Washington with impunity while American influence in Tokyo remains minimal.

Japanese agents have infiltrated virtually every institution of American government, including the White House, gathering the most sensitive inside information with which to use against Washington during negotiations, subverting policies that serve American over Japanese interests, and mobilizing apologists in the mass media, think tanks, and universities in a systematic continuing public relations campaign while isolating critics, blackballing appointees to high federal positions, and financing favorable political campaigns.

Another source of political power is the ability to create a simple image and sell it to an undiscerning mass public. Japanese lobbyists and public relations agents continue to repeat the false, but highly effective refrain that Japan's economy is the world's most open and the only reason why foreigners do not sell more in Japan is because they do not try hard enough and their goods are inferior. Likewise, Japan runs immense trade surpluses with virtually all other countries not because of dumping, export subsidies and other predatory trade tactics, but because Japanese goods are superior and Japanese corporations try harder.

The estimated $400 million Japan's bureaucracies and corporations spend on buying influence in America's political system may seem immense, but is actually insignificant when compared to continuing annual trade surpluses that enrich Japan at America's expense and increasing investments in the United States. Japan's trade surplus was $41 billion and its investment in the United States over $300 billion in 1990. Meanwhile, the United States continues to provide the bulk of Japan's defense. Tokyo's lobbying efforts bring enormous economic and military returns to Japan.

Japan's growing power over the global political economy in general and that of the United States in particular flows directly from its neomercantilist world view and policies, just as America's declining power reflects its continued reliance on liberalism to shape its world view and policies. Japan's government and business carefully manage all markets to maximize the benefits and minimize the costs of both co-operation and competition, while its policymaking process remains largely impervious to foreign influence. Japan's corporations have an increasing weight in shaping the political agendas and policies of all countries, including the United States. Tokyo's close partnership with Japan's corporate world gives it an enormously powerful foreign policy weapon to arm-twist foreign government into conceding Japanese interests.

Japanese are the world's best poker players. Although as an economic superpower, Japan obviously has a concrete basis for extracting political economic concessions from its opponents, much of Japan's power is psychological, the power to bluff. Time after time Tokyo has responded to the White House's attempts to reduce Japanese neomercantilism with the threat that reciprocity would harm the bilateral relationship. And time after time the White House has meekly bowed to that threat and tossed away any opportunity to promote American rather than Japanese interests. Tokyo and Washington have edged close to the brink of trade war numerous times, but have always backed off because both sides knew the result would be disaster for their nations' economies. If, for example, Japanese stopped buying American treasury bills, the resulting stock market crash would drag both countries into recession. Tokyo, however, has been highly effective in its brinkmanship, trading largely symbolic concessions while continuing to enjoy $40–50 billion trade surpluses. No matter how blatant Japan's protectionist or predatory trade practices, Tokyo always deftly drags out negotiations and then agreed to remove one barrier or rein in one dumping assault while simultaneously building up other more insidious barriers or export offensives.

The Japanese have stacked the deck against the United States in every political economic struggle. Given this reality, it is no surprise that the Americans lose virtually all the time and their few victories are either too little too late or Pyrrhic. Japon's steady rise and America's decline as globle economic superpowers will continue as long as America's leadership meekly tolerates these vast inequities.

6 American Policy Toward Japan: The Sisyphean Dilemma or What is the Sound of One Hand Clapping?

On 16 May 1991, the White House threatened Japan with trade sanctions. Was it because after decades of negotiations, a doubling of the yen's value since 1985, and Tokyo's ten "market opening packages" of the 1980s, the United States continued to suffer immense and intractable trade deficits with Japan? If America's $41 billion trade deficit with Japan in 1990 had instead been balanced, 1 435 000 more Americans would have been employed, and the country's economic development, creation of wealth, and ability to deal with a range of socioeconomic problems would have been greatly enhanced.[1] But, tragically, the efforts of American companies to sell or invest in Japan continue to be obstructed by a bewildering web of barriers. During the Spring of 1991, Tokyo continued to stall in negotiations over Japan's cartelized construction and semiconductor markets. Meanwhile, Japanese corporations enjoyed virtually unlimited access to American markets. By early 1991, Japan's automobile makers had captured 30 per cent of the American market, contributing to the $3.2 billion in losses for United States producers over the preceding year with no upturn in sight.

So, given all these grim realities, had the White House finally awakened to the reality of America's rapid decline and Japan's rise into a global hegemon? Would it now demand that Japan genuinely open its markets, eliminate the trade deficit, and accept responsibilities for helping manage the global political economy commeansurate with Japanese power?

Not quite. At stake was not America's future, millions of jobs and hundreds of billion of dollars in wealth. At stake instead was the Hawksbill turtle which was threatened with extinction by Japanese manufacturers of eyeglass frames, combs and jewelry which use tortoise shell. The White House threatened to impose duties or outright ban imports of Japanese fish and other wildlife products, which in 1990 ammounted to $353.8 million, unless Tokyo agreed to phase out the tortoise shell industry.

Predictably, Japanese shrilly denounced the threatened sanctions as one more example of "Japan bashing." In addition to pride, at stake for Japan was a $125 million industry employing 2000 in the Nagasaki region. Some angry Japanese declared that the United States was dropping "another atomic bomb on Nagasaki".[2] In constrast, most Americans and nature-lovers worldwide applauded the White House threat. The tortoise shell industry is grisly even by hunting standards. Turtles are roasted alive over an open fire until their shells are soft enough to be ripped off. The naked turtle is then flung back into the sea where it will soon die. A few days before sanctions would have taken effect, after bitter grumbling, Tokyo finally promised to eliminate the industry, although it did not present any timetable. The White House, as usual, unquestioningly accepted Tokyo's promise and lifted the sanction threat.

Most people sympathize with the plight of the sea turtles, porpoises, whales, elephants and other species which have been decimated, particularly due to Janpanese consumer demand, and are relieved when the United States and other concerned countries come to their rescue. But it is certainly symbolic of the disarray and misguided priorities of White House policymakers when saving sea turtles rather than eliminating the $41 billion deficit is the focus of American policy toward Japan.

The sea turtle "crisis" of May 1991 is no anomaly. American policy toward Japan has been inconsistent and contradictory from the relationship's beginning. Presidents continually tout the bilateral relationship as "the world's most important, bar none" while privately expressing concern about Japan's rise into a global economic superpower. Is Japan America's greatest ally or threat? Are its markets open or closed? Do or do not Japanese firms dump their products overseas to destroy American and other foreign rivals? Will the 21st century be America's or Japan's? And if Tokyo does systematically follow neomercantist policies designed to capture the throne of global hegemony from the United States, what should Washington do to counter this threat?

The inability of Washington to resolve these conflcting visions with a comprehensive, systematic policy that serves American interests is the source of most bilateral problems. The United States has continually put its geopolitical interests in maintaining an alliance with Japan ahead of its geoeconomic interests in asserting a level playing field. Perhaps the major reason for this lopsided policy has been the belief that the American way of politics and business is surpreme and all other nations will emulate the United States if given an opportunity. The neoclassical economists who determine American policy cannot conceive of any economic success without free markets and have refused to accept the possibility that Japan's neomercantilism even exists, let alone has succeeded in creating and distributing wealth much more rapidly than the United States. Yet, reality in the form of worsening trade deficits and Japan's leapfrogging of the United States in one industry after another continues to interrupt these liberal visions. Periodically, Washington will respond to domestic pressure and temporarily shift to asserting American interests in a specific trade issue. But without any comprehensive strategy for asserting America's geoeconomic interests, these fleeting tough positions simply aggravate tensions without resolving the vast gap between American liberalism and Japanese neomercantilism. This chapter analyzes the tradeoff between geopolitical and geoeconomic interests in America's policy toward Japan.

COLD WAR ALLY AND TRADE WAR ENEMY

Japan has been the cornerstone of American policy toward the Pacific Basin ever since Commodore Perry first steamed his gunboats into Tokyo Bay in 1853. President Fillmore dispatched Perry to Japan to open trade, secure coaling stations, and ensure the protection of shipwrecked sailors which washed ashore. Although it got the coaling stations and protection for its sailors, Washington has been futilely banging its head against Japan's closed trade doors ever since. Trade conflicts were complicated by Japan's rise into an imperial power at the turn of the century. The White House now had to figure Japan prominently into its calculations of the Pacific's balance of power and American interests. The War Department's "Plan Orange" of 1907 actually projected American strategy to counter a Japanese attack on the United States. Relations survived conflicts over Tokyo's meddling in China, immigration to the United States, and naval limitations until Japan's invasion of Manchuria in 1931, then steadily worsened with the march of Japanese imperialism across East Asia until its decisive defeat in 1945.

Washington's planning for postwar relations began in 1942 and deepened over the next three years. The Administration was united in wanting to eliminate Japanese imperialism, but was divided over the best means of doing so.[3] Softliners maintained that Japanese aggression could best be tempered through appeasement – Japan would be stripped of its empire but allowed to retain its imperial system while Japanese corporations would be allowed unlimited access to American markets. Hardliners argued that militarism was intricately entangled in Japanese culture, and thus could be contained only by destroying Japan's imperial and industrial means to wage war. The moderates proposed both extensive demilitarization and democratization, but would have allowed light industry and a figurehead emperor to remain.

America's seven year occupation of Japan (1945–52) passed through three phases characterized by a different mix of the moderate and softline positions – none of the hardline positions ever became policy. Moderates won out in the short-run (1945–47). The United States gave Japan $2.2 billion in food, medicine, and industrial aid – Washington's largest amount to any one country during the early postwar era. Japan's imperial system was scrapped and replaced with a parliamentary system which guaranteed human rights. The Japanese military was completely disbanded, and war criminals were tried and lesser offenders purged. Japan's economy was completely revamped with land, labor, industrial and administrative reforms that formed the foundation for its later "economic miracle."

The emergence of the Cold War brought the Occupation's first phase to an end. Washington now needed Japan as an ally, and the emphasis was shifted from the moderates' emphasis on demilitarization and democratization to the softliners' push for economic revival. Japan would be converted into Asia's workshop and engine of growth. The softline position was clearly pushed by George Kennan who spoke openly of a need to create for Japan a new "empire to the South . . . We have got to get Japan back into . . . the old co-prosperity sphere".[4]

MacArthur's headquarters, the Supreme Command for Allied Powers (SCAP), then created a range of institutions and laws that have guided Japan's phenomenal economic growth ever since. Japan's Ministry of International Trade and Industry (MITI) was created in 1949 with the responsibility for acting as Japan's "economic general staff", and was armed with such neomercantilist institutions as the Export–Import Bank, Japan Development Bank, and Fiscal Investment and Loan Program (FILP), and powerful laws like the Export Law (1949) and Foreign Investment Law (1950). At the same time, inspired by the recommendations of Chicago banker, Joseph Dodge, SCAP pushed through a sweeping reform of Japan's macroeconomic policies in February 1949 which forced Tokyo to: (1) balance the budget; (2) increase tax collection efficiency; (3) tighten credit; (4) reduce wage and price increases; (5) control trade; (6) allocate surpluses to favor exporters over those manufacturers producing solely for the domestic market; (7) establish a single exchange rate of 365 yen to the dollar, well below the 330 rate at which most Japanese industries would be competitive; and, (8) decrease the amounts of new currency. The United States not only opened its own vast market to Japanese exports but attempted to convince other countries to import Japanese goods as well. Washington actually tied some American aid to Southeast Asia to Japanese exports.

These economic reforms were an enormous success in stimulating growth and exports. The budget deficit of 160 billion yen in 1948 became a surplus of 260 billion in 1949. The currency increased by only 20 billion yen in 1949, compared to 100 billion in 1948. Real wages rose 35 per cent and economic growth 11 per cent in 1949. The proportion of net government expenditures to gross national expenditures rose from 51 to 53 per cent in 1950 but then dropped dramatically to 34 per cent in 1951. Japanese exports increased 270 per cent between 1949 and 1951, while production increased 70 per cent.[5] Triangular trade between the United States, Japan, and Southeast Asia became firmly established.

The Occupation's third phase started with the Korean War's outbreak in June 1950. The Korean War was a godsend for Japan's economy, stimulating a massive demand for Japanese goods and services. The United States pumped $1.565 billion into Japan's economy between 1950 and 1952, causing Japan's industrial production index to leap from 90 in 1950 to 140 in 1953.[6] American procurements helped fuel Japan's economy throughout the 1950s and into the 1960s, reviving Japan's heavy industry and creating the demand for its high technology industries. Japan's earnings from special procurements totaled $5.6 billion from 1950 to 1959, which, when the expenditures of American troops and their dependents in Japan are added constituted 37 per cent of all foreign exchange receipts in 1950–52, and 11 per cent as late as 1959–60. Japan's net trade deficit of $2.729 billion from 1960 to 1967 was offset by American special procurements of $2.646 billion during the same period.[7]

Until the Korean War, Washington unconditionally accepted its responsibiity for defending Japan. With messianic zeal, MacArthur convinced Tokyo to adopt a no-war clause in its 1947 Constitution which, if literally interpreted, forbade Japan's maintenance of any military forces or even the right of self-defense. Then, as the Cold War deepened, MacArthur resisted Washington's pressure on him to force Japan to rearm. But it was not until the Cold War burst into a hot war in Korea that Washington ordered MacArthur to form a paramilitary Japanese "national police force". In 1951, Secretary of State Dulles told Prime Minister Yoshida that a peace treaty would only be signed in conjuncture with a military alliance. Yoshida agreed, but resisted Dulles' attempts to increase Japan's military forces from 150 000 to 350 000 men. Peace and alliance treaties were simultaneously signed in September 1951 and went into effect a half year later. In 1954, Tokyo officially formed the Self Defense Force (SDF). By the Occupation's end in 1952, the United States had achieved all its objectives of transforming Japan into a reliable, properous, stable ally. But Washington continued to help integrate Japan within the global political economy by sponsoring its membership in the UN, GATT, IMF, and OECD, and pressuring other countries to lower their barriers to Japanese exports.

The relationship was not without frictions. The first skirmish in the economic war broke out in 1955 when Washington complained of Japanese dumping of "dollar" blouses and other textiles in the United

States. Tokyo responded with its classic temporary restraint tactic after
the Japanese producers had already seized large chunks of the market.
Other trade disputes soon followed, and steadily increased in intensity
after 1965 when Japan began running continuous trade surpluses with the
United States. The White House not only tried to defend the United
States from Japanese dumping of textiles, televisions, steel and microelectronics, but increasingly to open Japan's markets to American exports.
Despite Japan's growing power and the worsening deficit, Washington
continued to put its geopolitical interests before its geoeconomic ones with
Japan. Washington, preoccupied with its Cold War obsessions and
commitments, deepening Vietnam quagmire, and trade off with Tokyo
of free American markets for Japanese bases, failed to devise any policy to
deal with Japan's rapidly growing economy and penetration of American
and other markets around the globe. Tokyo continually succeeded in
sidestepping periodic complaints by Washington.

The "textile wrangle" of 1969 to 1971 was the economic war's first
major battle, and was managed ineptly by both sides.[8] President Nixon's
tough response to Japan's dumping of textiles in the United States was
part of his overall strategy to realign American commitments and power
amidst the tremendous changes in the global power balance – detente
with the Soviet Union and China and burden sharing among allies were
the central pillars of Nixon's foreign policy. At a November 1969 summit,
Nixon thought that Prime Minister Sato had promised to resolve the issue
in return for Okinawa's reversion to Japan. Sato had replied to Nixon's
offer of a quid pro quo with the words "*Zensho shimasu*", which literally
means "I will take care of it" but actually means that "I acknowledge the
situation and will look into it but don't guarantee anything". The
bilateral relationship has been plagued by countless examples of the
inability of translators to accurately convey the often wide gap between
the literal meaning of Japanese promises and the reality that they are
simply gestures designed to patch over animosities. Unfortunately, American ignorance and Japanese insincerity combine to deepen the harsh
feeling over real issues. The dumping dispute was only resolved in the
autumn of 1971 after Nixon threatened on 15 October to impose quotas
under the "Trading with the Enemy Act". Although Tokyo complied
with export restraints, the resolution left deep bitterness on both sides.

The textile climax followed Nixon's 15 August 1971 declaration of his
New Economic Policy which, among other things, included a temporary
across-the-board surcharge on tariffs, the withdrawal of the United States
from the gold standard, and attempts to devalue the dollar. Under the
Smithsonian Agreement of 18 December 1971, the dollar was devalued
against other major currencies and 17 per cent against the yen. Japanese
bitterly denounced the yen's revaluation from 360 to the dollar to 308,

despite the reality that the old rate had lasted for twenty-two years during which Japan's economy had steadily grown more powerful, in part because of the increasingly undervalued yen. Yet, Nixon's efforts failed to revive America's relative economic decline or its growing deficit with Japan which was $1.2 billion in 1970 and rose in a roller coaster pattern to $9.9 billion in 1980.

Bilateral trade conflicts follow the same pattern. After ignoring complaints for sometimes years, the White House will finally respond to pressure by beseiged American industries and their Congressmen to do something about Japanese neomercantilism. It will begin negotiations with Japan over that specific industry. Tokyo's negotiating strategy has changed little since 1854: "Consistent with their view of Japan as an open economy . . . Japanese officials always responded to these cases as isolated incidents . . . problems were attributed as a matter of course to 'misunderstandings', a characterization followed by long, tedious haggling over arcane bureaucratic regulations, each of which the Japanese claimed was integral to Japanese culture".[9] Tokyo compounds the White House policy disarray by adeptly setting the parameters of any negotiations so that both countries have to make concessions despite the fact that Japan continues to run immense trade surpluses with the United States. In Prestowitz's words, "the purpose thus shifted from opening Japan to mutual opening, and the United States found itself on the defensive trying to explain why it did not import even more than it did so that its trade deficit could be larger".[10] Meanwhile, Tokyo digs in its heels on any concessions for months and sometimes years while the pressure grows in Congress and elsewhere for tough measures. In return for Washington's concessions, Tokyo will finally "give in" and, with great fanfare, present Washington with a list of "significant" market opening steps that make "Japan the world's most open economy". The White House points to the list in justifying its often considerable concessions, and the American resentment subsides until the next year's trade statistics reveal that Japan's surplus has either actually risen or remained the same despite the claim that Japan's markets are wide open. Japanese cannot conceive of markets – at least in Japan – as being open in the Western sense of the word. Japan "think of openness as removal of restrictions case by case, as the bureaucratic giving of permission, and have not the generic Western concept of an absence of the need for permission".[11]

Washington's efforts to dismantle Japan's endless trade barriers are similar to Hercules' fight with the Hydra – two barriers seem to arise from the neck of every one lopped off. Japanese excuses for preventing competitive American products from reaching Japanese consumers frequently could be dismissed as laughable, if the barriers did not represent hundreds of billions of dollars worth of business that is being diverted to enrich Japan at the expense of the United States. Tokyo's favorite excuse is to claim that because "Japan is unique" the foreign products cannot be sold in Japan. For example, "in 1978 the Japanese government refused to permit imports of American-made blood analyzers because, it asserted, the Japanese have 'different blood'. In 1986, foreigners were not allowed to participate in the land reclamation portion of the Kansai Airport because Japan has 'different dirt'. That same year, MITI attempted to prevent American and European ski manufacturers from offering their products in Japan because Japan has 'different snow'. In 1987, American garbage disposals were kept out of the Japanese market because Japan has a 'different sewage system'. Also that year, American beef imports there were limited because Japanese intestines were longer than those of other people. In 1990, Japan tried to keep out American lumber exports, alleging the wood could not withstand Japanese earthquakes – which are 'different' from those here".[12] American grapefruits were officially denied entry because: (1) Japanese did not like grapefruit; (2) Japanese tangerine sales (and farmers) would be drastically hurt, an event that might upset the social stability of rural constituencies, on which the ruling LDP depended, and even contribute to Communist Party victories; and (3) Japan was merely a "small, island country with few natural resources", making what headway it could in a cold, cruel world. The officials did suggest that a few grapefruits might be admitted as a sign of "sincerity".[13] One can only wonder at the Japanese response if American negotiators requested that only a token number of Japanese steel, semiconductors, or automobiles would be admitted to the United States as a sign of American "sincerity." Washington's attempts to pry open Japan's cigarette monopoly elicited similar Japanese "logic". MITI minister Michio Watanabe argued that the "reason we don't smoke foreign cigarettes isn't their high price; it's that they don't taste good", a particularly absurd statement since Japan imports most of the tobacco used in domestically manufactured cigarettes.[14]

Every foreign firm which has tried to penetrate Japan's import barrier laybrinth has its own horror stories. Bureaucratic catch-22s that would make Kafka smile are a highly effective Japanese barrier. For example, Tokyo restricted American baseball bats from Japan by insisting that only bats stamped with an official seal could be sold, but only stamped bats from Japanese producers. It took three years after this discrimination became a trade issue in 1980 for American manufacturers to finally receive seals. Yet, Tokyo's agreement to stamp the bats was a complete smokescreen since the distribution system was still cartelized. Today, American bat manufacturers have only a 1 per cent market share. Glenn Fukushima, a USTR official who for five years was engaged in most of the bilateral trade talks, recounts a story that reveals that foreign firms are discrimated against in even the smallest ways, the accumulative effects of which are to make significant market share virtually impossible for all but the most specialized foreign products.[15] An American firm tried to place an advertisement in two Japanese trade journals, but was turned down not because there was no space or the American firm could not afford to pay the price, but because the firm's Japanese competitors had pressured the journals not to accept the advertisement and the journals meekly complied. The American firm complained to the American Embassy, and Fukushima requested MITI officials to do something. Within a week MITI had pressured the journals to run the advertisement, which months later actually appeared. Fukushima points out the absurdity that "it required the intervention of the USTR and MITI, potential congressional involvement, and one year of frustrated effort for a major, well-established and well-endowed American company even to place an ad in two Japanese trade journals".

THE REAGAN–BUSH ERA: GEOECONOMIC STRUGGLES

The Reagan Administration's policy toward Japan was anything but revolutionary – it simply reflected the contradictions and mismanagement which have characterized Washington's policies toward Tokyo since 1945. Prestowitz's account of the Reagan administration's first meeting on the trade crisis with Japan provides deep insights into some of these flaws:

> Although billed as a strategy session, this meeting . . . produced little discussion of strategy and no comment on objectives. While it was understood that our objective was to open the Japanese market, we did not address what was meant by open, whether it was realistic to believe we could open the market, and whether if we got what we wanted, the trade deficit would decline. Even less consideration was given to the likely Japanese response to certain initiatives. And no consideration was given to the staple issue of all negotiations: how to use a judicious mixture of carrots and sticks to achieve the objective.[16]

The conflict between economic ideologues and realists split the policy-making toward Japan, with the realists being continually undercut by the free trade ideologues. Any attempt by the Commerce Department or USTR to reorient negotiations into areas like "reciprocity" or "results" were defeated by a coalition of the State Department, Council of Economic Advisors, and the National Security Council. For example, in October 1982, for the first time ever, the US Trade Representative in a report to Congress identified Japan's industrial policies and keiretsu system as trade barriers. Then, in December 1982, Lionel Olmer, the Undersecretary of Commerce for International Trade formally presented a study to President Reagan and the Cabinet arguing that Japan would leapfrog then widen its lead over the United States in technology, manufacturing and financial power unless the White House dramatically shifted its policy toward Japan. Unfortunately, while President Reagan was reported to have dozed off, Olmer and Commerce Secretary Baldrige were overruled by the economists in the Cabinet who maintained that the White House would continue to operate under the neoclassical economic dogma that only visible tariffs and quotas could be considered significant trade barriers, and that any government management of an economy would inhibit rather than promote economic development. This despite overwhelming evidence that the American economy was being ravaged by Japan's neomercantilist policies. Malign neglect of America's geoeconomic security would have been bad enough, but the White House actually colluded openly with Tokyo to defeat protectionist or retaliatory Congressional measures, efforts which reached a climax in 1987 when even the USTR helped orchestrate Japan's lobby against tough trade legislation.[17]

The White House did occasionally intervene to protect particular industries beseiged by Japan's neomercantilism, but there was no grand strategy within which those interventions took place and one must question the Reagan Administration's priorities. For example, while America's semiconductor, machine tool and automobile industries, to name a few, were being devastated by Japanese dumping assaults, the White House devoted tremendous resources, time and energy to forcing Tokyo to increase its import quotas for beef and oranges. Upon receiving Tokyo promises to increase its quotas for beef and oranges the White House shifted its attention to baseball bats. After enduring at least a half year of numbing negotiations and Japanese footdragging on changing its "lot" inspection method for American baseball bats which effectively excluded any of them from competing in Japan's markets, on March 1983, Tokyo formally changed the law. Of course, changing one administrative procedure does not affect the half dozen or so other barriers to American baseball bats which continue to have a miniscule market share.

Fishing is hardly a strategic industry. Yet, in the spring of 1982, Washington used the 1980 Fisheries Management Act to restrict Japan's fishing rights within the American Economic Enterprise Zone (EEZ) extending out to 200 miles from the coast. The Act's goal was to build up America's fishing fleet by forcing Japan's fleet to buy from it. The policy worked as Japan bought not only fresh fish but refined products, thus keeping jobs and profits in the United States. One can marvel with Prestowitz at the irony that while the United States used an "industrial policy to build up its fishing fleet, it deemed such policies as inappropriate and inefficient for high technology industries".[18] Yet, despite this agreement, scores of Japanese fishing drift net factory ships are violating America's poorly patroled waters and threatening to wipe out America's fisheries.

Strangely, in 1983 the Reagan Administration agreed to a Harley Davidson petition for import relief, even though there was no claim of unfair Japanese trade. Motorcycles are hardly a strategic industry and Harley's 3 per cent market share compared to the Japanese motorcycle producer's 95 per cent share. Why the Reagan Administration chose to protect Harley and not the machine tool industry remains a mystery. The tariff protection, however, did save some American jobs and wealth; by 1986, Harley was turning a profit and had actually requested the withdrawal of the tariffs. Temporary relief from Japanese dumping can mean the difference of life or death for American industries.[19]

One American industry that did not survive Japan's neomercantilist onslaught was hydrogenerator industry, which converts water power into electricity. The combined effects of Japan's closed and carefully managed markets and the rotation of low bids in the United States among Hitachi, Toshiba and Fuji Electric eventually destroyed the hydrogenerator divisions of GE, Westinghouse and Siemens-Allis. When Commerce official Clyde Prestowitz revealed the strategy and destructive effects of Japan's dumping on American industry, the Council of Economic Advisors replied with the neoclassical doctrine that the United States benefited from the lower priced machines. Unheeded were Prestowitz's arguments that the short term savings from Japan's dumping of hydrogenerators might eventually translate into much higher prices in the long term as the cartel's monopoly could charge any price it wanted, plus the fact that the industry profits and employment were transferred from the United States to Japan.[20]

American producers have a large comparative advantage in soda ash, and immense market shares in virtually every significant world market, yet only a miniscule share of Japan's huge market – in 1980 only 60 000 tons out of 1 million tons consumed. Were Japanese trade barriers to blame? While Japan has no tariffs or quotas on soda ash imports, a buying and distribution cartel effectively keeps soda ash imports to a tiny market share. Toko Terminal, Japan's buying cartel, would allocate a different trading company to each American producer, which would be limited to annual imports of 12 000 tons. The Japanese trading firms were jointly owned by Japan's soda ash producers. The ash was sold at the same price as domestic ash thus giving all the Japanese firms enormous profits. By allowing this cartel, Tokyo forced American soda ash producers to subsidize their Japanese rivals. Tokyo allowed the cartel to use a range of other nontariff barriers to develop Japan's soda ash industry and damage America's. When the American firms tried to outflank the import cartel and sell direct to consumers, potential buyers were warned not to buy; when the American firms tried to build a plant in Japan they were forbidden land and construction permits.

In 1982, Washington pressured Tokyo to investigate charges that it was discriminating against American soda ash producers. MITI denied the existence of a cartel, and echoed the same contradictory cliches that American producers did not sell more because they were not trying hard enough and the quality was poor, and that anyway, Japan could not buy more because there might be a strike or something in the United States that could delay shipments. Unfortunately, for whatever reasons, American negotiators do not point out the inconsistency in such Japanese excuses. If the market were open, Japanese consumers would buy from the lowest cost source, regardless.

Continued pressure finally led Japan's Fair Trade Commission to seize the records of Japan's producers in August 1982. It found that a soda ash cartel had operated since 1974 and ordered it to stop. American sales rose rapidly to 220 000 tons then leveled off even though they would have dominated the market had it been completely free. The cartel simply continued to exist behind the scenes. Sumitomo Trading Company, which did not have a soda ash producer in its group, tried to sell the American ash at a price below that of Japanese producers, which, of course, is how a competitive market operates. But in the summer of 1984, the other groups pressured Sumitomo to restrict its imports while Tokyo warned that continued large quantities of imports "would not be good for Japan".[21] American soda ash sales remain locked at about 25 per cent of Japan's market despite an almost 50 per cent drop in the dollar's value after 1985. Japan's cartel persists despite Tokyo's claims to the contrary.

Conflict over Japanese service industry barriers is increasing. Japan's law cartel of lawyers, judges and prosecutors (Nichibenren) has been as effective as its counterparts throughout Japanese industry in ensuring Japan's legal market is tightly managed. Although Tokyo continually claims that Japanese values of harmony and cooperation account for the virtual lack of litigation, in reality, Tokyo prevents litigation by strictly limiting the number of judges, prosecutors, lawyers, and penalties, while stretching out the court time for even the most minor issues for years. Japan's legal system serves national rather than individual needs. Aspiring lawyers must study seven or eight years before passing the examination. Japan has only one law school, the government run Legal Training and Research Institute, from which 500 students graduate as lawyers annually. Many of America's best minds go into law while Tokyo severely restricts

Japan's law system – Japan has only 14 000 lawyers while the United States is overun with 760 000 lawyers.

Japan's law cartel fears the loss of Japanese lawyers to high paying foreign legal firms. In the postwar era, foreign lawyers were first banned from practicing in Japan in 1955. Washington first protested Tokyo's ban on foreign lawyers in 1973. Tokyo only allowed foreign lawyers a limited access in 1987, after fifteen years of intermittent pressure. Foreign lawyers remain severely discriminated against. Like Japan's other "significant market opening steps", those affecting the legal industry are a sham. Although they are allowed to give advice on foreign law they are forbidden to discuss Japanese law, form partnerships with Japanese law firms or hire Japanese lawyers, may not use the names of the law firms they have worked for at home, must follow stringent guidelines when listing their names on stationary, signs, and business cards, and must have worked for five years in their home country before being allowed to work in Japan. Since 1987, 67 foreign lawyers have been granted access, about two-thirds of them American.

The Administration attempted to target Japan's bureaucratic trade barriers, but again, not in any systematic way. In 1983 the White House proposed that Tokyo adopt a transparent policymaking process. While American economic policymaking operates in a fishbowl, Japanese policymaking in the ministries, policy councils and Diet is conducted behind firmly closed doors. This asymmetry gives Tokyo yet another advantage over Washington. Among other things, Japanese negotiators can monitor an American bill's progress and thus lobby against it in advance; American negotiators lack that luxury. The White House pressed for foreign access to such institutions as MITI and the Industrial Structure Council. In January 1984, Washington succeeded in getting Tokyo to agree to make MITI's policymaking process more "transparent" by allowing foreign businessmen to sit on and address the Industrial Structure Council. Dispite these actions, Japanese policymaking remained as veiled as ever.

In late 1984, Washington finally got Tokyo to agree to conduct Market Oriented Specific Sector (MOSS) negotiations in such strategic industries as telecommunications, electronics, forest products, and medical equipment and pharmaceuticals. Negotiations followed the familiar path of Japanese stonewalling for as long as possible and then granting token concessions. Although Tokyo made concessions in all four areas, as of 1992, severe barriers continued to impede foreign sales.

It was not until the mid–1985, that the White House adopted a clearer two track policy in which it simultaneously attempted to negotiate the reduction of import barriers under GATT with Japan and other countries. President Reagan articulated this policy when he said: "we will accelerate our efforts to launch a new GATT negotiating round . . . to reduce barriers for trade in agricultural products, services, technologies, investments and in mature industries . . . But if these negotiations are not initiated or if significant progress is not made, I am instructing our trade negotiators to explore regional and bilateral agreements with other nations".[22]

Yet, this two track policy was no more successful. Representative John Dingell of Michigan articulated the dismay of many with the Reagan Administration's irrational trade policies when he said:

> all the companies and workers of this country ask for is a level playing field. Yet, with few exceptions, this Administration continues to turn the other cheek when country after country targets industry after industry . . . First the intellectual property of our industry is stolen, then our foreign markets are flooded with counterfeit goods, profits are used to dump in the US market. Finally our firms are driven out of business, or close to it – and all the while, their markets are insulated from meaningful competition.[23]

Despite its two track policy, the Reagan Administration continued to emphasize macroeconomic solutions to the trade deficit, assuming that the trade deficit would decline rapidly following the September 1985 Plaza Accord to devalue the dollar. Between 1985 and 1989, the dollar devalued by a yearly average of 26.5 per cent against all other key currencies, 42 per cent against the yen in nominal terms, and 29 per cent against the yen in real (inflation adjusted) terms. From the yen's point of view, it appreciated by 73 per cent in nominal terms and 59.3 per cent in real terms.[24]

The Administration was partially right. As one would expect, the dollar's devaluation had a positive effect on America's trade balance. Overall, America's exports grew by 67 per cent and imports by 41 per cent. The initial J-curve during which the trade deficit actually worsened peaked at $169.9 billion in 1987 then dropped to $100 billion in 1990. Between 1985 and 1990, America's trade deficit of $27 billion with the European Community was transformed into a $4 billion surplus, and America's deficit with Canada was halved. The deficit with Japan, however, dropped only slightly, from $59 billion in 1985 to $42 billion in 1990, even though the yen appreciated over 100 per cent from 260 to 125 yen to a dollar during that period. The stronger yen did affect Japan's trade; Japanese exports increased by 55 per cent and its imports by 63 per cent, with its trade surplus dropping from $96 billion in 1987 to $77 billion in 1989.

What explains these widely differing results? The answer, of course, is neomercantilism. The European Community and Canada largely operate their economies along free market principles, and thus their markets respond to shifts in currency values. Japan, in stark contrast, carefully manages its economy to maximize its development and the creation of wealth. After enjoying windfall profits and the conquest of enormous market share through the mid–1980s, Japan's corporations then used the strong yen to buy up American and other foreign assets while Tokyo continued to protect its markets.

Since coming to office in January 1989, the Bush Administration has simply continued the Reagan Administration's schizophrenic policies of sectoral negotiations, proclamations that the relationship was sound, and outright collusion with Tokyo to defeat Congressional retaliation initiatives. Glen Fukushima, former USTR official, wrote that in Bush's second year, "we have yet to form a Japan policy. Some will claim that we do have a policy; a minimal role for government in the US domestic economy, coupled with sporadic efforts to open the Japanese market. But this represents more a philosophical outlook than the well-directed policy required to address the problems in the bilateral relationship. Philosophical blinders limit our ability to consider the full range of policy options available to the United States. A rigid adherence to neoclassical economic theory leads many Americans to assume that the world operates on textbook economic principles and that any attempt by the government to shape market forces will lead to economic inefficiency".[25]

Tokyo only responds to sincere threats of retaliation; polite requests for Tokyo to open its markets are contemptuously rejected. In May 1989, the USTR designated Japan, India and Brazil "unfair traders" under Super 301 of the 1988 trade law. Tokyo's response to Washington's action was intense anger. At first Tokyo refused to even negotiate but eventually grudgingly agreed to talk, even as it swore it would never give in to Washington's threat of retaliation. The stalemate dragged on throughout the summer. On 27 August 1989, only three weeks after taking office, Prime Minister Kaifu set his Administration's parameters for bilateral economic relations with the United States in a very tough, stern speech which encapsuled the classic Japanese trade position. The primary warning was that any Washington attempt to resort to "managed trade" to overcome the persistent $50 billion deficit with Japan was "foolish" and would seriously harm the US–Japan military alliance. Kaifu rejected Japan's designation as an "unfair trader" as unfair, and warned Bush to reject the growing pressure in Washington for him to use the "Super 301" clause of the 1988 Omnibus Trade Act granting the president enhanced power to retaliate against neomercantilist nations. He downplayed the importance of the negotiations scheduled for 7–11 September on Japan's closed markets for satellites, lumber and supercomputers. Tokyo could not guarantee any significant concessions in those areas because they would involve deeprooted economic and cultural issues. Washington's claims that America's persistent trade deficits with Japan resulted from Japanese neomercantilism were dismissed as a mere "misunderstanding". Once again it was claimed that Japan's markets were completely open, American and other foreign corporations did not sell more in Japan because they did not try hard enough, and Washington's budget deficit was the main reason for the persistent deficit. Any trade friction would dissolve if only Washington would cut its deficit and increase savings and international competitiveness. Kaifu urged Washington to forget the deficit and instead embark on a "global partnership" with Japan designed to deal with problems of poverty and environmental degradation. He promised greater Japanese foreign aid, help on Mexico's heavy debt burden, and efforts on environmental problems. Meanwhile, Foreign Minister Taro Nakayama said Tokyo was prepared to discuss a greater spending contribution for American troops stationed in Japan.[26]

Tokyo, of course, sidestepped the question that if Japan's markets really were open and misguided American macro-economic policy was the deficits' real cause, then the yen's doubling in value between 1985 and 1988 would have resulted in the elimination of the deficit just as the dollar's weakening against European currencies turned a huge deficit with Europe in 1985 into a small surplus in 1990. Kaifu repeated once more the central contradiction of Japan's trade position that while its markets were the world's most open any attempts to open closed markets in sectors like satellites, lumber and supercomputers would severely disrupt Japan's economic and cultural system, would constitute unaccepted interference in Japan's internal affairs, and would thus severely damage the bilateral relationship. Tokyo dismissed the deficit as unimportant while playing up greater Japanese contributions to defense and global issues. Of course, no concrete commitments were aired, only promises to discuss those issues.

Once again, Washington's response was contradictory. The White House's immediate response was to avoid confronting Tokyo on its contradictions and outright distortions. Fear that the security relation would be harmed and Japanese capital to finance the deficit would dry up forced the White House to not only meekly and unquestioningly accept Tokyo's position, but to try to sell it to Washington and the American people. The one way free traders and Japan apologists in the White House again won out over the revisionists, arguing that Washington should abandon a market results approach and instead try to enlist Tokyo's support in backing the United States position at the Uruguay trade talks. In a statement on 9 September Trade Representative Carla Hills tried to defuse the growing tension by backing off from the 1986 agreement that Japan allow American semiconductor firms a 21 per cent market share by 1991.

Congress rejected the White House appeasement policies toward Japan and Tokyo's latest public relations offensive. Instead, Congressional leaders continued to argue that the only sensible way to dismantle Japanese neomercantilism was to retaliate with trade sanctions – it was clear that Tokyo had no intention of genuinely liberalizing its policies and economy. Nebraska Senator James Exon wrote Hills a strong letter pointing out that it was "her obligation to uphold the US position" on the semiconductor agreement, while Senator Frank Murkowski revealed that once again Japan's financial institutions and the Finance Ministry were colluding on fixing prices in deposit rates.

Under Congressional fire, the White House then adopted a tougher stand, authorizing Hills to talk if not act tough against Japanese neomercantilism. On 27 October Hills called on Tokyo to enforce its antitrust laws, uphold its promise to grant American semiconductor makers a 21 per cent market share by 1991, buy more American beef and soda ash, and employ more contruction firms. She pointed out that while American semiconductor makers had 50 per cent of markets elsewhere, Tokyo continued to limit them to a mere 11 per cent market share in Japan despite the promise to increase their share to 21 per cent. Hills said that even the 21 per cent share would "sell ourselves short" and said it should be the "floor share". She also pointed out that while the Justice Department investigated 200 antitrust violations in 1988 alone, Tokyo had not fined any antitrust violators since the early 1970s. Yet, Hills avoided discussing specific retaliation actions if Japan failed to soften its neomercantilist policies in supercomputers, satellites, lumber, and, countless other sectors, and simply called on Tokyo to become an import rather than export superpower to prevent a contraction in trade and weakening of the global economy. It was clear that without threatening any specific retaliation, Hill's remarks were targeted on relieving Capital Hill's anger rather than Tokyo's neomercantilism.[27]

Washington also asserted a get tough posture in regard to other countries accused of engaging in similar neomercantilist policies. For example, on 1 November 1989, it warned Brazil, India, Mexico, China, Thailand, Malaysia and Turkey that they would face retaliation if they did not curb their firms' pirating of American films, records, pharmaceuticals, software, and other intellectual property. Washington lauded Saudi Arabia, South Korea and Taiwan for making progress on the intellectual property issue. It is estimated that the pirating of American products costs the United States $61 billion in lost revenues, or almost half of the American trade deficit.[28]

After a half year of tough negotiations, in April 1990 Tokyo promised to open its markets in the three designated areas, supercomputers, satellites and lumber. Supercomputer sales are expected to increase $500 million following Tokyo's agreement to use practical benchmarks to choose among machines instead of the hypothetical standards used to undercut American sales. In addition, Japan agreed to buy all commercial and operational satellites on the basis of open competitive bidding, an action which could lead to $200 million in additional sales. Lumber was the last sector negotiated with Tokyo agreeing to reduce product certification procedures, product standards, building codes and tariffs. If fulfilled, these promises could lead to more than $700 million in new lumber sales.

The costs of this agreement for the United States were enormous. Japan did not guarantee increased sales, only promised that it would open those three markets. Theoretically, opening these three markets could lead to as much as $1.4 billion in additional American exports to Japan. But American exporters are advised to keep their champagne on ice until their cash registers start ringing; Tokyo is notorious for reducing more obvious barriers while building invisible barriers like cartels and obstruction by individual bureaucrats. In return, the White House agreed not to cite Japan as an unfair trader in 1990, negotiate any conflicts behind closed doors, and essentially give up its retaliatory powers granted by Super 301. Once again, the White House agreed to unilaterally disarm itself in return for token gestures by Tokyo. Trade disputes over semiconductors, amorphous metals, construction contracts, and telecommunications equipment remain on the negotiation frontburner, with no progress in sight. Ambassador to Japan, Michael Armacost, ventured the contradictory observations that it was best to concede to Tokyo's pressure to abandon the threat of retaliation while admitting that "it is undeniably apparent that much of the (liberalization) movement has come near these deadlines" and the accompanying threat of retaliation.[29]

On 25 April 1990, Trade Representative Hills claimed before the Senate Finance Committee that the "unfair trader" label should be lifted because Japan had agreed to open its supercomputer, satellite, and lumber markets. Two days later, on 27 April 1990, President Bush officially bowed to the enormous pressure by Tokyo and its lobbying army in Washington, and declared that he would drop Japan from the list of unfair trading countries. Instead, the White House kept India on the list for its refusal to open its insurance market. The logic behind the White House decision was mystifying. Japan got off the hook despite its $49 billion surplus in 1989, while India's trade surplus was only $851 million; Japan's per capita income was $19,500 while India's was $450. In other words, Japan is an economic superpower whose neomercantilist policies are severely damaging America's economy while India is a poor country in need of temporary advantages. Not everyone in Washington agreed with Bush's action. Senator Lloyd Bentsen claimed he was "a skeptic" in regards to Japan's "free trader" status while Senator Carl Levin of Michigan declared that keeping India on the list while dropping Japan "makes a mockery of Super 301 and the US trade policy".[30] Levin and Senator Arlen Specter of Pennsylvania promised to introduce legislation mandating that Japan be designated an unfair trader, but to date no action has been taken.

Between 1988 and 1990, in the midst of these other negotiations, Tokyo and Washington conducted two rounds of Structural Impediments Initiative (SII) talks, in which Washington essentially called on Japan to become a liberal rather than neomercantilist country; to make its consumers rather than producers king. In particular, Washington pressed Tokyo to lower consumer prices by enforcing its antitrust laws, streamlining the distribution system, boosting public investments, and promoting imports. Tokyo's demands for American reforms were reasonable – cutting the budget deficit, increasing savings, investments and research and development, promoting exports, improving worker training and education, allowing greater business cooperation – and if implemented would improve America's competitive position in the global economy. The reforms, however, would have no significant effect on America's trade deficit with Japan which operates on neomercantilist principles. Tokyo simply used the proposals as a smokescreen to obscure attention from its own continued protectionism.

In early July 1990, the second of two SII talks was concluded. Tokyo promised a variety of new policies including spending 430 trillion yen on public works between 1991–2000, reforming the Large-Scale Retail Law in shorten the approval rating for large department stores, enforcing its antitrust laws in regards to cartels and the keiretsu, raising penalties for construction bid rigging (*dango*), requiring detailed securities reporting to inhibit insider trading, eliminating the accusor's burden of proof requirement in antitrust cases, and reducing the average waiting period for the granting of patents from its current 37 to 24 months. In return, Washington agreed to cut its deficit, stimulate R & D, and increase its export efforts.[31]

Tokyo's signing of the SII Accord was simply one more token gesture designed to stave off Washington pressure on Japan to abandon neomercantilism. Only a month earlier in June 1990, Tokyo clearly demonstrated the difference between rhetoric and reality when Finance Minister Ryutaro Hashimoto embraced an advisory council report advocating that Japan indefinitely continue to run international payments surpluses of at least 2 per cent of GNP. On 12 June Trade Representative Carla Hills responded to this latest official espousal of continued Japanese neomercantilism by arguing that "it is one thing to come upon a surplus because of currency swings . . . it is quite another thing to have a policy to maintain a 2 per cent surplus. It's that which creates dislocation in the trading system".[32]

Tokyo agreed to the SII accord partly with an eye to smoothing relations before the Houston summit of the seven advanced industrial nations on 9–11 July. The summit proved to be another resounding Japanese diplomatic victory. Kaifu succeeded in arm-twisting representatives at the annual Group of Seven industrial countries meeting in Houston to agree to Japan's 810 billion yen loan package to China. Although the European representatives questioned why Japan wanted to aid China which had crushed the pro-democracy movement the previous year yet had no plans to aid the Soviet Union which was then undergoing significant liberalization and surrendering its empire over Eastern Europe, Tokyo's proposed loan to China was approved with no resistance. The answer to the European question, of course, is that profits rather than abstract moral issues guide Tokyo policies, and Japanese businessmen stand to make much more money from China than the Soviet Union. Tokyo was also able to table any discussion of Japan's closed agricultural markets.[33]

SII's follow up meeting on 15 October 1990 was characteristically unproductive and often surreal. Washington complained that the 3 per cent penalty for Japanese cartel practices was too low – never mind that Japan's Fair Trade Commission (FTC) remains as toothless as ever in enforcing existing anti-monopoly law, made a bizarre accusation that Japan's growth was slowing when all indicators pointed to rates as high as 6 per cent for 1990, and pushed for greater public investments. Tokyo, of course, claimed that it had implemented all its promises, that Japan's markets were the world's most open and foreign businessmen just do not try hard enough. Tokyo then counterattacked by demanding that Washington reduce its deficit and improve industrial efficiency and education.

The Bush Administration colluded with Japan's charade. Its 1990 trade strategy aimed at staving off Congressional attempts to manage the trade crisis with Japan by allowing Tokyo to make purely symbolic "concessions" while the United States made a genuine effort at successfully concluding the GATT's Uruguay Round. Thus, the White House tabled Congressional attempts to designate Japan an unfair trader and retaliate for Japan's continued neomercantilism under the trade law's Super 301 provisions. Instead, the White House put all its eggs in the GATT Uruguay Round negotiations, claiming that greater liberalization through GATT was the best way to increase American exports. USTR Hills claimed that agreements on all pending issues would result in $125 billion from greater American exports and $60 billion to American entrepreneurs that are annually lost from intellectual property theft.[34] But, as usual, the Bush Administration's dreams of trade liberalization were misplaced. GATT's Uruguay Round ended in December 1990 after five years of bitter negotiations when representatives of 107 countries failed to agree on resolving differences over reducing agriculture subsidies and general tariffs, and protecting intellectual property. The Round, however, was not a complete loss for American industry. Ironically, although the Bush Administration continually blasts any suggestion of "industrial policy" or "managed trade", it did talk GATT into excluding four sectors – shipping, civil aviation, telecommunications, and banking – from any liberalization measures agreed to at the Uruguay Round.[35]

Bush's multilateral strategy played right into Tokyo's hands. While the White House was focused on the Uruguay Round, Japanese industry and agriculture continued to enrich itself at the expense of its American and other foreign rivals. Tokyo is trying hard to shift the intense bilateral negotiations with Washington into multilateral forums where both accusations and concessions can be diluted. Tokyo succeeded in diverting Washington's periodic demands that Japanese rice markets be opened into the GATT negotiations in Brussels where the issue was lost amidst the morass of other pressing issues and is attempting to force any future "structural initiatives" into the OECD where it can similarly distract attention from Japan by pointing the finger at the 24 other members.

Follow up meetings to SII in January and May 1991, revealed that Tokyo had made no significant progress in fulfilling its SII promises. Tokyo did promise in January that it would seek legislation that would allow foreigners more opportunities to penetrate Japan's keiretsu system by increasing the amount of non-keiretsu shares and allowing foreigners access to corporate boards proportionate to their stock ownership. Tokyo set aside its promises and severely criticized Washington at the May meeting where both sides issued economic report cards on SII's progress. A Japanese official claimed that Japan had lived up to 65 per cent of its promises while he graded the United States only a 20 per cent. Deputy USTR Linn Williams called the Japanese report a "bum rap" that was "just an attempt by some to avoid focus" on the persistence of Japanese monopolies and cartels.[36] Tokyo made yet more promises on 14 July 1991, when it published a new regulation forbidding firms from colluding to fix prices, blocking potential competitors from entering the market, driving competitors out of the market, prohibiting distributors from selling rival products, or blocking imports. Of course, whether these newest "market opening steps" will be more than mere symbolic gestures remains to be seen. Will Japan's Fair Trade Commission ever be more than the lapdog of the economic ministries and *zaikai*?

The trade imbalance will not be significantly affected even in the extremely unlikely event of Tokyo sincerely fulfilling all these promises. Decades of protection and promotion have entrenched Japan's industries so deeply at home and abroad that these reforms will be just another case of too little too late. Tokyo, of course, has signed hundreds of agreements over the past thirty years which theoretically committed itself to abandon neomercantilism and embrace liberalism. More likely, as in the past, Tokyo will simply use these agreements as expressions of more principles (*tatemae*) while its web of trade barriers (*honne*) is made more subtle but no less effective. Tokyo never saw SII as anything more than a forum with which to delay any results oriented concessions. Furthermore it used SII to attack the United States for its own inefficient policies. As always, Tokyo arm-twisted Washington into backing off by claiming that any attempts to achieve a results oriented agreement would "seriously undermine" the security relationship and dry up Japanese financing of the budget deficit, thus sending American interest rates soaring and the economy into depression.

Washington again cut itself off at the knees by appealing to neoclassical liberal economic principles (consumer rights and free trade) and failing to back up its positions with retaliation against Japan's neomercantilist policies. It failed to present any specific timetables or figures for the increased American sales in Japan it claimed would follow from these reforms. Overall, America's SII further inflamed anti-American feeling among Japanese without achieving any concrete results. Japanese resented what they believed was interference in Japan's internal affairs. What Washington failed to help Japanese understand is that any nation that maintains neomercantilist policies in an interdependent global political economy has given up its right to claim internal affairs to justify those actions. Neomercantilism adversely affects the prosperity of other nations, and those nations harmed have a right to protest the neomercantilist's policies.

THE REAGAN–BUSH ERA: GEOPOLITICAL STRUGGLES

Since its inception in 1952, the Washington–Tokyo military alliance has been overwhelmingly successful in achieving the objectives of each partner. The United States gained bases on an "unsinkable aircraft carrier" which have been a vital link in America's containment policy, allowing Washington to contain the Soviet Pacific fleet within the Japan Sea, support US troops in Korea, and maintain a stable balance of power in Northeast Asia. Like NATO with Germany, the bilateral security treaty also serves the unspoken objective of suppressing any possible revival of Japanese militarism, a belief that, for some, apparently remains as deeply entrenched as ever. In return, the United States cloaks Japan with a nuclear and conventional defense that allows Tokyo to concentrate on maximizing economic growth.

As Japan's global power soared and American power declined throughout the 1980s, Washington pressured Tokyo to assume more of the defense burden while it tried desparately if futilely to dismantled Japan's web of trade barriers. Just as it succeeded in reducing some of Japan's seemingly endless trade walls, Washington has succeeded in getting Tokyo to concede some greater responsibility for its own defense. In 1981, Prime Minister Suzuki agreed to defend sea-lanes up to 1000 miles from Japan, while Prime Minister Nakasone agreed in 1983 to share Japanese defense technology with the United States and breached the one per cent spending increase level in 1987.

Yet, as with trade, Japan's efforts have been largely symbolic. Tokyo has cynically used Article 9 of its Constitution to counter any Washington pressure for a greater defense role. Literally interpreted Article 9 forbids not only any Japanese military but even the right of self-defense; politically interpreted it allows a "self defense force" to ensure the "sovereign right of self-defense". A 1977 White Paper acknowledged that Japan's military could only hold out for a few days against a Soviet attack without massive American intervention. To date Japan's navy has not been significantly increased to fulfill its increased sealane defense, only three insignificant technology transfers have occurred, and the 1987 defense spending budget increased to only 1.004 per cent of GNP. Cynics point out that the only significant Japanese technology transfers were to the Soviet Union, not the United States, when Toshiba sold top secret technology to Moscow that will enable the Soviets to make their submarines to run silently – an advantage that will cost the United States an estimated $30–40 billion to overome. Arms manufacturing is only 0.5 per cent of Japan's GNP.

Yet, despite its firm resistance to any greater "burden sharing", Tokyo has largely if vaguely addressed such essential defense questions as: Where does the defense of Japan begin? Which countries pose a military threat to Japan? How much money and what kind of military should Japan devote to its defense? Until 1990, Japanese Defense White Papers consistently pointed to the Soviet Union as the only country posing a military threat to Japan. Although the alliance allowed Tokyo to keep defense spending below one per cent of GNP (1.6 per cent if NATO's accounting procedure is used), the immense size of Japan's GNP, however, meant that Japan's $30 billion defense budget in 1990 made it the world's third largest in volume after the United States and Soviet Union, although at the same time it was only one-tenth the size of America's and is unlikely to get much larger. Japan remains overwhelmingly dependent on the United States for protection.

Japan continues angrily to resist any pressure for greater contributions to the alliance. In 1989, Tokyo contributed $3 billion of the $7.6 billion in total operating costs of the 63 000 American military forces in Japan. These contributions included the partial costs of Japanese employees at the bases, compensation to local communities, and rent. That year, Tokyo outright rejected a Congressional resolution calling on Japan to raise its financial support for American forces based in Japan to 100 per cent. Tokyo justified its refusal to assume any more of its defense burden by claiming it would entail revision of the existing US–Japan Status of Forces Agreement, which could in turn touch off an unwanted new debate on the alliance which, given the Cold War's finale, could cause the Japanese public to reject it.[37]

The Gulf crisis of 1990–91 highlighted Japan's neomercantilist obsession and "fire on the river's far side" attitude toward international tragedies. Although oil comprises 70 per cent of Japan's energy consumption and 70 per cent of that comes from the Gulf, Tokyo and most Japanese believed President Hussein's imperialism should be appeased rather than confronted militarily or economically. It makes no difference, according to Japanese, who owns Gulf oil as long as it keeps flowing. Even if Hussein acquired control over Saudi Arabian as well as Kuwaiti oil, thus giving him 65 per cent of proven reserves, he would still have to sell it in order to make money from it. War, on the other hand, can severely destroy production capacity thus interrupting the flow and raising the price.

In contrast, although only 7 per cent of America's oil is imported from the Gulf region, Washington and most Americans felt that Hussain's conquest of Kuwait and pressure on Saudi Arabia and the other Gulf states gave him the power to threaten not only the global economy's propriety but Israel's survival. For the first time since the American Revolution when it received French and Dutch aid, Washington passed the hat to its allies to contribute troops and cash to an alliance. With the world's most dynamic economy and heavy dependence on Gulf oil, Japan was targeted for particularly heavy contributions. After four weeks of pressure, on 29 August Tokyo finally agreed to contribute $1 billion to the Gulf Alliance.

The White House and Congress, however, agreed that Tokyo's pledge was far too measly considering Japan's wealth and dependence on foreign oil. Throughout September, diplomatic and Congressional pressure mounted on Tokyo both to contribute more to the Coalition and American troops in Japan. The House of Representatives passed a bill demanding that Tokyo pay the full cost of American forces in Japan or else Washington would withdraw all 63 000 American troops in Japan at a rate of 5000 men a year. Meanwhile, in September, 70 members of Congress wrote to Secretary of State Baker complaining that "defense experts on both sides of the Pacific agree that comprehensive coverage of the vast area Japan has agreed to defend requires between 12 to 14 Awacs planes and at least 20 tankers". The Senate approved the House bill in October.

Most Japanese responded with intense anger that Congress would ask for a larger Japanese contribution to their own defense. Defense Agency Director General Yozo Ishikawa vividly expressed the feelings of most Japanese when he angrily retorted that "The US forces are not here because we asked them to be here. If they want to leave, I would like to say, 'Please go ahead and leave'".[38] As always, cooler heads prevailed, Tokyo grudgingly agreed that starting in April 1991 it would foot half the costs of underwriting the American military force in Japan. Any contributions higher than 50 per cent, however, were dismissed as "impossible", a stance that was justified by LDP Foreign Affairs Division Director, Takamori Itoh with the "logic": "We should be careful not to offend the feelings of American troops in Japan by paying too much for them".[39] And after adamantly refusing to contribute more than the $1 billion already pledged, Tokyo agreed to extend a second aid package worth $4 billion, of which half would go to the alliance and the other half as aid to Turkey, Egypt, and Jordan. Japanese were split over the amount with 39.3 per cent saying it was about "right", 9.5 per cent that it was "too little", only 30.9 per cent said it was "too much".[40]

Japan was overwhelmingly opposed to the dispatch of even unarmed military forces or minesweepers to the Gulf. On 8 September Kaifu dismissed fears that Japan would dispatch troops to the Gulf by arguing that the government has "to observe the constitution. I don't plan to contribute to the UN operation with armed forces".[41] But pressure was building within the government and LDP for at least dispatching a token unarmed military contingent to the Gulf. On 23 September 1990, Japan's Defence Agency openly split with the government and called for the dispatch of noncombat troops to the Gulf, and pressures built up within several LDP factions for Japan to make a symbolic contribution. Most supporters of a military contribution were concerned mostly about Japan's international image as a "free rider". LDP leader Kiichi Miyazawa candidly admitted the hypocrisy of supplying money but not blood and sweat, pointing out that during World War II:

> we shed blood believing our cause was just . . . (a mistake) that was so serious that we decided not to resort to bloodshed anymore. Thus the Japanese haven't dealt with the question of whether we will even shed

blood for freedom . . . It is clear to (Western People) that freedom and peace should be achieved at any cost, including blood. For the Japanese the question has been taboo. If it had been taken up earlier, we feared, it could have turned the country to a backward direction. Now we are asked that taboo question. We haven't found an answer.[42]

LDP Secretary General Ichiro Ozawa was the most articulate spokesman for the dispatch of Japanese troops to the Gulf.[43] Ozawa strongly asserted that "Japan should assume responsibilities commensurate with its international status, not only in terms of finances but also of manpower. This is necessary for Japan's own survival". Ozawa admitted the hypocrisy of sending money but not troops to protect Japan's interests in the Gulf and elsewhere: "the world has been unable to understand Japan's stance and the principles it uses in determining how it will assume its responsibilities in the international community". According to Ozawa, Japan's choice is clear: "We have to decide whether to say 'Japan is special and we can only give money', or devise more comprehensive assistance through the United Nations that does not go beyond the bounds of the constitution . . . In the past we have somehow muddled through various difficult times without touching the issue. But Japan is finding it impossible to further evade the issue with the onset of Iraq's invasion of Kuwait".

Finally, on 16 October the LDP approved a plan to dispatch an unarmed Peace Cooperation Corps composed entirely of 1000 volunteers to join the Gulf Alliance. The plan was contained in the UN Peace Cooperation Bill submitted to the Diet. The government argued that the dispatch of troops to the Gulf was constitutional under the notion of collective security, which it distinguished from the unconstitutional notion of collective defense. What is the difference between collective security and collective defense? Apparently the UN sanction of the Gulf Alliance makes it a "security" rather than "defense" action, and thus the constitution allows Japanese participation. Under the plan, Japanese troops would be limited to a purely support role and would only carry sidearms. But this action contradicted the official policy that Article 9 forbade any dispatch of troops overseas.

The plan's announcement provoked widespread protests. Despite Japan's economic superpower status, dependence on Gulf region oil for 70 per cent of its total oil needs, and existence of over 300 Japanese hostages in Iraq and Kuwait, the Japanese public remained largely opposed to sending Japanese troops to join the multinational force in Saudi Arabia to protect Japanese interests. Some 38.4 per cent opposed and only 23.1 per cent supported the proposed UN Peace Co-operation

Bill which would have provided the legal basis for sending Japanese troops overseas under UN auspices. The parties were spilt over the LDP's Peace Co-operation Bill. The JCP and JSP were opposed to sending any Japanese troops overseas, and the CGP wanted to restrict any personnel to medical officers without SDF status, and the DSP favored only the unarmed dispatch of Japanese military troops to the Gulf. All the East and Southeast Asian nations protested Tokyo's plan to dispatch troops to the Gulf, with the loudest protests coming from Beijing, Seoul, Singapore and Manila. It was claimed that Japan's action could lead to the reemergence of Japanese imperialism. Given the viciousness of Japan's conquest during World War II, East and Southeast Asian fears of a revival of Japanese imperialism are understandable. The LDP itself remained deeply divided over the bill. Uncertain whether the bill would pass, Kaifu withdrew it from consideration on 5 November 1990. Tokyo's token efforts to the Gulf coalition did not prevent it from looking out for Japanese interests. On the same day Kaifu withdrew his bill, former Prime Minister Nakasone flew to Baghdad aboard a chartered Boeing 747 to negotiate the release of the Japanese hostages. Hussein agreed to free 78 of the 305 Japanese held hostage, along with 31 other hostages from other countries.

The see-saw struggle in which Washington calls on Japan to contribute more and Tokyo eventually responds with token concessions continued. Shortly after Kaifu withdrew his bill, Congress passed a nonbinding resolution calling on Japan either to assume 100 per cent of the costs of American forces in Japan or face the annual pullout of 5000 of those forces. On 20 December 1990, Tokyo finally agreed to raise its contribution from 40 per cent to 50 per cent of the total costs within five years. Why not 100 per cent? Japanese spokesmen claimed with straight faces that "there are some things it would be inappropriate to have subsidized by another country. The United States is a sovereign country and it should supply its own fuel for its aircraft and ships. Its soldiers cannot be mercenaries or hired guns paid by others".[44] Tokyo maintains these views, of course, despite the fact that Congress has clearly and repeatedly stated that it wants Japan to assume full responsibility for operating costs and the assertions of Japanese prime ministers throughout the 1980s and into the 1990s that they want an "equal partnership" with the United States.

In January 1991, Congress introduced a Trade Agreement Compliance Act mandating sanctions against countries that do not meet their military commitments. Although these actions evoked bitter Japanese protests, on 25 January 1991, Kaifu urged the Diet to approve an additional $9 billion for the Gulf War, bringing Japan's total contributions to $13 billion, and the use of Japanese planes to evacuate refugees from the Gulf region. Kaifu claimed that failure to contribute more would lead to "Japan's international isolation". The opposition parties continued to claim that the financial contributions violated the constitution. Congress upped the ante. On 10 February 1991, a bill was introduced uging the State Department to begin negotiating with Tokyo the purchase of additional airplanes and fulfillment of Japan's promise to defend a radius of 1000 miles from Japan. The Bush Administration responded that it did not want to pressure Tokyo at a time when its promise of an additional $9 billion to the Gulf region was subject to the Diet's approval. The LDP and CGP reached an accord for co-operation in the Upper House. The CGP agreed to support the $9 billion contribution to the Gulf Alliance if the LDP promised it would not be used for arms or ammunition, would be funded by spending cuts elsewhere, and that Tokyo abandon its plan to use military transport planes to evacuate refugees from Jordan. The LDP agreed and the bill passed.

Japan eventually paid its $9 billion contribution, but Washington's concerted pressure intensified ill-feelings on both sides of the Pacific. Japan's only real contribution was financial. Japan could muster no more than 14 volunteers of the 100 medical workers it promised for the Gulf Alliance, and virtually none of the 1000 civilian volunteers it promised for the much-trumpeted Peace Co-operation Corps which would serve in non-combat support positions. On 24 April 1991, a month after the fighting ended, Tokyo announced that it would send six ships, including four minesweepers to the Gulf region, the Japanese military's first overseas mission since World War II. Tokyo dispatched the flotilla in response to a Saudi Arabian request for help in clearing the channels and justified the action by claiming that it did not constitute a military mission but was merely an attempt to clear sealanes for Japanese shipping.

What is the future of Japan's military and alliance with the United States? The 1989 "Defense of Japan" published by Japan's Defense Agency succinctly captures Japan's continuing military strategy: "It is impossible for Japan to establish its own defense system capable of coping with any conceivable developments ranging from all-out warfare, involving the use of nuclear weapons, to aggression in every conceivable form using conventional arms. Therefore, Japan makes it a policy to ensure its own security by not only possessing an appropriate scale of defense capability, but also maintaining security arrangements with the United States".

Japan will continue to enjoy a cheap if not free defense ride, with the annual diversion of only one per cent of GNP to the military compared to an average 3 per cent for NATO members and 6 per cent for the United States. Japan's defense buildup will continue in the 1990s, although its projected 3 per cent annual rate increase for 1991–95 will be below the 5.4 per cent rate of 1986–90. Despite the continued budget increases, uncompetitive pay and poor working conditions have prevented the SDF from reaching its quota of 180 000 personnel from its current complement of 153 000. Tokyo will use its procurement policies to boost technology and manufacturing advances. Subsidies to America's 63 000 troops in Japan will not exceed 50 per cent of their total costs. The economic advantages of low defense expenditures are as true today as in 1960 when Prime Minister Ikeda told the Diet that ". . . our country has the lowest defense expenditures in the world today with which it has been able to maintain . . . remarkable economic development that is the foundation of the successive conservative party administrations".[45] Tokyo continues to justify low defense spending and responsibilities by pointing to Article 9 of its constitution which literally interpreted outlaws any military and to opinion polls in which about 85 per cent of Japanese are opposed to any increase.

Tokyo has mixed feelings over the Cold War's demise. Japanese fear that with the loss of the Soviet threat the United States may devote more resources to economic development and confronting the Japan threat. Thus, Tokyo is continuing to cry wolf about the "Soviet threat" in Northeast Asia and call for a continued massive American military presence to contain it. At the June 1990 seven nation summit in Houston, Prime Minister Kaifu expounded on the Soviet threat and refused to commit Japan to any significant aid to Moscow until it had returned the four northern territories. In June 1990, Foreign Ministry Shintaro Abe celebrated the security treaty's 30th anniversary in Washington with a speech proclaiming the alliance "a framework for security, stability, and development in the Asia–Pacific region". An article by Vice-Minister Takakazu Kuriyama in *Gaiko Forum* (Diplomatic Forum) described the alliance as the "crucial pillar" for Washington's commitment to the region and deterrence of the Soviet Union. He added the promise that Japan would never become a great military power. MFA officials echoed these remarks, expressing fears that Washington's budgetary problems would cause a cutback in America's commitment to the Pacific, particularly in South Korea and the Philippines. On 18 September 1990, Defense Agency Director General Yozo Ishikawa submitted a defense White Paper to the Cabinet which, while acknowledging that the Soviet threat had diminished, did call for a continued Japanese military buildup to offset the qualitative improvments Moscow had made for its Far East forces.[46]

If evoking the specter of a rapidly vanishing "Soviet threat" cannot scare Washington into continuing its obsession with geopolitics, Tokyo is hoping that fears over a revival of Japan's military ambitions might perform the same trick. After all, many believe that the bilateral alliance's mission was as much to contain Japan as the Soviet Union. The classic Japanese response to Washington's periodic attempts to pressure Tokyo to build up its military and fulfill more responsibility for maintaining the alliance is to evoke images of past Japanese aggression and claims that the government might not be able to control a larger Japanese military. For example, Japan's ambassador to Thailand, a respected strategist, proclaimed that "if the Japan-US alliance is broken, Japan will tilt toward the right and become a military power within six months".[47]

These fears, of course, are completely irrational. Neomercantilism, democracy and pacifist values are firmly entrenched in Japan. Virtually all Japanese understand that, in an interdependent world, imperialism is completely self-defeating as a means of achieving national interests. Even if the public did support Japanese imperialism, just where would the Japanese military invade? During the 1930s, Japan's armies and navies filled the power vacuum in East Asia. Although it tried to justify its imperialism to counter what it claimed was an encirclement by the ABCD powers – America, Britain, China and the Dutch – in reality the three Western countries were preoccupied with domestic economic problems while China was torn apart by civil war. There was no threat to Japan during the 1930s. In contrast to the power vacuum of the 1930s, there is now a stable balance of power throughout East Asia. So fears of a revival of Japanese imperialism are baseless.

Irrational as these fears are, they present wonderful insights into Japanese psychology. A central aspect of Japanese political economic culture is finding a scapegoat for failure – someone or something that will take responsibility for defeat while allowing everyone else to carry on their lives. Traditionally, someone committed *seppuku* (suicide) for defeat, nowadays, someone merely resigns his post. The Japanese military has become the scapegoat for the defeat of Japanese imperialism between 1931 and 1945. Japanese have convinced themselves that they had nothing to do with the imperialism that left 20 million East Asians and 3.1 million Japanese dead and the region devastated – it was all the military's fault. Japanese either conveniently forget or never learned that only a few hundred Japanese – mostly communists and socialists – protested Japanese imperialism while the population was completely mobilized for the war and prepared fanatically to fight to the last old man, woman, and child had not the atomic bombings made an Allied invasion unnecessary. But evoking such fears has become an important tactic of Japanese neomercantilism. Tokyo's message is that its trade partners had better tolerate continued massive trade and payments deficits and Japanese trade barriers because the possible alternative, Japanese militarism, is much worse.

CONCLUSION

On 24 March 1991 the National Association of Manufacturers asked President Bush to review America's relationship with Japan, with the central question being: "If these present relationships continue, what will happen to the United States with respect to living standards, leading-edge technologies, research and development intensive exports, and per capita income in the year 2000 and beyond?"[48] The question is the most important one facing the United States and cuts to the heart of America's decline and Japan's deepening hegemony over the global political economy. The Bush Administration, like its predecessors, will undoubtedly fail to even acknowledge that question, let alone attempt systematically to address it.

White House efforts to open Japanese markets throughout the 1980s were unsystematic and only partially successful. Washington and Tokyo have edged close to the brink of trade war numerous times, but have always backed off because both sides knew the result would be disaster for both nation's economies. If, for example, Japanese stopped buying American treasury bills, the resulting stock market crash would drag both countries into recession. Tokyo, however, has been highly effective in its brinkmanship, trading largely symbolic concessions while continuing to enjoy a $41 billion trade surplus. Tokyo has successfully extracted concessions from Washington in virtually all the issues negotiated. No matter how blatant Japan's protectionist or predatory trade practices, Tokyo always skillfully dragged out negotiations and then agreed to remove one barrier or rein in one dumping assault while simultaneously building up other more invidious barriers or export offensives. Although Tokyo granted ten "significant market opening steps" during the decade, and, following each, claimed Japan was now the world's most open economy, American negotiators and businessmen often felt like Hercules fighting the hydra– two new barriers seemed to spring up from every one they chopped off. Tokyo points to the growing percentage of manufactured imports as a percentage of total imports to claim that its markets are open. In reality, most of these imports are from Japanese subsidiaries which are simply using cheap overseas labor and subsidies as export platforms for Japan and other global markets. Foreign corporations with competitive advantages for their products find Japan's markets just as impenetrable as before.

Cohen states bluntly that "none of Japanese concessions made between 1969 and 1989 significantly increased US market share in Japan for a major manufactured good or allowed US industries to emerge from the shadow of superior Japanese competition. Japanese liberalization packages have been political crisis management tools rather than levers of economic change".[49] The Japanese have mastered the art of playing off elements of America's fragmented policymaking system against the others, and have become particularly adept at coopting the White House to take its side in the battles, particularly in the Reagan Administration with its dogmatic adherence to "free markets". The Japanese continually use the liberal assumption that only pure free markets can explain economic success, and thus Japan's success was based on free markets. The result of this clever Japanese strategy was, according to Prestowitz:

> Implicitly we were linking ourselves in common cause with the Japanese and creating a false sense that free-traders on both sides were fighting against the black hats in Congress. The negotiation thus changed direction: originally a matter of US government requests (on Japan), it became one of mutually calibrating just how much action would be necessary to keep Congress leashed. Instead of a negotiator, the US trade team became an advisor to the government of Japan on how to handle the US Congress.[50]

Examples of government trade officials defecting to the Japanese, sometimes amidst negotiations, have become increasingly common. Under Ambassador Mansfield's tenure, embassy cables to Washington critical of Japanese neomercantilism were censored.[51]

If something unbelievable is repeated enough, some people may eventually set aside their initial skepticism and accept it as the truth. Japanese spokespeople continue to endlessly repeat the mantra that Japan's markets are the world's most open and foreigners do not sell more because their goods are inferior and they do not try hard enough – despite all evidence to the contrary. According to Japanese, foreign claims that Japan's markets remain carefully managed to minimize foreign penetration while its corporations dump their products overseas to destroy their foreign rivals is all a big misunderstanding. During Prime Minister Kaifu's July 1991 summit meeting with President Bush, Foreign Ministry official Taizo Watanabe captured the essence of Japan's position when he asserted that: "We have solved so many problems, the only thing that is remaining is the problem of the perception gap".[52] In other words, if only you Americans and other foreigners would accept our position, then there would be no problems.

Watanabe's claim occurred only weeks after a scandal involving almost a billion dollars in kickbacks from the Big Four securities firms to other corporations and organized crime leaders revealed that Japan's economy remains characterized by massive systematic collusion, insider trading, and discrimation against outsiders. For knowledgeable observers, Japan suffers from the "little boy who cried wolf" syndrome. Tokyo and its army of spokespeople have made so many unfulfilled promises and claims over the decades that Japan is now haunted by a "legitimacy deficit".[53]

American decline and Japanese ascendance over the global economy has been accelerated by Washington's massive and Tokyo's light defense burdens. While America's military alliance with Japan benefits both countries geopolitically, it has undermined America's geoeconomic security. Essentially the alliance is based on American access to bases in Japan in return for Washington turning a largely blind eye to Japanese neomercantilism. Has Japan enjoyed a free ride on defense? If not free it has been incredibly cheap! With its defense ensured by Washington, Tokyo can concentrate its financial, industrial, technological and manpower resources on enriching itself. Masaki Nakajima, a senior advisor at the Mitsubishi Research Institute, estimates that Japan has saved $1 trillion since 1945 by sheltering under America's nuclear and conventional umbrella – money that has been mostly invested into making Japan's strategic industries world champions.[54] The 1983 Mutual Defense Assistance Agreement was trumpeted at the time as a means whereby the United States could license military technology from Tokyo. There have only been two such transfers since the agreement was signed – one for cleaning ship hulls and the other for drydock upkeep. This is hardly the technology cornucopia that the Americans hoped they were tapping into when they signed the agreement.

Although over three decades Washington has conducted endless rounds of negotiations with Tokyo involving virtually all aspects of Japanese neomercantilism, the effects have been to nibble around the edges rather than exert the focus and power necessary to slash decisively through the Gordian knot of Japanese trade barriers.

The reasons for America's failure at the negotiating table and the larger failure to maintain its power in a rapidly changing world, are complex. But fundamentally, the United States has been less the victim of Japanese neomercantilism than of its own misguided liberal ideas. No one should fault the Japanese for so vigorously, single-mindedly, and skillfully pursuing their own national interests. There would be no significant problems with Japan if since 1945 Washington had based its policies on the real world rather than on abstract economic theories and an obsession with a Soviet "threat" that never came close to living up to its billing. The United States will continue steadily to decline and Japan just as steadily to expand its global power as long as Americans believe that the world must mirror the United States rather than that the United States must adapt American values, institutions, and policies to a rapidly changing world.

7   The Mature Industry Front

Tokyo extensively protects virtually every Japanese industry, but for different reasons.[1] Industries like microelectronics, steel, machine tools or automobiles are obviously promoted because of their strategic importance. Tokyo carefully protects a range of industries like agriculture, construction, and distribution for their political rather than economic importance. Tens of millions of farmers, builders and distributors and their families give the ruling LDP votes in return for protection and heavy subsidies. This in turn allows the LDP to remain in office and continue supporting both strategic and political industries. The losers are of course Japanese consumers who pay inflated prices for even basic goods and foreign producers whose profits and often livelihoods are lost to Japanese neomercantilism. If Tokyo had followed free market rather than neomercantilist policies for the seven industries analyzed below, none would have achieved their present level of development, and some might not have survived. Japan's steel, automobile, television and machine tools industries may well have been wiped out by competitive imports while its agriculture, construction and distribution industries would be severely limited in size and scope. Japan's economic growth would have been considerably lower while other countries with a comparative advantage in those industries would be wealthier.

Washington has battled Tokyo by either trying to stem the dumping and/or opening the markets of all seven industries below, with varying degrees of success or failure, depending on one's outlook. As in other economic fronts, Washington's attempts to counter Tokyo's neomercantilist policies in these industries have followed a familiar pattern. Battered American industries pressure Washington for relief from Japanese dumping and/or closed markets. The White House first tries to ignore the pressure but eventually succumbs after Congress lines up with the industry. The White House then attempts to pressure Tokyo for relief. Tokyo at first denies any wrongdoing, then, after considerable delay and enormous American pressure, grudgingly agrees to negotiations, which often drag on for years. Caught between Japanese stonewalling and Congressional fire, the White House eventually allows the Japanese to "settle" the dispute by making cosmetic concessions. Washington was too late to save America's television industry, and only barely saved America's machine tool and automobile industries from complete destruction. But the quotas the White House negotiated with Tokyo for machine tools and automobiles helped the Japanese producers as much and perhaps more than the Americans. Quotas guaranteed the Japanese huge market shares in the United States and allowed them to raise prices and reap windfall profits which were then reinvested in those industries. The White House's attempts to open up Japan's agriculture, construction, and distribution markets have failed – all three markets remain carefully controlled by Japanese cartels with foreigners allowed only token market shares.

TELEVISION

Japan's television manufacturers dominate virtually all the world's markets. In the international zero sum trade game Japan's gains in wealth and employment from the television industry have been synonymous with America's loss. Japanese producers used their mastery of television technology and profits to eventually dominate the entire consumer electronics industry. Japan became the global television leader in little more than a decade. In 1964, the United States produced over 1 million color television sets while the Japanese produced only a few thousand; by 1977, Japanese televisions held a 42 per cent global market share and 37 per cent American market share, while American firms produced less than 10 per cent of the global total.[2] There were 27 American television producers in 1960, 17 in 1970, 3 in 1980 (GE, RCA and Zenith) and in 1991 there was only one (Zenith).

What happened? As with so many other industries, Japan would not have a television industry if its policymakers had used liberal rather than neomercantilist policies. Japan's television producers became world leaders because Tokyo rejected free market principles and supplied them with a range of cartels, technologies, subsidies and protection that enabled them to systematically target, destroy, then take over America's television industry within a decade. According to Choate, Tokyo nurtured Japan's television industry with "an anti-competitive cartel and then (reinforced it) with diplomacy, fraud, and the influence of Washington insiders in a direct assault on the American consumer electronics industry".[3] Choate reveals that in addition to leading a cartel of Japanese television producers which dumped their products in the United States, the Japanese succeeded in further undermining America's television industry by making illegal payments to American importers, converting over twenty high-ranking federal officials into Japanese agents, buying secret information about White House strategy, and using its power to arm-twist the White

House into accepting a secret trade agreement which forced the government to work with Japan against America's own television industry.

Tokyo's predatory policies date back to 1956, when it helped organize Japan's consumer electronic producers into the Home Electric Appliance Market Stabilization Council, a cartel which set minimum price levels for domestic and foreign sales; established profit margin levels for retailers (22 per cent) and wholesalers (8 per cent); boycotted nonmembers; and denied foreign companies critical access to Japan's distribution system. The government reinforced this cartel by erecting a range of tariff and nontariff barriers. MITI forced Japan's Fair Trade Commission (FTC) to back down from charges it filed in 1956 and 1966 against all the major consumer electronic producers, except the outsider Sony, for illegally cartelizing the Japanese market, enforcing industry-wide high price levels, collusively setting rebates and profit margins for distributors, and collectively boycotting nonaffiliated wholesalers.

Meanwhile, Japan's government and electronic industry closely coordinated their efforts to ensure virtually no American television sets were sold in Japan. The government entangled American imports with webs of red tape while the Japan Electronics Industries Association organized an import cartel in which Japanese wholesalers refused to buy American televisions. MITI helped forge and then approve the industry agreements on the cartelized prices, production, and markets. Prevented from selling in Japan, and with Tokyo playing off one corporation against the others, in the early 1960s, the American consumer electronic makers, RCA, GE and Westinghouse licensed their black and white television technology to their Japanese rivals, and RCA even licensed away its color television technology. Although this technology sell-off seems incrediably shortsighted, the only alternative in a free market system was for the American producers to lose the sale to their domestic rivals. As doorkeeper, MITI manipulated American firms against each other to ensure that the Japanese firms could obtain the technology at the lowest possible price. Japan's television industry was built on over 400 licenses. American technology sell-offs would never occur if Washington replaced liberal with neomercantilist policies whereby American producers could form technology cartels to prevent any transfers while the government erected trade barriers in retaliation for Japan's trade barriers.

After building up Japan's industry through cartels, trade barriers, and technology transfers, the next step in Tokyo's systematic neomercantilist television policy was to launch a concerted dumping campaign against America's television industry. In 1963, the producers formed the Television Export Council to coordinate their dumping campaigns in the United States and other foreign countries by dividing markets and fixing prices. Japanese sets that sold for $350 in the United States cost Japanese consumers at least $700. Japan's producers reinforced their dumping with secret rebates to American importers to make up for the low selling prices.

The concerted Japanese offensive and inability of the United States to defend itself, let alone retaliate, resulted in the devastation of America's television industry. American television producers had a comparative advantage during the 1950s through the mid–1960s. But faced with Japan's dumping assault, American jobs were halved between 1966 and 1970, dropped another 30 per cent between 1970 and 1977, and a further 25 per cent between 1977 and 1981. The six remaining American manufacturers in 1976 accounted for only 2 per cent of the televisions sold in the United States and only 500 of the 5 million sets sold in Japan.

How did Washington respond to Japan's systematic destruction of America's television industry? Washington unwittingly colluded with Tokyo to destroy American industry. Antitrust laws prevented American producers from collaborating on manufacturing or marketing, while unreciprocated free trade policies allowed Japanese producers unlimited access to American markets while American producers were denied access to Japan's markets. Japan's producers could collude on market share and high prices in their protected home market while dumping their televisions in the United States at prices designed to drive their American rivals out of business.

Prevented from using its rivals' tactics, America's industry had only one option – to sue. Between 1962 and 1981, American producers filed twenty unfair trade cases involving dumping, fraud, and antitrust violations with Washington, but little was done to stop Japan's trade offensive. In 1968, the US Electronics Industries Association filed an anti-dumping petition with the Treasury Department. Treasury's investigation dragged on until 1971 when responsibility for defending the United States against foreign predatory trade practices was transferred to the International Trade Commission (then called the Tariff Commission). In March 1971, the government ruled that the Japanese corporations had indeed dumped their products in the United States since 1966, but that levies would only be applied from 7 September 1970, the date that the ITC's dumping appraisal was issued, and no actual figure was levied.

The government's failure to defend America's television industry led the National Union Electric Corporation (NUE) and Zenith to file private antitrust suits with the Treasury Department in 1970 and 1974, respectively. It was not until 1976, after years of pressure from the remnants of America's television industry, that the Treasury Department took up the case again. But the Justice Department tossed out the NUE and Zenith cases, having found "no evidence of concerted predatory conduct intended to destroy and supplant the US color TV industry".[4] Zenith continued to struggle on, petitioning the Supreme Court to rule on Japan's dumping and television cartel. In April 1978, the Supreme Court bowed to Tokyo's warnings that an adverse ruling would damage both bilateral and global trade, and ruled against Zenith. By March 1978, the Customs Service had calculated that the Japanese duties on televisions dumped between January 1972 and April 1977 alone came to $382 million, and were scheduled to be collected by 31 March 1978, which, according to the law, had to be collected before litigation procceeded. But Japan's lobbying army in Washington stalled the procedings and forced the Treasury Department to overule the Customs Service and instead assesed the penalties at only only $46 million, of which Japanese firms ended up paying only $600 000 by 1979. Congress rejected this amount and transferred responsibility for dumping cases to the Commerce Department. The case was finally "resolved" in 1980 when Commerce levied fines on the Japanese firms of $76 million for dumping and $10 million for fraud, of which only $16 million was ever collected. If the government had enforced the law, the fines would have amounted to over $1 billion for the entire 15 year span of Japanese dumping. Commerce's action was, as in so many other American industries, too little too late. Japan's television producers had already destroyed America's industry.[5]

Despite all this, Zenith and the Committee to Preserve American Color Television (COMPACT) renewed their struggle. The Justice Department retaliated by harassing Zenith with a range of legal obstacles including forcing it to post $11.5 million as security for its antitrust suit. In 1986, the Court of International Trade ruled in Zenith's favor, and a Justice Department appeal was overturned and the lower court ruling upheld by the Court of Appeal in July 1987. The Justice Department went so far as to file a "friend of the court" brief on behalf of the Japanese producers who asked the Supreme Court to overule the Court of Appeals decision! The Supreme Court ruled 5–4 in 1987 that there was no Japanese cartel.

Why was the American government so reluctant to retaliate against Japan's predatory trade policies? Although Nixon was the first postwar president to have resisted Japanese neomercantilism, even he eventually bowed to Tokyo's skillful diplomacy and political economic power. In August 1972, the Nixon Administration appears to have struck a deal with Tokyo on a range of bilateral trade conflicts in which in return for a Japanese promise to restrain textile exports and buy more than $1 billion of American goods, the United States would not retaliate against Japan's dumping of televisions.[6] In other words, the White House essentially said "you can only devastate one of two industries you are currently assaulting".

The Carter White House played even more notoriously into MITI's hands. In 1977, Washington and Tokyo negotiated an Orderly Marketing Agreement (OMA) in which Japan would only export 1.75 million televisions annually for three years. The OMA was yet another example of "too little too late", the equivalent of applying a Band Aid to a severed limb – America's television industry continued steadily to hemorrhage to death. The quotas also allowed the Japanese television manufacturers to raise prices and recoup the losses sustained earlier during their dumping offensive.

And, as usual, after agreeing to a quota which the Japanese had desired all along, Tokyo extracted immense concessions from the White House. The Carter Administration secretly promised to limit the ITC investigation of the Japanese cartel, appeal an earlier ruling by the Customs Court in favor of Zenith, quickly end the anti-dumping duties, ignore cartel charges against Japanese corporations when they were acting domestically in accordance with Japanese government directives, and quickly inform Tokyo of any ITC findings on Japanese dumping![7]

Why did the Carter Administration completely sell out American interests to Japan? One reason was the inexperience and ignorance of Special Trade Representative Robert Strauss. Another was the White House view that its main trade efforts should be focused on the multilateral GATT talks currently underway rather than bilateral conflicts. Yet another, the fact that the chairman of the ITC, Daniel Minchew, was then a paid Japanese lobbyist. Finally Tokyo's hiring of such influential ex-administration officials as Harald Malmgren to champion its case helped render the Carter Administration's sellout inevitable.

America's television producers were not blameless for their own destruction. Reich and Magaziner argue that American firms "ultimately failed because they invested in lawsuits, offshore production bases, and cosmetic features rather than in basic product design, process improvements, and export market development".[8] However, while Japan's television producers should be lauded for their productivity and quality gains, these did not occur in a vacuum. By protecting Japan from foreign television imports or investments, Tokyo untied American television technology from its production. The only money American producers could make in Japan's vast market came from technology licenses. At the time, American firms were competing mostly with each other, so it was a question of selling out to potential Japanese rivals before their rivals did. American antitrust laws prevented American producers from colluding to prevent any technology sell-off or at least to negotiate higher licensing fees.

Washington must ultimately take responsibility for the loss of America's television industry. Even if America's television producers had invested more money in research and development and less in lawsuits, their demise was inevitable given the reality that their Japanese rivals were massively supported by both Tokyo and Washington. Choate succinctly sums up the government's response to Japan's price, market, dumping, and import cartels:

> When confronted with Japanese subsidies, the federal government opposed its own industry's efforts to apply countervailing duties. When faced with the cartel's anti-competitive behavior, the American government refused to mount an antitrust suit and it actively opposed those filed by private American companies. When presented with clear evidence of a kickback scheme and Customs fraud, the federal government scuttled an ITC investigation. When the Japanese cartel engaged in massive dumping, the federal government took twelve years to provide relief to American companies – and then settled their claims for less than two cents on the dollar. Moreover, at critical moments, the federal government repeatedly leaked vital information to the Japanese government – information that it withheld from American companies and Congress.[9]

Choate points out that this incredible sellout by the American government to Japanese interests was in no small part influenced by the fact that by 1989 over twenty former government officials with some responsibility for the television case had been hired directly by the Japanese or their lobbying arms in the United States to promote Japanese national interests at the expense of American national interests.

The last remaining American television producer, Zenith, may well be on the ropes. In 1990, Zenith lost $52.3 million on sales of $1.4 billion. In March 1991, Zenith sold 5 per cent of its shares to the Korean company Goldstar to seal a closer manufacturing, technology, research and development, and marketing collaboration between the two companies in a desparate attempt by both to fight off the Japanese behemoths.

STEEL

Reich and Magaziner concisely capture the multiplier effects of Washington's failure to conceive and implement a rational steel policy:

> In the 1950s, US steelmakers produced almost 50 per cent of the world's steel. They had the world's largest, most efficient steel producing facilities. While the US had the world's highest wage rates, it was the world's lowest cost producer of steel, and the world's largest exporter. The combination of high productivity and access to good low cost raw materials gave the US a significant competitive advantage. Today (1980), the US produces only 16 per cent of the total

world steel output and exports less than one-tenth of the amount
exported by the Japanese . . . Declining (steel) productivity has had a
wide ranging impact. US producers of automobiles, appliances, ships,
and other steel-using products have been put at a serious disadvantage
by having to buy higher-priced American steel. In 1977 and 1978,
companies manufacturing cars in the US had to pay 25 to 30 per cent
more for their steel than did their Japanese counterparts.[10]

Unlike their Japanese rivals, American steel manufacturers failed to
invest in new technology such as basic oxygen furnaces and continuous
casting, and had to buy higher priced, poor quality domestic iron-ore
while Japanese firms bought from the cheapest and best quality from
global sources. American steel factories were located in the Great Lakes
region while Japan's were set up on the coasts for easy access to foreign
sources of raw materials and markets.

But was the rapid decline of America's steel industry solely attributable
to a failure to invest in cutting edge technology? Once again, Japan would
probably not have any steel industry, let alone be the world's global
leader, if Tokyo had not designated steel a strategic industry and systematically nurtured it with the familiar range of cartels, technology infusions,
subsidies, trade barriers, and foreign dumping campaigns. Cartels remain
central to the steel industrial policies. The power to create and regulate
cartels dates to 1952 when MITI pushed through the Iron and Steel
Demand Law as a supplement to the Antimonopoly Law. As in many
other strategic industries, the steel industry has been shaped by a series of
five year plans, and steel production has generally exceeded the targets.
Japan's steel industrial plans are made by the Iron and Steel Association,
approved with adjustments by MITI, and then largely implemented by
the Association itself. The Japan Iron and Steel Federation has a typical
three tier pyramid structure. The Big Five steelmakers – Nippon Steel,
Nippon Kotan, Kawasaki Steel, Sumitomo Metals and Kobe Steel – enjoy
80 per cent of the market and dominate the Association. All the Big Five
are keiretsu members with Nippon Steel shared by the Mitsui and
Mitsubishi keiretsu. There are almost 70 firms which have semi-inte-
grated steelmaking and rolling operations, including eight using open
hearth furnaces and over 60 using electric furnaces. Finally, there are
about 170 small rolling mills.

As in virtually all other industries, Japan's steel producers achieved vast
economies of scale through largely uninhibited access to America's huge
market combined with exclusive access to Japan's market. The United
States first imported large amounts of steel in 1959 when a 116 day strike
in the domestic industry forced consumers to look elsewhere. That year
the United States imported 4.4 million tons of steel, or 6.1 per cent of total

sales, and has had a large inbalance in its steel trade ever since. In 1965 foreign producers captured 10.3 per cent of the market, 16.7 per cent in 1969, and have averaged around 15 per cent through today. During this period Japanese imports rose from 17.9 per cent of foreign sales in 1960 to 55.6 per cent in 1976, and have averaged around 40 per cent of the market through today.[11] The importance of the American market to Japanese producers rose steadily from 21 per cent of exports in 1958 to peak at 57 per cent in 1968, and then steadily declined to 17 per cent in 1980 as Japanese producers expanded their exports to all corners of the world.[12]

The eventual result of the rapid surge in Japanese exports to the United States and other countries was a series of "voluntary export restraints" (VERs) imposed on Japanese producers. The United States responded belatedly to this surge of imports, signing its first VER with Japanese and European producers in 1969. The agreement mixed a quota of 5.5 million tons for each with a trigger price mechanism that went off when prices dropped below a certain point, and annual increases in imports of five per cent between 1970 and 1974.

These restrictions were ineffective. In the late 1970s, there was another round of bitter trade negotiations between Tokyo and Washington as American steel producers accused their Japanese rivals of dumping underpriced steel during a recession. Japan's share of foreign imports rose from 48.6 per cent in 1975 to 55.9 per cent in 1976. According to the criteria of the 1974 Trade Act, dumping occurs when the price of imports is lower than production costs, whose "constructed fair value" was estimated to be the full costs plus an eight per cent profit margin. The documentation on Japanese dumping was extensive. In February 1977 Gilmore Steel Corporation filed an antidumping petition claiming that Japanese producers had dumped carbon steel plate to capture huge market shares and drive out American producers. Later that year the American Iron and Steel Institute published a White Paper documenting Japanese dumping. US Steel Corporation filed an antidumping petition in September against six Japanese carbon steel products – an extensive report which cost several million dollars and thousands of manhours to prepare. The Treasury Department then published a preliminary report in October which estimated a 32 per cent dumping margin on Japanese plates, but later downgraded the dumping margin to 7 per cent in March 1978. In October 1977 the Council on Wage Prices and Price Stability also documented massive Japanese steel dumping. In January 1978 the Federal Trade Commission (FTC) finally published its own report revealing a large cost gap between the production costs and selling price of Japanese steel in American markets. As a result, the FTC used the trigger price mechanism to set uniform prices for all importers, whether they had dumped or not. As in other cases of Japanese dumping, Washington's policy of ordering Japanese producers to raise prices simply rewarded them with massive windfall profits after having captured huge market shares. In addition, the Carter Administration in 1977 initiated the trigger-price mechanism for steel imports, which imposed restrictions whenever imported steel fell below a certain price.

The White House quotas and trigger price mechanism did save America's steel industry from what would most assuredly have been its destruction had Japan's dumping campaign continued unhindered. But the steel industry continues to erode under persistent Japanese pressure. Having severely damaged America's steel industry during the 1960s and 1970s through continuous dumping campaigns, Japan then moved in to buy up the pieces during the 1980s. Japanese steel producers are surmounting their 5.8 per cent quota of America's steel market by either forming joint ventures with or outright buying American steel corporations. The joint ventures include NKK Corporation and National Steel Inc., Kobe Steel and USX Corporation, Nisshin Steel and Wheeling Pittburg Steel, Nippon Steel and Inland Steel Inc., Kawasaki Steel and Armco, and Sumitomo Metal and LTV.[13]

Despite their success in undermining America's steel industry, the operating costs of Japan's steel producers are about 20 per cent higher than those of South Korea's steelmakers, the world's lowest cost producer. Meanwhile Japan's share of the American market is officially frozen by the VER at 5.8 per cent, and Japanese steel manufacturers have had trouble fulfilling even this small quota throughout the late 1980s. In 1988, Japan exported 4.1 million tons of steel to the United States, considerably lower than the 5.6 million tons allowed. The major reasons for the decline are the rapid expansion of Japan's domestic economy which the steel industry has had trouble keeping up with and the fact that American steel is now cheaper than Japanese steel.[14]

Japan's import barriers against steel have loosened considerably recently. The steel cartel used to be iron-tight with officials actually tracing the origin of trucks carrying imported steel then boycotting the offender. Japan's huge trading firms still discriminate against steel imports, leaving the field to smaller trading firms with their tiny distribution networks. Since the yen's doubling after 1985, Japan has increasingly imported low-value bulk items like pig iron and steel and steel billets. Japan's exports, meanwhile, declined steadily from 27 million tons in 1987 to 17.555 million in 1990, while it imported 7.555 million tons of crude steel.

Although these challenges will continue to linger, Japan's steel industry will remain one of the world's most efficient and profitable. Massive investments in the most advanced technology will bring costs down and

profits up, even if production remains stagnant or even declines. Diversification will further swell the coffers of the steel corporations as they
become the centers of their own *keiretsu*, all the while enjoying the cozy
relations of membership within one of the Big Six *keiretsu*. Import barriers
– formal and informal– will continue to protect higher value and speciality
steel, although they will be gradually reduced at the lower end of the
market. MITI's industrial policies have been an enormous success in
transforming a weak industry that would have been swept away in a free
market into the world's leader.

America's steel industry, meanwhile, continues to strengthen. It invested $14 billion in new technology over the 1980s and shed dozens of
obsolete facilites. By 1990, America's steel industry had surpassed that of
Japan by several indicators including only 5.3 manhours to produce one
metric ton of cold-rolled steel compared to 5.6 in Japan, and foreign
penetration had fallen from 30 to 19.5 per cent. The average cost of
producing a ton of steel is about $535 in the United States versus $614 in
Japan. Claiming that America's steel industry was now globally competitive, President Bush has vowed not to renew the steel VER which has
held imports at less than 20 per cent of the market since 1984 when it
expires in March 1992.

Yet America's steel industry is still weak. Only about 70 per cent of
America's steel capacity is being utilized, while only 65 per cent of
American producers use the continuous casting method compared to
Japan's 93 per cent. Foreign steelmakers, mostly Japanese, own 19 per
cent of America's steel production. Japan's steelmakers invested over $4
billion in about 30 buyouts or joints ventures in the United States during
the late 1980s. The 1990–91 recession battered America's steel industry. In
the second quarter of 1991, America's Big Six lost an average $28 on each
$430 ton of steel shipped, or a combined total of almost $1 billion. Japan is
still the free world's largest producer with 110.333 million metric tons of
steel output in 1990 compared to 89.918 million for the United States.
American steel's fate rests with the policies of Washington and Tokyo.

MACHINE TOOLS

Few industries match the strategic importance of machine tools. In 1956,
America's machine tool industry, with 75 000 employees and $1.4 billion
in sales, was the world's largest producer and exporter. Three decades
later, in 1986, Japan surpassed the United States to become the world's
largest machine tool producer. Today, about half of the machines sold in
the United States and over 85 per cent of the numerically controlled
machines are Japanese made.

How did this tremendous power shift in the machine tool industry occur? As in most of its other strategic industries, America's machine tool industry has been largely shaped and finally undermined by an irrational industrial policy that combined Pentagon interference and an unreciprocated domestic free market. Washington's export restrictions prevented sales to both the Soviet bloc and American allies. Yet, much of American machine tool technology, including numerical controls, leaked into Japanese and other foreign hands. Japanese and other foreign producers were free to sell and often dump their products in the United States while American producers were locked out of Japan by a web of restrictions including cartels, tariffs, quotas, and regulations.

If Tokyo had relied on a free market to develop its industry, it would not have a machine tool industry; America's comparative advantage in machine tools in the 1950s and 1960s would have wiped out the Japanese industry. Although Japan's machine tool industry, like all other Japanese industries, had always been protected, in March 1957 MITI presented a comprehensive plan for developing the industry. There is considerable controversy over the effectiveness of MITI's machine tool policy, with some arguing that the industry grew in spite of MITI's efforts while others maintain that MITI's hand was decisive.[15] Specific MITI policies may not have been as effective in promoting Japan's machine tools as they were in other industries. Yet the important point is that Japan's machine tool industry would not have survived in a free market. MITI's policies creating or permitting a web of import restrictions, cartels, subsidies, and export incentives allowed the industry to not only survive but become the world leader while simultaneously battering America's industry.

MITI and the Japan Machine Tool Builders Association allocate production and market share for the industry. Import and investment barriers simultaneously protected Japan's machine tool industry and forced foreign manufacturers to sell out their technology. Machine tool imports dropped steadily from 30 – 50 per cent of the market in the 1950s to 5 per cent in 1983. During the 1950s, machine tool manufacturers were actually given import subsidies – matching funds and write-offs – to buy machines necessary to make other machines. After Japanese firms mastered the production of these types of machines, import tariffs were imposed to protect the industry. The tariffs varied according to the perceived importance of the product to Japan's growing industry: machines not produced in Japan were subject to a 10 per cent tariff, those competing with infant Japanese products were slapped with a 15 per cent tariff, while strategic products suffered a 25 per cent tariff. As the industry steadily strengthened, the government slowly reduced these tariffs under persistent foreign pressure. Tariffs ranged from 4 to 7.5 per cent throughout the 1970s and were completely eliminated in 1983.

Foreign technology sales, particularly in numerically controlled (NC) technology, were a vital boost to Japan's machine tool industry; between 1952 and 1981, there were over 160 joint ventures and over 220 technology licensing agreements. Virtually all of Fanuc's (the world's largest machine tool maker) basic technology came from such agreements. In the 1950s and 1960s, MITI used its licensing powers to squeeze out the best deal for Japanese firms. Japanese machine tool makers first made NCs in the early 1960s by copying American designs, but enhanced their value by concentrating on small-scale flexible manufacturing operations, a market ignored by their American rivals. By 1981, NC tools accounted for 51 per cent of total Japanese production.

MITI's decisive contribution was in getting Japan's machine tool-makers to focus on mastering the production of NC tools. According to Sarathy, this government support fortuitously came at just the decisive moment. Working closely together, government and business

> chose a product niche – standardized NC machine tools – where US competition was less well entrenched, developed a low-cost and large volume/scale economies producer position, and then took advantage of a market opportunity – US economic recovery, booming demand for machine tools, and rising backlogs – to supply their product on quick delivery terms; they priced aggressively due to their cost advantage and a favorable yen/dollar exchange rate; sold to a dissatisfied and neglected customer segment, the small US job shops that needed less expensive tools of a standardized and simple nature, with short delivery time, so that the profit opportunities could be exploited; and built up overseas stockpiles and an international distribution network in the US, so as to supply customers in satisfactory manner with both product and after sales-service. Finally, they followed up their market break-throughs in the US by gradually establishing a US manufacturing presense, whether through wholly owned subsidiaries or joint ventures, so as to consolidate their US market gains.[16]

As in other Japanese industries, the machine tool makers achieved vast economies of scale by capturing foreign markets. Exports did not take off until the mid–1970s, peaking at 44 per cent of production in 1978. Japan's market share in high technology numerically controlled tools rose from 5 per cent in 1976 to almost 50 per cent by 1980, and its global market share rose from 13 per cent to 50 per cent in the same period.[17] By the late 1970s exports accounted for more than 40 per cent of production, and 70 per cent of exports were NCs.

This massive dumping campaign was not challenged until 1982, when the American industry recorded its first payments deficit – which came to over $1 billion. The Machine Tool Builders' Association accused Japanese firms of predatory trade tactics including dumping and export cartels organized by Tokyo, and called for import relief. But the American firms lost out not so much from Japanese dumping, as from a combination of the Reagan Administration's high dollar policy which acted like an import subsidy and export penalty, the industry's fragmentation with few firms big enough to resist the Japanese, and the industry's blindness to the NC market. The American industry was fragmented between smaller firms that produced standardized equipment and larger firms that could afford to produce specialized tools. The smaller firms were quickly overrun during Japan's machine tool invasion starting in the late 1970s while the larger firms continued to retreat up market to increasingly specialized products.[18]

On 3 May 1982, Houdaille Industries, a large American producer, filed a dumping petition with the US Trade Representative, detailing Japan's neomercantilist machine tool policy, and requesting that the White House revoke the tax credits which further subsidized the sale of Japanese machine tools in the United States. The Japanese did everything they could to block Houdaille's petition and investigation. Tokyo went so far as to deny a visa to the Houdaille lawyer who was going to develop evidence in Japan.[19]

Once again, the Reagan Administration was torn between the one way free trade ideologues in the Treasury, State, Defense and Justice departments, and the Council of Economic Advisors, and the political economic realists in Commerce and USTR who feared that the destruction of America's machine tool industry would be a severe blow to American national security. Two independent studies both concluded that Tokyo's industrial policies had been mostly responsible for the global power of Japan's machine tool industry.[20] Yet, despite all of this evidence, eight months later, on 22 April 1983, President Reagan, citing his friendship with Nakasone, rejected Houdaille's petition.

Although deeply discouraged by Reagan's indifference to their plight, America's machine tool makers continued to resist the Japanese onslaught. In March 1983, the National Machine Tool Builder's Association petitioned the Commerce Department for protection from Japanese dumping under Section 232 of the Trade Law empowering the President to protect defense industries under foreign attack. The Commerce Department studied the question for a year, then concluded that there were several machine tool sectors, including numerically controlled tools, which should be protected. In 1985, President Reagan finally agreed to negotiate an agreement with Japan's producers rolling back their market share to the fifty per cent conquered in 1983. Tokyo readily agreed to the market share since that would allow Japan's producers to raise prices to recoup earlier losses sustained during their offensive's dumping phase.

As in other Japanese industries, the vast dumping campaign by Japan's machine toolmakers was only the first phase of its strategy to destroy and take over America's machine tool market. In the late 1980s, when the government finally began to respond to the Japanese dumping assaults, Japan's machine toolmakers began setting up screwdriver assembly operations in the United States. The deficit remained just as bad since the Japanese toolmakers would import all the value-added components. This investment rush began in 1987 when major producers such as Okuma Machinery Works Ltd and Hitachi Seiki Co. invested to circumvent a strengthening yen and threats of retaliation. Tokyo's 1988 decision to reduce exports of machining center (MC) and numercially controled (NC) lathes to a 35 per cent market share prompted a second wave of Japanese investments by such Japanese producers as Osaka Kiko Co and Kitamura Machinery Co. It is estimated that the production from Japanese investments in the United States will exceed exports by 1991.[21]

Japan is now the world's leading machine tool maker, a position Tokyo achieved by extending subsidies, protection, and cartels to the industry, which reinforced advantages to the Japanese producers from the American industry's fragmentation and inability to take advantage of new product areas like NCs. Japan's machine tool industry will remain the global leader for the indefinite future. In 1991, MITI renewed the VER limiting Japan's machine tool exports to 50 per cent of America's market. Japan's machine tool market remains tightly closed against competitive imports. In 1989, foreign machine tools were held to a 6 per cent market share in Japan while they made up 50 per cent of Germany's market.[22]

In Fall 1991, the Bush Administration decided not to renew the five year VER on machine tools. There were good arguments against the VER – it simply guaranteed the Japanese producers market share at inflated prices, it gouged consumers, and impeded the advances of Taiwanese, Singaporean and South Korean producers which could compete more fiercely against the Japanese. The quotas did offer a reprieve to the surviving American producers which embarked on a severe cost-cutting campaign. Between 1986 to 1991, American machine tool revenue rose from $2.7 billion to $2.9 billion, exports from $520 million to $910 million, while employment in the industry dropped from 68 000 to 60 000. Yet, the future of America's machine tool industry is bleak. Japanese already enjoy a 50 per cent market share for the computerized lathes and machining centers which represent the high technology end of the industry, and their domination will deepen into the future. Japan's machine tool policy was highly successful and America's an abject failure.

AUTOMOBILES

Japan's growth into the world's greatest automobile producer was extremely rapid. In 1951, the United States produced 76 per cent of the world's vehicles – over 8 million vehicles compared to Japan's production of only 38 490! Japan first surpassed West Germany to become the world's second largest automobile producer in 1974. Two years later in 1976, stimulated by foreign, and particularly American, demand for small cars following the 1973 oil crisis, exports reached 50 per cent of Japan's automobile production. In 1980, Japan surpassed the United States as the world's largest automobile manufacturer and accounted for 25 per cent of American's total automobile market and 67 per cent of all imports. That year Japan produced 11 042 884 units and the United States only 6 377 667 units, down 25 per cent since 1979.[23] Japan has held the "number one" title ever since. In 1989, Japan produced 13.2 million vehicles of which it exported 5.5 million while the Americans produced only 10.1 million of which they exported 668 000. Five of the world's top ten automobile firms are Japanese, lead by Toyota at number one and Nissan at number three.

How did Japan's automobile industry grow so rapidly? Although every one of Japan's eleven automobile firms in the 1980s except Honda was founded before 1945, a Japanese automobile industry would never have survived either before or after 1945 without massive government protection, subsidies, forced foreign technology transfers and cartels. Import barriers were probably the most important factor; Japan's automobile industry was saved from destruction by low priced imports in both the 1930s and 1950s.

Yet, Tokyo's targeting of the automobile industry was not inevitable. Throughout the late 1940s, Japan's economic policymakers were split over whether to develop or abandon the automobile industry. The opposing arguments were most clearly articulated at a policy council meeting on 13 September 1949. Bank of Japan President Ichimada championed the free trade cause by arguing that "since Japan should develop its trade on the basis of an international division of labor, efforts to develop the automobile industry would be futile. As we can get inexpensive motor vehicles of excellent quality from the United States, why don't we rely on them".[24] MITI countered with the neomercantilist argument that "since development of the automobile industry to a high level will lead to the modernization of the machinery industry and, consequently, all other industries, it is desirable to concentrate all possible efforts on raising its productivity and international competitiveness so that it can catch up with other advanced nations and can contribute to the growth of our national economy".[25]

MITI won. At the time, however, MITI's victory seemed hollow since Japan's economy remained depressed and its automobile industry barely alive. The Korean War saved Japan's automobile manufacturers from an uncertain and possibly bleak future. Between July 1950 and February 1951, the United States ordered 7079 trucks worth $13 million from Japanese firms to use in the Korean War, an infusion of capital and scale economics which proved to be decisive to the revival of Japan's automobile industry.[26] On the day the Korean War began, Toyota Motor Sales Company President Kamiya Shotaro arrived in the United States in hopes of salvaging his foundering firm by negotiating a tie up with the powerful Ford Motor Company of Detroit. Ford expressed only a moderate interest in the offer and the Defense department opposed cooperation as a diversion from domestic production. However, the flood of subsequent procurement orders proved to be, in Kamiya's words, "Toyota's salvation". The company's profits from truck orders and development of new production techniques allowed it to resume profitable passenger car production on a national and then international basis.[27]

MITI's industrial policy took full advantage of the Korean War procurements and nurtured Japan's automobile industry into a global giant over the next three decades with a range of subsidies, import barriers, cartels, technology infusions, and export incentives. MITI understood that a dynamic automobile industry depends on an equally dynamic automobile parts industry. The parts industry was designated a strategic industry by the 1956 Machinery Industry Promotion Act. MITI's goal was to reduce production costs by 20 per cent from 1956 to 1960, to be achieved through a 1.8 billion yen JDB loan, further subsidies and tariff waivers on purchases of vital foreign machinery, and the grouping of subcontractors with one key manufacturer. Between 1951 to 1971, over 300 technology licensing agreements were signed with foreign manufacturers, with American producers accounting for 54.2 per cent.[28] As a result of these policies, Japan's automobile industry is structured along the classic three tier pyramid of almost all other Japanese industries. The manufacturers sit atop a small army of subcontractors, which in turn subcontract some of their work to even smaller manufacturers. In 1971, Toyota had 202 members of its subcontractor association, Nissan 115, Toyo Kogyo 88, Mitsubishi 337, Isuzu 231, Fuji Heavy 162, Daihatsu 180, Hino 164, Suzuki 82 and Nissan Diesel 64.[29] The clubs meet twice a year during which time the automobile manufacturer sets the part cost reductions for the upcoming year. If any subcontractor fails to abide by the price reduction order, it loses membership and business.

Cartels remain an important industrial policy tool. These cartels are administered by the Japan Automobile Industrial Association and Japan

Small Automobile Industry Association. Perhaps the best indicator of the degree to which Japan's markets are carefully managed by cartels is the comparison of the market shares of Japanese producers at home and abroad. In 1987, Toyota sold 1 876 000 cars in Japan for a 54 per cent market share, Nissan 1 028 000 for a 30 per cent market share, and Honda trailed with 547 000 or a 16 per cent share. The lock of Toyota and Nissan on the best marketing locations in Japan explains much of this discrepancy. Honda's 2400 dealers and 8200 salesmen are a David against the Goliath of Toyota's 4000 dealers and 41 000 salemen. Honda, however, was the number one Japanese manufacturer in America's free market with 738 000 units sold for a 39 per cent share, Toyota followed with 630 000 or 33 per cent share, and Nissan sold 547 000 or 28 per cent share.[30]

A web of import barriers protected Japan's automobile industry from competitive imports. As in other industries, Tokyo gradually reduced its overt trade barriers under steady foreign pressure, but only in areas in which Japanese firms had acquired a comparative advantage. The first "liberalization" occurred when Tokyo removed its restrictions on foreign buses and trucks in April 1961 as part of the admission price it was negotiating to eventually enter the OECD in 1964. In 1965, it removed similar restrictions on passenger cars. The average tariffs on motor vehicle imports was reduced from from 35 per cent in 1967, to 8 per cent in 1972, and all tariffs were removed in 1978. Meanwhile, in 1970, Tokyo finally agreed to allow foreign car manufacturers to invest in Japan while in 1971 it supposedly allowed foreign parts makers free access. These "market opening steps" had absolutely no effect on foreign car sales in Japan which rose slightly from 1 per cent in 1977 to 1.3 per cent in 1979, then dropped to 0.7 per cent between 1981 and 1983. In 1988, foreign automobile manufacturers captured only a miniscule 2.5 per cent market share despite the yen's doubling in value over the previous three years.

In reality, little had changed; the overt barriers were dropped while even more powerful nontariff barriers were bolstered behind the scenes. Japan's sole agent system prevents foreign manufacturers from exporting directly to buyers, since only registered agents can file import applications. In 1989, only 180 of 3206 maker-affiliated dealers in Japan imported foreign cars. Most of the import dealers are associated with Suzuki and Isuzu, which both have joint ventures with General Motors – more than 60 per cent of Isuzu's dealers and 30 per cent of Suzuki are selling General Motors cars.[31] These agents are organized in the Japan Automobile Importers Association, which was founded "to establish orderly and cooperative marketing in import transactions so as to promote the development of the automobile import business".[32] In reality, the association acts as an import cartel, ultimately subject to MITI's administrative guidance. Although 51 import firms are members of the association, half the market is controlled by four firms – Yanase, Kintetsu Motors, Toho Motors, and New Empire Motors. Like other importers, the Automobile Importers Association has a vested interest in taking huge markups off a low volume with broadly agreed upon market shares. Commodity and weight taxes are designed to severely discriminate against foreign firms, and were only revised in 1989.

As if the sole agent system were not debilitating enough, foreign automobile manufacturers face a bewildering web of other nontariff barriers. In a classic "catch-22" regulation which Japanese officials have developed into a high art, each imported car must be individually inspected unless the sales volume is comparable to a domestic make, at which time a type certificate can be issued. It was only in 1988 that Tokyo changed its regulated insurance rates that severely discriminated against foreign automobiles. Of course, because of these and other nontariff barriers, it is impossible for any foreign automobile to achieve any significant market share since the average price is pushed up two to three times that same car's price in free third markets. As in other industries, the dynamism of Japan's automobile industry has depended on the scale economies acheived through massive exports. Even before OPEC's quadrupling of oil prices stimulated the explosion of demand for the small, fuel efficient cars at which the Japanese excelled, exports rose steadily throughout the 1960s. Between 1961 and 1971, passenger car exports grew 113 times, from 11 500 to 1 300 000, while exports of other types of vehicles rose 12 times from 44 500 to 480 000, an annual growth rate of 60.6 per cent and 27.7 per cent, respectively. In 1971 Japan's shares of exports in total production was 34.9 per cent, less than West Germany's 60.6 per cent, France's 47.6 per cent, Britain's 36.1 per cent, or Italy's 36.1 per cent. But each of those countries had to export more because they only had half Japan's domestic market size, and the common market did not assure a captured home market. As in Japan's other industries, most of these exports went to the vast, wide-open American market. In 1971, the United States absorbed 50.3 per cent of Japan's exports, which captured a 6.7 per cent share of a 9 729 000 unit market and 44.6 per cent of foreign passenger imports of 1 466 000 units. As a percentage of Japan's total value of exports, motor vehicles climbed from from 0.3 per cent ($6 353 000) in 1955 to 9.9 per cent in 1971 ($2.37 billion), following iron and steel 14.7 per cent and textiles 11.5 per cent.[33]

Despite these gains, Japan's automobile industry might still not have overtaken that of the United States and dominated world markets without OPEC's quadrupling of oil prices which led millions of Americans to switch from big American gas-guzzlers to small fuel efficient Japanese models. Between 1973 and 1981, the global automobile trade was truly zero-sum, with one producer's gains offset by the loss of others. Of the world's major motor vehicle makers, only Japan produced more cars during this period – all others lost market share. Japan's share of total world production increased from 18 to 30 per cent, with its exports tripling from 2.1 million to almost 6 million units. In 1981 Japan's producers accounted for 41 per cent of world exports; excluding the intra-North American or European trade, Japanese exports were 71 per cent of world exports.[34]

As in Japan's other successful export industries, dumping played an important role in the ability of Japan's automobile industry to conquer foreign markets. Euphemistically described as the "bleeding export" or "export that makes no profit", Japan's auto executives were quite candid about using dumping to capture huge chunks of the American market, with automobiles priced at least 20 per cent below those in their domestic market.[35] Detroit retreated upmarket with the Japanese in hot pursuit. After capturing the small car market and enjoying its huge economies of scale in the mid–1970s, the Japanese producers have steadily marched upmarket to compete in virtually every automobile category.

And, as in its other targeted industries, Japan's neomercantilist policies of maximizing automobile exports and minimizing imports threatened to undermine the global automobile market. Dunn writes that "the extent of liberalism in the auto trade regime depends on the relationship between how fast Japan learns to play by the rules and how much political leverage the West is willing to apply to affect the speed and extent of Japan's learning process".[36]

By the late 1970s, America's automobile industry was on the ropes, having plunged from $5.6 billion in profits in 1978 to a $3.9 billion loss in 1980, of which General Motors lost $750 million, Ford $1.5 billion, and Crysler $1.7 billion – the largest ever loss for a US corporation. These losses resulted from domestic sales dropping 30 per cent from 9.3 million units to 6.2 million, with sales down 33 per cent for General Motors, and 24 per cent for Ford and Crysler. The industry altogether lost 500 000 jobs in parts, steel, and other supplies. In the zero-sum trade war, America's loss directly translated into Japan's gain – Japanese sales increased from 800 000 units in 1975 to almost 2 million in 1980; by February 1981 they had captured 24 per cent of market.[37] On 12 June 1980 the United Auto Workers filed a petition with the United States Trade Representative (USTR) for temporary import relief under Section 201 of 1974 Trade Act, followed on 4 August 1980 by a similar petition by Ford. The USTR turned down both petitions.

This economic disaster and the relief petitions it spawned posed a political and philosophical challenge for the newly elected Reagan Administration which was dedicated to keeping American markets open at all costs. Any further American losses would sink the economy into recession, which would ravage the Administration's popularity rating and allow the Democrat controlled Congress to block key provisions of the "Reagan revolution". Clearly some restraints had to be imposed but without a favorable USTR ruling the President was unauthorized to issue an orderly marketing agreement.

During March and April, the Reagan Administration negotiated a "voluntary export restraint" with Japan. Tokyo announced on 1 May 1981 that it would voluntarily restrict automobile exports to the United States for the next three years at 1.68 million units a year beginning 1 April 1981. Eventually the VER was extended for a fourth year. Belying Tokyo's claims that it had no power over business, MITI administered the quota by issuing written directives to each automaker stating the maximum number of exports allowed. The individual quotas were based on that firm's market shares for the previous two years. The directive was backed up with the threat to deny export licenses under Foreign Trade Control Law and Article IV of the Establishment Law, both of which give MITI the power to restrict or prohibit exports or imports.

The quotas allowed both Japanese and American producers to enjoy billions of dollars in windfall profits at the expense of American consumers, who paid an estimated $4.3 billion extra each year as prices were raised $400. Japanese manufacturers scooped up an extra $1000 for every car sold. Detroit's carmakers went from record loss to record profits while the import share dropped from 28 to 23 per cent.[38] On 1 March 1985, President Reagan, citing the "wisdom of maintaining free and fair trade for the benefit of the world's consumers", announced that his Administration would not ask Tokyo to renew its "VER" of 1.85 million automobiles to the United States.[39] Given the mountainous profits Japan's automobile makers were banking, it was hardly surprising when MITI announced later that month that it would continue to restrict exports, but at a higher level of 2.3 million units.

Japan's automobile industry continued to expand despite these American and European restrictions and the doubling of the yen's value between 1985 and 1988. In 1988, Japanese carmakers exported 6.3 million units while selling 6.0 million at home. Over half of Japan's exports went to the United States, 20 per cent to Europe and 10 per cent to East and Southeast Asia. The short-term strategy was to hold on to market share at all costs while maintaining prices, cutting costs, and opening new markets elsewhere. Meanwhile, the automobile producers began opening both assembly and parts plants in their most important foreign markets. This strategy of "Japanese investment in the manufacturing industries of advanced countries . . . is designed to secure markets previously acquired through exports and avoid protectionism".[40]

During the 1980s, eight of Japan's eleven automakers opened plants in the United States. Although the transplants were originally welcomed as a way to cut America's trade deficit with Japan and preserve American jobs, the effect has actually been the opposite. Japan's foreign investment strategy has been described as a "Trojan horse" whereby "Japanese plants in America are for stamping and final assembly. Basic manufacturing will remain in Japan, as will high value-added operations such as engineering and research and development. Under present plans no Japanese producer will have even 50 per cent domestic content. This fits the broad pattern of Japanese foreign investments".[41] These investments are beachheads in which the assembly and parts manufacturers squeeze out local producers and inspire even greater Japanese imports. In the United States, the Japanese have set up 10 plants which are highly automated, efficient, and mostly nonunionized. The result is an average 10 per cent cost advantage ($700) over Detroit. It is estimated that every Japanese automobile produced in the United States will displace one imported and two Detroit automobiles. Japanese "transplants" took 12.9 per cent of the market in 1989, up from 8.6 per cent in 1988, with that share expected to expand steadily in the future.[42] The eight Japanese assembly plants that opened in the United States in the 1980s were offset by the closure of eight American owned plants between 1987 and 1990. Between 1985 and 1988 the number of unionized automobile workers dropped from 596 000 to 525 000.[43] Some of Japan's producers have promised to export automobiles from their American transplants back to Japan by the mid–1990s: Honda claims it will export 50 000, Toyota 40 000, and Mazda 60 000.[44] The US Ambassador to Japan, Michael Armacost, remains skeptical of these promises. Armacost fears they are simply yet another Japanese public relations stunt and warns he will wait until "the cash registers start ringing" in Japan before he expresses pleasure at the promises.[45] By 1991, the Japanese will produce 2.9 million automobiles in the United States on top of 2 million direct exports. This would raise Japan's market share from its 1988 share of 22 per cent to 30 per cent.[46]

There is considerable evidence that Japanese automobile manufacturers have engaged in extensive racist and sexist hiring practices at their American plants. On 24 March 1988, the Equal Opportunity Commission announced that Honda had agreed to pay 370 blacks and women $6 million in back pay in penalty for discriminating against them. Honda may not be an isolated example of discriminatory practices by Japanese firms. A study by Robert Cole and Donald Deskins found that Japanese firms, in contrast to American automobile firms, consistently had a lower percentage of blacks employed than would be expected from the local labor market, and these employment patterns may well be conscious discrimination by Japan's automobile executives.[47] At Honda's Marysville plant, only 2.8 per cent of the workforce is black when 10.8 per cent would be employed if no discrimination occurred; Nissan's plant has 14 per cent black employees of 19 per cent expected; and Mazda's only 14.1 per cent of 29 per cent expected. At 91 Japanese assembly and parts plants surveyed, blacks made up only 8.5 per cent of 11.7 per cent expected given the local population.[48] Black ownership of Japanese automobile dealerships fare even worse. Although about 12 per cent of Americans are black, only eight of the over 5000 Japanese automobile dealerships were owned by blacks, including one of Nissan's (0.1 per cent of the total) and three of Toyota's (0.3 per cent of the total). Of American automobile producers, Ford has 170 minority owned dealerships (3.4 per cent of their total), and GM has 204 (2 per cent of the total).[49]

Meanwhile American partsmakers are losing business with the American automobile manufacturers since the Japanese simply buy from each other. The autoparts market is worth $200 billion, larger than the $175.2 billion automobile market in 1987, and Japan's partsmakers have already captured 25 per cent of it.[50] The wave of Japanese partsmaking investments started in the mid–1980s when the yen strengthened. Although few Japanese parts investors have been able to turn a profit, they are steadily pushing American partsmakers out of business. In 1988, American – produced Japanese cars had an average domestic content of 38 per cent compared to 88 per cent for the Big Three. About 90 per cent of the parts and components that go into cars manufactured by the transplants come from Japan or from Japanese-owned suppliers with factories in the United States. Japanese partsmakers are not only supplying Japanese producers but are wooing America's automobile manufacturers as well. In 1987, Nippondenso alone sold $350 million in parts to the Big Three, up from $60 million in 1983. Stanley Electric Co. is selling to all three American manufacturers, which in 1990 accounted for 30 per cent of its American sales of $83 million.[51] There are currently over 240 Japanese parts manufacturers in the United States employing 41 000 workers, none of whom belong to the United Automobile Workers Union.[52] The transplants actually exacerbate the trade deficit since the cost of importing all the parts is more than a finished automobile.

As Japan's partsmakers rose, America's fell. The number of American partmakers steadily declined by 500 over the 1980s to 2225 at present while between 1985 and 1988 the number of unionized automobile workers dropped from 596 000 to 525 000. The General Accounting Office reported on 24 November 1990, that, because of their greater efficiency and tendency to buy from Japan's components producers, Japan's automobile manufacturers in the United States cost Americans 25 000 jobs in 1988 and 11 000 in 1989. Japan's factories in the United

States produced 1 131 000 cars in 1989, an activity which produced 66 000 jobs but displaced 77 000 other jobs, for a net loss of 11 000 that year, and bought only 50.5 per cent of their components from American sources. The auto part deficit is expected to reach $22 billion in 1994.[53]

Joint ventures between American and Japanese partsmakers have proved to be a Trojan horse whereby Japanese soon take over that industry as they have in virtually every other industry: the "alliance" dissolves as soon as Japanese manufacturers have milked it to master what little technology remains to the Americans. Of the 126 American auto part manufacturers that formed joint ventures with the Japanese, almost all are losing money and technology to their rivals.[54] Harsh complaints by American partners abound, such as the Japanese "buy Japanese" policy whereby they insisted that the American partner continue to import products from Japan even after the yen doubled in value between 1985 and 1987. One disillusioned American executive bitterly pointed out that joint ventures boil down to "How can you help us take over your market".[55]

Toyota claims that 60 per cent of the parts used in cars manufactured in the United States are locally produced, although only 1 or 2 per cent of the parts it uses in cars made in Japan are foreign made. On 30 October 1990, Toyota gathered 100 executives of American automobile parts manufacturers and severely condemned them for higher prices and defective parts "100 times" higher than Japanese partsmakers. Toyota contrasts the failure rate of 1000 of 1 million (0.10 per cent) of all American parts compared to only 10 of 1 million of Japanese parts (0.001 per cent). The American executives later quietly argued that Toyota's claims were greatly exaggerated.[56]

American parts manufacturers have been pressuring Japan's auto giants to follow GM's lead and make 75 per cent of their purchase from American plants. Honda's local content is typical for Japan's transplants. In 1989, only 20 per cent of the parts in Hondas built in America were from American producers, while about 48 per cent were imported and 32 per cent came from Japanese producers who had set up shop in the United States. Nissan made the news in September 1990 when it agreed to purchase 100 000 fuel injection pumps from Toyota's Nippondenso to supply its Tennessee factory, thus marking the first time it had not bought parts from one of its own subcontractors. Nissan's purchase from Nippondenso's plant in neighboring South Carolina rather than one of its Japan-based subsidiaries at once scored public relations points and saved the company the transportation costs of its own parts from Japan.[57]

Japan's automobile makers have proven just as adept as their counterparts in other Japanese industries in arm-twisting the White House into surrendering yet more concessions. For example, starting in spring 1988, Tokyo began a campaign to prevent the Customs Commission from its intention of shifting its classification of certain Japanese vehicles from that of automobiles subject to a 2.5 per cent tariff to light trucks subject to a 25 per cent tariff. Tokyo convinced two Congressmen with heavy Japanese investments in their districts – Jame Inofe and William Dannemeyer – to sponsor a petition to then Commissioner of Customs, William von Raab, to stop the designation change. By July 1988, more than thirty Representatives and eleven Senators had signed the petition and sent it to Customs, and van Raab himself was called to Capitol to justify the change. Meanwhile, Tokyo hired several lobbying firms to pressure the administration to prevent the change. Reasoning that the light trucks were clearly light trucks, the Customs Commission ruled on 4 January 1989 that they could not be classified as cars. Tokyo did not give up but instead pushed for a reversal of the policy at a group of seven leading industrial nation finance minister meeting later that month. US Treasury Secretary, Nicholas Brady, meekly complied with the pressure and promised to suspend the ruling. But to kill any possibility of it being enacted, Tokyo's Washington lobby met with the White House and related departments while Japanese automobile makers and American importers launched a massive public relations campaign. As always when Washington attempted to favor American over Japanese interests, Tokyo hinted broadly that the ruling could damage bilateral ties. In early February, the Treasury Department not only agreed to classify the trucks as automobiles, but to allow them to be reclassified as trucks for sale once they were in the United States in order for them to meet government fuel efficiency, emmissions, and safety requirements. As a result, The US Treasury was denied an annual $500 million in extra tariffs – a not inconsiderable sum given Washington's need to finance its deficit, American manufacturers were hit with even more unfair competition, and Tokyo as usual was "neither forced nor asked to make a single trade concession of its own".[58]

Japanese producers claim that they won fair and square, that America's car makers simply did not try hard enough and made inferior products. Until recently, American quality control was a severe problem. As late as 1988, an extensive survey of 30 000 new American car owners revealed that there were 1.44 of every Japanese car, up from 1.29 in 1987, compared for 1.76 of 100 American cars, down from 177, and 259 for every 100 European cars, up from 1.90.[59]

Japan's automobile industry will steadily grow more powerful for the indefinite future while America's industry just as steadily weakens. Japan's global automobile capacity soared from 10 million units in 1979 to 17 million in 1991 including 1.7 million in the United States, and is expected to rise to 19 million worldwide in 1995. The result will be increased trade tensions as this excess production is dumped overseas. There is plenty of room for Japanese producers to grow at home while the opportunities for growth abroad are virtually limitless. Japanese producers will continue to enjoy 97.5 per cent of Japan's huge market while Japan's foreign trade investment policies will rapidly take over foreign markets. In 1991, Japan's automobile giants held a 31 per cent share of America's market, of which 18 per cent are exports and 13 per cent transplants. Honda enjoyed a 9.3 per cent market share, higher than both Chrysler's 9.2 per cent and Toyota's 9.1 per cent shares.[60] Although Japan's annual exports to the United States have dropped from 2.6 million in the early 1980s to 1.6 million at present, an increasing amount of Japanese cars are being produced at factories set up in the United States. Japanese automobile makers continue to expand production despite an ever-growing global glut in manufacturing. In 1990, Nissan and Honda added facilities for 240 000 additional automobiles, Toyota for 120 000, and Mazda for 150 000.[61]

Japan exports about 55 per cent of its production, and those exports plus transplants will steadily take over foreign markets. Japan's automobile manufacturers reached a 31 per cent share of America's market in 1990, a share that is expected to steadily increase to 35 per cent over the decade.[62] Japan's automobile hegemony is clearly one of MITI's greatest success stories.

In the zero sum game of international trade, Japan's gains mean American losses. In 1990, the United States suffered a $31 billion automobile trade deficit, of which one-fourth of that amount was parts. America's Big Three automobile makers collectively dropped $3.7 billion into the red in 1990–91, while the industry was using only 60–65 per cent of capacity. Despite these losses, only Chrysler has petitioned the White House for across-the-board relief – Ford and GM claim they can make it on their own. However, on 2 June 1991, the Big Three American automobile makers filed a joint petition with the Commerce Department and USTR accusing Japan's producers with dumping minivans in the United States. This was the first time that the Big Three ever filed a joint dumping petition.

America's automobile industry is teetering on the brink of collapse. If Japanese automobiles capture a 40 per cent market share, Chrysler will be bankrupted and Ford mortally wounded. The Bush Administration has ignored the plight of America's automobile industry. President Bush rejected a plea by Chrysler's President Lee Iacocca to cut Japan's truck and car exports by 500 000 just to maintain their 31 per cent market share for 18 months or until America's automobile makers "regain their footing". Chrysler also pleaded with Mitsubishi to buy a $300 million stake in their Diamond Star Motors joint venture in Illinois, which would reduce Chrysler's equity stake from 50 per cent to 25 per cent, as well as a stake in Chrysler Financial Corporation. Chrysler is also considering selling off its remaining 11 per cent stake in Mitsubishi, already down from its previous 25 per cent peak, Mitsubishi, however, has let Iacocca twist in the wind in retaliation for his previous criticism of Japanese neomercantilism. A Nissan spokesman expressed Japan's view when he said: "He (Iacocca) talks so long about how America can live without Japan. Maybe he should try it".[63]

The automobile parts industry is just as vulnerable and dependent as the automobile industry. In 1990, Japan exported $11.4 billion in parts to the United States while American producers exported only $893 million to Japan! Japan's parts surplus is expected to rise to $22 billion by 1994. The industry's two associations, the Motor Equipment Manufacturers Association (MEMA) and the Auto Parts Advisory Committee (APAC), are split over whether to pressure the White House to retaliate against Japan's neomercantilist policies. MEMA wants to continue turning a blind eye against Japanese neomercantilism, fearing that an outcry would cause the Japanese to retaliate against what few sales the Americans already have. APAC asked the White House on 22 June 1991 to use Section 301 of the Trade Law to retaliate against Japanese parts dumping in the United States and web of barriers in Japan. The Bush Administration refuses to act without a united front of American parts manufacturers. The White House policy on auto parts may well be shaped by the fact that one of President Bush's senior campaign advisors, James Lake, is a lobbyist for the Japan Auto Parts Industry. Another senior Bush advisor, Charles Black, was an advisor to Eitaro Itoyama, an LDP Dietman.

The Bush administration finally succumbed to the automobile industry's persistent pressure when it invited the Big Three presidents to join the entourage to Tokyo in December 1991. While the President attended various diplomatic functions, heated negotiations took place between Japanese and American negotiators on a range of trade issues, including automobiles and auto parts. Tokyo finally promised to "encourage" its automobile products promised annually to help sell 200 000 American cars in Japan, double their imports of American car parts to $19.1 billion by 1994, and raise the domestic content of their American transplants from 50 per cent to 70 per cent.

How significant were these agreements? Even if Tokyo should fulfill its promise, always an uncertain prospect, it is questionable how many American firms will actually benefit from the increased sales. Japanese autoparts' transplants will likely gobble up virtually all of the business. But, as expected, Tokyo backpeddled from its "promises" shortly after Bush and his delegation returned to the United States. On January 20, 1992, Prime Minister Miyazawa announced that his government had not made a commitment to buying more American parts and automobiles, they had simply made a forecast.

Tokyo tacked with the winds once again on March 19, 1992 when it extended what it hoped would be a campaign present to President Bush who was sinking rapidly in the polls. As of April 1, MITI would lower its quota on Japanese exports to the United States from 2.3 to 1.65 million. This may seem like a significant drop to those unfamiliar with the Japanese or the trade deficit. The reality, as always, is quite different. Japan's automobile exports to the United States in 1991 were 1.76 million so that with the new target, exports would at most drop 110 000 units. But Japan can more than make up for any lost imports with more sales from its transplants in the United States, and of course more sales of auto parts to those transplants. Japan's total automobile share will remain at least 36 per cent. With classic Japanese sophistry, Tokyo hoped to kill two birds with one stone, giving the illusion of significantly cutting back Japanese exports and thus helping President Bush get re-elected while all along Japan's automobile share would remain the same, or even expand.

Three-quarters of America's deficit with Japan continues to be in automobiles or auto parts. In 1991, Japan imported only 35 000 American cars, of which 20 000 came from Japanese transplants in the United States. While American automobiles were confined to 0.3 per cent of Japan's market, Japan's market share of the United States, included joint venture transplants, exceeds 36 per cent! Ironically, Japan's automobile industry could never have survived, let alone become the global champion, if Washington had insisted that bilateral trade relations be based on reciprocity. Instead, Washington continued to allow Japanese manufacturers virtually unlimited access to America's market while tolerating Japan's vast web of trade barriers. Washington failed to devise rational trade and industrial policies to counter those of Japan. As a result, Japan's hegemony over the global automobile and other markets will only deepen in the decades ahead.

AGRICULTURE

Japan's industrial policies have in part rested on forcing its consumers to subsidize its producers through high prices. Import barriers and cartels extract from consumers prices sometimes two or three times world prices for even the most basic goods and services. No Japanese industry is more carefully protected than agriculture. Tokyo forces Japanese to spend over 35 per cent of their disposable income on food compared to 20 per cent for Americans. In 1987 Japanese consumers paid an estimated $65 billion more than world market prices for their food, a subsidy equal to four per cent of personal consumption. About 60 to 70 per cent of all agricultural products receive price supports. A United States Department of Agriculture report found that Tokyo's trade barriers on eight major food products were as high as 2 per cent of GNP.[64] Despite the yen's doubling in value since 1985, Japanese still pay five to seven times the world prices for rice, beef, and grain. If Tokyo opened its agriculture markets, Japanese would enjoy at least 15 percentage points of income with which to either spend or save, thus vastly stimulating both the domestic and world economy.

Tokyo is unlikely to genuinely open its agriculture markets despite continuing pressure by Washington. The LDP's most solid electoral pillar of support rests in the countryside – about 200 of the 445 LDP Dietmembers come from predominately rural districts. The Occupation land reforms converted Japan's perennially exploited, resentful peasants into middle class, conservative farmers, while the electoral district lines have remained unchanged since they were first drawn in the late 1940s when Japan's cities were emptied and countryside filled with refugees. The result is the most iron of political triangles. LDP politicians are continually re-elected from Japan's overrepresented rural electoral districts with the promise to continue protecting farmers, specific protection and subsidies are mapped out by the Ministry of Agriculture, Forestry, and Fisheries (MAFF), while Japan's farmers keep up the pressure by being tightly organized into the national lobbying federation (*Zenno*). For the LDP to accede to Washington's demands for open agriculture markets would be to commit political suicide.

And, anyway, Japanese consumers actually support high food prices – surveys consistently reveal that between 70–75 per cent of Japanese consumers do not mind paying higher prices to protect Japanese agriculture.[65] These attitudes are in part shaped by the prominent publication of statistics that show Japan's food self-sufficiency ratio dropped from 90 per cent in 1960 to about 65 per cent today, while the country has a severe trade imbalance in agricultural goods – in 1989, Japan imported $29.671 billion and exported only $1.646 billion, a deficit of $28.035 billion. But these attitudes are also shaped by a systematic government public relations campaign that equates many imported food products with a foreign invasion. Over one third of Japan's consumer groups are actually fronts for agriculture and industry and keep up a steady drumbeat in the minds of Japanese that import barriers protect Japan's culture as well as economic livelihood from foreign infection.

Although Japan's food markets remain tightly protected, there have been considerable changes in Japanese agriculture over the past two generations. In 1960, there were over 15 million farmers on 6.1 million farms; in 1988 there were less than 6 million farmers on 4.3 million farms. About 92 per cent are part-time farmers, and over 75 per cent of all farmers receive the bulk of their income from other sources. The average farm family enjoyed savings of 1 million yen on a total income of 9 million yen, of which only 2.9 million came from farming. As a result of double cropping, greater productivity, and urbanization the total planted area decreased from 8.1 million hectares in 1960 to 5.7 million in 1977.[66] Although only 8 per cent of all farmers, full-time farmers produce nearly 70 per cent of all livestock and 65 per cent of all vegetables, but only 20 per cent of the rice, while their average farm size is 2.3 hectares or twice the size of that of part-time farmers. Because of the high financial returns, relative ease in growing and harvesting, and guaranteed market most part-time farmers concentrate on rice farming.[67] The farm population is steadily aging as young people migrate to more desirable jobs and lifestyles in the cities.

Yet, agriculture's iron triangle remains virtually impregnable for several reasons. Although the number of farm families fell from 30.1 million in 1965 to 19.2 million in 1988, one out of six Japanese is still at least partially dependent on the farm economy.[68] Less than 1 per cent of Japan's workforce are full-time farmers with an additional 7 per cent part-time farmers, yet about 20 per cent of the electoral districts, 30 per cent of the Diet seats, and 200 of the LDP's 445 Diet members are agrarian-based. The farm lobby continually warns the LDP that any genuine food import liberalization could result in the loss of 80 seats in the next election. The LDP is thought to have already lost 30 seats through its limited orange and beef liberalization.[69]

No Japanese industry is as thoroughly cartelized as agriculture. There are four separate, complementary national farmers co-operatives: the National Federation of Agricultural Co-operative Associations (Zenno), the National Farm Co-operative Bank (Noringinko), the Central Union of Agricultural Co-operatives (Zenchu), and the National Chamber of Agriculture. With 7.7 million members organized into 57 prefectural unions, and over 7000 local farm co-operatives (nokyo), Zenno is the largest of these national farm federations, and by controlling the production and marketing of almost all rice, 90 per cent of vegetables and fruit, 80 per cent of eggs, pork and beef, and providing farmers with 90 per cent of their fertilizer and feed, 75 per cent of their pesticides and machinery, and even 70 per cent of their consumer durables, has actually formed Japanese agriculture into a vast cartel.[70] In addition, Zenno helps the Nokyo to export farm products and import required energy, fertilizer, chemicals and technology. The scale of these activities makes Zenno Japan's sixth largest trading company. Noringinko is Japan's second biggest bank; only the postal savings system has a larger pool of savings. The bank extends credit to farmers and funds local infrastructure projects. While Zenno dominates farm production and marketing, and Noringinko finance, Zenchu is agriculture's powerful political arm. Zenchu's lobbying branch is Noseiren, whose efforts revolve around pressuring the various

Dietmen and party agricultural committees. For example, in early July of each year during the rice price deliberation, Noseiren mobilizes thousands of farmers in mass demonstrations in Tokyo in favor of higher subsidies, and throughout the year organizes similar mass protests to pressure the government not to give in to foreign market opening demands. Finally, the National Chamber of Agriculture has branches in every city, town, and village throughout Japan, and, among other activities, aids joint ventures between the nokyo and local business.

Almost every farm family in Japan is a member of a local nokyo, which consists of 50 to 100 farm households, and performs such economic functions as the allocation of irrigation water or equipment and such political functions as mobilizing voters behind the LDP during elections. There are both multipurpose and specialized nokyo. Multipurpose nokyo help their members market, purchase and process agricultural products, and extend credit, insurance, warehousing and technology. Specialized nokyo usually promote a particular product such as rice, beef, or citrus. In addition to these functions nokyo also help administer government programs by distributing subsidies, building infrastructure, and sharing technology. The pattern of very carefully managed competition and co-operation is as prevalent among nokyo as in every other sector of Japan's political economy. Just as different nokyo compete very fiercely against other nokyo for government subsidies, they will co-operate just as fiercely when confronted with a common enemy. For example, beef and citrus nokyo have strongly united to pressure the government against granting any concessions during its trade talks with the United States.

Japan's postwar agricultural policy has been thoroughly neomercantilist, and built around the largely successful achievement of five goals: (1) self-sufficiency in food production to the highest possible degree; (2) food security through stockpiling and diversified imports of essential commodities; (3) modernization of agriculture; (4) equality between farm income and that of other sectors; and (5) preservation of a viable farm sector. An April 1980 unanimous Diet resolution succinctly captured the ends and means of Japan's agriculture policy: "it is imperative that Japan secure a stable food supply by improving its self-sufficiency in food, the level of which is far behind that of other developed countries . . . in the interest of national security, the Japanese government must institute proper measures to improve the capacity for self-sufficiency in food and to increase productivity in the agriculture and fishery industries".[71]

Although Japan's food self-sufficiency ratio is only about 65 per cent, such measures as the diversfication of imports, stockpiling, and acquisition of foreign farm land and infrastructure within a world of increasingly complex interdependence have ensured Japan's food security. The average farm size may remain only 1.2 hectares, but mechanization, biotechnology and extensive rural infrastructure building have thoroughly modernized Japanese agriculture to the point where less than one per cent of the workforce are full-time farmers. Huge subsidies, protection, modernization policies, and second jobs for 85 per cent of farmers have ensured equality between rural and urban incomes, as well as the cultural and political goal of maintaining a large farming population. Yet, agricultural output as a percentage of GNP has fallen from about 10 per cent in 1960 to about 4 per cent at present. Currently only 5.2 per cent of Japan's 4.6 million farm households would be considered "viable" without any government support.[72]

As in other areas of Japan's economy, any farm "market opening steps" have been largely token, and only followed after years of foreign and largely American pressure and negotiations. As in other bilateral issues, while the number of sectors and amount of pressure targeted by Washington has steadily increased over the years, its agricultural policies toward Japan have been largely ad hoc and ineffectual. Japanese "market opening steps" in agriculture go back to the Kennedy Round of trade negotiations (1964–67), during which Tokyo promised to reduce tariffs on $240.4 million of American agricultural imports, which consisted of 28 per cent of the total amount of agricultural agreements reached by the Kennedy Round. Altogether Tokyo cut tariffs on about 90 items an average 53 per cent. But this affected only 31 per cent of agricultural imports at this time. Tokyo refused to reduce tariffs or quotas on such items as tobacco, soybean meal, citrus fruits, honey, and chicken.[73]

Although these negotiations were relatively low-key, the bilateral relationship received a shock in 1973 when President Nixon announced an embargo on soybean exports to prevent a growing shortage in the United States that was helping to fuel inflation. Despite the declared embargo, Washington did not cut off its soybean exports to Japan and in fact kept them at previous years' levels. Unfortunately, the embargo's announcement alone sent Japanese consumers and producers of soybean products into a buying frenzy, creating shortages and boosting prices. The "soybean incident" was a tremendous psychological blow, sparking a feeling of vulnerability to America's arbitary policies and an instable world economy. The real blow, however, came with OPEC's quadrupling of oil prices and embargo in November 1973; Japan's economic growth in 1974 declined for the first time since the war and the average annual growth rate since has continued to be half its pre-1973 level. These trade disruptions hardened the view among Japanese that the country should achieve food self-sufficiency.

In the late 1970s, Tokyo bolstered its food security by signing a number of agreements with Washington ensuring a steady supply of vital agricultural imports while slightly lowering tariffs on over 150 food products. In 1975, Tokyo and Washington concluded an agreement whereby the United States set minimum annual exports of wheat, feed grains, and soybeans to Japan for the following three years. During the Tokyo Round (1973–79) of trade liberalization negotiations involving finance minsters from over 100 nations, Japan agreed to reduce tariffs and quotas on 14 American imports worth $809 million, of which 95 per cent of the tariff reductions worth $770 million involved only one product – soybeans. Of the rest, Tokyo promised to cut tariffs on 150 other items an average of 35 per cent, but refused to reduce barriers on beef and citrus fruits.[74]

During the 1980s, as America's trade deficit with Japan grew from about $8 billion in 1980 to peak at over $60 billion in 1987, Washington's efforts to genuinely open all Japan's economic sectors, including agriculture, grew steadily more intense and systematic. In each sector, Tokyo's response to American pressure and negotiations has followed a similar pattern: drag out negotiations as long as possible, limit any promises to mostly symbolic gestures, all the while encouraging Japanese firms to buy up foreign food production, processing, and infrastructure to reinforce Japan's food security and profits.

The Tokyo–Washington beef negotiations epitomized this strategy. Like so many other economic sectors, Japan would not have a livestock industry if it were not thoroughly protected by a range of cartels, subsidies, quotas, tariffs, and other non-tariff barriers. There are about 270 000 cattle producers with an average herd of only 9.7 cows.[75] This inefficient industry means Japanese consumers must pay prices five or more times higher than Americans for beef, in part because beef producers have to pay grain prices 30 per cent higher than world market rates because of similar protection extended to Japanese grain producers. Until 1988, Japanese quotas allowed in only 274 000 tons of beef a year through 36 officially sanctioned trading firms, 80 per cent of which were auctioned through the semi-public Livestock Industry Promotion Corporation.[76] Washington negotiated a gradual rise in the share American producers received from this quota on foreign beef imports from 15 per cent in 1977 to about 30 per cent or $750 million in 1988.[77]

The Reagan Administration's first successful beef negotiations occurred in 1984, when the two nations signed a four year agreement that slightly raised America's beef import quota. Eight rounds of bilateral beef negotiations ending on 3 May 1987 had similar limited results. But as the bilateral trade deficit deepened, Congress exerted greater pressure on the Reagan Administration to take a stronger stand against Japanese trade barriers. In early 1988, the United States along with Australia and Argentina took Japan's agricultural barriers before GATT; in March GATT ruled that Japanese import quotas on ten of twelve farm products were illegal. The Reagan Administration followed up the ruling by calling for the removal of 24 Japanese farm quotas within two years.

As a result of this powerful foreign pressure, on 8 April Tokyo finally agreed to completely open both its beef and orange markets by 1993, although it reserved the right to unilaterally intervene to prevent "excessive competition". In reality, the bureaucrats simply replaced one set of highly restrictive barriers with another. Although the government monopoly, the Livestock Industry Promotion Corporations (LIPC), no longer controlled imported beef, the 25 per cent tariff and subsequent drastic distribution markups it imposed on imports have been replaced by 70 per cent tariffs in 1989, 60 per cent tariffs in 1990, and 50 per cent tariffs in 1993.

Despite these concessions, Japan's markets in both sectors will remain largely closed. Beef and oranges are small parts of Japanese agriculture and by 1993 Japanese firms will have bought up enough cattle ranches and orange groves in North America, Australia, and Argentina to ensure that, no matter where those products originate, the profits will remain in Japan. MAFF estimates that these market-opening steps will result in Japan's beef self-sufficiency ratio dropping from 64 per cent in 1988 to 36 per cent by 2000, the volume of imports quadrupling to 1.1 million tons, wholesale prices dropping 30–40 per cent, and the total volume of beef in the market increasing to 1.84 billion from 861 000 in 1987.[78] These statistics are misleading since Japanese producers will continue to dominate virtually all beef sales in Japan; by gobbling up foreign cattle ranches more Japanese beef will be produced abroad than at home, but it will still be produced, processed, and sold by Japanese corporations. By 1987 Japanese corporations had made only 15 foreign acquisitions worth 5000 acres; in 1988 alone they made 42 purchases of 65 000 acres. These purchases included a 31 000 acre ranch in Colorado by Otaka International, Marubeni's 1 billion yen feedlot operation in Australia, Zenchiku Corporation's Selkirk Ranch in Montana, Nippon Meat Packers' two ranches in Australia totaling 5000 hectares, while Nichimen Corp. and Fujichiku Co. expanded their long-standing ties with California's Harris Ranch Beef Co., a feedlot and processing operation.[79] In 1988 at least 40 Japanese agricultural corporations had processing and production investments in the United States.[80]

The recent "opening" of Japan's tobacco market followed a similar pattern. The government monopoly, the Japan Tobacco Corporation, is legally empowered to buy all Japanese tobacco at three times world market prices, control cigarette prices throughout the 270 000 store distribution network, and handle other products including liquor, rice and drugs. With such protection and benefits, the tobacco monopoly enjoys immense profits; in 1987 pretax profits of 100 billion yen on cigarette sales of 2.8 trillion yen, plus 2 trillion yen to government coffers from the sales tax.[81]

Until 1985, foreign cigarette sales were limited to only 15 per cent of outlets, and were priced 50 per cent higher than domestic brands even though they were about 50 per cent lower in price in world markets. After years of negotiations, Tokyo announced the "privatization" of the Tobacco monopoly, and agreed to slightly reduce the tariff on foreign cigarettes and sell them in all the outlets. Even though foreign cigarette prices remained higher, they achieved a 11.5 per cent market share in 1988. Negotiations continued and in 1988 the government announced that it would decrease its administrative guidance of the industry, and in 1989 reduce tobacco acreage from 40 000 to 34 000 acres.[82] Again, these are largely token gestures; the Japan Tobacco Corporation is busy buying up foreign tobacco manufacturers and diversifying into new businesses while foreign cigarette-makers are limited to a 15 per cent market share.[83]

Trade barriers remain completely intact around only one sector of Japan's farm economy – rice. In 1988 Tokyo spent $4.4 billion subsidizing the production of 5.5 million tons of rice, of which 2.3 million tons were in storage.[84] Although the rice market is monopolized by the Nokyo which sell 95 per cent of the crop at fixed prices, government buys less than half the crop while a "voluntary distribution" (*jishu ryutsu*) and black market accounts for 44 and 20–30 per cent, respectively, of total sales.[85]

Although one of the justifications for protecting rice is it is a central aspect of national culture, Japanese themselves are increasingly eating less rice with total annual per capita consumption today less than half the amount in 1960.[86] Rice grows on about half of all Japanese farmland, and because it is relatively simple to produce, part-time farmers who have full-time jobs elsewhere grow about 80 per cent of Japan's rice crop.[87] Ironically, it has only been since 1945 that most Japanese could afford to regularly eat rice. Perhaps in part because their incomes have steadily risen as they eat less rice, most Japanese do not mind continuing to subsidize rice. A 1988 *Nihon Keizai Shimbun* survey found that although 84 per cent favored some liberalization of Japan's rice market, only 29 per cent wanted prices lowered to global market prices while 60 per cent favored only a partial liberalization that would not hurt Japanese rice-growers.[88] Japan's annual rice market is worth $35 billion. Japanese rice retails at a price seven times higher than American rice. A free rice market would allow much more efficient American and Thai rice farmers to wipe out Japanese producers.

Washington has always been sensitive to the feelings of Japanese about rice, and only raised the issue of Japan's closed rice markets after strong pressure by the American Rice Millers' Association. For example, although the government sells rice to consumers at a price seven times international market levels, it began exporting rice in 1979, in part to reduce the levels accumulating in warehouses. Washington acted on protests by the American Rice Millers' Association and denounced Japan's subsidized exports. After long negotiations, Tokyo agreed not to export more than 400 000 tons a year.

In 1986 the American Rice Millers' Association filed petitions with the International Trade Representative to investigate Japan's barriers against rice imports. In both years, the White House bowed to Tokyo threats and rejected petitions from the American Rice Millers' Association to retaliate against Japan's closed rice market. The White House rejected the Rice Millers' appeals by claiming that the issue could be more effectively addressed at the Uruguay round of GATT talks, thus avoiding the inevitable storm of anti-American emotions if Washington had directly confronted Tokyo over its blatant protection of rice. Only if the White House succeeds in having a GATT panel rule against Tokyo's neomercantilism, it was reasoned, then it would be justified in retaliating.

As expected, the Japanese stonewalled the negotiations. In 1988, the Rice Millers once again petitioned the USTR against Japan's locked rice markets. In September USTR Clayton Yeutter gently suggested that Tokyo grant American producers a 3 per cent market share, while the following month, on 28 October he rejected the Rice Millers' petition that they receive a 10 per cent share. Although during the Presidential campaign, Bush promised California and Texas rice-growers that he would try to open Japan's rice market, the White House avoided opening direct negotiations during Emperor Hirohito's lingering death.[89]

Tokyo launched a massive assault against this effort to open Japan's markets. A 29 September 1988 letter from three Liberal Democratic Party leaders – Shintaro Abe, Masayoshi Ito and Michio Watanabe – to President Reagan claimed that even if the matter was discussed, "grave political problems would arise and cause serious anxiety and confusion among the Japanese people. Furthermore we believe that, should this happen, the long standing friendship between the United States and Japan would be impaired".[90] Nokyo's lobbying organization, Zenchu, mounted a sustained campaign to turn American agriculture and media in Japan's favor. Zenchu threatened to restrict sales of American agriculture in Japan if any effort was made to open Japan's rice market. As a result, the American Agricultural Movement, North Dakota Wheat Commission, and Colorado Wheat Administrative Committee publicly opposed the Rice Millers' petition while other agricultural associations were silent.

Tokyo, as always, tried to avoid tough bilateral negotiations and instead defuse pressure in a multilateral GATT setting. At the Uruguay Round on 28 October 1988 Foreign Minister Uno said that "Japan would not refuse to join discussion on the market access of rice at the multilateral Uruguay Round of talks".[91] But MAFF vice minister Yasuo Goto immediately and accurately interpreted Tokyo's policy as not "involving rice imports". As in other agricultural sectors, Tokyo's rice strategy has been to stonewall negotiations as long as possible while Japanese corporations buy up foreign riceland. Only then will Tokyo accept a token amount of imports which will probably be used for food processing. Foreign rice remains illegal in Japan despite the fact that repeated blind tastings show that Japanese consumers actually prefer foreign rice.

The talks dragged on for over two years. The final proposal Washington submitted to GATT on 15 October 1990 for opening Japan's rice markets seemed modest – Japan should open 3 per cent of its market to imports in 1991 and 5.22 per cent within ten years, before replacing its quota with tariffs no higher than 30 per cent. In fact, the proposal would lead to a complete opening of Japan's markets since foreign rice would vastly undersell Japanese rice even when hit with a 30 per cent tariff. As expected, claiming that continued protection of rice and other crops is essential for its "food security", Tokyo adamantly refused to make any concessions on rice. Tokyo did propose that all nations cut their farm subsidies 30 per cent before 1996, a percentage well below Washington's call for 70 per cent cuts. As always, Tokyo's strategy was to drag out any talks for as long as possible without giving anything away. The Uruguay round concluded in November 1990 with Tokyo still steadfastly refusing to make any significant rice concessions.

Japan's protection of rice continues, sometimes to the point of complete absurdity. Japanese rice is sold at prices six to ten times global market prices. During the mid–1980s, Tokyo's rice protection cost Japan $60 billion annually – $15 billion from the national treasury, $15 billion from local governments, and $30 billion from Japanese consumers.[92] The pettiness and ultranationalism of Japanese officials was exemplified when MAFF officials angrily demanded that American trade officials withdraw a ten pound bag of American rice from the annual Chiba food trade show in March 1991, claiming that the display violated the Staple Food Control Law which bans commercial rice imports. The officials claimed that anyone found guilty of importing rice could be sentenced to up to two years in prison and fined three million yen ($22 000). American officials replied that the rice diplay was intended not for sale but to educate the public.

As usual, the law counts for little in Japan's political economy. There would have been no legal basis for the arrest of those displaying the rice. Japan's Food Control Law explicitly allows the display of food for educational purposes, and American officials armed themselves with copies of that law in a futile attempt to ward off Japan's food police. Undaunted, during each day of the fair, Food Control agents demanded angrily that the United States Rice Council withdraw its rice sample. Finally, on 16 March MAFF Minister Motoji Kondo warned the American embassy that everyone associated with the display would be arrested if the rice were not removed. The Rice Council finally caved in to this threat of criminal prosecution and withdrew the rice later that day. David Graves, the president of the Rice Millers' Association commented that "we removed it under threat of arrest, but I think we made our point. It is ridiculous that Japan's 10 million ton rice industry should feel threatened by ten pounds of American rice".[93]

Tokyo's refusal to genuinely open its agricultural markets is not unreasonable. Free agricultural markets would wipe out most Japanese farmers, which would also result in the LDP being voted out of government during the next election as its key voting blocs shifted their support to the opposition camp. Tokyo also claimed that it must retain some measure of agricultural self-sufficiency. Japan's food dependence on the United States has actually risen from about 30 per cent in 1954 to about 40 per cent at present. Japan depends on the United States for 95 per cent of its soybean imports, 96 per cent of its live cattle, 95 per cent of its citrus fruit, and 82 per cent of its corn. In all about 15 per cent of all American agricultural exports annually go to Japan. Japan is the number one buyer of American meat and meat products (33 per cent), feed grains (20 per cent), and tobacco (20 per cent), and the second leading importer of wheat and flour (10 per cent), fruits and vegetables (15 per cent), oilseeds (14 per cent), and cotton (19 per cent). Meanwhile the United States imports only 0.5 per cent of its agriculture from Japan, most of which consists of specialty food products and highly processed nonfood items.[94]

Throughout the 1980s, the White House spent enormous energies trying to pry open Japan's agricultural markets. What has been accomplished? Were these efforts well placed? There have been limited openings of all agricultural products except rice, but only at a pace and degree in which Japan's farmers were not hurt. Although American farmers have benefited from some increased sales, America's huge trade deficit with Japan has not been significantly affected. American agricultural exports have increased. American exports of fruits and vegetables increased from $0.21 billion in 1987 to $0.90 billion in 1990; tobacco from $0.83 billion to $1.62 billion; meats from $0.67 billion to $1.56 billion; and fish from $0.85 billion to $1.65 billion.

America's present and future prosperity and security depends on producing the best computers, automobiles, and machine tools, not the cheapest wheat, corn and rice. A more rational policy would have involved Washington negotiating a quid pro quo with Tokyo based on the concept of comprehensive security. Washington could have recognized the political, economic and security reasons for Tokyo's continued protection of agriculture if Tokyo recognized the same reasons for Washington's promotion of its automobile, machine tool, and microelectronics industries.

DISTRIBUTION

Japan's distribution system is the most inefficient of the industrialized countries. But like the agricultural and construction industries, there is a powerful political if not economic rationale for Japan's inefficient distribution system. Japan has over 1.3 million retailers which together employ over 5 million potential political supporters. Although there are over two to two and a half more stores per capita in Japan than in the other key industrial countries, the distribution of sales is far greater. In Japan there is one retailer with an average of 3.7 employees for every 68 people compared to one with an average of 7.0 employees for every 120 in the United States, and one for every 160 in both Britain and West Germany. In Britain, the top four retailers accounted for a quarter of all sales; in Japan it took the top 200 retailers to capture 27 per cent of all sales. About 92 per cent of all retail outlets are "mom and pop" stores that account for almost 80 of Japan's sales.[95]

Virtually all these retailers are dependent on a wholesaler to carry inventory and extend credit. About 83 per cent of all stock to retailers comes from wholesalers, only 15 per cent direct from producers, and about 2 per cent from foreign producers. In 1982 Japan had twice as many wholesalers per capita than West Germany; over 367 000 Japanese wholesalers with 3.7 million employees compared to 110 000 with 1.2 million in Germany, while wholesale sales were 380 per cent of retail sales in Japan versus 165 per cent in Germany and 113 per cent in the United States. One fifth of Japanese wholesalers employ only one or two people, one fourth less than ten, and only 0.7 per cent employ more than 100 people. The ranks of wholesalers swelled steadily between 1968 and 1982 from 235 000 to 428 750. In 1988, Japan's wholesale-retail turnover ratio of 4.2 times was twice America's 1.9 times, making Japan's system half as efficient and twice as inflationary.[96]

Only two major groups are hurt – consumers and foreign producers. Consumers continue to pay inflated prices for goods, particulary foreign goods, despite the doubling of the yen value between 1985 and 1988, which allows Japanese producers to enjoy windfall profits. The distribution system also serves as a vast non-tariff barrier that keeps the volume of imports low and the prices high. Foreign products that have a comparative advantage in world markets remain overpriced in Japan, allowing

Japanese corporations immense scale economies and windfall profits in the huge market of 120 million people. At 128.3 yen to the dollar an IBM personal computer cost $2295 in the United States, $3452.88 in Japan; a Black and Decker steam iron is three times higher in Japan ($99.77) than in the United States; likewise for a Revereware frying pan, $18 in the United States, $65.47 in Japan; and double for a pair of Levi's jeans, $62.35 in Tokyo, $32 in New York. The average price of a consumer good in Japan is 48 per cent higher than in the United States and 55 per cent higher than in Britain.[97] Of 109 large American and European firms operating in Japan and surveyed by MITI in 1982, 53 said Japan's marketing and distribution routes were "closed to foreign products", 91 said "Japanese marketing routes are long and complicated" compared to their own country" causing 52 to "suffer damage", and 66 believe such practices should be ended.[98] Even more firms might have admitted the closed nature of the system and the fact that they were hurt by it if they were not afraid of retailation.[99]

How did Japan's distribution system become so inefficient? MITI manages the distribution system through its small and medium sized business bureaus, and has protected the system through a series of laws dating back to the 1950s. The 1956 Department Store Law empowered MITI to approve all proposed new department stores and expansion of existing ones of more than 3000 square metres in the seven largest cities and 1000 square metres elsewhere, but MITI was required to consult extensively with local retailers before making a decision. In addition, MITI regulated the store opening hours and days and restricted the practice of large outlets of providing free transportation to customers. The 1974 Large-Scale Retailer Law further strengthened protection for small retailers. MITI now approved new stores or expansion of old stores larger than 3000 square metres in the top 11 cities and 1500 square meters elsewhere. MITI was further empowered to "recommend" reductions of proposed floor space, to postpone of a new store's opening, and to restrict opening hours or days. As if this were not enough, local small stores were given a veto power over the opening of any large stores. A 1979 amendment extended these powers to all stores over 500 square meters, about the size of a large convenience store. The 1981 Temporary Measures to Adjust Retailing Commerce and the Small and Medium Retail Business Promotion laws reinforced all these laws. It now takes up to seven years for MITI's final approval of new outlets.[100] The annual expansion of floor space for large stores steadily fell from 12 per cent to 2 per cent from 1979 to 1987, and then jumped 5 per cent in 1988.[101]

As a result of these laws and MITI administrative guidance, the number of new stores larger than 1500 square meters dropped from over

600 in 1979 to only 150 in 1980 and was still only 203 in 1987.[102] This shackles even the largest department stores into choosing between squeezing imports into their limited space or continuing to sell only Japanese goods. Even if a store decides to display a token amount of imported goods, the prices will be exorbitant. Thus, if a foreign good jumps the manifold hurdles of such direct government trade barriers as tariffs, quotas, arbitrary standards, and red tape, it still faces indirect government trade barriers caused by protecting an inefficient distribution system. Of course, small retailers have no room to sell any foreign goods. Since Japanese consumers do not have an opportunity to buy foreign goods at the same price as foreign consumers, they believe the constant refrain from their government and business spokespeople that foreigners do not sell more in Japan because their goods are inferior and they do not try hard enough.

As if these barriers are not enough, the government sponsors yet other distribution barriers to ensure a minimum penetration of foreign goods. The monopolistic Sole Agent Law forces foreign producers to sell through only one designated import agent who enjoys exclusive marketing rights for that product, including the distribution outlets, price and quantity. Most agents sell Japanese products that compete directly with the foreign goods, and thus are inclined to limit foreign sales in order to protect the domestic manufacturer, which already enjoys large sales and thus can pass on more profits to the agent. Competition between wholesalers is prevented by outlawing sales to any retailer other than a sole designated retail agent. The result of the Sole Agent Law is the proliferation of wholesalers.

Although Japan has strong anti-trust laws, it deliberately does not enforce them in order to allow administrative guidance of the almost 500 legal cartels and hundreds of extra-legal cartels currently existing in Japan. Many of these are distribution cartels, of which some of the more prominent are in automobiles, consumer electronics, cosmetics, pharmaceuticals, and cameras.[103] The consumer electronics market for example, is extensively monopolized by distribution keiretsu. From 60–80 per cent of each of the top 12 electronics manufacturer's sales are through their own respective keiretsu. Matsushita and Toshiba alone have 27 000 and 14 000 wholesalers and retailers, respectively.[104]

Manufacturers create vast networks of exclusive dealerships by buying stock in the outlet, extending cheap credit, rebates, personnel and technology, and allowing return of unsold stock or delayed payments. In return, a dealer agrees to sell only within a small market designated by the manufacturer, is either entirely prevented from selling competitive products or else can only sell token amounts, and must sell only at a price determined by the manufacturer. Prices, thus, are determined not by the market but by collusive relationships.[105]

Japan's automobile market provides a good example of the effects of distribution keiretsu. Toyota and Nissan consistently enjoy about 70 per cent of all automobiles sales in Japan while Honda has about 15 per cent market share. Why the difference? As Japan's oldest automobile firms, Toyota and Nissan have been able to build up both vast distribution cartels as well as political support which translates into a range of special economic priviledges. In contrast, as a postwar, entrepreneurial firm, Honda must accept its sliver of Japan's managed markets even though, with over 50 per cent of the Japanese automobile market in the United States, its products clearly have a comparative advantage. Foreign producers suffer doubly for being newcomers and foreign, and thus must be content with less than a 3 per cent market share.[106]

One way for foreign firms to overcome all these government trade barriers would be to simply buy up distribution chains and market their goods directly. But another direct effect of Tokyo's cartel policies is the inability of foreign firms to buy up Japanese firms because they are caught in webs of cross-share holdings by other Japanese firms. American financier T. Boone Pickens discovered that when in March 1989 he paid $770 million for 20 per cent of Koito Manufacturing Corporation, a Toyota subsidiary. At first Koito would not even register Pickens' stock, and only reluctantly did so after MOF ruled there was nothing illegal about the purchase. Koito then refused to grant Pickens board seats and bigger dividends while a court ruled in favor of Koito's refusal to give him tax information.[107]

Will Japan's vast, inefficient system ever be rationalized? Since 1985 there have been six "unofficial" US–Japan talks on the distribution system and related issues, but MITI remains unabashedly protectionist in the face of growing foreign demands that the system be liberalized. In response to an April 1989 call by Washington for Japan to reform its distribution system, MITI's Director for Commercial Affairs, Michinao Takahashi, adamantly refused and instead served up the classic Japanese defense of their system by saying:

> We won't accept unilateral American demands to change our marketing system just for the sake of increasing American imports. We intend to make the upcoming meetings (13–14 June 1989) a place to offer information on Japan's distribution system, not a place of negotiation. Japan's distribution system doesn't block entry of competitive foreign products. Even if the current system is changed into a simpler and more rational one, American consumer products wouldn't sell.[108]

In other words, MITI is still singing the same tired old refrain that Japan's markets are completely open and foreign firms do not sell more because their products are inferior and they do not try hard enough.

After two rounds of negotiations called the Structural Impediments Intiatives (SII), Tokyo agreed to several basic reforms of its economy, including the distribution system. There are some signs of change. MITI approved 1400 applications for large scale retail stores in 1990, up from 800 in 1989.[109] Meanwhile, Toys R Us and Tower Records are the first huge American chains to venture into Japan's carefully managed markets since the conclusion of SII, while Sears and Bloomingdales are also considering opening branches. Toys R Us, with global sales of $5 billion and 580 stores, is making a major push to establish a presence in Japan. It plans to open 100 stores, built upon a strategy of collaboration with McDonald's for access to land, sites in undeveloped neighborhoods and near highways away from local shops, and only after close consultation with the local community. As expected, Japan's toy store cartels have launched concerted attacks against the American distributors. Japan's toy stores have declined from 8000 to 6000 since 1985, and would rapidly decline should the superefficient Toys R Us become established.

Yet, Tokyo's promises, even if sincere, will be extremely difficult to implement. It is not clear that the new policy will either result in the increased competition that could bring prices down for Japan's suffering consumers or open more floor space to imported goods. MITI must overcome protectionist laws in 105 cities and towns restricting all stores over 500 square meters. And even if larger stores are opened, there is no guarantee that they will use their store space to sell more foreign goods. Nor would foreign chains be able to quickly establish branches. Foreign department stores will have to join the end of the 1100 applications currently pending, many of which have been delayed for over a decade. Distibutors provide a large chunk of LDP urban support and threaten massive defections should any liberalization occur. There was a typical response to the Summit supermarket and department store in Tokyo's Nakano district when it posted a notice in 1990 announcing that from now on it would stay open another hour. Within hours scores of local shopowners and their supporters were picketing the store complaining that Summit was being "deceitful" for changing their policy without consulting the other businesses.[110] Japan's distribution system is just as carefully managed by nongovernment rules such as no big sales promotions that lead to sales wars, no negative advertizing, limited introductions of new products which might cause "confusion in the marketplace". Japanese claim a free distribution system would put tens of thousands of small shops out of business, thus creating severe socioeconomic problems in every Japanese neighborhood. Japan's cartelized distribution system will remain virtually impregnable for the forseeable future.

If Tokyo were sincere about its claims to support open markets, it would abolish such trade barriers as the Large-scale Retail Law, sole agent retail and commission fee wholesale system, and distribution keiretsu. But Tokyo will not reverse these trade barriers which have proved to be an enormous success in protecting small retailer and wholesaler employment, as well as squeezing out competitive foreign goods and allowing Japanese corporations continued economies of scale and windfall profits at the expense of Japanese consumers and foreign producers. Japan's 2.5 million retail and wholesale outlets employ well over over 10 million people, and represent a very important voting bloc. The LDP have pushed through laws protecting these workers from the "excessive competition" of a free market. In addition to helping keep the LDP in office, the system prevents massive unemployment and thus serves as a form of indirect welfare. The LDP enjoys and is increasingly dependent on the votes and financial contributions of these protected sectors. Japan's distribution system will remain highly protected and protectionist for the indefinite future.

CONSTRUCTION

The construction industry is yet another area where Tokyo's neomercantilist policies have tipped the playing field decisively in Japan's favor. In 1989, Japanese construction corporations won $2.8 billion of projects in an American market worth $435 billion, while American firms won barely $100 million of Japan's estimated $550 billion industry.[111]

Japan's construction market is the world's largest – worth $442.6 billion in 1987 compared to America's $397 billion. Japan's 520 000 construction firms employ over 5.3 million workers and support a further 20 million people when family members are included. In 1988, the construction market rose to $485 billion or 15 per cent of GNP.[112] As in other high employment voting blocs like farming and distribution, Japan's construction industry is almost completely closed to foreign firms. In 1987, despite having a huge comparative advantage in many construction projects, American firms won only $20.5 million worth of projects in Japan, while Japanese firms won $2 billion worth in the United States.[113] Most of the American work was enjoyed by one company, Otis, an elevator manufacturer.[114]

The travails of Reynolds and Taylor Inc. in Japan epitomizes Tokyo's industrial policies toward the construction industry.[115] In 1985, Reynolds, the world's leading producer of aquarium glass, submitted the lowest bid on a Tokyo acquarium park worth 8.8 billion yen, scheduled for completion in 1989. The Tokyo authorities immediately passed on the "secret" bid to a joint venture between Mitsubishi and Sumitomo, which immediately submitted a new bid lower than that of Reynolds and thus received the project. A Reynolds spokesperson said that it was clear Tokyo was not interested in seriously considering a non-Japanese contractor. Instead "Mitsubishi and Sumitomo jointly dumped and offered the same price. It was a conspiracy and unfair business conduct".

Reynolds protested to the American embassy which in turn pressured the Tokyo metropolitan government to re-evaluate the bid. The American position was that Reynold's was clearly the world's leading manufacturer of aquarium glass, had won prizes for similar projects in the United States, Europe, and Australia, and submitted the best product for the lowest price. If Japan's markets were truly open Reynolds would have won the bid. Instead, a cartel between Mitsubishi and Sumitomo sponsored by the Japanese government unfairly discriminated against Reynolds. The Japanese claimed that there was no discrimination and that the reason Reynolds lost the bid was because its windows were inferior and more expensive. Furthermore, piling one absurdity upon another, Kenji Suzuki, manager of Hazama Gumi with overall charge of the project, justified rejecting Reynolds with the words: "What should we do if there is a delay in delivery due to a walkout by unionized US longshoremen or a sinking of a cargo ship".

The Japanese tried to console Reynolds by arguing that if it formed a joint venture with a Japanese construction firm and shared technology and production, it might get some of the business. But a Reynold's representative rejected a joint venture, saying: "We have a very good product that is far better than theirs". Clearly Reynolds was familiar with the classic Japanese strategy of forcing foreign firms with superior technology to form joint production ventures with Japanese firms before being allowed to enter Japan's managed markets. In the short term, a joint venture allows the foreign firm to pick up business that would ordinarily be completely denied; in the long-term the Japanese partner uses the joint venture to master technology with which to eventually attack the foreign firm. It is experiences like that of Reynolds that cause many foreign firms with a comparative advantage for their products to avoid Japan's markets; why take the money and time to bid on projects or promote exports to Japan when the market is so thoroughly rigged against foreigners?

Japan's construction industry is as thoroughly politicized as the farm economy. As many as 80 per cent of the 445 LDP Diet members have close ties with the construction industry. In 1986, official construction industry political contributions were 340.5 billion yen, second only to the banking industry, a figure that averages out to 20 million yen per politician. As if these financial ties were not enough, family members of ranking LDP politicians have married into the industry. For example, Nakasone's daughter married the hier apparent to Kajima Construction, Japan's largest construction firm, while Takeshita's youngest daughter married the son of Takenaka Komuten, owner of the third largest construction firm, while his oldest daughter married the son of Diet member Shin Kanemaru, the head of the 40 member construction zoku.[116]

Policymaking is lead by the Ministry of Construction (MOC) which co-ordinates the rigged bidding system (*dango*) and bails out weak companies, but MITI also intervenes through its Small and Medium Enterprise Agency, the Ministry of Transportation (MOT) on projects like air-ports, highways, railroads and bridges, and occasionally the MFA when Japanese firms need help winning overseas projects, or more recently resisting the attempts of foreign firms to break into Japan's cartelized markets. As in all other economic sectors, Japanese bureaucrats informally influence the construction industry by retiring into high ranking executive positions in the corporations they had previously been regulating. In December 1987 about 40 Diet members and 10 ranking members of the Ministry of Construction formed the National Land Construction Re-search Conference, which ostensibly acts as a construction industry policy council but mostly lobbies for the industry and channels funds to politicians.

The construction industry has a classic dual structure. The industrial association is called the Federation of Contruction Contractors, whose president, Hajime Sato, is close friend of Takeshita. The industry is dominated by the "Big Five", Kajima Corp., Ohbayashi Corp., Shimizu Corp., Taisei Corp., and Takenaka Komuten Co. all of which are about the same size. They preside over half a million small- and medium-sized firms (*shitauke*), of which 99 per cent are capitalized at less than 100 million yen and most of which are tired directly to a parent construction firm. As much as 5 per cent of construction contracts are received by firms run by gangsters (*Yakuza*). It is estimated that Yakuza-run firms will earn 20–30 billion yen from the Trans–Tokyo Bay project alone, mostly by supplying cheap labor.[117]

Of Japan's almost half a trillion dollar construction market in 1988, 31.6 per cent was for private housing, 22.7 per cent for private non-housing construction, 9.5 per cent for private engineering works, 1.4 per cent for government housing, 5.0 per cent for government non-housing, and 29.8 per cent for government engineering works. Government projects acount for more than 35 per cent of the market.[118] Virtually all the bidding for both government and private projects was rigged (*dango*). The government carefully manages Japan's construction market so that only certain contractors can bid on public works, while the construction industry rotates bidding on private projects. Firms are rated from A to E based on such factors as the number of jobs they have completed, their equity capital, number of employees, ratio of capital to fixed assets, ratio of net profits to total capital, and operating years. Projects are also classified from A to E, and in turn subdivided along the same range so that only firms from one class can bid on a project with the same classification. As if this collusion were not enough, winning bids are rotated so that every firm gets at least enough work to stay in business. The government also supports small firms by organizing them into "co-operatives" – over 700 in 1987 alone seeded with over 2.24 billion yen. Like the larger cartels, the co-operatives rotate or share contracts and fix bids.[119] The government has also formed Technology Exchange Plazas in each prefecture to enable construction firms to share technology.

According to Japan's antitrust laws, these construction cartels are as illegal as any of the almost five hundred other "legal" cartels and hundreds of "extralegal" cartels currently operating. But the government turns a blind eye to its own antitrust laws and instead organizes and presides over many of the cartels. Until 1988, foreign firms were formally excluded by the catch-22 regulation that they were not allowed to bid in Japan without experience, and of course could not gain experience without winning a bid. Although this obvious trade barrier has been removed, the rigged bidding will continue to restrict foreign access to all but the most token projects. All the while, whenever foreigners criticize the rigged construction or other managed "markets", Japanese government and business spokesmen will continue to repeat the mantra that Japan's markets are the world's most open and foreign firms do not win bids because their technology is inferior and they do not try hard enough.

The experience of the American construction firm, PAE International, clearly reveals how futile even the most strenuous of foreign efforts can be.[120] For over 34 years PAE has operated in Japan as a military contractor, and until 1988, along with Bechtel and General Electric Technical Service, was one of only three American firms licensed to work in Japan. President of PAE, Theodore Ury, said that even after over three decades his firm was still excluded from all but the smallest projects. Even when PAE wins a bid it has trouble hiring local contractors because of the unspoken blacklist. At construction sites subcontractor workers disguise themselves as regular PAE workers to avoid retribution from other firms. Ury points out that "behind the scenes, they'll support us, but they're still not willing to take that step forward and work openly with foreigners". PAE's most recent job was underbidding Japanese competitors to build two toilets at the American military base at Yokosuka, the first bid at the base in ten years since PAE workers were beaten up going to a roofing project at the base. The firm's only other job in the past three years was installing the plumbing for five Mrs. Field's cookie shops. PAE's three decades of failure is certainly not for lack of trying.

Meanwhile, the United States has had enormous difficulties with the Japanese firms it is forced to rely on for military base contruction. On 23 November 1989, Washington announced that 99 Japanese construction corporations had agreed to pay it $32.6 million to settle accusations that they had rigged bids on a variety of American bases in Japan. The case was initiated by American pressure on the Fair Trade Commission to investigate extensive collusion on construction projects. In December 1988 the FTC ruled that 140 companies had colluded to rig bids between April 1984 and September 1987 for a range of projects at the Yokosuka Naval Base. Typically, the FTC let off the violators with a mere warning and did not impose any fines. Progress resulted only after the American embassy threatened to sue the violaters and bar them from further work from the American government. The remaining 41 firms named by the FTC continue to refuse to pay any compensation.

As in other sectors of Japan's economy, protectionism allows Japanese construction firms to enjoy immense economies of scale and windfall projects at home, which in turn gives them the financial war chests to dump bids on foreign projects. Within Japan's huge protected markets, the ranks of construction firms tripled in number from about 150 000 in 1960 to 488 520 in 1980, then grew more slowly to 510 844 by March 1987. The largest construction growth during the 1980s was overseas, when contracts awarded Japanese firms doubled in value from 511 billion yen in 1980 to 1.029 trillon yen in 1985. In 1986, Japanese companies won 41.3 per cent of new orders in the United States, and three firms were among the ten largest construction firms. But the profit margin for Japanese firms averaged less than 1 per cent of the total contract value, implying that they dumped their bids.[121]

Of course, both consumers and foreign producers suffer from Japanese protectionism at home and dumping abroad. But the domestic industry itself has become so bloated and inefficient that, like the farming and distribution sectors, any genuine liberalization would create widespread bankruptcies and unemployment. The government must avoid "excessive competition", as always the code word for free markets, at all costs. It is estimated that if Japan's construction industry operated on free market principles, hundreds of thousands of small firms would go bankrupt, and the industry's ranks would be "reduced from half a million to several thousand". Rationalization of the construction industry would have similar effects as in the farming or distribution sectors – massive unemployment and the subsequent defection of a vital LDP voting bloc to opposition parties during the following election.

Washington did not challenge Japan's protection of its construction market until 1985 when the Reagan Administration requested that American firms be allowed to bid on the proposed $8 billion Kansai airport and $6 billion Trans–Tokyo Bay projects. Tokyo agreed to allow American bids but none were rewarded. Under increasing pressure from Congress to confront America's worsening trade deficit, Commerce

Secretary Verity, in November 1987, asked for guaranteed shares of the projects. Tokyo refused to extend to foreigners the same priviledges Japanese producers have always enjoyed, and instead said further talks should be conducted at GATT. Between 1984 and 1987, Japanese construction firms won almost $2 billion in contracts in the United States while foreign firms remained virtually locked out of Japan. On 30 December 1987, Congress attached a rider to an appropriations bill which refused to accept bids on public construction projects from firms whose countries discriminated against American firms.

Tokyo only concedes when faced with genuine retaliation against its neomercantilist policies. On 6 January 1988 during his visit to Washington, Prime Minister Takeshita announced that bids from American firms with extensive overseas experience would be allowed on six projects with a total value of $140 billion – the projects included Tokyo Bay development, Akashi Straits Bridge, Port of Yokohama expansion, Hiroshima airport expansion, Kansai academic and science city, and a coastal redevelopment project. He warned, however, that the chances of winning bids would improve if the American firms formed joint ventures with Japanese firms.

The reaction to Takeshita's promises were negative on both sides of the Pacific. Takeshita was heavily criticized at home for granting his "concessions" and not getting anything in return – an ironic position considering Japan's over $50 billion trade surplus with the United States. MOC argued that aside from the fact that foreign firms do not try hard enough and anyway lack a comparative advantage, "if the (fixed bid, *dango*) practice is changed, smaller construction firms will go bankrupt one after another and things will be plunged into confusion. If big firms are allowed to participate in the bidding for smaller projects, the number of construction firms will be sharply reduced from the present half a million to several hundred".[122]

Meanwhile American politicians and businessmen treated Takeshita's announcement with extreme skepticism, reasoning that it was yet another public relations attempt to allay criticism while Japan's construction market would remain firmly shut. The skeptics were right. Despite Tokyo's "opening" of six projects, it continued to discriminate against foreign firm. For example, Bechtel, one of the world's most dynamic construction firms, won only 9 billion yen worth of projects in 1988. It did win some token work as one of a 10 firm consortium bidding on Tokyo's Haneda Airport.

Anger mounted in Washington. Prominent Congressmen talked of invoking Section 301 of American Trade Law allowing retaliation against unfair foreign traders. In March 1988 the Reagan Administration refused to accept the participation of a consortium lead by Kajima Corp. on a subway tunnel and station in Washington, DC. The Japanese government, business and press reacted to the rejection of Kajima's participation with outrage, with MOC Minister Sako angrily demanding that the Reagan Administration reverse its decision. But, faced with retaliation, on 14 May Tokyo extended the list of approved projects to a total of 14, and eliminated the requirement that foreign firms need experience in Japan before they can bid. The MOC itself publically requested that Japanese firms help foreign firms with their bids. Public corporations like the Japan Highway, Housing and Urban Development and Tokyo Metropolitan Expressway were given permission to accept foreign bids.

Discrimination continued. Bechtel, for example, was judged unqualified to bid alone on the 1.15 trillion yen ($8.5 billion) Trans–Tokyo Bay Highway, a 15 km bridge, tunnel, and causeway. Bechtel was not the only foreign firm to lose out on the Trans–Tokyo Bay Highway, one of the 14 projects supposedly "opened" to competitive bidding. All foreign firms were excluded on the grounds that they lacked the experience building earthquake resistant structures on reclaimed land; 74 Japanese firms, however, are participating on the project.[123]

Negotiations continued. In fall 1989, Washington got Tokyo to agree to establish a regulatory agency to guard against collusion and allow foreign firms to bid without a Japanese partner. These "concessions" did not result in any greater business for American firms. In March 1990, Trade Representative Carla Hills removed a five year ban on Japanese bids for contracts on American airports. In return, Tokyo finally agreed to allow American construction firms to bid on 17 projects worth $26 billion. Since 1988, American firms have won $310 million of the total.

As usual, Tokyo bowed only to strength. On 17 April 1991, the Trade Policy Group representing sub-Cabinet officials from trade related agencies and departments unanimously recommended that the United States bar Japanese firms from work on federal construction projects. On 26 April 1991, USTR Hills officially cited Japan as an unfair trader in construction under Section 301 and set a 31 May deadline for sanctions that would have forbidden Japanese construction firms to receive federal projects if Tokyo did not significantly open its market. The administration's action, however, was mostly bluff – in 1989, Japanese firms won only $100 million of the $14 billion federal market while they enjoyed $2.7 billion in private projects. Tokyo protested the threatened sanctions, claiming that it could not find any projects "suitable" for foreign firms, and tried to call Hills' bluff by warning that if the sanctions took effect it will bar American firms from the 17 projects they are currently allowed to bid on. The American embassy responded by drawing up a list of hundreds of projects on which American firms should participate, then narrowed the list down to 30 big projects. On 1 June the day after the deadline passed and as American officials prepared to imposed sanctions, an intervention by Prime Minister Kaifu allowed Tokyo to agree to increase its original limit of 10 new projects to 17, which Washington quickly agreed to after abandoning its original request for 30 projects. Washington then cancelled its planned sanctions.

Have these "significant market opening steps" been genuine (*honne*), or were they simply public relations stunts to deflect foreign pressure (*tatemae*)? To date, the bilateral construction trade remains lopsided; Japanese firms continue to gobble up public and private projects in the United States while even the largest, most experienced American construction firms are given only small, token projects in Japan. As of mid–1990, Tokyo had granted licenses to only 26 foreign firms, of which 23 had tied up with their Japanese competitors. Japan's construction market remains essentially closed. Projects continue to be rewarded to established Japanese firms, whether or not they have the best technology to do the job. For example, the Japanese firm that won the contract to build the Tokyo Dome, Takenaka Komuten, had to buy the membrane technology from Geiger Berger Associates of the United States.[124] Within a few years, Takenaka Komuten, having mastered that technology, will be winning bids on similar projects around the world while Geiger Berger Associates will watch its projects and profits steadily dwindle.

Tokyo's construction policies have been an immense success. Japanese firms continue to monopolize the immense profits and economies of scale of the world's largest construction market. Forbidden to freely operate in Japan's carefully rigged market, foreign construction firms sell out their technology to their Japanese rivals either through licensing deals or joint ventures. With the immense profits from their own closed market and easy access to foreign technology, the largest Japanese firms are rapidly taking over foreign markets. Meanwhile, in return for continued protection, the half a million small construction firms continue shelling out large amounts of cash and votes to the LDP. The MOC is probably correct in arguing that a free market would cut the number of construction firms from half a million to a few hundred. The political and economic costs of a free market would be disastrous, and no government will ever consider genuine reforms.

CONCLUSION

Trade is largely a zero sum game. In all seven industries examined, the Americans lost heavily against the Japanese. Washington's liberal outlook and decentralized political system aborts any attempts to construct systematic industrial policies that could have achieved a level playing field for all these American industries, thus keeping the wealth and dynamism in the United States that continually drains away to Japan.

The tardy, reactive, ad hoc, Band Aid policies that the White House did eventually push with these industries generally proved to be too little too late. Somtimes, as with the television and machine tool industries, the White House actually worked with the Japanese against the American industries. In steel and automobiles, Washington's reaction was insufficient to prevent significant Japanese inroads into the market. Washington's efforts to open Japan's closed agriculture, distribution and construction markets have had varying degrees of success or failure. The biggest success has been in agriculture where the White House has negotiated away a range of overt Japanese barriers. The White House has failed to force Tokyo to dismantle significantly either the distribution or construction industries. American losses in its economic war with Japan are often devastating and its victories Pyrrhic.

8   The Foreign Investment Front

On 17 January 1991, the White House approved the huge Japanese robot and machine tool producer Fanuc's purchase of a 40 per cent controlling interest in Moore Special Tool Inc., the last American producer of precision tools used, among other things, to make nuclear weapons. The decision followed a half year review by the Committee on Foreign Investment set up by the 1988 Exxon–Florio Law. The Administration was deeply divided over the purchase, with the Defense, Commerce and Energy Departments arguing that to allow Moore to fall into Japanese hands would represent a major national security breach, and the State and Treasury Departments characteristically advocating open American markets at any cost. Besides, the free marketeers argued, no American purchaser could be found and the choice was either Japanese control over Moore or its bankruptcy. Chairman of the House High Technology Committee, Mel Levine, lamented that "failure to stop this sale sends a clear signal that everything, no matter how vital to our interests, is for sale in the United States".[1] Worried by Congressional criticism, Fanuc announced on 10 February 1991 an abandonment of its takeover attempt.[2]

T. Boone Pickens became the largest shareholder in Koito Corporation in 1988 when he bought 20 per cent of its stock, a position he later strengthened to 26 per cent. In Japan, however, owning a large percentage of a company's stock does not translate into influence if the owner happens to be foreign. Pickens' request for directorships for himself and three others was rejected at the annual general meeting in June 1989, while the Tokyo District Court rejected his request for access to the company's books and an increase in dividends. Toyota owns 19 per cent of Koito's stock, a position bolstered to a 63 per cent share when the shares of five other related institutional investors are included. Toyota supplies Koito's president, vice-president and a director, and effectively controls the price, delivery period, and profits of Koito's products. If Koito's profit is too large, Toyota will reduce it the next year by discounting its profits. Toyota has adamantly refused to allow Pickens even a peek at Koito's books, let alone consider granting him any board seats.[3] On 29 April 1991, after two years of struggle to get on Koito's board, Pickens finally admitted defeat and announced he would sell his 26.4 per cent share.

Pickens originally paid $1.01 billion for the stock; it was worth $844 million when he sold it.

Fanuc's proposed takeover of Moore Special Tool and T. Boone Picken's frustrated attempts to gain board seats at Koito starkly contrast the successes of Japanese neomercantilism with the failures of American liberalism – and their respective impacts on Japanese and American power. Washington's irrational industrial policies, ill-concealed under the rubric of liberalism, were responsible for the steady destruction of America's machine tool industry under Japanese assault during the 1980s. America's machine tool industry evolved on its own without government guidance, although stimulated by massive government procurement. Thus the industry's hundreds of small firms lacked the financial depth to develop new products or markets, or to protect themselves from take-over. The White House's failure to respond to Japan's dumping of numerically controlled machine tools in the late 1970s and throughout the 1980s resulted in the devastation of America's machine tool industry just as similar sustained Japanese dumping of televisions, steel, automobiles and semiconductors had ravaged those American strategic industries. Faced with the stark choice of bankruptcy or Japanese takeover, many American machine tool producers choose the later. The White House's acquiesence to Fanuc's proposed takeover of Moore Special Tool represents the culmination of its policy of malign neglect. Hobbled by a liberal mindset, the White House apparently never considered arranging Moore's takeover by an American firm or resuscitating Moore with a capital infusion. The White House Committee on Foreign Investment, which was empowered with the responsibility for carefully screening all proposed foreign investments to ensure no strategic American firms fell into foreign hands, turned out to be a paper tiger. The Committee rejected only one of 517 foreign investments over three years – the Chinese purchase of Mamco Manufacturing Co., which makes aircraft components.[4]

Tokyo would never allow foreign competition to capture significant market share let alone to take over outright any industry, from its most economically strategic high technology, manufacturing or financial industries to politically strategic industries like agriculture, construction or distribution. The reason is that Tokyo views virtually every industry as being either economically and/or politically strategic to Japan's political economy. Tokyo carefully nurtures all Japanese industries into either economic champions garnering vast wealth by dominating global markets or political champions which employ vast numbers of Japanese and thus votes for the ruling party. The near bankruptcy of a strategic jewel, like Moore Special Tool, would be inconceivable in Japan. If the firm had not been spun off from the corporation of a powerful keiretsu, the government would have managed its acquisition by a keiretsu, then encouraged the other key keiretsu to create similar companies of their own, if they had not already done so. Likewise, Koito's denial of board seats to Pickens is simply neomercantilist business as usual in Japan where widespread cartels, insider trading, and heavy government interference are designed to maximize Japan's accumulation of wealth and power.

Yet, Fanuc's eventual abandonment of its attempt to take over Moore represents a temporary caution among Japanese investors. Congressional criticism and mounting public concern have slowed Japan's vast spending splurge of the late 1980s. Tokyo advised Japan's corporations to target smaller, less known but strategic high technology firms like Moore rather than landmark purchases like Rockefeller Center and MCA. This strategy has been successful. Although the attempted takeover of Moore was heavily criticized, similar purchases of America's small high technology firms continue unabated. While the Japanese purchase of a flagship company like Columbia or building like Rockefeller Center may make the news, the average deal in 1990 was only $8.5 million, down from $23 million in 1988. Of Japan's total direct investments between 1985 and 1990, investments in small American high technology firms represented the largest number, of which 127 deals worth $3.049 billion were in computer firms, 23 deals worth $1.176 billion were in electronics firms, and 37 deals worth $1.176 billion were in instruments and control equipment.[5] The exact amount of foreign investment is unknown, but is undoubtedly much larger. Many deals are never disclosed, and the United States has no central office for tabulating foreign investments in the country.

The United States is not the only target of Japanese investments. Japan's corporate behemoths are rapidly reinforcing their massive global market shares by investing in key markets around the world. Japan surpassed both the United States and Britain to become the world's top foreign investor in 1989. Japanese corporations directly invested $44.1 billion of that year's total $197.9 billion in global foreign investment. Although Japan's outstanding investment balance of $154.4 billion accounted for 12.2 per cent of the total global balance of $1.263 trillion, it remained third behind the United States and Britain. Japan's growth in total net overseas assets has been extraordinarily rapid: from $10.9 billion in 1980 to $240.7 billion by the end of 1987. Astonishing as these figures are, they downplay the actual magnitude of Japan's capital outflow: from 1982 to 1986 Japan's gross overseas assets surged from $227.7 billion to $1.07 trillion. Nomura Securities conservatively estimates that Japan's net overseas assets will triple to $550 billion by 1995, but this may be a considerable underestimation. In 1988, of Japan's total foreign assets of $1.469 trillion, $832.669 billion (private $728.168 billion, government $104.501 billion) were long-term and $636.678 billion (private $538.802 billion, government $97.876 billion) were short-term assets, while of

Japan's total liabilities of $1.177 trillion, $311.625 billion (private $268.431 billion, government $43.194 billion) were long term and $865.976 billion (private $850.968 billion, government $15.008 billion) were short term.[6]

The United States was the choice investment country for not just Japanese, but from many other countries. Foreign investment in the United States quadrupled during the 1980s, from about $500 billion to over $2 trillion in 1990. Britain was the largest investor with over $122.1 billion or 32.4 per cent of the total, with Japan second with $70.6 billion, or 17.6 per cent. At current investment rates, over 1 million Americans will have Japanese bosses by the mid-1990s, which translates into enormous political clout. Recently, Japan's investment surge into the United States has slowed. Only $10.5 billion in new direct investments entered the United States between April and October 1990, less than 30 per cent during the same period a year earlier.[7] Rising Japanese interest rates and caution over a possible Congressional backlash are causing Japan's investors to keep their money at home. The lull will not last long – Japanese investments in the United States will surge again.

Meanwhile, despite repeatedly claiming that its markets are the world's most open, Tokyo continues to manage their fierce resistance against any significant foreign penetration. There is a severe investment imbalance between the United States and Japan: in 1990, while Japan's corporations were profiting from over $70 billion in direct United States investments, American firms had only invested a total of $7 billion in Japan. This imbalance reflects the relative success of liberal and neomercantilist policies in promoting a nation's geoeconomic interests. This chapter explores the foreign investment front in the geoeconomic struggle between the United States and Japan.

AMERICAN INVESTMENT POLICY AND POWER

What is the real impact of this investment flood? Neoclassical economists applauded this huge influx of foreign investments, claiming it represents foreign confidence in America's economy and will increase American jobs, technology, and wealth. Political economists, however, have a much more sophisticated view of foreign investment, pointing out that in real life there are always tradeoffs. They distinguish between different types of foreign investment and different investment settings, in which foreign investments can have either a net positive or negative effect on a country's political economy. Foreign investments can have a positive effect if they stimulate rather than destroy local industry. But there is often a vicious cycle between increases in foreign investment and the trade deficit. Japanese investors in particular tend to import Japanese made components rather than buy American products while the total influx of foreign capital increases the demand for dollars and thus its value which simultaneously lowers the price of foreign goods and raises the price of American goods. Both these forces exacerbate the trade deficit which in turn attracts more foreign investment and ultimately even larger American trade and payments deficits. In addition, most profits return overseas. In 1984 55 per cent was repatriated and in 1985 as much as 79 per cent fled the United States.[8] In 1987, for example, foreign corporations invested $41 billion in the United States, of which $236 billion bought up existing corporations ($16 billion of which took over manufacturing firms) while only $5 billion was invested in new businesses.[9]

There is a significant difference between the inflow of foreign capital today and that of the late 19th century.[10] Foreign capital in the late 19th century was invested in economic infrastructure and industries, and the major foreign investors – Britain, Germany and France – liquidated their holdings during World War I to pay for their war effort. Had it not been for World War I, America's economic development might have remained largely in foreign hands and thus much more stunted than the historic rate. In contrast to the productive investments of the 19th century which by good fortune were eventually transferred to American ownership, most foreign capital in the 1980s and 1990s has merely financed America's consumer frenzy, deepening debt, and decline and foreign takeover of strategic industries, thus exacerbating America's economic development problems.

Like virtually all American economic policy, Washington's investment policy simply reflects the prevailing White House attitude of malign neglect and veto of any attempt by Congress to assert a more rational policy. No government agency is responsible for creating and implementing investment policy. Instead American policymakers remain engaged in fratricidal turf wars at the expense of a coherent policy. At least sixteen federal agencies collect information on foreign investments, but according to Representative John Bryant, "the information is so limited, hidden in bureaucratic quagmires, or actually kept secret by law – even from Congress – that we often don't know who is investing here or whether they are from friendly nations like Canada or hostile ones".[11]

Part of the 1988 Exxon–Florio law set up the interagency Committee on Foreign Investment, which is supposed to screen foreign investments to ensure none endanger America's geoeconomic or geopolitical security. Yet, like all the other trade-powers Congress has granted the president, the Exxon–Florio law is a toothless tiger if the president refuses to use it to retaliate against foreign predatory trade and investment attacks. Since 1988, of 517 reviews of foreign takeovers and 12 full-scale reviews by the interagency Committee on Foreign Investment in the United States, President Bush has blocked only one foreign sale – the purchase by the China National Aero-technology Import and Export Corporation of Mamco Manufacturing Inc. which supplies aircraft components.[12]

Congress and the public moan when the news breaks of such Japanese purchases as the Rockefeller Center or the Yosemite concessions or E.T., yet have no significant policy impact. It is unclear, however, how many potential Japanese purchases of America's strategic economic assets have been blocked by Japanese fears of an American backlash. Worried by the negative publicity generated by Sony's purchase of Columbia Pictures and Mitsubishi's of Rockefeller Center, in 1989 Tokyo and Keidanren warned Japan's corporations to back off from other headline purchases of American assets to soften any building American reaction against Japanese neomercantilism. Japanese business dutifully complied, the most conspicuous example of which was the collapse of a Japanese plan to buy the Sears Tower in Chicago.

To date, the only notable Japanese retreat other than the attempted purchases of Moore and the Sears Tower, was Fujitsu's 1986 attempt to buy Fairchild Semiconductor Corporation which annually sells more than $100 million of high-speed circuitry to the defense industry. It was Fairchild Semiconductor's founding by engineering and managerial wizard Robert Noyce which led to the birth of Silicon Valley as the dynamic core of America's microelectronic industry. When wind of the pending purchase was released, the protests by Commerce Secretary Malcolm Baldridge, Defense Secretary Weinberger, and other concerned politicians and analysts that the United States was becoming too dependent on foreign technology caused Fujitsu to withdraw its offer. Ironically, Fairchild was already owned by a French firm so that one foreign firm would have simply replaced another. Japanese cite the Fairchild case to bolster their assertion that American fears of Japanese investments are based on racism. In reality, the worry in the Fairchild case was not foreign ownership, but the solidity of Tokyo's lead in microelectronics which it had achieved by the sustained dumping of its products in the United States while maintaining webs of trade barriers against similar foreign products in Japan. To have allowed Fujitsu to purchase Fairchild without protest would have simply been one more American reward for Japanese neomercantilism.

The Bush Administration's approval of the sale of Semi-Gas Systems to Nippon Sanso K.K. in July 1990 was typical. The union of Semi-Gas, which controls 40 per cent of America's market for speciality gas distribution equipment which is used to produce advanced computer chips, and Nippon Sanso K.K., a subsidiary of Nikon and the largest Japanese producer, would give the Japanese firm a 51.9 per cent global market share. Sematech and other American firms dependent on Semi-Gas products strongly protested to the Justice Department which agreed to attempt to block the sale on anti-trust grounds, and the probability that the Japanese would either cut off or delay the sales of vital equipment to the Americans. Although the Justice Department agreed to champion the American case, on 26 March 1991, a Federal District Court overruled the Justice Department's attempt to block Matheson Gas Co., a subsidiary of Nippon Sanso K.K., from buying Semi-Gas Systems. The Bush Administration did not fight the decision.

Many in Washington are deeply concerned about the sell-out of America's technological and manufacturing jewels. The Defense Department's Defense Science Board Task Force on Foreign Ownership and Control of Foreign Ownership, issued a report on 1 May 1990 calling on the government "to actively intervene to maintain American ownership of industries critical to national security." This defense of critical industries would include gathering accurate information on strategic industries, encouraging them to remain in American hands, and improving the oversight of foreign investments in the United States. If the proposals are adopted, the government would, "after it makes appropriate investigations and before weak firms are put up for sale, actively intervene to help negotiate US mergers, provide refinancing, or offer other support to assist the critical industry." The report noted Hitachi's 1989 purchase of Ceraclad Corporation, a small ceramics firm which, before its purchase, had been chosen as one of two American subcontractors to supply highly specialized ceramic chips for a fourth generation ceramic single memory chip carrier. Two months after Hitachi bought the firm, it stripped Ceraclad of its technology and shut it down. Also noted was Minebea's 1985 purchase of New Hampshire Ball Bearings which produces ball bearings critical to many weapons systems. Likewise, with Sony's 1989 purchase of MRC, the United States lost its last important producer of specialized equipment to make semiconductors. The report criticized the Interagency Committee on Foreign Investment for taking a shortsighted view of foreign investments as alleviating the international payments deficit and not a long-term view that these purchases represent a serious drain of American manufacturing and technological dynamism, and the wealth it creates.[13] To date, nothing has been done to implement these policy recommendations.

Japan's government and business is an increasingly powerful player in setting America's policy agenda and policies. For example, foreign lobbyists, led by the Japanese, succeeded in killing the National Cooperative Production Amendments of 1990, which would have relaxed antitrust laws for joint manufacturing ventures, extended a current exemption for research and development ventures, and reduced penalties from triple to single damages. Joint ventures would not be eligible if any partner were more than 50 per cent foreign owned, or if the venture were outside of the United States.

In America's liberal system the consumer, not producer, is king – most of the time. Consumer complaints about Japanese investments in the United States abound. The Greenlining Coalition, a group of minority and women's organizations, has lobbied US officials and Japanese corporations against the latters' repeated violations of the 1977 Community Reinvestment Act by engaging in discriminatory loan and investment practices. In response to these criticisms, the Federal Reserve is increasingly scutinizing Japanese financial practices in the United States. Under the Community Reinvestment Act the Board can initiate an investigation when it receives an application from a bank for approval of an acquisition or new branch opening, and can reject the application if it decides that the bank violates criteria detailed in the Act. In 1990, the Board blocked a proposed capital tie-up between Mitsui Taiyo Kobe Bank and Security Pacific Corporation when it found the Japanese giant guilty of neglecting housing loans, low interest loan funds, and engaged in discriminatory hiring practices against women and minorities. Mitsui had to submit a report by 20 July documenting its compliance with the Act or its merger could not go through. But Japan's financial giants are attempting to sidestep these restrictions by setting up showcase projects for minorities and other disadvantaged groups. For example, in June 1990 four Japanese trust banks in New York organized a fund which channeled housing loans to low-income earners.[14] The efforts of the Federal Reserve Board to regulate Japan's financial offensive in the United States is a classic example of too little, too late, and for the wrong reasons. Although the complaints of minorities and women against Japan's investment practices are legitimate and should be rectified, the government's priority should be to ensure that the country is not selling off its manufacturing and technological future.

While Washington fiddles, the states and cities, starved for American investments, engage in fierce bidding wars to attract foreign investments to their districts, which include offering such incentives as tax holidays, bonds, low cost loans, infrastructure, and political lobbying assistance. This free for all between states and cities in attracting foreign investments results in foreign corporations receiving an immense range of subsidies often denied to American corporations. In effect, the United States is subsidizing the attempts of foreign corporations to drive American corporations out of business. The Tolchins write that the "states are engaged in economic fratricide. They vie with each other to see who can offer the most tax abatements, grants, real estate, and loans, while the foreign multinationals sit back and wait for the best bargain. While other industrialized nations carefully co-ordinate and control their own policies toward foreign investment, the United States has embarked on a free-for-all that can only make it less competitive in the long run if it continues to dissipate its resources in this way".[15] Even the Japanese have criticized the incentives when they created a local banklash. The Tolchins quote a Nissan executive as exclaiming: "You people are crazy with incentives . . . Our company located here and you gave them sewers, roads, and curbs. When people from the surrounding community . . . looked around, they said, 'We haven't got roads, curbs, and sewers.' The resentment gave us a lot of trouble".[16] Or, in Senator Jim Sasser's words: "Why are we using taxpayers' money to help Komatsu beat Caterpillar's brains out!"[17]

The Tolchins relate scores of cases of states giving away the store to attract foreign investments. For example, Tennessee provided a range of low interest loans, job training, and land improvements to attract Nissan Motor Company. The town leaders of Lewisburg, Tennessee lured Kanto Seiki, which manufactures automotive instrument panels, by helping it obtain an $820 000 Urban Development Action Grant (UDAG), sold them the land at a subsidized price, provided biligual education in the schools, and a ten year tax holiday. Toyota invested in Kentucky after being given $112 million in new roads, employee training programs, grants and low-cost loans, and 1500 acres of free land. It cost Kentucky taxpayers $40 000 for each of the 3000 Toyota positions. The final cost to Kentucky, however, could be as high as $325 million by the year 2006 when the cost of land, highway improvements, site preparation, and education are tallied. Chatanooga gave away $20 million of tax free loans, federal grants, property tax deferrals, $500 000 of employee training programs, the promise of reducing import tariffs by moving Komatsu into a subzone of a foreign trade zone, and special Japanese educational programs to Komatsu in exchange for a factory that employed 250 people and helped undermine Caterpillar. Between 1982 and 1985 Caterpillar lost close to $1 billion and reduced its labor force from 89 000 to 54 000.[18] The Tolchins point out: "While Tennessee justly cheers the promise of 250 jobs, who is mourning Caterpillar's loss of 35 000 jobs".[19]

Former Colorado Governor Richard Lamm succinctly sums up the dilemma: "There are all kinds of Faustian bargains made in economic development. Even though you get 250 jobs, the net effect on your community is negative because you've given away the show".[20] Many analysts echo Lamm's warning of a Faustian bargain. Former Central Intelligence Agency (CIA) Director William Casey was one of the more prominent government leaders to describe Japanese investments in American computer firms and other high technology companies as "a Trojan Horse" – although he apparently did nothing to prevent it.[21] Nabraska Senator Bob Kerrey also points out foreign investment's dark side: "Technology drain is a major concern . . . Reciprocity is a major concern. They bring in jobs and money . . . but we find ourselves importing their products. The trade deficit creates a major employment problem for us".[22] Some governors are well aware of the Faustian bargains being struck by other states and refuse to give in. Virginia Governor Lenkey complained bitterly about Tennessee flying "four hundred people to Japan for training, and the county bought property and leased it to next to nothing to Nissan. In Virginia, there are no concessions to foreign firms. Our governor and tax commissioner won't play that game. It's not fair to our own companies".[23] Ironically, the result of these give aways is that after being vastly subsidized and protected by their own government Japanese firms enjoy additional benefits in the United States which are denied to American firms. It can be argued that, "the pattern of government interventions . . . looks as if the United States practices industrial policy for foreign multinationals while practicing free market philosophy" for American firms.[24]

How do Americans feel about Japan's buying spree in their country? Surveys indicate widely different views of Japanese investments. Japanese surveys generally claim that most American business and the general public have positive feelings toward Japanese investments while international polls indicate just the opposite, that most Americans view with alarm Japan's inroads into America's economy. A December 1989 Nihon Keizai Shimbun poll of 407 American CEOs claimed that most respondants overwelmingly favored Japanese investments in the United States: 69.1 per cent thought Japanese investments would strengthen America's economy and only 13.6 per cent thought it would have weaken the economy and 17.3 per cent gave no opinion; 59.6 per cent thought those investments would bring advanced technologies and better quality control compared to 14.6 per cent who disagreed and 25.7 per cent who gave no opinion; 46.0 per cent said these investments would not give the Japanese too much control over the American economy, 41.0 per cent thought they would, and 12.4 per cent ventured no opinion; and, finally, 76.8 thought the frictions over Japanese investments reflected some American cultural bias while 11.6 per cent disagreed and 11.6 per cent gave no opinion. The American CEOs survey did agree (89.9 per cent) that it was harder for foreign firms to invest in Japan than in the United States (5.4 per cent disagreed and 5.7 per cent did not answer); Japanese investments could give them access to sensitive American technology (46.4 per cent agreed, 30.9 per cent disagreed, and 22.7 per cent gave no answer); and the investments will cause more bilateral frictions (68.9 per cent agreed, 17.1 per cent disagreed, and 15.1 per cent gave no answer).[25]

In contrast, a January 1990 Roper poll asked 1 994 Americans about their feelings on Japanese investment, of which 44 per cent thought it undermined America's economy while only 27 per cent felt it had a positive effect. Of those who agreed that Japanese investments were bad, 42 per cent cited possible Japanese control over American industry.[26] Japanese spokespersons would like Americans to believe that Japanese investments in the United States are a wonderful gift and that any criticism of their investments is simply based on racism. They base their assertion of racism on pointing out that Britain's total investments remain larger than Japan's and yet there is no significant criticism of British investments.

In reality, criticism of Japanese investments is based not on racism, but on the nature of Japan's investments themselves, and Tokyo's overall neomercantilist policies. One reason for the outcry against Japanese investments is the pace of those investments. Japan's investments in the United States more than quadrupled during the 1980s while British firms have slowly built up their presence since the late 19th century. The frenzied onslaught of Japanese firms in the past decade and subsequent disruption to American firms has naturally created animosities. But, more importantly, Americans increasingly recognize Tokyo as an economic adversary that uses a neomercantilist strategy to strengthen Japan's economy at the expense of America's. It is Tokyo's refusal to allow American firms the same opportunities to trade and invest in Japan even though Japan is an economic superpower that is the basis of most criticism. Japanese investments are perceived as Trojan horses which drive American firms out of business and open the flood gates to yet further Japanese products and investments, thus deepening Japan's trade and investment surpluses while excerbating America's deficits and economic decline. Japan enjoys enormous economies of scale and profits that would have remained in America had Washington pursued similar neomercantilist policies. Japan's government and corporations invest most of those profits to increasing Japanese productivity and capturing more market share, while other funds are diverted to buy off America's political leadership and public opinion to back policies that further aid Japan at the expense of the United States.

Although Japanese and neoclassical adherents claim that foreign investment creates jobs, the reality is that Japanese investments in the United States, just like their exports, destroy American jobs. About 95 per cent of all jobs "created" by Japanese investments were were simply transferred from American owned to Japanese owned factories; only about five per cent of the jobs were actually new.[27] But overall jobs are lost from Japanese investments for two reasons: Japanese affiliates buy 250 per cent more components from Japanese sources than do American companies, while the greater efficiency of Japanese investments means fewer workers are required than in an equivalent American factory.

There is also considerable evidence that Japan's investments really are "Trojan horses" which conquer America's high technology markets. As Jim Bryant points out, the Japanese "have invested heavily in our high tech industries and own more than 32 000 US patents. They are draining us of our technology, while denying us access to theirs".[28] Although the Japanese acquisitions of Rockefeller Center and MCA made front page news, Japan's corporations are increasingly targeting low profile yet strategic high technology firms for conquest. Kubota, for example, after doubling its market share against Caterpillar in the 1980s through dumping, then set up factories in the United States and bought five American software and supercomputer technology companies. In 1988, Kubota produced its first mini-supercomputer. In 1987, Minebea paid $110 million to purchase its key American competitor, New Hampshire Ball Bearings. Following the footsteps of Motorola and VLSI Technology, National Semiconductor became the latest American firm to abandon its efforts to develop a one megabit chip because the investment costs had simply become too vast and it sold out its semiconductor manufacturing plant to Matsushita for $100 million.

Sony took over Columbia in 1987 partly in hopes of creating a synergy between Japanese hardware and American software. Although Akio Morita and his Sony Corporation like to project an "international" image, the reality is that Sony is as nationalistic and closed as other Japanese corporations. For example in October 1989, when Sony announced its acquisition of Columbia, its press conference was closed to non-Japanese journalists. Sony's strategy forced Matsushita, which had pursued a conservative stay-at-home, hardware strategy, to follow suit with its purchase of MCA. It is believed that the winner of the race to develop HDTV will be a corporation that manufactures both hardware and software for HDTV sets. MCA, with 1989 sales of $3.38 billion, owns Universal Studios, Universal Pictures, MCA Records, theme parks, the G.P. Putnam Sons publishing house, and the concessions at Yosemite Park. Yet, with Matsuhita's keiretsu of 87 firms, 1989 revenues of $45 billion, $12 billion in cash, and $13 billion in short-term securities, MCA's purchase at $66 a share or $6.13 billion, was an easy matter. Matsushita's 1990 revenues were expected to rise to $55 billion.[29]

Japan's corporations have acquired a nasty reputation for overworking and underpaying their employees, discriminating against women and minorities, and denying American managers significant responsibilities or advancment opportunities. The joint venture between Toyota and GM at Fremont, California, for example, has a higher productivity and quality rate than any GM factory, although a recent book by two former workers argues that this was achieved simply by speeding up the assembly line and playing off workers against each other.[30] Kawasaki has earned a particularly bad reputation for labor abuse. Rudy Oswald, chief economist of the AFL–CIO, points out that "some foreign companies operate much worse than the worst US companies. You'd have to be hard pressed to find someone worse than Kawasaki".[31] The National Labor Relations Board (NLRB) found Kawasaki guilty of a range of unfair labor practices, including intimidating and outright dismissing union organizers. Kawasaki threatened to move its production to existing factories in Japan if a union were created, an ironic threat since Kawasaki's Japan-based factories are all unionized.[32] Sumitomo Shoji was sued in a class-action suit by thirteen female secretaries who claimed that the company's practice of hiring only Japanese citizens to fill executive, managerial and sales posts violated the Civil Rights Act. Sumitomo claimed that if such practices existed, they would be protected under United States–Japan trade treaties. The Supreme Court disagreed, ruling in Sumitomo Shoji Inc. v. Avagiliano that the purpose of such treaties "was not to give foreign corporations greater rights than domestic companies, but instead to give them the right to conduct business on an equal basis without suffering discrimination based on their alienage . . . The local subsidiaries are considered . . . to be companies of the country in which they are incorporated; they are entitled to the rights, and subject to the responsibilities, of other domestic corporations".[33] Six years after the Court decision, Sumitomo finally settled the ten year case by agreeing to spend $2.8 million to pay, train and promote its female employees.

American managers for Japanese firms probably suffer the most abuse. Leah Nathan conducted an extensive investigation of some of the 25 000 American managers now working for Japanese managers and concluded that

> by and large they seem to be an unhappy and demoralized lot. The Japanese need American executives' expertise to sell their products in the United States and are willing to pay top salaries to get them. But in company after company, the Americans complain about a system of subtle and debilitating discrimination in which they are treated as necessary but inferior outsiders – without the authority to get things done and without upward mobility . . . Japan's vaunted management methods, while generally successful on the factory floor, are a dismal failure in the executive ranks . . . . American managers have to contend with the traditional xenophobia of the Japanese and their belief in their own superiority.[34]

Nathan points out that "every American manager has a Japanese counterpart – or "shadow" – who officially serves as the communications liaison with the company in Japan but whose real job is to watch over the

American and get headquarters approval for decisions made ... the actual decision-making cuts out the Americans altogether".[35] In 1990, Matsushita, Sumitomo and NEC Electronics were among scores of Japanese corporations which settled discrimination suits brought against them by disgruntled American managers. The common complaint in the suits was that there is an glass ceiling to advancement by Americans, that all major decisions and responsibilities are held by Japanese staff, and that American managers are simply figureheads while real power lies in Japanese "shadows." Japan's corporations are topheavy with Japanese expatriates, with often four times more than other foreign firms.

Japan's discriminatory practices are causing a boomerang effect. Japanese companies are having difficulties recruiting skilled American managers for their American operations. The widespread knowledge that Japan's corporations use shadow Japanese managers to keep a close watch on the figurehead American management, whose advancement and decision-making possibilities are extremely limited, means the best American managers avoid working for Japanese corporations or drop out as soon as a better offer arises. Japan's management policies thus become a self-fulfilling prophecy, in which American managers are assumed to put themselves before the company, so their power and advancement opportunities are limited, thus forcing out the more skilled and ambitious.[36]

Japanese corporations are notorious for using every conceivable device for evading payment of US taxes. American tax law requires parent firms to charge their subsidiaries the same prices that would be paid in an open market, or so called "arm's length prices." In 1990, the US Internal Revenue Service charged that hundreds of Japanese subsidiaries vastly underreported their income in the United States between 1984 and 1987. Japanese corporations milked their American subsidiaries by charging excessive prices for goods, services and technology, thus reducing reported profits and channeling those immense profits back to Japan. During those four years, the amount of Japanese corporations' net income from their American operations steadily dropped from $1.85 billion in 1984 to $219 million in 1987, while gross receipts almost tripled from $65.5 billion to $172 billion. The American subsidiaries of Toshiba Corp., Hitachi Ltd., and Matsushita Electric Industrial Co., for example, received notices from the IRS that they are being investigated for having underpaid taxes by as much as 50 billion yen. But Japanese corporate tax evasion is nothing new and is, in fact, standard operating procedure. The first big IRS case occurred in 1978 when Honda Motor Co. was ordered to pay $21 million in back taxes for excessive prices on its exports to reduce its tax liability. Bowing to Japan's lobbying power, the Reagan Administration dropped the charge in 1984. The Nissho Iwai Corp. also beat the IRS out of charges that it had to pay $485 000 in additional tax in 1972–75 for undercharging the costs of timber sold to its Japanese parent.[37]

Japanese government and corporate spokesmen, of course, dismiss the IRS charges as mere "Japan-bashing" and a violation of the US–Japan Tax Treaty which calls for equal treatment of foreign and domestic companies. According to Tokyo, Japanese corporations are model businesses and any charges of tax evasion are simply a result of "misunderstandings" of Japanese business operations. It is claimed the strong yen, corporate emphasis on market share rather than profit, and influx of smaller firms from 1 422 in 1984 to 2 165 in 1987 undercut profits during this period despite the almost tripling of gross operating revenues.[38] As usual, there is an immense gap between Japanese rhetoric and reality. The US–Japan Tax Treaty provides a classic example of Tokyo's endless ability to outfox Washington. The Treaty requires Tokyo to reimburse any Japanese corporations which are caught evading taxes and must pay back taxes. As a result, the Japanese government ends up subsidizing the tax evasions of Japanese corporations – or at least those that are caught. Thus with nothing to lose and everything to gain, the Treaty encourages Japanese corporations to evade taxes.

The Japanese purchase of American communications conglomerates raised troubling questions of possible censorship. Matsushita, for example, hired such top gun lobbyists as Robert Strauss (former Democratic Chairman) and Jody Powell (former Carter White House press secretary) to undercut any protests that key outlets of American mass culture were falling into foreign hands or could lead to censorship. Matsushita president, Akio Tanii, was asked several times if MCA's purchase would mean the censorship of films and books critical of Japan. Tanii first ducked the questions with the cryptic words, "MCA's management had common sense and fairness in their powers of judgement", but then later angrily remarked: "I could never imagine such a case so I cannot imagine such a question . . . Our new co-operation with MCA is part of broader US–Japan co-operation as countries. So I believe that such a movie will not be produced".[39]

In other words, Japan's economic power to buy up America's strategic industries, or "co-operation" as Mr Tanii describes it, will be translated into the political power to censor any filmed or written works critical of Japanese neomercantilism. Hiroshi Ishikawa, a social psychology professor at Seijo University, warned that "Japanese companies are very, very careful about their (corporate and national) image." The Japanese takeover of American mass entertainment firms could usher in "an age of subtle cultural censorship, and it could be very dangerous. It is hard to think of Matsushita making a movie in which the hero is killed by the Japanese army".[40] Tokyo has continually attempted to censor school textbooks and films that run counter to the myth that Japan was the victim rather victimizer during World War II. For example, Tokyo cut out newsreels from Bernardo Bertolucci's film "The Last Emperor" which depicted Japanese mass executions of Chinese, claiming that such scenes would cause "discomfort" to Japanese and might "cause unnecessary confusion in the movie theaters".[41] The American-made movie "Mishima", released in 1986 to highly favorable reviews, was prevented from being shown in Japan for similar reasons. The virtuous cycle of economic and political power will accelerate: Japan's power to censor combined with the power to shape American policies will, in turn, strengthen Japan's economic power, which will further enhance its political power, and so on.

Japanese inroads into other sectors of the American economy have also been criticized. The United States not only does not restrict the foreign purchase of American real estate, but, except for farm land, does not require the dislosure of foreign real estate assets. As a result, the official tallying of foreign owned American real estate may be only half the actual amount. And, as in other United States economic sectors, foreign corporations enjoy advantages denied to American firms. For example, foreigners can avoid capital gains taxes on stock sales while American firms must pay up.[42] Although the 1978 Agricultural Foreign Investment Disclosure Law required the disclosure of foreign farm ownership, loopholes allow foreigners to avoid disclosure by setting up three levels of dummy incorporations while the Department of Agriculture lacks the manpower to investigate potentially phony claims. In contrast to Washington's *laissez-faire* policy, twenty-nine states have some restrictions on foreign ownership of farmland.

Yet, popular fears about foreigners buying America may be exaggerated. In 1986, foreign investors owned only $209 billion or less than one per cent of the $12 trillion in American business and private real estate.[43] Despite this low percentage of total American real estate, foreign purchases were concentrated in highly visible sectors. For example, in 1987, foreign investors owned half of all commercial real estate in downtown Los Angeles, almost a quarter in New York, and more than a third in Houston.[44] In 1985, foreigners owned 12.1 million acres or less than 1 per cent of the total American farmland. About 51 per cent of this foreign ownership was in forest, 17 per cent cropland, 27 per cent in pasture and other agricultural land, and 5 per cent unreported. Only 38 per cent of all American agricultural land is actually used for food production; the rest is either in forestry or disuse.[45] Thus, even if foreign farm ownership were underreported by half, it would hardly represent a threat to American agricultural sovereignty.

Japan has the largest foreign direct investments in American real estate, and its assets grew astronomically throughout the late 1980s. Between

1983 and 1988, Japanese-owned real estate in the United States rose almost twenty times in value from $515 million to $10.017 billion, and in 1990 the Japanese officially owned $71 billion in American real estate.[46] But the real figure is much larger since much of the investment in mortgage financing shows up as debt and not ownership. Japanese own more real estate in the United States than all the European Community members. And the cash rich Japanese corporations have paid some staggeringly high prices: In New York, Japanese corporations paid $610 million for the Exxon building, $250 million for the Mobil building, $175 million for the ABC building, $670 million for 37 floors of the Citicorp building. Mitsubishi Estate Corporation bought a 51 per cent stake in Rockefeller Center in October 1989 for $846 million, a drop in the bucket of Mitsubishi's global assets valued at $84 billion, of which 90 per cent is located in Tokyo.[47] Japanese corporations own 25 per cent of Los Angeles' skyline, and paid $620 million alone for the Arco Plaza.[48]

Nowhere have the Japanese bought up more American real estate than in Hawaii. In 1988, Japanese tourists accounted for $3.7 billion and Japanese investors $1.6 billion of Hawaii's gross state product of $21.3 billion. Japanese investors now own all but one of the seafront hotels in Waikiki, and altogether 92 per cent of the deluxe hotel rooms and 57 per cent of luxury class rooms in the entire state are Japanese owned. Between 1989 and 1992, 14 additional Japanese owned top-class hotels will open in Hawaii. Over 70 per cent of the $3.3 billion Japanese invested in Hawaiian real estate in the fifteen months up to March 1988 was targeted on seven largely residential areas. Much of this tide of speculation was fueled by the Tokyo property magnate, Genshiro Kawamoto, who bought more than 170 properties.[49]

As elsewhere, Japan's investment tidal wave has caused problems. House prices in affluent neighborhoods like Kahala doubled while even lower priced homes increased in value as a side effect of Japan's widespread and concerted speculation. After buying the Turtle Bay country club, the Japanese owners sent a letter to all local members that their memberships would be terminated at the year's end. The growing dependence of Hawaii on Japanese capital, the land speculation and inflation, and the "Japanese only" policies of Japanese owned golf courses and clubs led to growing resentment among Hawaiians. A May 1988 poll revealed that 78 per cent objected to foreigners buying homes and 72 per cent favoring banning foreign acquisitions.[50]

Japan's real estate buying splurge was stimulated by the huge cash oceans acquired during the mid-1980s. But a combination of poor returns on their investments, the collapse of the real estate market, and the stock market crashes of 1987 and 1990 which sharply cut back financial reserves forced Japan's real estate speculators to sell off some of their investments.

Japan's real estate investments peaked at $17.5 billion in 1988, then dropped to $14.8 billion in 1989, and to $10 billion in 1990.[51] Now Japan's real estate investors have been accused of "dumping" the sales of leases. Renters are lured from other properties with promises that their rent on the remaining lease will be paid.[52] Whether they buy up or sell out, Japan's corporations cannot seem to escape criticism.

JAPAN'S INVESTMENT POLICIES AND POWER

Japan's ability to buy up its battered overseas rivals is not reciprocated. Tokyo's neomercantilist policies toward foreign investments in Japan contrasts sharply with Japan's neomercantilist investment policies. "Liberalization" has only occured after systematic foreign pressure by governments and multinationals. Yet, despite a series of "investment opening steps", Tokyo maintains a web of restrictions that dramatically raise the cost of foreign investment in Japan, make an outright purchase of a Japanese firm extremely difficult, and a hostile takeover impossible. After carefully analyzing Japan's foreign investment policies one can only conclude that "no other country has so adamantly denied multinational corporations (MNCs) access to domestic markets".[53]

Yet, having hurdled the seemingly endless investment and market obstacles, many foreign firms thrive after they have finally become established. The average profit to sales ratio of 6.8 per cent for foreign firms was much higher than the average for Japanese firms in Japan of 2.8 per cent. Those foreign investments also helped alleviate some of immense trade deficits their home countries suffered from Japan – they imported 3.198 trillion in yen of products and exported 1.495 trillion yen in 1988, and imported on average seven times as much as the average Japanese company and they export much less from Japan.[54] As surprising is the fact that American firms actually employed more Japanese (345 500) and were more profitable ($3.205 billion), than Japanese firms Americans (284 600) and profits ($484 million). These official profit figures may be meaningless, however, since Japanese corporations are so skilled at underreporting overseas profits to avoid taxation. American firms also invested in more manufacturing enterprises ($7.136 billion) which were more profitable ($1.967 billion), and employed more Japanese (222 400) than Japanese firms made manufacturing investments ($5.345 billion), profits ($6000), or employees (81 600).

The trouble, of course, is getting in and, more importantly, at what price. The Faustian bargain often involves the foreign surrender of technology for access. Tokyo traditionally held a pistol to the head of any foreign firm requesting access: the admission price included sharing key technology and forming joint ventures with the firm's Japanese rivals. The Japanese "partner" milks the venture for all its technological juices then dumps it.

Japan's systematic restrictions on foreign investment date to the Occupation. The American Occupation reinforced Japan's traditional xenophobia toward foreign investment by enacting two laws which gave MOF and newly created MITI vast controls over the economy and trade. The 1949 Foreign Exchange Control Law (FECL) and 1950 Foreign Investment Law (FIL) granted the government virtually total control over any capital inflows and outflows. Any foreign investments within Japan had to improve Japan's international payments, essential industries or public enterprises, or technological resources. The only foreign investors allowed were those which promised not to remit any profits. All proposed investments were screened by the Foreign Investment Deliberation Council (Gaishi Shingikai, FIDC) staffed by MITI and other concerned ministries. Most proposals were flatly rejected while those few excepted had to agree to numerous restrictions. Wholly owned subsidiaries were rarely allowed. Most foreign firms were not only forced to accept minority or equal partnership joint ventures with their current and future Japanese rivals, but also license them their technology. The investments were often prevented from entering related or new industries, and could not increase their capitalization from abroad, raise capital locally, or remit profits, and limited in capital or resource imports. All investments licenses had to be periodically renewed.

The admission price for Japan's membership in the International Monetary Fund (IMF) in 1956 and Organization for Economic Co-operation and Development (OECD) in 1964 theoretically included financial and investment deregulation. Tokyo's adept diplomacy enabled it to join these prestigious organizations with a tremendous discount – unlike other members, Japan did not have to liberalize its markets. Although Tokyo made vague promises to eventually liberalize its trade, investment, and financial markets, after obtaining OECD membership, Tokyo actually tightened its foreign currency restrictions, including limiting remittances and new investments, and closed off the yen company route to investment. Between 1956 and 1963, Tokyo had allowed a second category of foreign investment called a "yen-based company", in which there were no restrictions except the remittance of profits. The mass media worked in harness with the government and business to inhibit foreign investment by continuing running lurid sensa-tionalistic stories equating foreign investment with the loss of sovereignty and destruction of Japanese culture, which seem particularly ironic now when Tokyo is making a concerted public relations campaign to convince Americans of the completely beneficial results of Japanese investments in the United States. As a result of these restrictions, between 1945 and 1952, only 90 foreign investments worth $20 million were allowed in Japan, and between 1953 and 1960, only 101 foreign investments worth $59.7 million. Just 289 yen-based companies with total investments worth about $500 million were permitted between 1957 and 1963, of which 161 were more than 95 per cent majority owned. In addition, there were about 150 companies with total assets at 235 million by 1963 that did not have national treatment.[55]

Tokyo succeeded in forcing many foreign firms which invested simply to foster their future rivals. For example, Singer Sewing Machine, the prewar market leader, was allowed back in only after agreeing to severe production quotas and a joint venture with its competitor, Pine. The restriction ensured the transfer of Singer's technology and eventually global leadership to Japan. Coca Cola's fifteen years efforts to gain a foothold in Japan should be cited everytime a Japanese spokesperson repeats the mantra that foreign firms do not succeed because they do not try hard enough. Although Coca Cola had had an office in Tokyo since 1945, reformed the office into a yen company in 1957, and formed a joint venture with Kirin Brewery in 1958, its sales were minimal until MITI finally allowed that venture to produce the Coke concentrate in 1960.

IBM's horror stories are just as revealing of Japanese neomercantilism. In 1961, after four years of tough negotiations, MITI finally granted IBM a license allowing limited production and markets in return for IBM granting its key technology to its rivals. Sahashi Shigeru, Deputy Director of MITI's Heavy Industries Bureau, clearly declared Japan's objectives and strategy: "We will take every measure possible to obstruct the success of your business unless you license IBM patents to Japanese firms and charge them no more than a 5 per cent royalty. We need only time and money to compete effectively".[56] Washington's inept policies were almost as troublesome to IBM as MITI. IBM deliberately choose not to gain Embassy help in its efforts for fear that it might incite American antitrust action when it was discovered that its Japanese competitors had to pay a higher royalty than its domestic competitors.[57]

Texas Instruments (TI) suffered similar horrors in its attempts to invest in Japan and achieve protection for its intellectual property. A Japanese patent for TI's semiconductor technology was granted in 1990 – thirty years after TI first filed for patent protection in 1960. For three decades, TI's competitors capitalized on the stolen property to the point where they have seriously devastated America's semiconductor and microelectronic industries. In 1964, TI applied to become IBM's main semiconductor supplier both through exports from the United States and investments in Japan. After four years of bitter negotiations, approval was finally granted in 1968. The cost for TI was extreme. Once again

MITI used its power to shut off both trade and investments and play off foreign corporations against each other to force TI to grant three concessions which eventually devastated America's microelectronics industry. First, TI was forced to establish a joint venture with one of its Japanese rivals – it settled on Sony. Second, it had to "consult" with MITI about its Japanese production levels and market shares. Finally, it had to license its key technology to its Japanese rivals for a set licensing fee. The result was that once again, Japan's government and "companies had controlled the timing and substance of a foreign corporation's entry into the home market and in the process had extracted from that foreigner a high price for entry. In exchange, however, TI gained market access that was denied to other foreign, less technologically advanced competitors, who were still held at bay by tariff barriers, capital controls, technology restrictions and other such regulations".[58]

IBM and TI only were only granted investment access because of their technological prowess and global market share, and the bargaining power it gave those firms; other American semiconductor makers were simply forced to license their technology to their rivals or prevented from investing in Japan. For example, Fairchild and National Semiconductor attempted to evade Japan's investment barries by setting up plants in Okinawa. But after Okinawa was returned to Japan in 1972, MITI forced the American producers to choose between either forming a joint venture with their rivals or shutting down. National Semiconductor choose to abandon its operation while Fairchild made a joint venture that collapsed in 1977 after its "partner" had squeezed the venture of its technology and production benefits.

MITI's nefarious and cynical tricks combined with its continual pressure on American high technology firms like TI to surrender their technology to their rivals stimulated a tougher American policy. In 1966, Washington made a concerted effort to force Tokyo to liberalize by using such forums as the Joint US–Japan Committee on Trade, Economic Affairs and the American Chamber of Commerce in Japan (ACCJ), the OECD Business and Industrial Advisory Council, the OECD Committee on Invisible Transactions, and the Commerce Department. The government and Keidanren continued to reject liberalization as "too early", with MITI claiming that fully 90 per cent of Japanese industry was not "sufficiently competitive" to permit foreign investment inflows.[59]

Eventually, however, Tokyo did agree to a series of "investment opening packages", upon whose completion, it was claimed, Japan would be "completely open to foreign investment".[60] In June 1967, the government announced that beginning on 1 July the FIDC would grant "automatic approval" for wholly owned investments in 17 product groups, minority or equal partnerships in 33 other product groups, and up to 20 per cent equity spread among three or different shareholders in Japanese firms. The trouble was that none of the 17 product groups supposedly open to wholly owned foreign investments provided economically viable opportunities. For example, cement was one of the 17 groups listed. But the cement industry, which held a monopoly over limestone deposits and the distribution system, was already suffering from severe overcapacity. On paper the industry was "100 per cent liberalized"; in reality, it was effectively 100 per cent closed to either foreign investments or imports. As a result, from July 1967 to April 1968, no foreign investments were made in these 60 product areas supposedly completely liberalized, and from April 1968 to April 1969, there were only four applications totaling less than $2.2 million. Japanese, of course, claimed that the lack of investments showed that foreign corporations simply did not try hard enough or take a long term view. The reality is that Tokyo's "liberalization" measures were simply public relations stunts designed to obscure continued severe neomercantilist policies.

In April 1968, the second "liberalization" allowed "automatic approval" for wholly owned foreign investments in 44 product groups and up to equal partnerships in 160 other product groups. Once again, the "liberalization" was economically virtually meaningless – only 15 subsidiaries or joint ventures totaling $1.7 million occured during the second phase. In September 1970, the third "liberalization" phase allowed foreign equity as high as 25 per cent in Japanese firms – although it still had to be spread among three or more different shareholders, wholly owned investments in 77 product groups and up to equal partnerships in 447 product groups. Only 47 investments worth $9 million were approved during the third phase. In April 1971, the FIDC designated 228 wholly owned product groups and allowed individual foreign shareholders up to 10 per cent equity in a Japanese firm. The fifth package was announced in 1973 "liberalized" all but 27 industries on the negative list. Yet, by 1974, only 2 per cent of America's foreign investments were in Japan, and only one out of ten foreign investments in Japan were wholly owned. Although the number of American investments in Japan doubled between 1974 and 1980, they did so from a very low base and continued to be fought at every step by Japan's bureaucratic industrial complex. As if continued discrimination against competitive foreign investments was not enough, the government stepped up its efforts to promote cartels, intercorporate cross-sharing, mergers, and joint ventures among Japan's microelectronics corporations. In addition, it encouraged Japanese firms to limit the number and voting rights of foreign investors or board directors.

In 1980, Tokyo eliminated the FIL and many formal controls on foreign investment within Japan. From now foreign investments could proceed after simple notification rather than approval of an application.

The government, however, retained its power to prevent any foreign investments that would adversely affect any domestic industries, the payments balance, or the economy. As in Tokyo's other "liberalization" measures, there is a wide gap between the principles espoused (*tatemae*) and the continuing protectionist reality (*honne*). According to Johnson, Japan's "liberalization" of its rules governing foreign investment is simply "a strictly pro forma acquiescence in international conventions", while in reality multinationals trying to invest are still trapped "in a vast tangle of rules and procedures".[61]

Since 1980, the restrictions on foreign investments have largely shifted from government to industry administered. Japanese corporations use their market, production, price, and distribution cartels to make any investment prohibitively expensive for all but the largest foreign corporations. Japanese claim that American and other foreign firms do not sell or invest more in Japan because they don't try hard enough. In reality, Japan is protected by a web of overt and subtle trade and investment barriers that make significant foreign share of Japan's markets virtually impossible. For example, when Cargill Inc., an American agribusiness, tried to build a livestock feed plant in Shibushi it faced the classic run around that any competitive foreign corporation faces when it wants to invest in Japan: it could not buy the land without permission of the local government, which in turn claimed it could not give permission without Tokyo's approval. It was only after Senator John Danforth pressured the USTR, who in turn pressured Tokyo that Cargill was allowed to open its plant.

Government policies and private cartels severely restrict Japan's mergers and acquisitions (M & A) market. The Securities and Exchange Law requires someone to notify MOF ten days before it conducts a tender offer if the value of the stock is more than 10 per cent of the targeted firm's equity – which gives that firm considerable time to prepare a defense. Foreign firms or individuals suffer even greater discrimination in that they must appoint a securities house as agent and then wait at least 30 days after MOF accepts their filing before they can buy any shares – a waiting period that can be arbitrarily extended if the acquisition is believed to harm national security or competitiveness. M & A activity in Japan, like virtually all other economic transactions, occurs behind closed doors. Unlike in the United States where such a deal can only occur with the consent of a majority of stockholders, Japan's shareholders are the last to know. M & A activity has slowly increased during the 1980s from a very low base. In 1984, 140 deals were announced of which the values of only two deals were revealed, a total of 1.490 billion yen. In 1988, 223 deals were announced of which the values of only 69 deals were revealed, a combined total of 109.018 billion yen.[62] The attitude of Japanese toward

M&A is revealed by the vocabulary describing such deals: the Japanese word for takeover is *nottori* (hijack) and divestiture is *mi-uri* (selling one's body).

Thus, while Japanese firms can buy almost any American corporation it is still virtually impossible for American and other foreign firms to buy a Japanese firm. Foreign ownership is outright forbidden in some economic sectors. Japan only permits foreign ownership of up to 50 per cent in its energy corporations and 25 per cent of its "technologically innovative companies" – a term so vague as to apply to most Japanese corporations, and outright bans ownership in agriculture, forestry, fisheries, mining, petroleum, leather and leather products. Foreign investors can finance up to 100 per cent of their purchases of American assets while American investors may not be able to borrow more than 50 per cent.(63) Elsewhere in the economy, foreign takeovers of Japanese companies are extremely rare and never hostile. In 1984, there were six deals of which the values of only two were publically announced – a total of 3.857 billion yen. In 1988, there were 17 deals of which the values of only 7 were revealed – a total of 69.811 billion yen. Japanese companies are not similarly burdened in the United States. For example, in 1986 Japanese firms acquired 44 American firms worth $1.6 billion. In contrast, the sole American attempt to takeover a Japanese firm in 1985 – Minabea Holdings – was defeated.[64] The inability to takeover Japanese firms severely hobbles the competitive power of American firms. Abegglen points out that "American companies have traditionally entered European markets via acquisition. An acquisition of a successful company solves at one stroke problems of establishing a capable management and staff, effective government relations, physical plant and equipment, and distribution system. Unfortunately, Japanese only accept acquisition when a company is bankrupt".[65]

Japan's cartels aside, foreign firms are often denied the protection of Japanese law. Japan's shareholders have clear legal rights varying according to what percentage of a company's stock they own. Anyone with 1 per cent of a company has the right to vote at shareholder's meetings, inspect the register of shareholders, or propose any action for consideration at a meeting. Three per cent of a company's shares entitles the holder to convene a shareholders' meeting. Ten per cent allows the holder to inspect and make copies of accounts and other company records. Ownership of one third of a company's shares confers veto power which can only be overidden by a two-thirds majority, half the shares gives the power to appoint directors and two-thirds the power to remove directors, change articles of incorporation, approve mergers and transfers of substantial assets. As always, things in Japan are rarely as they seem. Despite these clear legal quidelines the Tokyo District Court rejected T. Boone Picken's right to examine the tax records of Koito even though with 20 per cent of the company's stock, he had twice the percentage of shares necessary to excercise such a right.

JAPAN'S FOREIGN INVESTMENT POLICY AND POWER

In stark contrast to the web of restrictions which continue to entangle any foreign firm attempting to invest in Japan, is the genuine freedom with which Japanese firms can invest overseas. Japan's accumulated direct foreign investments between 1951 and 1988 was $186.356 billion, up $47.022 billion from 1987, of which $49.843 billion or 26.7 per cent was in manufacturing, $131.999 billion or 70.8 in non-anufacturing, and $3.919 billion or 2.1 per cent in opening or expanding branch offices. Of this total, $71.860 billion, or 38.6 per cent was in the United States, $32.227 billion or 17.3 per cent in Asia, $31.617 billion in Latin America, $30.164 billion or 16.2 per cent in Europe, $9.315 billion or 5.0 per cent in Oceania, $4.604 billion or 2.5 per cent in Africa, and $3.338 billion or 1.8 per cent in the Middle East.

As of 1988, although Japan's overseas investments were an estimated 10.7 per cent of the world total, behind America's 31.7 per cent and Britain's 17.8 per cent, Japan's net assets were the world's highest. The growth of Japan's net foreign investments throughout the 1980s was extraordinary, increasing from less than 1 per cent of GNP in 1981 to more than 4 per cent in 1986, with its accumulated net foreign holdings of $180 billion in 1986 far surpassing America's $133 billion peak in 1981, and by 1988, Japan's total net assets had soared to $291.746 billion.[66] In 1987, direct foreign investments made up only 14 per cent of Japan's capital outflows; in the first half of 1990, it made up an astonishing 70 per cent. In the first nine months of 1990 alone, Japanese corporations took over 328 foreign companies in the first nine months of 1990, about half of which were American firms.[67] In 1988, America's payment's deficit with Japan was $128.5 billion ($156.3 billion credits, $284.8 billion liabilities).

Japan's foreign investments have surged in three waves since the 1950s, with each wave more powerful and diverse than the preceding. The first wave started slowly in the 1950s, gathered volume throughout the 1960s, and peaked in 1974. During this time, using its vast powers under the 1949 Foreign Exchange Control Act, MOF carefully screened every foreign investment proposal, allowing only those which would not harm Japan's international payments balance. The total value of Japan's foreign investments from its first in 1951 until 1962 was only $545 million, most of which consisted of the re-establishment and expansion of trade offices or small scale extraction and manufacturing operations. MOF slowly loosened its reins throughout the 1960s as foreign pressure for liberalization, and Japan's labor costs, pollution problem, land costs, and annual international payments surpluses all rose steadily. MOF finally instituted five liberalization stages between 1969 and 1972 which rapidly accelerated Japan's foreign investments. The value of Japan's foreign investments rose ten times between 1962 to $4.435 billion in 1972, then shot up to $12.664 billion in 11,614 projects in 1974 as the last restrictions were removed. About 70 per cent of all the manufacturing and resource investments were located in Asia, and most of these in Taiwanese and South Korean export processing zones, and most of these were joint ventures with local firms.[68] About 42 of all Japan's foreign investments were made by small- and medium-sized companies.[69]

OPEC's quadrupling of oil prices in 1973 forced Tokyo to dramatically revise its foreign trade and investment strategy. Up until then Tokyo had procured over 95 per cent of its energy and raw materials through long term purchase agreements with the cheapest international sources, a highly successful strategy until OPEC proved its vulnerability. Thus Tokyo initiated its comprehensive security whereby it spread its foreign sources of markets, energy, and raw materials as widely as possible while making those sources dependent on Japanese finance, technology, machine tools and managerial skills. According to Tokyo, the optimum numbers of sources for raw materials was three, enough to play them off against each other for the lowest price and long term agreements yet concentrated enough to realize large-scale development and transportation scale economies.

Japan's corporations were encouraged to invest in massive schemes like the Asahan project in Indonesia, which involved dozens of Japanese corporations investing billions of dollars in mines and factories, and such infrastructure as a huge dam for hydroelectric power, railroads and ports. Tokyo reinforced these huge investments with cheap loans and grants to both Japanese firms and the host country. Japan's government and corporations used the "Asahan formula" for similar projects in Brazil, Iran, Saudi Arabia, and elsewhere. This strategy allows Tokyo to control key economic sectors in the host country. According to Ozawa:

> The Japanese will help to buld deep water ports, automated warehouses, roll-on-off facilities for transferring supplies to giant purpose bulk vessels (which will be Japanese built and Japanese owned) . . . Japanese imports and shippers will control the rate of shipments, the rate of shipping arrivals, the levels of onshore inventories – and thus have considerable influence over any prices which the Japanese think are improper. This could give them considerable political, as well as overwelmingly commercial, weight in these areas . . . The control of logistics rather than that of resource projection itself serves to palliate

economic nationalism in the resource producing country, simultaneously enables Japan indirectly to exercise controls over the supply of resources, and reduces the risk, as well as the potential cost, of nationalization, because Japan's capital is not tied up, and the vessels can be easily withdrawn. The facilities and mode of transportation that are uniquely custom-made to fit the specific technical requirements of Japan's logistics alone will give Japan a monopsony position hindering the entry of other resource importing nations . . . A substantial reduction in transportation cost is crucial for Japan not only to acquire resources at a lower cost but also to diversify the supply sources".[70]

By the early 1980s, three decades of sustained neomercantilist policies had converted Japan's corporations and keiretsu into global giants floating atop enormous oceans of cash and assets. Japan's corporations then embarked on a global buying spree to consolidate their power over farflung markets captured by earlier dumping offensives. Having acheived control over strategic Third World markets and raw materials sources and facing increased protectionism from other industrial democracies under seige from Japan's neomercantilist policies, much of Japan's most recent investment wave descended on the United States and Europe. This trend became evident by 1986, when 46.8 per cent or almost half of that year's Japanese foreign investments flowed into the United States, and an additional 15.5 per cent to Europe. From 1985 through 1989, Japan's foreign investments amounted to a staggering $689.26, of which $570.47 billion was in portfolio investment and $118.79 billion direct investment. Bonds have financed 70.8 per cent or $403.80 billion of these foreign investments, loans and trade credits $90.34 billion or 15.8 per cent, and foreign equities only $46.35 billion or 8.1 per cent. Most of these investments were targeted on the United States and Europe: American and offshore dollar accounts absorbed 61.3 per cent of Japan's international bond investments, while European markets took another 37.1 per cent.[71] While Japan's largest corporations targeted other industrial countries, Asia remained the target for 65.6 per cent of the investments by small- and medium-sized firms, while North America took in 25.6 per cent, Europe 6.2 per cent, and other countries 2.6 per cent.

Japan's third investment wave built steadily throughout the 1980s and into the 1990s as financial and other service industries joined manufacturing and resource corporations in a frenzy of overseas investments. In 1988, 32.4 per cent of Japan's new foreign investments were in finance and insurance, followed by 17.9 per cent in real estate, 17.1 per cent in manufacturing, 8.7 per cent in other services, 8.6 per cent in natural resources, 8.3 per cent in commerce, and 7 per cent in other categories. The ratio of new direct foreign investments to indirect purchases of foreign stocks and bonds by institutional and private investors shifted from five ($109.7 billion) to one ($22.3 billion) in 1986 to two ($74.4 billion) to one ($33.4 billion) in 1987.[72]

What is behind Japan's investment wave across the United States and around the world? Japan's overseas investments are the last stage of Tokyo industrial policies which first target a strategic industry for development, then nurture it with a range of subsidies, cartels, and technology infusions behind a web of import barriers, thus allowing the corporations in those industries to dump their products overseas and drive their foreign rivals out of business. Denied access to Japan's vast market and underpriced at home, the foreign corporations are pushed into a vicious cycle of declining market shares, profits and investments which eventually brings them to the brink of bankruptcy. In the zero sum game of international trade, the foreign firms' losses mean gains for Japanese corporations which enjoy global sized economies of scale production from their investments and profits. The Japanese corporations then set up assembly operation overseas when the foreign country threatens to retaliate against the Japanese dumping onslaught. These "screwdriver assembly plants" allow the Japanese to keep value added production in Japan and increase their trade surplus through transfer payments on the parts ships overseas. Direct foreign investments allows the Japanese corporations to administer the coup de grace to their foreign rivals, and thus establish global hegemony for their products. Japan's textile, television, steel, consumer electronic, automobile and semiconductor industries have all followed this pattern, to varying means of success, against the United States. Markets are the primary objective of Japan's corporations. A 1985 MITI survey of Japanese businesses revealed that their primary reasons for investing in industrial countries was capturing markets (86 per cent) and information collection and market study (54 per cent), while their objectives in developing countries were to capture markets (55 per cent) and cheap labor (46 per cent).[73]

Increasingly, having either bankrupted or mortally wounded many of their American rivals, Japan's corporate behemoths are now largely battling each other in the United States. The long-term rivalry between postwar upstart Sony and established Matsushita is reflected in the former's $5 billion purchase of Columbia in 1987 and the latter's $7.5 billion acquisitions of MCA in 1990. Japan's steel industry is surmounting its 5.8 per cent market quota of America's steel market by either forming joint ventures with or outright buying American steel corporations. The joint ventures include include NKK Corporation and National Steel Inc., Kobe Steel and USX Corporation, Nisshin Steel and Wheeling Pittburg Steel, Nippon Steel and Inland Steel Inc., Kawasaki Steel and Armco, and Sumitomo Mental and LTV.

The enormous outflow of Japanese capital during the 1980s was staggering and unprecented. Yet, Tokyo has been very careful to ensure that most value-added production remains in Japan. Most foreign direct investment has been "screwdriver assembly plants" which actually increase Japan's trade surpluses with the host nations since it exports components whose total value exceeds that of the finished product.

CONCLUSION

White House policy towards foreign investment remains based on the neoclassical dogma that all foreign investments are by definition positive and thus any restrictions negative. To date, Washington has not blocked the purchase of any American corporation by Japanese investors. Unfortunately, few of these foreign investments have lived up to the economists' promises of revitalizing America's economy with new technology, productivity, finance, and managerial skills. More often than not, foreign investments drive American firms out of business and increase unemployment, while America's trade and balances payments go further in the red as the foreign investors import all the value-added parts at inflated prices to be assembled in their American plants, then send most of the profits back home.

Washington's policy of malign neglect toward foreign investment means that policy is actually set by the states and cities rather than the national government. The Tolchins write bluntly that state "policy has become national policy, since federal officials, supposedly the guardians of the national interest, have abdicated to state leadership".[74] The scramble of states and cities to attract foreign investment gives foreign investors an advantage over their American rivals in setting up shop in the United States. The foreign investor plays off one local government against the others to maximize the investment incentives, then can use its threat to withdraw its investments to further armtwist the local government into conceding other concessions. Thus, the most destructive foreign investments occur when local governments, often desparate for any new business in their district and neglected by national government, agree to a range of expensive subsidies with foreign corporations to attract investments. A state or city's incentives are a bonus to foreign investors who usually look at the location's overall investment climate and may well have invested anyway. Economic power is then translated into political power as state and national representatives, heavily financed by the foreign investor, champion yet more benefits for their "constituent".

Japanese corporations invest in the United States because it fits into their overall export policy. Jobs, either their creation or loss, is central to any American discussion of economics. Japanese corporations always try to emphasize the new jobs that will be created by their investments. Japanese investments at once allay criticism of the trade deficit since "American rather than Japanese workers are making the product" while deepening it since the firm buys most of its parts from other Japanese firms. Japanese justify their acquisitions by rightfully arguing that they are all invited. Criticism of such sell-offs of America's high technology and manufacturing jewels should be leveled against America's liberal political economic system, characterized by a war of all American firms against each other, which allows foreign corporations freely to pick up the pieces. In contrast, Tokyo's neomercantilist policies carefully manage domestic and often foreign markets to prevent such fratricide. When a Japanese corporate jewel experiences financial difficulties, the government arranges a marriage with a suitable Japanese firm – foreign takeovers are severely restricted.

While liberal policies further unravel America's economy, Tokyo's neomercantilist policies continue to deepen the power of Japan's corporations over the global political economy. The Japanese have a double standard in regard to foreign investment, just as they do all other aspects of international relations. Tokyo denies American corporations the same benefits in Japan that Japanese corporations enjoy in the United States. Before the 1970s, only firms with a strong patent position were allowed to invest in Japan. The entrance price, however, was exhorbinant. IBM and TI surrendered vital technologies; Coca Cola vast marketing skills – and the profits that went with them; Chrysler, Ford, and General Motors, global distribution systems and political protection for their partners. After setting up their operations, the foreign firms were allocated token market shares. Yet, foreign firms usually did not protest because they knew Tokyo and its cartels would cut away what little share they had, and could then simply buy from yet another rival. Many foreign firms still made a profit because the cartel gouged Japanese consumers with prices usually twice that of foreign markets. Most joint ventures, however, have failed. The Japanese partner invariably entered the venture with the sole short-term objective of appropriating its "partner's" technology. The venture usually folds after the Japanese absorbs the targeted technology. Until recently about 70 per cent of all foreign firms attempted to enter Japan's markets through a joint venture; the rate has fallen to 50 per cent as firms realize that the costs of joint ventures often far outweigh the benefits. Some foreign firms are avoiding such pitfalls by forming joint ventures with other foreign firms already established in Japan. For example, Toys R Us formed a partnership with McDonalds to gain access to sites and officials. Recently, changes have occurred – Japan's neomercantilist investment policies are now largely administered by businessmen rather than bureaucrats. Formal restrictions have been removed while informal barriers like cartels have become more important. These changes have occured at a pace and degree that would strengthen rather than weaken Japan's corporations. Washington and other foreign pressure had little impact on Japan's "liberalization" policies, while

> economic and political pressures initiated by American MNCs forced the Japanese government to grant limited concessions to individual corporations and, later, more general liberalizations to broader classes of firms . . . The Japanese state seldom reacted to the direct pressure of the MNCs but responded instead to foreign pressures aggressively mediated by those Japanese oligopolists who typically sought the assets and skills that foreign firms controlled . . . Japanese oligopolists deftly manipulated foreign demands both to their domestic advantage over local competitors and the state and to their foreign advantage over those who (in retaliation for Japanese restrictions) would restrict Japanese export markets and overseas investments.[75]

Encarnation and Mason conclude that foreign pressure "may have influenced the form of Japanese policy but not its substance".[76] Given the qauntlet of obstacles and restrictions foreign investors must run to set up and sustain operations in Japan, the low investment rate is not "a result of their own 'benign neglect' of the Japanese market, as a consensus forged among numerous scholars on Japan would have us erroneously believe. Instead . . . hostile government policy, not 'benign neglect,' principally explains the low levels of foreign investment in Japan".[77]

What should be done?

The Tolchins ask some very tough questions about the consequences of America's free market toward foreign investors: Should American foreign investment policy simply be the sum total of a *laissez-faire* national outlook and fifty separate state policies? Should states be allowed to lure foreign manufacturing or financial firms which put American firms out of business? What should American policy be if a foreign government is subsidizing foreign investments with the intention of driving American firms out of the business? Should foreign firms be allowed to buy America firms which own state of the art technology?[78]

What alternatives are there to America's present irrational policies? The Tolchins advocate a foreign investment policy which systematically addresses the issue, and which includes the following: (1) reciprocity in opportunities for foreign investors here and American investors in those countries; (2) restrictions on foreign investments which threaten American geoeconomic security; (3) asserting national policy over the fifty state policies.[79] These policies should be guided by such important questions as: Even if there was evidence that merely publicizing information about who is investing what in the United States inhibits further investments (and there is absolutely no evidence supporting that contention), should that prevent American citizens from being fully informed? If selective restrictions on foreign investment adversely affect a nation's economy, why do virtually all nations employ such restrictions? Just what do the states' bidding wars to attract foreign investment cost taxpayers and the American economy? Perhaps the key question, according to the Tolchins, is rather "than ask whether Bridgestone should be allowed to take over Firestone, we should instead be asking why Firestone was allowed to fail".[80] Tokyo would have never let a strategic firm like Bridgestone to fail, and in fact by administering a range of subsidies, cheap credit, cartels, import barriers and export incentives is largely responsible for Bridgestone's success.

The implementation of any comprehensive policy toward foreign investment is unlikely. The White House adamantly opposes even a bill requiring all foreign investors to reveal their assets in the United States, arguing that it would scare away potential investors. Japan's lobbying army is mobilized against that bill and any other policies regulating foreign investment. Apparently a free one-way flow of investment is valued more highly than the free flow of information. Senator Tom Harkin asks if a bill to force foreign firms to disclose their assets in the United States were so bad, then "why would US investors continue to invest in Japan despite disclosure, preclearance requirements of joint ventures, and everything else".[81] Washington is unlikely to create and implement a rational investment policy that protect and promotes America's geoeconomic security any time soon. The Bush Administration, like its predecessor, clings to liberal economic notions that have no real world basis and refuses to utilize the array of powerful weapons Congress has supplied the White House to deter foreign neomercantilism. And even if a new administration takes office devoted to America's economic renewal, any measures taken then may be too little too late.

9   The High Technology Front

Technologically, Japan is rapidly leapfrogging the United States by virtually every measurement.[1] The CHI Research Inc. annually analyzes global technology trends by examining a range of indicators including patents, scientific paper citations, and innovations.[2] According to CHI Research, Japan has either surpassed or is running neck and neck with the United States in virtually every technology area, while Japanese corporations have clearly leapfrogged their American rivals in many key sectors: Japan's automobile giants surged past America's producers in the late 1970s, Fuji overcame Kodak in 1984, and Hitachi surpassed IBM in 1985, to name a few. Although America's 104 541 patents in 1990 were larger than Japan's 76 984, Japan's corporations led in the ability to turn inventions into mass consumer products.

And Japanese have not hesitated to convert their growing technological power into political power. On 27 May 1991, Tokyo protested Washington's proposed cutbacks in its space station program in which Japan agreed to build a critical $2 billion space laboratory, and threatened to withhold participation from other joint technology ventures, including the $8.4 billion dollar supercollider project, if Congress cut out its project.[3] Washington faces a dilemma. The United States is broke, yet Washington continues to spend hundreds of billions of dollars on projects of often dubious military or scientific worth. Estimates for the space station's cost alone run from $85 billion to $185 billion. The United States has become so dependent on Japanese capital and technology for its "big science" projects that a Japanese withdrawal would cripple those projects. And if Washington bows to Tokyo and continues to fund the space station it will deepen America's debt and diversion of its best scientific brains and facilities to outer space rather than America's deteriorating big cities and industries.

These dilemmas will become more frequent. As Japan's technology power grows so will its political power. According to Paul Kennedy, there is a clear relationship between "the shifts . . . in the . . . economic and productive balances and the position occupied by individual powers in the international system".[4] Kennedy maintains that shifts in national power are

312

driven chiefly by economic and technological developments, which then impact upon social structures, political systems, military power, and the position of individual states . . . Different regions and societies across the globe have experienced a faster or slower rate of growth, depending not only upon the shifting patterns of technology, production, and trade, but also upon their receptivity to the new modes of increasing output and wealth. As some areas of the world have risen, others have fallen behind – relatively or (sometimes) absolutely.[5]

According to Christopher Freeman, "Japan is opening up a new 'technology gap' . . . related not simply or even mainly to the scale of research and development, but to other social and institutional changes".[6] There is a dynamic relationship between technology and society; technological advances both shape and are shaped by society. The source of Japan's economic and technological power is a system of innovation and expansion which encompasses the entire country, from its industrial policies, ministries, and ruling party to its factories, grade schools, research laboratories and industrial groups – all are permeated by Japan's cultural values of conformity, groupism, hierarchy, xenophobia, and fierce drive to excel. Within this vast, complex, socioeconomic system, Japan masters clusters of technologies which transform the entire economy and deepen Japan's power over the global political economy.

How is American and Japanese technology policy created and implemented? What technology disputes have arisen? How, if at all, have they been resolved? And in whose favor? Will Japan's technology leadership widen in the 21st century? Or can the United States halt and even reverse its technology decline? If so, what policymaking and industrial restructuring reforms are essential for any serious attempt to regain global leadership?

AMERICAN TECHNOLOGY POLICY

America's technology policymaking disarray and inept, self-destructive policies are captured in the deeply divided attitudes over the destruction of America's consumer electronics industry. Japan now dominates the global consumer electronics market, one that symbolically began with Thomas Edison's invention of the phonograph in 1887, and rapidly evolved with a succession of other American inventions including the cathode ray tube (1897), radio (1900), radio broadcasting (1920), television receivers (1923), magnetic wire recorders (1946), the transistor (1947), color television (1954), portable radios (1954) and home videocassette recorders (1963). America's domination of mass consumer electronics peaked around 1970 when it held a 90 per cent American market share for phonographs, 90 per cent share for color television, 65 per cent share for black and white television. In 1990, American producers held only 1 per cent of the phonography, 10 per cent of the color television, and 1 per cent of the black and white television markets. From 1984 to 1987 alone, Japan's electronics production rose 75 per cent compared to 8 per cent in the United States.[7]

The Bush Administration and neoclassical economists see the destruction of America's mass consumer electronics industry as good, arguing that if other countries can produce such products cheaper and better, then American consumers should buy their products while American entrepreneurs should shift into products which they are better at producing. However, as Inman and Burton point out, liberal economists fail to see the strategic links between low-tech mass consumer goods and high-tech microelectronics. Conceding the low end of the technology scale allows Japanese producers to amass enormous profits, learning curves, and markets from which they march steadily upscale, similarly destroying their American competitors in those fields as well.[8]

The Commerce Department clearly recognizes this danger, but is prevented by the White House from acting. Commerce released a two year study on 8 June 1990 warning that the annual $200 billion American microelectronics industry will probably be eclipsed in the early 1990s by Japan's just as its consumer electronics industry was destroyed in the 1970s. According to the report, Japan's strategy of systematically targeting and capturing vital technology links such as silicon wafers, semiconductors, telecommunication network switches, X-ray lithography, optical storage devices and flat panel displays was having a termite effect on America's microelectronics industry, and would inevitably destroy it if a comprehensive strategy to revive the industry were not devised and implemented. Among the proposals for rescuing America's microelectronics industry were tax credits for research and development, antitrust exemptions for joint manufacturing consortiums, relaxed export control regulations, and cuts in the capital gains tax to reduce capital costs. Commerce's comprehensive plan for reversing America's technology decline will not be implemented in the forseeable future, if at all. The White House rejected the report, claiming that only markets and not government can pick winners and losers.

Yet, nine months later on 25 April 1991, to the surprise of many, the White House departed from its policies of malign neglect and issued a report identifying 22 technologies "critical to the national prosperity and to national security".[9] The list included: materials processing, electronic and photonic materials, ceramics, composites, high-performance metals and alloys, flexible computer integrated manufacturing, intelligent processing equipment, micro- and nano-fabrication, systems management technologies, software, microelectronics and optoelectronics, high performance computing and networking, high definition imaging and displays, sensors and signal processing, data storage, computer simulation, applied molecular biology, medical technology, aeronautics and energy technologies. The report was only issued because it was required by the Congressional Defense Authorization Act. And, as usual, defense and commercial technology were linked in arguing for development of those technologies: "We most recently have been reminded by the spectacular performance of US coalition forces in the Persian Gulf, of the crucial role that technology plays in military competitiveness. It is equally clear that technology plays a similar role in the economic competitiveness among nations".

Although the report encouraged those deeply concerned with American competitiveness, prosperity and security, it remains to be seen whether there will be any systematic government attempt to nurture these industries. President Bush seems simply to be continuing the Reagan Administration's disavowal of any responsibility for American geoeconomic power and prosperity. The administration is deeply split between realists and idealists, with the latter dominating with their assertions that the government cannot pick winners and losers. The Bush Administration's inner circle is controlled by neoclassical economists like Chief of Staff John Sununu, Budget Director Dick Darman, and Council of Economic Advisors head Michael Boskin who smash any suggestion for abandoning America's irrational industrial policies for rational efforts that will stimulate rather than hobble American economic and technological growth. Yet, economic realists fill many positions elsewhere in the cabinet and at lower levels throughout the administration. As in other industrial sectors, responsibility for creating and implementing America's high technology industrial policies is scattered throughout government in twelve executive agencies, and thirteen congressional appropriations committees for civilian projects alone. The White House Office of Science and Technology Policy is supposed to coordinate these government efforts, but its budget is small, personnel loaned from other agencies, and it has no real powers.

American firms are trying hard to shape rational Washington industrial policies for the high technology industries. The American Electronics Association, which represents 3500 electronics and information processing firms, is the most important domestic interest group lobbying for a rational technology industrial policy. The Semiconductor Industry Association with 37 members and the Semiconductor Equipment and Materials International with over 800 members are becoming increasingly active in lobbying Congress for protection and subsidies similar to those enjoyed by the Japanese. These lobbying efforts have had mixed success. After years of lobbying, Commerce did finally protest Japanese semiconductor dumping in 1985, initiate an in-depth investigation into its extent, and negotiate an agreement signed in September 1986. But like most such price agreements, the semiconductor accord may have benefited the Japanese more than the Americans.

America's technology policies thus result from the multipoled tug of war between these vastly different institutional and ideological interests. As in America's other industrial policies, those few rational technology initiatives come from the Defense Department, or more specifically the Pentagon's Defense Advanced Research and Development Agency (DARPA). About half of DARPA's 1990 $1.4 billion budget was invested in dual-use technologies. DARPA is the major source of funding for such government-private industry collaborations as Sematech and the National Center for Manufacturing Sciences and has targeted such technologies as X-ray lithography for development. DARPA's very high speed integrated circuit, gallium arsenide, software, and strategic computing projects were initiated during the 1980s as a direct responses to similar Japanese efforts, but still the commercial spinoffs were minimal. Another Pentagon project is the Defense Intelligence Agency's Project Socrates which was created in 1988 to build an accurate data base of the world's most advanced technologies to help assess the status of America's high technology efforts compared with foreign rivals. The program focused on tracking advances in such fields as microelectronics, exotic structural materials, superconductors, high performance computers, HDTV, and a range of classified fields.

Consumed with its liberal economic dogma, the Bush Administration succeeded in gutting these programs. The date 20 April 1990 represented a huge leap backwards for American competitiveness. The Administration fired Craig Fields, DARPA's Director, for his continued push for a rational industrial policy and the funding of key technologies. Fields had previously allocated $30 million to HDTV research. The White House responded by diverting $20 million of those funds elsewhere. Fields was finally fired when he allocated $4 million to a company developing a radiation resistant gallium arsenide chip as a substitute for silicon, a technology in which the Japanese are well ahead. In protest of Fields' firing and the planned cancellation of Project Socrates, Michael Sekora, its director, resigned that same day. Robert Costello, former Undersecretary for Pentagon procurement under the Reagan Administration, was dismayed at the proposed cancellation of Project Socrates: "They're terminating the only data base on industrial policy that the nation has. You have to have this kind of information to even know how to lay out your research and development money".[10] Responding to

Fields' firing, Dr. William Schreiber, an MIT engineering professor and member of the Pentagon's High-Resolution Systems Task Force, argues that "the belief that the market always gives the right answer is a kind of economic religion based on faith and not on reason".[11]

These projects may or may not be better than nothing at all. America's military industrial complex is like a black hole which sucks in vital finance, facilities, technologies, and expertise. Pentagon technology projects thus may actually be detrimental to America's high technology development since they drain many of the best scientists, engineers, and technicians from commercial firms, while any technological breakthroughs are locked up into military applications. In 1990, nearly 70 per cent of all government R&D funds went into the military – up from 50 per cent in 1980. As a percentage of GNP, Washington funds far less commercial projects than Japan and other industrial countries.

Okimoto and Saxonhouse write that America's large government R&D efforts may actually benefit Japan

> if the spillover effects from military to commercial spheres are low or if there are finite supplies of skilled R&D manpower. Of the large industrial states, Japan may be the only one capable of concentrating its finite resources almost exclusively on commercial applications of technology . . . If the Japanese government spends less, it takes more initiative than the US government in microindustrial management through the use of industrial policy. Not only does it identify and target key technologies for Japan's economic future, it also coordinates intra-industry efforts at building a binding consensus within industry and between government and industry.[12]

They go on to argue that there is a difference between technological innovation and commercial application of technological innovation. The United States has excelled at the former; Japan at the latter. Despite the low ratio of government funding of Japanese research and development, the government plays a key role in ensuring that no Japanese firm gains a monopoly over important technology; instead the government aids the distribution of technology to all viable firms in a relevant industry. Two thirds of Japan's technological investments are carried out by private sector firms, and almost all of this is oriented towards applied rather than basic research and development.

Senator George Mitchell's best response to President Bush's 1991 State of the Union address was: "If we can make the best smart bomb, why can't we make the best VCR".[13] The reason, of course, is that while America's array of high tech weaponry was conceived, developed, and produced according to systematic rational, industrial policies, the VCR and other consumer electronic industries were battered by irrational, short-sighted policies that often gave more benefits to Japanese than American producers. Commercial success depends on quickly producing cheap high quality products while military success simply depends on producing high quality products regardless of cost or time. One would hope that after spending over $9.5 billion on development of the cruise missile since 1972 that the missile would work well. American spy satellites may be able to photograph a piece of paper a hundred miles below, but it is the Japanese who dominate the world's camera markets. American computer chips may be radiation resistant, but it is the Japanese who dominate the world's semiconductor markets.

Yet, even many of the weapons that were so effective in the Persian Gulf are based on obsolete technology. For example, the cruise and patriot missiles were developed over a decade ago and their technology is less advanced than that found in the average personal computer today. Costello admitted that "Defense is not a leader. In many cases it's not even a user of the latest technology".[14] Military "spinoffs" into commercial products were always few, and are steadily decreasing. Military procurement did get the computer and semiconductor industries off the ground, but nowadays military technology is dependent on commercial technology. In the 1960s, the military bought 70 per cent of semiconductors, in 1990, 8 per cent. And nowadays, with America's consumer electronics industry destroyed by Tokyo's neomercantilism and Washington's incompetence, the military is becoming increasingly dependent on Japanese components.

There are some limited government initiatives targeting commercial industry for development. NASA is the government's most important agency whose impact is mostly commercial, while the Commerce, Agriculture, and Energy Departments all have their own small technology projects. But government funding of civilian research and development as a percentage of GNP peaked at 1.1 per cent in 1965, declined rapidly to an average 0.6 per cent in the 1970s, and then dropped to a 1980s average of 0.4 per cent.[15]

Many of these technology projects, however, are controversial. "Big science" projects are valued at over $100 million, but exclude overtly military projects like the Strategic Defense Initiative. The Reagan and Bush Administrations emphasized a dozen "big science" projects whose construction costs are budgeted for $64.8 billion and maintenance costs could be another $100 billion to maintain over the life of the projects. These projects include the $1.5 billion Hubble Space Telescope, $3 billion plan to map the human genetic structure, $8 billion supercollider, and $120 billion space station. The particle beam project will cost an annual $313 million just to operate. On 11 June 1991, the National Space Council chaired by Vice President Dan Quayle published a report which advocated completion of the space station and plans to return to the moon by 2005 and reach Mars by 2014, whose combined cost would be over $500 billion. Apparently, the sole excuse for spending half a trillion of increasingly scarce dollars in space rather than in America's crumbling factories, research laboratories, infrastructure, or crime-filled, poverty-stricken cities, was simply "because it is there". The Council did not justify the projects in terms of American competitiveness or security.

Critics argue that the immense cost drains vital funds and expertise from small-scale basic and applied research projects. Scientist Dr Rustum Roy warns that "Big science has gone berserk. Good minds and a lot of money are going into areas that are not relevant to America's competitiveness, or even the balanced development of American science". Dr George Chapline of Lawrence Livermore National Laboratory notes that "it is very questionable whether these projects will contribute much to stopping America's industrial decline, and may even exacerbate it".[16] Like military weapons programs, the big science projects continually run far beyond initial estimates. For example, when the Reagan Administration unveiled its proposed space station in 1984, it claimed the project would cost only $8 billion; in 1990, NASA confessed that the final price tag could exceed $120 billion, and even then would not achieve the projects original objectives! Dr James Allan points out that although the space station is "advertised as the world's greatest invention . . . it's scientific uses are pretty dubious. Those uses could easily be accomplished on a much less grandoise scale". Even President Reagan's science advisor, George Keyworth, told Congress in 1983 that a space station would "be a most unfortunate step backwards".[17] Over $4 billion has been spent on just the space station's design and prototype parts – the program's final design must still be decided. The big projects take so long to complete that they are often obsolete once they become operational, but their sheer economic and political clout ensures that they will defeat any attempt to devise cheaper, more efficient projects that accomplish the same goals.

Are the lobbyists for big science projects aware of their programs' flaws and the opportunities forgone to employ those vast sums of money, facilities, and experts in more productive ventures? Big science is big porkbarrel in which scores of Congressmen are allowed to ladle out contracts and other benefits to countless supporters in their districts. As with military weapons programs, advocates deliberately underestimate the costs of big science projects and exaggerate the benefits to receive approval. Projects are sometimes conceived, not so much as ends in themselves, but to justify the development of other related projects. For example, James Biggs, NASA's former Director, admitted that the space station was conceived as a means of keeping the agency in business: "The feeling was that unless we could get a station the manned activities would truncate and we'd run out of mission".[18] Of course, many argue that all the manned flights from the Apollo mission to put a man on the moon to the recent space shuttle flights may boost American prestige but diminish America's real power. The hundreds of billions spent on those programs of dubious scientific value could have been diverted into building a range of strategic consumer and intermediate industries, and refurbishing the country's economic and human infrastructure. Once again, an institution's need to survive and expand overrode national interests to employ its vast but ultimately limited resources most productively.

Meanwhile, countless science projects that could achieve major technological and economic advances atrophy, starved of funds, facilities, and expertise, and hobbled by red tape. These projects lack the glitter of Star Wars or the Space Station, but often represent opportunities to achieve significant advances in science and technology. Past small science projects of enormous applications were the transitor, laser, and antibiotics. During the 1980s, of ten Nobel Prizes for Physics, one went to pure theory, three to big projects, and six to small projects; the prizes in chemistry, medicine and physiology all went to small projects.

Budget allocations simply do not reflect the importance of these small projects. In 1990, the proposed budget for the space station alone was $2.5 billion, higher than the entire National Science Foundation budget of $2.4 billion which helps fund many small but vital science projects. Prices for setting up labs, hiring personnel, buying materials, ensuring environmental and worker safety, and other related costs tripled in the 1980s while government assistance to small science projects rose modestly from $7.3 billion in 1980 to $10.7 billion in 1989 in constant 1990 dollars. While the National Science Foundation, which funds many small projects, grew from $2.6 billion to $4.1 billion, contributions from civilian agencies that assist science dropped considerably from $728 million in 1976 to $562 million in 1987 in constant 1982 dollars. The emphasis on big science has sharply cut back the number of federal grants for new and continuing research from 6446 in 1987 to 4633 in 1990.[19]

Congressional support is growing for the creation of a civilian version of DARPA that can rationalize all these projects. A 1988 bill sponsored by Senator Ernest Hollings created a Technology Administration within the Commerce Department, whose responsibility is to assess and help develop technology. The Technology Administration's Advanced Technology Program (ATP), which co-ordinates government-business ventures in strategic technologies, has the potential to become the civilian equivalent of DARPA, but is hampered by a tiny budget and continual White House pressure to suppress such efforts. Robert White, the Technology Administration's Director, is treading lightly for fear of provoking the sort of outburst from the White House neoclassical ideologues that earlier caused Fields and Sekora to depart from heading DARPA and Project Socrates, respectively. On 6 March 1991, the Commerce Department announced its granting of $9 million to 11 American firms for projects designed to foster innovative civilian technologies and restore American competitiveness. Congress allocated an additional $35.9 million for 1991, and President Bush requested the same amount for 1992.[20] These grants, however, are a mere drop in the bucket when compared to the hundreds of billions of dollars and concentrated, comprehensive efforts actually needed to regain America's technology lead.

As if the unco-ordinated, inefficient, underfunded government initiatives were not enough of a burden to America's high technology industry, the government actually forces America to give away its technology. American government laboratories are required by law to publish and sell to anyone all non-classified technology they create or enhance. Under US antitrust law, AT&T was forced to sell its technologies to any interested party, domestic or foreign. It was Sony's purchase of Bell Lab's transitor technology that enabled Sony to become one of the world's leading consumer electronic corporations. Every year over 325 Japanese scientists engage in advanced research in biotechnology at the National Institute of Health, a program that amounts to a enormous technology give away in one of the few fields in which the United States still clings to a small lead. Washington allows joint production of its military equipment such as aircraft to strengthen alliances and standardize equipment. The Defense and State Departments approve these co-production agreements; the Labor and Commerce Departments have no influence on the policy. As a result, Washington gives away technology, jobs and profits to foreign governments with no discernable gain to the United States. The foreign government can then turn around and sell that technology to the United States. For example, Japan used the speed brake of the F–15 which is composed of carbon composites for a range of commercial projects including the Shikansen bullet train and a Mitsubishi corporate jet which is exported to the United States since it is not allowed in Japan.[21] With this technology give away, it is not surprising that Japan continues to import far more technology from the United States than it exports. Between 1 April 1986, to 31 March 1987, Japanese bought $1.34 billion of technology from the United States and sold only $479 million.

The White House has always subordinated America's genuine geoeconomic security needs to its perceived geopolitical needs. Washington's creation of the Co-ordinating Committee on Multilateral Export Controls (Cocom) in 1950 to restrict high technology sales to Soviet bloc and other communist countries was a sensible but poorly executed policy. Washington has been very vigorous in curbing any strategic American exports to the Soviet bloc while its allies have more often than not turned a blind eye to the exports of its own firms. The most notorious example was the 1984 revelation that Toshiba had exported technology to the Soviet Union that would enable their submarines to run silently, a development which could cost the United States as much as $40 billion to overcome.

The split in American policy between geopolitical and geoeconomic ends and means surfaced in March 1991 when Washington began negotiating with Tokyo over an expansion of a secret 1984 agreement limiting supercomputer sales to Eastern Europe or the Third World. When the 1984 accord was signed, only Cray Research, Control Data, and Hitachi produced supercomputers. But supercomputers have been used to design supercomputers, and the use of parallel processing with very high speed microprocessors has enabled other Japanese corporations to master the technology while firms from Britain, Germany, France, and possibly the Netherlands and Italy are posed to unveil their own super-computers. Washington is urging a new agreement that will include these other producers. A secondary American objective is to ensure a "level playing field" between American firms and their foreign rivals. Although both sides believe the agreement should be renewed, they differ over how to define supercomputers, with Washington pressing for relatively lower calculation speed of 800 million calculations a second which would include many computers under the designation and Tokyo holding out for the much higher standards of 2 billion calculations a second that would allow Japan's corporations to export a wider range of advanced computers.[22]

One of Washington's few recent positive initiatives towards America's high technology industries was passage of the 1984 Co-operative Research Act. The Act allows businesses to co-operate on basic research, and since it was passed over 140 co-operative ventures have been set up. The pioneering American computer consortium was the Microelectronics & Computer Technology Corporation (MCC) formed and capitalized in 1983 at $65 million by a dozen small firms. Although largely unsuccessful, MCC did inspire many of the others formed since. The most ambitious consortium was Sematech, a joint venture formed in 1987 of 14 of both chip makers like Motorola, Intel and Texas Instruments and computer makers like IBM, Digital and Hewlett-Packard. The consortium spends $200 million annually, and has a staff of 700, one third of which are on loan from its members. The members and the government split the costs. The goal is to emulate Japan's success in spurring technology development. Although Sematech took nearly a year before it found its first chief executive, Robert Noyce, co-inventor of the integrated circuit and former vice-chairman of Intel, it picked up steam under his leadership and actually began to test a 4m DRAM prototype. While Sematech has not accomplished its goal of restoring American supremacy in semiconductors, it helps individual semiconductor firms inprove their products and research. Of particular concern is propping up those few American producers of semiconductor making equipment which are rapidly succumbing to the Japanese onslaught. About half of Sematech's budget goes to the equipment makers, between 20 to 30 of which have been saved from bankruptcy by these efforts. But perhaps Sematech's major accomplishment has simply been the co-operation among American firms which normally would be fiercely competing with each other.[23] Sematech is scheduled to disolve in 1992, but plans are being drawn for a Sematech II. American consortia are a positive step, but may be too little too late. Japan's corporations have enjoyed a four decade lead time in enjoying all the benefits of consortia and outright cartels. To date, none of the American consortia have enjoyed a fraction of the success of their Japanese rivals.

America's higher education system reflects the self-destructive effects of Washington's irrational policies. In 1990, there were over 1500 vacant engineering faculty positions in American colleges and universities, while there were over 60 000 vacant math and science positions in America's secondary schools. These shortages will worsen in the 1990s as a wave of retirements sweep America's education system from professors originally hired in the 1950s and 1960s when the system rapidly expanded.[24] It was against this background of a gutted science education system that the Massachusetts Institute of Technology agreed in December 1990 to teach Japanese scientists how to replicate its Media Laboratory in which researchers are developing futuristic entertainment and education products, including vital HDTV technology. MIT's $1.6 billion endowment will be increased a measly $10 million for this strategic technology and expertise transfer to Japan. The Japanese are not required to publish their research results as is MIT. The Media Lab was created in 1985 and Japanese firms finance about $1.5 million of its annual $10 million budget. Dr Andrew Lipman, the Media Labratory's associate director, justified the deal with the liberal argument that the world and United States would be better off if foreign scientists appropriated MIT techniques and technology: "it's unfortunate that the media lab is unique in the breadth and scope of what it's doing. More media labs can only be better".[25] No Japanese or neoclassical economic spokesperson could have said it better.

JAPANESE TECHNOLOGY POLICY

One constant theme of Japan's public relations campaigns is that Tokyo's rational industrial policies in which strategic industries and products are targeted with an array of cartels, technology infusions, import barriers, subsidies, and export incentives no longer exist. Japan's markets are the world's most open while its government plays no stronger role in the economy that does Washington.[26]

The reality, as always, is quite different. Yamamura maintains that MITI's role in the high technology sector of Japan's economy is actually strengthening, noting that "MITI officials . . . often exert leadership quite openly . . . MITI officials are exhibiting a strong sense of 'mission' and unusual zeal in promoting joint R&D activities and are playing a much more visible, as well as important, role in determining the research agendas than they ever did in promoting the technological capabilities of the major industries during the rapid growth period".[27] The Temporary Law for the Promotion of Specific Machinery and Information Industries (1978–85) alone identified 88 specific technologies for development, and through a variety of means MITI succeeded in promoting almost all of them. As foreign pressure forced Tokyo to discard such industrial policy tools as tariffs, quotas, foreign exchange and investment controls, export subsidies, and technology licensing, MITI has simply focused on other methods like co-operative R&D programs and cartels to target key technologies for development.

As in other industrial policy areas, MITI is the most important but by no means not the only ministry creating and implementing technology policy. As in all industrial policy areas, the Ministry of Finance (MOF) has the final say over tax and budget policies, while the Science and Technology Agency (STA), Ministry of Posts and Telecommunications (MPT), and Ministry of Education (MOE) continue to challenge MITI over a range of high technology turf issues, and have played vital roles in developing key sectors of Japan's high technology industries. Public financial institutions like the Japan Development Bank (JDB) or Export Import Bank, semi-public enterprises like Nippon Telephone and Telegraph (NTT) or Japan Electronic Computer Corporation (JECC), national business federations like Keidanren, Nikkeiren, and Keizai Doyukai, the keiretsu, policy advisory councils, and industrial associations have all played important roles in helping shape and implement policy.

Japan's microelectronics industry is composed of huge keiretsu which co-operate extensively with each other on R&D and markets. According to Fong, "the industrial structure of Japanese electronics provides secure 'investment' risks around which to form public policy. Their large size, diversified product lines, and oligopolistic market positions reduce their exposure to competitive failure. More important . . . dependence upon external financing . . . translates into dependence upon the Japanese government".[28] The industry is further organized in a number of very powerful industrial associations. The Electronics Industry Association of Japan (EIAJ) represents the largest high technology industrial association and is lead by an ex-MITI official. The diverse interests and often fierce competition among its over 600 members makes it difficult for EIAJ to easily reach agreement on issues and enjoy a powerful influence on policy. More influential are smaller associations representing specific product areas like the Japan Electronics Industry Development Association (JEIDA) with 100 member computer firms, the Japan Software Industry Association (JSIA) with 140 members, and the Japan Industrial Personal Computer Association (JIPCA) with 150 members. More important than the industrial associations are the two high technology policy zoku – the Information Industries Promotion Caucus (IIPC) and the Knowledge Industries Promotion Caucus (KIPC) – organized by MITI among leading Tanaka and Fukuda faction members, respectively, in the early 1970s to forge an LDP concensus behind its 1972 vision to transform Japan from a heavy industrial into a knowledge intensive postindustrial economy. The IIPC concentrates on computers while the KIPC promotes a range of other high tech industries like robotics, aerospace, and biotechnology.[29]

Government laboratories have also played an important role in technology policy. Each high technology ministry has its own laboratories. Until its "privatization" in 1985, NTT was controlled by MPT. The four NTT laboratories employ 3000 scientists, engineers, and researchers with a 1988 budget of nearly $800 million, of which about half was spent on four key technology projects: information processing, digital switching, large scale integrated circuits, and satellites. Althogether the NTT labs have taken out over 10 000 patents, including the development and diffusion of the 64k RAM, 256K RAM and 1m ROM without which Japan would not have become the world's leading semiconductor manufacturer. The NTT labs have no production facilities but license production to its "family" of firms lead by NEC, Oki, Fujitsu, and Hitachi which in turn act as "big brother" to 300 other firms. STA has the Electrotechnical Laboratory which conducts key microelectronics research and the Research Development Corporation of Japan which has sponsored the Exploratory Research for Advanced Technology project from 1981 to co-ordinate university and corporate research. The latter project has launched over 20 joint projects, each running for five years and funded between $10–15 million. The forerunners of the STA and NTT laboratories, the Electrical Laboratory and Electrical Communications Research Laboratory, respectively, laid the basis for the microelectronics industry when they jointly lead Japan's development of commerical applications of the transistor throughout the 1950s. More recently, the government passed the Key Technology Research Facilitation Law in

1985 which led to the creation of 14 technolopolises (Key Technolopy Centers) throughout Japan, with each specializing in three or four high technologies. The centers are funded from sales of NTT stock, and are allocated through MITI and MPT, with additional support from JDB.[30]

Tokyo's most important policy involved extracting technology from Japan's foreign and largely American rivals. Unable to sell or directly invest in Japan's immense markets, foreign producers usually chose to license their technology to their Japanese rivals before a more advanced foreign rival did. As a result, Japan was able to gather vital technology at a fraction of what it would have cost in time, money, and personnel if Japanese firms had had to develop it themselves. Between 1950 and 1980, Japan signed 42 000 foreign licensing arrangements worth $17 billion, or about 17 per cent of America's annual research and development budget. Abbegglen writes that the vast technology giveaway "has nurtured competitors who have now entered or threaten United States markets. Thus, foreign technology that might have been a lever to enter the Japanese market has been surrendered, and with it the advantage that might have made entry successful".[31] According to Prestowitz, Japan's strategy to force American firms to license their technology to their Japanese rivals had three consequences: it hastened the closing of the technological gap between the United States and Japan; helped lock American producers into producing mostly for domestic consumption; and thus prevented them from realizing economies of scale and learning curves efficiencies (in most industries, every doubling of cumulative volume yields a cost decline of 20 to 30 per cent.[32]

MITI played the central role in arm-twisting technology away from its foreign proprietors. Chalmers Johnson writes that,

> before the capital liberalization of the late 1960s and 1970s, no technology entered the country without MITI's approval; no joint venture was ever agreed to without MITI's scrutiny and frequent alteration of terms; no patent rights were ever bought without MITI's pressuring the seller to lower the royalties or make other changes advantageous to the Japanese industry as a whole; and no program for the importation of foreign technology was ever approved until MITI and its various advisory committees had agreed that the time was right and that the industry involved was scheduled for "nurturing".[33]

During the catch-up phase between 1945 and the 1980s, most Japanese technological advances were based on simply improving technology licensed from abroad, mostly from the United States. Licensed technology costs only 10 per cent the costs and time of development. Many of these came from AT&T's Bell laboratory which is legally required to license its technology to anyone. Some argue that without this compulsory licensing system Japan would have never achieved its present position of being able to technologically leapfrog the United States.[34] Okimoto writes that almost "all the breakthrough technologies and revolutionary new products – the transitor, integrated circuit, microprocessor, vacuum tube computers, super-, mini-, and microcomputers, fiber optics, office automation equipment, and basic software programs – bear the label "Invented in America".[35] Weinstein argues the same point even more forcefully: "Japanese industry has benefited from a "free ride" on US R&D: American companies have borne the burden of designing new products, and supporting the basic research that makes those products possible, while the Japanese, emphasizing the development of process technology that enables them to replicate or adapt US designs at low cost and high quality, have often been able to capture a large share of the market in a relatively short time".[36]

Despite its technological prowess, Japan still pays out 3.3 times more for licenses, patents and royalties than it earns, and half of all licenses imported are in high technology fields of which 70 per cent are for computer-related knowhow. About one-quarter of all Japanese research and development costs remain licensing, while Japan continues to import four times more American technology than it exports to the United States. A typical year 1981 was: of 2,076 new technology agreements worth $537 million, 977 (47 percent) were with the United States, 244 (10.8 pecent) with France, 219 (8.4 percent) with West Germany, and 119 (5.7 percent) with Britain. Of these agreements, 603 involved the licensing of patents.[37]

Import barriers were yet another means of nurturing Japan's high technology industries. For example, NTT continues to refuse to buy any significant amounts of foreign products, even if they are of superior quality. One method NTT uses to justify its discrimination is to refuse to provide specifications to foreign producers so they cannot adapt their products to Japan's needs. For example, the loose tube optical fiber cable that Siecor, a joint venture between Seimens and Corning, developed was superior to anything the Japanese made but cost only one third the price NTT was paying. NTT rejected the Siecor product with the claim it did not meet its specifications, then refused to submit those specifications until the Japanese corporations had not only copied Seicor's technology and created a similar product, but began dumping it overseas. Corning sued for patent infringement in both the United States and Canada. Although Corning won its Canadian suit, the International Trade Commission ruled that since the infringement was not causing Corning any significant loss of sales or profits, the Japanese dumper, Sumitomo, would not be penalized.

Japan's patent policies simultaneously impede foreign access to Japan's markets and nurture Japanese firms: "Western nations think of patents as just another form of property to be exchanged in the marketplace; in the hands of Japanese patents become blunt weapons to be used to gain comparative advantage".[38] The Japanese patent system is blatantly rigged against foreigners and designed to expropriate their technology. The entire application to reward process takes between five to seven years, with additional delays of up to nine months between permitting and actually issuing patents. In the United States the entire process rarely takes more than one and a half years. MITI controls the Patent Office and has consistently seen patents as a public rather than private good, and thus created a system which encourages Japanese firms to easily acquire technology and quickly disseminate that knowledge throughout the economy. Japan's first to file system allows a firm to apply for a patent even if the firm did not invent it (which rewards industrial espionage). If two or more firms make the same application on the same day they must split the royalties. The Patent Office's loose requirements for prototypes and easy amendments of the application during the first 15 months encourages firms to file ideas rather than specific inventions.

By delaying foreign market access until Japanese corporations can produce and market similar products, Tokyo effectively prevents foreign corporations from ever achieving any significant market share. The patent application itself is open to public viewing 18 months after it is submitted in contrast to the United States where it is publically aired only after the patent is granted. During this time anyone can copy the idea and use it for commercial purposes. If a rival firm makes an improvement on the invention during that time both firms must split the royalties when the patent is eventually issued. If the patent holder has not used its invention for three years, the government can force it to license the patent to rival firms. Like Japan's legal system in general, the patent system was designed so that any litigation would be more trouble than it was worth. Tokyo keeps the number of judges, lawyers, and clerks to a minimum to ensure that both applications and litigation will drag on for years. For example, between 1977 and 1987 the amount of applications increased from 161 006 to 341 095 while the number of officials rose from 2309 to only 2323.[39]

Examples of predatory patent practices by Japanese firms are legion. For example, in 1975 Fusion Systems, an American firm, applied for 20 patents on a high intensity microwave lamp. Two years later, shortly after the publication of the patent application, Mitsubishi Electric flooded the Patent Office with 200 applications for a similar lamp. Since mounting a challenge would be expensive and failure to do so could result in infringement, Fusion had no choice but to cross-license its technology. Corning Glassware experienced a similar theft of its property. The Patent Office told Corning that its patent would be granted if it specified the percentage of an ingredient in a vital chemical compound. It was no surprise when shortly thereafter a Japanese competitor was granted a patent with a one-percentage point difference of the same ingredient. The slight difference had no effect on the product while allowing the Japanese rival to avoid infringing Corning's patent.[40]

Between 1985 and 1988, American firms submitted 28 patent infringement suits against Japanese firms before the United States International Trade Commission. The results have been mixed: Intel lost its suit claiming that NEC had stolen key microprocessor technology, while IBM received huge damages from both Hitachi and Fujitsu for copying its computer software, and Corning Glass won its suit against Sumitomo Electric for the infringement of its fiber-optic patents. These suits, however, are only the tip of the iceberg in terms of Japanese firms stealing American technology. A 1988 report by the International Trade Commission (ITC) concluded that inadequate foreign intellectual property protection cost American firms $24 billion in lost sales in 1986, and targeted Japan as the most serious violator.[41]

Japan's most notorious example of using the patent application process to expropriate foreign technology was revealed on 21 November 1989 when, 29 years after filing its claim, Texas Instruments finally received Japanese patent rights for its integrated circuit. Japan's microelectronic firms had taken full advantage of the intervening three decades by exploiting Texas Instrument's technology for all it was worth. If Texas Instruments had been granted a patent within an internationally accepted timeframe without its rival's open access to the blueprints, it is unlikely that Japan's semiconductor industry would have gotten off the ground. Although Japan's chipmakers must pay royalties on almost all chips produced in Japan from 30 October 1989 through 27 November 2001, the estimated $120–200 million in annual royalties will be only 0.4–0.6 per cent of Japanese chip sales, and will have no adverse impact on Japan's semiconductor industry.[42]

Japan's technology policy has been an enormous success. Yet, some argue that Japan's strength in applied research is offset by its weak basic research efforts. A 1988 MITI White Paper admitted this weakness, noting four concerns: (1) government investment in basic research remains below that of other industrial nations; (2) Japan has a large pool of researchers, but few hold doctorates or master degrees; (3) the Japanese research environment is not as creative or flexible as that of the United States or Europe; (4) Japan lags behind other countries in large-scale research facilities. MITI concluded by calling for a strong government push in all four areas.[43]

Japan's huge corporations are attempting to bridge this basic research lag by using their vast cash mountains to simply buy up foreign, and largely American, basic research facilities. Immense amounts of Japanese corporate money – twice the amount given to Japanese universities – is flowing into American universities every year, "donating" laboratories, endowing chairs, and making other "gifts" to American universities to tap into the rich vein of minds, ideas and facilities devoted to basic research. Since 1988, Hitachi Chemical Ltd opened a lab at UC Irvine, Otsuka Pharmaceutical at the University of Washington, NEC at Princeton, Kobe Steel at North Carolina State University, Matsushita in San Francisco, Canon in Palo Alto, and Mitsubishi at MIT, while Fujitsu and Ricoh are considering several sites.

America's universities and even corporations simply cannot compete with the huge salaries the Japanese corporations are offering. Typical offers were $250 000 for senior scientists and $70 000 for fresh Ph.Ds. Few Americans can resist salaries 20–30 per cent higher than any competing American firm or university, as well as a chance to work with Japan's new equipment. Critics complain that Japan's research institutes in the United States are fraying America's already hard pressed, thin line in basic and applied research. As a result, American scientists who jump on board are helping Japan destroy America's high technology industries. MIT's computer expert, Charles Ferguson, describes the Japanese inroads as "near the end of the world" for America's computer industry.[44]

Are Japan's neomercantilist technology policies changing? Yes, they are changing, but they are definitely not being liberalized. In 1984 MITI attempted to change the proprietary rights to software from 50 to 15 years to enable Japanese software producers the same opportunity to expropriate foreign software ideas that other Japanese industries enjoyed with appropriate foreign technology. If passed, the law would have been retroactive, thus giving the Japanese government the right to compel foreign software patent holders to license their technology to their Japanese rivals. Fortunately, Washington pressured MITI to table its proposed legislation. In 1987, Tokyo did strengthen patent protection for the pharmaceutical and chemical industries, but only after its own industries had achieved a comparative advantage and needed patent rather than import protection. After decades of Japanese firms using Japanese patent laws to expropriate foreign technology, Patent Office Commissioner Fumitake Yoshida declared in November 1988 at a Trilateral Meeting in Tokyo that the patent "misunderstanding" would be completely resolved within five years.[45] Meanwhile, Tokyo made two concessions: a single application can now cover a group of related technologies while rejects must be given detailed explanation for their rejection. However, that will not stop Japanese corporations from continuing to copy foreign technology.

NTT continues to largely "buy Japanese" despite its privatization and claimed liberalization in the mid-1980s. In 1980, NTT purchased only about 4 per cent of some $3.3 billion in communications equipment through open bidding, and foreign companies sold only a minute 0.5 per cent of the total. At the end of 1980, Japan agreed, as part of the negotiations on the GATT Government Procurement Code, to allow Americans to participate in about $3 billion worth of NTT business each year, including an opportunity to bid on about $1.5 billion a year in high technology telecommunications equipment. Yet, the first year, American firms sold only about $1.5 million worth of mostly small items, which rose to $30 million in 1983, despite the reality that the United States has a comparative advantage in telecommunications equipment. NTT still gives preference to its family.[46]

Equally impotent have been Washington's attempts to extract more technology from Tokyo. The 1980 US-Japan Science and Technology Agreement, since amended in 1985, 1987 and 1988, is also designed to reverse this lopsided technology flow, plug leaks in defense technology outflow from Japan such as the Toshiba Machine sell-out to the Soviet Union, protect American intellectual property rights, and open up government-funded projects to American researchers. In 1982, MITI agreed to allow foreigners to lease government patents, but made the procedures so difficult that it was not until 1985 that IBM was able to negotiate an agreement for access to government computer patents. The 1983 Japan–US Mutual Defense Assistance Pact was supposed to open Japan's military technology gates to America's defense industry, but to date there have been only three relatively minor transfers. A 1986 law made it possible for foreigners to receive research positions at national institutes and become department or section heads. Although recently, Japanese bureaucracies have been inviting foreign participation in Japanese research consortia, the membership is rigged so that foreigners must give up far more technology than they gain. The result is that few foreign firms join. For example, in 1987 MITI opened the International Superconductivity Technology Center, but all 44 members were Japanese. That same year the STA New Superconductor Materials Forum atracted 140 firms, of which only one was foreign. In 1988 the National Science Foundation published a list of 123 Japanese firms willing to accept foreign researchers, but to date there have been few participants. Foreign firms remain locked in the catch-22 where if they do not attempt to devote immense time, energy, and money breaching Japan's carefully defended markets, they are accused of not trying hard enough, whereas if they do make an effort they usually end up losing more than they gain no matter how hard they try. MITI first opened its research and development consortia to foreign membership in 1990, and is currently organizing a Center of Excellence (COE) that will included domestic and foreign scientists working together on basic research projects. MITI has been

criticized for limiting foreign membership to the United States and
European Community, while excluding South Korea and other industrialized countries. MITI reasons that Japan can still learn from the
United States and European Community while limiting the technology
outflow; it will keep its labs closed to other industrialized countries,
particularly the South Koreans, so as to not groom future competitors.

Unable to gain any significant penetration of Japan's research facilities,
Washington has attempted to elicit Japanese technology by inviting
participation in major projects including SDI and the space station. In
May 1990, Washington asked Tokyo to invest $2 billion and take a
leading management role in building a $8 billion superconducting super-
collider in Texas. Congress will contribute $5 billion and Texas $1 billion
to the project, and the rest would come from foreign countries. To date,
Tokyo is hesitating on joining the project since it is considering building its
own supercollider. Many scientists, bureaucrats, and politicians are
opposed to any participation in the project because they fear it will
drain funds away from a range of Japanese research initiatives.

COMPUTERS

If Tokyo followed free trade rather than neomercantilist policies, Japan
would not have any computer industry, let alone be a global computer
leader. MITI targeted computers for development in the mid–1950s, and
over past four decades has continually nourished it with of "a combination
of protectionism, financial assistance, and co-operative projects to encourage and guide the industry's development without squelching the
individual initiative of each company".[47]

Government subsidies have been vital to nurturing a Japanese computer industry, particularly in the 1960s and 1970s. Edward Lincoln
maintains that Japan's computer industry has "received heavier and
more consistent assistance than any other high technology industry . . .
(and is) a prime example of an industry that may actually owe . . . its
success to the existence of government policy".[48] Between 1961 and 1969,
the government injected $269.44 million in interest free loans 1961–69,
and $132.6 million in subsidies and tax benefits which combined equaled
46 per cent of private investments; if government low interest loans are
included the total aid of $542.8 million was almost double (188 per cent)
that of private investments. Even between 1970 to 1975 the $636.55
million in government subsidies and tax breaks were still 57 per cent of
what firms were investing, while the total aid of $1.88 billion was 169 per
cent. There was a relative decline in government aid between 1976 to
1981 as the $1.03 billion in subsidies and tax benefits declined to 25.2 per

cent and total aid was $3.74 billion or 91.6 per cent of private efforts. These subsidies doubled the cash flow to strategic firms, without which none of them could survived since they could not have gotten enough from private sources. Government funds remain an important carrot. For example, between 1976 and 1982 government research and development subsidies to the computer industry were $355 million; from 1983 to 1989 they were $992 million, in both periods about 10 per cent of the industry total.[49]

During this time, MITI organized Japan's once small computer makers into research and development consortia which attempted to match each new IBM advance with a Japanese advance. MITI has continually attempted to upgrade Japan's computer industry with a series of joint government–private efforts including the Very Large Scale Intergration Project (VLSI, 1975–80), Pattern Information Processing System (1971–80), Flexible Manufacturing Using Lasers (1977–85), Software Automation (1976–81), supergrid components integrated circuits (1981–89), three dimensional integrated circuits (1981–89), environment-resistant ICs (1981–88), and High Speed Scientific Computer (1981–89), and Fifth Generation Computer Project (1982–92), all of which represented vital steps in the industry's evolution.

Japan's Fifth Generation Computer Project fell short of its ambitious goal of creating a computer that reasons like a human being at speeds thousands of times faster than present computers. Yet, to date the project has succeeded in making major advances in such key technologies as Josephson junctions as well as producing the Personal Sequential Inference Machine which by using parallel processing can compute three or four times faster than existing machines, thereby stimulating an immense technological leap in Japan's computer industry during the 1980s similar to the effects of the VSLI project during the 1970s.

Tokyo is currently embarked on a vast, decade long Sixth Generation Computer Project (1990–2000) to develop three interrelated technologies, a "massive parallel processing" computer with over 1 million separate processors that can simultaneously attack a problem, microscopic lasers shooting beams of light rather than electronic pulses to fuel the computer, and the software to manage the computer. The project will be funded with at least $300 million in government funds with matching funds from participants. On 14 March 1991, MITI publically invited American and European computer makers to contribute to its Sixth Generation Computer project and sweetened the offer by rescinding several highly protectionist policies. Japan's intellectual property law previously allowed the government to own all inventions conceived of by its projects, which Tokyo then shared only with Japanese firms. The law has been amended to now allow foreign partners a 50 per cent share in any resulting technology.[50] Foreign corporations thus face the dilemma that has plagued them since the 1950s when Tokyo first systematically asserted its neomercantilist technology policies. If they refuse to join the project, other firms may benefit from what funds and technology the project provides. If they do join they will probably end up surrendering far more technology to their Japanese rivals than they receive. American universities, however, will not feel so inhibited and will happily sell out their technology for access to Japanese funds.

Although MITI's hardware projects have been enormously successful, its software projects have been less so. For example, only about 20 per cent of the software packages developed during the Software Development Project (1976–80) were marketable while the Fourth Generation Project (1979–83), Sigma Project (1982–87), and the Optoelectronic IC Project (1981–86), achieved only modest results. Unable to develop Japanese software, in 1983 MITI tried its previously successful strategy of forcing foreign firms to surrender their technology. MITI promoted a bill designed to reduce copyright protection for computer software from fifty to fifteen years, and in addition require registration and compulsory licensing at MITI's discretion. MITI justified the harsh measures by rejecting the idea that software is a work of literature or music, and instead argued that software is like any mass produced product and just deserved patent rather than copyright protection. MITI's bill would have resulted in the wholesale expropriation of foreign software technology, one of the few areas of the computer industry in which the Japanese lagged. Fortunately, for once, the White House set aside its one way free trade ideology, and succeeded in pressuring Tokyo to abandon the bill.

Japan's computer efforts have focused on surpassing IBM in market share, products, and technology, while destroying the lesser American computer firms, a goal which has largely been accomplished. MITI has used every means and opportunity at its disposal to damage IBM. It only allowed IBM to set up shop in the early 1960s after forcing it to sell its technology to fifteen of its Japanese competitors, limiting the number and type of IBM machines sold, and requiring permission before IBM could introduce a new model. This managed trade agreement lasted at least until 1979. Although IBM proved too powerful to force into a joint venture, MITI did succeed in forcing Sperry Rand to sign with Oki, RCA with Hitachi, General Electric with Toshiba, TRW with Mitsubishi, and Honeywell with NEC, all of which have since either completely or mostly dropped out of the computer industry as their "partners" took their technology and soon produced a range of competitive products.

What Japanese firms cannot license they often attempt to steal. Washington was successful in helping contain a 1984 MITI attempt to strip software of even copyright protection. Success came when Washington played off one ministry against another, in this case the Ministry of Education, which argued that copyrights were part of its turf, against MITI. Washington's hand was bolstered by Congressional reciprocity legislation mandating retaliation against the imports of any country which pirates American technology. But it was not until 1 January 1986 that Tokyo granted copyright protection to computer software. For three decades until that date, Japanese pirated foreign software with impunity. Yet, the new copyright law offers only a fig leaf to foreign software manufacturers. A copyright protects only the form, not the concepts of a work thus allowing pirates to employ the concepts in a new form. Patents, in contrast, protect both the form and concepts, but for a much shorter time, usually fifteen rather than fifty years.

As if government discrimination were not enough, foreign firms must continually guard against industrial espionage and patent theft from their Japanese rivals. The extent of this espionage became apparent in 1982 when 17 ranking officials from Hitachi and Mitsubishi were arrested for buying what they were told were stolen IBM secrets. MITI itself handled their defense and guided an out of court settlement with IBM. The United States government had an airtight criminal case; after trying to deny the charges, the Japanese gave in and plea-bargained the charges down, so as to keep publicity to a minimum. Despite this, the Japanese felt it was they, and not IBM, that were being victimized. During the trial, trucks equipped with loudspeakers appeared outside IBM Japan President Shiina's house, blaring messages that he was a traitor, calling him "Yankee Shiina" and ordering him to "Go back to America".[51]

Far more damaging was the civil case later brought against Hitachi by IBM which was settled in a way that mortified the Japanese. In November 1988, IBM won a three count settlement in the American Arbitration Association that Fujitsu had infringed some of its software copyrights. According to the settlement Fujitsu paid a lump sum of $833.2 million to IBM plus $25.7–51.3 million every time it wants to look at IBM's new software technology. IBM does not have to show Fujitsu how the software works, only what it does – Fujitsu must figure out its own software – and the settlement covers only existing not future IBM product lines. Other recent lawsuits include Motorola v. Hitachi over the the theft of microprocessor technology; Texas Instruments v. NEC over the theft of software technology; Union Carbide v. Komatsu and other firms which conspired to keep it out of the Japanese market for polysilicon.

Yet, the IBM decisions and other court cases represent relatively minor victories in a long, debilitating economic war that the Americans are steadily losing. Japan's sustained efforts have devastated America's computer industry. IBM's once dominant market share in Japan has been steadily carved away until it now has only a 10 per cent share behind

NEC and Fujitsu. Although IBM Japan still enjoys the largest share of Japan's mainframe computer market, that share has steadily declined from 42.2 per cent in 1978 to 24.4 per cent in 1989, compared to its 51.8 global market share. Overall, however, in 1990 IBM Japan held on to a mere 15.7 per cent market share behind Fujitsu's 23.1 per cent and NEC's 18.6 per cent, but still ahead of Hitachi's 11.2 per cent, Mitsubishi's 6.0 per cent, and Toshiba's 3.5 per cent. In 1986, the combined research budgets of Hitachi, Fujitsu and NEC were twice IBM, and have doubled since. But the Japanese firms have steadily undermined IBM's global strength, they have all but wiped out the other American computer firms. Between 1980 and 1991, America's share of the global computer market dropped from 80 per cent to 38 per cent, while Japan's rose from 10 per cent to 42 per cent.[52] Many American companies have not only failed to compete, but have even sold out to their Japanese rivals in other computer sectors targeted by the Japanese. For example, RCA licensed its patents to Hitachi, while GE sold its machines through a licensing arrangement with Toshiba. Honeywell entered into arrangements with Nippon Electric, and RemRand with Oki Denki. Other players – such as TRW, Bunker Ramo and Westinghouse – developed reciprocal agreements with Mitsubishi. Fujitsu's 1990 acquistion of International Computers Ltd allowed it to leapfrog Digital Equipment to become the world's second largest computer corporation after IBM. Control Data was forced to drop out of its supercomputer production in April 1989 because of its lack of access to Japan's huge potential market.

IBM is the only firm powerful enough to offer the Japanese any significant resistance. Yet on 11 March 1991, even IBM succumbed to a highly risky "if you can't beat 'em, join 'em" strategy, in which it agreed to license its software technology to its bitter Japanese rivals, Hitachi, Fujitsu, Mitsubishi, Sony, Sharp, Sanyo, Ricoh, Oki and Canon, in an attempt to cut down NEC's enormous lead. Designed to boost its current dismal 10 per cent market share in Japan, the strategy could backfire if the Japanese rivals simply use the technology to attack IBM rather than NEC. Japan's computer makers will now achieve an overwhelming comparative advantage for their products if they become IBM compatible.[53] Meanwhile, IBM is trying to leapfrog Japan's semiconductor giants by mastering X-ray chip etching machines, which are powered by giant superconducting synchrotron storage rings. The Japanese, however, are in hot pursuit, having created several research consortia and built 10 of their own sychrotron rings, with more scheduled for opening.

Japan's computer behemoths have captured strategic technological and product segments, from whence they launch Pac Man like attacks on yet other segments until they capture the entire industry. For example, Japanese corporations have capitalized on their manufacturing ability in calculators, watches, walkmans, and miniature televisions and seemingly bottomless financial pockets to produce and then dump cheap portable computers in Japan and overseas markets. Many American laptop manufacturers such as Apple, Tandy, Texas Instruments and Compaq, have surrendered to the Japanese onslaught and now either jointly produce or simply import laptops from their rivals. Japan's computer giants are far ahead in the race to produce one pound palmtop computers that can transmit and receive data from anywhere, and dispense with keyboards for handwritten notes. It is estimated that by 1994, 40 per cent of personal computers will be portables, up from 14 per cent now. Japan currently holds only a 9 per cent global share, but with their new products they are expected to expand their share to well over half.[54]

Supercomputers, which can be used to design, among countless other things, nuclear weapons and advanced missiles, are yet another key segment being steadily taken over by the Japanese. Cray sold its first two supercomputers to Japan in 1980. MITI's industrial policies prevented Cray from selling another supercomputer in Japan until 1987, when Tokyo finally agreed to open its bidding to foreign firms after years of bilateral government negotiations. In 1981, MITI targeted supercomputers for development. Hitachi, NEC and Fujitsu unveiled their owns supercomputers in 1983, 1985 and 1986, respectively, and have continually upgraded them since. In addition to a cartelized market, the big three enjoy immense government subsidies which reached $200 million in 1988 alone which in turn allows them to offer discounts as high as 86 per cent to national universities.[55] Today there is a severe imbalance of power between the small independent David Cray with 1989 worldwide sales of $784 million and the three Goliaths, Fujitsu, Hitachi and NEC with their combined worldwide sales of $30 billion! While Cray's supercomputers continue to be far superior in software, the Japanese snatch sales away by dumping their products in Japan and elsewhere – the seemingly bottomless pockets of the Japanese enable them to offer discounts of 80 and even 90 per cent. Japanese government purchases were conducted behind closed doors and often even the bids were not announced ahead of time. In November 1987, MIT canceled its plans to buy a NEC supercomputer for one-third the normal price only after the Commerce Department warned of a possible antidumping violation. By the late 1980s, Japan's producers had not only mastered the technology and dominated Japan's market, but were dumping their products overseas in an attempt to destroy Cray.

Japan's supercomputer industrial policy has been an enormous success. While the supercomputer industry has grown from a $89 million market in 1980 to a $1.1 billion market in 1990, Cray Research's global market share fell steadily from 90 per cent to 54 per cent, while Japan's market share rose from nothing to 28 per cent.[56] In 1989, Fujitsu had a 50.9 per cent Japan market share, Hitachi 16.7 per cent, Cray 15.7 per cent, and NEC 14.8 per cent. The number of supercomputers in the United States has fallen from 81 per cent of the world's total in 1980 to 50 per cent in 1990, while Japan's number of supercomputers rose from 8 to 28 per cent.[57] Although Cray still clings to a dominant market share around the world, comparative advantage counts for little in Japan's huge, carefully managed market where Japan's big three supercomputer makers enjoy a 85 per cent share. Without access to these potential sales and lacking similar government support, Control Data was denied vital economies of scale production, and in Spring 1989 announced that it had to abandon its supercomputer line. Control Data dropped out because of lack of access to Japan's huge market while the future of Cray is in doubt. As if the onslaught of NEC, Hitachi and Fujitsu against Cray were not enough, Sony, Toshiba, and Sharp are leading in the race to develop a a portable supercomputer called a Dynabook.

With the nearly total destruction of America's semiconductor makers, Cray and other American industries are becoming increasingly dependent on Japanese components. And the Japanese have not hesitated to use that dependence to further weaken America's economy. Prestowitz reveals that at least one leading Japanese supplier delayed delivery of certain new kinds of components that Cray had actually designed, thus giving its own computer group a one-year lead time in designing them into its own machines. In order to lessen its dependence on the Japanese giants, Cray then began working with Fairchild Corporation. Fujitsu's aborted buyout of Fairchild would have killed two American birds with one stone.[58]

Although Japan's destruction of America's supercomputer industry has made business page headlines, its takeover of several smaller fields may be just as important. If the Japanese succeed in conquering the machines which make computers, they will be in a position to deal America's remaining computer industry a death blow by either outright refusing to sell such vital equipment, or more likely by jacking up the prices and delaying shipments so that Japan's producers can deepen their lead. In 1988 worldwide sales of this capital equipment were only $15 billion. Yet, this equipment is used to produce $50 billion worth of chips which in turn supply the guts of the annual $700 billion worth of computers and other electrical equipment. As in most other sectors of the computer industry, the market share of American firms in the capital equipment sector plunged from 62 per cent in 1982 to 45 per cent in 1987 while Japan's share rose steadily from 29 to 44 per cent. Today, only Applied Materials continues to thrive, although there is a good chance it will picked off by a Japanese buyer.

Yet another strategic sector is X-ray lithography manufacturing technology which, when it becomes operational in the mid–1990s, will produce chips with so much data storage capacity that all the power now available in the largest IBM mainframe will be stored in a chip the size of a fingernail. A lithography production plant will cost over $1 billion compared to the $200 million plant employing current technology, something only the cash rich Japanese can afford. The Japanese are already well ahead in developing this technology, lead by a government–industry consortium of 20 firms that will spend $1 billion over the next five years. The consortium already has 10 synchrotron storage rings which are essential for developing the technology, with five additional rings currently being built. In contrast, the Americans are talking about creating consortia to develop the technology, but nothing concrete has emerged. IBM cannot build such synchrotron rings alone and is offering to share its existing technology with participating firms. But, again, the development costs and Japanese lead are prohibitive. It seems that this strategic sector will be conceded to the Japanese without a fight.

Washington's response to Japan's threat to destroy America's computer industry has been a typically ad hoc and inconsistent. Only the Defense Department is making any attempt to offset Japan's sustained offensive, and its efforts have been desultory and mixed at best. DARPA did give $300 million for a dozen firms involved in its Very High Speed Integrated Circuit (VHSIC) project, and in 1983 contributed $250 million for the Strategic Computing Program (SCP), to develop "superintelligent" computers that deal with symbols rather than numbers. These projects were created to offset Japan's VSIC and Fifth Generation computer projects, respectively. Other efforts to offset Japan are sporadic at best. For example, in 1981, Fujitsu was the low bidder for an 776 mile AT&T fiber optic cable system connecting Boston and Washington. But Congressional pressure forced AT&T to give the job to a domestic firm. Fujitsu's planned purchase of Fairchild in 1986 was also prevented by a Congressional outcry.[59]

A government study published in April 1991 found that a Congressional proposal for a $1.9 billion program to improve supercomputers will generate $10 billion in additional revenue for the industry and increase American GNP by six-tenths of a per cent. The study recognized the strategic importance of supercomputers as the stimulus for dozens of related industries, including microelectronics, aerospace, chemicals, and pharmaceuticals. The centerpiece of the Congressional program would help create a national data highway which would link the nation's supercomputers at speeds greater than a billion bits of data a second. But like countless other studies which attempt to revive America's economic decline, this one has not been implemented. As in all other industrial sectors, only the White House has the power to cut through the Gordian knot of Washington politics and decisively counter Japan's onslaught. The White House, however, still refuses to accept this responsibility.

SEMICONDUCTORS

Semiconductors are to high technology industries as steel is to heavy industry. Like scores of other basic technologies, the semiconductor was invented in the United States but has since been mastered by Japan. All along, Washington's industrial policy toward the semiconductor industry has been typically ad hoc and irrational, and, as in so many other American industries, largely shaped by the Pentagon. Semiconductors were created almost simultaneously in 1959 by two Americans, Jack Kilby of Texas Instrument and Robert Noyce of Fairchild, and were immediately pressed into military service. In 1962, defense accounted for 40 per cent of total semiconductor production and 100 per cent of integrated circuit production, figures which had dropped to 12 and 7 per cent, respectively, in 1977.[60]

But although Pentagon procurements steadily declined as a percentage of total sales, the Pentagon's VHSIC program from 1979 to 1988 represented Washington's largest government microelectronics initiative. The $1 billion program involving 25 firms was designed to create new generations of technology which could be applied to "smart weapons" employed against the Soviet Union. Research projects included lithography, circuit design, wafer processing and fabrication, chip packaging and testing, computer aided design, and computer architecture and software with immediate applications toward radar, guidance, communications, and other military systems. The project was not designed to promote the industrial competiveness of American microelectronics producers, and, in fact, the Pentagon requirements for radiation hardness and package strength divert the industry's focus on practical consumer needs. Intel was one of several American microelectronics firms which protested the Pentagon's policy, charging that it would divert human, capital and technological resources away from commercial applications, thus ultimately weakening America's microelectronics industry. Prestowitz writes that although "defense and NASA procurements provided a large market for American chipmakers in the 1960s, the government did not concern itself with the structure of the industry, with who did or did not get venture money, with who could or could not expand production, or with any special tax or financial measures aimed at especially promoting this industry. Moreover, it did not protect US companies from foreign competition".[61]

In contrast, Japan's semiconductor policy was typically rationally conceived and executed toward the goal of Japan's eventual domination of the world's semiconductor industry. Tokyo skillfully extracted semiconductor technology from the Americans by a variety of means. IBM and Texas Instruments were only allowed to manufacture in Japan after agreeing to license key patents to their competitors and agreeing not to take more than a ten per cent market share. Firms like Motorola and Fairchild which did not have the strong patent position of TI and IBM were outright barred from Japan's markets. Those American technologies that were not licensed were stolen. The extent of Japanese pirating is unknown, but is sometimes revealed when the Japanese copied the mistakes of the American chips. Intel, for example, recognized the same flaw in a NEC chip that had recently been corrected in its own 8086 microprocessor.[62]

MITI nurtured Japan's semiconductor industry through a range of collaborative efforts, the most important of which was the Very Large Scale Integration (VLSI) from 1976 to 1980 and designed dramatically to accelerate Japan's integrated circuit technology. The project was funded with $300 million, 40 per cent of which was government money and the rest corporate, and included Japan's leading microelectronics firms – Fujitsu, Hitachi, Mitsubishi, NEC, and Toshiba. The firms divided into two teams, Fujitsu, Hitachi, and Mitsubishi at the Computer Development Laboratories and NEC and Toshiba at the NEC-Toshiba Information Systems. All five firms worked at MITI's research institute, whose over 100 scientists and engineers were divided into six teams, each of which was headed by a different company: three on lithography and one each for crystal, process, and device technology. The project targeted such technologies as fine-line lithography, circuit design, wafer processing and fabrication, chip packaging and testing, and computer aided design. The program was an attempt to strengthen Japan's microelectronics industry which had been weakened by the 1973–74 recession and faced IBM's continuing domination. The project produced over 1000 semiconductor patents, of which about 160 were joint inventions and the rest by individual companies. The VLSI Technology Research Association, composed of MITI, NTT, and industry representatives, co-ordinated the project and made all major policy, technical, and financial decisions.

Another decisive boost to Japan's semiconductor industry has been NTT procurement, which Weinstein argues was decisive for the development of a Japanese semiconductor industry: the "role of NTT as a major consumer of semiconductor memories was probably crucial. In the early 1970s, NTT's need for large quantities of 16k RAMs was a major stimulus to the Japanese semiconductor industry, and NTT established quality standards that were very high even for Japan".[63] NTT sources 70 per cent of its purchases from its "family" of NEC, Fujitsu, Hitachi, and NEC and their "children" of 300 subcontractors. The family is turn in dependent on NTT to buy 60 per cent of its telecommunications production. NTT provided a \$13.5 billion market between 1965 and 1975 alone. Three related laws privatizing NTT, liberalizing regulations, and modifying 100 related laws were passed on 24 December 1984. Starting with the sale of 12.5 per cent of NTT's stock in November 1986 at \$7,500 a share, MPT subsequently launched a series of sales with the price per share eventually reaching a height of \$21 000, nearly 200 times earnings, just before the October 1987 stock market crash. Since privatization NTT has created over 100 subsidiaries, including a range of businesses closed to AT&T including leasing, engineering services, travel services, telemarketing, market research, credit card systems, "intelligent building" services, and security services. Despite this "privatization", NTT continues to base its purchases on its family rather than free markets. In 1988 foreign suppliers sold only \$366 million to NTT, less than 5 per cent of all hardware purchases.[64]

By 1981, as a result of these concerted industrial policies, Japan's semiconductor corporations had achieved technological and manufacturing parity with the United States, and were thus now ready for a massive, sustained dumping campaign designed to devastate America's semiconductor industry. At the beginning of that year, Japanese firms held 80 per cent of their own market but only 20 per cent of the world market. But by dropping the price of their 64k RAM chips 80 per cent and dumping them overseas, aided by the Reagan Administration's policy whereby the dollar rose 50 per cent, Japanese market share increased steadily until its 38 per cent global market share surpassed America's 35 per cent in 1987. Japan's chipmakers steadily moved their dumping attack upmarket, for example selling their 256k RAMs for two dollars although they cost three dollars to produce.[65]

In the largely zero sum game of international trade, Japanese gains in profits and development time equaled American losses. Battered by Japan's dumping offensives, American producers lacked the resources to develop commercial 256k RAMs even though IBM and AT&T had first developed them. Instead, the American producers abandoned the 256k RAMs and retreated up market to more sophisticated microprocessors and EPROMs (electrical programable read only memories). Yet, in 1985 the Japanese makers were dumping EPROMs as well. A glimpse into the specific tactics of Japanese dumping was revealed when a memo was leaked from Hitachi's US subsidiary for its salesmen to concentrate on destroying Intel and Advanced Micro Devices, Inc. by cutting prices by increments of 10 per cent until they had taken over the market, while guaranteeing distributors a 25 per cent profit.[66]

The effects of Japanese dumping were devastating to America's semiconductor industry. Throughout the mid–1980s it lost over $2 billion and 25 000 jobs and was completely knocked out of the memory chip market. American industry lost $900 million over the lifetime of the 256k D-RAMS alone. Japanese producers lost over twice as much as the Americans, but, in effect, used its $4 billion losses in the 1980s to "buy" the American market.[67]

The result was Japan's domination of the world's semiconductor market. In 1988, the world's three top firms (NEC, Toshiba and Hitachi), and six of the top ten semiconductor firms were Japanese. In contrast, Motorola and Texas Instruments were number four and five, respectively, while Intel was number seven. Japanese firms now have 90 per cent of the global market for the 64k, 128k and 256k chips, and have an early lead in the leap into 1M-bit or 1 048 576-bit chips and 4M-bit chips, and have produced prototypes of 16M-bit chips. Meanwhile, the market share of American firms in Japan dropped to 8.5 per cent by 1986 and has since risen to only 11.1 per cent despite a 1987 gentleman's agreement that Japan would allocate American firms a 20 per cent market share by 1991. The Japanese enjoy a 24.3 per cent share of America's market.[68]

Despite the devastation wrought by Japan's sustained dumping offensive, it proved extremely difficult forging a policy consensus between the US Trade Representative, Council of Economic Advisors, the National Security Council, the Office of Management and Budget, and the Departments of State, Labor, Treasury, Commerce and Defense. The Trade Representative was the only organization that initially wanted to resist Japan's dumping attack, all the other key economic policymakers were either cemented to the idealist concept of free trade or the primacy of the military alliance with Tokyo over economic conflicts. Prestowitz writes that the State Department and National Security Council "would not even allow – even as a tactic – the suggestion of any retaliation if Japan did not respond favorably for fear that the overall relationship between the two countries might be harmed . . . the invocation of free trade doctrine by most of the US government agencies made it impossible to negotiate for concrete results".[69]

The policy disarray was complicated by mixed messages from the private sector. Although the semiconductor industry was screaming for protection from the Japanese onslaught, the more dependent other American industries became on Japanese chips, the more they resisted any administration efforts to stop Japanese dumping. Thus, the deadlock between trade realists and idealists within the administration continued. Finally, the American Semiconductor Industry used Section 301 of the 1974 US Trade Act to file a dumping action against Japanese chipmakers on EPROMs and a blanket unfair trade petition including claims that

Tokyo had reneged on the two previous agreements, although the ultimate aim of the American producers was equal access rather than protection. Only then did the White House begin exerting pressure on Tokyo to stop dumping.

Tokyo's response to Washington's pressure was classic – deny any wrongdoing while delaying any negotiations for as long as possible. Tokyo proposed forming a High Technology Working Group to deal with semiconductors and related conflicts. The result was the First Semiconductor Agreement of November 1982 which simply set up a monitoring system on chip shipments. Obviously, simply observing Japanese chipmakers destroy America's industry through dumping was not enough. Washington's negotiators pressed MITI to give "guidance" to Japan's chipmakers to restrain dumping just as it had the automobile industry. In the Second Semiconductor Agreement of November 1983, MITI secretly promised to "encourage" (a euphemism for "give guidance to") the Japanese chipmakers to buy more American chips and develop long term relations with American producers.

Although the dumping continued despite MITI's promise, the Reagan Administration did nothing until June 4, 1985, when Commerce Under-secretary Lionel Olmer first warned Tokyo against predatory pricing and asked it to completely open its markets after the latest free fall in prices over the previous few months threatened to wipe out America's survivors. Nine months later, on 13 March 1986, the Commerce Department published a study revealing the extent of Japanese dumping. At a fair market price of 100 per cent, it was found that Mitsubishi Electric's price at 108.72 per cent was the only Japanese firm not guilty of dumping, while Fujitsu's 74.35 per cent, Toshiba's 49.5 per cent, Hitachi's 19.8 per cent, and the other producer's average price of 39.68 per cent revealed the massive short-term losses those firms were willing to sustain in order to destroy their American rivals and enjoy windfall profits in the long run.[70] Two months later the House of Representatives voted 408 to 5 to urge the President to retaliate against Japan if no agreement were reached. Finally, in mid-1986, under the weight of all the dumping evidence and Congressional and private pressure, the Reagan Administration agreed to open its own dumping case on 256k RAMs as well as the private initiatives on 256k RAMs and EPROMs, and the 301 unfair trade case against the Japanese. Tough, bilateral negotiations throughout the summer resulted in the Japan–US Semiconductor Trade Agreement of 17 September 1986, under which Tokyo officially promised that Japanese producers would sell chips at a fair market value based on floor prices established for each firm, with no dumping in third markets, and in a secret side letter promised to grant American producers a 20 per cent share of Japan's market by 1991. Tokyo also agreed to actively help

American producers sell in Japan while monitoring the costs of Japanese products to the United States and elsewhere to prevent dumping. In return, the White House agreed to drop its dumping and unfair trade cases. The agreement expires in June 1991.

Tokyo signed the 1986 Agreement simply to create a smokescreen behind which Japanese producers could continue conquering huge market shares and profits, all the while battering their American rivals. The floor price agreement allowed Japanese producers to raise prices and enjoy windfall profits, while ensuring their huge market shares remained unchanged. American semiconductor producers did get a breathing spell, but their share of Japan's protected markets rose only slightly from 8.6 per cent in 1986 to 11.6 per cent in 1991; the US Semiconductor Industry Association charged in 1988 that Tokyo removed obvious trade barriers only to erect more insidious ones behind the scenes.[71]

Dumping continued despite the agreement. The 1986 trade deficit with Japan reached $50 billion, and Congressional pressures were building on the White House for decisive action. Finally, on 27 January 1987, the White House once again succumbed to domestic pressure and gave Tokyo sixty days to prove it was in compliance with the agreement. Tokyo, of course, denied any dumping but all the evidence pointed to a massive violation of the agreement. Thus, on 17 April 1987, the White House imposed 100 per cent tariffs on Japanese personal computers, color TVs and power tools, for a total of $300 million annually, or $180 million, $90 million and $30 million, on each industry, respectively. Although these trade sanctions were the first against Japan since 1945, they were a mere slap on the wrist compared to the damage done. Japanese products assembled in the United States were not affected by the tariffs. Tokyo protested vigorously to GATT, voicing the predictable claims that Japan's semiconductor markets were the world's most open and American producers simply were not trying hard enough. But, as usual, the Administration threw in the towel before it had achieved any concrete results. Reagan agreed to drop tariffs on $51 million of Japanese imports just before meeting with his "friend Yasu", Prime Minister Nakasone, at the June 1987 Group of Seven meeting at Venice. The Reagan Administration reduced the tariffs a further $84 million in November 1987. These conciliatory gestures werepredictably unreciprocated.

Instead, Tokyo backed up its continued dumping with a two pronged attack. It cried foul to GATT, which on 4 May 1988 ruled that the agreement was a restraint of trade, that Tokyo must abolish its monitoring system on Japanese semiconductor sales to third markets and replace it with a mechanism to ensure there was no more dumping. Meanwhile, Tokyo followed its usual "divide and conquer" strategy. In 1987 and

1988, Japan's semiconductor producers colluded to restrain sales to pressure American users against American semiconductor makers. MITI went so far as to offer one US chip manufacturer access to Japan's closed market in return for its agreeing to publicly denounce the bilateral semiconductor accord.

In March 1988, when he found out about the nefarious schemes of MITI and Japan's semiconductor industry, Senator Pete Wilson of California threatened to sponsor new sanctions against Japan if the blackmail and artificial chip shortage did not stop. MITI then announced that it was sure that the shortage would soon lift, and not long after there was an adequate supply.[72] The effectiveness of Senator Wilson's threat in overcoming such blatant Japanese neomercantilism makes one wonder what would happen to the trade deficit and America's relative economic decline if there were a White House dedicated to serving American rather than Japanese national interests. Much of Japan's power is psychological, the power to bluff.

The Bush Administration sought a new semiconductor agreement to replace the old accord which would expire in June 1991. The foreign share of Japan's semiconductor remained stalled at 13.1 per cent in 1990, of which American chipmakers had 11.5 per cent, well below the 20 per cent share promised by 1991. But the White House undersold its case when it negotiated the 1986 agreement. USTR Carla Hills complained that the real American market share would be be two or three times that if a genuine free market existed.[73] The Japanese excuse for reneging on its agreement is that the promise is invalid because it was only made by one ministry, not the government. In October 1990, the US Semiconductor Industry Association (SIA) and the Computer Systems Policy Project jointly called for a new agreement that would allow for a 20 per cent American share of Japan's market by December 1992, but Tokyo has dug its heels in on an agreement.

Meanwhile, what is the fate of America's semiconductor industry? Those American producers that have survived like Texas Instruments and Micron have retreated upmarket to specialize in sophisticated products like complex logic systems, microprocessors, software, or custom chips, and are shifting from production of individual components to entire systems. Between 1986 and 1988, in a "if you can't beat 'em, join 'em" frenzy, nine American firms formed 31 joint ventures with their Japanese opponents. The most dramatic joint ventures were the November 1987 agreement between Toshiba and Motorola and the December 1988 agreement between Texas Instruments and Hitachi in which the American firms agreed to exchange their microprocessor technology for aid in developing 16–megabit D-RAMs. In 1989 alone, there were ten additional tie-ups between Japanese and American chipmakers. Other firms are selling off their assets to their Japanese rivals. In 1990, National Semiconductor and Advanced Micro Devices sold factories to Matsushita and Sony, respectively. These joint ventures and sell-outs are a classical Faustian bargain whereby the American producers may gain licensing fees in the short run but will eventually be overrun by the Japanese as they master and use the technology to create yet more innovative products.

In July 1991, Washington and Tokyo signed a new semiconductor agreement. Originally Washington had pushed for a five year extension of the current rules governing the prices charged by Japan's chipmakers while Tokyo first refused any extension. They compromised at a three year extension. The new agreement also suspends the remaining $155 million in sanctions on Japanese imports for violations of the previous agreement and states that the 20 per cent foreign share of Japan's market would be a goal and not a requirement. Difficulties remained over just how to count chip sales, with each side counting differently Japanese chips made in the United States under an American brand name, or chips made in the United States for subsidiaries of American companies in Japan.

Meanwhile, American firms continued trying hard to shape rational Washington industrial policies for the microelectronics industry. Industrial associations like the Semiconductor Industry Association with 37 members or the Semiconductor Equipment and Materials International with over 800 members are becoming increasingly active in lobbying Congress for protection and subsidies similar to those enjoyed by the Japanese. These lobbying efforts have had mixed success. After years of lobbying, Commerce did finally protest Japanese semiconductor dumping in 1985, initiate an in-depth investigation that its extent, and negotiate an agreement signed in September 1986. As we have seen, though, like most OMA agreements, the semiconductor accords may have benefited the Japanese more than the Americans.

As in so many other American industries, all this may be too little too late. The Japanese are circling in for the kill, with Tokyo in the driver's seat. According to Prestowitz, "MITI is now the arbiter of the world semiconductor industry. By controlling Japanese production, it determines world prices and the availability of critical devices . . . (Meanwhile) the United States is now so dependent on Japan that it cannot move unilaterally to strengthen its own industry".[74] Industrial and technology targeting continues unabated. In 1989, for example, the government launched a ten year research cartel project designed to produce a superconductive chip, which, when achieved, will revolutionize computers and communications.

Japan's microelectronics corporations are in the last stages of a systematic war to take over America's semiconductor industry. Japan's Big Seven are rapidly developing 1 megabit and 4 megabit chips, and custom chips called application-specific integrated circuits (ASICs), and already enjoy about 90 per cent of the market shares for all three products, while the South Koreans hold another five per cent.[75] It costs over $200 million to build just one fabrication line for a 4 megabit chip – a price tag beyond the reach of most American producers. IBM, TI, and AT&T currently manufacture 1 megabit chips, but even those giants are hesitating to invest in 4 megabit production with the Japanese so far ahead.

Japan's microelectronics firms have even more thoroughly ravished America's semiconductor production equipment industry. American semiconductor equipment maker shares dropped from 75 per cent of global sales in 1980 to 48 per cent in 1988 while Japan's sales rose from 18 to 39 per cent.[76] The industry is on the brink of being revolutionized by synchrotron technology which can etch the chips about 0.1 micron (one thousandth the width of a human hair), which theoretically would allow up to four billion transitors to be crammed into each microchip. In contrast, the standard etching process today can achieve no more than 1 micron (one-hundredth the width of a human hair), enough for one million transitors. Congress had originally helped Brookhaven National Laboratory acquire the nation's first synchrotron, but Japan's efforts to perfect synchrotron technology far surpass America's. Washington's response to these developments was typically confused. Over the Bush Administration's objections, Congress succeeded in allocating $30 million in 1990 to the industry and doubled the amount for 1991. But, again, it will probably be another example of too little too late.[77]

History's "what ifs" provide not just interesting parlor games but possible insights into future policies. Japanese never give anything up without a fight, and only then if faced with no alternative. Prestowitz points out that if Washington had in 1982 "simply limited the Japanese share of the US market to that obtained by the US companies in Japan, the superiority of the US industry could probably have been maintained. Without the sales volume generated in the US market, Japanese costs would have risen and become uncompetitive".[78] America's semiconductor industry and the country itself today would enjoy more wealth, diversity, and competitive power. Tragically, the White House's missed opportunity in semiconductors is merely one of countless flawed policies which have collectively undermined American power and promoted Japan's.

AEROSPACE

Aerospace remains one of the few areas in which the United States retains a comfortable lead. Despite being targeted as a strategic industry, Japan's aerospace industry remains a generation or so behind that of the United

States. In 1989, Japanese firms held only six per cent of the global aerospace market, while the Japanese government's aerospace budget was only one-thirteenth that of the United States and one-third that of the EC. The Americans have a particularly immense lead in the aircraft industry. In 1988, airlines around the world placed orders for 1050 aircraft worth $48 billion. Boeing and McDonnell Douglas captured 80 per cent of that market while the European Airbus took most of the rest.[79]

Yet, despite these odds, Tokyo is determined to create an aerospace industry that will eventually rival that of the United States.[80] MITI officially targeted the aerospace industry for development with the Aircraft Industry Promotion Law of 1954 which cartelized the industry under its leadership. In 1953, MITI formed both the Japan Jet Engine Consortium and a "national policy company" (*kokusaku gaisha*) called the Nippon Aircraft Manufacturing Consortium whose aim was to create a Japanese aerospace industry. The government contributed 50 per cent of the equity and organized scores of Japan's leading heavy and high technology firms behind the effort. The consortium succeeded in producing Japan's only commercial aircraft to date, the YS–11 of which less than 200 were sold after it appeared in 1957. But the consortium eventually folded in the 1970s as its losses averaged four times its capitalization.

Tokyo then shifted its strategy from making its own jets from scratch to forcing Washington to license the production of its advanced aircraft. Military aircraft account for about 85 per cent of all Japanese aircraft production. Of the 36 aircraft that the JDF employs, nine were bought from the United States, sixteen were co-produced, and eleven were copies of American aircraft.[81] Japan's defense budget is the world's third largest of which 40 per cent of all procurements is spent on aircraft. About 1500 firms annually receive Japan Defense Agency (JDA) procurement orders. Japan's three biggest military contractors are Mitsubishi Heavy Industries, Japan's aerospace industry, however, is dominated by the four giant heavy industry divisions of Mitsubishi, Kawasaki, Fuji, and Ishikawajima, of which Mitsubishi controls over half of the contracts, while Japan's microelectronics giants like Mitsubishi Electric, Nissan, Toshiba, NEC, and Hitachi also play a vital support role.

The Japanese have been very successful in exploiting production licensing agreements of American military aircraft for their commercial spinoffs. In each licensing project, the Japanese eventually mastered the technology and production techniques, and moved on to independent projects. Most spinoff applications have been limited to specific types of technology, such as adapting the braking system of the F–4 Phantom jet to the Shinkansen bullet train. Some spinoffs, however, have involved the entire system. Japan's BK–117 helicopter was a direct spinoff from the HSS–2 anti-submarine helicopter of the early 1960s, and has been competing with commercial American helicopters ever since. More recently, Mitsubishi used parts of the F–86 and F–4 Phantom to produce the MU–300 medium-size business jet which has been competing with American producers since 1981. A 1981 joint licensing venture between Mitsubishi and MacDonnell Douglas allowed the Japanese to produce 147 of 155 ordered by the JDF. Part of the deal included Mitsubishi's procurement of the sophisticated fire control technology, and Mitsubishi has since adapted the sophisticated avionics for the F–15 to make first a military trainer and then a commercial jet.[82]

Tokyo's independence grows with Japan's mastery of aerospace production and technology. Tokyo built its only indigenous fighter, the F–1, when Washington refused to co-produce another fighter and instead urged Japan to buy existing American fighters. Tokyo refused and eventually deployed 83 F–1s between 1977 and 1983, but military experts rate the aircraft as extremely poor.[83] By 1986, Tokyo had also developed and deployed its own XT–4 trainer jet, on schedule and budget. Japan would have produced its FSX fighter plane if Washington had not negotiated a joint production agreement.

Aside from licensing production of military aircraft, MITI has also skillfully created a dependence of American civilian aircraft producers on Japan's aerospace firms for a steadily expanding range of technology and production. As in other industries, Japan's aerospace producers are skillfully using their comparative advantage in a few key technologies to win large chunks of joint production agreements. MITI has played a divide and conquer strategy with the American manufacturers, whereby it warns them that Japan's corporations will work with and buy from the Europeans if not the Americans. It, of course, tells the European producers the same thing. MITI then either directly negotiates or directs from behind the scenes the subsequent agreements. The American producers give in not just because of reliance on key Japanese technology and sales but Japanese capital as well. Thus, it is not surprising that the Americans are selling out large chunks of their technology and production to the Japanese. Japan's strategy of playing the American and European aerospace manufacturers off against each other was consisely expressed by a high ranking MITI official: "We (Japan and the US) had better co-operate in the commercial aircraft business in order to keep ourselves competitive with our European rival. Now that the US has a very powerful competitor, Airbus Industrie, it would be better for the US to make Japan a partner".[84]

Using this strategy, MITI in 1986 succeeded in arm-twisting Boeing into accepting a partnership with the Big Three Japanese aerospace corporations – Mitsubishi, Fuji and Kawasaki heavy industries. A Boeing spokesperson admitted the firm had no choice: "had the Japanese developed a partnership with Airbus instead of us, they would be flying

Airbuses today instead of our airliners".[85] This partnership gave the Big Three a 25 per cent stake in the development of the 7J7, a 150–seat turboprop jet. About 115 Japanese engineers were allowed access to Boeing's R&D centers, a number that was cut back to about 40 when the project was scrapped for lack of a market. Boeing has already used Japanese subcontractors for previous projects including the 737, 747, and 757, but never previously included the Japanese firms as full partners. In 1989, Boeing cut a deal with Japan's three largest aerospace companies – Mitsubishi, Fuji, and Kawasaki heavy industries – to provide $1 billion of its $4 billion project to build the proposed 300 seat 767X passenger plane. Boeing is gambling that the financial and possible technology imputs of its Japanese investors will outweigh the inevitable drain of Boeing technology to Japan. In addition, the Big Three received 17 per cent of the airframe production for the Boeing 767. In January 1990, Boeing announced that the Japanese aircraft manufacturers were given a 20 per cent production share of Boeing's new B777, a next generation 350 seat aircraft, and will also share in marketing and servicing the aircraft. MITI allocated 803 million yen in 1991 to help the three corporations develop their parts of the project. Meanwhile, Japan's aerospace firms have been busy cutting deals with other American and European producers. Mitsubishi formed a joint venture with Germany's Daimler Benz AG to develop projects involving space-related technology, supersonic transport, passenger aircraft, and jet engines. Japanese firms own 23 per cent of the V2500 jet engine project with Rolls Royce, Pratt Whitney, and other firms.

Boeing has come under increasing criticism from knowledgeable American political economists for cutting these deals with Japanese producers; a development that was met with consternation by knowledgable American political economists. Boeing dismissed those concerned that Japan's participation in its projects will be yet another "Trojan Horse" used to take over an American industry with the laconic statement that "integrating an automobile and integrating an aircraft are a magnitude apart".[86] Yet, on 13 April 1990, Boeing announced that it would proceed with its development of the 777 jet without Japanese capital, although it would still procure about 15–20 per cent of the parts from Japanese sources. The announcement was clearly a setback for the Japanese corporations which desperately wanted to gain the vast technology exchange from being a joint owner of the project, but had bowed out fearing the controversy would cause another FSX-style conflict. American aircraft parts manufacturers, on the other hand, which are already facing a recession from military budget cuts, were overjoyed at the news.[87]

But Japan's aerospace industry has developed so quickly that now MITI is leading its own projects. In 1988 MITI announced that it had earmarked $225.6 million for a six firm consortium that would lead the development and production of a hypersonic spaceplane to be completed in 2006. The spaceplane would be fast enough to travel from Tokyo to New York in three hours. Like its threats to scrap the FSX agreement and produce its own fighter-jet, Tokyo's claims to be ahead of similar spacejet efforts by Boeing and MacDonald Douglas are largely a bluff, used to win large development and production shares of joint ventures with foreign manufacturers. Tokyo approached both British and French aerospace firms for a joint venture in which the Japanese, with such key technologies as new materials like carbon fibers, microelectronics, and supercomputers, and seemingly bottomless pit of financial assets, would be the senior partner. By December 1989, four foreign firms – General Electric, Pratt & Whitney, Rolls Royce and Shecma (France) – had joined Ishikawaji-ma-Harima Heavy Industries, Kawasaki Heavy Industries, and Mitsubishi Heavy Industries in submitting applications for research money from MITI for the engine that will propel the "hypersonic" jet. The catch of course is that the foreign firms must share their technological advances with their Japanese rivals, thus possibly repeating the pattern which the Japanese have mastered in exploiting foreign technology to leapfrog and thus ravage their foreign rivals. In February 1991, MITI opened up its hypersonic airplane, designed to fly five times the speed of sound, to foreign investors. General Electric, Pratt and Whitney, and Rolls Royce promptly jumped on board, excited by the chance to tap into Japan's massive financial reserves.

What is Washington doing about Tokyo's systematic efforts to catch up to then leapfrog America's aircraft industry? Washington has increasingly taken a tougher stand on giving away its technology and production to Japan. Although it essentially gave away the F–4 and F–104 fighters to Japan, Washington has tightened up its licensing of production and technology on subsequent aircraft as Japan's industry expanded. About 40 per cent of the technology for the F–15 was "blackboxed" so the Japanese could not reverse engineer it.

Washington, however, did not take a tough stand on Japan's expropriation of American technology until Tokyo proposed to build the FSX, the F–1's successor. The battle over the FSX fighter plane in the late 1980s provides an illuminating case study of Japan's aerospace strategy. Most analysts conclude with Inman and Burton that: "Japan's ultimate objective was not military, but commercial. The FSX deal would help Japan achieve its goal of launching a civilian aerospace industry that might well take jobs and profits from the United States".[88]

The FSX (now called the SX–3) will be an extensively modified version of the F–16. In April 1987, Tokyo rejected Washington's request that it buy the F–16s off the shelf. Japan argued that the F–16 was an obsolete airplane and that instead Japan wanted to develop its own advanced fighter jet. Negotiations then began over the terms on which the United States would sell its F–16 technology to Japan. In November 1988, an agreement was signed in which Tokyo conceded 40 per cent of the FSX's development work but retained 100 per cent of production. Congress protested and the White House pressured Tokyo for a significant share of production work as well.

Washington's refusal simply to give away its production and technology as in the past provoked Japanese anger and protests which were as irrational as they were bitter. When Prime Minister Takeshita visited Washington in February 1989, he pleaded with Congress to separate defense and trade issues and approve the transfer of F–16C technology.[89] He attempted to justify his position by arguing that Tokyo had originally planned to develop the FSX on its own, and only reluctantly agreed to share the development and production after massive Washington pressure. In Japanese eyes, Washington's demand to share development and production, and refusal to turn over technical information is a glaring example of "techno-nationalism". Takeshita claimed that it would be years before Japan's aerospace industry could compete with America's, and threatened to develop the FSX completely on its own if Washington did not surrender the technology, a position which somewhat undercut his argument that it needed the technology in the first place. Shinji Otsuki, a senior defense expert with the Asahi Shibun, trotted out the classic Japanese claim that the issue was all a big American misunderstanding: "opposition to the FSX deal in Congress and the US media was a graphic example of the information and awareness gap between Japan and the United States".[90] Shintaro Ishihara, argued in the March 1989 issue of the monthly magazine *Bungei Shunju*, that:

> Deployment by Japan alone of a fighter craft Japan built itself with its own advanced technology would give it absolute authority over its own airspace, and this would alter both the meaning and the value of the Japan-US defense alliance. The United States would then be unable to continue patronizing Japan in the area of defense . . . Creating its own weapons systems using its own leading-edge technologies would . . . display in a very dramatic fashion Japan's latent power in international politics and give Japan greater capacity to resolve world tensions and compel the military powers to compromise and co-operate with Japan.[91]

After continued tough negotiations, an agreement was signed on April 28, 1989. The FSX deal was a triumph of American diplomacy – for once Washington did not give away to Japan more than it gained. Although Tokyo will gain access to some important American technologies,

Washington negotiated the right to take any Japanese improvements free of charge and license any Japanese technology used for the aircraft. Japanese radar, electronic countermeasures, inertial reference systems and computer hardware, will be transferred to the United States, while Tokyo also promised not to transfer the technology to third countries without Washington's permission. In addition, American firms will split both development and production 40–60 with their Japanese rivals. American patents will be held in secret at the JDA rather than openly at MITI. A New York Times editorial pointed out that the FSX issue represented a "milestone in relations between the United States and Japan, symbolized Washington's new concern over the economic dimension of national security. Under pressure from Congress, the Administration was compelled to expand the definition of national security to include trade and economic objectives, as well as military and strategic concerns".[92]

Japan's aerospace ambitions do not just involve aircraft. Tokyo is determined to launch Japanese into space itself. As in other industries, Japan's space industry development depends on access to American technology and goodwill. Japan's first giant space step took place in 1969 when the Scienc and Technology Agency (STA) created the National Space Development Agency (NSDA), with the initial goal of launching a satellite, a goal which it achieved the following year. As always, most of the technology came from the Americans, although over the next fifteen years under strict government guidance the domestic content rose from about 10 per cent to its present nearly 100 per cent. According to the 1969 agreement in which Washington authorized the transfer of rocket and satellite technology to Tokyo, Japan cannot launch satellites for other countries unless it uses a 100 per cent Japanese-made rocket.

Japan has almost achieved independence in space technology. In a 1980 "vision", MITI designated aerospace a strategic industry equivalent to the information and nuclear industries, and began funneling subsidies into aerospace equal to those for computers and greater than telecommunications. A 1982 government white paper entitled "Long Term Vision for Space Development" clearly outlined the goal to build and eventually export satellites. In 1983, Japan launched its first commercial communications satellite at a total cost only three times more than an American satellite. Two years later, in 1985, NSDA launched the H–1 three-stage rocket, whose guidance and first and second stage boosters were 100 per cent Japanese technology. The H–1 sent out two probes which rendezvoused with Haley's comet. By 1988 NDSA had launched a total of 17 scientific satellites for space observation, and 19 application satellites for such purposes as broadcasting, engineering and materials tests. Unlike the

American or European space efforts, all of Japan's were successful. The space industry had grown 17.2 per cent over the previous year, and of total sales of $1.56 billion in 1988, 38.3 per cent was for satellites, 30 per cent for ground facilities, 24.3 per cent for rockets, and the rest for such items as software, data processing analysis and research on development of space stations.[93] On 24 January 1990, Japan launched a $41 million rocket toward the moon, the first venture since a similar Russian venture in 1976.

Tokyo plans to achieve very ambitious goals in the 1990s. An important symbolic step was taken in 1991 when the first Japanese was launched into space when a NDSA astronaut joined an American space shuttle flight. During the flight he conducted materials processing and microgravity experiments in co-ordination with similar experiments by US astronauts on other flights in 1991 and 1993 using the US International Microgravity Laboratory. This experience will prove invaluable not only for Japan's new materials research but for Japan's manned space flights. NDSA plans to launch its own manned space shuttle in 1995. If Congress allows the project to procede, in the late 1990s the Japanese Experimental Module, a permanent laboratory for microgravity experiments operated by Japanese astronauts will be attached to Freedom, the US international space station. Meanwhile, Japan's satellite program will roar ahead. In 1992, the H–2 rocket, entirely built from Japanese technology and capable of putting a 2.2 ton satellite into orbit, will be launched initiating Japan's entry into the world commercial market for communications and broadcasting satellites.

What is Washington doing about Japan's space offensive? As in so many other Japanese industries, if there were a free satellite market, Japan would not have a satellite industry. In the zero sum game of international trade, every Japanese satellite sale represents a potential lost sale to an American or other satellite producer. In May 1989, USTR Carla Hills designated Japan an "unfair trader" in satellites because its government and industry continued to "buy Japan" despite the much higher quality and cheaper price of American satellites. Washington complained that Tokyo protects its domestic satellite market to nurture it eventually into a global champion. It demanded that Tokyo open up its National Space Development Agency of Japan (NASDA) satellite procurement process to competitive bidding and allow American participation in the 90 billion yen CS4 satellite project being developed by MPT, NASDA, and such microelectronics giants as NEC, Mitsubishi Electric and Toshiba. Finally Washington pressured Tokyo to license the Satelite Japan Corporation, a Sony subsidiary, which intends to buy several American satellites after it is licensed to begin business. Hills argued that Washington "does not intend to interfere with Japan's satellite development projects. What we want is equal access for foreign firms to government procurement of commercial satellites".[94]

In a classic Japanese contradiction, Tokyo rejected all of Washington's requests. With one breath Tokyo claimed that the satellite market is completely open while with the next it argued that it must keep out foreign satellites in order to promote a Japanese satellite industry. It claimed that private firms are allowed to purchase American satellites. According to Tokyo, the CS4 project is purely a research and development project despite the fact that NTT will use three of the five transponders and 90 per cent of the satellite's capacity for commercial purposes, and refused to allow American participation in the CS4 project. Finally, Tokyo has agreed to grant a license to the Satelite Japan Corporation, but will only allow it to purchase foreign satellites on a case-by-case basis. Then, after a year of tough negotiations, on 3 April 1990, Tokyo agreed to allow foreign satellites to compete with Japanese satellites for government procurements, a promise that if sincerely fulfilled will result in all sales going to the American producers with their cost only half those of Japanese satellites. Japan currently has 43 satellites of which only 5 were bought from the United States.[95] Although the United States still enjoys a comfortable lead, MITI is rapidly developing Japan's aerospace industry. As in other industries, Japan's aerospace industry has been built on taking and mastering American technology. But the balance of aerospace technology power is shifting steadily toward Japan's favor, revealed by Tokyo's ability to produce the FSX. A Defense Department official revealed that "the Japanese made it very clear that the American side needed to recognize the world had changed considerably . . . When we proposed yet another co-production project the Japanese calmly urged us not to be so 'nostalgic.' They insisted that the era of co-development is upon us".[96] Japan leads the world in such technologies as advanced materials, microelectronics and radar. America's dependence on Japanese technology is deepening, thus raising Tokyo's bargaining clout to elicit yet greater concessions from Washington at the expense of America's aerospace industry.

Yet, despite these dramatic gains, Japan's aerospace industry faces considerable difficulties. Twice as many jet aircraft are sold to the military than the commercial sector. Tokyo's ban on military exports prevents its aerospace producers from enjoying scale production, thus also undercutting potential foreign and domestic commercial sales. Tokyo will undoubtedly overcome these development obstacles as it has so many others. If Washington does not create and implement a comprehensive policy, America's aerospace industry may eventually find itself surpassed by Japan's.

HIGH DEFINITION TELEVISION

High definition television (HDTV) can revolutionize the entire micro-electronics industry. With double the number of lines, HDTV produces sparkling clear images which in turn will create a market estimated to be worth $30 billion in the industrialized countries by 2000 and potentially $150 billion if the entire world switches over. The spinoffs of HDTV throughout the electronics industry will be even more profitable as entire new generations of semiconductors, computers and VCRs emerge. HDTV will become the world's largest consumer of chips, microprocessors and signal processing chips, which in turn will stimulate new graphics and screen technology for computers, medical and printing equipment.

All these fields are currently dominated by American firms but will be taken over by Japanese firms if they are the first to develop HDTV. The American Electronics Association (AEA) calculates that if American firms capture less than 10 per cent of the world's future high definition television market it will lose half its share of the personal computer and chip markets, and even to maintain its current strength in the computer industry it will need to control half the HDTV market.[97]

The Japanese are presently far ahead of the Americans in HDTV research and development, by some estimates as much as 20 years. Japan's HDTV policy began in the early 1970s as MITI and Japan's national broadcasting network (NHK) formed consortia and spread generous subsidies, while total R&D expenditures have topped $1 billion. In 1987 MITI, supported by the 126 Dietmember Federation for the Promotion of High Definition Television (Yuseizoku), reinforced these efforts by launching a 20 year program to perfect and market HDTV worldwide. In early December 1990, Sony, Matsushita and Hitachi began selling the first HDTVs in Japan, priced at $34 000 each. Within five years sales are expected to reach 1 million while the price drops to $7500, giving the Japanese manufacturers profits, scale economies, and learning curves that should allow them to dominate the industry indefinitely. Even if European or American manufacturers are able to hobble into the race, they will still depend on Japanese technology and components. Sony's acquistion of CBS records in 1988 and Columbia Pictures in 1989, and Matsushita's takeover of MCA, Universal Studio's parent, in 1990 were key aspects of grand strategies designed to merge Japan's hardware expertise with America's software technology. Sony opened an HDTV production facility with Columbia in 1991 and has begun filming movies and TV shows with HDTV in order to build a market. Matsushita is expected to soon follow suit. Both Sony and Matsushita hope to use their market power to force Washington to accept their production standard for the United States, thus cementing their domination of the industry.

The American response to this latest Japanese challenge is typically ad hoc, unco-ordinated, and lead by the military. The Reagan and Bush Administrations refused to support America's fledgling HDTV industry, parroting the liberal mantra that only the market and not the government can pick winners or losers – despite the overwelming evidence that Tokyo has mastered the art of picking and developing winners that would have failed to develop if the market had prevailed. Despite these attitudes, in December 1988, DARPA announced two HDTV-related contracts worth $30 million (Sony was one of the applicants). In January 1989, 16 firms including IBM, AT&T, Apple, and Motorola formed a research consortium designed to license technology and maybe even make HDTV sets. Yet, HDTV did not become a heated political issue until 1 February 1989 when two dozen industry, academic, and interest group experts testified largely in favor of HDTV research and development before the House Telecommunications and Finance Subcommittee, followed by similar Senate Commerce Committee hearings on the subject in May during which the American Electronic Association presented a plan calling for the creation of a public–private consortium and funded with $1.3 billion in government loans for research. During February 1989 subcommitte hearings on HDTV, Commerce Secretary Mosbacher called HDTV a top development priority. In July 1990, the White House reacted to these efforts by turning down a request by the American Electronics Association to provide $100 million for basic research and protested Congress' $75 million appropriation for DARPA to invest in developing high-resolution flat-panel video displays. DARPA Director, Craig Fields, resigned in protest in 1990 after the White House criticized him for attempting to nurture an American HDTV industry.

In 1990, Congress overode the Bush Administration objectives and appropriated $75 million for DARPA to spend on HDTV flat-panel video displays. As usual, the gesture may be far too little too late. Like countless other technologies, flat-panel display technology was first developed in the United States and is now mastered by Japan. The market for flat-panel displays is estimated to grow from $3.4 billion in 1990 to $10.2 billion in 1997. Flat-panel technology spills over into other product areas including active-matrix liquid crystal displays and giant glass integrated circuits. Over the last ten years, massive dumping by Japan's flat-panel displays forced at least a score of American flat-panel display firms into bankruptcy including the divisions of such large corporations as AT&T, IBM, Control Data, Burroughs, GE, GTE and Texas Instruments. Only a dozen small American firms continue to cling tenaciously to the panel display market, while, with the higher resolution of its active-matrix technology, Xerox remains the only viable competitor against the

Japanese. In 1989, eight American manufacturers of flat screens filed an as yet unresolved anti-dumping suit against their Japanese rivals.

Two recent developments may have put the United States back into the HDTV development race. Stimulated by a 1988 Federal requirement that high-definition technology be available for local broadcasting, American companies have complied, thus giving them the edge over their Japanese and European rivals which transmit only by satellite. The Federal Communications Commission (FCC) orchestrated these developments by sponsoring a competition among American firms to develop a transmission system. In June 1993, the FCC will choose among the six designs submitted as the standard for use in the United States. Whether these breakthroughs will allow the United States to catch up, however, is questionable. The Japanese firms hold an overwhelming lead in the development of high resolution video screens and will have little difficulty incorporating the American technology into their products. Japan's strategy of exploiting basic American research may well repeat itself in HDTV. Inman and Burton write that "the federal response to HDTV has emphasized traditional policy measures centering around military applications and basic research. Efforts to develop policies for commercial applications have been hampered by lack of institutions capable of dealing with issues related to commercial technology".[98] HDTV represents the economic disasters that result when the United States abandons a low-tech mass consumer industry like television to the Japanese which uses the vast profits, scales economics, and learning scales to jump into a range of related high technology fields.

TELECOMMUNICATIONS

The United States annually suffers a two or three billion dollar deficit in telecommunications even though it has a comparative advantage in most products.[99] The industry is directed by Nippon Telephone and Telegraph (NTT), which is in turn is overseen by the Ministry of Posts and Telecommunications (MPT). NTT annually buys $5 billion in equipment mostly from an oligopoly, or "family", of some of Japan's largest microelectronic corporations including NEC, Fujitsu, Oki Electric and Hitachi. Tokyo began "privatizing" NTT in April 1985 when it sold the first lot of two thirds of total shares earmarked for private Japanese investors. As Johnson reminds us, Japanese "privatization" is not synonymous with "liberalization".[100] Foreign producers of superior telecommunications equipment are still denied significant entry to Japan's carefully managed telecommunications markets.

Washington first tried to break into NTT's "family" in 1978–80. After two and a half years of tough negotiations, in December 1980 Tokyo finally agreed to sign the "NTT Procurement Procedures Agreement" which theoretically promised that NTT would consider buying some foreign products. The agreement's significance, however, was soon revealed by NTT's president Akikusa, who swore that "the only thing NTT would buy from the United States was mops and buckets". Although sales rose from $11.6 million in 1980 to $130 million of $2.9 billion of NTT procurements in 1984, they did not reflect the shares that American firms would have won if the market had been free rather than carefully managed. Japan sold the United States ten times more telecommunication equipment than it bought. In mid-February 1983, USTR Brock began another round of pressure and negotiations to open up Japan's telecommunications markets. The stalemate continued until January 1985 when Prime Minister Nakasone promised President Reagan that Japan would eventually comply with a GATT code that Tokyo had signed in 1979 pledging to drop nontarriff barriers protecting the telecommunications industry. Later that year, Tokyo aceded to Washington's demand for greater transparency and allowed several foreign representatives to sit in on the Telecommunications Deliberation Council attached to MPT. In 1985, Tokyo and Washington signed an agreement which supposedly opened Japan's telecommunications markets. "Fairness" was "guaranteed" when Tokyo created a new agency to take over the product certification process from NTT and sold off some of NTT to Japanese investors over the next five years – foreigners are prohibited from owning any NTT stock.

Washington's efforts to open Japan's telecommunications market were aided by turf battles between MITI and MPT for control over the industry which began in 1981 when MITI blocked an MPT bid for enhanced powers over computer-connected telecommunications circuits then spread to battles over value-added networks (VANs) through 1982 and seven separate issues in 1984–85. Since MPT proposed restrictions on foreign products and investments in all these areas, MITI used Washington's demands to bolster it own efforts to contain MPT. The most egregious barriers were in VANs, naturally the area in which American firms held their largest comparative advantage. In February 1990, Washington asked Tokyo to further open its telecommunications market by the end of March. It specifically requested Tokyo to permit the sales of circuit terminal equipment – data servicing units (DSU) – technology, to common carriers, and to scrap two general and special categories for value added networks (VANs) type 2 operators. Tokyo categorically rejected these American requests. Despite all Washington's efforts, Japan's markets remain carefully managed so that foreign producers do not capture more than tiny market slivers no matter how great their competitive advantage.

Motorola has suffered continual and systematic discrimination from Tokyo in a variety of telecommunications products with which it enjoyed comparative advantage but no opportunity to sell freely in Japan. For example, although Japan's automobile and cellular phone market was theoretically liberalized in July 1988, Tokyo prevented Motorola from freely selling its palm size Micro TAC cellular telephone until 1990, by which time its Japanese competitors had captured enormous market share. Japanese consumers are not allowed to buy direct from the manufacturer but instead must lease their phones from one of three Japanese telecommunications carriers, of which NTT has a 77.3 per cent market share. Thus NTT can still buy on the basis of old connections with Japanese firms rather than from the most competitive source.

MPT impeded Motorola by a variety of means. It outright banned Motorola from Japan's most lucrative submarket – the Tokyo–Nagoya corridor whose market will expand from 250 000 to 4.5 million throughout the 1990s. MPT also employed a classic Japanese non-tariff barrier, arbitrary standards that favor domestic producers, in order to protect Japan's inefficient producers. Motorola had to sign up customers even before it applied for a license to sell, a regulation tailor made for Motorola since none of its Japanese competitors were required to do so. As a result, although the number of automobile and cellular phones sold in Japan doubled from 242 900 in 1988 to 489 600 in 1989, Motorola took only a 6–7 per cent share.[101]

If unchallenged, Tokyo will use any neomercantilist device to boost Japanese firms and undermines foreign firms. Until 1989, because the criticisms were not backed by clout, Tokyo shrugged off American accusations that these discriminatory policies represented a blatant violation of a 1986 US–Japan trade pact on telecommunications guranteeing "mutually advantageous marketing opportunities". Although Congress has granted the White House enormous power to counter Japanese neomercantilism, administrations hesitate to use it. The 1988 US Trade Act included section 1377 which was drafted specifically to pry open Japan's closed telecommunications market and live up to its 1986 agreement, authorizing the USTR to retaliate if the barriers remained. Under this new threat MPT dropped the regulation that Motorola had to sign up customers even before it applied for a license and conceded that Motorola could attach an adapter to its telephones for use in the Tokyo–Nagoya corridor. But aside from raising costs, the adapters can only be used in car phones while 90 per cent of mobile phones are used in trains. Motorola estimates that it will not only lose $2 billion over the next decade unless the market is opened, but will also lose comparative advantage to Japanese producers which will soon achieve economies of scale and high quality standards within their protected market.[102]

Motorola continued to pressure Washington to pressure Tokyo, a lobbying effort aided by Motorola's strong contacts within the Republican Party. Washington's pressure did cause the MPT on 24 May 1990 to select Motorola's product as the standard for the next generation digital cellular phone while NTT allowed Motorola to join nine other firms which will co-develop the next generation digital car phone. Although MPT emphasized that its choice was made on purely technical criteria, the decision was reached in a highly charged political atmosphere. Motorola was only allowed to submit its design after over a year of Washington pressure, which resulted in an agreement that Japan open its telecommunications market. But, as expected, despite a comparative advantage and tremendous export efforts, Motorola gained minimal benefits from Tokyo's reduction of barriers to its automobile phone market. Sales of automobile and cellular phones, like virtually every other product sold in Japan, continue to be largely based on connection and obligation rather than price or quality. Motorola has held on in Japan's managed markets not only on the basis of its products and marketing savvy, but because it has powerful allies in Washington. Few other American firms enjoy political power equal to the comparative advantage of their products.

AMORPHOUS METALS

Amorphous metals conduct electricity much faster than conventional materials and could form a new foundation of the vast electricity transformer industry, allowing tremendous savings in money and energy. None of Japan's 7.15 million commercial transformers use amorphous metals. The world's leading amorphous metals or metaglas producer is the American firm Allied Signal, which has developed a new metal alloy that cuts energy losses in electrical transformers by 70 per cent, which if installed could annually save Japan 25 million oil barrels. Allied Signal spent over 15 years and $100 million developing the alloy for what is estimated to be an annual $2.5 billion market.

MITI has launched a concerted effort to simultaneously create a Japanese amorphous metal industry and destroy Allied Signal. MITI ordered Japan's utilities to hold off buying the product until Allied Signal's patents expire and sat on top of Allied Signal's applications for two vital patents for over a dozen years before grudgingly granting them in 1984. Meanwhile, MITI formed a consortium of 34 corporations led by Nippon Steel to capitalize on the technology lifted from Allied Signal during the period its application languished in Japan's Patent Office. Allied Signal's patents expire in 1993 and 1997, respectively, by which time Nippon Steel, which already holds half the global market share for conventional silicon-steel transformer cores, is expected to market its own metaglas.[103]

How has Washington responded? In early 1990, the White House briefly considered then rejected the idea of using Tokyo's blatant discrimination against Allied Signal to list Japan as a "priority country" for investigation under Section 301. Instead Washington embarked on what became five months of intense negotiations which were finally concluded in September 1990. Washington agreed to drop its request that Tokyo extend patent protection for Allied Signal in return for Tokyo's promise to allow it to sell to Japanese utilities firms and form joint ventures with Japanese corporations. Tokyo conceded short term sales for Allied Signal with the knowledge that it had bought time and technology to nurture Japan's amorphous metals industry into a global champion. A decade from now, like so many other American corporations whose hamstrings are cut by irrational American and neomercantilist Japanese policies, Allied Signal will no doubt have joined the ranks of hundreds of other American firms which have either gone out of business or been bought up by one of its Japanese rivals.

SUPERCONDUCTORS

Superconductors are yet another strategic industry founded by Americans that is rapidly being taken over by Japan. In 1986, two scientists in an IBM Zurich laboratory were able to use exotic new ceramic compounds to increase the temperature at which superconductors work from −459.7 degrees Fahrenheit below zero to −230 degrees. If superconductors could be developed to operate at room temperature, the savings in energy would be enormous.

Tokyo recognized the strategic importance of superconductors and immediately began organizing a Japanese effort. In January 1987 MITI created a consortium of 50 firms paying $800 000 for membership into an International Superconductivity Technology Center. There are now over 85 firms in the consortia, none of them foreign. MITI has sponsored dozens of other consortium through its Electrotechnical Laboratory exploring different aspects of superconductor research. Other bureaucracies have joined the superconductor development race, including the STA's National Research Institute for Metals which is sponsoring its own consortium and MOE which is funneling $14 million into university research toward development of a magnetically levitated train.

For once, Washington responded with a rational policy to support the fledgling industry rather than its typical benign neglect which plays right into Tokyo's hands. In July 1987, President Reagan unveiled an eleven point superconductor initiative closed to non-Americans which he promised would achieve America's lead in the field and allocated $43 million for those efforts. Unfortunately, Washington's efforts characteristically remain focused on basic rather than applied research.

The superconductor policies of the United States and Japan reflect their vastly different approaches to industrial policy. While MITI, STA, and MOE are solely concerned with commercial applications, the Reagan Administration assured a largely military orientation for America's efforts by allowing the Defense and Energy departments to lead the effort. Total R&D spending is about the same, with Japan's $258 million in 1987 slightly higher than America's $256 million, but Japan committed much more private capital than the United States – $147 million versus $97 million, respectively, and also more scientists – 1,066 and 625, respectively.[104]

Japan is clearly leading the estimated 15 year race before room temperature superconductors are commercialized. The Japanese strategy of deluging patent offices around the world with applications in order to pre-empt rivals has been extremely successful. Of outstanding superconductor patent applications by mid–1988, 82 per cent of the processing techniques, 49 per cent of the electronic devices, and 40 per cent of the electrical applications were Japanese. In 1988, of over 2000 patents filed worldwide, Sumitomo Electric alone gathered 700, putting it in an excellent position to horse-trade technology through licensing or joint ventures with other firms. With its better organized consortia and lock on patents, Japan's lead will steadily widen in the years ahead. While there are currently over 75 Japanese firms committed to superconductor research, only four American firms have stayed in the race.[105] Whether they stick it out until the end or not, Japan will clearly dominate superconductor technology just as it has so many other technologies.

OTHER HIGH TECHNOLOGY FIELDS

Tokyo's neomercantilist policies are systematically destroying a range of other less known but strategically vital American industries and companies. Washington's response to these other threats has been characteristically inconsistent; the response has invariably depended on the threatened industry's political clout rather than any objective assessment of its strategic importance.

Victims of Japanese neomercantilism are endless. A few examples can illustrate how Tokyo systematically continues to destroy American and other foreign firms despite claims that its markets are the world's most open. Corning Glass developed fiber optics technology in the late 1960s. Understanding the significance of this new technology, Tokyo targeted fiber optics for development, delayed issuing patents to Corning for over a decade, formed a development cartel among Japanese corporations whose products were bought by NTT, imposed import barriers on competitive foreign products, and subsidized the development. Although the US ITO eventually found that Japanese corporations had infringed Corning's patents, it was no more than a furtile gesture that did nothing to reverse the enormouse transfer of technology, manufacturing prowess, and wealth from the United States to Japan. Monsanto is another victim. Starting in 1985, Monsanto was prevented from selling its silicon wafers in Japan until its Japanese competitors could produce and market their own version. Monsanto was later forced to sell its silicon wafer division, claiming that Tokyo's neomercantilist policies effectively prevented any posibility of success.

Micromachines are machines less than 0.0001 of an inch across, so tiny that they could fit in an artery and can eventually be used in medical operations, mining, and machinery repairs, and, conceivably, could be a vital stepping stone to manipulating matter at the subatomic level, or nanotechnology. American scientists first invented the micromachines. Bell Laboratories created the first micromachines in 1987 and U.C. Berkeley devised its own machine in 1988. The National Science Foundation and DARPA have since spent $2.5 million to develop the industry.

But, tragically, micromachines may be yet another industry that the American scientists founded and Japanese scientists mastered. In 1989, Toshiba and Hitachi formed a joint venture to develop microrobots. In 1990, MITI announced a five year $167 million project which targets microrobots – motors, sensors, and other devices as wide as a hair's width – which can be used to repair everything from nuclear power plants to the human body. Most of Japan's leading microelectronic firms like Hitachi, Nippon Steel, Nikon, Toshiba, NTT and NEC have joined MITI's consortium.

Yet another strategic technology being promoted vigorously by Tokyo and neglected by the White House is diamond coating, which has revolutionized the machine tool, chemical processing, electronics, optics, and military weapons by radically improving the quality of coating. Although the National Research Council recently called diamond coating "one of the most important technological developments of the past decade", the White House refuses to aid the project with anything more than $5 million annually to ten American projects while, since the early 1980s, Tokyo has contributed $150 million annually to a field that has expanded to over 100 ventures.[106]

The Commerce Department announced on February 14, 1991 that it was imposing dumping duties of 1.46 per cent to 4.6 per cent on Japanese liquid crystal display makers for dumping their products in the United States. Japan's sustained dumping had destroyed most American crystal display makers, thus making American personal computer makers dependent on Japanese products. IBM, Apple and other personal computer makers protested Commerce's action by claiming that it would drive up the price of their products. Like voracious Pac Men, Japanese industries have gobbled up their American rivals, one by one up the technology chain.

"Virtual reality" may well become yet another high technology field founded by Americans but taken over by Japanese. Virtual reality simulates computer models of anything in not only three dimensions but all five senses! The market for virtual reality products in education, research, entertainment, and manufacturing could be as high as $1 trillion by 2000! While the United States has no comprehensive program to develop the field, MITI's Agency for Industrial Science and Technology (AIST) has funded several virtual reality fields since 1983 while MITI itself organized and funded with $200 million a 30 firm consortium in 1991. As usual, small, underfunded, entrepreneurial American companies have developed the industry, but lacking government or corporate support, are selling out to the Japanese. The attitude of Audio Cybernetics president, Christopher Currell, is typical. Currell's firm has operated on a $500 million Japanese loan since 1989, and he says: "I don't care who owns the patents – whether they are Japanese, American . . . I just want to see my dream come true".[107]

CONCLUSION

To paraphrase Lenin, America's transfer of its leading technology to Japan since 1945 is the equivalent of selling Japanese the economic rope with which to hang the United States. Until the late 1980s, American antitrust law prevented American firms from collaborating on research, though it did not prevent American firms from collaborating with foreign firms. American corporations sold at nominal costs, their Japanese rivals such key technologies as the transitor, laser, television, optical fiber, computer and VCR. Japan now leads the world or is rapidly demolishing America's lead in all these technologies. Although the United States continues to excel at basic research, it lags in applying its inventions to mass produced consumer goods. Washington's free technology market policies allow foreigners to capitalize on American basic research and thus save billions of dollars in their own research and earn billions of dollars more in profits from the mass consumer products. The Japanese are rapidly capturing America's basic research as well as, in a familar pattern, innovative but small and underfinanced American firms license their technology to the Japanese: Sun Microsystems to Fujitsu and MIPS Computer Systems to NEC.

America's microelectronics industry remains fragmented with little integration. While defense gobbles up huge R&D resources and some of the best and brightest American scientists and engineers, few commercial benefits trickle down to the economy, in complete contrast to Japan's R&D efforts which are concentrated on commercial applications. There are literally hundreds of small American firms with microelectronic technology superior to anything their Japanese rivals have. The problem is they lack the financial resources necessary to develop and market such technology into viable products that enrich both those firms and the United States. No American financial institution wants to invest in these small firms with Japan's corporate behemoths arrayed against them. Having been severely bashed by Japan's waves of dumping campaigns throughout the 1980s, America's remaining high tech firms are surrendering to their rivals through joint ventures and technology licensing, and often the only recourse is to sell out completely to their Japanese rivals. Even America's big high technology firms are succumbing to the Japan's systematic attack. In January 1991, IBM–Japan reversed its long-standing policy of rejecting any relations with companies that produced IBM clones and now invites its Japanese rivals to join its Open Architecture Developers Groups (OADG) in which members jointly develop software and machines. Later that year, AT&T formed a joint venture with Marubeni for the latter to produce laptop personal computers under the AT&T label. Without Japanese style industrial policies, increasing numbers of American producers will succumb to the "escalating costs of new plant and equipment, faster rates of equipment obsolescence; higher costs of skilled labor; contracting product life cycles; rapid product replication and second-sourcing; shorter periods, therefore, within which firms can first market and then recoup 'up front' investments; greater costs, risks, and uncertainties associated with state-of-the-art intensified price competition; and stepped up competition in all areas".[108] The Japanese will systematically continue to target and take over one strategic high technology sector after another.

Washington policymaking and policies continues to be largely ad hoc, unco-ordinated, and military-led. Washington continues to shoot its industries in the back with self-defeating policies. At the root of America's high technology failures is the same basic problem that plagues all of America's policies – a narrow view of national security. While key American technologies and firms are starved for funds, Washington continues to channel billions into military and space projects of questionable importance. Originally, military industries "spunoff" products and technologies to the commercial sector. Now, it is a much more advanced commercial sector that is spinning off products to the military industrial complex. Given the long lead times and high performance standards such as being able to survive a nuclear attack, military technology has fallen further behind the more dynamic, competitive commercial sector. The Patriot and Cruise missiles that seemed to work so spectacularly in the Persian Gulf War were actually based on technology from the 1970s and early 1980s. President Reagan was a soft touch for big science projects like Star Wars and the Space Station. Duped by promises of creating an "antinuclear shield" over the United States or the romance of a permanent space station, Reagan eagerly embraced such projects while rejecting those of less than Hollywood image and proportion. Yet, overall, federal spending for science and technology, including military projects, has remained stagnant; in 1990, it was only $48.2 billion, little more than the $46 billion in current dollars spent in 1967 at the Apollo program's height. Government-funded small science projects, in contrast, have declined in value since 1988.

The balance of technology power is shifting decisively in favor of Japan, and Washington is only belatedly and unsystematically attempting to do anything about it. Although the United States has given away technology through formal agreements and its own open domestic system to Japan since 1945, Tokyo has resisted any Washington efforts to license any significant technology to the United States, even if it is only designated for military use. After years of negotiations, Tokyo finally signed an agreement in November 1983 allowing the transfer of dual-use (military or commercial) technology to the United States. In 1987, Tokyo reluctantly agreed to join the SDI project. It had resisted because it was felt Japan's technology was more advanced and there would be nothing to gain. After two years of bitter negotiations, Tokyo agreed to share production as well as development of the FSX with American firms. Yet, despite these limited gains, American policy toward Japan remains fatally flawed. American negotiators continue naively to believe Japanese promises that they will open their markets instead of extracting agreements for specific, growing market shares in Japan for American products similar to increases in third markets. Yet, even when Washington does pry a specific market quota from Japan, such as the 1985 promise to allow American semi-conductors a 20 per cent market share by 1992, Tokyo does not honor its promise.

Japan's corporations have at times seemed to be much more willing to extend technology and assistance to America's enemies than to the United States. For example, on 5 July 1991, it was revealed that Japan Aviation Electronics Industry Ltd, an NEC subsidiary, had secretly repaired

American designed missile-guidance systems and sold other gyroscopes used in American sidewinder missiles and military technology worth $250 000 to Iran during its war with Iraq. The case is full of ironies. Honeywell had invented the gyroscopes, but licensed the production to Japan Aviation, and was completely unaware of the transaction. Once again, American firms transfer not just future American wealth and jobs when they license technology to Japan, they also potentially sell secrets to America's geopolitical adversaries. If the production had stayed in American hands, the sellout to Iran would probably not have occurred. Like the earlier Toshiba case, the Japan Aviation technology transfer was revealed by American intelligence. Japanese officials claim to have known nothing about the transactions, a surprising claim considering how deeply entwined are Japan's public and private sectors. Somehow the annual parachuting of hundreds of bureaucrats into top private management jobs, and the pervasive "administative guidance" and constant information gathering of the ministeries failed to uncover the transactions. Although the action violates Japan's own laws on exporting military technology, Japan Aviation will escape any penalties because of a five year statute of limitations on such cases.

Japan's claims that it has opened its markets are completely untrue. For example, between 1973 and 1990, despite a series of Japanese "market opening steps", yen revaluations, and American comparative advantage for the first decade, and a market sharing agreement in 1986, America's penetration of Japan's semiconductor market has remained roughly 10 per cent. Tokyo claimed to have made three "liberalization" market opening steps in integrated circuits between 1973 and 1975; NTT claimed to have opened its procurement practices in 1981; Japan's tariff on semiconductors was reduced to 4.2 per cent in 1982 and eliminated in 1985; the Japanese yen strengthened rapidly in the late 1970s and late 1980s, and fell rapidly in the early to mid-1980s; under a 1986 bilateral agreement Tokyo agreed to restrain Japanese dumping and promised a 20 per cent American share of Japan's market by 1991; Washington imposed sanctions on $300 million of Japanese electronics imports in 1987. Yet, despite all these seemingly largely favorable developments for American semiconductor makers, their share of Japan's markets hovered at around ten per cent. Meanwhile Japan's share of global markets soared from 27 to 52 per cent between 1980 and 1989, while America's plunged from 57 to 35 per cent. Why? The overwhelming circumstantial evidence is that Japan's government and semiconductor industry massively conspired to hold America's share to 10 per cent. However, as in Japan's other carefully managed markets, smoking guns of cartelization are hard to find.

The United States is becoming increasingly dependent on Japanese technology. America's deepening technology and financial dependence on

Japan was revealed in early June 1991 when Tokyo warned that any Washington cutbacks in the space station, to which Japan would contribute a laboratory module, would result in a cutoff in Japanese funds for all other American projects in which it was a participant, including the supercollider. Another example occurred in July 1990, when seven small American flat screen makers, which call themselves the Advanced Display Manufacturers of America, brought a dumping case against the Japanese screen makers. They were opposed not only by the Japanese, but by American computer makers which argued that a dumping penalty would raise the price of their products, and threatened to move their production overseas in laptop and notebook computers, the industry's fastest growing segment which uses the screens. The Commerce Department faced a dilemma. If they allowed the Japanese panel makers to continue dumping in the United States, it would eventually lead to the destruction of one more vital link in America's high technology food chain, with the accompanying loss of wealth, jobs, and economic security. If it imposed penalties it would weaken the competitive advantage of American computermakers which have become dependent on the dumped Japanese products. Even greater economic losses could occur if America's hardpressed computer making were driven under. Meanwhile, many have written off the American screen maker industry. As in other high technology segments, the American producers are small, independent, and underfinanced, while they face immense Japanese rivals which are members of vast industrial groups with seemingly bottomless pockets for financing R&D and marketing. A panel factory costs $100 million to set up, and even the biggest American firms hesitate to invest that amount when Japan's producers are already so far ahead. On 8 July 1991, the Commerce Department proposed levying dumping penalties on Japan's active matrix liquid crystal computer screens.

Tokyo is systematically attempting to take over one link in America's high technology food chain after another until it dominates all important industries. America's technology seedbeds have been gutted by waves of Japanese dumping attacks followed by outright buyouts of the battered firms. Japan's technology will deepen steadily into the 21st century while the United States falls further behind. Silicon Valley will probably remain the world's leading high technology center since it has the immense "critical mass" of facilities, experts and money. But Japan will continue to buy up the Valley's leading scientists, inventions, and corporations. And American firms, starved of finance and bashed by Japanese neomercantilism and American liberalism, will continue to sell their technology and even themselves to their Japanese rivals.

10 The Financial Front

Probably no industry is more strategic than that which peddles cash, stocks, bonds, and other money-making schemes. All other industries depend on finance for their investments in research and development, production and marketing. Where they obtain the finance, how much, and at what terms is a vital factor in that industry's future. Money-lenders in turn obtain intimate understandings of a firm's operations, strategy and strengths and weaknesses. Those nations which achieve the most virtuous savings/investment cycles enjoy the most dynamic economies, greatest wealth, and accompanying power. The most potentially powerful nation in an interdependent world is the largest lender. The power to grant or deny loans to foreign governments or corporations, or set the terms at which loans are granted is the power to shape other nations' economic destinies. Likewise, the weaker a state's financial system, the weaker its entire economy and the more dependent it is on global bankers to finance development. Thus virtually all countries carefully regulate their financial sectors to prevent bankruptcy or foreign control, and to achieve virtuous savings/investment cycles. The means by which nations achieve these ends vary considerably from one nation to the next. Some nations like Japan have been extremely successful in creating powerful financial and industrial systems that minimize their dependence on foreign credit; other nations like the United States have followed disastrous policies which produce chronically weak financial and industrial systems which have left it addicted to foreign capital.

The world's balance of financial power shifted decisively in 1985 when the United States became the world's greatest debtor with a $35 billion net deficit and Japan the world's financial superpower with a $64 billion net surplus. America's debt and Japan financial superpower's status have deepened steadily since. In 1990, Japan enjoyed a $350 billion net financial surplus while the United States suffered a $412 billion net deficit. Although the Reagan administration's inept overvalued dollar and spend and borrow policies vastly accelerated America's decline and have made any revival all but impossible, Japan's rise into a global financial superpower would have been inevitable regardless. The only question was when the balance of financial power would shift decisively toward Japan. As always, American liberalism simply cannot compete

371

against Japanese neomercantilism. The financial systems of the United States and Japan are both carefully regulated, but with a decisive difference – Washington's regulations attempt to maximize competition and the ability of ambitious entrepreneurs to set up financial shop while Tokyo has focused on nurturing a handful of financial corporations into global giants.

These opposing strategies created completely different financial systems. Today, America has 12 926 banks while Japan has only about 80. Washington's decentralization policies have hobbled the ability of America's financial firms to compete against Japan's financial behemoths. The world's seven largest banks, and twenty-five of the top fifty banks are Japanese. In stark contrast, the United States has only two banks in the top fifty – Citibank ranked second and Chase thirty-sixth. Japan also has the world's four largest securities firms and largest insurance firm, while its ubiquitous trading firms play an important role by financing international trade and investments. Japanese banks own about 25 per cent of California's banking system and 12 per cent of America's. Japan's securities firms annually finance a quarter to one third of America's government debt and are major players on the New York stock exchange. Meanwhile, Tokyo has allowed America's financial firms only a symbolic presence in Japan's financial markets.

Even worse, Washington's policies have led to the virtual collapse of America's financial system – the bankrupt savings and loan industry will cost a half trillion taxpayer dollars to bail out while the banking and insurance industries are at the brink of insolvency. The financial wizards of Japan's Ministry of Finance (MOF) can only shake their heads in disbelief at the ineptitude of America's financial system and the policies and people which guide it. MOF has carefully nurtured its financial system into the world's most powerful through policies which emphasize the best rather than worst of both competition and co-operation.

American and Japanese policies toward the financial industry will be analyzed through a section on each, with a third section on Washington's efforts to crack Japan's carefully managed financial cartel system.[1]

AMERICAN FINANCIAL POLICY: STRAITJACKETED LIBERALISM

Washington tends to overreact in a crisis, often with cures worse than the original malady. America's present financial system is shaped by the worst elements of regulation and free markets. By straitjacketing the industry with the Glass–Steagal Act of 1934, Washington attempted to prevent another huge speculative bubble like the one which burst in 1929 with the stock market crash and subsequent run on the banks and Great Depression. In the sixty years since Glass–Steagal became law, America's finance industry has been strictly segmented by a series of firewalls which outlaw any interstate banking or bank ownership of manufacturers. Yet, any ambitious entrepreneurs can start a bank or savings and loan. The result is the industrial world's most decentralized, unstable, and open financial system.

America's financial system has been structurally weak since 1934, but it took the global debt crisis of the 1970s and 1980s, the rise of Japan, and Reagan's reckless policies to bring it to its knees. Reagan Administration "spend and borrow" policies are the reason for America's conversion from the world's greatest creditor into the world's worst debtor. Taxes were cut 25 per cent between 1981 and 1983 while spending actually increased from 24.5 per cent to 25.6 per cent of GNP, thus causing America's national debt to rise from 27 per cent of GNP in 1980 to 42 per cent in 1986. Interest payments on the debt in 1986 represented 14 per cent of the budget, a figure which cost taxpayers $67 billion or $200 per capita. The White House and Federal Reserve then compounded these problems with policies designed to attract foreign investors to help finance the growing debt ocean. The Federal Reserve raised interest rates while the White House wrote a clause into the 1984 Deficit Reduction Act which allowed foreigners which purchased American bonds and securities to eliminate the 30 per cent withholding tax on interest earned by their investments. The Treasury Department then offered $1 billion in new tax-free three year, eleven month notes. Many foreigners switched from Treasury Bills to the new notes to avoid taxes, thus forcing the Department of Treasury to raise the rates to attract back investors. The result of both actions was to attract a short term injection of foreign capital while simultaneously deepening America's debt and raising taxes for Americans. Other industrial countries like Britain and Germany which experienced an outflow of capital toward these American accounts were compelled to offer similar investment incentives, thus undercutting their own economies. The Reagan Administration justified these give aways to foreign investors by arguing that without foreign capital to finance the deficit interest rates would rise and America's economy would fall into a deep recession. What the Reagan Administration did not address were its irresponsible policies which had doubled America's national debt within five years and almost tripled it in eight years.

As if America's conversion from the world's greatest banker to worst debtor were not enough, the country's savings and loan industry became bankrupt by the late 1980s while the banking and insurance industries are threatened with insolvency. The savings and loan crisis was the result of bad policy decisions taken by the Carter, Reagan and Bush Administrations which undermined existing structural weaknesses. The savings and loan industry was established in the late 19th century to provide home mortgages, from which banks shied away. From then until the early 1980s, the industry was run by sound, conservative management which took in deposits and re-lent them as mortgages. This steady business largely survived the 1930s; although 40 per cent of the nation's banks failed, only 5 per cent of savings and loans went under. The seeds of the present crisis, however, were sown during this time when Congress pushed for deposit insurance guaranteed by the government. President Roosevelt was opposed to deposit insurance, reasoning that it would encourage unsound banking practices, but bowed to Congress and signed legislation insuring deposits up to $5000, a limit which has since been raised to $100 000. But to attract depositors, interest rates were fixed at a half point above that of the banking system.

The system continued to operate smoothly until the late 1970s when the Federal Reserve pushed short-term interest rates as high as 20 per cent to curb the inflation set off by OPEC's quadrupling of oil prices in 1973 and further doubling in 1979. The result was a crisis in the savings and loan industry as depositors took their money to higher yielding accounts elsewhere, leaving more than two-thirds of the industry technically insolvent. In 1980, the Carter Administration attempted to relieve the savings and loan crisis by raising the deposit insurance ceiling from $40 000 to $100 000, expanding the industry's ability to make consumer loans, and phasing out interest rate limits. In 1982, the Reagan White House, waving its free market banner, allowed the industry to make unsecured business loans and invest large amounts in commercial real estate, while it sharply cut back government regulatory policies and its number of regulatory officials in half. "All in all", Reagan declared as he signed the 1982 bill deregulating the industry, "I think we've hit the jackpot".[2]

But free market principles did not apply to the savings and loan industry since the government and not private industry bore most of the financial risks. The combination of deposit insurance and interest rate deregulation permitted depositors to seek the highest interest rates without worrying about whether or not the institution were sound, and allowed those institutions to make investments regardless of risk. The result was rampant speculation by most savings and loans, particularly in the high rising real estate, oil and stock markets of the mid–980s. The speculative bubble, however, burst for real estate and the oil market in 1986, and the stock market in 1987. As if the reckless investments were not bad enough, fraud has been found in 60 per cent of the institutions investigated, and included countless cases of phoney appraisals, self-dealing, loans to family and associates, kickbacks and payoffs. Indictments, however, are unlikely because the line between mismanagement and outright fraud is blurred. The industry suffered a net loss of $6 billion in 1987, $11 billion in 1988 and $20 billion in 1989.

How did President Reagan and Congress respond to this deepening crisis? Essentially, they stuck their heads in the sand hoping it would go away. The "Keating Five" and scores of other Congressmen who accepted large contributions from the industry co-operated in allowing the problem to fester. For example, former House Speaker Jim Wright delayed a key reform bill in 1986 which would have raised $15 billion to address the industry's financial hemorrhage, during which time the bail out costs continued to spiral, while the Keating Five delayed a government takeover of Lincoln Savings and Loan for over two years while it continued to lose money. The Reagan White House also kept sweeping the problem under the rug, hoping that it would stay put at least until after the 1988 elections. John Bowsher, named Comptroller General in 1981 for a fifteen year term, declared frankly that "the Administration played ostrich right through 1988. They didn't want the problem to be recognized until after Reagan left town".[3]

Sure enough, it was not until the Bush Administration was safely installed in the White House that any systematic attempt was made to bail out the system. How much will it cost? Estimates vary considerably, with the standard cost at about $500 billion over the next 30 years, or about $5000 for every household. But a Stanford Law and Policy Review study based on OMB and GAO statistics estimates that the eventual cost could be as high as $1.369 trillion, with $456.3 billion incurred between 1989 and 1990 alone, and the rest over the next three decades. It is estimated that more than 1000 institutions or 40 per cent of the industry may eventually be seized, adding considerably to the total costs.[4]

The bail out must be paid for with borrowed money, burying the country ever deeper in debt. Incalculable are the losses from the lower economic growth, higher interest rates, lower unemployment, and forgone development opportunities had all that money been invested in cutting edge industries, infrastructure, or education. What could $250 billion buy? It could address a range of deepening problems including fully funding every existing government program for education for the next four years, or provide universal health insurance and long-term care for the elderly for four years, or fund a 20 year nation-wide hazardous waste clean up.[5]

As Tom Wolfe's novel, *Bonfire of the Vanities*, brilliantly depicted, if anything the 1980s were about making a quick buck. No one did better than the junk bond dealers. The Reagan Administration's deregulation policies contributed to the rise of the junk bond kings of Wall Street and the wave of leveraged buyouts (LBOs) in which dynamic corporations were taken over and often broken up with their parts selling for more than the whole. Proponents of the LBO frenzy declared that the takeovers made those firms and thus America's economy more efficient, reflected by the rise in stock prices. Paul Krugman, however, asks "why, if corporate restructuring is so beneficial, the great wave of restructuring since 1980 hasn't had a more noticeable effect on America's economic growth. Hundreds of billions of dollars have been added to stock prices through such deals. Yet productivity growth remains hardly faster than during the 1970s, and America's economic and technological standing in the world continues its inexorable decline".[6] Krugman then contrasts the pre-LBO era of the 1960s when there were annual productivity rates of 3 per cent, rapidly rising living standards, and American technological predominance, with the LBO era of the 1980s characterized by "one per cent productivity growth, stagnant living standards, and relative decline". Although most corporations escaped the raiders, the defensive measures they were forced to adopt, like stock buybacks, consumed enormous financial, human, energy, and time resources while global competition from their Japanese and other foreign rivals worsened.

Junk bonds in themselves are not necessarily detrimental to America's economy. They are potentially useful for the 95 per cent of American corporations that do not enjoy high credit ratings. One fifth of all corporate debt issues involve junk bonds, and about half of the junk bonds were used for capital investments and other corporate needs. The controversy is over the use of junk bonds to finance the takeover of other companies. To abolish junk bonds would severely harm the ability of most American corporations to raise capital. A sensible alternative would be to simply outlaw the use of junk bonds to take over other companies, while continuing to allow their use for capital investments and other internal needs.[7]

America's entire banking industry – from thousands of one town banks to the country's largest like Citibank, Chase Manhattan, Manufacturers Hanover, Chemical, First Chicago and Security Pacific – is threatening to collapse. Federal Deposit Insurance Company (FDIC) losses for the 1992 recession are estimated to range anywhere from $32–62 billion, and bank failures to reach at least 440. In late March, Treasury Secretary Brady and FDIC Chairman Seidman asked Congress for $70 billion to bail out the industry. Disturbing as Seidelman's warnings are, the real severity of the banking crisis may not be revealed until after the 1992 election, much as the seriousness of the savings and loan scandal did not emerge until Bush was safely in the White House in 1988.

Will the banking industry follow the savings and loan industry into public ownership? The industry's insurance program has been losing money since 1987 and the debt is expected to deepen to $23 billion in 1995, with premiums rising from the current 19.5 cents for every $100 to

23 cents.[8] As in so many industries, Washington actually gives foreign corporations and governments advantages in banking in the United States and acquiring American financial institutions that interstate banking laws deny to American firms. Domestic firms are not allowed to operate across state lines while foreign banks can, thus enjoying vast economies of scale. Domestic banks must adhere to strict antitrust laws; foreign banks can extend their cartel arrangements to the United States. Large American banks are forbidden to buy other large or medium-sized banks; large foreign banks are free to do so. Most foreign banks operate on much lower capital requirements, ratio of asset/liability mix to deposits, and profitability than American banks, thus giving them a powerful comparative advantage in interest rates and dividends. Foreign banks are shielded from inspection by government regulators while American banks must open wide their account books. American banks cannot own other corporations or engage in the securities business; foreign banks can. Only Vermont and Maine outright ban foreign bank operations.

William Seidman, chairman of the Federal Deposit Insurance Corporation (FDIC) is one of many who recognize the absurdity of Amerian banking policy, but is impotent to change it. He admits that hobbling American financial institutions while allowing foreign banks free access to American financial markets is "damaging our banks and our banking system. They're the factor in the decreased earnings of our banks. Our banks are going downhill. They're getting less business. They have to compete with people who are less regulated than we are".[9]

Periodic attempts by concerned political leaders to reverse the steady foreign takeover of America's financial industry have been defeated by combinations of the White House's *laissez-faire* outlook and foreign lobbying. For example, the International Banking Act of 1978 attempted to address these inequalities favoring foreign banks by requiring that they adhere to the same interstate banking restrictions as American banks. Unfortunately, a grandfather clause in the Act exempted all foreign banks which already had interstate banking operations on or before 27 July 1978 when the law took effect. Thus 63 foreign banks continued to enjoy immense advantages denied to American banks. The Act also does not require foreign banks engaged in retail business to obtain deposit insurance. Thus in 1980 only 14 of 126 foreign banks operating in the United States had applied for FDIC insurance and were thus subject to FDIC regulation and inspection.[10]

Protectionist efforts continued, to little avail. In 1980 the Comptroller General issued a report to Congress entitled, "Despite Positive Effects, Further Foreign Acquisitions of US Banks Should Be Limited Until Policy Conflicts Are Fully Addressed". In response, Congress issued a three month moratorium on foreign purchase of American banking interests but neither Capitol Hill nor the White House did anything to rationalize American banking policy in that breathing space. In 1984 Senator Jake Garn introduced legislation which would have forced reciprocity on foreign countries discriminating against American banks. Citing its free trade ideology, the Reagan White House succeeded in killing the bill.

Foreign-owned banking assets in the United States rose from $32 billion in 1973 to $445 billion in 1986 when about 17 per cent of America's total banking assets of $1.7 trillion were foreign owned. This was a substantial rise from a 3.8 per cent foreign ownership in 1973 and 11.9 per cent in 1986. Of the $445 billion in foreign controlled banking, $11.3 billion was represented by foreign bank ownership of US banks, $23 billion by foreign individual and corporate ownership of US banks, while the remaining $310.8 billion represented the assets of US branches and agencies of foreign banks. Japanese banks accounted for $170 billion, or about one third of the total foreign ownership, over three times the next largest bank owner, Britain, with $54 billion. In New York foreign banks make over half of all commercial and industrial loans.[11]

Although the McFadden Act and Douglas Amendment which prevent domestic banks from interstate banking will be abolished in 1992, the bill may be about two or three decades too late. Unfortunately, in the meantime foreign banks will already have cornered about 25 per cent of the market, and with it enormous power over America's economy.

JAPANESE FINANCIAL POLICY: NURTURING GLOBAL CHAMPIONS

Tokyo has carefully managed Japan's financial system toward two interrelated ends: (1) to finance Japan's manufacturing and technology development; and (2) to transform the financial industry itself into a global champion. These policies have been in effect since the 1920s when Tokyo abandoned a largely free market policy and began to take an increasingly powerful role in developing the economy. Japan's banking structure has since been transformed from a free market with over 1800 banks into a financial cartel system. In 1921 MOF Minister Takahashi Korekiyo, arguing that "the key feature of the management of the . . . system was the prevention of excess competition", ordered the forced amalgamation of small regional banks. The 1927 Banking Law gave MOF vast legal powers over the banking system, powers that remained unchanged until 1981. As a result of this managed market policy, between 1921 to 1945 the number of trust banks fell from 422 to 7 and national and regional commercial banks from 538 to 61. Today, the number of trust banks remains unchanged at 7 while the number of national and regional commercial banks has increased slightly to 80. There has not been a bank failure since 1945.[12]

As in other sectors, the American Occupation reforms created the new institutions and policies vital for Tokyo to develop Japan's manufacturing and financial industries into world leaders. SCAP strongly boosted MOF's powers in 1947 by sponsoring the the Securities and Exchange Law which strictly segmented the banking and securities markets and gave MOF extensive control over each. Then, later that year, SCAP pushed through the Temporary Interest Rate Law which empowered MOF to dictate bank deposit and short-term bank loan interest rates, both of which are linked to MOF's official discount rate. But, as with the other ministries, MOF's greatest power is "administrative guidance", or the ability to regulate the industry through ordinances (*shorei*) and notifications (*tsutatsu*) not subject to Diet approval.

MOF and the BOJ have achieved the world's most virtuous savings/ investment cycle. From the 1940s through the 1980s, households faced extremely high interest rates on loans, inadequate welfare and social security, high prices for goods and education, and only a limited range of investment opportunities, all of which offered extremely low interest rates. Japanese thus saved an enormous amount of their disposable income; during the 1950s almost one third and even during the 1990s, when credit has eased, about 15 per cent – three times America's household savings rate. MOF then channeled this enormous savings pool to its strategic industries at rock bottom interest rates. MOF and MITI work closely together to determine which industries should be targeted as strategic and how much they should be subsidized. The BOJ lends to Japan's dozen commercial banks which in turn lend the money to keiretsu members. BOJ's "window guidance" gave the government enormous leverage over determining winners and losers, and thus enforcing its industrial policies. Other money is allocated through Japan's public financial corporations and can be divided between those relatively free from political pressure like the Bank of Japan (BOJ 1949), Japan Development Bank (JDB 1951), and Export Import Bank (Eximbank 1951), and those which are locked into iron triangles of public officials, private businessmen, and LDP Diet members like the People's Finance Corporation (1949), Housing Loan Corporation (1953), Small Business Finance Corporation (1953) or Agriculture Forestry and Fisheries Finance Corporation (1953). Although loans remain important, as Japan's corporations have become more competitive, they have increasingly relied on retained earnings for most of their capital.

MOF has more subtle ways of regulating the finance industry and preventing foreign financial institutions from winning any significant market share or introducing new products in which they enjoy a comparative advantage. After retiring from MOF, many officials parachute down into lucrative jobs (*amakudari*) in other public financial institutions, the private financial sector or the LDP. The BOJ governor and deputy governor are always former MOF officials. In 1980, for example, there was one retired MOF officer in a public or private financial institution for every five MOF officials, while 52 LDP Diet members were former MOF officials, about 10 per cent of the Diet's total membership. That year 189 former MOF career officers parachuted into executive positions in private financial institutions, about 80 per cent of which were in regional banks, mutual banks, and credit associations. A relatively small number entered city banks and long-term credit banks since these larger institutions already had the expertise and did not want the interference.[13]

MOF has nurtured Japan's finance industry into the world's most powerful. The competitive power of Japanese banks is based on their access to cheap funds and protection from foreign competition through Japan's regulated, cartelized financial markets, and thus their ability to offer razor thin profit margins. Japan's banks grew rapidly throughout the 1980s, like the rest of Japanese industry, in part by relying on ever rising stock and real estate markets to finance their rapid overseas expansion, and capturing huge chunks of foreign markets by dumping cheap ("kamikaze") loans. Japanese banks can own up to 5 per cent of an industrial firm and count 45 per cent of the value of those stocks as capital. In 1988 and 1989, Japan's banks raised $60 billion from securities markets and used their stock shares to cover the Bank for International Settlements requirement that at least 8 per cent of deposits be covered by March 1993.

In 1990, Japan's banking behemoths had to regroup after a series of minor setbacks. When the stock and real estate market bubbles burst in 1990, Japan's banks drastically reined in their operations. The stock market fall in particular cut deeply into the hidden reserves of Japanese banks, causing four banks to fall below the capital-to-asset ratio of 8 per cent required by the Bank for International Settlements (BIS). Even the banks above the 8 per cent margin are likely to cut back some of their international lending. The stock market crash particularly affected the new-issues markets for equity and equity linked securities such as convertibles and warrant bonds which had been vital sources of capital for Japan's corporations. As if the stock and real estate market crashes were not bad enough, the greater exposure of Japanese banks to Third World debt has cut into their profits. For example, on 1 April 1990, the 12 city banks announced total losses of $3.95 billion on Mexican loans for the previous fiscal year.[14] To make matters worse, Tokyo raised interest rates throughout 1990 and 1991 to combat growing inflation, thus slightly undercutting the competitive advantage Japanese corporations have enjoyed by having access to cheap capital. By Autumn 1990, real interest rates in Japan were nearly 3 per cent higher than in the United States. Bank profits dropped an average 30 per cent in 1990.

As a result of these setbacks, Japan's banks have cut back their loans, particularly the "kamikaze loans" – which often had a spread of only 0.25 percentage points over the cost of their funds – they dumped in the late 1980s which stirred fierce protests from foreign banks. Japanese banks are planning to cut the annual growth of their overseas lending to only 10 per cent from the previous heights of 15–20 per cent. Tokyo is encouraging the banks to raise their return-on-assets from 1 per cent to 4–5 per cent. Japan's banks and other corporations will not be able to dump cheap loans in global markets during the 1990s as easily as they could during the late 1980s. Japanese banks are increasingly relying on the Euromarket and other offshore funds to finance international lending. Tokyo is trying to postpone the March 1993 deadline for the 8 per cent deposit rate.

Yet, for Japan's banking industry, these setbacks are merely temporary adjustments after their massive global expansion in the 1980s. The bruises Japan's banking system suffered with the global economic turndown in the early 1990s is nothing compared to the massive hemorrhaging America's banking system has experienced for over a decade. Japan's banks will quickly regroup and launch a massive, sustained assault on world financial markets during the 1990s which will deepen their hegemony and further batter America's industry.

MOF has been just as successful in nurturing Japan's security industry into the world's largest if not the most competitive. Despite their vast size, Japan's security giants are not omnipotent, and in the early 1990s have also been regrouping after a decade of dazzling expansion. All were hurt by the 1987 and 1990 stock market plunges and the steady increase in Japanese interest rates. Japan's purchase of American securities in 1990 plunged as the previously higher interest rate differential with Japanese securities vanished, the dollar slid, and Tokyo Stock Exchange dropped 40 per cent, thus wiping out a good chunk of Japanese paper wealth. Until the stock market plunge, Japan's life insurance companies and other investors could cover their foreign exchange losses with their Wall Street gains. Nomura's 1990 profits, for example, plunged 60 per cent to $2.1 billion. Although it retained its number one ranking for underwritings in the Euromarket, its market share was cut in half to 9 per cent. After having devoted about 20 per cent of its assets to attacking Wall Street during the late 1980s, Nomura had little to show for its efforts – in 1990 it received only 4 per cent of its total revenues and made only $20 million in pre-tax earnings from its Wall Street investments. Japan's "big four" securities corporations remain mostly stock peddlers, and have had trouble mastering sophisticated Wall Street style financial instruments like computerized trading, mortgage backed securities, lease financing, mergers and acquisitions, and others. Nomura still depends on commissions for 41 per cent of its earnings compared to only about 15 per cent at Shearson and Merril Lynch, and a miniscule 2 per cent at Salomon Brothers.[15]

But, like Japan's banking industry, its securities corporations will quickly regroup, master new financial products and money-making techniques, and launch another massive assault on global markets during the 1990s. Joint ventures with American securities firms will be Trojan horses designed to acquire skills and markets. By the late 1990s, Japan's securities firms will have surpassed their American rivals to the same degree that Japan's banks did during the 1980s.

The Tokyo Stock Exchange (TSE) is the world's largest and provides immense cash oceans for Japanese firms and profits for investors. On the surface the TSE appears to operate by market principles. Since 1945, Japan's stock market has experienced three long, sharp bull runs, in 1954–61, 1965–73, and 1982–89. Each bubble expanded about five times over a seven year period before the inevitable collapse, then languished for a half decade before surging again past its previous high. The TSE peaked at 38 915.87 on 29 December 1989, then fell in a series of plunges throughout 1990 to reach a low of 20 983 on 28 September 1990, for a total fall of 46 per cent. This drop wiped out about $1.8 trillion in value, bringing the era of ultra-cheap Japanese money to a close. Dramatic as the 1990 stock market crash was, it will have only a limited effect on Japan's economy. The crash will probably knock only a half percentage point off economic growth, cause a higher than usual bankruptcy rate and credit squeeze on many smaller firms as interest rates climb.[16] But Japan's first rate corporations are still floating happily atop vast cash oceans, and are thus insulated from the interest rate hikes.

This last bull market was pushed up by the immense cash oceans that flowed into Japan throughout the 1980s. The stock and real estate markets rose simultaneously, and investors borrowed against their real estate holdings to finance more stock purchases. Japanese firms issued more bonds at cheap rates to invest in more productive capacity and buy off old loans. In 1980, Japan's banks and insurance firms held an average ratio of bonds to equity of 2.5 to 1; in 1990, the ratio was 0.7 to 1. The gap between bond yields and earning rose steadily from 3 per cent in 1982 to 5 per cent in 1989. In 1989, Japanese corporations offered stock dividends of only 0.38 per cent, one tenth the 3.7 per cent rate paid by American corporations. But Japanese investors did not mind the low rates as long as the stock values continued to rise. The stock market underwrote $162.4 billion in overseas investments from 1986 to 1989, including the Japanese purchase of foreign corporations. For example, Sony's $3.4 billion buy out of Columbia Pictures was partly financed by the issues of bonds with rates as low as 0.3 per cent.[17] Why did the crash occur? In 1989, Tokyo withdrew some of the tax advantages which had helped fuel the real estate boom, while the BOJ began steadily to raise interest rates throughout 1990. Then came the lemming effect as increased numbers of investors bailed out of a steadily dropping market, thus turning the retreat into a rout.[18]

The Tokyo Stock Exchange's rises and falls reflect classic market principles, right? Have not foreign securities firms failed to achieve more than a 5 per cent market share because their financial products are inferior and they do not try hard enough? As in Japan's other markets, widespread collusion and transactions based on connections rather than prices continue to make the stock market conform to neomercantilist rather than neoclassical economic principles. Knowledgable observers describe Japan's stock markets as thoroughly "rigged" whereby "the Japanese government uses the market and is able to direct it" . . . . in an association among "big brokers, banks, corporations, and Finance Ministry and Bank of Japan bureaucrats all bent on achieving three primary goals: a sky-high savings rate, lofty stock prices, and cheap funds for economic growth. Japan has a managed market, why shouldn't financial markets be managed too?"[19] An aide to former Prime Minister Tanaka, admitted that Japan "is an insider society. It is not unusual for us to share this kind of information with friends. The brokers who do this don't feel they are doing anything wrong. Even to my eyes it's not a matter of right and wrong, or morals, but difference in our two cultures. Put more frankly, Japan is a society of insider dealings".[20]

The Recruit and Kotani stock scandals of the late 1980s reveal how Japan's stock market and political system really operate. The Recruit Scandal involved the Recruit corporation giving shares to Japan's political, bureaucratic, mass media, and opposition party elite – eventually 169 recipients were identified – before it went public, thus allowing the recipients to sell the stocks for an enormous profit. In return, the recipients allowed Recruit several advantages in Japan's managed markets. The Recruit Scandal was soon followed by the Kotani Scandal, in which Mitsuhiro Kotani was indicted for stock manipulation that directly implicated three of Japan's largest financial institutions: Sumitomo Bank, Mitsui Trust and Banking and Daiwa Securities. Like the Recruit Scandal, Kotani's operations entailed politicians and other members of Japan's elite enriching themselves through insider stock trading. Kotani was caught passing on the inside information and manipulating share prices. Sumitomo Bank's chairman, Ichiro Isoda, resigned when it was revealed one of his branch managers funneled $175 million in illegal loans to Kotani to conduct his operations.

There are some limits to insider trading. After all, it is illegal and scandals result in resignations for some and embarassment for all concerned. But the threshold for Japan's tolerance of insider trading is vastly higher than in other industrial countries. By continuing to turn a blind eye to all but the most outrageous of such dealings, the government essentially condones it, and thus gives Japanese firms enormous advantages over their foreign rivals.

AMERICAN-LED DEREGULATION OF JAPAN'S FINANCIAL MARKETS

Although Washington has been pressuring Tokyo to deregulate its financial markets since the 1970s, there is a large difference between deregulation and liberalization. After digging in its heels on each financial sector or instrument, Tokyo has eventually grudgingly deregulated, but only in areas and at a pace whereby Japanese financial institutions gain the advantage over their foreign rivals. Wright characterizes Japan's financial deregulation as "wrapped in terms of hard fought concessions to foreigners but shrewdly crafted to derive maximum benefits to Japanese. They only deregulate areas in which they already have a comparative advantage, still protect weak sectors, stretch out the change timetable by subdividing major concessions into small manageable parts, making changes on a individual case basis, and by simply taking time to "study" the matter further".[21]

Tokyo has made a succession of deregulatory steps since 1975 which have gradually expanded the types of financial products available to investors. Tokyo, in 1975 began to float large amounts of long-term bonds to finance the deepening budget deficits; in 1977 it allowed Japanese to aquire short-term foreign securities and lifted the ban on short-term foreign currency loans; in 1979 it introduced negotiable bank certificates of deposit paying interest at market rates; in 1980 it revised the Foreign Exchange Control Law so that all financial transactions were now "free in principle", and allowed securities firms to offer new instruments similar to money market mutual funds, which began attracting a growing number of small investors because of their higher yields and liquidity than bank time deposits. Throughout this five year period Japanese financial institutions steadily increased their overseas operations while foreign firms were allowed increased access to the domestic yen bond market. Yet, since these steps were geared to promote Japan's financial industry rather than create a level playing field for foreign financial institutions, they reflected neomercantilist rather than liberal policies.

The Reagan Administration pressured Tokyo to increase both the pace and types of deregulation, but no genuine progress was made until the mid-1980s. MOF's May 1984 report entitled "Japan's Financial Deregulation and the Yen's Internationalization: Present and Future Prospects" presented a deregulation timetable for the 1980s in which Tokyo promised that by 1986 it would decontrol the interest rates on at least 25 per cent of the deposits at the 13 city banks, and introduce money market certificates with interest rates linked to those on bank certificates. The following year in March 1985, under the US–Japan Working Group on the Internationalization of the Yen, Tokyo promised to liberalize the yen, the Euroyen bond market, and its long-term Euroyen loans. The Plaza Accord of the Group of Five industrial countries in September 1985 committed Japan to strengthening the yen. The Treasury Department successfully used the Bank for International Settlements to negotiate uniform and relatively high capital requirments for all banks in the system. This agreement helped alleviate some of the enormous advantage Japanese banks had over American banks through their lower capital requirements. The Bank for International Settlements requires that capital ratios should be at least 7.25 per cent by March 1992 and 8.0 per cent by March 1993.

Japan's financial system has been significantly deregulized. For example, in 1988, only 37 per cent of the city banks deposits 'interest rates were market determined; by 1990, Tokyo had liberalized about 50 per cent of its bank deposits, including 60 per cent of the city banks, 45 per cent of the regional banks, and 30 per cent of the small shinkin banks deposit rates. MOF promises that by 1992, 85 per cent should be market determined. On 1 April 1990, Tokyo reduced the minimum size of money market certificates from 3.05 million yen (around $20 000) to 1 million yen.[22]

Yet the effects of "liberalization" on foreign market share are insignificant. As in manufacturing industries, most of Tokyo's financial "market opening steps" involved lowering more obvious barriers while creating more subtle barriers. Tokyo virtually forces foreign banks and securities firms to form joint ventures with their rivals, prevents them from buying a Japanese bank, and limits their access to Japan's vast pool of funds. Although foreign banks have been allowed a tiny market share since the 1950s, they were limited to supplying foreign exchange through long term tied loans and trade financing, and their market shares steadily fell as Japanese banks acquired reserves and expertise. The 123 foreign banks in Japan compete fiercely for a tiny 3 per cent market share despite so called liberalization. Foreign securities firms are even more tightly controlled. Although their ranks rose from three in 1980 to 124 in 1990, they also cling to a 4 per cent share. For example, until recently, foreign firms were completely excluded from the underwriting syndicates. After years of foreign pressure, 15 foreign firms were first allowed into Japan's underwriting syndicate in 1984. As in Japan's other markets the foreign firms were given a token share – foreign firms rarely receive more than 5 per cent of new issues of 10-year bonds – while the bids remain thoroughly managed: "the government did not set the coupon rate and issuing price of the ten-year bonds by competitive bid, but through negotiations with the underwriting syndicate, which distributed the remaining 80 per cent of the issue in the usual way. For the auctioned 20 per cent, all that could be bid for was quantity; and then a ceiling of 1 per cent of the total issue was imposed for each bidder . . . This . . . gives foreign firms about 2.5 per cent of the total amount of a ten-year issue".[23] Although 20-year government bonds are now auctioned in a free market, 97 per cent of the 10–year government bond market is still reserved for Japanese firms.[24]

Japan's underwriting cartel controls corporate bonds even more thoroughly than government bonds. Foreign firms currently hold only 0.5 per cent of the average issue. It was big news, for example, in 1987 when Morgan Stanley was allowed to participate in 10 million of 200 billion yen convertible bond issue by Matsushita.[25] Likewise foreign firms are prevented from easily raising funds in Japan's capital markets: "The Japanese system of dual underwriting, requiring bank collateralization of corporate security issues, adds a layer of fees that generally makes it uneconomic for foreign corporate treasurers to raise capital directly in the Tokyo capital market".[26] Costs are pushed up further since the registration time for transactions or preparations to float a bond issue takes up to a month in Japan compared to two or three days in Europe.

Recently, the president has reluctantly received considerable powers to retaliate against Japan's neomercantilist financial policies. The 1990 passage of the Riegle–Garn Fair Trade and Financial Services Act gives the president the financial equivalent of the Super 301 Trade Act, empowering him to retaliate against Japan's financial institutions if Tokyo fails to ensure reciprocity. Under the Act, the Treasury Department would designate as "unfair" any country that denies American banks the same privileges that that country's foreign banks enjoy in the United States. The Treasury Department would then be authorized to negotiate with the neomercantilist country. If the negotiations fail to remove the restrictions, the president would be authorized to retaliate against that country's financial firms in the United States. The bill was prompted by the Federal Reserve's refusal to comply with the 1988 Trade Bill and withdraw primary dealer status from Japanese institutions trading in US securities in retaliation against continued Japanese discrimination against American financial houses in Japan.

The bill's passage prompted Tokyo to make several concessions at the bilateral financial talks ending on 22 May 1990. It agreed to expand the ceiling on overseas accounts for individuals, allowed foreign securities firms to sell some foreign currency products without having to go through Japanese banks, and deregulated sales of some securities products. MOF also promised that by October 1990 it would reduce the minimum size for large-lot time-deposits, which offer floating rates, from 10 million yen to 7 million yen. Tokyo, however, stonewalled on three important issues. Firstly, it fiercely resisted Washington's pressure to liberalize its deposit markets within a year, claiming that the resulting "excessive competition" (read free markets) would wipe out as much as 20 per cent of city bank profits, sharply reduce earnings of the 140 regional banks and 452 small shinkin banks by as much as three quarters, and possibly wipe out many of the 3700 agricultural co-operatives and 400 credit co-operatives. Tokyo refused to set a specific timetable for lifting protection on them. Secondly, Tokyo refused to eliminate a withholding tax on treasury bills which inhibited foreign corporate and individual investors. Lack of demand for Japanese treasury bills means less demand for yen and thus a weak currency and higher Japanese exports. Thirdly, Tokyo adamantly refused to present a timetable for the liberalization of interest rate controls.[27]

The controversy over free deposit markets gives Washington an excellent opportunity for some tough horse trading. Washington could concede that, recognizing the disruptions that liberalization of Japan's deposit market could cause, the liberalization could be postponed. However, Japan would have to compensate by, say, fulfilling its promise to raise the American semiconductor market to 20 per cent, or allowing a genuinely free market for satelites or supercomputers, and accept the losses Japan's corporation would endure if faced with free markets in those goods. Unfortunately, the White House liberal blinders and administrative disarray prevents it from devising any comprehensive trade policy.

What, if anything, has Tokyo done in response to Washington's pressure to rein in the pervasive insider trading and create a more level playing field for foreign securities firms? On 1 April 1989, the Securities and Exchange Law was revised to strengthen penalties against insider trading. The revision represented a classic Japanese symbolic gesture which will have absolutely no effect on Japan's insider trading. MOF's Securities Bureau, which is responsible for guarding against insider-trading, is as much of a lapdog for the firm securities industry as the FTC is for Japan's entire economy. The Bureau's 400 personnel regulated 270 securities houses. Security Bureau Director-General, Masahiko Kadotani openly admitted that the bureau "is not set up to expose insider trading. Our role is to prevent it . . . We have not found a single case of stock price manipulation".[28] It is extremely difficult to catch insider traders in the act, and can only be achieved through sting-type operations involving secret surveillance and informants, which are banned under Japanese law.

In July 1990, the foreign firms share of Tokyo Stock Market trading was only 7.3 per cent, although it had risen five times its 1.5 per cent in 1986. Foreign brokers are harassed by a variety of means. The mass media and corporate rumor mills claim that foreign program trading is responsible for every stock market drop. The government continually tries to reign in those sectors in which foreign brokers excell. In April 1990, the government used "administrative guidance" to stop foreign firms from issuing the popular put and call warrants traded in the United States which bet on moves in Japanese stocks. The government justified the repression by claiming that the practice was somehow causing volatility in the Japanese market. Fearing that they could lose those miniscule gains they have made, foreign brokers refuse to protest most of the government and business harrassment.

MOF's response to the bankruptcy of the Japanese operations of the American firm, Drexel Burnham Lambert, in April 1990 reveals how entrenched Japan's bureaucratic power and protectionist policies remains. When Drexel's Tokyo president, Mashiko Yamamoto informed MOF that he would be shutting down his operations he was simply told he could not do so since Drexel had "responsibilities to take care of".[29] Yamamoto said that the MOF officials just "couldn't understand how something like this could be allowed to happen. MOF Deputy Director Nokuchika Mori said "We license you – you can't simply close. We have to give you permission. When we license a securities firm it has certain responsibilities, and we work with them to see things are done properly". Apparently MOF still does not understand how free markets work, an ignorance that has been essential for Japan's transformation into an economic superpower, but means continued conflict with its free trade oriented foreign rivals.

Salomon Brothers suffered a barrage of mass media criticism in early 1990 when it underwrote some bonds for Mitsui Toatsu. The critics claimed that the action led to a steep slide in share prices. Japan Inc. rallied around the flag again later that year when Salomon Brothers became the lead manager on two big offerings of convertible bonds in the Euromarkets for Oji Paper and Fujisawa Pharmaceutical, thus threatening the monopoly Japan's security houses hold on underwriting the yen securities of Japanese firms. Salomon Brothers was publicly blasted for daring to challenge the Japanese monopoly while Oji and Fujisawa were pressured to drop the deal. Salomon Brothers Managing Director, Kunihiko Kumagai, lamented the reality that even though the American firm offered "good technology and some good market opportunities . . . the cultural or invisible factors can be the most important part of doing business".[30] Of course, Japanese spokespeople will continue to claim that American firms just do not try hard enough.

Meanwhile, despite the reality that Japan's economy was the world's most dynamic, Japan's trade surplus continued to be fueled in part by a severely undervalued yen which dropped from its height of 121 yen to the dollar in 1988 to nearly 150 yen to the dollar in Spring 1990. Although the lack of evidence of official Japanese complicity in the yen's weakening does not rule it out, most analysts said speculation and psychology were the major reasons for the yen's fall.[31] The Tokyo stock market's continued fall stimulated an outflow of capital from Japan, thus weakening the demand for yen.

Tokyo's neomercantilist policies remain the major reason for the under-valued yen and Japan's intractable export surplus. Although Tokyo promised to switch its economic growth from largely export- to domestic-led, it continues to allow Japanese producers to gouge Japanese consumers. Although the yen has doubled in value since the Group of Five aggreement in September 1985, importers kept most of the profits to themselves and passed on only a fraction of the revaluation to consumers. A 1988 survey indicated that only 7.9 per cent felt they were benefiting from the high yen, and in fact only 11 trillion yen of 29 trillion yen ($230 billion) in lower prices since 1985 has been passed on to consumers. Aside from importers, producers greatly benefited by the strong yen, as raw materials and energy prices dropped almost in half. In 1986 for example, Japan paid $40 billion less for oil which dropped as a percentage of imports from 43.1 per cent in 1985 to 29.8 per cent in 1986.[32]

Japan's carefully managed financial markets, targeted credit, and artificially low interest rates help keep the yen severely underdemanded and thus undervalued. Japan's short-term money markets remain limited. Old instruments like certificates of deposits have been increased and new instruments like treasury bills, secondary markets, commercial paper, and yen-denominated bankers acceptances have been created, but all remain restricted to varying extents. Tokyo consciously limits the yen's use as an international currency – only about 40 per cent of Japan's exports and 10 per cent of its imports are yen denominated. If Tokyo abandoned its neomercantilist yen policies – if the BOJ stopped supporting the dollar and MOF genuinely liberalized its capital markets and denominated most of Japan's trade in yen, Japan's yen would quickly rise in value beyond 100 yen to a dollar and its interest rates to global levels, thus undercutting the comparative advantage for most Japanese products, and Japan's huge trade and payments surpluses with its trade partners would disolve into equilibrium.

Despite several decades of Washington pressure on Japan to embrace liberalism and Tokyo promises to comply, Japanese neomercantilism continues as intensively as ever. A Treasury Department report issued on 10 December 1990 condemned Tokyo for continuing to use a range of legal and informal means harshly to discriminate against foreign banks and securities firms. The report noted the slow dismantlement of Japan's web of formal restrictions against foreigners, but argued that these were merely replaced by more insidious government and business practices. Discriminatory measures include excluding foreigners from the inexpensive short-term loans from the Bank of Japan, administrative guidance, underdeveloped money market and securities instruments in which foreigners excell, new instrument only accepted after Japanese financial firms have mastered them, exclusion from such huge markets as managing pension funds and investment trust, exclusion from foreign currency trading, pervasive insider stock trading, market, price, and product cartels, and general collusive Japanese business practices.

CONCLUSION

Washington's efforts to force open Japan's financial markets will never genuinely succeed in achieving a level playing field. Although Japan's financial markets have experienced considerable superficial change over the past fifteen years, most sectors remain carefully managed by government-business cartels and the playing field remains sharply tilted in favor of Japan's financial industry. Robert Kuttner of *Businessweek* writes that MOF "restricts access to areas where outsiders might gain toeholds. New products that foreign bankers wish to introduce such as cash-managment accounts, are prohibited by a web of Japanese regulations" while those miniscule foreign financial market shares "result from a Japanese decision to throw foreigners a bone rather than from genuine market competition. In effect, Japan has simply treated capital as yet another product to export. And as usual, the companies that get to manage that export and profit from it are primarily Japanese. This is . . . not true internationalization".[33] As in Japan's other industries, Tokyo's careful management and protection of financial markets and products allows its financial industry to soak consumers at home and "dump" its products overseas. Because Tokyo rather than markets determine interest rates, Japanese corporations can raise money at regulated rates while American banks cannot.

A financial scandal that broke in the summer of 1991 revealed that Japan's financial system continues to be characterized by cartels, insider trading, kickbacks, and corruption despite Tokyo's repeated claims that its markets are the world's most open. In June 1991, a tax office investigation revealed that the Big Four Securities firms had kick backed $930 million to 229 favorite clients, including organized crime leaders, to cover losses on the stock market. Even this massive amount was thought to be the iceberg's tip. These kickbacks violate Articles 58 and 125 of the Securities and Exchange Law which prohibit soliciting business by offering guarantees against losses, fraud, and manipulative practices, and make violators criminally punishable for up to three years at hard labor, and Article 126 which allows compensation to people damaged by such crimes.

The scandal belies assertions that Japan's financial markets are open and foreigners do not do better because they do not try hard enough. Massive insider trading and collusion continue to characterize all of Japan's markets; government officials do not regulate the market, they collude with corporate leaders to maximize the industry's power and wealth. These practices remain an "open secret", winked at by government and corporate leaders, while Japanese spokespeople continue to claim that they do not exist. The Asahi Shimbun, one of Japan's largest daily papers, admitted ruefully that "this scandal lends credence to those who argue that Japan is an unfair society whose economy operates solely by insider collusion, to the exclusion of would be foreign participants".[34]

Once the scandal was revealed, the government moved fast to limit the damage and revelations of more massive irregularites. At first, those business leaders and government officials involved in the scanal denied any wrongdoing. MOF officials tried to dismiss the scandal as the result of poor judgement, and withheld information on the scandal's extent and participants in order to protect the quilty. Big Four spokesmen first denied that the kickbacks had occured, but later admitted the practice with the excuse that it was not illegal because they had received MOF permission. Deeply embarrassed by the disclosures, Tokyo apologized and tried to reassure a disbelieving global financial community that the scandal was, in Prime Minister Kaifu's words, "a rare case", the exception to the rule of unfettered Japanese markets.[35]

Despite the severity of the scandal, Tokyo characteristically refused not only to launch a sweeping investigation that would uncover all those involved in these crimes, but tried to dismiss the problem through extralegal administrative guidance rather than the law. Those involved in the scandal got off with a slap on the wrist. MOF officials involved in the scandal remained uncensored, although several top officials promised to take ten per cent pay cuts. Tokyo fined Nomura, whose pre-tax profits in 1990 were $1.74 billion, a piddling $116 000, and in addition forced the Big Four to "restrain" the trading of their headquarters offices with their largest clients for four days. All other offices would enjoy business as usual. The presidents of Nomura and Nikko retired while each of the Big Four announced pay cuts of 10–20 per cent for participating officials. There was no talk of imposing huge penalties or suspending the licenses of the Big Four, let alone sending anyone to jail for three years at hard labor.

Japan's political system then quietly attempted to forget the whole scandal and return to business as usual as quickly as possible. There were no demands in the Diet for a thorough investigation of the scandal, or for more stringent laws to protect small and foreign enterprises from Zaikai collusion, or for an end to the parachuting of MOF officials after retirement into high paying sinecures in the industry they were supposedly regulating. A Japanese businessman colorfully characterized the differences between American and Japanese government policy: "In the United States the regulators are theoretically supposed to be like cops standing on street corners policing traffic. In Japan the regulators are in a patrol car with the light flashing on the top, leading the charge through red lights".[36] Charles Stevens, writing in the New York Times, points out a Japanese saying that "the law is like a family's heirloom sword. The family brings it out to emphasize its distinguished lineage, but would never dream of using it on anyone".[37] Japan will continue to be ruled by men rather than laws; its markets by Japanese insiders rather than competition; foreigner firms, no matter how competitive their products, will remain outsiders.

The White House's reaction to the scandal was as predictable as Tokyo's. The Bush Adminstration's reaction was not strongly to condemn the continued existence of Japan's fixed financial markets that have discriminated against foreign firms for so long and helped Japan become the world's financial hegemon; there were no demands that the system be genuinely liberalized once and for all. Instead, on 27 July 1991, Treasury Secretary Nicholas Brady expressed concern that the scandal would force the resignation of his counterpart, Ryutaro Hashimoto! Brady asserted that "Mr Hashimoto has been a pretty good friend of the United States amd we hope he'll be all right".[38] Brady went on to laud Japan's financial contributions to the Gulf War. When asked about if he was as worried about the fate of American's financial institutions, Brady replied, "To the extent that Americans want to be fairly treated when they go to Japan, that's important to us". He then added, "To be honest with you, it has seemed to far away to do anything about". Brady's statements reflected classical Washington thinking about Japan and the world – Japan's value as an ally far outweighs its challenge as an economic rival.

Just as Washington cannot force open Japan's carefully manipulated markets no matter how hard it trys, any attempts to reform America's financial system are unlikely to reverse the country's decline. But America's deepening financial crisis and Japan's rising financial super-power have been decades in the making. Although battles will continue to be fought indefinitely, Japan's finance industry has essentially vanquished American's. The United States will continue to be the world's greatest debtor nation and Japan's the global economy's banker for the forseeable future.

Part III

What Is To Be Done?

11 America and Japan into the 21st Century

As the world moves closer to then into the 21st century, the future seems filled with a twirling collage of bright and bleak possibilities. Cures for cancer and AIDS are offset by the greenhouse effect, the peaceful democratic revolutions sweeping away one dictatorship after another around the world by vicious civil wars, mass affluence by mass poverty and starvation, longer lifespans by population explosions, the Cold War's end by economic nationalism.

And what fate awaits the United States? Will America continue steadily to deteriorate, with the most noticeable growth in the gap between rich and poor, its cities, bridges, and roads crumbling, its youth jailed, drugged, indifferent, its real income falling and debt and health costs rising, its people consumed by consumerism, greed and flashy images? Will America's factories continue to shut down or be sold out to foreign rivals? Will Japanese and other foreign powers play an increasingly significant role in shaping America's economic policies and destiny? Will America's leaders continue to fiddle while their country burns?

This vision is a genuine possibility. The United States has simply not adapted to the dramatic changes that have swept the world over the past half century. Consumed with the Cold War struggle and belief that the "American way" is the best way, America's leaders and public have failed to understand and respond to the challenge of Japanese neomercantilism. Under the rubric of "comprehensive security", the Japanese have mastered a superior way of creating and securing wealth throughout the world. Japan is now the world's economic superpower, and its ability to shape international relations in its favor will deepen as its economic power grows.

Can America's economic decline be reversed, and if so, how? Given the shift in economic power between the two countries, a solution of the trade crisis with Japan would by synonymous with the reversal of American economic decline. The stakes in this crisis are enormous. If Tokyo continues to surge ahead while America's financial, manufacturing, and technological prowess continues to drain away and its budget, trade, and account debts accumulate, the United States will find itself a second rate economic power within a generation.

The United States is down but not out. It remains the world's largest economy and retains enormous human and technological resources. Most Americans also have the will to overcome the myriad of problems pulling down their country. But the United States lacks two essential ingredients for a revival of American power – a consensus over what must be done and a single-minded focus on doing it. What follows is an analysis over what must be done to revive American wealth and power.[1] Ultimate success or failure depends on the willingness of America's leaders to lead, to mobilize the vast energies and resources vital for overcoming the Japanese challenge which were earlier deployed against the Soviet challenge.

In meeting the Japanese challenge, the United States must drastically overhaul three interrelated policies – toward the global political economy, its own economy, and its direct relations with Japan. The first policy in reviving American power is to acknowledge and adapt to the tremendous shift in the nature of international politics. Split second communications and jet age transportation tie the world together in an increasingly dense web of trade in goods, services, people and ideas. Interdependence turns the traditional concept of national security inside out. A nation's security once rested on a powerful military protecting and often enlarging that nation's frontiers. Today and increasingly into the future, a nation's security rests on its ability to master the creation of wealth and the power to promote that wealth. A nation's conquest of global markets in heavy, high technology and financial products is the economic basis of national security in an interdependent world. The objective is to penetrate as thoroughly as possible strategic markets and production around the world, and entangle those countries as deeply as possible in the exporting nation's products, technology, finance, services and investments while minimizing any economic dependence on that country. Economic penetration allows political dominance, which enhances economic penetration. In the post-Cold War world, the balance of international economic power surpasses the balance of military power in importance, and the state which is most adept at manipulating that balance in its own favor will be the most successful in garnering wealth and power for its country.

The second related policy is for Washington to abandon obsolete notions of how to create wealth and wield power in the contemporary world. Every nation faces the challenge of either maintaining or enhancing three vital interests: geoeconomic and geopolitical integrity, economic growth, and a large middle class with a high standard of living. Governments achieve these national interests by using rational industrial and trade policies to give their economies a manufacturing, technological, and financial edge over their rivals. Wealth must be distributed as well as created. There is a dynamic relationship between enhancing economic growth and a large middle class; the larger the middle class the greater the production and learning scales for that nation's industry, which in turn can be invested in stimulating even more economic growth. America's relative economic decline can only begin to be reversed when Washington learns how to manage its economy and nurture its strategic industries as skillfully as do the Japanese.

The success of adapting a geoeconomic strategy for international relations and rational industrial policies to stimulate rapid industrial and technological development depends ultimately on achieving a level playing field with Japan the third policy area. America's relationship with Japan is a zero sum game in which Tokyo constantly outfoxes Washington in one issue after another with the result that Japan's wealth and power continues rapidly to grow at America's expense. Neomercantilist fire can only be fought with neomercantilist fire. America's vast trade deficit with Japan will continue to persist, despite strenuous, continual efforts by American negotiators and businessmen to penetrate Japan's labyrinth of nontariff trade and investment barriers, as long as Washington's trade and industrial policies continue to be shaped by liberal economic principles. Washington and the American business community must realize that to continue to pursue *laissez-faire* policies when powerful foreign rivals use neomercantilist policies is an act of unilateral economic disarmament. The United States will only begin to turn around its relative economic decline when it begins to play hardball with Tokyo and insist on reciprocity in trade, investment and other political economic opportunities.

THE NEW WORLD ORDER

A new world order is emerging. Military power is increasingly irrelevant in resolving international conflicts while the costs of simply maintaining a vast military industrial complex will steadily undermine a nation's economic power. The world is converging politically and economically, and power in the contemporary and future world will depend on how skillfully nations create and wield economic power. A democratic revolution is sweeping away authoritarians governments while states are abandoning both central planning and free markets for managed markets in which private ownership prevails. International cooperation grows steadily in dealing with such crises as the greenhouse and depletion of the ozone layer effects, widespread poverty, disease, the population explosion, and international violence.

The Cold War is over. The Soviet empire and communism are rapidly crumbling. Neither the Soviet Union nor China, despite their respective vast populations, territories, natural resources and military forces, pose any threat to the United States. President Gorbachev faced, and Premier Deng and his successors continue to face, the paradox that to "reform" communism may mean eventually abandoning it. The Soviet and Chinese reforms unleashed political and economic forces that will increasingly undermine the authority of communist rule; the genie of rising popular frustrations has been let out of the bottle and can only be appeased through increased state concessions to economic and political pluralism. In August 1991, a failed coup by hardline communists in the Soviet Union forced President Gorbachev to suspend the communist party, grant independence to those Soviet Republics that requested it, turn over most political powers to the Republics, and embark on sweeping economic reforms. By 1992, the Soviet Union broke up into fifteen independent non-communist states. The "Soviet Threat" and Cold War disappeared. Twenty years from now, China may also be in the last stages of a rocky, crisis ridden evolution into a mixed economy and multiparty system. In the end, Washington's victory over the Soviet Union and communism in the Cold War may be as complete as its victory over the Axis powers during World War II.

The costs of winning the Cold War have, however, been devastating to the United States. The diversion of trillions of dollars and America's best minds into the promotion of weapons rather than consumer goods has been a major reason for America's dramatic relative economic decline. Washington is only now awakening to the reality that it has been engaged in not one but two "wars" since 1945, the Cold War with the Soviet Union and the economic war with Japan for supremacy over the global political economy. In its single-minded devotion to winning the Cold War with the Soviet Union, Washington may have lost a much more difficult and subtle war with Japan, a war that it was not even aware it was engaged in until late in the struggle. The United States has suffered constant defeats and is falling further behind in the economic war with Japan. While the United States maintains a stable balance of military power with the Soviet Union, it is suffering from an increasingly severe imbalance of economic power with Japan.

Like Dr Frankenstein's creation, Japan has turned against the country which was responsible for its dramatic transformation from early postwar poverty into present political economic superpower. The United States revolutionized Japan's political economy during the postwar occupation (1945–52). Then, while the United States focused its energies on winning the Cold War, Japan, basking under the protection of America's nuclear umbrella, and with virtually unlimited access to America's huge market and a continually expanding global economy, used neomercantilist industrial and trade policies to achieve a growth rate four times that of America's before 1974 and twice its rate since.

Japan has achieved a dynamic virtuous cycle of political economic power over the United States. Tokyo can use America's growing dependence on Japan's technological, financial and manufacturing power to arm-twist Washington into maintaining the asymmetrical relationship between the two countries, whereby Japanese corporations are allowed virtually unlimited access to America's free political and economic markets while Japan's remain all but closed to competitive American corporations. Japan will become ever more politically and economically powerful, and thus can extract even more concessions from a increasingly decrepit United States. The reach of Tokyo and Japanese corporations is now global, although it varies considerably from one country and region to the next. And, if unchecked, Japan's power and wealth will continue to deepen and expand indefinitely, often at the expense of others.

There are limits to Japan's power. Japan's economic threat will never become a military threat. The Japanese were the first to understand that military power is increasingly obsolete in an interdependent world, and that diverting enormous resources from consumer to military production actually undermines a nation's wealth and power. The government and public are united in opposing any significant increase in the size, let alone the mission of Japan's military. Japanese spokespeople, however, do use the threat of remilitarization to scare foreign governments off from hardline positions on Japanese neomercantilism.

Nor will Japanese culture, with its emphasis on groupism, conformity, and sacrifice, ever challenge the universal appeal of American individualism, opportunity, and creativity. The chauvinistic Japanese belief that no foreigner can understand let alone become a member of Japanese society and culture obviously limits its appeal in contrast to the American belief that anyone can become American by simply embracing the culture. Related to the parochial nature of Japanese culture is the inability of Tokyo to construct any sort of appealing international ideology that it could use to influence foreign leaders and publics and thus strengthen Japan's position. The constant refrain by Japanese spokesmen and their foreign collaborators that Japan is the world's most open market and foreign manufacturers do not sell more because they do not try hard enough is not an ideology but simply a public relations stunt. Perceptive foreign observers know well that Japanese policy remains single-mindedly neomercantilist despite all the hoopla surrounding the ten "significant market opening steps" of the 1980s. As long as the Japanese touting of "liberalism" or "internationalism" remains just a public relations smokescreen obscuring continued neomercantilism and nationalism, Tokyo will never be able to produce a credible ideology with universal appeal.

But Tokyo may not need to do so. Having a culture and ideology with universal appeal obviously enhances a nation's power, but it is not essential. The bottom line of power in an increasingly interdependent global political economy is economic, and Japan's manufacturing, technology and financial hegemony will continue to deepen even if Japan lacks a culture or ideology with universal appeal to bolster it.

The world political economy seems to be evolving into domination by three economic blocs to which the rest of the world will be loosely tied. The European Community's (EC) twelve members and European Free Trade Association's (EFTA) seven members will dismantle all significant internal trade barriers in 1992, thus creating a united market of 380 million prosperous consumers, and may well adopt a common currency by the mid-1990s. ETFA members like Austria and Sweden and other European countries are lining up to join the EC ranks. Promising as these remarkable developments are, the EC still faces tough political and economic divisions. While the EC has been evolving for over four decades, a North American free trade zone is much more recent development. Washington's signature of free trade agreements with Canada in 1988 and Mexico in 1992, may eventually create a market of over 400 million consumers. The Bush Administration has hopes of eventually extending this free trade zone throughout the entire Western Hemisphere. But given the vast economic differences among those states, a hemispheric free trade zone will not emerge any time soon, if ever. Meanwhile, Tokyo is steadily cementing its economic domination of East an Southeast Asia with more powerful political economic ties. Given, however, persistent anti-Japanese sentiments, the vast economic gulf between Japan's 1990 per capita income of $23 000, Taiwan or Singapore's $7500, Thailand's $1500, or China's $450, and Tokyo's own preference for subtle behind the scenes political manipulation, the region is unlikely ever to be formally united by an international organization. Yet, those same economic differences can be a source of regional strength since they complement more than compete with each other.

None of these trade blocs could ever become autarkic. Although an increasing amount of trade occurs within each bloc, they are still economically bound together almost as intricately. The United States remains the centerpiece of relations between the three blocs. The American and Japanese blocs are intricately tied together in the Pacific Basin, whose trade and investment volumes are now greater than Atlantic Basin economic relations. Japanese–European Community economic ties remain much less important, but are steadily increasing. The conflicting need to both compete and co-operate with each other will complicate relations between the blocs. Such world crises like the debt problem, greenhouse effect and ozone depletion, political and economic revolution in Eastern Europe and elsewhere, mass starvation in central Africa and elsewhere, and threats to the Gulf region, can only be managed through co-operation by Washington, Tokyo and Brussels. Yet, relations will continue to be strained by predatory trade and industrial practices. Trade relations will undoubtedly become increasingly managed as the United States and European Community adapt Japan's neomercantilist strategy in order to compete with Japan's growing economic power.

The shifting balance of economic power will be the dominant mechanism for determining the outcome of economic conflict in an increasingly interdependent world just as the balance of military power shaped past territorial and ideological conflicts. A balance of power between three blocs is the most unstable of any arrangement because of the fear that the other two will combine against the third. There are three possible scenarios for the global political economy. Perhaps the most probable scenario is each bloc's continued development and steady management of conflict with rival blocs. Meanwhile, although Tokyo will deepen its technological, manufacturing, and financial power over both the East Asian and global political economy, Washington and Brussels will remain in the race by adopting rational industrial and managed trade policies. This stable balance of power may lead to a second possibility, the eventual dissolution of the blocs into a genuine global free trade system. But this can only occur if Japan genuinely transforms itself from a neomercantilist into a liberal political economy – a highly unlikely development considering how deeply entrenched Japan's neomercantilist system remains and how successful it continues to be in amassing political and economic power. It is possible, however, that growing trade and investment conflicts will result in either two blocs uniting against the most predatory of the three, or, the least likely possibility, the continued trade conflicts dissolving into trade war between all three blocs and the subsequent collapse of the global political economy.

Just what are America's national interests and how should they be promoted in the post-Cold War world? Washington must recognize that national security is ultimately based on technological, financial, manufacturing and trade prowess rather than military might. In today's increasingly interdependent world, all nations must "export or die". A trade and payments balance of power should be considered as vital to American security today as a military power balance was in the Cold War, and Washington must become as skilled in manipulating the former in America's favor and it is the latter. The principle for balancing both military and economic power is the same: the rival of my rival is my ally.

America's military must be vastly restructured and redeployed to deal with geoeconomic as well as geopolitical conflicts. The Cold War's demise gives the United States an opportunity to address its relative economic decline, and all the attendant problems such as crime, drug abuse, poverty, bad education, crumbling infrastructure, and low investments and savings. Without a Soviet or even communist threat to worry about, Washington's policy agenda will not be dominated by such at one time seemingly important matters as civil wars in Central America, Africa, Southeast Asia, and elsewhere which consumed trillions of dollars and countless human resources that could have been invested at home.

The Bush Administration plans to cut defense spending a mere two per cent annually through 1997, resulting in an annual budget about 10 per cent lower than the current $285 billion. Altogether, American military spending will be reduced from 6.3 per cent of GNP in 1987 to 3.6 per cent in 1996, the lowest level since 1941. The military will be reduced from its post-Vietnam peak of 2.17 million personnel in 1987 to 1.65 millon in 1995, a reduction of 521 000 or about the amount deployed in Operation Desert Storm. American troops in Europe will be cut from their current level of 325 000 to 180 000. Although under the Bush plan, the army would be reduced from 18 to 14 divisions, reserves from 10 to 8 divisions, aircraft carriers from 14 to 12, and air force tactical wings from 36 to 28, such projects as the stealth B–2 bomber, mobile MX, SDI, and midgetman programs would continue to consume hundreds of billions of dollars.[1]

It is questionable whether the United States needs to maintain such an immense defense program when the Russian threat and American economy continue to crumble. In conjuncture with equivalent Soviet reductions, the United States should slash its defense by 50 per cent over the next decade until it reaches only 1 per cent of America's GNP. Throughout the 1990s, without a Soviet threat, American forces in Europe and the Far East can be stripped to skeleton forces, both defense spending and the number of army regular and reserve divisions halved, strategically wasteful and unnecessary programs like the B–2, SDI, mobile MX, and midgetman canceled, and America's nuclear forces cut up to 70–80 per cent without any loss of deterrence. All these reductions, however, should only be made if Russia agrees to make equivalent drastic cuts in its own forces. Half of all the annual savings of $150 billion could then be used for reducing the budget deficit and the other half in rebuilding America's economic and human infrastructure and targeting strategic industries and technologies.

Redeployment and restructuring of American military power is as important as cutting it back. America's military has overwhelming power to deter a potential Soviet attack on the West or defeat a regional aggressor like Iraq, but is powerless to stop drug shipments or illegal aliens from entering the United States or the poaching of fish from American waters. Drugs, illegal aliens, and poaching undermine American security, and part of the military must be redeployed and restructured to combat those threats. Meanwhile, the European Community and Japan should be asked to take care of their own defense, with the United States playing only a supporting role in the extremely unlikely event of Russian attack. The United States would still provide the most troops and equipment in military actions elsewhere around the world, although each NATO member and Japan would be assessed a quota of troops and/or finance for any operations. The construction and maintenance of supply depots, bases, airfields, and ports in strategic areas like the Gulf region, Panama Canal, or Northeast Asia would allow allied troops to deploy rapidly in an emergency.

In the Third World, only the Gulf region will remain a vital geopolitical interest. America's economy, along with most of the rest of the world, was bashed by OPEC's quadrupling of oil prices in 1973 and further doubling in 1979. In 1991, the United States led an alliance of 37 nations in a short but fierce war against Iraq after it tookover Kuwait in an attempt to control 40 per cent of global oil reserves. Free trade's short-term advantages and long-term disadvantages for consumers are exemplified by global oil markets. Americans are estimated to save $60 billion a year for every $10 decrease on an oil barrel. But the price could drop to a low as $7–8 dollars a barrel if a free market emerges in the years following the Gulf War as Iraqi and Kuwait oil begin surging into already oversupplied global markets. While cheap oil puts more money into the pockets of American individual and business consumers, a cheap oil addiction bankrupts domestic oil and alternative energy producers, impedes conservation measures, increases pollution and deepens American dependence on foreign energy sources. Any future oil price jump would thus make the resulting recession and the payments deficit all the more devastating. Over 4600 American oil rigs were pumping when the price was $30 a barrel in 1981, while only 1000 rigs are operating at the present oil price.[2]

Washington and its allies must continue to be prepared to defend the global political economy against any threats to its vital access to the Gulf region's oil. The Middle East will remain unstable and conflict prone for the foreseeable future. Washington should continue to alleviate tensions by helping negotiate a regional peace treaty which simultaneously guarantees Israel's survival and grants the Palestinian people political autonomy. Meanwhile, the United States could dramatically reduce its dependence on foreign oil and immense trade deficits through a concerted program of conservation, energy efficiency, and diversification of energy sources. A sensible oil policy would seek a roughly $25 a barrel price, which would cost consumers $1.50 at the pump. That price would be high enough to encourage domestic energy producers and low enough to check inflation. That level could be achieved by imposing a dollar tax on all domestic and foreign oil sales. The tax receipts could be used to reduce the deficit. A tariff could be levied on foreign imports whenever the price falls below that level and the proceeds used to develop alternate energy sources and pollution control.

But stable oil prices are less important than gradually reducing America's dependence on oil. Amory and Hunter Lovins, directors of the Rocky Mountain Institute, estimate that a comprehensive policy of boosting energy conservation and efficiency, and diversifying energy sources could allow America's present economy to run on one-fifth the oil that is now required. Today's new cars average 29 miles per gallon while the American fleet averages a mere 20 miles per gallon. A fleet improvement of three miles per gallon, could eliminate all American imports from Iraq and Kuwait, and an additional improvement of nine miles per gallon would eliminate the need for any Persian Gulf oil. Automobile prototypes exist which get anywhere from 67 to 138 miles per gallon. The Lovins recommend the use of "feebates", in which buyers would pay a fee or get a rebate when they register a car, depending on its efficiency.[3] Conservation and alternative energies rather than military deterrence will provide the best security against any threat to America's oil supplies or steady price.

The focus of American foreign policy, however, should be on overcoming the Japanese challenge. Washington's policies toward Japan continue to be self-defeating. Governments which follow liberal trade policies in a neomercantilist world will eventually destroy their economy. The United States continues to wave its free trade banner when most other states have hoisted their national flags. America's one-sided free trade policies have allowed foreign competitors advantages in the United States that American producers lacked overseas. In the immediate postwar era, Washington's toleration of foreign trade barriers was vital for those countries' economic growth and the prosperity they enjoy today. But when foreign industries strengthened to the point where American producers began to lose their comparative advantage, "free trade" undermined American security and prosperity. Thus, as Chalmers Johnson points out "we are having our economy shaped by the policies of others rather than the impersonal operations of the marketplace. Our adherence to a *laissez-faire* philosophy under these conditions would mean that the structure of American industry is being determined, not by market forces, but by the industrial policies of others".[4]

Washington must substitute the policy of "fair trade" for "free trade" in its relations with other advanced industrial countries, allowing no other OECD country advantages in the United States that are not reciprocated to American manufacturers in its own market. When a trade asymmetry is identified, Washington must insist that it be removed. If the asymmetry persists, the United States should retaliate by closing off either an equivalent or similar domestic market to the offender. The concept of fair trade or reciprocity applies to the concept of deterrence to trade. Reciprocity deters any nation from launching or permitting an export offensive against the American market. It allows comparative advantage, not trade barriers, to determine market share.

Although protectionist policies are anathema to liberal economists, in reality, according to Paul Krugman,

> protectionism does not cost our economy jobs, any more than the trade deficit does: US employment is essentially determined by supply, not demand. The claim that protectionism caused the Depression is nonsense; the claim that future protectionism will lead to a repeat performance is equally nonsensical . . . The combined costs of these major restrictions (autos, steel, textile quotas) . . . are . . . less than three quarters of one per cent of US national income. Most of the loss, furthermore, comes from the fact that the import restrictions, in effect, form foreign producers into cartels that charge higher prices to US consumers. So most of US losses are matched by higher foreign profits . . . the negative effects of US import restrictions on efficiency are therefore much smaller–around one quarter of one per cent of US GNP . . . The cost to taxpayers of the savings and loan bailout alone will be at least five times as large as the annual cost to US consumers of all US import restrictions.[5]

Krugman sees the costs of protectionism in reduced efficiency rather than employment, since each country would simply produce at home what it previously imported. According to Krugman, the imposition of 100 per cent tariffs in a trade war between American, Japanese, and European trade blocs which

> cut international trade in half, and which caused an average cost of wasted resources for the displaced production of, say, 50 per cent, would therefore cost the world economy only 2.5 per cent of its income . . . roughly the cost of a one per cent increase in the unemployment rate, and it is the result of an extreme scenario, in which protectionism has a devastating effect on world trade. If the trade conflict were milder, the costs would be much less. Suppose that the tariff rates were only 50 per cent, leading to a 30 per cent fall in world trade. Then 3 per cent of the goods originally used would be replaced with domestic substitutes, costing at most 50 per cent more.[6]

But these scenarios are extreme. The threat of retaliation to open foreign markets will have no noticeable effect on world trade if they fail, and a positive effect if they succeed.

Japan is clearly America's greatest geoeconomic rival. Washington can enhance its bargaining position with Tokyo and contain Japan's geoeco-

nomic threat by allying with the European Community and the East
Asian economies. Washington's efforts to develop a North American free
trade zone will give it the ability to counter any possible protectionist
policies from Brussels. Washington can then use the power of its North
American free trade zone to negotiate an Atlantic Basin free trade region.
Meanwhile, Washington should use the dependence of the East Asian
NICs on America's vast market to play them off against Japan. This
would force the NICs to choose between access to American markets or
Japan's unreciprocated, increased penetration of their own political
economies. Faced with this choice, Seoul, Taipei, Beijing and Singapore
would have to side with Washington over Tokyo. East Asian compliance
with the coalition can be further bolstered by the reduction of Washington's military commitment to Japan. Virtually all the East and Southeast
Asian countries favor the continued presence of American military forces
in the region to contain Japan, even as they understand that America's
vast defense burden has been partially responsible for economically
crippling the United States. An economic coalition, it can be argued,
will replace the bilateral alliance as the means of containing any possible
revival of Japanese militarism. Washington has the opportunity to play
the "China card", and Korean, Taiwan, and Thai "cards" as skillfully
against Japan as it once did against the Soviet Union.

What should be the objectives of such a grand coalition spanning the
Atlantic and Pacific oceans? Nothing less than Tokyo's abandonment of
neomercantilism and embrace of liberalism. All these countries suffer deep
trade deficits and lower economic growth from Japanese neomercantilism.
It is in their collective interests to force Tokyo to genuinely liberalize its
economy. By what means would the coalition achieve Japan's liberalization? Market access for Japanese products could be either allowed or
restricted depending on Tokyo's degree of liberalization.

The coalition's tough line against Japan can be justified by GATT which
includes several "escape clauses" which allow contracting parties temporarily to erect import barriers to offset damage to domestic industries, the
balance of payments, or national security. Of the several GATT articles
which allow temporary relief for nations suffering balance of payments or
foreign predatory trade practices, none is more central than Article XIX.
States can retaliate with higher tariffs or quotas if they can prove that as a
result of unforeseen developments and GATT obligations, imports are
increasing either in terms of greater market share (relatively) and/or
volume (absolutely), and are either causing or threatening to cause injury
to domestic industries. States can then suspend GATT obligations for that
product or industry for the time necessary to prevent or remedy the injury.
GATT, however, softens the retaliation by requiring that unless "critical
circumstances" in injury are present, the importing nation must negotiate

with the predatory country(s) before erecting trade barriers, and allows that exporting country(s) the right to suspend similar obligations should no agreement emerge.[7] Other articles reinforce the ability of a state to withdraw from MFN duties. GATT Article XXVIII goes so far as to allow injured nations to permanently withdraw tariff advantages. Nations can justify exceptions from MFN responsibilities under Articles XII and XVIII for predatory foreign practices, under Articles XII, XIII, and XIV for balance of payments problems, under Articles XVI for predatory foreign subsidies, and under Articles XXI for national security considerations, and receive an official GATT waiver under Article XXV. GATT's vague criteria and numerous categories for nations to evoke escape clauses makes it very easy for them to do so.[7]

Obviously, Tokyo will not meekly stand idle while such an economic coalition is forged against it. Tokyo has already deeply tied the East and Southeast Asian economies with its own, and will use its vast economic power over the region to create its own economic bloc. Meanwhile it will attempt to weaken any American or European resolve by exploiting its increasingly powerful political economic inroads into both. Tokyo will attempt to retaliate by strengthening its current drive to increase its political economic clout in Mexico, Brazil and other Latin American countries. Washington's free trade pacts with Mexico and Canada and America's continued strong political economic position throughout the region will limit Japanese inroads into its back yard. Tokyo may also attempt to enlist Moscow against any coalition designed to counter Japanese neomercantilism. The Soviets are in desperate need of massive financial, technological and manufacturing resources and Japan is obviously a prime potential source. Moscow may be eventually give up the four disputed islands north of Hokkaido in return for a massive Japanese investment commitment. Yet, any Japanese commitment, no matter how large, could not offset Moscow's dependence on the European Community and United States. Ultimately, Tokyo will be forced to abandon neomercantilism if Washington implements a firm, comprehensive containment policy.

THE REVOLUTION AT HOME

The United States has fallen behind as much by its own liberal policies as from Japanese neomercantilism. The revival of American power depends on a complete restructuring and reorientation of America's economic policymaking and policies. But no reforms can occur until a consensus is reached over why the existing system and policies have undermined rather than promoted American wealth and power. Such a consensus, however, will be extremely difficult to forge.

A number of analysts have attributed America's political economic weaknesses to a decline in American virtue. Benjamin Friedman writes that "the radical course upon which United States economic policy was launched in the 1980s violated the basic moral principle that had bound each generation of Americans to the next since the founding of the republic: that men and women should work and eat, earn and spend both privately and collectively, so that their children and their children's children would inherit a better world. Since 1980 we have broken faith with that tradition by pursuing a policy which . . . we are living well by running up our debt and selling off our assets".[8] Pat Choate asserts that "American weakness . . . is not a result of villanry by the Japanese or any other foreign interest. America's foreign competitors merely use the legal opportunities and services presented in America by Americans to maximize their economic and political advantage here . . . Any indignation about undue foreign influence in America's internal affairs . . . should focus on those Americans who have supported the progressive cheapening—even the fundamental corruption – of the value of national service that used to guide the conduct of our public life".[9] Paul Krugman confesses that the "lack of protest over our basically dreary economic record the most remarkable fact about America today . . . it is astonishing how readily Americans have scaled down their expectations in line with their performance, to such an extent that from a political point of view our economic management appears to be a huge success . . . We live in an 'age of diminished expectations', an era in which our economy has not delivered very much but in which there is little political demand that it do better".[10] These ideological and ethical obstacles to reforming America's policymaking system and policies will be formidable.

There is a chicken and egg relationship between the system's institutional and ideological inertia, and public apathy. Despite all the evidence that rational industrial policies and managed trade promote a nation's wealth and power much more rapidly and efficiently than free trade policies. America's policymaking system and policies continue to be permeated with liberal dogma. This outlook was concisely expressed in the 1990 President's Economic Report touting free trade: "Over the past 40 years, the world has learned that excessive government involvement in the economy leads to unsound decisions . . . slows growth, and costs jobs".[11] The converse, however, is equally true. Inadequate government involvement in the economy also leads to unsound decisions, slows growth and costs jobs.

But the choice is not this black and white. Japan and other countries have found a middle way between inadequate and excessive government involvement in the economy. Reich and Magaziner argue that a "*laissez-faire* approach is both naive and dangerous for a national economy with slow growth and for a nation within an interdependent world economy that is prone to sharp and often sudden changes in supply, demand, technology, and politics. Active government policies are necessary to enable the economy to respond quickly and efficiently to worldwide structural changes".[12]

Any comprehensive attempt to overhaul America's system should be geared toward recapturing American financial, manufacturing, and technological leadership, and should include: (1) a reorganized policy-making regime which creates and implements (2) rational macroeconomic, industrial, trade, technology and investment policies. America's industrial, trade and investment policies are shaped by an anarchy of political forces at the national, state, and even local level. Senator Llyod Bentsen describes the process as "shaped not systematically, but almost by accident. It is the least common denominator worked out, as some have so aptly put it, by a kind of guerrilla warfare among the Departments of State, Treasury, Agriculture, Commerce, the Fed, and a whole host of other executive branch agencies".[13] Stephen Cohen uses words like "adhoc" and "inconsistent" to describe the same process. He continues:

> Key US international economic policy has been made on a highly idiosyncratic basis. Some were quickly devised in crisis situations, others grew by inertia . . . All too often policies have been reactive. There is an inability to get the problem identified far enough in advance. Policy makers are on the defensive putting out a series of brush fires. There is a lack of any firm guidelines from the White House and the bewildering array of coordinating committees, working groups, and task forces complicate the problem. The result is a cumbersome system in which an inordinate amount of time and energy is consumed in intragovernment debates which pass through a multi-stage process.[14]

Trade policy alone is shaped by a half-dozen departments and twelve Congressional committees; antitrust policy by a tug of war among the Justice Department, Federal Trade Commission, and Senate and House Judiciary committees.Perhaps the biggest reason for this policy making morass is the fact that international economic policy making has traditionally fallen between the respective realms of the Treasury Department's domestic economic policy and the State Department's foreign policy making, and both have been largely subordinate to the overall focus on containing the Soviet Union. More often than not, international economic policy is a result of the tug of war between these two departments with their own constituencies, values, and personalities. In the words of Senators Russell Long and Abraham Ribicoff: "It's time to end the bureaucratic separation of international issues with parts of each specific issue scattered throughout the government machinery without any sense of overall purpose and general guidance from the top".[15]

The solution that cuts this Gordian knot of decision making is to implement House Majority Leader Richard Gephardt's plan to create a Department of International Trade and Industry (DITI) and a civilian counterpart to the Defense Department's Defense Advanced Research Projects Agency. The United States is the only major industrial country that does not have a separate ministry charged with the overall direction of trade and industrial policy, a reality that has been a major handicap in America's economic and trade development. DITI could absorb the Commerce Department, the USDA, the National Science Foundation, the Office of the Special Representative for Trade Negotiation, and the international statistical and policy staffs of the Departments of Labor, Treasury, State and Agriculture. DITI would have responsibility for both trade and industrial policy, and, rather than the Department of Treasury, would represent the United States in all international economic forums. It would identify, nurture, and promote strategic heavy and high technology industries by supplying them with tax credits, infrastructure and R&D research funds. In addition, DITI would be the watchdog for the military–industrial complex, making sure there was optimum resource allocation, efficiency, and competition. The DITI secretary would be a permanent member of the National Security Council.

America's intelligence system should be completely overhauled and reorientated to deal with the new challenges the United States faces into the 21st century. The system costs $30 billion annually and is geared mostly toward the Soviet Union. Critics charge that the intelligence system has repeatedly failed to predict major events like the rapid destruction of the Soviet empire and Iraq's invasion of Kuwait. Furthermore, journalists and academics often have access to human intelligence and provide analysis that rivals and often surpasses the CIA in quality. The overlapping missions of the different agencies mean considerable waste of energies, personnel and resources.

A clear division of labor within the intelligence community should enable the United States to deal with its twin challenges, the rapidly receding Russian and ever more powerful Japanese threats. The DIA should focus on geopolitical conflicts with an emphasis on the Russian threat while the CIA concentrates on geoeconomic conflicts centered around the Japanese threat, while the eavesdropping National Security Agency supplies vital information to both agencies. The agencies would then be completely reorganized to fulfill these responsibilities, with an emphasis on different in-house rather than between-house perspectives on these conflicts. Project Socrates, the government agency designed to assess the global balance of technology power and share that intelligence with policymakers and private industry, must be revived and made part of the CIA. Geoeconomic intelligence must be considered as vital to national security as geopolitical intelligence.

The creation of DITI and reform of the Japan policy and intelligence communities will give the White House a centralized international economic policy making and intelligence capacity roughly equal to Japan's Ministry of International Trade and Industry (MITI). But if the reforms end here, the United States will still have severe handicaps in its economic rivalry with Japan. The US Export–Import Bank (Eximbank) can be a powerful tool for promoting American exports and deterring unfair export subsidies by foreign competitors. The Eximbank provides direct loans, loan guarantees, insurance of repayment, and a discount facility for export loans held by private banks to American exporters. It should be endowed with sufficient resources to match below market terms offered by foreign governments to their exporters. The Eximbank is not a budgetary cost to the United States and has, in fact, been a net earner of revenues.[16] About two-thirds of total US exports financed by the bank represent sales that might not otherwise have been made.[17]

In 1980, total US exports topped $220 billion. Yet, according to the Commerce Department, only 200 firms supplied 75 per cent of these exports. The rest were supplied by 20 000 firms, mostly small and medium sized. It is estimated that another 20–25 000 medium and small firms could be exporting but are not. An important goal of American international economic policy must be to get those potential exporters to actually begin exporting. This would be a major boost to the domestic economy. The Domestic International Sales Corporations (DISC) is designed to encourage exports by deferring indefinitely increased export sales over the previous year. More than 14 000 firms had created DISCs in 1981. It is estimated that in 1979 American exports were between $4.5 and $7 billion higher than they would have been without DISC. In addition, DISC is estimated to actually return $1.24 to the treasury for every dollar of tax incentive given.[18] DISC's funding should be vastly increased and its services extended to all potential exporters.

No large Japanese style trading companies exist in the US. Instead small and medium sized American firms who cannot afford to have their own international trade department have recourse to over 3800 export management firms (EMFs). More than 90 per cent of EMFs employ less than five people and limit their lines to specialized products or geographical areas. While Japanese trading companies have debt equity ratios of 10–1 or 20–1, American EMFs are confined to a 6–1 leverage.[19] A major reason for this is the 1934 Glass–Steagal Act that outlawed co-operative arrangements among banks, manufacturers, and traders. The Glass–

Steagal Act should be replaced with a new law allowing banks to invest in one or more trading companies up to an amount equal to 5 per cent of the bank's capital. Another major trade promotion effort could involve advertizing the provisions of the Webb-Pomerene Act of 1918, which allows American firms to form export cartels as long as they do not restrain domestic competition. The Act should be extended to include such service industries as accounting, banking, insurance, air transport, management consulting, construction, engineering, and architectural activities. Another reform should be targeted against tax laws that discourage trade. For example, price cutting by American exporters to capture market share is viewed as an attempt to displace income to a different tax jurisdiction. There should be a major overhaul of corporate tax codes to remove all disincentives to exports. The United States is currently the only country which makes it illegal to give "presents" to foreigners to promote business deals, denying the reality that in many areas of the world local customs dictate making "presents" to brokers and agents. The repeal of the 1977 Corrupt Practices Act would remove a major disincentive to American overseas investment and trade. These actions all represent major steps in increasing American trade and prosperity.

Likewise, the anti-trust laws need to be completely rewritten to strengthen American industry within the United States. The anti-trust legislation enacted at the turn of the century was an important promoter of domestic competition when the American market was relatively isolated from the world and few multinational corporations existed. But today, antitrust regulations are a severe handicap for American business, and actually contribute to the trade deficit. For example, GM can legally form a joint venture with Toyota, the world's largest automobile firm, but is barred from any co-operative arrangement with another American automobile firm. The laws should be rewritten to allow more co-operation between American companies, particularly if their foreign rivals enjoy similar arrangements. The Antitrust Division could be converted from a prosecutorial body under the Justice Department into a regulatory agency under DITI with the power to issue legally binding decisions. Under the new arrangements firms would file complaints rather than suits, thus avoiding the great time and expense of trials. The DITI Antitrust division should take international competition into account when determining if a monopoly situation exists.

Pat Choate in the conclusion to his book, *Agents of Influence*, advocates a range of policies to reform the current revolving door system whereby former and sometimes current administration officials can serve foreign interests. He advocates permanently prohibiting all ranking White House officials such as the USTR, Director of Intelligence, and Secretary of State from becoming a foreign agent or lobbyist for domestic companies while instituting a longer period of five to ten years before lower ranking officials could go through the revolving door. Choate argues that "those who refuse to serve in government because of such a limitation certainly are not the kind needed to tend the public's affairs".[20] Choate also advocates such additional reforms as requiring the full disclosure of all those who represent foreign countries, forbidding any foreign participation, including American subsidiaries of foreign firm, in any American election, providing public funding for the full costs of presidential libraries so the former presidents do not have to go begging to foreign countries for the funds, and prohibiting foreign gifts or compensation to ex-presidents.

These policymaking reforms must be matched by policy reforms. Irrational macro-economic and industrial policies largely account for America's relative economic decline. Rational macro-economic and industrial policies should: (1) promote a high savings/investment cycle; (2) achieve a dollar-yen exchange rate in which there is a trade and payments balance between the United States and Japan; and (3) target strategic industries and technologies for global leadership.

The high dollar policy has continually undercut America's economy and promoted foreign exporters. Before 1971, the dollar's value was fixed, and Washington failed to readjust its value as America's economy steadily weakened and its rivals correspondingly strengthened. Even after Nixon devalued the dollar in 1971 and abandoned the fixed for a floating currency system in 1973, the dollar remained overvalued, and a drag on America's economy and subsidy for foreign producers. In the 1980s, the Reagan administration grossly overvalued the dollar through its spend and borrow policies. Unable to finance its deficits through domestic savings, the White House raised interest rates to attract foreign capital, an action which simultaneously slowed economic growth and boosted the dollar's value as demand for the currency grew. The result of these inept policies was America's trade deficit with Japan deepening dramatically from $8 billion in 1980 to $59 billion in 1987.

A rational policy would be based on the dollar's devaluation until a trade and payments balance, overall and with Japan, is achieved. The benefits of a devalued dollar are immense while the costs are insignificant. According to Krugman, although a 30 per cent reduction in the dollar against the yen theoretically means that American wages fall 30 per cent relative to Japanese wages, "it is not the same as saying that US wages fall by 30 percent: They probably fall by no more than 1.5 per cent. Why? Because even now most of the goods and services we consume are made at home, and a fairly large part of our imports tend to be priced in dollars, too".[21] A trade balance can only be achieved after the dollar declines by an average 20 per cent against other leading currencies, and perhaps as much as 40–50 per cent against the yen.

Washington's high dollar policy is only the most obvious irrational macroeconomic policy. America's low savings/investment ratio is another important reason for the wretched economic growth. Easy credit, taxes on savings, and other policies encourage consumption over savings. America's savings rate has consistently been three to four times lower than Japan's. The lower the savings rate, the higher the interest rates and thus the lower the investment rate and economic growth. If demand for savings exceeds the domestic supply, then investors must borrow from foreign sources. A rational policy would tax consumption and reward savings through tax reductions, thus allowing for more savings, lower interest rates, less dependence on foreign capital, a lower dollar and higher economic growth.

America's vast debt remains an enormous drag on the economy. To reduce the national debt the government must spend less and tax more while the country must import less and export more. But the best way to pay back the national debt is to run continual trade and payments surpluses for the indefinite future, which could only be achieved if the White House abandoned liberal and adopted neomercantilist policies. Balanced annual government budget and international payments will lower interest rates and thus boost growth. Annual budget and payments surpluses will lower interest rates and raise national wealth even further.

But America's economic revival cannot depend on rational macroeconomic policies alone. The United States must target and develop strategic industries as systematically as does Japan. Reich and Magaziner state bluntly that America's relative economic decline cannot begin to be addressed without "a coherent and coordinated industrial policy whose aim is to raise the real income of our citizens by improving the pattern of our investments . . . Our country's real income can rise only if (1) its labor and capital increasingly flow toward businesses that add greater value per employee and (2) we maintain a position in these businesses that is superior to that of our international competitors . . . Without government support, American business will find it increasingly difficult to achieve competitive leadership in today's international environment . . . The competitive strength of the economy . . . requires a coherent set of public policies for improving competitive productivity in industry".[22] In addition, only government can make the immense investments in industrial infrastructure and basic research which are beyond the financial means of even the largest consortia, let alone individual firms.

Despite its importance, the concept of an "industrial policy" has only recently received much public attention. Chalmers Johnson provides some concise definitions of industrial policy:

a summary term for the activities of government that are intended to develop or retrench various industries in a national economy in order to maintain global competitiveness . . . it is first of all an attitude, and only then a matter of technique. It involves the realization that all government measures . . . have a significant impact on the well being or ill-health of whole sectors, industries, and enterprises in a marketing economy . . . changes of industrial structure are only poorly accomplished through the market mechanism. The workings of the market are commonly preempted by political action. Rather than leaving such political interventions solely to pressure groups and other well organized interests, industrial policy seeks to solve problems before they arise . . . It can mean anything from economic warfare to the ad hoc consequences of government regulatory decisions.[23]

The United States must abandon its existing ad hoc, inconsistent, often contradictory industrial policy, and must instead establish a rational industrial policy that identifies, nurtures, and promotes strategic future growth industries. There are severe obstacles to the rejection of America's politically shaped industrial policies in favor of those which target strategic industries for development. America's industrial policy debate is characterized as "more ideological than pragmatic, framed in terms of the ideal relationship between governments and markets rather than in terms of the hard realities of international competition".[24]

Although free trade ideologists deny it, the United States has had policies which favor some industries over others since the beginning of its history. The trouble is, as William Diebold points out, that American industrial policies have rarely been rational in promoting growth industries of the future, but have instead tended to be "political" props to declining industries.[25] These industrial policies largely fail because they are products of an irrational policymaking system and the free trade ideology that guides it. American industrial policies have been described as "irrational and unco-ordinated . . . comprised of 'voluntary' restrictions on imports, occasional bailouts of for major companies near bankruptcy, small sums spent for job training and relocation, a huge and growing program of defense procurement and defense-related research, and a wide array of subsidies, loan guarantees, and special tax benefits for particular firms or industries. It is an industrial policy by default".[26] The discrepancy between American free market ideals and realities is often vast: Washington "has clung tenaciously to the notion that government can and should be 'neutral' with regard to market adjustments. The vast array of US tariffs, quotas, 'voluntary' export agreements, and bail-outs for declining businesses are viewed as isolated exceptions to this rule of neutrality; its defense related expenditures, tax breaks, and assorted subsidies for other industries are seen as somehow unrelated to industrial development or to market dynamics. Consequently, the US has neither neutrality nor rationality".[27] When Washington protects an industry, it never makes that protection contingent on that industry's restructuring. The Reagan Administration's record on industrial policy was decidedly schizophrenic. On one hand, the Reagan White House continually lauded the "magic of the market place" and dismissed industrial policies with the false argument that government cannot pick winners and losers. But the Reagan Administration applied a number of Band Aids to some of the more pressing of countless wounded American industries, including automobiles and semiconductors. The Bush Administration has been more consistent–in both rhetoric and deed, it rejects any attempts to reform America's irrational, politically-shaped, industrial policy system.

An important aspect of rational industrial policies are rational trade and investment policies which should: (1) be based on reciprocal opportunities for American corporations overseas; (2) negotiate the opening of foreign product and investment markets from strength – in other words, threatening the restriction of access by that country's firms unless it agrees to reciprocity; (3) link all bilateral economic, military, and political issues to reciprocity; (4) ensure full disclosure of all foreign assets in the United States; (5) identify strategic American industries and firms which are off limits to foreign ownership.

The President already has the power to implement virtually all of these goals. Article 1, section 8 of the Constitution specifically empowers Congress to "regulate commerce with foreign nations". Prior to 1934, Congress did take the lead in forming international economic policy. But since then there has been a transition period when control over international economic policy was delegated to the executive branch. A series of trade acts (1964, 1974, 1984 and 1988) have completed this transfer of trade policy from Congress to the President. Each act enhanced the executive branch's power to retaliate against unfair foreign trade practices, and thus strengthen world trade. The President's responsibilities are identified by Section 301 of the 1974 Act which authorizes the President to retaliate against "unjustifiable, unreasonable, or discriminatory acts of foreign governments that burden or restrict US commerce, including "dumping" and export subsidies. Retaliation includes the ability to impose import restrictions for a maximum of five years, to phased out beginning with the third year. These import restrictions can be renewed for one three year period if necessary. The Trade Act of 1984 gives the President the additional power to initiate actions while trade distorting foreign government practices are in place, but before injury to US firms has occurred. Retaliation may include the form of curtailing previous trade concessions, imposing import duties, and otherwise restricting imports, or, conceivably providing countervailing domestic subsidies. Frustrated with President Reagan's failure to adequately respond to repeated Japanese trade offensives, Congress enacted the 1988 Trade Act to transfer the power to retaliate from the White House to the United States Trade Representative, and make retaliation mandatory in some cases. Although the Reagan Administration originally vetoed the bill based on the charge of neoclassical economists that it was protectionist, it eventually gave into the overwhelming support from big business and others for the bill and signed a revised version in September 1988. Under the new law, the administration would be required to negotiate with any country that consistently launches export offensives against American producers while continuing to close off its own markets. If negotiations fail to stop the foreign trade offensives and barriers, the Trade Representative is legally forced to retaliate. The President, however, is allowed to waive retaliation on grounds of national security. What is lacking is a President with an understanding of America's economic decline and the will to reverse it.

With the Cold War over and the economic war at a fever pitch, the United States must drastically overhaul its technology policies. The development and funding emphasis must shift from arcane military weapons to cutting edge technologies of tomorrow that can be applied to mass consumer goods. Also important are policies designed to prevent the foreign pirating of American technology, which was estimated to have cost the United States 750 000 jobs in 1987 and $60 billion in exports.[28]

There are plenty of proposals for reforming the technology policy-making system and policies, but they are sidelined or distorted by the system itself. Bobby Inmann and Daniel Burton, members of the Executive Committee of the Council on Competitiveness decry "the absence of government institutions capable of dealing with complex technological issues that have both commercial and military implications and that cut across several industries".[29] They call on the government to target four areas for development: (1) strengthening America's manufacturing base; (2) improving the technology policymaking process; (3) rebuilding the nation's technological infrastructure; and (4) encouraging greater R&D efforts. Several important bills which could implement parts of Inman and Burton's proposals are tied up in Congress, including Senator Albert Gore's bill which would provide $1.75 billion for the development of advanced computers, software, and networks, Representative Mel Levine's bill that would establish a Technology Corporation of America, which would aid joint technology ventures with $50 million annually, Senator John Glenn's bill allocating $100 million annually for an applied research program called the Advanced Civilian Technology Agency. Other proposals include expanding financing of the Advanced Technology Program, currently receiving $10 million annually or setting up an Electronics Capital Corporation funded with $5–10 billion to aid microelectronics research. The House Democrat High Technology policy offers a sweeping reform package. The policy includes increased funding of $400 million over the next three years for the Commerce Department's Advanced Technology Program which provides matching grants to firms or joint ventures trying to commercialize technologies, and an additional $80 million to the Pentagon to develop dual use technologies. It remains to be seen whether these policies will become law or remain some of countless important but neglected proposals for reviving American power.

Washington's macro-economic, industrial, trade, investment and technology policies have an enormous impact on the decisions reached in America's corporate boardrooms. A low dollar and interest rate obviously give businesses an opportunity to expand just as a high dollar and interest rate penalizes American business. Irrational industrial policies help the squeaky wheels with political clout in Congress while diverting resources from strategic industries; rational industrial policies on the other hand directly help the targeted industries, and indirectly aid all American business by accelerating economic growth, tax receipts and lowering interest rates.

Although the government can help or hinder business, ultimately, American businesses are responsible for their own survival. Each corporation or firm has its own strengths and weaknesses, yet share many characteristics. American firms are often hobbled rather than helped by the free market system. Money, or its high cost and limited supply, is the most important reason behind the difficulties so many American firms have in competing with their Japanese and foreign rivals. The obsession with maintaining quarterly profits straitjackets America's corporations as they use creative bookkeeping rather than build better and cheaper products to maintain profits. Likewise, when bashed by a foreign dumping attack, American corporations maintain prices and sacrifice market share just to keep up short-term profits, even though this strategy's long-term result is financial ruin. But the short-term emphasis simply reflects a free market economy. If America's firms were protected by webs of cartels, import barriers, technology infusions, and export incentives like their Japanese counterparts, they could take an equally long-term investment and market perspective.

America's vast open market spoils domestic corporations. It is too easy to sell at home and concede foreign markets, particularly Japan's 120 million protected market. But this strategy is ultimately self-defeating if that firm is targeted for destruction by a foreign dumping attack. American firms are criticized for moving their manufacturing operations to countries with cheap labor, thus weakening America's economy. But this practice is encouraged by America's high dollar policy. American technology sell-offs are also severely criticized. But again, if American corporations were allowed to form technology cartels like their Japanese counterparts, they would gain far better deals when they do sell technology, and limit what they sell. In the existing free market system, foreign governments following neomercantilist policies can play off one American firm against the others, and thus take technology on easy terms. Finally, while Japan's corporations strive to achieve "zero defects" quality standards, American producers maintain a "acceptable quality level" quality standards. Again, the contrast is between a short- and long-term outlook. Although the zero defects strategy is more costly in the short-run, it saves money in the long-term. A complete reform of Washington's economic policymaking system and policies will provide a level playing field for American corporations to succeed or fail on their own merits rather than fall victim to Japanese neomercantilism.

AMERICAN POLICY TOWARD JAPAN

Ronald Reagan frequently used to remind his listeners that the "Soviets aren't ten feet high". In other words, Washington should not cower indecisively before the Soviet threat – tough, unyielding policies would eventually cause the Soviet empire and communism to crumble. Forty-five years of a sustained American commitment to containment combined with communism's vast economic, social, and political failures and Gorbachev's sweeping policies resulted in the Soviet system's rapid destruction.

The collapse of the Soviet geopolitical threat was inevitable given America's containment policies and communism's deep flaws. Japan's geoeconomic threat to the United States may be far more difficult to contain, let alone overcome. The United States always enjoyed military and ideological superiority over the Soviet Union. Japan, however, is rapidly leapfrogging the United States financially, technologically, and productively, and unless Washington drastically revises its outlook and policies, Japan's vast political economic power and America's subsequent dependence will continually deepen. Yet, despite Japan's increasing lead, American policymakers and the public should start reminding themselves that the Japanese are not ten feet tall. Japan is still vulnerable in many areas and Washington can exploit those vulnerabilities to chip away at Japan's lead.

But what then should be America's policy toward Japan? No one doubts the bilateral relation's importance. It can be said without exaggeration, as former ambassador to Tokyo, Mike Mansfield frequently does, that the "bilateral relationship between the United States and Japan is the most important in the world, bar none". Seizaburo Sato, a leading LDP advisor, asserts that "divorce in the Japanese–American alliance would be economically impossible, militarily impractible, and politically unthinkable, in this century anyway but for the incipient 21st century, as well".[30] The two countries' combined GNP is over one-third of global GNP and their continued trade and economic expansion is vital for the world economy's prosperity. Nothing should be done to jeopardize this relationship. Instead both countries must work hard to strengthen their bilateral ties and joint responsibility for acting as engines of growth for the world economy.

But a healthy relationship between the United States and Japan must be an equally beneficial relationship. A lopsided relationship whereby one country benefits at the expense of the other threatens not just their bilateral ties but the prosperity of the entire world economy. Unfortunately, as America's continued trade deficits with Japan clearly reveal, the relationship is strongly skewed in favor of Tokyo. Japan is now the world's greatest financial power while the United States is the world's largest debtor nation. This rapid and startling shift in power occurred largely because Washington continued to allow Tokyo to dump its goods and finance in American markets while severely restricting the access of American goods and finance to Japanese markets. This was a rational policy in the 1950s when Japan was still a relatively weak economic power and needed to maintain trade barriers and export offensives to develop its economy. A politically stable and economically dynamic Japan was a vital pillar of Washington's interrelated policies of rebuilding the world economy and containing the Soviet Union.

But after the mid–1960s when Japan began to continually run larger annual trade surpluses, Washington should have insisted that Tokyo immediately allow foreign firms the same benefits in Japan that Japanese and other foreign firms enjoyed in the vast American market. It should have been clear by this time that Washington faced not one but two challenges – a military challenge from the Soviet Union and an economic challenge from Japan. While Washington had achieved a stable balance of power with Moscow, the economic balance of power was rapidly tilting in Tokyo's favor. Unfortunately, however, Washington policymakers continued to devote vast human, technological and financial resources to containing the Soviet Union while neglecting to counter Japan's growing economic threat. The Reagan Administration's huge military buildup and largely free market policies were responsible for tipping the economic balance decisively in favor of Japan during the 1980s.

Washington has spent several decades sporadically trying to crack open Japan's markets and curb Japan's dumping attacks. Yet, many of the tactics Washington has used against Japanese neomercantilism have been dismal failures. The United States suffers from the "little boy who cried wolf" syndrome. Washington has repeatedly warned of retaliation against Japanese neomercantilism but has rarely taken any meaningful action. In virtually every negotiation with the Japanese, the Americans commit the equivalent of geoeconomic disarmament. The powerful retaliatory weapons at the President's disposal continue to rust away inside the scabbard. As a result, Tokyo continues to pursue neomercantilist policies that enrich Japan at America's expense, secure in the knowledge that, despite all its bluster, Washington will continue meekly to turn the other cheek.

Another failed tactic is Washington's "good cop/bad cop" routine, which often makes Americans appear like a bunch of Keystone cops. Both the Reagan and Bush Administrations used the threat of Congressional initiatives to extract concessions from Tokyo. The trouble was that the White House unquestionably accepted largely symbolic "concessions" in return for promoting the Japanese position against that of Congress. If the White House would abandon this "good cop/bad cop" routine and instead work carefully with Congress to create and implement a rational policy toward Japan, it would serve rather than undermine American geoeconomic interests.

It is not clear whether the Bush Administration really believed that the Structural Impediments Initiatives (SII) talks of 1990–91 "would really make Japan more like us" or cynically used the negotiations as a smokescreen to deflate Congressional pressure for substantial retaliation against Japanese neomercantilism. SII consumed the time, energy, and efforts of America's trade team for over a year. The Japanese as always promised liberalization; as always no substantial changes occurred.

The naïveté of the White House's strategy in SII of serving as the Japanese consumer's "liberator" provokes a mixture of tears and laugher. Japanese producers, not consumers, shape Japan's industrial and trade policies. Japanese consumers are fatalistic about high prices and lack of choice, and fiercely nationalistic and anti-American, attitudes which both reflect and enhance their powerlessness. Washington's meddling simply further enflames the ferocity of their nationalism and anti-Americanism. Naoichi Takeuchi, President of the Consumer Union of Japan, dismissed Washington's "liberation" efforts, pointing out that the "US government seems to think the Japanese people will rush to buy goods, especially imported goods, if they are only cheaper".[31] According to liberal economic theory, people consume more when prices are cheaper. But Japan is different. Neomercantilism, not liberalism, is intricately interwoven throughout Japan's institutions and psychology. Japanese willingly sacrifice their individual interests, including the interest in enjoying as many products as possible for the cheapest prices possible, for a stronger, wealthier Japan. At least one third of consumer groups are simply front organizations for Japanese industries. Japanese neomercantilism will never be blunted much less transformed as long as head-in-the-clouds neoclassical economists rather than hardnosed political economists with a in-depth understanding of Japan shape policy. Washington should be playing to the ministries rather than the mass public. Johnson writes that American "pressure on Japan was never decisive unless it happended to coincide with the interests of a major domestic player, in which case it could be quite effective".[32]

Of all its Quixotic policies, Washington's efforts to force open Japan's rice markets are the most misguided. Farm interests are so deeply entrenched that nothing short of a revolution (a rather unlikely prospect) could uproot them. Even if Japan's rice markets were completely open (an impossible dream), and American and other foreign producers dominated, the bilateral trade deficit would be reduced by only several billion dollars. Washington's demands that Tokyo open its rice markets are completely futile and divert attention from infinitely more important sectors and problems as well as fuel the flames of Japanese nationalism.

Tokyo repeatedly claims that continued protection of its rice industry is essential for Japan's national security, culture, and LDP rule – which are often seen as synonyomous. Washington should wholeheartedly agree. "Fine", America's negotiators should reply, "You are completely right. Some industries are essential for a nation's security, and thus should be protected by whatever means considered necessary. Globally competitive automobile, computer, semiconductor, machine tool industries – to name a few – are essential for American national security, and as such, Japan's penetration of those markets will be limited to the same percentage that those American industries penetrate Japanese markets. In other words, if American semiconductor manufacturers capture only 11 per cent of Japan's markets, that is roughly how much Japanese manufacturers will be allowed in the United States, after account has been taken of differences in market size and volume."

Balance must be restored to America's policy and its relations with Japan. In Fukushima's words, "a new Japan policy should be based on a pragmatic and realistic mix of philosophies that acknowledges where US–Japan interests converge and where they diverge. It should recognize economic and technological strength as vital to national security. And it should understand fully the strategic linkage between trade, investment, technology, and financial power".[33] Prestowitz maintains that "we must develop a new structure based on comprehensive guidelines that cover the whole relationship – military, political and economic".[34]

The first step in achieving a balanced, rational policy toward Japan is to completely reform the Japan policy network. Glenn Fukushima, a former USTR official, writes that "even before US trade negotiators sit down with their Japanese counterparts, interagency squabbles reduce the US negotiating position to the lowest common denominator. The trade agencies are hobbled by the diplomats, who attach primary importance to the US–Japan military security relationship, and by the pure economists, who insist that economic matters be left entirely to the "market".[35] The appeasers' domination of American policy toward Japan is not total. Articulate, intelligent, uncorrupted realists like Clyde Prestowitz, Glenn Fukushima, and Kevin Kearns struggled hard when in government to serve American interests and give disturbing insider accounts of the bankruptcy of the administration's policy making process and policies. What can be done to break the appeasers' grip on policy? DITI's creation will tip the balance of power from the appeasers to the realists, but the realists' influence should be reinforced by implementing the proposal of Kevin Kearns, a State Department maverick, that a special "B–Team" of revisionist Japan experts be formed to counter the current dominance of Japan apologists (the "Chrysanthemum club"). The B–team can work with DITI to shape rational policies toward Japan.[36]

Just what specific objectives should govern America's policy toward Japan? How can Washington achieve these objectives? The primary goal of American policy toward Japan should be the achievement of a trade, payments and manufacturing import balance. How can the United States achieve trade reciprocity with Japan?

Washington will never convince Tokyo to abandon the neomercantilist policies that have brought Japan such wealth and power. The product by product approach to prying open Japan's markets has had no significant effect on the trade deficit, and only increases frustrations on both sides. Despite an almost 50 per cent drop in the dollar's value over the past two years, American's 1990 trade deficit with Japan was $42 billion dollars. The only solution to the persistent trade deficit with Japan is for the White House to simply announce that the situation has become intolerable and that if Tokyo does not reduce the deficit by $10 billion a year for the next four years until it is balanced the United States will retaliate with tariffs and quotas on finished Japanese products until there is a trade balance. This can be accomplished by Japan either restraining exports, buying more imports, or a combination of the two, but the burden will thus fall on Tokyo to arm-twist industry into buying American products. Tokyo could quickly reduce its trade surpluses if it were sincerely interested in doing so. An export tariff would cut down the comparative advantage for most Japanese products. The revenue could be invested in such desperately needed quality of life infrastructure for the Japanese people as parks, and better sewage, and housing.

Once Japan agrees to the deficit timetable, the two countries must work together to reduce the deficit. The most important way the deficit can be reduced is through a steady strengthening of the Japanese yen. Although the yen has already risen almost 50 per cent in value against the dollar since September 1985 when the Group of Five countries began an active intervention, and is currently hovering at around 135 yen to the dollar, the trade deficit has barely been touched. Washington and Tokyo should agree on a timetable whereby the yen strengthens 12 yen a year for three years until it rises to between 100 and 90 yen to the dollar. This slow, steady appreciation each year will enable Japanese industry to adapt without major disruptions of the Japanese economy, and will give Japanese producers an economic rationale for buying American components and Japanese consumers a rationale to demand American finished goods.

The stronger the yen becomes, the stronger the comparative advantage of American goods in both domestic and foreign markets. It is estimated that there is a $3 billion decrease in the trade deficit for every 1 per cent devaluation of the dollar.[37] But a strong yen benefits Japan as well. The stronger the yen becomes, the smaller the percentage of exports necessary to finance essential imports. As Japan's industrial structure increasingly shifts into a high technology service economy, the need for massive imports of raw materials and energy will decline further. Washington should emphasize, however, that American products not assets are for sale. Temporary restrictions on Japanese purchases of American corporations should be imposed to prevent Japanese corporations from using their immense reserves of strong yen to buy up strategic firms at bargain basement prices as they have in the past. Washington would, however, encourage Japanese purchases of American property such as land and buildings to free up more American capital for hopefully more productive investments.

Tokyo will not easily agree to a trade balance and yen revaluation. Japanese only respect strength and will only yield if faced with overwhelming odds, and even then only after a long hard struggle. The Achilles heel of Japanese power is the vulnerability of its trade and investments in the United States. Japan's corporations sell over 45 per cent of its exports and 70 per cent of their overall trade surplus to the United States while American firms sell only 22 per cent of their exports to Japan. Forty-five per cent of Japan's direct foreign investments are in the United States, and Japan's combined direct and portfolio investments in the United States are twenty times those of America's in Japan. Japan's ratio of exports to GNP is 18 per cent, compared to about 12 per cent for the United States. Since Japan sends about twice as many billions of dollars worth of goods to the United States than it receives, it is extremely vulnerable to American retaliation.

If Washington simply announced that it would impose 100 per cent tariffs on Japanese products unless the trade deficit annually declines by $10 billion until there is a balance, Tokyo would have no choice but to comply. If Tokyo threatened to counter by withdrawing its assets, Washington could simply freeze them. Tariffs on unfinished goods should not be imposed because many American manufacturers are dependent on Japanese components. A higher price on these components would force

American manufacturers to raise their prices and thus make their products less competitive both at home and abroad. The tariffs would remain until the deficit reduction target is reached. It would be Tokyo's choice whether to reduce the deficit by increasing imports of American goods, decreasing Japanese exports to the United States, or some combination. Past strategies dealing with specific barriers and products, or structural barriers like the keiretsu and distribution systems fail to achieve any significant liberalization of Japan's markets.

A results oriented strategy backed by the clear capacity and will to retaliate would cut the Gordian knot of Japan's web of trade barriers with one decisive blow. Such a straight forward retaliation against Tokyo's neomercantilism would certainly cause very loud wailing and gnashing of teeth in Japan, but the clamor would not be much greater than the response to Washington's past, largely inept attempts to pry open Japanese markets. America's economy would greatly benefit from the tens of billion of dollars of increased sales at home, in Japan, and elsewhere which would set off a virtuous cycle of increased jobs, profits and tax revenues which would further economic growth. Meanwhile Japan's consumers would experience windfall savings that previously had accrued to its corporations.

The White House has a range of legal provisions to back up its threat to retaliate against Japanese neomercantilism. Super 301 works! Tokyo bitterly condemns Super 301 as unfairly making Washington the prosecutor, judge, and jury of trade disputes, and claims it will never negotiate under its rubric. Yet, armed with Super 301, Washington can bring Tokyo to the negotiating table. For example, Tokyo agreed to take up the amorphous metals conflict just a few days before the 30 April 1990 deadline for the designation of unfair traders and conceded in opening more construction projects on 30 May 1991, the eve of a threatened White House retaliation. The Foreign Ministry's chief spokesman, Taizo Watanable, understatedly admits that the "unfair trader" label "is rather embarrassing to us", and forces Tokyo to make concessions and negotiate specific sectors.[38] Super 301 exposes as a fraud Tokyo's careful public relations campaigns built on the image that Japan's economy is the world's most open and that foreign firms do not sell or invest more because they do not try hard enough.

Why are Japanese manufacturers such effective exporters? High quality products are important, but protected home markets, "laser beam" trade tactics, and artificially cheap capital infused into strategic industries are the most important reasons. Japanese exporters concentrate on one sector in the lower end of a foreign market and through price cuts try to destroy the opposition. After capturing a dominant market share in that product (e.g. small cars, semiconductors) the Japanese concentrate on the next product within the industry, and then advance up the product scale until they dominate the entire industry. After achieving a predominant market share, Japanese firms raise prices to recoup losses sustained from the original dumping offensives.

Because of the vast scale and openness of the American market, the United States generally bears the brunt of these offensives. After achieving a dominant market share in the American market and, subsequent economies of scale, the Japanese firms then turn to other world markets. The first anti-American postwar Japanese export offensive took place in the 1950s and was directed against America's textile market. In the past 30 years, subsequent offensives have occurred in a wide range of products including televisions, steel, automobiles, VCRs and semiconductors. Soon, as Japan's next generation of targeted industries begins to emerge, Japanese industries such as supercomputers, biotechnology, new materials, industrial ceramics, robotics, microelectronics, and optical fibers will assault their American rivals.

Washington's reaction to Japanese export offensives is generally ineffective and delayed. Most Japanese dumping is unhindered, but occasionally, if the targeted industry has enough political clout Washington will negotiate "voluntary export quotas" with Tokyo. This usually only occurs long after Japanese firms have already captured huge market shares. Quotas are eagerly sought after by the Japanese because they allow Japanese producers a secure market share after which prices can be raised to recoup the short-term losses incurred from dumping. For example, Tokyo's quota on automobile imports to the United States allowed windfall profits of $2.2 billion to Japanese firms and only $2.6 billion to American firms. Meanwhile, American consumers had to pay an additional $4.8 billion for new automobiles.[39]

Instead of quotas, Washington should use tariffs to retaliate against foreign dumping and other unfair trade practices. With tariffs both American business and government benefit. In the automobile example, the $2.2 billion that went to Japanese producers could have flowed into a special government budget which assists American producers. A "tariff trigger system" that automatically imposes a 20 per cent tariff when producers from any one foreign country increase their market share more than 10 per cent in one year would discourage the dumping that is now encouraged by the widespread use of quotas.

It is much more difficult to open Japan's markets than to deter Japanese dumping. Japan's markets have been going through a series of "liberalization" phases since Japan joined the OECD in 1964. Throughout the 1980s, Tokyo made ten "significant market opening steps", after each of which it was proclaimed that Japan's markets were now the world's most open and foreign producers did not sell more because they did not try hard enough and their goods were inferior. Market liberalization was theoretically enhanced by the yen's doubling in value after the September 1985 Plaza Accord where the Group of Five industrial giants – the United States, Japan, Germany, France, and Britain – agreed to devalue the dollar. Most Japanese will echo former Prime Minister Suzuki's stance that, "our market in Japan is as open as American or European markets", or Sony Chairman Akio Morita, "I believe Japan's market is very easy for foreign countries to enter. I cannot understand why this wonderful market is left untouched. I believe that foreign industry should be more serious and make a real effort to sell in Japan".[40] It argues that Japan's economic power and America's decline are simply the result of Japan's ability to master the "four fundamentals – outsave and outinvest, outwork, out-manage, and outstudy".[41]

Tokyo's proclaimed goals of liberalizing and internationalizing Japan seemed to make considerable progress during the late 1980s. Japan's trade and payments surpluses peaked at $101 billion and $87 billion, respectively, in 1987, then fell rapidly to $35.8 billion and $63.8 billion, respectively, in 1990. Alas, as so many observers have remarked, in Japan things are seldom as they seem. The yen's doubling in value accounted for much of the surpluses' decline. A flood of Japanese overseas investments and tourists exploiting the strong yen were the most important reasons for payment surpluses' reduction. Although Japanese aid surpassed that of the United States to reach $10 billion in 1990, its yen value represented a less significant rise, but still helped nudge down the payments surplus. Japanese imports did increase, although they did not necessarily represent significant sales increases for foreign producers. Much of the imports came from Japan's overseas investments. Likewise, Japan's exports are not rising as rapidly in part because they were partly replaced by sales from those Japanese overseas factories. For example, about half of the 2.6 million Japanese vehicles sold in the United States flow from Japanese factories in the United States. A 35 per cent increase in oil prices in the second half of 1990 accounted for much of Japan's trade surplus decline. With oil prices back to their pre-invasion of Kuwait levels, Japan's trade surplus will rise again. Meanwhile, Japan's much vaunted internationalization and the yen's doubling in value between 1985 and 1987 did not translate as promised into a better life for Japan's much abused consumers. Distributors enjoyed windfall profits. Nor has the quality of life improved for most Japanese. Schools, parks, housing, sewage, and other public infrastructure remain woefully inadequate by OECD standards. As always, the oceans of cash have simply been reinvested in further developing Japan's industrial superpower.

From a strictly neoclassical economic point of view, Japan's markets are among the world's most open; Japanese tariffs are now the lowest of any industrial country, and the number of quotas are comparable to most other OECD countries. It is the bewildering, Kafquesque maze of non tariff barriers (NTBs) which foreign producers must overcome that makes Japan's markets the most carefully regulated and closed of any industrial country. These NTBs include both direct government policies and broader political economic barriers that are indirectly influenced by government policy. These include the various forms of "administrative guidance" whereby bureaucrats use such extra-legal methods as sponsorship of cartels in weak industries (there are currently about 500 legal cartels and hundreds of others winked at by officials), arbitrary foreign product testing and approval, "buy Japan" procurement policies, a range of government subsidies, grants, and cheap loans to industry, weak anti-trust and patent protection laws, laws that encourage an inefficient distribution system that discriminates against foreign products, and the industrial groups (keiretsu) which buy largely from other firms within the group, and negative consumer images of foreign mass consumer goods. Japan's market remains only open to foreign products in which Japanese firms already have a comparative advantage. Japan willfully, consistently, and outrageously violates GATT's rules on national treatment which maintains that once "imported goods have entered the internal stream of commerce, no government regulatory measure should assist the purchase of the domestic goods without likewise doing the same for imported goods". [42]

Washington has attempted to crack open these barriers for decades, with mostly disappointing results. Washington's policy to overcome these trade barriers must be realistic. It must abandon its goal of converting Japan to free market capitalism. For the last twenty years, Japan has repeatedly promised to open its markets and accept more international responsibilities. But to date most Japanese actions have been cosmetic – delaying actions while its firms continue to pile up massive profits at the expense of their foreign competitors. Japan remains highly protectionist and miserly in its contributions to the world economy and certainly will not voluntarily give this up based on Washington's idealistic appeals to free trade.

The White House should immediately adopt the recommendations of the February 1989 report of the Advisory Committee on Trade Policy and Negotiation (ACTPN), comprised of some of America's most experienced corporate leaders. The "blue ribbon" committee called for establishing sector-by-sector priorities with Japan and defining successful outcomes for each, using Super 301 to ensure Tokyo's compliance. [43] Although it refuses to admit it, the White House already manages trade in many industries. For example, on 11 March 1991, Washington and London reached an airlines agreement that both sides found mutually beneficial. The agree-

sense that they can survive without them and usually produce reasonably
good substitutes at home. They could just as well stop buying from
Japan".[46] Tokyo's agreement to increase its imports of manufactured
goods by 10 percentage points a year for the next three will overcome its
present discrimination. Again, the threat of retaliatory tariffs will force
Japan to comply.

Reciprocity must also extend to technology exchanges. Japan would
never have become an economic superpower if it had been denied
virtually unlimited access to America's state of the art technology at
bargain basement prices, before the 1980s largely through licensing and
since then often by directly buying out America's high techology firms. In
1990, Japan's direct foreign investments in the United States were valued
at $78 billion, more than ten times the $7 billion American investments in
Japan. Washington has failed to demand investment reciprocity in two
broad areas. Unable to sell or invest in Japan for a quarter century after
1945, American and other foreign corporations felt compelled to license or
sell their technology to their Japanese rivals. Although such sales boosted
American corporate earnings in the short run, the Japanese corporations
eventually used the technology to undermine their American rivals – a
development that would have never occurred if Washington had demanded American access to Japan's markets similar to what they enjoyed
in Europe. Another severe mistake was Washington's agreement to set up
joint production or development of aircraft rather than simply sell them
directly to the Japanese. These ventures gave away technology vital to
Japan's development of its own aerospace industry which will steadily eat
into America's lead.

Broad targets for the reduction of the trade deficit, strengthening of the
yen, and percentage of manufactured imports should be the basis of
Washington's trade policy toward Japan. These targets, and the threat
of retaliation if they are not reached, will finesse the traditional method
whereby American negotiators spin their wheels negotiating for years over
isolated sectors of Japan's economy. Washington will never get Tokyo to
reform the keiretsu system so that firms buy on the basis of price rather
than "*kone*" (relationships). There is no real alternative to the "*amakudari*"
system whereby bureaucrats retire into plush jobs in public and private
companies. Washington cannot alter bank control over companies that
prevents their foreign acquisition. The distribution system will remain a
bewildering maze. American companies may have to live with the cartel
arrangements of Japanese industries which agree on "proper" market
share and avoid "excess" competition. It will be difficult to break down
the discriminatory attitudes of Japanese consumers towards foreign
products. If Tokyo will not agree to base its economy on liberal rather
than neomercantilist principles, then Washington must negotiate with

Japan on the best way to manage bilateral trade so that it is based on reciprocal benefits while strengthening the world economy as a whole.

Any policies designed to reverse the unequal relationship between the United States and Japan must take into account the fact that Tokyo is America's military ally as well as its economic rival. Thus Washington must place its demands for trade reciprocity in the context of the common interests of both countries in promoting a continued expansion of the world economy and containment of Russia. Given its enormous economic power Japan should be considered an equal partner in contribution to both these goals. Reciprocity and the elimination of America's trade deficit with Japan should be viewed as the major but not the only means to these related ends. Until now Japan has enjoyed all the benefits of an expanding world economy while making largely symbolic contributions to maintaining the system; the burden of upholding continued world economic expansion remains on Washington's shoulders despite its own economic decline.

Thus, in addition to an elimination of the trade deficit, Washington must convince Tokyo to accept its economic superpower responsibility for supporting the global political economy. There must be reciprocity between Washington and Tokyo over the amount of GNP the two countries devote to defense and foreign aid. Washington currently spends 6.7 per cent (6.5 per cent military, 0.20 per cent aid) of its GNP while Tokyo spends only 1.30 per cent of its GNP (1.0 per cent military, 0.30 per cent aid) on its global responsibilities. Tokyo adamantly rejected Congress's October 1990 resolution that Japan should underwrite the entire cost of maintaining American forces, even though Japan continues to enjoy an annual $42 billion trade surplus. Japan did contribute $9 billion to the Persian Gulf alliance, but only after months of sustained pressure by Washington and the other allies who continually pointed out the reality that Japan depends on the Persian Gulf for 60 per cent of its oil needs.

Tokyo argues that for it to contribute more money for American forces based in Japan or in the Persian Gulf would be "inappropriate" because it would convert those troops into "mercenaries". Nothing could be further from the truth. Washington's acceptance of financial contributions from its allies would not alter American control over its own forces or its treaty obligations. The mercenary argument is simply a classic Japanese smokescreen device designed to hide the real issue – that Japan continues to enjoy a cheap defense ride despite the reality that it enjoys a persistent trade surpluses with the United States which was $42 billion in 1990, and is the world's most dynamic economic power.

Should Washington continue to tolerate a continued cheap if not free Japanese defense and aid ride? Given the Japanese government and public's resistance to any increased military force within Japan, let alone send even a token unit of troops to help defend its Gulf interests, just what defense obligations, if any, should Washington attempt to wring from Tokyo?

Washington must abandon the current "division of labor" whereby the United States plays global "cop" while Japan reaps continually greater economic expansion and profits. Any nation's financial contributions to the protection and development of the global political economy can be measured by determining the combined defense and aid budget as a percentage of GNP. Tokyo continually calls for an equal partnership while Congress demands reciprocity. Perhaps the time has come to create a full partnership with Tokyo. The two countries should agree to both devote 4 per cent of their respective GNPs to defense and foreign aid within five years. Each country could determine what mix of defense or aid they would allocate. Tokyo would have to abandon its neomercantilist policy of tying its aid to the recipient's purchase of Japanese products. All aid should be untied and distributed through multilateral organizations. Assuming Tokyo does not increase its defense spending to more than 1.5 per cent of GNP, it would take years for Japan to increase its aid budget from 0.30 to 2.0 per cent of GNP. A decade would be a reasonable period within which to expect Tokyo to fulfill its obligations. As long as Japan's financial contributions are untied to purchases of Japanese products, Tokyo should be given responsibilities in any international organizations equal to its contributions. In addition, Tokyo should follow Washington's lead and continually run trade deficits with developing countries while acting as an engine of growth during periods of world economic stagnation through expansionary fiscal policies. A massive, untied Japanese aid contribution, if carefully targeted and administered (always a questionable assumption), and complete dismantlement of Japanese trade barriers and a Japanese commitment to emulating the United States and European Community by running trade deficits with developing countries could prove a decisive boost to Third World development. Washington can reward Japan's compliance with these policies by extending a full partnership in helping lead the global political economy. Establishing a full partnership with Tokyo in resolving the world's deepening problems such as the debt crisis, greenhouse effect, and underdevelopment would at once ease America's enormous defense and aid burden and help divert Japan's attention from the phased reduction of its immense, persistent trade surplus with the United States.

How relevant is America's security treaty with Japan in the post Cold War world? The treaty would have allowed American forces to bottle up the Soviets inside the Japan Sea in the event of a war. But the war never occurred. Is it still in America's interests to maintain 63 000 troops in Japan to defend that country against a Soviet military threat which no longer exists – if it ever did? Should Washington continue annually to spend over \$5 billion underwriting the cost of its troop's presence in Japan and spend tens of billions of dollars and thousands of lives defending Japanese interests in the Gulf region when the bilateral trade deficit remains stuck at around \$40 billion, and Japan's per capita income is several thousand dollars higher than that of the United States while its growth rate is nearly three times higher?

The White House believes that the security treaty remains important despite the Cold War's end. On 23 February 1990, Defense Secretary Cheney said in Tokyo that without a continued massive American military presence in the Western Pacific "a vacuum would quickly develop (which would result) . . . in a series of destabilizing arms races and an increase in regional tension . . . We would want to be engaged in the Asia-Pacific region even if the Soviet Union were not".[47] According to Harrison and Prestowitz, the White House believes that Japan "will eventually dominate Asia militarily as well as economically unless the United States maintains countervailing power. China and Japan, it is argued, are likely to be rivals, and the United States should play a balancing role".[48] Harrison and Prestowitz, however, sharply reject the White House assessment: "The concept of a vacuum that has to be filled smacks of the colonial era and the "white man's burden" mentality. It reflects a lingering self-image of the United States as a world policeman . . . Cheney's assumption that 'regional arms races' would follow Soviet and American force reductions is open to question. In the case of China and Japan, many indications suggest that an economic partnership with aspects of a defense alliance is more likely than a military rivalry. In any event, it cannot be taken for granted that Japan would step up defense spending in direct proportion to Japan related US force reductions".[49]

Fears that an American pullback will spark a revival of Japanese militarism are completely unfounded. Tokyo encourages every Pacific Basin country, particularly the United States, to believe that latent Japanese militarism can only be placated by continued foreign toleration of Japan's neomercantilist policies and Washington's responsibility for Japan's defense. In reality, Japan's public remains adamantly opposed to any significant increase in the size or deployment of Japan's military. The public overwhelmingly rejected Prime Minister Kaifu's proposal in October 1990 to send a token force of 1000 unarmed Japanese troops to serve behind the lines in Saudi Arabia. It is inconceivable that, given Japan's alleged "nuclear allergy" and the united opposition of all Pacific Basin countries, that Tokyo would ever consider employing nuclear missiles. The security treaty has guaranteed Japan's military security at minimal cost and, even more importantly, helped divert Washington's attention from the increasingly severe impact of Tokyo's neomercantilist policies. Tokyo will continue to strongly resist both any suggestion of American troop reductions in Northeast or Southeast Asia and pressure for contributing more to the alliance.

Even if the impossible happened and Japanese public opinion magically changed from being overwhelmingly opposed to overwhelmingly in favor of creating a powerful conventional and nuclear military, just what would such a force be used for? Imperialism is obsolete. Interdependence allows states to gain infinitely more cheaply from trade those resources which were formerly the object of conquest. Even if Tokyo did want to embark on its old imperialist path, just where would the path begin? Unlike the power vacuum in East Asia during the 1930s which encouraged Japanese aggression, there is now a stable balance of power in the region. The world would respond to, say, a Japanese thrust into a chaotic Philippines with an economic embargo and military alliance that would devastate Japan. Given Japan's relatively small size with 45 per cent of its population concentrated on two per cent of its land area and 90 per cent in urban areas, any nuclear retaliation against the Japanese use of nuclear weapons would wipe out the Japanese people.

What should be done? Washington's Pacific rim defense strategy worked well during the Cold War. Soviet, Chinese, and North Korean ambitions were militarily contained and diplomatically played off against each other. Meanwhile, Japan, South Korea, and Taiwan were developed into the East Asian powerhouses of the Pacific Basin political economy. Yet the strategy was flawed by two American policies. Washington's departure from this deft containment strategy in Vietnam proved a tragic and costly disaster. Even more debilitating has been Washington's inability to creatively respond to the Japanese challenge. Washington continues to trade open American markets and closed Japanese markets for military bases in Japan. As recently as 1989 the direct and indirect costs of America's military commitment in the Far East was an estimated $42 billion.[50]

The simultaneous rise of a Japanese "threat" and collapse of a Soviet "threat" have rendered Washington's Pacific rim strategy obsolete. Geopolitical threats in the Pacific and Indian basins are minimal in the post Cold War. Russian forces do not threaten either Northeast Asia or the Pacific Basin while there is a stable balance of power on the Korean peninsula. Continuing instability in the Gulf region, however, will require a continued American military commitment and access. America's geopolitical interests in the post Cold War can be served by a mid-Pacific defense strategy with key bases at Anchorage, Guam and Hawaii linked with stepping stones, in Singapore and Australia, to the Gulf region. While the formal military alliances with Tokyo and Seoul should be maintained, the United States does not need more than token forces in

Northeast and Southeast Asia. Washington's six bases in the Philippines will be turned over to Manila while troop levels in South Korea and Japan will be steadily reduced to token forces. As the amount of American military resources committed to the region declines, Tokyo's ability to hold Washington psychologically hostage to the alliance will also diminish. Rather than diverting attention from pressing geoeconomic realties, the alliance with Tokyo and continued willingness to defend Japan's access to Gulf oil can give Washington more clout to address the devastating effects of Japanese neomercantilism.

CONCLUSION

During the mid-1980s, Japan replaced the United States as the world's greatest economic superpower and is rapidly deepening its control over the global political economy. Tokyo's neomercantilist policies have given Japan control over vital global sources of capital, markets, raw materials, technology, and energy. Japan is the world's greatest banking country while the United States in the worst debtor. Japan's corporations have leapfrogged and often outright destroyed their American rivals in a range of industries and technologies, and are busy buying up companies, banks, technologies, and real estate around the world. While the United States continues to wallow in $100 billion dollar trade deficits, Japan enjoyed a $130 billion trade surplus in 1992. Japanese are richer than Americans and Japan's affluent population of 120 million people represents the world's second largest mass consumer market.

Japan has achieved all this through industrial policies which nurture Japanese firms and products through both competition and co-operation within Japan until they have developed the scale economies and product quality sufficient to take over foreign markets. After twenty years of "liberalization" Japan's market remains protected by a maze of nontariff barriers, despite repeated Japanese claims that their market is the world's most open. The Japanese government has consistently traded token concessions of domestic market access for genuine overseas market access. Japan's lack of domestic natural resources has proven to be a blessing in disguise. Japanese firms can take advantage of international markets to find the cheapest sources of raw materials, while other industrial countries with significant natural resources must pay a much higher price because of higher labor costs. This has given Japanese firms a tremendous price advantage. Since the late 1950s, Japanese multinational corporations have invested extensively in overseas raw material sources. In an open international trade system, it is better for an industrial country to own foreign rather than domestic raw materials. Japan has control over cheap, diversified, dependable supplies of most natural resources.

An important factor behind Japan's rise to hegemony has been its ability to limit defense spending. In the postwar era, the United States has had to devote an average of 7 or 8 per cent of its GNP to defense while Japan spent about 1 per cent of its GNP. Whereas many leading American manufacturing and technological industries and firms are tied to defense work that produces goods with limited export or "spin off" potential, Japan's can concentrate on producing mass consumer goods with which to flood the world's markets. Military force is almost irrevelant to contemporary international economic relations. Comparative advantage and skillful diplomacy, not gunboats, provide overseas market access. Japan can continue to rely on the United States to provide a deterrent against the Russian threat.

Tokyo is extremely adept in constantly setting the parameters of any negotiations so that both countries have to make concessions despite the fact that Japan continues to run immense trade surpluses with the United States. In Prestowitz's words, "the purpose thus shifted from opening Japan to mutual opening, and the United States found itself on the defensive trying to explain why it did not import even more than it did so that its trade deficit could be larger".[51]

Japan's massive public relations campaign is becoming increasingly successful in shaping both official and popular American views of the relationship. Increasing numbers of influential Americans are mouthing the false notion that Japan's economic prowess is simply a matter of hard work, superior products, better education, and greater savings, while industrial policies, trade barriers and export dumping either no longer exist or have no effect on Japan's economy – instead, Japan has the world's most open markets.

Can anything be done to counter Japan's ever more formidable economic and political power? Will the United States continue to deteriorate with its economic future increasingly shaped by Tokyo rather than Washington? What obstacles prevent the policy prescriptions articulate earlier from being adopted and implemented?

Realistically, it is extremely unlikely that America's leaders can muster the understanding of what must be done to reverse American decline and the will to implement those policies. American administrations continue to cling to anachronistic concepts of trade, national security, and industrial policy. With its liberal ideology, fragmented, adversarial political economic system, and citizens lulled by the illusion of prosperity, security, and American omniscience, the United States will likely succumb to rather than rise to the Japanese challenge.

America's relative economic decline will continue. There appears to be no escape from their vicious cycle of irrational economic policies, stagnant productivity, deteriorating infrastructure and real wages, debilitating trade and budget deficits, and low savings and investments. These problems are further exacerbated by Japan's virtuous cycle of rational neomercantilist trade and industrial policies, and high savings and investments in technology infrastructure, and productivity. The threat, however, is not just to the United States but to the entire global trade system. Japanese neomercantilism is eating away at the global economy's foundations and could destroy it just as American neomercantilism did in 1930. Perhaps only then will America's leaders wake up and respond to the Japanese challenge.

Notes

Introduction

1. *State of the Union Address*, January 29, 1991.
2. Ibid.
3. *Newsweek*, March 11, 1991.
4. *Businessweek*, June 23, 1991.
5. *Businessweek*, July 6, 1991.
6. *New York Times*, June 13, 1990; Pat Choate, *Agents of Influence*, p. xvi.
7. *New York Times*, June 9, 1990.
8. *New York Times*, March 8, 1991.
9. Robert Gilpin, *The Political Economy of International Relations*, Princeton, NJ: Princeton University Press, 1987, p. 77.
10. Samuel P. Huntington, "The U.S. – Decline or Renewal?", *Foreign Affairs*, 67 (Winter 1988/1989), p. 84.
11. Joseph Nye, *Bound to Lead: The Changing Nature of American Power*, New York: Basic Books, 1990, p. 73.
12. Ibid, p. 108.
13. Paul Kennedy, "Fin de Siecle America", *New York Review of Books*, June 28, 1990, pp. 37–38.
14. Ibid, p. 39.
15. See William Nester, *Japanese Industrial Targeting*, London: Macmillan, 1991.
16. *Businessweek*, April 1, 1991. .
17. Clyde Prestowitz, *Trading Places*, New York: Basic Books, 1988, p. 22.
18. Seig Harrison and Clyde Prestowitz, "Pacific Agenda: Defense on Economics?", *Foreign Policy*, no. 79, Summer 1990, pp. 56.
19. George Friedman and Meredith Lebard, *The Coming War with Japan*, New York: St. Martin's Press, 1991.

1 Power and the Changing Nature of International Relations

1. Hans Morganthau, *Politics Among Nations: The Struggle For Power and Peace*, 5th ed., New York: Knopf, 1973, p. 9.
2. Karl Deutsch, *Analysis of International Relations*, Englewood Cliffs, NJ.: Prentice Hall, 1968, pp. 21–39.
3. Leez Maoz and Narin Abdolai, "Regime Types and International Conflict", *Journal of Conflict Resolution*, vol. 33, March 1989, pp. 3–36.
4. Joseph Nye, *Bound to Lead*, p. 27.
5. Ibid, p. 62.
6. Paul Kennedy, *The Rise and Fall of the Great Powers*, New York: Random House, 1987, p. 439.
7. Ibid, p. xv.
8. See Robert Kuttner, *End of Laissez-Faire*, New York: Alfred A. Knopf, 1991, for the best critique of liberal economic theory; see my *Japanese Industrial Targeting: The Neomercantilist Path to Economic Superpower*, for a related discussion.
9. Adam Smith, *Wealth of Nations*, 1776.

10. Quoted in Peter Kenen, *The International Economy*, Englewood Cliffs, NJ.: Prentice Hall, 1985, p. 6.
11. Paul Samuelson, *Economics*, New York: McGraw Hill, 11th ed. 1980, p. 651.
12. Milton Friedman, Robert Eisner, Herbert Stein, Robert Barro, Robert McKinnon, Robert Mundell, Jude Wanniski, and Jagdish Bhagwati are leading liberal theorists.
13. Henry Clay quoted in Kuttner, p. 7.
14. Ibid, p. 141.
15. Freidrich List quoted in John Spanier, *Games Nations Play: Analyzing International Politics*, New York: Holt, Rinehart & Winston, 1984, p. 354.
16. Ibid, p. 355.
17. Quoted in Scott and Lodge, p. 94.
18. Ibid, p. 94.
19. Chalmers Johnson, John Zysman, Laura Tyson, *Politics and Productivity: The Real Story of Why Japan's Economy Works*, chapter 1.
20. One cannot help but wonder how many neoclassical economists would persist in their quaint beliefs if all the world's countries had the good sense to get rid of their economists by dumping them in the United States. Economists might literally be worth a dime a dozen and American consumers of the product would enjoy windfall savings.
21. Selig Harrison and Clyde Prestowitz, "Pacific Agenda: Defense or Economics?", *Foreign Policy*, no. 79, Summer 1990, pp. 56–57.
22. Robert G. Gilpin, *The Political Economy of International Relations*, Princeton, NJ: Princeton University Press, 1987, p. 59.
23. Hugh Patrick, and Larry Meissner, eds, *Japan's High Technology Industries: Lessons and Limitations of Industrial Policy*, Seattle: University of Washington Press, 1986, p. xiii; Chalmers Johnson, ed. *The Industrial Policy Debate*, San Francisco: ICS Press, 1984, p. 3.
24. Scott and Lodge, op. cit. pp. 80–95.
25. Robert Reich, "Beyond Free Trade", *Foreign Affairs*, Spring 1983, p. 789.
26. Joshua S. Goldstein, *Long Cycles: Prosperity and War in the Modern Age*, New Haven, Conn.: Yale University Press, 1986, p. 88.
27. Robert North and Julie Strickland, "Power Transition and Hegemonic Succession" (paper delivered at the meeting of the International Studies Association, Anaheim, Calif., March–April 1986), p. 5.
28. See Keohane, *After Hegemony*, pp. 34, 39.
29. G. John Ikenberry and Charles A. Kupchan, "Socialization and Hegemonic Power", *International Organization*, vol. 44, no. 3, Summer 1990, p. 283.
30. Ibid, p. 286.
31. Ibid, p. 289.
32. George Modelski, *Long Cycles in World Politics*, Seattle: University of Washington Press, 1987.
33. Robert Gilpin, *War and Change in International Politics*.
34. Keohane, op. cit. p. 33.
35. Gilpin, op. cit. p. 134.
36. Jackson, p. 53.
37. Kostecki, "Export-restraint Arrangements and Trade Liberalization", *World Economy*, vol. 10, 1987, pp. 425, 429.
38. Nye, op. cit., p. 107.
39. Immanuel Wallerstein, "The United States and the World 'Crisis,'" in Terry Boswell and Albert Bergesen, eds, *America's Changing Role in the World System*, New York: Praeger, 1987, p. 17.

40. Richard Rosecrance and Jennifer Taw, "Japan and the Theory of International Leadership", *World Politics*, vol. 42, no. 2, January 1990, pp.190–191.
41. Ibid, p. 191.
42. Taken from George Modelski, "Is World Politics Evolutionary Learning?", *International Organization*, vol. 44, no. 1, Winter 1990, pp. 2–24. Immanuel Kant distinguished between the warlike tendencies of democratic and authoritarian countries almost two hundred years ago, when he argued that democratic nations, tied together by trade and a respect for international law, would be unlikely to go to war. In his 1795 essay entitled "Perpetual Peace", Kant asserts that "if the consent of citizens is required in order to decide that war should be declared . . ., nothing is more natural than they would be very cautious in commencing such a poor game, decreeing for themselves the calamities of war . . . In a constitution which is not republican, and under which the subjects are not citizens, a declaration of war is the easiest thing in the world to decide on", Immanuel Kant, "Perpetual Peace", in Peter Gay, ed, *The Enlightenment*, New York: Simon & Schuster, 1974, pp. 790–92.
43. Stern, p. 132, in Krasner.
44. See Spanier, *Games Nations Play*; and Robert Keohane and Joseph Nye, *Transnational Relations and World Politics*, pp. 229–230.
45. See Levy, pp. 186–187 in Thompson; Stern, p. 135, in Stephen Krasner, *Structural Conflict*; and Robert Keohane, *After Hegemony*, p. 66.
46. Gilpin, op. cit., p. 40.
47. Keohane and Nye, op. cit., pp. 12–15.
48. Rosecrance, op. cit., p. 62.
49. Nye, op. cit., pp. 181, 189.
50. Brown, op. cit., p. 242.
51. Spanier, op. cit. p. 301.
52. Jack Levy, "Domestic Politics and War", *Journal of Interdisciplinary History*, vol. 18, no. 1, Spring 1988, pp. 661–62.
53. Levy, op. cit., p. 661.
54. Micheal Doyle, "Kant, Liberal Legacies, and Foreign Affairs", *Philosophy and Public Affairs*, vol. 12, no. 2, Summer 1987, p. 325.
55. Gilpin, op. cit., p. x.
56. Richard Betts, *Nuclear Blackmail and Nuclear Balance*, Washington, DC: Brookings Institution, 1987.
57. Nye, op. cit., p. 100.
58. Ibid, p. 185.
59. Herbert K. Tillema, *Appeal to Force: American Military Intervention in the Era of Containment*, New York: Thomas Crowell, 1973, chapter 5.
60. Barry Blechman and Stephen Kaplan, *Force without War: U.S. Armed Forces as a Political Instrument*, Washington, DC: The Brookings Institution, 1978), chapter 4.
61. Nye, op. cit., p. 29.
62. Pat Buchannan was probably the most vociferous in protesting the U.S. military buildup.
63. Quoted in Kennedy, op. cit., p. 415.
64. Ibid.
65. G. Blackburn, *The West and the World since 1945*, New York: Praeger, 1985, p. 96.
66. Quoted in John Jackson, *The World Trading System*, p. 10.

67. Gary C. Hufbauer and Jeffrey J. Schott, *Economic Sanctions Reconsidered*, Washington, DC: Institute for International Economics, 1985, pp. 45–55.
68. Keohane, op. cit., p. 106.
69. Quoted in Scott and Lodge, op. cit., p. 133.
70. Charles Maynes, "America without the Cold War", *Foreign Policy*, no. 78, Spring 1990, p. 3.
71. Rosecrance, op. cit., p. 160.
72. Harrison and Prestowitz, op. cit., p. 37.

2 American Liberalism: Triumph and Tragedy

1. See William Nester, *Japan's Growing Power over East Asia and the World Economy*, London: Macmillan Press, 1990.
2. Alexander Hamilton, *Report on Manufactures*, p. 163; for a concise history of American industrial policies, see William Diebold's, "Past and Future Industrial in the United States", in Pinder, *National Industrial Strategies and the World Economy*.
3. Hamilton, op. cit., p. 159.
4. Jacob Viner, *Dumping: A Problem in International Trade*, p. 40.
5. Kenen, pp. 224–232.
6. *New York Times*, September 19, 1990; October 10, 1990.
7. *New York Times*, April 25, 1990.
8. *New York Times*, September 19, 1990.
9. *New York Times*, March 18, 1991.
10. Glenn Fong, "State Strength, Industry Structure, and Industrial Policy", *Comparative Politics*, vol. 22, no. 3, April 1990, p. 276.
11. Stephen Cohen, *The Making of United States Economic Policy*, p. 58; see also Richard Pious, *The American Presidency*, p. 298; and Louis Koenig, *The Chief Executive*, pp. 264–265.
12. Pat Choate, *Agents of Influence*, pp. 19. 13.
    New York Times, December 16, 1990.
14. Congress extended the President's trade powers either temporarily or permanently in 1937, 1940, 1943, 1945, 1948, 1951, 1954, 1955, 1958, 1962, 1974, 1979, 1984, 1986 and 1988. Jackson, p. 66.
15. Ibid, pp. 157–158.
16. Choate, op. cit., p. 26.
17. Clyde Prestowitz, *Trading Places*, pp. 270–271.
18. Congressional Record, 98th Congress, 2nd session, vol. 130, no 132, Washington DC, October 9, 1984, p. 1.
19. Ibid.
20. Ibid.
21. Jackson, op. cit., p. 246.
22. Ibid, p. 212.
23. Ibid, p. 106.
24. Fisher and Steinhardt, "Section 301 of the Trade Act of 1974: Protection for U.S. Exporters of Goods, Services, and Capital", *Law and Policy in International Business*, vol. 14, 1982.
25. Jackson, op. cit., pp. 156, 157.
26. Ibid, p. 228.
27. Clyde Prestowitz, op. cit., p. 134.
28. Jackson, op. cit., p. 251.

29. Quoted in Robert Tucker and David Hendrickson, "Thomas Jefferson and American Foreign Policy", *Foreign Affairs*, vol. 69, no. 2, Spring 1990, p. 137.
30. Ibid.
31. Wilson, quoted in Arthur Link, *Wilson the Diplomatist: A Look at his Major Foreign Policies*, New York: New Viewpoints, 1974, p. 96.
32. Wilson quoted by Arno Mayer, *Politics and Diplomacy of Peacemaking: Containment and Counterrevolution at Versailles, 1918–1919*, New York: Knopf, 1967.
33. Quoted in Tucker, op. cit., p. 138.
34. Ibid, p. 147.
35. For an interesting account of Roosevelt's foreign policy, see Frederick Marks, Wind over the Sand: *The Diplomacy of Franklin Roosevelt*, Athens: University of Georgia Press, 1991.
36. Krasner, in William Avery and David Rapkin, *America in a Changing World Political Economy*, p. 31.
37. Robert Gilpin, *U.S. Power and the Multinational Corporation*, pp. 103–104.
38. George Kennan, *Foreign Affairs*, 1947.
39. Quoted in Gaddis, *Strategies of Containment*, p. 280.
40. *Frontline*, PBS, April 16, 1991.
41. Benjamin Friedman, *Day of Reckoning*, p. 4.
42. Ibid, p. 5.
43. Both quotes from ibid, p. 239.
44. Unless otherwise noted all the statistics come from Friedman.
45. Ibid, pp. 110–115.
46. Some economists claim that budget deficits do not matter. Friedman counters that the budget crisis may actually be even worse than it seems because the federal budget "systematically understates costs by failing to incorporate the growing liabilities for future payments for the pensions of federal employees and military personnel. At the same time, the budget systematically overstates costs by including all interest that the Treasury pays on its outstanding securities, while failing to allow for the shrinking real value of those securities due to inflation. And there are many other omissions and mismeasurements", ibid, p. 80. America's net debt would be even greater if it counted its shaky loans at the market prices these loans were traded at, for example, fifty-three cents to the dollar for Mexico, forty-seven cents for Argentina, thirty-nine cents for Brazil, and twenty-eight cents for Nigeria; ibid, p. 228.
47. Both quotes from ibid, p. 256.
48. Ibid, p. 265.
49. Barry Bluestone and Bennett Harrison, *The Great U-turn, Corporate Restructuring and the Polarizing of America*, New York: Basic Books, 1988, p. 127.
50. *Economist*, February 25, 1989.
51. Friedman, op. cit., pp. 86–87.
52. See Steve Chan, "The Impact of Defense Spending on Economic Performance: A Survey of Evidence and Problems", *Orbis*, Summer 1985, pp. 407–412; Paul Craig and John Jungerman, *Nuclear Arms Race: Technology and Society*, New York: McGraw-Hill, 1986.
53. Kennedy, op. cit., pp. 444–445.
54. Nye, op. cit., p. 90.
55. Charles S. Maier, "The Two Postwar Eras and the Conditions for Stability in Twentieth Century Western Europe", *American Historical Review*, vol. 86, no. 2, 1981, pp. 342–43.

56. *New York Times*, March 5, 1992.
57. Richard Solomon, "Asian Security in the 1990s: Integration in Economics: Diversity in Defense", address to the University of California at San Diego, October 30, 1990, official text from the American Embassy, Tokyo, November 1, 1990, p. 2.

3 Japanese Neomercantalism: The New Hegemony

1. Quoted in *OECD Annual Report*, Paris, 1972.
2. Quoted in Scott and Lodge, op. cit., pp. 95, 138.
3. For extended discussions of Japan's culture, sociology, and psychology see: William Nester, *Japan's Growing Power over East Asia and the World Economy: Ends and Means*; William Nester, *The Foundations of Japanese Power*; Takeo Doi, *The Anatomy of Dependence*; Takie Sugiyama Lebra, *Patterns of Japanese Behavior*; Richardson and Scott Flanagan, *Politics in Japan*.
4. Quoted in Steve Schollsstein, *Trade War*, New York: Congdon & Weed, 1984, p. 104.
5. Chalmers Johnson, *MITI and the Japanese Miracle*, p. 241.
6. Ibid, p. 81.
7. Haru Fukui, in Scalipino, p. 35.
8. Clyde Prestowitz, *Trading Places*, p. 80.
9. Quoted in Stephen Cohen, *Cowboys and Samurai*, New York: HarperBusiness, 1991, p. 176.
10. Richardson and Flanagan, op. cit., p. 178.
11. Kanji Haitani, "The Paradox of Japan's Groupism", *Asian Survey*, vol. 30, no. 3, March 1990, p. 245.
12. *New York Times*, April 27, 1988.
13. *New York Times*, February 19, 1991.
14. Ibid.
15. Ronald Dore, *Flexible Rigidities*, Stanford, Calif.: Stanford University Press, 1986, p. 248.
16. Ibid, p. 244.
17. *New York Times*, November 12, 1990.
18. For the best analysis of Japanese democracy, see J.A.A. Stockwin, ed. *Dynamism and Immobilism in Japanese Politics*.
19. Ibid, p.10.
20. See Peter Cheng, "Japanese Interest Group Politics", *Asian Survey*, vol. 30, no. 3, March 1990, pp. 251–265.
21. Johnson, op. cit., pp. viii, 240.
22. Prestowitz, op. cit., p. 115.
23. Ibid, p. 119.
24. *Economist*, February 3, 1990; *New York Times*, January 29, 1990.
25. *Business Tokyo*, April 1990.
26. *Far Eastern Economic Review*, June 20, 1990.
27. *Japan Economic Journal*, April 14, 1990; December 15, 1990.
28. Chikara Higashi, *Japanese Trade Policy Formulation*, New York: Praeger, 1983, p. 114.
29. Boye De Mente, *Japanese Business Etiquette*, Englewood Cliffs, NJ: Prentice Hall, 1981, p. 125.
30. *Far Eastern Economic Review*, July 26, 1990.

31. *Far Eastern Economic Review*, June 21, 1990; *Japan Economic Journal*, May 19, 1990.
32. Kazuo Sato, "Saving and Investment", in Kozo Yamamura and Yasukichi Yasuba, *The Political Economy of Japan*, p. 140.
33. Horne, op. cit., p. 16.
34. John Campbell, *Contemporary Japanese Budget Politics*, pp. 20, 51.
35. *Far Eastern Economic Review*, October 11, 1990.
36. Johnson, op. cit.
37. Ibid, p. 29.
38. Ibid, 236–237.
39. Schmeligower, op. cit., p. 280.
40. Ibid.
41. Richard Wright and Gunter Pauli, *The Second Wave: Japan's Global Assault on Financial Services*, p. 86.
42. Shigeru Yoshida, *Memoirs*, pp. 119–120.
43. Ibid.
44. Krasner, p. 83.
45. Prestowitz, op. cit., p. 63.
46. Mordechai Keirenin, "How Closed is Japan's Market?", *World Economy*, vol. 11, no. 4, July 1989, p. 539.
47. U.S. Department of Commerce, "Japan Office Estimates", 1983.
48. Committee for Economic Development (CED), *Strategy for US Industrial Competiveness*, 1984, p. 30.
49. Quoted in Jon Woronoff, *World Trade War*, p. 197.
50. *Far Eastern Economic Review*, June 21, 1990.
51. Robert Lawrence, "Does Japan Import Too Little: Closed Minds or Markets?", *Brookings Papers in Economic Activity*, no. 2, Washington, DC, 1987.
52. *Far Eastern Economic Review*, June 21, 1990.
53. *Japan Economic Journal*, August 18, 1990.
54. Quoted in Stephen Cohen, *Cowboys and Samurai*, New York: HarperBusiness, 1991, p. 213.
55. Masayoshi Hotta, quoted in Schollssstein, op. cit., p. 105.
56. John Dower, *Empire and Aftermath*, p. 307.
57. Cited in Kenneth Pyle, "The Burden of Japanese History", in John Makin and Donald Hellman, eds, *Sharing World Leadership? A New Era for America and Japan*, Washington, American Enterprise Institute, 1989, pp. 61–62.
58. Marius Jansen, "Modernization and Foreign Policy in Meiji Japan", in Robert Ward, *Political Development in Modern Japan*, p. 153.
59. See Roger Hackett, "Political Modernization and the Meiji Genro", in Ward, pp. 65–97.
60. Quoted in Frank Langdon, *Japanese Foreign Policy*, p. 2.
61. Kenneth Pyle, "The Future of Japanese Nationality", *Journal of Japanese Studies*, vol. 8, no. 2, 1982, p. 225.
62. Ibid, p. 251.
63. Muthiah Alagappa, "Japan's Political and Security Role in the Asia-Pacific Region", *Contemporary Southeast Asia*, vol. 10, no. 1, June 1988, p. 48.
64. "Kokuryoku ni ojita na bijyon no keisei ni mukete", ("Toward a New Vision Commensurate with National Strength"), *Gaiko Forum*, October 1988, p. 10.
65. *Japan Economic Journal*, May 28, 1988.
66. *International Herald Tribune*, June 27, 1988.
67. Ibid.

68. *Business Tokyo*, August 1990.
69. *New York Times*, November 14, 1990.
70. *Far Eastern Economic Review*, October 11, 1990.
71. *Far Eastern Economic Review*, January 17, 1991.
72. Ibid.
73. *Far Eastern Economic Review*, July 12, 1990.
74. Kent Calder, "Japanese Foreign Economic Policy Formation", *World Politics*, vol. 40, no. 4, July 1988, p. 519.
75. Ibid, p. 518.

4 The Shifting Balance of Economic Power

1. Chalmers Johnson, John Zysman, and Laura Tyson, *Politics and Productivity: The Real Story of Why Japan's Economy Works*, pp. 43–50.
2. Ibid, p. 24.
3. Klaus Knorr, p. 16.
4. Ibid, p. 23.
5. Paul Kennedy, *Rise and Fall of the Great Powers*, pp. 357–358.
6. Joseph Nye, "Understating U.S. Strength", *Foreign Policy*, no. 72, Fall 1988, p. 123.
7. Unless otherwise indicated, all economic growth statistics have been taken from various issues of such sources as: *Japan, An International Comparison* (Keizai Koho Center), *Nippon Business Facts and Figures* (JETRO), *IMF Direction of Trade, World Bank Studies*.
8. *Bureau of Labor Statistics*, various issues.
9. *Wall Street Journal*, September 25, 1989.
10. *New York Times*, February 5, 1991.
11. R. Jaikumar, "Postindustrial Manufacturing", *Harvard Business Review*, vol. 64, 1986, p. 69.
12. *Businessweek*, July 15, 1991.
13. *Businessweek*, July 10, 1990.
14. *Businessweek*, October 15, 1990.
15. *Japan Economic Journal*, April 14, 1990; *New York Times*, June 15, 1990.
16. Unless otherwise indicated, all trade statistics have been culled from various issues of the *IMF Direction of Trade*.
17. *Newsweek*, April 2, 1990.
18. *Japan Economic Journal*, April 7, 1990.
19. Glen Fukushima, "Back to Business", *Business Tokyo*, July 1990, p. 40.
20. Laura d'Andrea Tyson, "Competiveness: An Analysis of the Problem and a Perspective on Future Policy", in *Global Competitiveness*, ed. Martin Starr, New York: W.W. Norton, 1988, p. 97.
21. *New York Times*, March 25, 1991.
22. The White House, Executive Office of the President, Office of the Press Secretary, September 9, 1983.
23. Martin and Susan Tochin, *Buying into America: How Foreign Money is Changing the Face of our Nation*, New York: Berkeley Books, 1988, pp. 5–7.
24. Russell B. Scholl, "The International Investment Position of the United States in 1986", *Survey of Current Business*, vol. 26, June 1987, pp. 38–45.
25. Benjamin Friedman, *Day of Reckoning*, p. 229.
26. *New York Times*, June 13, 1990; JETRO, 1989–90, *Directory: Japanese Affiliated Companies in USA and Canada*, JETRO, 1990. p. 25.
27. Tolchin, op. cit., p. 245.

28. *New York Times*, June 13, 1990; Pat Choate, *Agents of Influence*, p. xvi.
29. *Economist*, March 21–27, 1987, p. 94.
30. *Newsweek*, April 2, 1990.
31. *Far Eastern Economic Review*, December 17, 1987, p. 88.
32. *New York Times*, October 27, 1990.
33. *Wall Street Journal*, February 24, 1986. These figures have been attacked as meaningless by some who argue that they do not reflect the appreciation of American foreign investments made decades ago. One calculation based on the price of gold each year brought the deficit down to $281.4 billion. But a new Commerce Department approach, called the Current-cost Calculation, which attempts to factor in changed land, factory, and other asset values found a $463.9 billion gap. But whichever measure is used, the result is that the United States is suffering an immense and growing investment deficit that reflects America's steady relative economic decline. (*New York Times*, June 10, 1991.)
34. *Japan Economic Journal*, May 26, 1990.
35. *New York Times*, February 22, 1989.
36. Martin and Susan Tolchin, op. cit., p. 201.
37. *New York Times*, October 14, 1990.
38. James Ray, *Global Politics*, Boston: Houghton Mifflin, 1990, p. 275.
39. *Far Eastern Economic Review*, March 5, 1988; March 23, 1989; February 8, 1990; May 10, 1990.
40. Clyde Prestowitz, *Trading Places*, p. 210.
41. *New York Times*, June 10, 1990.
42. *Japan Economic Journal*, September 15, 1990.
43. *New York Times*, January 20, 1991.
44. *Businessweek*, July 1991.
45. Pat Choate, *Agents of Influence*, p. 22.
46. *New York Times*, March 10, 1991; *Businessweek*, September 7, 1987.
47. Al Alletzhauser, *The House of Nomura*.
48. *World Herald Tribune*, April 23, 1988.
49. William Nester, *Japanese Industrial Targeting*, p. 267.
50. *Japan Economic Journal*, April 28, 1990.
51. See William Nester, *Japanese Industrial Targeting: The Neomercantalist Path to Economic Superpower*, New York: St. Martin's Press, 1991 for an in-depth account of Japan's technology policies, from which some of the following statistics, information and exerpts have been culled.
52. Quoted in Kinmouth, p. 186.
53. National Science Foundation, *International Science and Technology Update*, 1988, Washington, DC: 1989, p. 92.
54. National Academy of Engineering, *Strengthening U.S. Engineering Through International Cooperation: Some Reconsiderations for Action*, Washington, D.C.: National Academy Press, 1987; Clyde Prestowitz, *Trading Places: How We Lost to the Japanese*, p. 37.
55. *New York Times*, March 20, 1991.
56. Wineberg, op. cit., p. 11; *New York Times*, June 9, 1990. The other two top ten winners were the Dutch firm Phillips (687) and German Siemens (539). Unless otherwise indicated, the following statistics on semiconductors, semiconductor equipment, and computers were obtained from *Dataquest*.
57. Inman and Burton, op. cit., p. 119.
58. *New York Times*, November 19, 1990.

59. Jay Stowsky, "Weak Links, Strong Bonds", in Zysman, *et al.*, *Politics and Productivity*, p. 267.
60. *Far Eastern Economic Review*, August 9, 1990.
61. *New York Times*, November 24, 1990.
62. Justin Bloom. "A New Era for US–Japan Technical Relations? Problems and Prospects", *Journal of Northeast Asian Studies*, Summer 1987, p. 17.
63. Prestowitz, op. cit. pp. 11, 27.
64. Kiyoshi Kojima and Terutomo Ozawa, *Japan's General Trading Companies*, Paris: OECD, 1984, p. 71.
65. *New York Times*, March 20, 1991.
66. *New York Times*, Deember 6, 1988.
67. *Independent*, May 26, 1989.
68. Japan Science Technology Agency, *White Paper*, 1983.
69. OECD, *Science and Technology Indicators*, Paris 1982.
70. *New York Times*, May 1, 1990.
71. *US News and World Report*, July 10, 1989; *Economist*, December 2, 1989, *New York Times*, December 7, 1988; *New York Times*, March 24, 1991, *New York Times*, September 4, 1990.
72. Hiraoka, op. cit., p. 12; *Economist*, December 2, 1989; *New York Times*, April 28, 1991; *Times*, November 1, 1989.
73. Charles Ferguson. "America's High Tech Decline", *Foreign Policy*, Spring 1989, p. 136.
74. *International Herald Tribune*, March 22, 1989.
75. Ibid.
76. *Japan Economic Journal*, March 11, 1989.
77. *Japan Economic Journal*, December 15, 1990.
78. Ferguson, op. cit., pp. 123, 125, 129.
79. Shitaro Ishihara and Akio Morita, *The Japan That Can Say "No"*, p. 18.

5 The Shifting Balance of Political Power: Hearts, Minds and Policies

1. Martin and Susan Tolchin, *Buying Into America: How Foreign Investment is Changing the Face of the Nation*, New York: Berkeley Books, 1988, p. vii.
2. Pat Choate, *Agents of Influence*, p. xi.
3. Ibid, pp. xi-xii.
4. Ibid, p. xii.
5. *New York Times*, Quoting Cylde Farnsworth, May 7, 1987.
6. Choate, op. cit., pp. xvii, xviii, xx; Pat Choate, "Money Talks", *Washington Post*, Outlook, June 19, 1988, p. 1.
7. *Newsweek*, December 22, 1986.
8. Choate, op. cit., p. 38.
9. Bob Woodward, *Veil: The Secret Wars of the CIA*, New York: Pocket Books, 1987, pp. 420–421, 444.
10. Choate, op. cit., p. 37.
11. Clyde Prestowitz, *Trading Places*, p. 265.
12. Choate, op. cit., p. 143.
13. Ibid.
14. Quoted in ibid, pp. 137–138.
15. Ibid, p. 111.
16. *New York Times*, May 7, 1987.

17. Choate, op. cit., pp. 113–114.
18. *New York Times*, November 24, 1991.
19. Willian Holstein, *The Japanes Power Game*, New York: Charles Scribner & Sons, 1990, p. 230; *New York Times*, March 3, 1991.
20. Choate, p. 61.
21. Ibid, pp. 69, 126–127.
22. Ibid, p. 175
23. Ibid, pp. 52, 56, 62.
24. Ibid, p. 180.
25. *Japan Economic Journal*, May 19, 1990.
26. *Japan Economic Journal*, February 9, 1991.
27. Choate, op. cit., pp. xi-xii.
28. Ibid, p. xx.
29. Ibid, p. 25.
30. Ibid, p. 42.
31. Quoted in Tolchin, op. cit., p. 215.
32. *Congressional Record*, Senate, July 17, 1987, pp. S 10154.
33. Quoted in Choate, op. cit., p. 8.
34. Ibid, p. 10.
35. *World Herald Tribune*, May 2, 1988.
36. Quoted in Choate, op. cit., pp. 10. 37.
    Quoted in Choate, 134.
38. Tolchin, op. cit., p. 75.
39. Ibid, p. 85.
40. Ibid, pp. 15–16, 46–47.
41. Ibid, pp. 94–118.
42. Ibid, pp. 112.
43. Ibid, p. 160.
44. Ibid, p. 118.
45. Ibid, p. 16.
46. Ibid, p. 20.
47. *New York Times*, June 13, 1990.
48. Quoted in Tolchin, op. cit., pp. 19, 20.
49. Ibid, p. 21.
50. Parts of this section are exerpted from my book *The Foundation of Japanese Power*, chapter 7.
51. Ibid, chapter 5.
52. See Kan Ito, "Trans-Pacific Anger", *Foreign Policy*, no. 78, Spring 1990, p. 133, for one of the milder attacks on the "gang".
53. *Business Tokyo*, September 1990.
54. Choate, op. cit., p. 39.
55. Glen Fukushima, "The U.S.-Japan Trade Conflict: A View from Washington", *Bulletin of the International House*, vol. 6, Spring 1986, p. 7.
56. Choate, op. cit., p. 40.
57. Ibid, p. 154.
58. For an in-depth discussion, see William Nester, *Japan's Growing Power over East Asia and the World Economy: Ends and Means*, London: Macmillan Press, 1990.
59. Grant Goodman, *The American Occupation of Japan*, p. 18.
60. Kevin Kearns, "After FSX: A New Approach to US–Japan Trade Relations", *Foreign Service Journal*, December 1989.
61. *Business Tokyo*, September 1990.

62. Ibid.
63. Quoted in *New York Times*, March 8, 1990.
64. Herbert Stein, "Don't Worry About the Trade Deficit", *Wall Street Journal*, May 16, 1989.
65. Herbert Stein, "Who's Number One? Who Cares?", *Wall Street Journal*, March 1, 1990.
66. Quoted in *New York Times*, September 3, 1990.
67. *New York Times*, May 2, 1990.
68. Ibid. The Foundation for International Economic Policy, founded by Representative Richard Gephardt, not only sees no danger in the opening of American branches in Japan, but actually encourages such investments as giving Americans a clearer view of Japan's political economy.
69. Choate, op. cit., p. 198.
70. Ibid, p. 191.
71. Ibid, p. 193.
72. *Japan Times*, November 14, 1986.
73. Choate, op. cit., p. 194.
74. *Businessweek*, July 11, 1988.
75. Ibid.
76. *Economist*, November 24, 1990.
77. Sugimoto and Mouer, *Japanese Society: Stereotypes and Realities*, pp. 7–29.
78. Both quotes are from Jon Woronoff, *World Trade War*, pp. 78, 94.
79. *New York Times*, March 23, 1991.
80. Ishihara Shintaro and Akio Morita, *The Japan That Can Say "No"*, xeroxed copy.
81. Ibid, pp. 8–14, 19–26, 52–60.
82. *Japan Economic Journal*, August 25, 1990.
83. *Japan Times*, November 26, 1936.
84. *New York Times*, October 18, 1990.
85. Paul Krugman, *The Age of Diminished Expectations*, Washington: The Washington Post Company, 1990, p. 69.
86. *Japan Economic Journal*, March 17, 1990.
87. *Newsweek*, April 2, 1990.
88. *Businessweek*, December 18, 1989.
89. *Japan Economic Journal*, April 7, 1990.
90. *Newsweek*, April 2, 1990.
91. *Japan Economic Journal*, May 19, 1990.
92. Washington Post/ABC New Poll, February 1989, *International Herald Tribune*, February 19, 1989.
93. *Businessweek*, September 3, 1990. 94. *Businessweek*, August 7,1989.
95. *New York Times*, June 6, 1990.
96. *Washington Post National Weekly Edition*, September 24–30, 1990.
97. *Economist*, November 24, 1990.
98. *Businessweek*, April 1, 1991.

6   American Policy Toward Japan: The Sisyphean Dilemma or What is the Sound of One Hand Clapping?

1. The unemployed figure was calculated by the standard economists' projection of 35,000 jobs lost for every $1 billion of a country's deficit.
2. *New York Times*, May 17, 1991.

3. For indepth discussions of these issues, see William Nester, *Japan's Growing Power over East Asia and the World Economy*, chapter 2; and *The Foundations of Japanese Power*, chapters 3, 4.
4. Quoted in Schaffer, p. 179.
5. Redford, op. cit., p. 79; Johnson, op. cit., p. 208.
6. Walt Rostow, *The United States and the Regional Organization of the Pacific*, p. 53.
7. Ibid, p. 67.
8. For the definitive account, see I.M. Destler, Haruhiro Fukui, and Hideo Sato, *The Textile Wrangle*, Ithaca, NY: Cornell University Press, 1979.
9. Clyde Prestowitz, *Trading Places*, p. 99.
10. Ibid, p. 278.
11. Ibid, p. 99.
12. Pat Choate, *Agents of Influence*, p. 44.
13. Pepper, op. cit., p. 77–78.
14. Ibid.
15. Glen Fukushima, "Back to Business", *Business Tokyo*, July 1990, p. 40.
16. Prestowitz, op. cit., p. 273.
17. Ibid, pp. 18, 281.
18. Ibid, p. 283.
19. Ibid, p. 236.
20. Ibid, p. 234.
21. Ibid, p. 163.
22. Quoted in Jackson, p. 148.
23. *International Trade Reporter*, 3, 1986, p. 1198.
24. *Japan Economic Journal*, September 15, 1990.
25. Glen Fukushima, "Back to Business", *Business Tokyo*, July 1990, p. 41.
26. *Japan Economic Journal*, September 7, 1989.
27. *New York Times*, October 28, 1990.
28. *New York Times*, November 2, 1989.
29. *New York Times*, April 27, 1990.
30. *New York Times*, April 27, 1990.
31. *Japan Economic Journal*, July 7, 1990.
32. *New York Times*, June 14, 1990.
33. *Japan Economic Journal*, July 21, 1990.
34. *New York Times*, September 19, 1990.
35. *New York Times*, October 28, 1990.
36. *New York Times*, May 23, 1991.
37. *Far Eastern Economic Review*, February 5, 1990.
38. *Japan Economic Journal*, October 27, 1990.
39. *Japan Economic Journal*, November 3, 1990.
40. *Japan Economic Journal*, October 20, 1990.
41. *Japan Economic Journal*, October 27, 1990.
42. *Japan Economic Journal*, November 3, 1990.
43. *Japan Economic Journal*, November 3, 1990.
44. *New York Times*, December 21, 1990.
45. Okimoto, pp. 129–130, in Weinstein, *Northeast Asian Security after Vietnam*.
46. *Japan Economic Journal*, September 29, 1990.
47. *Japan Economic Journal*, October 27, 1990.
48. *New York Times*, March 25, 1991.
49. Stephen D. Cohen, *Cowboys and Samurai*, New York: HarperBusiness, 1991, p. 147.
50. Prestowitz, op. cit., p. 260.

51. James Fallows, "The Japan Handlers", *Atlantic*, August 1987, p. 23.
52. *New York Times*, July 12, 1991.
53. See David P. Rapkin, "Japan and World Leadership", in D.P. Rapkin, ed., *World Leadership and Hegemony*, Boulder, Co.: Lynne Rienner Publishers; *International Political Economy Yearbook*, vol. 5, 1990, pp. 196–199.
54. *Business Tokyo*, June 1990.

7 The Mature Industry Front

1. Exerpts from chapters 3 and 4 of my *Japanese Industrial Targeting* appear throughout this chapter.
2. Robert Reich and IRA Magaziner, p. 169. Unless otherwise noted, all the information and statistics in the television section have been culled from Reich and Maginer, Pat Choate, *Agents of Influence* or Clyde Prestowitz, *Trading Places*.
3. Pat Choate, op. cit., pp. 77–105.
4. Ibid, p. 90.
5. Kozo Yamamura and Gary Saxonhouse, *Law and Trade Issues of the Japanese Economy*, Seattle: University of Washington Press, 1986, pp. 238–70.
6. Choate, op. cit., p. 84.
7. Ibid, pp. 88–89.
8. Reich and Magaziner, op. cit., p. 78.
9. Choate, op. cit., p. 104.
10. Reich and Magaziner, op. cit., p. 155.
11. Kawahito, 1981, pp. 222–34.
12. Ibid, p. 240.
13. *Japan Economic Journal*, August 19, 1989.
14. *Japan Economic Journal*, October 28, 1989.
15. Friedman, *The Misunderstood Miracles*, argues the industry grew in spite of MITI while Sarathy argues that MITI's influence was decisive. Unless otherwise noted, all statistics will come from Friedman's book.
16. Sarathy, op. cit., p. 153.
17. Ibid, pp. 133, 136.
18. Helen V. Milner and David B. Yoffie, "Between Free Trade and Protectionism: Strategic Trade Policy and a Theory of Corporate Trade Demands", *International Organization*, vol. 43, no. 2, Spring 1989, pp. 266–268.
19. Clyde Prestowitz, *Trading Places*, p. 223.
20. Cravath, Swaine & Moore, *Computer Aided Manufacturing: The Japanese Challenge*, submitted to the US International Trade Commission in Investigation no. 332–149 under 19 U.S.C. 1332 (b), Washington, D.C., 1982, p. 3; US Department of Commerce, *U.S. Competitiveness in High Technology Industries*, Washington, D.C., February 1983.
21. *Japan Economic Journal*, August 25, 1990.
22. *Japan Economic Journal*, April 7, 1990.
23. Chang, p. 64.
24. Ibid, p. 49.
25. Ueno, op. cit., pp. 148–49.
26. Kawai, op. cit., p. 179.
27. Schaffer, op. cit., p. 289.
28. Change, op. cit., p. 81.
29. Ibid. p. 77.
30. *Japan Times*, June 18, 1988.
31. *Japan Economic Journal*, June 17, 1989.

32. Ueno, p. 190.
33. Ibid, pp. 161–162.
34. Dunn, pp. 242–243.
35. Change, p. 102.
36. Ibid, p. 243.
37. Lochmann, op. cit., p. 101.
38. Ibid, pp. 109, 114.
39. Dunn, op. cit., p. 226.
40. Ibid, p. 244.
41. Ibid, p. 245.
42. *New York Times*, February 6, 1990.
43. *New York Times*, February 6, 1990.
44. *Japan Economic Journal*, December 9, 1989.
45. *New York Times*, October 12, 1989.
46. *Economist*, February 11, 1989.
47. Robert Cole and Donald Deskins, 'Radical Factors in Site Location . . .', *California Management Review*, vol. 31, no. 1, Fall 1989.
48. Ibid, p. 15.
49. Ibid, p. 17.
50. *International Herald Tribune*, June 8, 1988.
51. *Japan Economic Journal*, July 14, 1990.
52. *New York Times*, October 11, 1990; *New York Times*, February 6, 1990
53. *New York Times*, November 24, 1990.
54. *Businessweek*, July 24, 1989.
55. Ibid.
56. *New York Times*, November 1, 1990.
57. *Businessweek*, July 1, 1991. *Japan Economic Journal*, September 15, 1990.
58. Choate, op. cit., p. 6.
59. *Economist*, November 18, 1989.
60. *Japan Economic Journal*, December 1, 1990.
61. Ibid.
62. *Japan Economic Journal*, January 12, 1991.
63. *New York Times*, March 20, 1991.
64. Castle, op. cit., pp. 136, 321.
65. *Japan Economic Journal*, April 27, 1991.
66. *Economist*, February 27, 1988.
67. Castle, op. cit., p. 136.
68. *Economist*, August 20, 1988.
69. *Far Eastern Economic Review*, November 17, 1988.
70. George, op. cit., p. 411.
71. Castle, op. cit., p. 248.
72. Hillman, op. cit., p. 52.
73. Castle, op. cit., p. 70.
74. Ibid, p. 75.
75. *Japan Economic Journal*, April 16, 1988, July 2, 1988.
76. *Japan Economic Journal*, December 17, 1988.
77. *Far Eastern Economic Review*, April 7, 1988.
78. *Japan Economic Journal*, December 17, 1988.
79. Ibid.
80. *International Herald Tribune*, May 13, 1989.
81. *Japan Economic Journal*, December 10, 1988.
82. Ibid.

83. Ibid.
84. *Economist*, October 22, 1988.
85. *Japan Economic Journal*, February 27, 1988.
86. *Economist*, October 22, 1988.
87. *Japan Economic Journal*, October 15, 1988.
88. *Japan Economic Journal*, December 10, 1988.
89. *Japan Economic Journal*, October 15, 1988.
90. Quoted in Choate, op. cit., p. 10.
91. *Japan Economic Journal*, October 15, 1988.
92. Peter Gordon, "The Rice Policy of Japan's LDP", *Asian Survey*, vol. 30, no. 10, October 1990, pp. 946–947.
93. *New York Times*, March 18, 1991.
94. Castle, op. cit., pp. 64–67.
95. *Economist*, April 30, 1988.
96. Laumer, op. cit., p. 265. See also Mitsuo Wada, "Selling in Japan: Consumer Distribution", in Pugel, pp. 95–8.
97. *Economist*, January 28, 1989.
98. Laumer, op. cit, p. 257 in Pugel.
99. Ibid.
100. *Japan Economic Journal*, March 12, 1988.
101. *Economist*, January 28, 1989.
102. Douglas, p. 108.
103. Ishida, p. 323.
104. *Economist*, January 28, 1989.
105. Ishida, op. cit., pp. 323–340.
106. Ibid, p. 326.
107. *Businessweek*, May 8, 1989.
108. *Japan Economic Journal*, May 17, 1989.
109. *New York Times*, November 11, 1990.
110. Ibid.
111. *New York Times*, April 26, 1991.
112. *Economist*, April 29, 1989.
113. *Japan Economic Journal*, January 9, 1988, February 13, 1988.
114. *Far Eastern Economic Review*, March 24, 1988.
115. *Japan Times*, November 16, 1987.
116. *Far Eastern Economic Review*, January 7, 1988.
117. *Economist*, April 29, 1989.
118. Ibid.
119. *Japan Economic Journal*, January 30, 1988.
120. *Los Angeles Times*, April 3, 1988.
121. *Japan Economic Journal*, February 13, 1988.
122. *Japan Economic Journal*, January 23, 1988.
123. *Japan Economic Journal* June 10, 1989; *Economist*, April 29, 1989.
124. *Economist*, April 29, 1989.

8 The Foreign Investment Front

1. *New York Times*, January 18, 1991.
2. *New York Times*, February 20, 1991.
3. Pickens articles.
4. *New York Times*, January 18, 1991.
5. *Business Tokyo*, May 1991.

6. *Nippon 1990, Business Facts and Figures*, JETRO. All Japan's foreign invest-ment figures come from this source unless otherwise mentioned; *Japan Economic Journal*, January 5, 1991.

7. *New York Times*, June 13, 1990; *Washington Post National Weekly Edition*, October 15–21, 1990.

8. Tolchin, op. cit., p. 245.

9. Ellen Herr, "U.S. Business Enterprises Acquired or Established by Foreign Direct Investors in 1987", *Survey of Current Business*, May 1988, pp. 50–58.

10. See Benjamin Friedman, op. cit., for an interesting discussion of this theme.

11. US Congress, Committee on Energy and Commerce, Subcommittee on Telecommunications, Consumer Protection, and Finance, "Disclosure of Foreign Investment in the United States", May 8, 1986, Washington, DC, US Government Printing Office.

12. *New York Times*, March 26, 1991.

13. *New York Times*, June 1, 1990.

14. *Japan Economic Journal*, July 21, 1990.

15. Tolchin, op. cit., p. 245.

16. Ibid, p. 45.

17. Ibid, p. 64.

18. Ibid, pp. 22, 71–74, 256.

19. Quoted in ibid, p. 75.

20. Quoted in ibid, p. 3.

21. Quoted in ibid, p. 11.

22. Quoted in ibid, p. 44.

23. Quoted in ibid, p. 53.

24. Ibid, p. 87.

25. *Japan Economic Journal*, February 24, 1990.

26. Ibid.

27. Tolchin, op. cit., p. 207.

28. *New York Times*, October 14, 1990.

29. *New York Times*, September 27, 1990; *New York Times*, October 14, 1990.

30. Jane Slaughter and Mike Parker, *Choosing Sides*, reviewed in the *International Herald Tribune*, February 1, 1989.

31. Quoted in Tolchin, op. cit., p. 161.

32. Ibid, pp. 164–165.

33. Sumitomo Shoji Inc. v. Avagiliano, 457 U.S. 176, October 1981.

34. Leah Nathans "A Matter of Control", *Business Month*, September 1988, p. 49.

35. Ibid, p. 50.

36. See William Nester, *The Foundation of Japanese Power*, chapter 6.

37. *Japan Economic Journal*, August 11, 1990.

38. Ibid.

39. *New York Times*, November 27, 1990; *New York Times*, December 2, 1990.

40. Ibid.

41. Ibid.

42. Tolchin, op. cit., p. 144.

43. *Balance Sheets for the U.S. Economy*, 1947–86, Washington, DC Board of Governors of the Federal Reserve System, 1987; Anthony Down, *Foreign Capital in the U.S. Real Estate Markets*, New York, Salomon Brothers, Inc, 1987.

44. *Time*, September 14, 1987.

45. Peter DeBraal and T. Alexander Majchrowicz, "Foreign Onwership of U.S. Agricultural Land Through December 31, 1984", US Department of

Agriculture, 1985. The problem, however, is in Japanese ownership of American agriculture and its effect on bilateral trade. See Chapter 7 for details.

46. *New York Times*, November 1, 1989; *Business Tokyo*, May 1991. Japanese investors have run up prices in the art world as dramatically as they have those of New York and Los Angeles skyscrapers. At one Christie's auction alone in May 1990, Japanese paid $185.2 million of $286.2 million total sales for 23 of 58 artworks sold. Two days earlier a Japanese investor, Ryoei Sato, paid a record $160.6 million for two paintings, $82.5 million for Van Gough's "Portrait of Dr. Gauchet" and $78.1 million for Renoir's "At the Moulin de la Galette", *New York Times*, May 19, 1990.

47. *New York Times*, November 1, 1989.

48. *A Summary of Japanese Real Estate Investment and Development Activity in the United States, 1984–1987*, pp. 52–62.

49. *Far Eastern Economic Review*, August 3, 1989.

50. *Far Eastern Economic Review*, August 3, 1990.

51. *Japan Economic Journal*, November 24, 1990.

52. *Japan Economic Journal*, January 19, 1991.

53. Dennis J. Encarnation and Mark Mason, "Neither MITI nor America: The Political Economy of Capital Liberalization in Japan", *International Organization*, vol. 44, no. 1, Winter 1990, pp. 59–75.

54. *Economist*, March 21, 1987.

55. Encarnation and Mason, op. cit., p. 32, pp. 37–38.

56. Quoted in Chalmers Johnson, *MITI and the Japanese Miracle: The Growth of Japanese Industrial Policy, 1925–1975*, Stanford, Calif.: Stanford University Press, 1982, p. 245.

57. Encarnation and Mason, op. cit., p. 37.

58. Ibid, p. 45.

59. Ibid, p. 41.

60. See ibid, pp. 43–45 for details of this "liberalization".

61. Johnson, op. cit., pp. 278–79.

62. *Far Eastern Economic Review*, January 11, 1990. The Japanese word for takeover, "highjack" (*nottori*), and divestiture, "selling one's body" (*mi-uri*), give some idea of how dimly Japanese view the notion of a free market.

63. Tolchin, op. cit., p. 226.

64. *Far Eastern Economic Review*, January 11, 1990.

65. James Abegglen, *KAISHA*, pp. 127, 137.

66. Friedman, op. cit., p. 81.

67. *New York Times*, October 14, 1990.

68. Ozawa, *Multilateralism, Japanese Style*, p. 28.

69. Tsurumi, *The Japanese are Coming*, p. 78.

70. Ozawa, op. cit., pp. 189–190.

71. *Japan Economic Journal*, October 27, 1990.

72. *Japan An International Comparison*, Keizai Koho Center, 1990.

73. MITI Survey of Small- and Medium-sized Firms, July 1985.

74. Tolchin, op. cit., p. 63.

75. Encarntion and Mason, op. cit., p. 52.

76. Ibid, p. 44.

77. Ibid, op. cit., p. 52.

78. Tolchin, op. cit., pp. 31–32.

79. Ibid, pp. 249–254.

80. Ibid, p. 252.

81. Quoted in ibid, p. 222.

9 The High Technology Front

1. For a comprehensive analysis of the technology balance of power, see the technology section of Chapter 4.
2. *New York Times*, May 28, 1991.
3. Ibid.
4. Paul Kennedy, *The Rise and Fall of the Great Powers*, p. xxii.
5. Ibid, p. 439.
6. Christopher Freeman, *Technology Policy and Economic Performance*, p. 31.
7. Charles Ferguson, "America's High Tech Decline", *Foreign Policy*, Spring 1989, op. cit., p. 136.
8. Imman and Burton, op. cit., p. 118.
9. *New York Times*, April 25, 1991.
10. *New York Times*, May 10, 1990. Sekora has since set up a private company, Technology Strategic Planning, to provide American firms with a data base of foreign technology that the Bush administration had eliminated. The trouble is that no private firm can equal the intelligence facilities and sources of the DIA.
11. *New York Times*, May 28, 1990.
12. Okimoto, op. cit., in Yamamura, pp. 406–419.
13. *New York Times*, February 4, 1991.
14. *New York Times*, March 4, 1991.
15. *New York Times*, May 27, 1990.
16. Both Roy and Chapline are quoted in *New York Times*, May 27, 1990.
17. Both Allan and Keyworth are quoted in *New York Times*, June 10, 1990.
18. *New York Times*, June 10, 1990.
19. *New York Times*, September 4, 1990.
20. *New York Times*, March 7, 1991.
21. Prestowitz, op. cit., p. 140.
22. *New York Times*, March 1, 1991.
23. *New York Times*, April 18, 1991.
24. Inman and Burton, op. cit., p. 132.
25. *New York Times*, December 19, 1990.
26. See William Nester, *Japanese Industrial Targeting: The Neomercantilist Path to Economic Superpower*, New York: St. Martin's Press, 1991 for an indepth account of Japan's technology policies, from which some of the following statistics, information, and excerpts have been culled.
27. Kozo Yamamura, "Caveat Emptor: The Industrial Policy of Japan", in Paul Krugman, ed., *Strategic Trade Policy and the New International Economics*, Cambridge, Mass.: MIT Press, 1986, p. 192.
28. Fong, op. cit., p. 284.
29. Okimoto, pp. 119–120, op. cit., in Okimoto *et al.*
30. Ibid.
31. Abegglen and Stalk, *Kaisha: The Japanese Corporation*, pp. 121, 49.
32. Prestowitz, op. cit., p. 200.
33. Johnson, op. cit., p. 67.
34. *US News and World Report*, July 10, 1989.
35. Okimoto, op. cit., in Patrick, p. 35.
36. Weinstein, op. cit., in Okimoto *et al*, p. 37.
37. *Economist*, April 1, 1989; *Economist*, May 28, 1989; Teruo Doi. "The Role of Intellectual Property Law in Bilateral Licensing Transactions between Japan and the United States", in *Law and Trade Issues of the Japanese Economy*, p. 159.

38. Arthur Wineberg. "The Japanese Patent System: A Non-Tariff Barrier to Foreign Businesses?", *Journal of World Trade*, vol. 22, no. 1, Fall 1988. p. 12.
39. Earl H. Kinmouth, "Japanese Patents: Olympic Gold or Public Relations Brass", *Pacific Affairs*, p. 4; Doi, op. cit., p. 159.
40. David S. Guttman, "Protecting Intellectual Property: An American Viewpoint", *Speaking of Japan*, vol. 5, no. 41, May 1984, p. 18.
41. *Far Eastern Economic Review*, November 17, 1988; *Japan Economic Journal*, October 22, 1988.
42. *Economist*, April 1, 1989; *Japan Economic Journal*, December 9, 1989.
43. Inman and Burton, op. cit., p. 127.
44. *New York Times*, November 11,1990.
45. *Japan Economic Journal*, November 19, 1988.
46. Woronoff, op. cit., p. 92; Jones, p. 71, in Sigur.
47. Anchordoguy, p. 532.
48. Edward Lincoln, *Japan's Industrial Policies: What are they, Do they matter, and Are They Different From Those in the United States?*, Tokyo: Japan Economic Institute, 1984, pp. 34, 36.
49. Anchordoguy, pp. 521, 523; Daniel Okimoto, p. 101 in Daniel Okimoto, Takuo Sugano, and Franklin B. Weinstein, eds, *Competitive Edge: The Semiconductor Industry in the U.S. and Japan*, Stanford, Stanford: University Press, 1984, p. 102.
50. *New York Times*, March 15, 1991.
51. Sobel, pp. 168–170.
52. *International Herald Tribune*, April 20, 1989; *Economist*, December 2, 1989; *Japan Economic Journal*, September 15, 1990; *New York Times*, November 24, 1990; *New York Times*, June 3, 1991.
53. *New York Times*, March 12, 1991.
54. *New York Times*, November 24. 1990.
55. *Japan Economic Journal*, April 3, 1989.
56. *New York Times*, November 25, 1990.
57. *New York Times*, April 11, 1991.
58. Prestowitz, op. cit., p. 21.
59. Sobel, op. cit., p. 241; Davidson, op. cit., p. 224.
60. Fong, opl cit., pp. 280–281.
61. Prestowitz, op. cit., p. 32.
62. Ibid, p. 48.
63. Franklin Weinstein, p. 55 in Okimoto *et al.*
64. *International Herald Tribune*, June 26, 1989.
65. Prestowitz, op. cit., p. 57.
66. US Department of Defense, *Report on Semiconductor Dependency*, p. 74.
67. *Economist*, June 11, 1988; *Businessweek*, July 4, 1988.
68. Anchordoguy, p. 93; *Economist*, February 18, 1989; *Far Eastern Economic Review*, August 18, 1988; *Businessweek*, July 10, 1989.
69. Prestowitz, op. cit., pp. 52–53.
70. *Los Angeles Times*, March 14, 1986.
71. *Far Eastern Economic Review*, November 17, 1988.
72. Choate, p. 21.
73. *Businessweek*, August 6, 1990.
74. Prestowitz, op. cit., pp. 68–69.
75. *International Herald Tribune*, March 4/5, 1989.
76. *New York Times*, May 6, 1991.
77. *New York Times*, December 4, 1990.

78. Prestowitz, op. cit., p. 50.
79. *Far Eastern Economic Review*, April 6, 1989.
80. For in-depth studies see Richard Samuels and Benjamin Whipple, "Defense Production and Industrial Development: the Case of Japanese Aircraft", in Zysman *et al.*, *Politics and Productivity*, pp. 275–318.
81. Ibid, p. 293.
82. Kent E. Calder, "The Rise of Japan's Military-Industrial Complex", *Asia Pacific Community*, no. 17, Summer 1982, pp. 31–32.
83. Samuels, op. cit., p. 292.
84. *Japan Economic Journal*, October 27, 1990.
85. *New York Times*, November 11, 1989.
86. *Japan Economic Journal*, January 27, 1990.
87. *New York Times*, April 15, 1990.
88. Inman and Burton, op. cit., p. 123.
89. *Japan Economic Journal*, February 28, 1989.
90. Shinji Otsuki, "The FSX Problem Resolved?", *Japan Quarterly*, January–March 1990, p. 73.
91. Quoted in ibid, pp. 172–173.
92. *New York Times*, April 29, 1989.
93. *Far Eastern Economic Review*, March 9, 1989.
94. *Japan Economic Journal*, February 17, 1990.
95. Ibid.
96. Quoted in Samuel, op. cit., p. 304.
97. *Economist*, May 13, 1989.
98. Inman and Burton, op. cit., p. 126.
99. For an indepth overview of Japan's telecommunications policy, see Chalmers Johnson, "MITI, MPT, and the Telecom Wars", in Zysman *et al.*, *Politics and Productivity*, pp. 177–140.
100. Ibid, p. 183.
101. *Japan Economic Journal*, June 2, 1990.
102. *Economist*, May 13, 1989.
103. *Japan Economic Journal*, September 8, 1990.
104. *Businessweek*, September 19, 1988.
105. *Businessweek*, September 19, 1988; *Far Eastern Economic Review*, April 6, 1989.
106. *New York Times*, September 4, 1990.
107. *Business Tokyo*, February 1991.
108. *New York Times*, July 6, 1991.

10   The Financial Front

1. Parts of this chapter are taken from chapter 7 of *Japanese Industrial Targeting: The Neomercantilist Path to Economic Superpower*.
2. *Newsweek*, May 21, 1990.
3. *New York Times*, June 6, 1990.
4. *New York Times*, June 1, 1990.
5. *Newsweek*, May 21, 1990.
6. Paul Krugman, *The Age of Diminished Expectations*, p. 158.
7. *New York Times*, May 1, 1990.
8. *New York Times*, January 26, 1991.
9. Quoted in Martin and Susan Tolchin, *Buying into America*, p. 123.
10. Ibid, p. 127.
11. Ibid, pp. 120, 122, 263.

12. Crum in McCraw, p. 266.
13. Horne, pp. 201–207.
14. *Far Eastern Economic Review*, June 7, 1990.
15. *New York Times*, March 10, 1991.
16. *Far Eastern Economic Review*, April 16, 1990.
17. *Businessweek*, October 15, 1990.
18. *Japan Economic Journal*, April 14, 1990.
19. *Businessweek*, July 25, 1988.
20. *New York Times*, February 2, 1991.
21. Wright, op. cit., p. 36.
22. *Economist*, November 3, 1990; *Far Eastern Economic Review*, June 21, 1990.
23. *Economist*, July 9, 1988.
24. *Businessweek*, June 13, 1988.
25. *Japan Economic Journal*, April 30, 1988; *Far Eastern Economic Review*, May 5, 1988.
26. *Businessweek*, June 13, 1989.
27. *Japan Economic Journal*, June 21, 1990.
28. *Japan Economic Journal*, April 14, 1990.
29. *New York Times*, April 23, 1990.
30. *New York Times*, December 11, 1990.
31. See Fred Bergsten's remarks in the *Japan Economic Journal*, May 12, 1990.
32. *Economist*, January 28, 1989.
33. *Businessweek*, June 13, 1989.
34. Quoted in *New York Times*, July 9, 1991.
35. *New York Times*, July 9, 1991.
36. *Newsweek*, July 8, 1991.
37. *New York Times*, July 21, 1991.
38. *New York Times*, July 28, 1991.

11 America and Japan into the 21st Century

1. *New York Times*, February 14, 1991.
2. *New York Times*, March 12, 1991.
3. *New York Times*, December 3, 1990.
4. Chalmers Johnson, *The Industrial Policy Debate*, p. 164.
5. Paul Krugman, *The Age of Diminished Expectations*, pp. 103–104.
6. Ibid, p. 105.
7. Jackson, p. 155.
8. Friedman, p. 4.
9. Pat Choate, *Agents of Influence*, p. xiii.
10. Krugman, op. cit., p. xi.
11. *New York Times*, September 9, 1990.
12. Robert Reich and Magazines, p. 331.
13. Quoted in Stephen Cohen, *The Making of United States Economic Policy*, p. 103.
14. Ibid, p. 27.
15. Quoted in ibid, p. 63.
16. Timothy Stanley et al., *U.S. Economic Policy for the 1980s*, p. 00.
17. Fred Bergsten, *The United States in the World Economy*, p. 33.
18. M. Czinkota and G. Tesar, *Export Policy*, p. 72.
19. Stanley, op. cit., pp. 150–151.
20. Choate, op. cit., p. 201.
21. Krugman, op. cit., p. 100.

22. Reich and Magaziners, op. cit., pp. 4, 197.
23. Johnson, op. cit., pp. 7–8.
24. Reich and Magaziners, op. cit., p. 6.
25. See John Pinder, *National Industrial Strategies and the World Economy*, for a concise history of American industrial policies.
26. Reich and Magazines, op. cit., p. 255.
27. Ibid, p. 200.
28. David H. Brandin and Michael Harrison, *The Technology War*, New York: John Wiley, 1987, p. 61.
29. Inman and Burton, p. 126.
30. Quoted in Sylvia-Yvonne Kaufmann, "Political Role of Japan in World Affairs", *Korea and World Affairs*, vol. 14, no. 1, Spring 1990.
31. *Japan Economic Journal*, May 19, 1990.
32. Chalmers Johnson, "MITI, MPT, and the Telcomon Wars", in Zysman *et al.*, *Politics and Productivity*, p. 214.
33. Fukushima, op. cit., p. 41.
34. Clyde Prestowitz, *Trading Places*, p. 323.
35. Glen Fukushima, "Back to Business", *Business Tokyo*, July 1990.
36. Ibid.
37. *New York Times*, June 9, 1990.
38. *Japan Economic Journal*, January 15, 1991.
39. *Japan Economic Journal*, September 3, 1988.
40. Both quotes from Jon Woronoff, *World Trade War*, p. 96.
41. Kan Ito, "Trans-Pacific Anger", *Foreign Policy*, no. 78, Spring.
42. Jackson, op. cit., p. 190.
43. *New York Times*, October 11, 1989.
44. *New York Times*, March 27, 1991.
45. Prestowitz, op. cit., p. 324.
46. Woronoff, op. cit., p. 58.
47. Quoted in Harrison and Prestowitz, op. cit., p. 68.
48. Ibid, p. 68.
49. Ibid, pp. 68–69.
50. Harrison and Prestowitz, op. cit., p. 57.
51. Prestowitz, op. cit., p. 278.

Bibliography

Geopolitics and Geoeconomics: Theory and Reality

Adams, F. Gerald, and Lawrence Klein, (eds) *Industrial Policy for Growth and Consequences*, Lexington, Mass.: Lexington Books, 1983.

Altschiller, Donald, (ed.) *Free Trade Versus Protectionism*, New York: H.W. Wilson Press, 1988.

Ashley, Richard K., "The Poverty of Neorealism", *International Organization*, vol. 38, no. 2, Spring 1984 pp. 225–286.

Axline, W. Andrew, "Underdevelopment, Dependence, and Integration: the Politics of Regionalism in the Third World", *International Organization*, vol. 31, no. 1, Winter 1977 pp. 83–106.

Balassa, Bela, *The Newly Industrializing Countries in the World Economy*, New York: Pergamon Press, 1981.

Balassa, Bela *et al.*, *Developing Strategies in Semi-industrializing Countries*, World Bank Research Publication, Baltimore: John Hopkins University Press, 1982.

Balassa, Bela, "Dependency and Trade Orientation", *The World Economy*, vol. 9, no. 3, September 1986, pp. 239–258.

Baldwin, David A, "International Political Economy and the International Monetary System", *International Organization*, vol. 32, no. 2, Spring 1978, pp. 487–512.

Baldwin, Robert, *Trade Policy in A Changing World Economy*, Chicago: University of Chicago Press, 1988.

Bander, James and Barbara Spencer, "Export Subsidies and International Market Share Rivalry", *Journal of International Economics*, vol. 18, no. 1, 1985.

Baranson, Jack, *Robots in Manufacturing: Key to International Competitiveness*, Mt. Airy, Md.: Lomond, 1983.

Barfield, Claude E. and William Schambra (eds) *The Politics of Industrial Policy*, Washington, DC: American Enterprise Institute for Public Policy Research, 1986.

Bartel, Richard D., "Industrial Policy as an International Issue", *Challenge*, vol. 23, no. 6, January/February 1981.

Behrman, Jack, *Industrial Policy: International Structuring and Transnationalism*, Lexington, Mass.: Lexington Books, 1984.

Benjamin, Roger and Robert T. Kudrle (eds) *The Industrial Future of the Pacific Basin*, Boulder, Colorado: Westview Press, 1984.

Bergsten, C. Fred, "The World Economy After the Cold War", *Foreign Affairs*, vol. 69, no. 3, Summer 1990.

Bhattacharya, Anindya, *The Asia Dollar Market: International Offshore Financing*, New York: Praeger Publishers Inc., 1977.

Blake, David and Robert Walter, *The Politics of Global Economic Relations*, Englewood Cliffs, NJ: Prentice-Hall, 1983.

Block, Fred, *The Origins of International Economic Disorder: A Study of US International Monetary Policy from World War II to the Present*, Berkeley: University of California Press, 1977.

461

Bobrow, David and Robert T. Kudrle, "How Middle Powers Can Manage Resource Weakness", *World Politics*, vol. 39, no. 4, July 1987.

Boyd, Gavin (ed.) *Region Building in the Pacific*, New York: Pergamon Press, 1982.

Boyd, Gavin (ed.) *Regionalism and Global Security*, Lexington, Mass.: Lexington Books, 1984.

Brainard, Lawrence J., "Current Illusions about the International Debt Crisis", *The World Economy*, vol. 8, no. 1, March 1985, pp. 1–10.

Bressand, Albert, "Mastering the 'World Economy'," *Foreign Affairs*, pp. 745–772.

Brown, Clair, "When Does Union–Management Cooperation Work?", *California Management Review*, vol. 31, no. 4, Spring 1989.

Brown, William S., "Industrial Policy and Corporate Power", *Journal of Economic Issues*, vol. 19, no. 2, June 1985.

Brownlie, Ian, *Principles of International Law*, 3rd ed., Oxford: Clarendon Press, 1979.

Bueno de Mequita, Bruce, *The War Trap*, New Haven, Conn.: Yale University Press, 1981.

Buss, Claude A. (ed.) *National Security Interests in the Pacific Basin*, Stanford: Hoover Institute Press, 1985.

Buzan, Barry, "Economic Structure and International Security", *International Organization*, vol. 38, no. 4, Autumn 1984, pp. 597–624.

Calder, Kent E. and Roy Hofheinz, Jr, *The East Asia Edge*, New York: Basic Books, 1982.

Calton, Jerry M., "Industrial Policy, International Competitiveness, and the World Auto Industry", *Journal of Contemporary Business*, vol. 11, no. 1, June 1982.

Cannizo, Cynthia A., "The Costs of Combat: Death, Duration, and Defeat", in David J. Singer (ed.) *The Correlates of War II: Testing Some Realipolitik Models*, New York: Free Press, 1980.

Caporaso, James A., "Theory and Method in the Study of International Integration", vol. 25, no. 2, Spring 1972, pp. 228–253.

Caporaso, James A., "Introduction: Dependence, and Dependency in the Global System", *International Organization*, vol. 32, no. 1, Winter 1978, pp. 1–12.

Caporaso, James A., "Dependence, and Power in the Global System: A Structural and Behavioral Analysis", *International Organization*, vol. 32, no. 1, Winter 1978, pp. 13–44.

Chan, Steve, "The Impact of Defense Spending on Economic Performance: A Survey of Evidence and Problems", *Orbis*, vol. 29, Summer 1985.

Chen, Edward, *Hypergrowth in the Asian Economies*, New York: Holmes & Meier Publishers, 1979.

Cheng, Hang-seng, *Financial Policies and Reform in Pacific Basin Countries*, Lexington: Lexington Books, 1986.

Cohen, Benjamin J., "The Political Economy of International Trade", *International Organization*, vol. 44, no. 2, Spring 1990.

Cohen, Stephen and John Zysman, *Manufacturing Matters: The Myth of the Post-industrial Economy*, New York: Basic Books, 1987.

Conybeare, John A.C., *Trade Wars: The Theory and Practice of International Commercial Rivalry*, New York: Columbia University Press, 1987.

Cox, Robert, *Production, Power, and World Order: Social Forces in the Making of History*, New York: Columbia University Press, 1987.

Craig, Paul and John Jungerman, *Nuclear Arms Race: Technology and Society*, New York: McGraw Hill, 1986.

Cummings, Bruce, "The Origins and Development of the Northeast Asian Political Economy: Industrial Sectors, Product Cycles and Political Consequences", *International Organization*, vol. 38, no. 1, Winter 1984, pp. 1–40.

Cypher, James M. "Military Spending, Technical Change and Economic Growth: A Disguised Form of Industrial Policy", *Journal of Economic Issues*, vol. xxi, no. 1, March 1987, pp. 33–59.

Czinkota, Michael and George, Tesar, (eds) *Export Policy: A Global Assessment*, New York: Praeger Publishers, 1982.

Dell, Edmund, "Of Free Trade and Reciprocity", *The World Economy*, vol. 9, no. 2, June 1986, pp. 125–140.

Dewar, Margaret E. (ed.) *Industrial Vitalization: Toward A National Industrial Policy*, New York: Pergamon Press, 1982.

Diebold, William, *Industrial Policy as an International Issue*, New York: McGraw-Hill Book Co., 1980.

Downen, Robert and Bruce Dickson (eds) *The Emerging Pacific Community: A Regional Perspective*, Boulder, Colorado: Westview Press, 1984.

Doyle, Michael, "Kant, Liberal Legacies and Foreign Affairs", *Philosophy and Public Affairs*, vol. 12, no. 3, no. 4, Summer, Fall 1983.

Drysdale, Peter (ed.) *Direct Foreign Investment in Asia and the Pacific*, University of Toronto Press, Toronto, 1972.

Dunn, James A., "Automobiles in International Trade: Regime Change or Persistence", *International Organization*, vol. 41, no. 2, Spring 1987.

Duvall, Raymond D., "Dependence and Dependenica Theory: Notes Toward Precision of Concept and Argument", *International Organization*, vol. 32, no. 1, Winter 1978, pp. 51–78.

Evans, Peter B., Dietrich Ruseschemeyer and Theda Skocpol (eds) *Bringing the State Back in*, Cambridge: Cambridge University Press, 1985.

Fagen, Richard, "A Funny Thing Happened on the Way to the Market: Thoughts on Extending Dependency Ideas", *International Organization*, vol. 32, no. 1, Winter 1978, pp. 287–300.

Feld, Werner J., Robert S. Jordan and Leon Hurwitz (eds) *International Organizations: A Comparative Approach*, Praeger Publishers, New York: 1983.

Fong, Glenn, "State Strength, Industry Structure and Industrial Policy: American and Japanese Experiences in Microelectronics", *Comparative Politics*, vol. 22, no. 3, April 1990.

Freenstra, Robert (ed.) *Empirical Research in International Trade*, Cambridge, Mass.: MIT Press 1988.

Fukuyama, Francis, "The End of History?", *The National Interest*, no. 16, Summer 1989.

Gilpin, Robert, *War and Change in World Politics*, Cambridge: Cambridge University Press, 1981.

Gilpin, Robert G., "The Richness of the Tradition of Political Realism", *International Organization*, vol. 38, no. 2, Spring 1984, pp. 287–304.

Gilpin, Robert G., *The Political Economy of International Relations*, Princeton, N.J., Princeton University Press, 1987.

Glick, L.A., *Multilateral Trade Negotiations: World Trade after the Tokyo Round*, Totowa, NJ: Rowman and Allenheld, 1984.

Gold, Bela, "Some International Differences in Approaches to Industrial Policy", *Contemporary Policy Issues*, vol. 4, no. 1, January 1986.

Gordon, Bernard K. and Kenneth J. Rothwell (eds) *The New Political Economy of the Pacific*, Cambridge, Mass.: Ballinger Publishing Company, 1975.

Gowa, Joanne, "Hegemons, IOs and Markets: the Case of the Substitution Account", *International Organization*, vol. 38, no. 4, Autumn 1984, pp. 661–684.

Gowa, Joanne, "Cooperation and International Relations", *International Organization*, Winter 1986, vol. 40, no. 1, pp. 167–186.

Grady, Robert C., "Reindustrialization, Liberal Democracy and Corporate Representation", *Political Science Quarterly*, no. 3, 1986, pp. 415–432.

Guerrieri, Paolo and Pier Carlo Padovan, "Neomercantilism and International Economic Stability", *International Organization*, 1986, vol. 40, no. 1, pp. 167–186.

Helpman, Elhanen and Paul Krugman, *Market Structure and Foreign Trade*, Cambridge, Mass.: MIT Press, 1985.

Henkin, Louis, *International Law*, St. Paul: West, 2nd ed., 1987.

Holsti, K.J., "A New International Politics? Diplomacy in Complex Interdependence", *International Organization*, vol. 32, no. 2, Spring 1978, pp. 513–530.

Holsti, Kal J., "Politics in Command: Foreign Trade as National Security Policy", *International Organization*, Summer 1986, vol. 40, no. 3, pp. 643–671.

Holsti, Ole, Randolph Silverson and Alexander George (eds) *Change in the International System*, Boulder, Colorado: Westview Press, 1980.

Hopkins, Terrence and Immanuel Wallerstein, *World Systems Analysis; Theory and Methodology*, Beverly Hills: Sage Publications, 1982.

Ikenberry, G. John and Charles A. Kupchan, "Socialization and Hegemonic Power", *International Organization*, vol. 44, no. 3, Summer 1990.

Jackson, John and William Davey, *Legal Problems of International Economic Relations*, 2nd ed., St. Paul: West, 1986.

Jaikumar, R., "Postindustrial Manufacturing", *Harvard Business Review*, vol. 64, 1986.

Jones, T.M. *et al.*, "Industrial Policy: Influencing the International Marketplace", *Journal of Contemporary Business*, vol. 11, no. 1, 1982.

Katzenstein, Peter J, "International Interdependence: Some Long Term Trends Changes", *International Organization*, vol. 29, no. 4, Autumn 1975, pp. 1021–1034.

Kaysen, Carl, "Is War Obsolete?", *International Organization*, vol. 14, no. 4, Spring 1990.

Kegly, Charles and Pat McGowan (eds) *The Political Economy of Foreign Policy Behavior*, Beverly Hills: Sage Publications, 1981.

Kenen, Peter, *The International Economy*, Englewood Cliffs, NJ: Prentice Hall, 1985.

Kennedy, Paul, *The Rise and Fall of the Great Powers*, New York: Random House, 1987.

Keohane, Robert, *After Hegemony: Co-operation and Discord in the World Political Economy*, Princeton, NJ: Princeton University Press, 1984.

Keohane, Robert, "Reciprocity in International Relations", *International Organization*, Winter 1986, vol. 40, no. 1, pp. 1–28.

Keohane, Robert and Joseph Nye (eds) *Power and Interdependence: World Politics in Transition*, Boston, Mass.: Little, Brown and Company, 1977.

Kindleberger, Charles P., *The World in Depression*, London: Allen Press, 1973.

Kindleberger, Charles P., "Hierarchy Versus Inertial Cooperation", *International Organization*, Autumn 1986, vol. 40, no. 4, pp. 841–848.

Kolde, Endel Jakob, *The Pacific Quest: The Concept and Scope of an Oceanic Community*, Lexington Mass.: Lexington Books, 1976.

Krasner, Stephen (ed.) *International Regimes*, Ithaca: Cornell University Press, 1982.

Krasner, Stephen (ed.) *Structural Conflict: The Third World Against Global Liberalism*, Berkeley: University of California Press, 1985.

Krause, Lawrence and Sueo Sekiguchi (ed.) *Economic Interaction in the Pacific Basin*, Washington, D.C.: The Brookings Institute, 1980.

Krause, Lawrence, "Trade Policy in the 1990s: Goodbye Bipolarity, Hello Regions", *World Today*, vol. 46, no. 5, May 1990.

Krugman, Paul (ed.) *Strategic Trade Policy and the New International Economics*, Cambridge, Mass.: MIT Press, 1986.

Krugman, Paul, "Is Free Trade Passe", *Economic Perspectives*, vol. 1, no. 2, Fall 1987.(NT)

Krugman, Paul, *The Age of Diminished Expectations*, Cambridge, Mass.: MIT Press, 1990.

Kugler, Jacek and William Domke, "Comparing the Strengths of Nations", *Comparative Political Studies*, vol. 19, no. 1, April 1986.

Lake, David A., *Power, Protection, and Free Trade: International Sources of US Commercial Strategy*, 1887–1939, Cornell University Press, 1988.

Lavoie, Don, "Two Varieties of Industrial Policy: A Critique", *CATO Journal*, vol. 4, no. 2, Fall 1984.

Lawrence, Robert and Robert Litan, *Saving Free Trade: A Pragmatic Approach*, Washington, D.C.: Brookings Institute, 1986.

Laxer, James, *Decline of the Superpowers: Winners and Losers in Today's Global Economy*, New York: Praeger Press, 1989.

Levy, J.S., *War in the Modern Great Power System, 1495–1975*, Lexington: University Press of Kentucky, 1983.

Linder, Staffan, *The Pacific Century; Economic and Political Consequences of Asian–Pacific Dynamism*, Stanford: Stanford University Press, 1986.

Lipsey, Richard G. and Wendy Dobson (eds) *Shaping Comparative Advantage*, Policy Study no. 2, Toronto: C.D. Howe Institute, 1987.

Luard, Evan, *War in International Society*, London: I.B. Tauris, 1986.

Mack, Andrew, "Why Big Nations Lose Small Wars: The Politics of Asymetric Conflict", *World Politics*, vol. 27, no. 1, January 1975.

Maoz, Zee, *Paths to Conflict*, Boulder, Colo.: Westview Press, 1982.

Maoz, Zee, "Resolve, Capabilities and the Outcomes of Interstate Disputes, 1816–1975", *Journal of Conflict Resolution*, vol. 27, no. 2, June 1983.

Maoz, Zee, "Power, Capabilities and Paradoxical Conflict Outcomes", *World Politics*, vol. 41, no. 1, January 1989.

McCulloch, Rachel, "Points of View: Trade Deficits, International Competiveness and the Japanese", *California Management Review*, vol. 27, no. 2, 1984.

McGovern, Edmond, *International Trade Regulation*, Exeter: Globefield Press, 2nd ed., 1986.

McKenna, Regis *et al.*, "Industrial Policy and International Competition in High Technology", *California Management Review*, vol. 26, no. 2, Winter 1984.

McKeown, Timothy J., "Hegemonic Stability Theory and 19th Century Tariff Levels in Europe", *International Organization*, pp. 73–92, vol. 37, no. 1, Winter 1983.

Milner, Helen V., *Resisting Protectionism: Global Industries and the Politics of International Trade*, Princeton, N.J.: Princeton University Press, 1988.

Milner, Helen V. and David B. Yoffie, "Between Free Trade and Protectionism: Strategic Trade Policy and a Theory of Corporate Trade Demands", *International Organization*, vol. 43, no. 2, Spring 1989.

Modelski, George, "Is World Politics Evolutionary Learning?" *International Organization*, vol. 44, no. 1, Winter 1990.

Moran, Theodore H., "Multinational Corporations and Dependency: A Dialogue for Dependentistas and Non-dependentistas", *International Organization*, vol. 32, no. 1, Winter 1978, pp. 79–100.

Morrison, Charles E., *Threats to Security in East Asia Pacific: National and Regional Perspectives*, Lexington: Lexington Books, 1981.

Morse, Edward, *Modernization and the Transformation of International Relations*, New York: The Free Press, 1976.

Mowery, David, *Alliance Politics and Economics*, Cambridge, Mass.: Ballinger, 1987.

Mueller, John, *Retreat from Doomsday: The Obsolescence of War*, New York: Basic Books, 1989.

Nelson, Richard, *High-technology Policies: A Five Nation Comparison*, Washington, DC: American Enterprise Institute for Public Policy Research, 1984.

Nicolaides, Phedon, "Trade Policy in the 1990s: Avoiding the Trap of Regionalism", *World Today*, vol. 46, no. 4, May 1990.

Olsen, Mancur, *The Rise and Decline of Nations*, New Haven, Conn: Yale University Press, 1982.

Organski, A.F.K. and Jack Kugler, *The War Ledger*, Chicago: The University of Chicago Press, 1980.

Pinder, John (ed.) *National Industrial Strategies and the World Economy*, London: Croom-Helm, 1982.

Piore, Michal and Charles F. Sabel, *The Second Industrial Divide: Possibilities for Prosperity*, New York: Basic Books, 1984.

Pudaite, Paul R. and Gretchen Hower, "National Capability and Conflict Outcome", in Richard J. Stoll and Michael Don Wards (eds), *Power and World Politics*, Boulder, Colorado: Rienner, 1989.

Quo, F. Quei (ed.) *Politics of the Pacific Rim: Perspectives on the 1980s*, Simon Fraser University, Burnaby, BC: San Francisco University Publishers, 1982.

Ramsted, Yugue, "Free Trade Versus Fair Trade: Import Barriers as a Problem of Reasonable Values", *Journal of Economic Issues*, vol. xxi, no. 1, March 1987, pp. 5–22.

Reich, Robert B., "Making Industrial Policy", *Foreign Affairs*, Spring 1982, pp. 852–881.

Reich, Robert B., "Beyond Free Trade", *Foreign Affairs*, Spring 1983, pp. 773–804.

Reich, Robert B., "The Threat of the Global Corporation", *Canadian Business*, vol. 56, no. 8, August 1983.

Reich, Robert B., "What Kind of Industrial Policy?", *Journal of Business Strategy*, vol. 5, no. 1, Summer 1984.

Richardson, J. David, "The Politial Economy of Strategic Trade Policy", *International Organization*, vol. 44, no. 1, Winter 1990.

Rockman, Bert A., "Minding the State or a State of Mind?", *Comparative Studies*, vol. 22, no. 3, April 1990.

Rohrlich, Paul Egan, "Economic Culture and Foreign Policy: The Cognitive Analysis of Economic Policymaking", *International Organization*, Winter 1987, vol. 41, no. 1, pp. 61–92.

Rosecrance, Richard, *The Rise of the Trading State: Commerce and Conquest in the Modern World*, New York: Basic Books, 1986.

Rosecrance, R. *et al.*, "Whither Interdependence?", *International Organization*, vol. 31, no. 3, Summer 1977, pp. 425–472.

Rosecrance, Richard and William Gutowitz, "Measuring Interdependence: A Rejoinder", *International Organization*, vol. 35, no. 3, Summer 1981, pp. 553–556.

Rosenau, James N., "Hegemons, Regimes and Habit Driven Actors in World Politics", *International Organization*, Autumn 1986, vol. 40, no. 4, pp. 849–894.

Russett, Bruce, "Dimension of Resource Dependence: Some Elements of Rigor in Concept and Policy Analysis", *International Organization*, vol. 38, no. 3, Summer 1984, pp. 481–500.

Sabel, Charles F., *Work and Politics: The Division of Labor in Industry*, New York: Cambridge University Press, 1982.

Samuelson, Paul, *Economics*, 11th ed., New York: McGraw Hill, 1980.

Sato, Ryuzo and Paul Wachtel (eds) *Trade Friction and Economic Policy*, New York: Cambridge University Press, 1985.

Schmitter, Philippe and Gerhard Lehmbruch, *Trends Toward Corporate Intervention*, London: Sage Publications, 1979.

Schumpeter, Joseph, *Capitalism, Socialism, and Democracy*, New York: Harper, 1942.

Snidal, Duncan, "The Limits of Hegemonic Stability Theory", *International Organization*, Autumn 1985, vol. 39, no. 4, pp. 579–614.

Spanier, John, *Games Nations Play: Analyzing International Politics*, New York: Holt, Rinehart and Winston, 1984.

Staniland, Martin, *What is Political Economy?: A Study of Social Theory and Underdevelopment*, New Haven, Conn.: Yale University Press, 1985.

Stegeman, Klaus, "Policy Rivalry Among Industrial States: What Can We Learn from Models of Strategic Trade Theory?", *International Organization*, vol. 43, no. 4, Winter 1989.

Stein, Arthur A., "The Hegemon's Dilemma: Great Britain, the United States and the International Economic Order", *International Organization*, vol. 38, no. 2, Spring 1984, pp. 355–386.

Stern, Robert M. (ed.) US Trade Policies in *A Changing World Economy*, Cambridge, Mass.: MIT Press, 1987.

Strange, Susan (ed.) *Paths to International Political Economy*, London: George Allen & Unwin, 1984.

Tetreault, Mary Ann, "Measuring Interdependence: A Response", *International Organization*, vol. 35, no. 3, Summer 1981, pp. 557–560.

Tetreualt, Mary Ann, "Measuring Interdependence", *International Organization*, vol. 34, no. 3, Summer 1980, pp. 429–443.

Toffler, Alvin, *The Third Wave*, New York: Morrow, 1980.

Van Themaat and Pieter Verloren, *The Changing Structure of International Economic Law*, The Hague: Martinus Nijhoff, 1981.

Venables, Anthony and M. Alastair Smith, "Trade and Industrial Policy Under Imperfect Competition", *Economic Policy*, vol. 3, no. 1, October 1986.

Viner, Jacob, *Dumping: A Problem in International Trade*, New York: Kelly, 1966.

Ward, Michael D. and Lewis L. House, "A Theory of Behavioral Power of Nations", *Journal of Conflict Resolution*, vol. 32, no. 1, March 1988.

Whalen, Charles J., "A Reason to Look Beyond Neoclassical Economics: Some Major Shortcomings of Orthodox Theory", *Journal of Economic Issues*, vol. xxi, no. 1, March 1987, pp. 259–280.

Whalley, John, *Trade Liberalization* among *Major World Trading Partners*, Cambridge, Mass.: MIT Press, 1985.

White, John, *The Politics of Foreign Aid*, New York: St. Martin's Press, 1974.

Williamson, John, *The Open Economy and the World Economy*, New York: Basic Books, 1983.

Wrong, Dennis H., *Power: Its Forms, Bases, and Uses*, New York: Harper & Row, 1979.

Zimmerman, William, "Hierarchial Regional Systems and the Politics of System Boundaries", *International Organization*, vol. 26, no. 1, Winter 1972, pp. 18–36.

Zysman, John, *Governments, Markets, and Growth: Financial Systems and the Politics of Industrial Change*, Ithaca, NY: Cornell University Press, 1983.

Zysman, John and Laura Tyson (eds) *American Industry in Industrial Competition: Government Policies and Corporate Strategies*, Ithaca, NY: Cornell University Press, 1983.

United States–Japanese Relations

Abegglen, James C. and Thomas M. Hout, "Facing up to the Trade Gap with Japan", *Foreign Affairs*, Fall 1978, pp. 146–168.

Barnds, William (ed.) *Japan and the United States: Challenges and Opportunities*, New York University Press, New York: 1979.

Bergsten, C. Fred, "What to Do About the US–Japan Economic Conflict", *Foreign Affairs*, Summer 1982, pp. 1059–1076.

Bergsten, C. Fred, *The United States–Japan Economic Problem*, Washington, DC: Institute for International Economics, 1985.

Blaker, Michael, *The Politics of Trade: US and Japanese Policymaking for the GATT Negotiations*, New York: East Asian Institute, 1978.

Bloom, Justin, "A New Era for US–Japan Technical Relations? Problems and Prospects", *Journal of NorthEast Asian Studies*, Summer 1987.

Borden, William, *The Pacific Alliance: United States Foreign Economic Policy and the Japanese Trade Recovery, 1947–55*, Madison: University of Wisconsin Press, 1984.

Borrus, Michael *et al.*, *US–Japanese Competition in the Semiconductor Industry*, Policy Papers in International Affairs 17, Berkeley, California: Institute of International Studies, University of California, 1982.

Calista, Samuel, "Japanese Values and Perceptions of US Values", *Pacific Affairs*, vol. 16, no. 4, January 1984.

Castle, Emery and Kenzo Hemmi (eds) *US–Japanese Agricultural Trade Relations*, Washington, DC: Resources for the Future Inc., 1982.

Chang, C.S., *The Japanese Auto Industry and the US Market*, New York: Praeger Publishing Co., 1981.

Choate, Pat, *Agents of Influence: How Japan's Lobbyists in the United States Manipulate America's Political and Economic System*, New York: Alfred A. Knopf Inc., 1990.

Cleaver, Charles Grinnell, *Japanese and Americans: Cultural Parallels and Paradoxes*, Minneapolis: University of Minnesota Press, 1976.

Cohen, Jerome B. (ed.) *Pacific Partnership: United States–Japan Trade Prospects and Recommendations for the Seventies*, Lexington, Mass.: Lexington Books, 1972.

Cole, Robert E. and Taizo Yakushiji (eds) *The American and Japanese Auto Industries in Transition*, Tokyo: Technova Inc., 1984.

Cole, Robert E. and Donald Deskins, "Racial Factors in Site Location and Employment Patterns of Japanese Auto Firms in America", *California Management Review*, vol. 31, no. 1, Fall 1989.

Copper, John, "US–Japanese Relations", *Asia Affairs: An American Review*, vol. 10, no. 4, 1984.

Davidson, William H., *The Amazing Race: Winning the Technorivalry with Japan*, New York: John Wiley and Sons Inc., 1984.

Destler, I.M. and Hideo Sato (eds) *Coping with the United States–Japanese Economic Conflicts*, Lexington, Mass.: Lexington Books, 1982.

Doi, Teruo, "The Role of Intellectual Property Law in Bilateral Licensing Transactions between Japan and the United States", in Gary Saxonhouse (ed.) *Law and Trade Issues of the Japanese Economy*.

Duncan, William, *United States–Japan Auto Diplomacy*, Cambridge, Mass.: Ballinger Publishing Company, 1973.

Encarnation, Dennis and Mark Mason, "Neither MITI nor America: the Political Economy of Capital Liberalization in Japan", *International Organization*, vol. 44, no. 1, Winter 1990.

Feigenbaum, Edward and Pamela McCorduck (eds) *The Fifth Generation Computer: Artificial Intelligence and Japan's Computer Challenge to the World*, Reading, Mass.: Addison-Wesley Publishing Company, 1983.

Fong, Glenn R., "State Strength, Industry Structure and Industrial Policy: American and Japanese Experiences in Microelectronics", *Comparative Politics*, vol. 22, no. 3, April 1990.

Foreign Industrial Targeting and its Effects on US Industries, Phase I: *Japan*, USITC Pub. no. 1437, 1983.

Fried, Edward, Philip Treise and Shigenobu Yoshida, *The Future Course of US–Japan Economic Relations*, Washington, DC: Brookings Institute, 1983.

Guttman, David S, "Protecting Intellectual Property: An American Viewpoint", *Speaking of Japan*, vol. 5, no. 41, May 1984.

Harrison, Selig and Clyde V. Prestowitz, "Pacific Agenda: Defense or Economics", *Foreign Policy*, no. 79, Summer 1990.

Hiraoka, L.S., "US–Japanese Competition in High Technology Fields", *Technological Forecasting and Social Change*, vol. 26, no. 1, August 1984.

Holland, Harrison, *Managing Diplomacy between the United States and Japan*, Stanford: Hoover Institute, 1984.

Hollerman, Leon. (ed.) *Japan and the United States: Economic and Political Adversaries*, Boulder, Colorado: Westview Press, 1980.

Hostein, William, *The Japanese Power Game: What IT Means for America*, New York: Charles Scribner's Sons, 1990.

Hunsberger, Warren S., *Japan and the United States in World Trade*, New York: Harper & Row, 1964.

Ito, Kan, "Trans-Pacific Anger", *Foreign Policy*, no. 78, Spring 1990.

Kang, T.W., *Gaishi*, New York: Basic Books, 1990.

Kestler, W. Carl, *Japanese Takeovers*, Cambridge, Mass.: Harvard Business School, 1990.

Kim, Youn-Suk, "Prospects for Japanese–US Trade and Industrial Competition", *Asian Survey*, vol. 30, no. 5, May 1990.

Kiyuna, Kenneth, "Japanese and American Companies", *Asian Affairs*, vol. 10, no. 2, Summer 1983.

Langdon, Frank, "Japan-US Trade Friction: The Reciprocity Issue", *Asian Survey*, vol. 23, no. 5, May 1983.

Lincoln, Edward J., "Disentangling the Mess in US–Japan Economic Relations", *The Brookings Review*, Fall 1985, vol. 4, no. 1., pp. 22–27.

Lincoln, Edward, *Japan's Unequal Trade*, Washington, DC: Brookings Institute, 1990.

Matsushita and Repeta, "Restricting the Supply of Japanese Automobiles: Sovereign Compulsion or Sovereign Collusion", *Case Western Reserves Journal of International Law*, vol. 14, 1982.

McCraw, Thomas K. (ed.) *America versus Japan*, Boston: Harvard Business School Press, 1986.

Mowery, David C. and Nathan Rosenberg, "Commercial Aircraft: Cooperation and Competition Between the US and Japan", *California Management Review*, vol. 27, no. 4, Summer 1985.

Nakamura, Takafusa, "Japanese Perspectives on US–Japan Trade Relations", *Asia Affairs: An American Review*, vol. 12, no. 4, Winter 1985–86.

Nathan, Leah, "A Matter of Control", *Business Month*, September 1988.

Okimoto, Daniel, Takuo Sugano and Franklin B. Weinstein (eds) *Competitive Edge: The Semiconductor Industry in the US and Japan*, Stanford: Stanford University Press, 1984.

Okita, Saburo, "Japanese–American Economic Troubles: Lowering the Temperature", *International Security*, vol. 7, no. 2, Fall 1982, pp. 198–203.

Otsuki, Shinji, "The FSX Problem Resolved?", *Japan Quarterly*, vol. 37, no. 1, January–March 1990.

Patrick, Hugh and Ryuichiro Tachi (eds) *Japan and the United States Today: Exchange Rates, Macroeconomic Policies, and Financial Market Innovations*, New York: Columbia University Press, 1986.

Pepper, Thomas, Merrit E. Janow and Jimmy W. Wheeler, *The Competition: Dealing with Japan*, New York: Praeger Publishers, 1985.

Petri, Peter A., *Modeling Japanese–American Trade: A Study of Symmetrical Interdependence*, Cambridge Mass.: Harvard University Press, 1988.

Pierce, John *et al.*, "The New Environmental Paradigm in Japan and the United States", *Journal of Politics*, vol. 49, no. 1, February 1987.

Prestowitz, Cylde, *Trading Places: How We Allowed Japan to Take the Lead*, New York: Basic Books, 1988.

Pugel, Thomas (ed.) *Fragile Interdependence: Economic Issues in United States–Japan Trade and Investments*, Lexington Mass.: Lexington Books, 1986.

Roemer, John E., *US–Japanese Competition in International Markets: A Study of the Trade–Investment Cycle in Modern Capitalism*, Berkeley: University of California Press, 1975.

Rubinstein, Gregg, "Emerging Bonds of US–Japanese Defense Technology Cooperation", *Strategic Review*, Winter 1987.

Scalapino, Robert A., "Asia and the United States: The Challenges Ahead", *Foreign Affairs*, vol. 69, no. 1, 1989/90.

Schlossstein, Steven, *Trade War: Greed, Power, and Industrial Policy on Opposite Sides of the Pacific*, New York: Gongdon and Weed, 1984.

Sigur, Gaston and Kim Young, *Japanese and US Policy in Asia*, New York: Praeger Publishers, 1982.

Slover, John (ed.) *Government Policy Towards Industry in the United States and Japan*, New York: Cambridge University Press, 1988.

Sobel, Robert, *CAR Wars: The Untold Story*, New York: E.P. Dutton, 1984.

Sobel, Robert, *IBM v. Japan: The Struggle for the Future*, New York: Stein and Day, Publishers, 1986.

Spencer, Edson W., "Japan as Competitor", *Foreign Policy*, no. 78, Spring 1990.

Spencer, John, "Japan: Stimulus or Scapgoat", *Foreign Affairs*, vol. 62, no. 1, Fall 1983.

Striner, Herbert E., *Regaining the Lead: Policies for Economic Growth*, New York: Praeger, 1984.

Tarnoff, Peter, "America's New Special Relationship", *Foreign Affairs*, vol. 69, no. 3, Summer 1990.

Tasca, Diane (ed.) US–Japanese Economic Relations: Co-operation, Competition, Confrontation, *New York: Pergamon Press, 1980.*

Thayer, Nathaniel B, "Beyond Security: US–Japanese Relations in the 1990s", *Journal of International Affairs*, vol. 43, no. 1, Summer/Fall 1989.

Tolchin, Martin and Susan, *Buying into America: How Foreign Money is Changing the Face of our Nation*, New York: Berkley Books, 1988.

Tsurutani, Taketsugu, "Old Habits, New Times: Challenges to Japanese-American Security Relations", *International Security*, vol. 7, no. 2, Fall 1982, pp. 175–187.

Vernon, Raymond, *Two Hungry Giants: The United States and Japan in the Quest for Oil and Ores*, Cambridge, Mass.: Harvard University Press, 1983.

Vogel, Erza, *Come Back – Case by Case: Building the Resurgence of American Business*, New York: Simon and Schuster, 1985.

Wallace, "Redefining the Foreign Compulsion Defence in US Antitrust Laws: The Japanese Auto Restraints and Beyond", *Law and Policy in International Business*, vol. 14, 1982.

Ward, Robert E. and Sakamoto Yoshikazu (eds) *Democratizing Japan: The Allied Occupation*, Honolulu: University of Hawaii Press, 1987.

Weil and Glick, "Japan – Is the Market Open? A View of the Japanese Market Drawn from US Corporate Experience", *Law and Policy in International Business*, vol. 11, 1979.

Weinstein, Franklin (ed.) *US–Japan Relations and the Security of East Asia: The Next Decade*, Boulder, Colorado: Westview Press, 1978.

Weinstein, Martin E., *NorthEast Asian Security after Vietnam*, Urbana, Chicago, London: University of Illinois Press, 1982.

Welfield, John, *An Empire in Eclipse: Japan in the Postwar American Alliance System: A Study in the Interaction of Domestic Politics and Foreign Policy*, London: Athalone Press, 1988.

Wheeler, Jimmy W., *Japanese Industrial Development Policies in the 1980s: Implications for US Trade and Investment: Final Report*, Croton-on-Hudson, New York: Hudson Institute, 1982.

Williams, Justin, *Japan's Political Revolution under MaCarthur: A Participant's Account*, Athens: University of Georgia Press, 1979.

Wilson, Robert, Peter Ashton and Thomas Egan, *Innovation, Competition, and Government Policy in the Semi-conductor Industry*, Lexington, Mass.: Lexington Books, 1980.

Woodall, Brian, "Response to the Japanese Challenge", *Asia Pacific Community*, Winter 1985, no. 2, pp. 63–80.

Zielinksi, Robert and Nigel Holloway, *Unequal Equities*, Tokyo: Kodansha, 1990.

America's Political Economy and Policies

Alexander, Robert J., "Is the US Substituting a Speculative Economy for a Productive One?", *Journal of Economic Issues*, vol. xx, no. 2, June 1986.

American Agenda: Report to the Forty-first President of the United States of America, Camp Hill, Pa.: Book-of-the-Month Club, n.d.

Avery, William and David Rapkin (eds) *America in a Changing World Political Economy*, New York: Longman Inc., 1982.

Bailey, Martin Neil and Alok K. Chakrabarti, "Innovation and US Competiveness", *The Brookings Review*, Fall 1985, vol. 4, no. 1, pp. 14–21.

Baldwin, Robert, *The Political Economy of US Import Policy*, Cambridge, Mass.: MIT Press, 1985.

Bello and Holmer, "The Heart of the 1988 Trade Act: A Legislative History of the Amendments of Section 301", *Stanford Journal of International Law*, vol. 25, 1988.

Bergsten, C. Fred, "The New Economics and US Foreign Policy", *Foreign Policy*, pp. 199–221, January 1972.

Bhagwati and Irwin, "The Return of the Reciprocitarians: US Trade Policy Today", *World Economy*, vol. 10, 1987.

Choate, Pat, *Agents of Influence: How Japan's Lobbyists in the United States Manipulate America's Political and Economic System*, New York: Alfred A. Knopf Inc., 1990.

Cline, William, *A New Approach to World Trade Policy?*, Washington DC: Institute for International Economics, no. 2, 1982.

Cohen, Stephen, *The Making of United States International Economic Policy*, New York: Praeger Publishers, 1977.

Cohen, Stephen S. and John Zysman, "Can America Compete", *Challenge*, vol. 29, no. 2, May/June 1986.

Cohen, Warren. (ed.) *New Frontiers in American–East Asian Relations*, New York: Columbia University Press, 1983.

Destler, I.M., *American Trade Politics: System under Stress*, Washington, DC: Institute for International Economic Relations, 1986.

Diebold, William (ed.) *Bilateralism, Multilateralism, and Canada in US Trade Policy*, Cambridge, Mass.: Ballinger, 1988.

Final Report on the Defense Industrial and Technology Base, Department of Defense, October 1988.

Fisher and Steinhardt, "Section 301 of the Trade Act of 1974: Protection for US Exporters of Goods, Services and Capital", *Law and Policy in International Business*, vol. 14, 1982, p. 569.

Flamm, Kenneth, *Targeting the Computer: Government support and International Competition*, Washington, DC: Brookings Institute, 1987.

Friedman, Benjamin, *Day of Reckoning: The Consequences of American Economic Policy*, New York: Vintage Books, 1988.

Fulbright, "American Foreign Policy in the Twentieth Century Under a Eighteenth Century Constitution", *Cornell Law Quarterly*, vol. 47, no. 1, 1981.

Gadbaw, "Reciprocity and Its Implications for US Trade Policy", *Law and Policy in International Business*, vol. 14, 1982.

Gilpin, Robert, *US Power and the Multinational Corporation*, New York: Basic Books, 1975.

Green, Robert and James Lutz, *The United States and World Trade: Changing Patterns and Dimensions*, New York: Praeger Publishers, 1978.

Gressner, Julian, *Partners in Prosperity: Strategic Industries for the United States and Japan*, New York: McGraw-Hill Book Company, 1984.

Harrison, Selig S. and Clyde V. Prestowitz, "Pacific Agenda: Defense or Economics", *Foreign Policy*, no. 79, Summer 1990.

Henkin, Louis, "Foreign Affairs and the Constitution", *Foreign Affairs*, vol. 66, 1988.

Herr, Ellen M., "US Business Enterprises Acquired or Established by Foreign Investment in 1987", *Survey of Current Business*, August 1988.

Hyland, William G., "America's New Course", *Foreign Affairs*, vol. 69, no. 2, Spring 1990.

Inman, B.R., "Technology and Competitiveness: The New Policy Frontier", *Foreign Affairs*, vol. 69, no. 2, Spring 1990.

Kennan, George, "America and the Russian Future", *Foreign Affairs*, vol. 69, no. 2, 1990.

Kennedy, Paul, "Fin de Siecle America", *New York Review of Books*, June 28, 1990.

Kosobric, Richard (ed.) *NorthEast Asia and the US: Defense Partnership and Trade Rivalries*, Chicago: Chicago Council on Foreign Relations, 1983.

Krasner, Stephen, *Defending the National Interests: Raw Materials Investments and US Foreign Policy*, Princeton, NJ: Princeton University Press, 1978.

Krugman, Paul and G. Hatsopoulos, "The Problem of US Competitiveness in Manufacturing", *New England Economic Review*, January/February 1987.

Lawrence, Robert Z. and Robert E. Litan, "Living with the Trade Deficit: Adjustment Strategies to Preserve Free Trade", *The Brookings Review*, Fall 1985, vol. 4, no. 1, pp. 3–13.

Lee, Chae-Jin and Hideo Sato, *US Policy Toward Japan and Korea: A Changing Influence Relationship*, New York: Praeger Publishers, 1982.

Link, Arthur, *Wilson the Diplomatist: A Look at his Major Foreign Policies*, New York: New Viewpoints, 1974.

Magaziner, Ira and Robert Reich, *Minding America's Business: The Decline and Rise of the American Economy*, New York: Vintage Books, 1982.

Mayer, Arno, *Politics and Diplomacy of Peacemaking: Containment and Counterrevolution at Versailles*, New York: Knopf, 1967.

Maynes, Charles William, "America Without the Cold War", *Foreign Policy*, no. 78, Spring 1990.

Nau, Henry, *The Myth of America's Decline: Leading the World Economy into the 1990s*, Oxford: Oxford University Press, 1990.

Nivola, Pietro S., "The New Protectionism: US Trade Policy in Historical Perspective", *Political Science Quarterly*, no. 4, 1986, pp. 577–600.

Nye, Joseph, "The Misleading Metaphor of Decline", *The Atlantic*, March 1990.

Nye, Joseph S., *Bound to Lead: The Changing Nature of American Power*, New York: Basic Books, 1990.

Olsen, Robert, *US Foreign Policy and the New International Order*, Boulder, Colorado: Westview Press, 1981.

Reich, Robert, *The Next American Frontier*, New York: Times Books, 1983.

Rosecrance, Richard, *America's Resurgence: A Bold New Strategy*, New York: Harper & Row, 1990.

Schlesinger, "Congress and the Making of American Foreign Policy", *Foreign Affairs*, vol. 51, 1972.

Schlosstein, Steven, *The End of the American Century*, New York: Congdon and Weed Inc. 1989.

Scott, B.R., "National Strategy for Stronger US Competitiveness", *Harvard Business Review*, vol. 62, no. 2, March/April 1984.

Silk, Leonard, "The United States and the World Economy", *Foreign Affairs*, vol. 65, no. 3, Fall 1986, pp. 458–476.

Starr, Martin K. (ed.) *Global Competitiveness: Setting the US Back on Track*, New York: W.W. Norton, 1988.

Stern, R.M. (ed.) *US Trade Policies in A Changing World Economy*, Cambridge, Mass.: MIT Press, 1987.

Tarr, David and Morris Morke, *Aggregate Costs to the United States of Tariff Cuts and Removal of Quotas on Imports*, Washington, DC: Federal Trade Commission, 1984.

Tolchin, Martin and Susan, *Buying into America: How Foreign Money is Changing the Face of our Nation*, New York: Berkley Books, 1988.

Weil, F.A., "US Industrial Policy: A Process in Need of a Federal Industrial Coordination Board", *Law and Policy in International Business*, vol. 14, no. 4, 1983.

Wheelwright, S. and R.M. Hayes, *Restoring our Competitive Edge: Competing through Manufactures*, New York: Wiley, 1984.

Wonnacott, Ronald, *Aggressive United States Reciprocity Evaluated with a New Analytical Approach to Trade Conflicts*, Montreal: Institute for Research on Public Policy, 1984.

Woodward, Bob, *Veil: The Secret Wars of the CIA*, New York: Simon & Schuster, 1987.

Zysman, John and Laura Tyson (eds) *American Industry in International Competitiveness: Government Policies and Corporate Strategies*, Ithaca, NY: Cornell University Press, 1983.

Japan's Political Economy and Policies

Abegglen, James, *The Strategy of Japanese Business*, Cambridge, Mass.: Ballinger Publishing Company, 1984.

Abegglen, James, KAISHA, *The Japanese Corporation: The New Competitors in World Business*, New York: Basic Books, 1985.

Adler, Vernon R., "Who Says You Can't Crack Japanese Markets?", *Harvard Business Review*, January–February, 1987, no. 1, pp. 52–56.

Aichi, Kiichi, "Japan's Legacy and Destiny of Change", *Foreign Affairs*, October 1969, pp. 21–38.

Akao, Nobutoshi, *Japan's Economic Security*, New York: St. Martin's Press, 1983.

Akita, George, *Foundations of Constitutional Government in Modern Japan, 1968–1900*, Cambridge, Mass.: Harvard University Press, 1967.

Alagappa, Muthiah, "Japan's Political and Security Role in the Asia Pacific Region", *Contemporary Southeast Asia*, vol. 10, no. 1, June 1988.

Alexander, Arthur, *Barriers to United States Service Trade in Japan*, Hong W. Tan, Santa Monica, California: Rand Corporation, 1984.

Allen, George C., *Japan's Place in Trade Strategy: Larger Role in Pacific Region*, London: Atlantic Trade Study, 1968.

Allinson, Gary, "Japan's Keidanren and its New Leadership", *Pacific Affairs*, vol. 60, no. 3, Fall 1987.

Allinson, Gary D., "Politics in Contemporary Japan: Pluralist Scholarship in the Conservative Era", *Journal of Asian Studies*, vol. 48, no. 2, May 1989.

Ames, Walter L., "Buying a Piece of Japan Inc.: Foreign Acquisitions in Japan", *Harvard International Law Journal*, vol. 27, Special Issue, 1986.

Anchordoguy, Marie, "Mastering the Market: Japanese Government Targeting of the Computer Industry", *International Organization*, vol. 42, no. 3, Summer 1988.

Andrews, Kenneth R. and Malcolm S. Salter, "The Automobile Crisis and Public Policy", *Harvard Business Review*, vol. 59, no. 1, January/February 1981.

Armour, Andrew (ed.) *Asia and Japan: The Search for Modernization and Identity*, London: The Athlone Press, 1985.

Arnold, James, "Japanese Economic Nationalism: Protectionism versus Internationalism", *Canadian Review of Studies in Nationalism*, vol. 10, no. 2, Fall 1983.

Arnold, James, "Study of Japanese Economic Nationalism: A Bibliographical Essay", *Canadian Review of Studies in Nationalism*, vol. 10, no. 2, Fall 1983.

Asada, Sado (ed.) *Japan and the World 1853–1952: A Bibliographical Guide to Japanese Scholarship in Foreign Relations*, New York: Columbia University Press, 1989.

Atarashii, Kinju, "Japan's Economic Cooperation Policy Towards the ASEAN Countries", *International Affairs* (Great Britain), vol. 61, no. 1, Winter, 1984–85.

Baerwald, Hans, *Party Politics in Japan*, Boston: Allen & Unwin, 1986.

Baerwald, Hans, "Japan's 39th House of Representatives Election: A Case of Mixed Signals", *Asian Survey*, vol. 30, no. 6, June 1990.

Balassa, Bela, *Japan in the World Economy*, Washington, DC: Institute for International Economics, 1988.

Ballon, Robert J., *Foreign Investment and Japan*, Kodansha International Ltd., Tokyo, 1972.

Baranson, Jack, *The Japanese Challenge to US Industry*, Lexington, Mass.: Lexington Books, 1981.

Barnett, Robert W., *Beyond War: Japan's Concept of Comprehensive National Security*, Washington, DC: Pergamon Press, 1984.

Barnhardt, Michael, *Japan Prepares for Total War: The Search for Economic Security, 1919–1941*, Ithaca, NY: Cornell University Press, 1987.

Bedeski, Michael, "Japanese Foreign Policy Under Nakasone: The Dilemma of an Economic Superpower", *Etudes Internationales*, vol. 15, no. 2, June 1984.

Blaker, Michael, *Japanese International Negotiating Style*, New York: Columbia University Press, 1977.

Blumenthal, Tuvia and Chung H. Lee, "Development Strategies of Japan and the Republic of Korea", *The Developing Economies*, vol. 23, no. 2, September 1985.

Boger, Karl, *Postwar Industrial Policy in Japan: an Annotated Bibliography*, Metchuen, NJ: Scarecrow Press, 1988.

Boltho, Andrea, "Was Japan's Industrial Policy Successful?", *Cambridge Journal of Economics*, vol. 9, no. 2, June 1985.

Braddon, Russell, *The Other Hundred Years War: Japan's Bid for Supremacy*, London: Collins Press, 1983.

Bridges, Brian, "Japan: Business as Usual", *World Today*, vol. 46, no. 4, April 1990.

Bronte, Stephen, *Japanese Finance: Markets and Institutions*, London: Euromoney Publications, 1982.

Brooks, John and William Orr, "Japan's Foreign Assistance", vol. 25, no. 3, March 1985.

Bryant, William E., *Japanese Private Economic Diplomacy: an Analysis of Business–Government Linkages*, New York: Praeger Press, 1975.

Brzinski, Zbigniew, "Japan's Global Engagement", *Foreign Affairs*, January 1972, pp. 270–282.

Burkman, Thomas W, *The Occupation of Japan: The International Context*, Norfolk, Va.: Liskey Lithograph, 1984.

Burks, Ardath W., *Japan: A Postindustrial Power*, Boulder, Colorado: Westview Press, 1984.

Burnett, Robert W., *Beyond War: Japan's Concept of Comprehensive National Security*, McLean, Va.: Pergamon-Brassey's International Defense Publishers, 1984.

Burstein, Dan, *Yen! Japan's New Financial Empire and its Threat to America*, New York: Simon & Schuster, 1989.

Calder, Kent E., "Opening Japan", *Foreign Policy*, N0. 47, Summer 1982, pp. 82–98.

Calder, Kent E., "The Rise of Japan's Military-Industrial Complex", *Asia Pacific Community*, no. 17, Summer 1982.

Calder, Kent E., "Japanese Foreign Economic Policy Formation: Explaining the Reactive State", *World Politics*, vol. 40, no. 4, July 1988.

Calder, Kent E., *Crisis and Compensation: Public Policy and Political Stability in Japan, 1949–1986*, Princeton, NJ: Princeton University Press, 1989.

Campbell, John Creighton, *Contemporary Japanese Budget Politics*, Berkeley, University of California Press, 1977.

Chapman, J.W.M., R. Drifte and I.T.M. Row, *Japan's Quest for Comprehensive Security: Defense–Diplomacy–Dependence*, New York: St. Martin's Press, 1983.

Cheng, Peter P., "Japanese Interest Group Politics: An Institutional Framework", *Asian Survey*, vol. 30, no. 3, March 1990.

Christopher, Robert C., *The Japanese Mind: The Goliath Explained*, New York: Linden Press, 1983.

Clark, Gregory, "Japan in Asia: A Cultural Comparison", *Asia Pacific Community*, no. 17, Summer 1982, pp. 60–63.

Cole, Robert E. (ed.) *The Japanese Automobile Industry: Model and Challenge for the Future?*. Michigan Papers in Japanese Studies 3, Ann Arbor: Center for Japanese Studies, University of Michigan, 1981.

Curtis, Gerald, *The Japanese Way of Politics*. New York: Columbia University Press, 1988.

Cusumano, Michael A., *The Japanese Automobile Industry*, Cambridge, Mass.: Harvard University Press, 1985.

Czinkota, Michael and Jon Woronoff, *Japan's Market: The Distribution System*, New York: Praeger, 1986.

Dale, Peter, *The Myth of Japanese Uniqueness*, New York: St. Martin's Press, 1986.

Davis, John, "The Institutional Foundations of Japanese Industrial Policy", *California Management Review*, vol. 27, no. 4, Summer 1985.

De Mente, Boye, *Japanese Business Etiquette*, Englewood Cliffs, NJ: Prentice-Hall, 1981.

Doi, Takeo, *The Anatomy of Japanese Dependence*, Tokyo: Kodansha, 1981.

Donnely, Michael, "Setting the Price of Rice: A Study in Political Decisionmaking", in T.J. Pempel (ed.) *Policymaking in Japan*.

Dore, Ronald, *Flexible Rigidities: Industrial Policy and Structural Adjustments in the Japanese Economy*, London: Ther Athlone Press, 1986.

Dow, Tsung-I, "The Meaning of the Confucian Work Ethic as the Source of Japan's Economic Power", *Asian Profile*, vol. 11, no. 3, June 1983.

Dower, J. W., *Empire and Aftermath: Yoshida Shigeru and the Japanese Experience, 1878–1954*, Cambridge, Mass.: Harvard University Press, 1979.

Drifte, Reinhard, *Arms Production in Japan: The Military Applications of Civilian Technology*, Boulder, Colorado: Westview Press, 1986.

Drucker, Peter F., "Japan: the Problems of Success", *Foreign Affairs*, April 1978, pp. 564–578.

Dubhashi, F.R., "Economic Planning in Japan", *Indian Journal of Public Administration*, vol. 30, no. 3, August 1984.

Edelman, "Japanese Product Standards as Non-Tariff Barriers, When Regulatory Policy Becomes a Trade Issue", *Stanford Journal of International Law*, vol. 24, 1988.

Eguchi, Yujiro, "Japanese Energy Policy", *International Affairs*, vol. 56, no. 2, April 1980.

El-Agraa, A.M., *Japan's Trade Frictions: Realities OR Misconceptions*, New York: St. Martin's Press, 1988.

Emerson, John K., *Arms, Yen, and Power: The Japanese Dilemma*, New York: Dunellen, 1971.

Emery, Robert F., *The Japanese Money Market*, Lexington, Mass.: Lexington Books, 1984.

Encarnation, Dennis and Mark Mason, "Neither MITI nor America: The Political Economy of Capital Liberalization in Japan", *International Organization*, vol. 44, no. 1, Winter 1990.

Entwistle, Basil, *Japan's Decisive Decade: How A Determined Minority Changed the Nation's Course in the 1950s*, London: Grosvenor Books, 1985.

Feldman, Robert A., *Japanese Financial Markets: Deficits, Dilemmas, and Deregulation*, Boston: MIT Press, 1986.

Fletcher, Miles, "Intellectuals and Fascism in Early Showa Japan", *Journal of Asian Studies*, vol. 39, no. 1, November 1979.

Fletcher, William M., *The Search for a New Order: Intellectuals and Facism in Prewar Japan*, Chapel Hill: University of North Carolina Press, 1982.

Frank, Isaiah (ed.) *The Japanese Economy in International Perspective*, Baltimore, Md: Johns Hopkins University Press, 1975.

Frankel, Jeffrey A., *The Yen/dollar Agreement: Liberalizing Japanese Capital Markets*, Washington, DC: Institute for International Economics, 1984.

Franko, Lawrence, *The Threat of Japanese Multinationals: How the West can Respond*, New York: John Wiley and Sons, 1983.

Freeman, Christopher, *Technology Policy and Economic Performance: Lessons from Japan*, New York: Pinter Publisher, 1987.

Frenkel, Orit, "Flying High: A Case Study of Japanese Industrial Policy", *Journal of Policy Analysis and Management*, vol. 3, no. 3, Spring 1984.

Friedman, David, *The Misunderstood Miracle: Industrial Development and Policy Change in Japan*, Ithaca, NY: Cornell University Press, 1988.

Fukai, Shigeko, "Japan's Energy Policy", *Current History*, April 1988.

Fukui, Haruhiro, *Party in Power: The Japanese Liberal-Democrats and Policy-Making*, Berkeley: University of California Press, 1970.

Fukushima, Haruhiro, "Japan's Real Trade Policy", *Foreign Policy*, no. 59, Summer 1985.

Fukuzawa, Shiji, "A New Industrial Structure", *Speaking of Japan*, vol. 7, no. 73, January 1987.

Fullerton, Stuart, "International Trade: Reforming Japan's Trade Policy", *Harvard International Law Journal*, vol. 8, no. 4, December 1985.

Furuya, Kenichi, "Labor-Management Relations in Postwar Japan", *Japan Quarterly*, vol. 27, no. 1, 1980.

George, Aurelia, "The Japanese Farm Lobby and Agricultural Policymaking", *Pacific Affairs*, vol. 54, no. 3, Fall 1981.

Gerlach, Michael, *Alliance Capitalism: The Social Organization of Japanese Business*, Berkeley: University of California Press, 1990.

Gibney, Frank, "The View From Japan", *Foreign Affairs*, October 1971, pp. 97–111.

Gibney, Frank, *The Fragile Superpower*, Tokyo: Charles E. Tuttle, 1979.

Girling, John, "Agents of Influence", *Australian Outlook*, vol. 38, no. 2, August 1984.

Goble, Andrew, "Japan's America-Bashers", *Orbis*, vol. 34, no. 4, Winter 1990.

Goodman, Herbert, "Japan and the World Energy Crisis" in Dan Okimoto (ed.) *The Political Economy of Japan*.

Gordon, Peter, "Rice Policy of Japan's LDP", *Asian Survey*, vol. 30, no. 10, October 1990.

Government Decisionmaking in Japan: Implications for the United States, prepared for the Woodrow Wilson Center, Washington, DC, 1982.

Gregory, Gene, "Japan's Telecom Industry Rushes into the Information Age", *Telephony*, vol. 206, no. 20, May 1984.

Guttman, William, "Japanese Capital Markets and Financial Liberalization", *Asian Survey*, vol. 27, no. 12, December 1987.

Hadley, Eleanor M., *Antitrust in Japan*, Princeton, NJ, Princeton University Press, 1970.

Hadley, Eleanor M., "The Secret of Japan's Success", *Challenge*, vol. 26, no. 2, May/June 1983.

Hagiwara, Noguchi and Yasuhiro Masui, "Anti-Dumping Laws in Japan", *Journal of World Trade*, vol. 22, no. 4, 1988.

Haitani, Kanji, "The Paradox of Japan's Groupism: Threat to Future Competitiveness?", *Asian Survey*, vol. 30, no. 3, March 1990.

Haliday, Jon and Gavin McCorduck, *Japanese Imperialism Today*, New York: Monthly Review Press, 1973.

Hall, John, *Japan: From Prehistory to Modern Times*, New York: Delacorte Press, 1970.

Hall, John and Marius Jansen (eds) *Studies in the Institutional History of Japan*, Princeton NJ: Princeton University Press, 1968.

Hamada, Tetsuo, "Corporate Culture and Environment in Japan", *Asian Survey*, vol. 25, no. 12, December 1985, pp. 1214–1228.

Hamilton, Pamela, "Protection for Software Under US and Japanese Law", *Boston College International and Comparative Law Review*, vol. 7, no. 2, Summer 1984.

Harris, Robert, "Telecommunications Policy in Japan: Lesson for the US", *California Management Review*, vol. 31, no. 3, Spring 1983.

Hart, Jeffrey and Laura Tyson, "Responding to the Challenge of HDTV", *California Management Review*, vol. 31, no. 4, Summer 1989.

Hasegawa, Sukehiro, *Japanese Foreign Aid: Policy and Practice*, New York: Praeger Publishers, 1975.

Hayashi, Risuke, "Japanese Views", *Asia Pacific Community*, Summer 1979, no. 5, pp. 15–26.

Hayden, Eric W., "Internationalizing Japan's Financial System", *Japan's Economy: Coping with Change in the International Environment*, Boulder, Colorado: Westview Press, 1982.

Hayden, Lesbril, "The Political Economy of Substitution Policy: Japan's Response to Lower Oil Prices", *Pacific Affairs*, vol. 61, no. 2, Summer 1988.

Henderson, John, *Foreign Enterprise in Japan: Laws and Policies*, Chapel Hill: University of North Carolina Press, 1973.

Higashi, Chikara, *Japanese Trade Policy Formulation*, New York: Praeger, 1983.

Higashi, Chikara, *The Internationalization of the Japanese Economy*, Boston: Kluwer Academic Publications, 1987.

Hillman, Jimmy S. and R.A. Rothenberg, "Wider Implications of Defending Japan's Rice Farmers", *The World Economy*, vol. 8, no. 1, March 1985, pp. 43–62.

Hiraoka, Leslie S., "A History of Assimilation: Japan's Technology Trade", *Speaking of Japan*, vol. 7, no. 71, November 1986.

Hiraoka, Tatsuo, "Japan's Increasing Investments Abroad", *Futures*, vol. 17, no. 5, October 1985.

Hirasawa, Kazushige, "Japan's Emerging Foreign Policy", *Foreign Policy*, pp. 155–172, October 1975.

Hoffman, Arthur (ed.) *Japan and the Pacific Basin*, Paris: Atlantic Institute for International Affairs, 1980.

Hollerman, Leon, *Japan Disincorporated: The Economic Liberalization Process*, Stanford, Calif.: Hoover Institution Press, 1988.

Hollerman, Leon, "Distintegrative Versus Integrative Aspects of Interdependence: The Japanese Case", *Asian Survey*, vol. XX, no. 3, March 1980, pp. 324–348.

Horne, James, *Japan's Financial Markets: Conflict and Consensus in Policymaking*, George Allen & Unwin, London: 1985.

Horvath, Dezso and Charles McMillan, "Industrial Planning in Japan", *California Management Review*, vol. 23, no. 1, Fall 1980.

Hrebrenaur, Ronald J., *The Japanese Party System: From One Party Rule to Coalition Government*, Boulder, Colorado: Westview Press, 1986.

Ike, Nobutaka, *Japanese Politics*, New York: Alfred Knopf, 1973.

Ikle, Fred Charles and Terumasa Nakanishi, "Japan's Grand Strategy", *Foreign Affairs*, vol. 69, no. 3, Summer 1990.

Imai, K., "Iron and Steel: Industrial Organization", *Japanese Economic Studies*, vol. 3, no. 2, Winter 1974/75.

Inada, Nada, "One-hundred Million Japanese", *Japan Quarterly*, vol. 28, no. 1, January–March 1981.

Inagaki, Takeshi, "Rocket Readiness", *Japan Quarterly*, April–June 1988.

Inoguchi, Takashi and Tomoaki Iwai, *"Zoku Giin" No Kenkyu*, Tokyo: Nihon Keizai Shinbunsha, 1987.

Inoguchi Takashi and Daniel Okimoto (eds) *The Political Economy of Japan*: Volume 2, *The Changing International Context*, Stanford: Stanford University Press, 1988.

Ishida, Hideto, "Anticompetitive Practices in the Distribution of Goods and Services in Japan: the Problem of Distribution Keiretsu", *Journal of Japanese Studies*, vol. 9, no. 2, Summer 1983.

Ishida, Takeshi, *Japan's Political Culture: Change and Continuity*, New Brunswick and London: Transaction Books, 1983.

Ishida, Takeshi and Ellis S. Krauss (eds) *Democracy in Japan*, Pittsburgh: University of Pittsburgh Press, 1989.

Ishii, Ryosuke, *A History of Political Institutions in Japan*, Tokyo: University of Tokyo Press, 1980.

Ishizaki, Tadoa, "Is Japan's Income Distribution Equal?" *Japanese Economic Studies*, vol. 14, no. 2, Winter 1985/86.

Ito, Keiichi, "Japan's Defense Policy and Limited Budget", *Asia Pacific Community*, Summer 1985, no. 29, pp. 13–24.

Itoh, Hiroshi. (ed.) *Japan's Foreign Policy Making*, Buffalo: State University of New York: 1982.

Jain, Hem C., "The Japanese System of Human Resource Management", *Asian Survey*, vol. 27, no. 9, September 1987.

Japanese Industrial and Trade Collusion, prepared for the Subcommittee on Economic Goals and Intergovernmental Policy of the Joint Economic Committee, Washington, DC: 1986.

Johnson, Chalmers, *Japan's Public Policy Companies*, Washington, DC: AEI–Hoover Policy Studies,1978.

Johnson, Chalmers *MITI and the Japanese Miracle: The Growth of Industrial Policy*, 1925–1975, Stanford, California: Stanford University Press, 1982.

Johnson, Chalmers (ed.) *The Industrial Policy Debate*, San Francisco: ICS Press, 1984.

Johnson, Chalmers, "The Institutional Foundations of Japanese Industrial Policy", *California Management Review*, vol. 27, no. 4, Summer 1985.

Johnson, Chalmers, "Reflections on the Dilemma of Japanese Defense", *Asian Survey*, vol. xxvi, no. 5, May 1986, pp. 557–572.

Kabashima, Yasuo, "Supportive Economic Growth in Japan", *World Politics*, vol. 36, no. 3, April 1983.

Kabashima, Ikui and Jeffrey Broadbent, "Referent Pluralism: Mass Media and Politics in Japan", *Journal of Japanese Studies*, Summer 1986.

Kajima, Morinosuke, *Modern Japan's Foreign Policy*, Charles E. Tuttle Tokyo: 1969.

Kaplan, Eugene, *Japan: The Government–Business Relationship*, Washington, DC: Government Printing Office, 1972.

Kashiwagi, Yusuke, "Going Global: The Internationalization of the Yen and the Tokyo Financial Market", *Speaking of Japan*, vol. 8, no. 79, July 1987.

Katsuo, Satoh, "Japan's Economic Success: Industrial Policy or Free Market", *CATO Journal*, vol. 4, no. 2, Fall 1984.

Katz, Joshua and Tilly Friedman (eds) *Japan's New World Role*, Boulder, Colorado: Westview Press, 1985.

Kaufman, Sylia-Yvonne, "Political Role of Japan in World Affairs", *Korea and World Affairs*, vol. 14, no. 1, Spring 1990.

Kawahito, Kiyoshi, *The Japanese Steel Industry: with an Analysis of the US Steel Import Problem*, New York: Praeger, 1972.

Kawaii, Kazuo, *Japan's American Interlude*, Chicago: University of Chicago Press, 1960.

Kershner, Thomas, *Japanese Foreign Trade*, Lexington, Mass.: Lexington Books, 1975.

Kim, Young, *Japanese Journalists and their World*, Charlottesville: University of Virginia, 1981.

Kinmouth, Earl H., "Japanese Patents: Olympic Gold or Public Relations Brass", *Pacific Affairs*, vol. 61, no. 1, Spring 1988.

Koh, B.C. and Jae-ln Kim, "Paths to Advancement in Japanese Bureaucracy", *Comparative Politics Studies*, vol. 15, no. 3, October 1983, pp. 289–313.

Kojima, Kiyoshi, *Direct Foreign Investment: A Japanese Model of Multinational Business Operations*, London: Croom Helm, 1978.

Kojima, Kiyoshi, *Japan and A New World Economic Order*, Boulder Colorado: Westview Press, 1977.

Konosuke, Odaka, Kunosuke Ono and Fumihiko Adachi, *The Automobile Industry in Japan*, Tokyo: Kinokuniya Ltd., 1988.

Krause, Lawrence, *US Economic Policy Toward the Association of Southeast Asian Nations: Meeting the Japanese Challenge*, Washington, DC: The Brookings Institute, 1982.

Krause, Lawrence and Harumi Muramatsu, "Bureaucrats and Politicians in Japan-ese Policymaking", *American Political Science Review*, vol. 78, no. 1, March 1984.

Kubota, Akira, "Japan: Social Structure and Work Ethic", *Asia Pacific Community*, no. 20, Spring 1983.

Kubota, Akira, "Japan's External Economic Relations: Trade Barriers Versus Perception Barriers", *Asia Pacific Community*, no. 30, Fall, 1986, pp. 119–134.

Kuroda, Yasumasa *et al.*, "The End of Westernization and the Beginning of New Modernization in Japan", *Arab Journal of the Social Sciences*, vol. 2, no. 1, April 1987.

Langdon, F.C., *Japan's Foreign Policy*, Vancouver: University of British Columbia Press, 1973.

Langdon, Frank, "The Security Debate in Japan", *Pacific Affairs*, September 1985, vol. 58, no. 3, pp. 397–410.

Lebra, Takie Sugiyama, *Japanese Patterns of Behavior*, Honolulu: University of Hawaii Press, 1976.

Lebra, Takie Sugiyama and William Lebra, *Japanese Culture and Behavior*, Honolulu: University of Hawaii Press, East-West Book, 1974.

Lee, Ching, "Japanese Foreign Investment Theories", *Economic Development and Cultural Change*, vol. 32, no. 4, July 1984.

Lee, Chong-Sik, *Japan and Korea: The Political Dimension*, Stanford: Hoover Institute Press, 1985.

Lee, Jung Bock, *The Political Character of the Japanese Press*, Seoul: Seoul National University Press, 1985.

Lincoln, Edward J., *Japan: Facing Economic Maturity*, Washington, DC: Brookings Institute, 1988.

Linhart, Sepp, "From Industrial to Postindustrial Society", *Journal of Japanese Studies*, vol. 14, no. 2, Summer 1988.

Lochmann, Michael W., "The Japanese Voluntary Restraint on Automobile Exports, *Harvard International Law Journal*, vol. 27, no. 1, Winter 1986.

Loutfi, Martha F., *The Net Cost of Japanese Foreign Aid*, New York: Praeger Press, 1973.

Lynn, Loreta, "Japanese Robotics", *Annals of the American Academy of Political and Sociological Sciences*, vol. 470, November 1983.

Machizuki, Mike, "Japan's Search for Strategy", *International Security*, vol. 8, no. 3, Winter 1983/84, pp. 152–179.

MacIntosh, Malcolm, *Japan Rearmed*, New York: St. Martin's Press, 1986.

Magaziner, Ira C. and Thomas M. Hout, *Japanese Industrial Policy*, Policy Papers in International Affairs 15, Berkeley: Institute of International Studies, University of California, 1980.

Malik, Rex, "Japan's Fifth Generation Computer", *Futures*, vol. 15, no. 3, June 1983, pp. 205–211.

Mannari, Hiroshi and Harumi Befu (eds) *The Challenge of Japan's Internationalization, Organization, and Culture*, Nishinomiya, Japan: Kwansei Gkuin University, Kodansha, 1983.

Maruyama, Masao, *Thought and Behavior in Japanese Politics*, New York: Oxford University Press, 1969.

Matsuzaka, Hideo, "The Future of Japanese–ASEAN Relations", *Asia Pacific Community*, no. 3, Summer 1983, pp. 11–21.

McCormick, Gavan and Yoshio Sugimoto, *Democracy in Contemporary Japan*, Armonk New York: M.E. Sharpe, 1986.

McLean, Mick (ed.) *The Japanese Electronics Challenge*, New York: St. Martin's Press, 1982.

McLean, Mick (ed.) *Mechatronics: Developments in Japan and Europe*, Westport, Conn.: Technova, Quorum Books, 1983.

McMillan, Charles, *The Japanese Industrial System*, Berlin: De Gruyter, 1985.

McRae, Hamish, *Japan's Role in the Emerging Securities Market*, Occasional Paper no. 17, New York: Group of Thirty, 1985.

Minor, John, "Decision-makers and Japanese Foreign Policy", *Asian Survey*, vol. 25, no. 13, December 1985.

Mochizuki, "Japanese Search for Strategy", *International Security*, vol. 8, no. 3, Winter 1983–84.

Morita, Akio and Shintaro Ishihara, *"No" to Ieru Nihon: Shin Nichi-Bei Kankei No Kado*, Tokyo: Kobunsha, 1989.

Morse, Ronald (ed.) *The Politics of Japan's Energy Strategy*, Berkeley: Institute of East Asian Studies, 1981.

Morse, Ronald, "Japan's Search for an Independent Foreign Policy", *Journal of Northeast Asian Studies*, vol. 3, no. 2, Summer 1984.

Mowery, David C. and Nathan Rosenberg, *The Japanese Commercial Aircraft Industry Since 1945: Government Policy, Technical Development, & Industrial Structure*, Stanford: Stanford University Press, 1985.

Muldoon, Robert, "Japan and Deep Seabed Mining", *Ocean Development and International Law*, vol. 17, no. 4, 1986.

Najima, Tetsuo, *Japan: The Intellectual Foundations of Modern Japanese Politics*, Chicago: University of Chicago Press, 1980.

Nakamura, Takafusa, *The Postwar Japanese Economy*: ITS *Development and Structure*, Tokyo: University of Tokyo Press, 1981.

Nakane, Chie, *Japanese Society*, Berkeley: University of California Press, 1970.

Nakasone, Soridaijin, "Japan's Choice: A Strategy for World Peace", *Atlantic Community Quarterly*, vol. 22, no. 3, Fall 1984.

Nester, William, "Japanese Rearmament: Fact and Fiction", *Japan Times*, April 24, 1984.

Nester, William, "Japan's Policy to the Middle East, Tatemae and Honne", *Third World Quarterly*, January 1989, with Kweku Ampiah.

Nester, William, "Japan's Mainstream Press: Freedom to Conform?", *Pacific Affairs*, vol. 62, no. 1, April 1989.

Nester, William, "Japan's Corporate Miracle: Ideals and Realities at Home and Abroad", *Asian Profile*, vol. 18, no 4, December 1989.

Nester, William, *The Foundations of Japanese Power: Continuities, Changes, Challenges*, London: Macmillan, 1989; Armonk, New York: M.E. Sharpe, 1990.

Nester, William, "Japan's Governing Triad: Models of Development and Policy-making", *Asian Perspective*, vol. 12, no. 3, March 1990.

Nester, William, "Japan's Recruit Scandal: Government and Business for Sale", *Third World Quarterly*, vol. 2, Spring 1990.

Nester, William, "Japanese, Korean and Taiwan Development: Patterns and Process", *Korea Observer*, Summer 1990.

Nester, William, "Japan's Relations with the Third World", *Millennium*, vol. 18, no. 5, Winter 1990.

Nester, William, *Japanese Industrial Targeting: The Neomercantilist Path to Economic Superpower*, London: Macmillan, 1990.

Nester, William, *Japan's Growing Power over East Asia and the World Economy: Ends and Means*, London: Macmillan, 1990.

Nester, William, *Japan and the Third World: Patterns, Power, Prospects*, London: Macmillan, 1991.

Nishihara, "Expanding Japan's Credible Defense Role", *International Security*, vol. 8, no. 3, Winter 1983–84.

Noguchi, Yukio, "Public Finance", in Kozo Yamamura and Yasukichi Yasuba (eds) *The Political Economy of Japan: Volume 1, The Domestic Transformation*, Stanford: Stanford University Press, 1987.

Nukazama, "Yen for Dollars", *World Economy*, vol. 6, no. 3, September 1983.

Ohkawa, Kazushi and Gustav Ranis (eds) *Japan and the Developing Countries: A Comparative Analysis*, New York: Basil Blackwell, 1985.

Ohmae, Kenichi, *Japan Business Obstacles and Opportunities*, New York: McKinsey & Company, 1983.

Ohmae, Kenichi, *Beyond National Borders: Reflections on Japan and the World*, Homewood, Ill.: Dow Jones-Irwin, 1987.

Okazaki, Hisahiko, *A Grand Strategy for Japanese Defense*, New York: University Press of America, 1986.

Okimoto, Daniel, *Japan's Economy: Coping with Change in the International Environment*, Boulder, Colorado: Westview Press, 1982.

Okimoto, Daniel, *Between MITI and the Market Place: Japanese Industrial Policy for High Technology*, Stanford: Stanford University Press, 1989.

Okimoto, Daniel and Thomas Rohlen (eds) *Inside the Japanese System: Readings on Contemporary Society and Political Economy*, Stanford: Stanford University Press, 1988.

Okita, Saburo, "The Role of the Trade Ombudsman in Liberalizing Japan's Markets", *The World Economy*, vol. 7, no. 3, September 1984, pp. 241–256.

Olsen, Lawrence, *Japan in Postwar Asia*, New York: Praeger Publishers, 1970.

Organization for Economic Cooperation and Development, *The Industrial Policy of Japan*, Paris: OECD, 1972.

Oshima, Harry T, "Reinterpreting Japan's Postwar Growth", *Economic Development and Social Change*, vol. 31, no. 10, October 1982.

Ozaki, Hisahiko, "Japanese Security Policy: A Time for Strategy", *International Security*, vol. 7, no. 2, Fall 1982, pp. 188–197.

Ozaki, Robert, *The Control of Imports and Foreign Capital in Japan*, New York: Praeger Publishers, 1972.

Ozaki, Robert, *The Japanese: A Cultural Portrait*, Tokyo: Charles E. Tuttle, 1978.

Ozaki, Robert and Walter Arnold (eds) *Japan's Foreign Relations: A Global Search for Economic Security*, Boulder, Colorado: Westview Press, 1985.

Ozaki, Robert, "The Humanistic Enterprise System in Japan", *Asian Survey*, vol. 28, no. 12, December 1985.

Ozawa, Terutomo, *Japan's Technological Challenge to the West, 1950–74*, Cambridge, Mass.: MIT Press, 1974.

Ozawa, Terutomo, *Multinationalism, Japanese Style*, Princeton, NJ: Princeton University Press, 1978.

Ozawa, Terutomo, "Japan's New Resource Diplomacy: Government Backed Group Investment", *Journal of World Trade Law*, vol. 14, no. 1, January February 1980.

Passin, Herbert and Akira Iriye (ed.) *Encounter at Shimoda: Search for a New Pacific Partnership*, Boulder, Colorado: Westview Press, 1979.

Patrick, Hugh, "The Future of the Japanese Economy", *Journal of Japanese Studies*, Summer 1977.

Patrick, Hugh and Henry Rosovsky (eds) *Asia's New Giant: How the Japanese Economy Works*, Washington, DC: The Brookings Institute, 1976.

Patrick, Hugh and Larry Meissner (eds) *Japan's High Technology Industries: Lessons and Limitations of Industrial Policy*, Seattle: University of Washington Press, 1986.

Peck, Merton J., Richard Levin and Akira Goto, "Picking Losers: Public Policy Toward Declining Industries in Japan", *Journal of Japanese Studies*, vol. 13, no. 1, Winter 1987.

Pempel, T.J. (ed.) *Policymaking in Contemporary Japan*, Ithaca, NY:Cornell University Press, 1977.

Pempel, T.J., "Japanese Foreign Economic Policy: the Domestic Bases for International Behavior", *International Organization*, vol. 31, no. 4, Autumn 1977, pp. 722–774.

Pempel, T.J., *Policymaking in Contemporary Japan*, Boulder, Colorado: Westview Press, 1978.

Pempel, T.J., *Policy and Politics in Japan: Creative Conservatism*, Philidephia: Temple University Press, 1982.

Pempel, T.J., *Japan: The Dilemma of Success*, New York: Foreign Policy Association, 1986.

Pepper, Thomas, *The Japanese Challenge*, New York: Cromwell, 1979.

Peritz, Rene, "Japan's Foreign Policy at Mid-Decade: A Critique", *Asian Profile*, vol. 13, no. 1, February 1985.

Ping, Lee Poh, "Malaysian Perceptions of Japan Before and During the 'Look East' Period", *Asia Pacific Community*, Summer 1985, no. 29, pp. 25–34.

Pugel, Thomas, "Japan's Industrial Policy: Instruments, Trends, Effects", *Journal of Comparative Economics*, vol. 8, no. 4, December 1984.

Pyle, Kenneth, *The Making of Modern Japan*, Lexington, Mass.: D.C. Heath, 1978.

Pyle, Lucian, "The Future of Japanese Nationality", *Journal of Japanese Studies*, vol. 8, no. 2, Summer 1982.

Quo, F. Quei, "Japan's Role in Asia", *International Journal*, vol. 38, no. 2, Spring 1983.

Reading, Brian, *Investing in Japan*, Cambridge: Woodhead-Faulkner, 1978.

Redford, Lawrence (ed.) *The Occupation of Japan: Economic Policy and Reform*, Norfolk, Va.: The Memorial, 1980.

Reed, Steven, "Environmental Politics in Japan", *Comparative Politics*, vol. 13, no. 3, April 1981.

Reich, Robert B., "Beyond Free Trade", *Foreign Affairs*, Spring 1983, pp. 773–804.

Reichauer, Edwin, *The Japanese*, Toyko: Charles E. Tuttle Company, 1977.

Reynolds, Peter, "Foreign Investment in Japan: The Legal and Social Climate", *Texas International Law Journal*, vol. 18, no. 1, Winter 1983.

Rice, Richard, "Economic Mobilization in Wartime Japan", *Journal of Asian Studies*, vol. 38, no. 4, August 1979.

Richardson, Bradley and Taizo Ueda (eds) *Business and Society in Japan: Fundamentals for Businessmen*, Winter 1987, vol. 41, no. 1, pp. 61–92.

Rosecrance, Richard and Jennifer Taw, "Japan and the Theory of International Leadership", *World Politics*, vol. 42, no. 2, January 1990.

Sakoh, Katsuro and Philip H. Trezise, "Japanese Economic Success: Industrial Policy or Free Market?", *CATO Journal*, vol. 4, no. 2, Fall 1984.

Samuels, Richard, *The Business of the Japanese State*, Ithaca: Cornell University Press, 1987.

Samuels, Richard, "Consuming for Production: Japanese National Security, Nuclear Fuel Procurement and the Domestic Economy", *International Organization*, vol. 43, no. 4, Autumn 1989.

Sarathy, Ravi, "The Interplay of Industrial Policy and International Strategy: Japan's Machine Tool Industry", *California Management Review*, vol. 31, no. 3, Spring 1989.

Sato, Kazuo, "Saving and Investment", in Kozo Yamamura and Yasukichi Yasuba (eds) *The Political Economy of Japan: Volume 1, The Domestic Transformation*, Stanford: Stanford University Press, 1987.

Sato, Kazuo and Yasuo Hochino, *The Anatomy of Japanese Business*, Armonk, New York: M.E. Sharpe Inc. 1984.

Sato, Seizaburo and Matsuzaki Tetsuhisa, *Jiminto Seiken*, Tokyo: Chuo Koronsha, 1986.

Saxonhouse, Gary, "What is all this about Industrial Targeting in Japan?", *World Economy*, vol. 6, no. 3, September 1983.

Saxonhouse, Gary, "Japan's Intractable Trade Surplus in a New Era", *The World Economy*, vol. 9, no. 3, September 1986, pp. 239–258.

Saxonhouse, Gary and Kozo Yamamura, *Law and Trade Issues of the Japanese Economy*, Seattle: University of Washington Press, 1986.

Scalipino, Robert (ed.) *The Foreign Policy of Modern Japan*, Berkeley, University of California Press, 1977.

Schaller, Michael, *The American Occupation of Japan: The Origins of the Cold War in Asia*, Oxford: Oxford University Press, 1985.

Schmiegelow, Michele (ed.) *Japan's Response to Crisis and Change in the World Economy*, Armonk, New York: M.E. Sharpe, 1987.

Sekiguchi, Haruichi, "Myth and Reality of Japan's Industrial Policy", *World Economy*, vol. 8, no. 4, December 1985.

Sekiguchi, Sueo, *Japanese Direct Foreign Investment*, Montclair, NJ: Allanheld, Osmun & Co. Publishers, 1979.

Shapiro, Michael, *Japan: in the Land of the Brokenhearted*, New York: H. Holt, 1989.

Shibata, Tokue, *Public Finance in Japan*, Tokyo, University of Tokyo Press, 1986.

Shibusawa, Masahide, "Japan and its Region", *Asia Pacific Community*, Summer 1985, no. 29, pp. 25–34.

Shinkai, Yoichi, "The Internationalization of Finance in Japan", in Takashi Inoguchi and Daniel Okimoto (eds) *The Political Economy of Japan: Volume 2, The Changing International Context*, Stanford: Stanford University Press, 1988.

Smith, Robert, *Japanese Society: Tradition, Self, and the Social Order*, London: Cambridge University Press, 1984.

Spindler, J. Andrew, *The Politics of International Credit: Private Finance and Foreign Relations in Germany and Japan*, Washington, DC: Brookings Institute, 1984.

Stockwin, J.A.A., *Japan: Divided Politics in A Growth Economy*, New York: W.W. Norton, 1982.

Stockwin, John, "Understanding Japanese Foreign Policy", *Review of International Studies*, vol. 11, no. 2, April 1985.

Stockwin, J.A.A., *Dynamics and Immobolist Politics in Japan*, London: Macmillan, 1988.

Suzuki, Yoshio, *Money, Finance, and Macroeconomic Performance in Japan*, New Haven, Conn.: Yale University Press, 1986.

Tai, Chong-Soo, "The Relationship Between Economic Development and Social Equality in Japan, Korea and Taiwan: A Comparative Analysis Using Regression Models", *Asian Profile*, vol. 14, no. 1. February 1986.

Taira, Koji, "Colonialism in Foreign Subsidiaries: Lessons from Japanese Investment in Thailand", *Asian Survey*, April 1980.

Taira, Koji, "Labor Federation in Japan", *Current History*, April 1988.

Tasker, Peter, *The Japanese: A Major Exploration of Modern Japan*, New York: Dutton Press, 1989.

Tatsuno, Sheridan, *The Technopolis Strategy: Japan, High Technology, and the Control of the Twenty-first Century*, New York: Prentice Hall, 1986.

Taylor, R., *The Sino-Japanese Axis: A New Force in Asia*, New York: St. Martin's Press, 1985.

Tenderten, Gianni Fodella (ed.) *Japan's Economy in A Comparative Perspective*, Kent: Paul Norbury Publications, 1983.

Thurow, Lester, *The Japanese Management Challenge*, Cambridge, Mass.: MIT Press, 1985.

Trezise, Philip H., "Industrial Policy is Not the Major Reason for Japan's Success." *Brookings Review*, vol. 1, no. 3, Spring 1983.

Trezise, Phil, "Japan's Miracles Revisited", *Society*, vol. 22, no. 1, November–December 1984.

Tsuji, Kiyoaki (ed.) *Public Administration in Japan*, Tokyo: University of Tokyo Press, 1980.

Tsurumi, Yoshi, *The Japanese are Coming: A Multinational Interaction of Firms and Politics*, Cambridge, Mass.: Ballinger, 1976.

Tsurumi, Yoshi, *Technology Transfer and Foreign Trade: The Case of Japan, 1950–66*, New York: Arno Press, 1980.

Tung, Rosalie, *Business Negotiations with the Japanese*, Lexington, Mass.: Lexington Books, 1984.

Uchino, Tasuo, *Japan's Postwar Economy*, Tokyo: Kodansha, 1983.

Ueno, Hiroya and Hiromichi Muto, "The Automobile Industry of Japan", *Japanese Economic Studies*, vol. 3, no. 1, Fall 1974.

Uno, Masami, *Yudaya Ga Wakaru to Dekai Ga Miete Kuru*, Tokyo: Tokuma Shoten, 1987.

Viner, Aron, *The Emerging Power of Japanese Money*, Homewood, Ill.: Dow Jones-Irwin, 1988.

Viner, Aron, *Inside Japan's Financial Markets*, Homewood, Ill.: Dow Jones-Irwin, 1988.

Vogel, Erza, "Pax Nipponica", *Foreign Affairs*, vol. 64, no. 4, Spring 1986.

Wakaizumi, Kei, "Japan's Role in a New World Order", *Foreign Affairs*, pp. 310–326, January 1973.

Ward, Robert E. (ed) *Political Development in Modern Japan*, Princeton: Princeton University Press, 1968.

Wineberg, "The Japanese Patent System: A Non-Tariff Barrier to Foreign Businesses?", *Journal of World Trade*, vol. 22, no. 1, 1988.

Wolf, Marvin J, *The Japanese Conspiracy: The Plot to Dominate Industry Worldwide*, New York: Empire Books, 1983.

Wolferen, Karel B. Van, "Agreeing on Reality: Political Reporting by the Japanese Press", *Speaking of Japan*, vol. 5, no. 44, August 1984.

Wolferen, Karel B. Van, "The Japan Problem", *Foreign Affairs*, vol. 65, no. 2, Winter 1986/87, pp. 288–303.

Wolferen, Karel B. Van, *The Enigma of Japanese Power*, London: Macmillan, 1989.

World Trade Competition: Western Countries and Third World Markets, Center for Strategic and International Studies (ed.), New York: Praeger, 1981.

Woronoff, Jon, *World Trade War*, New York: Praeger Press, 1984.

Woronoff, Jon, *Japan's Commercial Empire*, Armonk, New York: M.E. Sharpe, 1984.

Woronoff, Jon, *The Japan Syndrome: Symptoms, Ailments, and Remedies*, New Brunswick: Transaction Books, 1986.

Woronoff, Jon, *Politics the Japanese Way*, London: Macmillan, 1988.

Wright, Richard and Gunter Pauli, *The Second Wave: Japan's Global Assault on Financial Services*, New York: St. Martin's Press, 1987.

Wu, Yuan-li, *Japan's Search for Oil: A Case Study on Economic Nationalism and International Security*, Stanford: Hoover Institute, 1977.

Yamamura, Kozo, *Economic Policy in Postwar Japan*, Berkeley: University of California Press, 1967.

Yamamura, Kozo (ed.) *Policy and Trade Issues of the Japanese Economy: American and Japanese Perspectives*, Seattle: University of Washington Press, 1982.

Yamamura, Kozo and Yasukichi Yasuba (eds) *The Political Economy of Japan: Volume 1, The Domestic Transformation*, Stanford: Stanford University Press, 1987.

Yamauchi, "Long Range Strategic Planning in Japanese R&D", *Futures*, vol. 15, no. 5, October 1983.

Yasutomo, Dennis, *Japan and the Asian Development* BANK, New York: Praeger Press, 1983.

Yoshida, Shigeru, *The Yoshida Memoirs: The Story of Japan in Crisis*, Westport, Conn.: Greenwood Press, 1962.

Yoshihara, Kunio, *Sogo Shosha: The Vanguard of the Japanese Economy*, New York: Oxford University Press, 1982.

Yoshino, Michael, *Japan's Multinational Enterprise*, Cambridge, Mass.: Harvard University Press, 1976.

Yoshino, Michael and Thomas B. Lifson, *The Invisible Link: Japan's Sogo Shosha and the Organization of Trade*, Cambridge, Mass.: MIT Press, 1986.

Yoshitani, Masaru, "An Appraisal of Japan's Financial Policy", *The World Economy*, vol. 6, no. 3, March 1983, pp. 27–38.

Yoshitsu, Michael, *Japan and the San Francisco Peace Settlement*, New York: Columbia University Press, 1983.

Young, Alexander, *The Sogo Shosha: Japan's Multinational Trading Companies*, Boulder, Colorado: Westview Press, 1979.

Yutaka, Matsumura, *Japan's Economic Growth, 1945–60*, Tokyo: Tokyo News Service, 1961.

Zimmerman, William, *How to Do Business with the Japanese*, New York: Random House, 1984.

Index

Aerospace 9, 312, 318–20, 348–57
Afghanistan 22, 53, 75
Africa 16, 36, 50, 304, 402
Agriculture 60–1, 202, 204, 214, 254–65
Akihito 95, 116
Amorphous metals 362–3
Asia 16, 24, 36, 111, 303
Asian Development Bank 113, 144
Asian Pacific Economic Cooperation 116, 117
Association of Southeast Asian Nations 115, 117, 118, 135
Atomic bombs 24, 188, 224
Australia 117
Automobile parts, 250–2, 253, 254
Automobiles 9, 243–54, 268

Bangladesh 116
Bank of Japan 103, 243, 380, 383, 389
Baseball bats 202–3
Bentham, Jeremy 16
Biotechnology 9
Blood plasma 202
Brazil 47, 50, 80, 138, 209, 211, 305, 407
Bretton Woods 37, 58, 72
Britain 15, 16, 19, 22–3, 25, 29, 30, 33, 35–7, 39, 40, 59, 72, 84, 109, 111, 114, 124, 131, 137, 144, 157, 224, 246, 266, 282, 284, 290, 373
Bush, George 1, 2, 12, 24, 56, 60, 61, 69, 76, 77, 163, 183, 184, 209–26, 254–5, 285–6, 287, 311, 314, 315, 316, 346, 358, 374, 375, 377, 392, 400, 402, 416, 421

Canada 19, 117, 135, 157, 209, 284
Carter, Jimmy 75, 76, 164, 230–1, 235, 374
Central America 75
Central Intelligence Agency 5, 50, 56, 65, 169–70, 288, 410–11

China 19, 21, 26, 27, 44, 50, 74, 75, 113, 117, 118, 135, 200, 211, 214, 224, 400
Clay, Henry 28
Cold War 1, 2, 11, 16, 17, 21, 45, 46, 54, 61, 73–6, 86, 87, 198–200, 200, 223, 396, 401
Computers 9, 318, 332–40
Conference on Security and Cooperation in Europe 45
Construction 202, 271–9
Consumer electronics 10, 314–16
Coordinating Committee for Export Controls 61, 321–2
Council of Economic Advisors 62, 65, 203, 205, 239, 315, 343

Denmark 43
Department of Agriculture 62, 65, 69, 255, 409
Department of Commerce 61, 62, 65, 66, 69, 163, 167–8, 203, 230, 239, 280, 285, 314, 320, 321, 343, 366, 370, 409
Department of Defense 62, 65, 239, 277, 283, 284, 315–17, 319, 320, 321, 339, 340, 343, 358, 409, 418
Department of Energy 277
Department of Justice 62, 230, 239, 286, 409
Department of Labor 62, 343
Department of State 64, 177, 203, 241, 279, 321, 343, 409
Department of Treasury 62, 64, 65, 68, 84, 229, 241, 252, 279, 343, 385, 409
Distribution 265–70
Dulles, John Foster Dulles 74
Dumping 32, 67

Eastern Asia 116, 117, 400, 406
Eastern Europe 44, 45, 47, 61, 169–70, 214
Economic Planning Agency 91, 104

Egypt 115, 219
Eisenhower, Dwight 74, 174
Europe 5, 7, 12, 15–16, 20, 39, 43, 54,
  73, 91, 107, 111, 114, 127, 135,
  210, 247, 304, 306, 350
European Community 1, 12, 21, 29,
  37, 38, 85, 116, 132, 208, 209,
  296, 349, 400, 401, 406
European Free Trade Association 1,
  400
Export–Import Bank 61, 69, 87, 411

Federal Bureau of Investigation 56
Federation of Economic Organizations
  (Keidanren) 98, 99, 300, 324
Federal Reserve 62, 80, 83, 167, 287,
  373, 374, 387
Federal Trade Commission 236
Fiscal Investment and Loan
  Program 198
Fishing 204–5
Ford, Gerald 75, 166
Foreign aid 6, 7, 32
Foreign investments 32
  American in Japan 279, 283,
    297–304
  Japanese in US 280–97, 304–11
Forestry and lumber 212
France 15, 19, 22, 33, 39, 43, 45, 49,
  59, 85, 109, 131, 132, 246, 284

General Accounting Office 63
General Agreement on Tariffs and
  Trade 1, 16, 25, 37–8, 60, 64,
    66, 67, 68, 72, 75, 113, 167, 199,
    207–8, 214–15, 233, 263, 345,
    406–7
Germany 1, 29, 33, 39, 40, 45, 84, 85,
  109, 118, 126, 127, 131, 132, 137,
  144, 144, 150, 216, 243, 246, 264,
  284, 373
Gorbachev, Mikhail 1
Greece 50, 73
Greenhouse effect 2
Group of Seven 116, 214, 225
Gulf War 2, 4, 11, 21, 24, 46, 51, 192,
  218–19, 400

Hamilton, Alexander 58–9, 70, 85
Hegemony 5, 6, 7, 8, 15, 17–18, 25,
  34–40

Hirohito, Emperor 112, 262
Hong Kong 84, 117
Hungary 50, 116

India 19, 47, 209, 211, 213
Indochina 116
Indonesia 304
Industrial policy 1, 2, 31, 32–5
Intellectual property 211, 215
Internal Revenue Service 293–4
International Monetary Fund 1, 16,
  25, 36, 49, 72, 144, 199, 298
International Trade
  Organization 37, 68
Iran 24, 47, 75, 114, 304
Iraq 2, 21, 24, 47, 48, 52, 53, 114,
  218, 220
Ishihara, Shintaro 153, 184, 353
Israel 21, 47, 50, 114
Italy 131, 132, 244

Japan Development Bank 104, 198,
  324, 326, 380
Japan Export Import Bank 104, 198,
  324, 380
Japan Fair Trade Commission 100,
  206, 214, 215, 230, 388
Japan, political parties
  Clean Government Party 98, 101,
    221, 222
  Democratic Socialist Party 98,
    101, 221
  Japan Communist Party 98, 101,
    220–1
  Japan Socialist Party 98, 101,
    220–1
  Liberal Democratic Party 9, 96,
    98, 99, 188, 202, 221, 222, 228,
    255, 269, 270, 272, 325, 380
Japan Self Defense Forces 11, 199
Japanese, policymaking and policies
  defense 9, 11, 116, 117, 216–27
  foreign 22, 23, 110–19
  foreign aid 113, 115–16
  foreign investments 303–8
  imperialism 20, 24, 110–11, 197,
    224
  industrial 8–9, 11, 54, 90–101,
    379–84
  macroeconomic 90–119

Japanese, policymaking and policies
(*cont.*)
  neomercantilism 6, 8, 11, 12, 16,
    25, 39, 40, 53, 54, 55, 58, 59,
    66, 71, 73, 89–119, 123–4,
    124–53, 226–78, 280ff, 312–71
Japanese power
  cartels 8, 100, 105
  comprehensive security 114
  corporations 4, 99–100, 128–30,
    215, 288–94, 304–8, 329–30
  debt 137–41
  energy 114
  financial 3–4, 7, 10, 141–4, 370–92
  foreign investments 136–7,
    304–8
  lobby power in US 9, 63, 286–7
  market 19–20
  national resources 114
  patents 145–6
  political power over US 154–84
  power 2–4, 115, 124–94, 195–225,
    228ff, 280ff, 312–70,
    371–92, 395
  research and development 149–50,
    311–70
  savings and investment 11, 124–8
  stock market 128, 143–4, 382–3,
    388–9
  technology 4, 10, 144–53, 311–70
  trade 3, 33, 119, 126–7, 129–35
Jefferson, Thomas 1, 61, 69, 85
Johnson, Lyndon 57
Jordan 219, 222

Kaifu, Toshiki 115, 117, 185, 188,
  209–10, 214, 219–20, 221, 228,
  391, 433
Kant, Immanuel 40, 44
Kennan, George 73, 198
Kennedy, John 46
Korea 111
Korean War 47, 74, 199, 244
Kuwait 2, 21, 47, 53, 218, 220

Latin America 43, 44, 303, 407
Lawyers 206–7
League of Nations 72
Liberalism 16, 27–32, 33, 90–1
Libya 48–9
List, Friedrich 29

MacArthur, Douglas 198, 199
Machine tools 238–43
Malaysia 117, 211
Manchuria 112
Market Oriented Specific Sector
  (MOSS) 207–8
Marxist Leninism 27, 44, 53, 73
Mercantilism 15–16, 33
Mexico 19, 50, 80, 138, 210, 380, 400,
  407
Microelectronics 10, 313
Middle East 16, 21, 46, 73, 114, 115,
  304, 403
Mill, John Stuart 16
Ministry of Agriculture, Forestry, and
  Fisheries 97, 255–60, 263, 264
Ministry of Construction 97, 277–8
Ministry of Education 166, 324, 335
Ministry of Finance 97, 101, 213,
  302, 304–6, 324, 372, 379–81,
  382, 387–9, 391
Ministry of Foreign Affairs 94, 116
Ministry of Health and Welfare 97
Ministry of International Trade and
  Industry 65, 90–1, 92, 94, 97–8,
  100, 102, 103–7, 114, 118, 166,
  167, 176, 180–1, 198, 203, 206,
  207, 230, 232, 235, 239–40,
  243–6, 253, 266–7, 268–9, 298,
  299–300, 324–5, 326, 328, 330,
  331–2, 332–40, 341, 344, 346,
  347, 349, 352, 354, 360
Ministry of Justice 97
Ministry of Posts and
  Telecommunications 97, 166,
  324, 325, 326, 342, 360, 361
Ministry of Transportation 97
Miyazawa, Kiichi 219
Motorcyles 205, 292

Nakasone, Yasuhiro 167, 181, 184,
  217, 221, 241, 345, 360
National Science Foundation 88
National Security Council 65, 203,
  343
Neomercantilism 6, 17, 32–51, 66, 68,
  89–119
Netherlands 15, 19, 35, 36, 39, 40, 43,
  137, 157, 224
New World Order 1, 2

Newly Industrializing Countries 7, 117, 118, 135, 190, 406
Nixon, Richard 58, 74–5, 84, 86, 133, 162–3, 182, 200–1, 231–2, 258
North America 116
North Atlantic Treaty Organization 45, 46–7, 74, 216, 222
North Korea 115
Norway 131
Nuclear power 45–6, 49

Oceana 301
Office of Management and Budget 62
Okinawa (Ryukyu Islands) 111, 200
Opinion polls 23
  America 1, 4, 10, 188–95, 289–90
  Japan 182–8, 255–6, 289–90
Organization for Economic Cooperation and Development 29, 107, 108, 113, 116, 126, 132, 199, 215, 245, 298, 404
Organization of Petroleum Exporting Countries 7, 20, 50, 58, 75, 113, 246, 247, 258, 304, 374

Pakistan 47, 115, 116
Panama 7, 48
Perot, Ross 82
Peru 116
Philippines 116, 117
Pickens, T. Boone 142, 163, 268, 280–1, 303–4
Plaza Accord 130, 208–9, 385, 390
Poland 47, 50, 115
Portugal 15, 19, 26, 30, 35, 36, 43, 50, 118

Reagan, Ronald 2, 12, 24, 46, 56, 57, 58, 60–1, 64, 66, 76–86, 87–9, 130, 133, 134, 136, 137–8, 162–3, 163–4, 167, 170, 173, 183, 203–9, 225–6, 241, 248, 259–63, 275–6, 293, 315, 318, 342, 344, 345, 358, 360, 368, 371, 373, 374, 375, 376, 378, 385, 413, 416, 421
Ricardo, David 16, 30, 90, 91
Robots 9
Roosevelt, Franklin 37, 57, 70, 71, 72–3, 86, 372

Romania 116
Russia 19, 35

Satellites 212
Sato, Eisaku 200
Saudi Arabia 211, 218, 220, 222, 304
Semiconductors 9, 10, 32, 285, 299–300, 316, 318, 322–3, 325, 329, 340–8, 369
Shipbuilding 9
Singapore 1, 17, 29, 50, 84, 242, 400
Skiing 202
Smith, Adam 16, 27, 28, 57, 90, 91
Soda Ash 205–6
South Africa 47, 50
South Korea 1, 17, 29, 50, 74, 84, 113, 114, 117, 132, 211, 237, 242, 348
Southeast Asia 21, 22, 113, 116, 400
Soviet Union 1, 8, 10, 11, 16, 22, 27, 38, 44, 45–6, 47, 48, 50, 53, 54, 61, 72, 73–6, 86, 87, 111, 200, 214, 217, 223–4, 322, 331
Spain 15, 36, 43
Steel 9, 32, 91, 234–8
Structural Impediments Initiative 100, 213–14, 215–16, 269, 421
Superconductors 9, 331, 362–4
Supercomputers 212–13, 291, 322, 337–8
Suzuki, Zenko 184, 217, 427
Sweden 43
Switzerland 43

Taiwan 1, 17, 29, 50, 84, 111, 117, 211, 242, 400
Takeshita, Noboru 116, 275, 276, 353
Technology 9, 26, 291, 297–8, 299–300, 312–70
Telecommunications 359–62
Television 229–34
  HDTV 289, 316, 323, 357–9
Textiles 60, 199–200
Thailand 115, 117, 135, 211, 400
Tortoiseshell 195–6
Truman 51, 54, 58, 73
Turkey 115, 211, 218

United States Constitution 56, 63, 64, 414

United States occupation of
    Japan 113, 197–200, 255, 298,
    379, 398
United States policies
    defense 9, 22, 24, 38–9, 45–8, 53,
        54, 79, 216–26, 402–3, 431–3
    foreign 7, 22–4, 25, 34, 3
        7–8, 39–40, 49, 50, 54, 118
    industrial 5, 57–89, 313–23, 371–9
    Japan 57–8, 73, 75, 83, 84–5,
        109–10, 196–25, 384–91,
        419–35
    liberalism 7, 16, 24, 28–31, 54–5,
        56–89, 126, 135–6, 178–9, 281,
        308, 343, 372, 388, 404,
        407–19
    trade 7, 16, 24, 28–31, 33, 57–89
    trade and investment law 12, 37–8,
        64, 65–9, 280, 284–5, 321, 322,
        343, 387, 416–18, 425–8
United States policymaking 8, 30, 31,
    33, 62–4, 366–70, 407–19
    Congress 24, 36, 58, 59, 60, 63–4,
        68, 72, 78, 204, 211, 212, 214,
        218–19, 221, 228–9, 232,
        261–2, 276, 280, 284, 285, 315,
        319, 335, 339, 344, 348, 353,
        374, 375, 409, 417–18, 421
    International Trade
        Commission 64, 67, 167, 171,
        229, 233, 329
    Supreme Court 63–4, 195–6, 232,
        291
    United States Trade
        Representative 62, 64–5,
        163–4, 166, 203–4, 209,
        210–11, 213, 214–15, 241,
        247–9, 262, 276–7, 302, 346,
        355–6, 365, 416–17

White House 36, 59, 62, 63–4,
    65–9, 193, 314–15
United States, other entries
    corporations 4, 81, 82, 128–9
    debt 2–3, 57, 75, 78, 87, 137–41
    financial 3–4, 57, 75, 119, 371–92
    foreign investments 135–7
    lobby power in Japan 164–6,
    patents 145–6
    power 2–4, 35–6, 72, 78, 124, 125
    research and development 149–50,
        317–18, 367
    savings and investment 11, 80
    socioeconomic problems 2–3,
        10–11
    stock market 143–4
    technology 4, 10, 140–1, 144–53,
        312–70
    trade 3, 9, 10, 57, 84–5, 129–35
United Nations 2, 21, 24, 38, 49, 50,
    72, 199

Versailles Conference 23, 69–70, 72,
    111
Vietnam 115
Vietnam War 21, 22, 24, 44, 47, 50,
    53, 71, 74, 75, 86, 200

Warsaw Pact 45, 46–7
Washington, George 56, 69, 70
Wilson, Woodrow 69–70, 72
World Bank 16, 37, 49, 72
World War I 23, 85, 111, 282
World War II 7, 16, 71–2, 117,
    118, 125

Yoshida, Shigeru 110, 113, 199